BACKGROUND READINGS FOR TEACHERS OF AMERICAN LITERATURE

BACKGROUND READINGS FOR TEACHERS OF AMERICAN LITERATURE

Venetria K. Patton

Purdue University

BEDFORD/ST. MARTIN'S   Boston • New York

For Bedford/St. Martin's
Developmental Editors: Stefanie Wortman and Kaitlin Hannon
Production Editor: Kendra LeFleur
Senior Production Supervisor: Nancy Myers
Marketing Manager: Adrienne Petsick
Copyeditor: Adam Groff
Text Design: Anna Palchik
Composition: Karla Goethe, Orchard Wind Graphics
Printing and Binding: Haddon Craftsmen Inc., an R.R. Donnelley & Sons Company

President: Joan E. Feinberg
Editorial Director: Denise B. Wydra
Editor in Chief: Karen S. Henry
Director of Marketing: Karen Melton Soeltz
Director of Editing, Design, and Production: Marcia Cohen
Managing Editor: Elizabeth M. Schaaf

Library of Congress Control Number: 2005934218

Manufactured in the United States of America.

0   9   8   7   6   5
f   e   d   c   b   a

For information, write: Bedford/St. Martin's, 75 Arlington Street, Boston, MA 02116 (617-399-4000)

ISBN: 0–312–44518–0
EAN: 978–0–312–44518–8

ACKNOWLEDGMENTS

Charlene Avallone. "What American Renaissance? The Gendered Genealogy of a Critical Discourse." From *PMLA* Vol. 112, No. 5 (October 1997): 1102–20. Copyright © 1997. Reprinted by permission of the Modern Language Association of America.

Sacvan Bercovitch. "The Puritan Vision of the New World." From *Columbia Literacy History of the United States* by Emory Elliot. Copyright © 1988. Reprinted by permission of Columbia University Press.

Lawrence Buell. "American Literary Emergence as a Postcolonial Phenomenon." From *American Literary History*, Vol. 4, No. 3 (Autumn, 1992); 411–42. Copyright © 1992. Reprinted by permission of Oxford University Press.

Philip Fisher. "American Literary and Cultural Studies since the Civil War." From *Redrawing the Boundaries: The Transformation of English and American Literary Studies,* edited by Stephen Greenblatt and Giles Gunn. Copyright © 1995. Reprinted by permission of the Modern Language Association of America.

Acknowledgments and copyrights are continued at the back of the book on pages 385–87, which constitute an extension of the copyright page. It is a violation of the law to reproduce these selections by any means whatsoever without the written permission of the copyright holder.

PREFACE

Anthologies are a mainstay for many literature instructors, but it can be difficult to find a suitable selection for our courses. Many of the current anthologies have become almost unwieldy in their attempt to include everything that an instructor might wish to teach. However, *The Bedford Anthology of American Literature* takes a very different approach by aiming for representation rather than comprehensive coverage. The anthology includes frequently-taught writers while also reflecting the gender and ethnic diversity of American literature. The editors also seek to provide crucial historical context for the selections by including brief introductions to the periods and writers. Yet, what I find most attractive about the anthology is the inclusion of clusters of related works found in the American Contexts sections and the brief Through a Modern Lens features, which put later writers in conversation with their predecessors. Because of my excitement about this new anthology, I was pleased to be asked to edit this companion essay collection on the challenges of teaching American literature.

In an era of canon expansion and even destruction, one of the clearest challenges is determining what constitutes American literature. With the increased emphasis on diversity, scholars are questioning why certain women and ethnic writers have been undervalued. Critics are also insisting that issues of sexuality and class be addressed in discussions of literature. The landscape has clearly changed and many instructors lack formal training in more recent critical approaches. While many of us use conferences and professional journals to keep up with the changing times, it can be hard to find time for such professional development. In addition to a more diverse body of literature, instructors are also faced with a more diverse student body, and instructors often require a variety of teaching methodologies in order to be successful in the classroom. It is to these challenges that this collection speaks. While one book cannot provide all of the answers, I do believe that this set of essays addresses some of the most pressing issues in the field and provides essential resources for teaching in the trenches.

I think many teachers are, like me, collectors. I am always looking for good ideas and resources for my classes. I have a sizeable collection of books related to teaching American and African American literature, but the vast majority is devoted to how to teach a particular text or provides contextual material to assist in the teaching of a particular text. I have nothing on my bookshelves that approaches the collection gathered here. My hope is that this text will fill a hole in the bookshelf of many an American literature instructor.

In thinking about how to approach this collection and how to organize the materials, I reflected on the numerous conversations I have had with colleagues over lunch, in the hallways, or even on the phone after a particularly rough class. My colleagues were struggling with many of the same teaching dilemmas that I faced: what should I include on the syllabus, how can I break the monotony of the classroom, how do I make the text accessible, how do I get students to talk about the reading, and what type of assignments should I use? As instructors, we like to appear calm and collected in front of our students, but amongst ourselves we often shake our heads, frown, and grimace about our teaching. Of course there are times when we beam with joy because a class went exactly as we planned or even better, but I have found that my colleagues tend to be type A personalities, who while pleased with success are troubled by the one student they did not reach.

Before discussing the aims of this collection, I would like to share a bit about some of my initial experiences teaching American literature courses. During my Ph.D. studies, while teaching composition at a nearby junior college, I was asked to substitute for an ill instructor who had been assigned to teach American Literature: 1865 to Present. Since I entered the class *in medias res*, I did not have to worry about how to cram a century of literature into sixteen weeks. My main concern was keeping the attention of my students and keeping the discussion flowing. In fact, my initial difficulty engaging students in discussion inspired me to assign study questions on a fairly regular basis. The questions served as both a reading check and a starting point for in-class discussion of the reading. My next foray into the teaching of American literature was the American Novel to Dreiser course, now known as American Novel I. Although I realized that my predecessors had tended toward a rather traditional approach to the class, I was not dissuaded from offering a more colorful approach to the American novel. I consciously selected more women and African American writers for my syllabus. While I wanted to shake up my students a bit by highlighting issues of race, gender, and nation building, I did not abandon the canon. However, I think some of my students suspected I had gone off the deep end; they questioned my notion of the American novel because I was not teaching what was expected.

Looking back on this experience, I suspect that I could have set things up better in order to build a case for the approach I was using. The course was essentially based on the primary texts and it could have benefited from some secondary sources. I had a vision for the course, but I didn't know how to share it with my students. I spent many a lunch hour with my colleagues moaning and groaning about that course. The moaning and groaning had a cathartic effect, but what I really needed was guidance — I needed this book.

American Literature: A Sourcebook for Teachers is the resource I needed as a beginning teacher, and can still use even as a seasoned, award-winning teacher. My intent was to create a book that would be essential for new teachers but also beneficial for veteran teachers. Moreover, I kept in the forefront of my mind the fact that we all have holes in our training, so someone completely at home with the Puritans might be at sea with Modernists. I have also found that sometimes instructors get into a bit of a rut once they discover what works for them, and they do not try new things. While I am open to trying what has worked for my colleagues, if I have not had success with something I am loathe to tweak it and try again. So this is why I have pulled together a mix of informative background readings as well as practical teaching suggestions to create this sourcebook. There is no other collection quite like this, as most books on teaching focus on a particular text or type of text, while this volume seeks to address a variety of concerns related to the American literature survey.

Chapter 1, Challenges of Teaching American Literature, serves as an overview of ongoing concerns within the field of American literary studies. The first two essays, by Cecelia Tichi and Philip Fisher, provide a nice overview of the two main periods of American literature, while Gregory S. Jay's essay addresses the impact multiculturalism has had on the field. Chapter 2, Considering Literary and Social Movements, highlights some of the earlier movements that are reflected in American literature survey courses. This is the section that I imagine as filling in the gaps for instructors teaching outside of their specialty.

Many instructors were trained before the emphasis on multiculturalism hit Ph.D. programs, while others may believe that discussions of the intersection of race, gender, and sexuality are no longer cutting edge. Regardless of one's particular camp, Chapter 3, Considering Identities, includes a wealth of information. David Palumbo-Liu's "Assumed Identities" sets the stage with regard to the continuing importance of considering identities. The essays that follow all address some aspect of race, gender, or sexuality. The essays on ethnic literature are meant to provide a broad overview for those who are less familiar with the particular fields. The essays on gender provide a nice balance to each other because one focuses on feminism, while the other addresses manhood. This construction destabilizes the notion that discussions of gender only pertain to women. The chapter concludes with an excerpt from Michael Ryan that addresses the intersection of gender studies and the study of sexuality.

Chapter 4, Considering the Geopolitical, looks toward recent concerns regarding the impact of political, geographic, demographic, and economic issues on our approach to American literary studies. Since this is a relatively new direction in the field, many instructors will benefit from reading these very different approaches to the geopolitical. These essays may inspire instructors to structure their courses differently or incorporate some different material.

The final chapter turns to the practical concerns of classroom practices. Chapter 5, Approaches in the Classroom, brings together a set of essays that provide very specific examples of classroom activities. While some might think that this section is meant for novice instructors, I encourage more senior instructors to peruse these pages as well. I found that I learned quite a bit during the process of selecting the material, and I am looking forward to trying out some of these practices. I hope that readers of this collection will find it as useful and informative as I intend.

In closing, I must acknowledge that this collection has benefited from the contributions and expertise of many people. The editors of *The Bedford Anthology of American Literature*, Susan Belasco and Linck Johnson, provided extensive and invaluable suggestions for this collection. I must thank my editor, Stefanie Wortman, for her excellent guidance throughout this process. I would also like to recognize other members of the Bedford/St. Martin's staff for their hard work on this project: Steve Scipione, Executive Editor; Maura Shea, Senior Editor; Laura Arcari, Editor; Kaitlin Hannon, Associate Editor; Kendra LeFleur, Production Editor; and Abby Bielagus, Editorial Assistant. I would be remiss if I did not also mention Anne Noyes, the associate editor with whom I began this venture before she left Bedford/St. Martin's. I must also extend my sincere thanks to the many reviewers who provided detailed feedback regarding the initial plans for this project: Joseph Alkana, University of Miami; Scott Ash, Nassau Community College; Peter J. Bellis, University of Miami; Robert Bergstrom, University of Nebraska–Lincoln; Donna Campbell, Washington State University; Paul Crumbley, Utah State University; William Merrill Decker, Oklahoma State University; Carole E. Henderson Belton, University of Delaware; Desiree Henderson, University of Texas at Arlington; Patricia L. Kalayjian, California State University, Dominguez Hills; Peggy Pritchard Kulesz, University of Texas at Arlington; Linda Leavell, Oklahoma State University; Richard M. Millington, Smith College; Sally Mitchell, Temple University; James Nagel, University of Georgia; Sandra Oh, University of Miami; Patricia Okker, University of Missouri, Columbia; Leland S. Person, University of Cincinnati; Connie L. Richards, Salisbury University; Joseph Urgo, University of Mississippi; Eric A. Weil, Shaw University; Cindy Weinstein, California Institute of Technology; Gary Williams, University of Idaho; and Susan Williams, Ohio State University. I would like to recognize my administrative assistant, Matilda Stokes, and our work study student, LaNese Chandler, who helped me in innumerable ways throughout this endeavor. Finally, I must acknowledge the support of my son, Hollis, who endured my long hours when necessary, but also reminded me of the importance of taking a break to play.

Venetria K. Patton

CONTENTS

1 Challenges of Teaching American Literature

One of the biggest challenges of teaching is determining what to teach — there always seems to be more material than time. However, this concern has been exacerbated since the 1970s, as the nature of American literary studies has been questioned. Just what is American literature? As Cecelia Tichi points out in "American Literary Studies to the Civil War," it is no longer just the literature of white men. Scholars have broadened our notion of canonical American literature by including the literature of women and people of color. However, this expansion of the canon was just the beginning of a major revolution within American literary studies. New theoretical approaches were developing, and some scholars were even talking about the end of American literature. However, the essays included in this section should put these changes in perspective.

Canonical shifts are apparent in recent anthologies that include more than the perfunctory woman author and slave narrative. Many newer anthologies are beginning with the oral traditions of Native Americans and include a much more representative sampling of African American, Asian American, and Latina/o literature. This greater inclusiveness is also apparent with regard to women writers, including ethnic women writers. Of course, for the instructor the more representative anthologies are a double-edged sword. While there is more great material to teach, there is also more to exclude, since our semesters or quarters have not been lengthened to accommodate these additional options.

Even after instructors have risen to the challenge of deciding what to teach, there is then the question of how to teach it. Should students be introduced to newer critical approaches or would they be better served by more traditional approaches? Perhaps they might benefit from studying very different readings of the same text? In her discussion of American literary studies up to the Civil War, Tichi notes the deceptively constant use of this rubric in what has become an ideologically complex understanding of American literary studies. In other words, we continue to maintain traditional trappings such as the existence of a literary canon and major wars as demarcations of literary periods, but their significance has changed. Not only are we reading women's texts, but we are often using feminist or gender theory. The study of oral traditions is enhanced by the use of rhetorical theory. However, as Tichi points out, these newer methodologies "have not come to the fore without a degree of resistance and hostility" (p. 21). Tichi concludes by noting the cyclical nature of literary studies.

Philip Fisher takes a slightly different approach in his essay, "American Literary and Cultural Studies since the Civil War." According to Fisher, the new generation of American studies scholars is moving from myth, a singular story, to rhetorics, a plural approach to culture. This pluralistic, dynamic approach to culture is reflected in what he terms "episodes of regionalism." Although Fisher and Tichi approach the changing theoretical terrain in different ways, they both point to the challenge for instructors who are typically not versed in all of the available critical approaches.

While many of us are still grappling with the changes within the field of American literary studies, some scholars have begun to question the very nature of the term *American*. Gregory S. Jay begins "The End of 'American' Literature: Toward a Multicultural Practice" by saying, "It is time to stop teaching 'American' literature" (p. 46). Jay argues for not just a revision of curriculum and pedagogy, but a dismantling of what he considers to be an "oppressive nationalist ideology" (p. 46). Jay would like the borders between the United States, Canada, and Mexico to be seen as the products of our history and not its origins. This revised approach to American literary studies would address the role of assimilation and translation within American literature and allow for more cultural exchange between cultural groups.

These essays by Jay, Fisher, and Tichi do not solve the challenges associated with teaching American literature, but they do contextualize major issues within the field. Fisher and Tichi make important connections between content and approach. The incorporation of new topics of study has necessitated new approaches and calls into question one-size-fits-all notions of literary criticism. The heterogeneity of the field demands a variety of methodologies. This may at times be disconcerting to students who often want "the" answer rather than several possibilities, but it can also be empowering as students are taught to engage the literature. Jay's essay includes a practical discussion of how his ideas might be transferred to the classroom. I can imagine an interesting unit on assimilation that would bring together a wide range of readings and perspectives. This might include an excerpt from Sarah Winnemucca Hopkins's *Life among the Piutes: Their Wrongs and Claims*, Saum Song Bo's "A Chinese View of the Statue of Liberty," Thomas Bailey Aldrich's "Unguarded Gates," Frederick Douglass's speech at the Columbian Exposition, Abraham Cahan's "A Sweat-Shop Romance," Paul Laurence Dunbar's "We Wear the Mask," Zitkala-Ša's "The School Days of an Indian Girl," and an excerpt from Jane Addams's *Twenty Years at Hull-House*. I might begin this unit with an excerpt from W. E. B. Du Bois's *The Souls of Black Folk*, using his concept of double consciousness as a starting point for our discussion of how one becomes an American. In an oft-quoted passage from the first chapter of his landmark book, Du Bois describes double consciousness as seeing oneself through the eyes of another and relates this to the African American's sense of "twoness" — of being African and American. Du Bois's notion of two ideals in one body serves as a nice introduction to a discussion of the construction of an American identity. Students may be able to easily relate this concept to ethnic identities because these are often thought of as hyphenated, but with some prodding students should also be able to link double consciousness to other forms of identity formation.

American Literary Studies to the Civil War

CECELIA TICHI

T aken from the collection Redrawing the Boundaries (1992), *Tichi's essay observes that beginning in the 1970s, scholars noticed that texts taught in American literature courses tended to focus on the Anglo-American experience to the exclusion of the perspectives of ethnic groups, women, and non-Anglo colonial powers. This recognition led to more representative anthologies, broader literary histories, and different literary approaches. These changes have prompted not only the study of new material, but also a rethinking of canonical works. For example, despite the revision of the American literary canon, New England Puritanism remains a hot topic for scholars. Thus Mary Rowlandson's captivity narrative remains a staple on Early American literature syllabi; however, Tichi asserts that since the 1990s Rowlandson's text has been "reread as an ethnographic juxtapositioning" (p. 9) of Anglo-American and Native American cultures rather than merely as an exemplar of Puritan doctrine. According to Tichi, this change in approach is in part related to poststructuralism's interest in gender, race, and class as categories of inquiry. She argues that New Historicism has led to a rereading of "classic" American authors as complicit with marketplace values rather than as critics of culture. Thus the contemplative attitudes of transcendentalists such as Emerson and Thoreau become products of economic history, and their visionary thinking is seen as the necessary outcome of capitalist alienation. Tichi notes that another recent trend in American literary studies is the application of reader-response theory to questions about the cultural shaping of interpretation and assessment.*

Tichi concludes with the caveat that recent changes in scholarship have not come without resistance and hostility from scholars trained in New Criticism. She considers the controversy associated with newer methods as a political struggle to control the meaning of literary works. Tichi cautions both camps to be aware of the shortcomings of their respective approaches, as neither historicism nor formalism is without blind spots.

From *Redrawing the Boundaries: The Transformation of English and American Literary Studies,* ed. Stephen Greenblatt and Giles Gunn (New York: MLA, 1992) 209–31.

For some twenty-five years, from the close of World War II through the 1960s, American Literary Studies to the Civil War seemed to be a clear, straightforward rubric. It performed — as it continues to perform — taxonomic service in classroom texts and in college texts and in college and university catalogs. Within the rubric a certain evolutionary literary coherence, even progress, was presumed to be demonstrable, as instructors and critics located in prose and poetry the growing expressions of democratic consciousness and of such values as individualism and self-reliance. Certain topics and themes were shown to undergo development — for instance, in the *from-to* model based on the notion of aesthetic or thematic incipience leading to fulfillment (e.g., from nature in Jonathan Edwards's *Personal Narrative* to Emerson's *Nature*). Thus it was in no way considered disruptive for teaching or scholarship to subdivide American literature to the Civil War into such areas as colonial, revolutionary, early national, transcendental, American Renaissance.

And if few scholars assented to the simplicity of the homogeneous melting pot, the acceptance of such formulations as the American Adam (Lewis) or the American Renaissance (Matthiessen) reinforced the importance of certain patterns of texts considered to be major because they demonstrated salient parts of the American identity and its aesthetic expression. "American" in those years seemed synonymous with "United States," and teachers and students were in the main untroubled by conceptual problems implied in a body of literature representing a developing nation-state but claiming the whole of two continents as its purview.

This postwar epoch in American literary study, however, began to undergo major revaluation in the 1970s, when scholars pointed out that the canonical texts thought to constitute American literature excluded the cultural record of indigenous peoples, ethnic and minority groups, women, and non-Anglo colonial powers. A post-1960s generation of scholars and editors, moreover, invoked the terms of this rubric with growing awareness of myriad complexities embedded in virtually every word. The term *American* began to seem hegemonic and inaccurately univocal, while the largely Marxist challenge to the belletristic tradition made *literary studies* itself a problematic category. If *Civil War* has often been read as a contradiction in terms, newer scholarship additionally would point out that, given Michel Foucault's arguments on social discipline, the phrase is a tautology. Suffice it to say that for the past twenty-five years, every term in the title of this essay and every ramifying subcategory has undergone dynamic, radical change.

"Always historicize!" begins Fredric Jameson's *Political Unconscious*. And that is one crucial heuristic enterprise of contemporary critics of American literature from the colonial era through the mid-nineteenth century. The other is a change of subject positions. The two are of course related. Historicizing, as Jameson comments, can follow two paths, of the object and of the subject (9). Critical theory, particularly deconstruction, has let critics do both. The critical byword has become "the social construction of —," the prepositional object of that phrase including not only texts but temporal periods, authorial careers, and scholars' own argumentative positions. No category of literary text, period, approach is considered to be a natural one, from Puritan New England to the reputation of Nathaniel Hawthorne to the mid-nineteenth-century American Renaissance; and the inquiry into the process of naturalization necessarily results in the vigorous decentering of all literary categories.

The classroom anthologies show this new decentering, from the once-standard *American Tradition in Literature* (Bradley, Beatty, and Long), which as recently as 1974 opened with a section called "The Puritan Culture," down to *The Harper American Literature* (McQuade et al., 1986), which repositioned the literary origins with the Renaissance discovery narratives, and now *The Heath Anthology of American Literature* (Lauter et al., 1990), which, committed to a multiethnic, multiracial, and doubly gendered canon, opens with a section entitled "Native American Traditions" and boasts the work of "time-honored favorite authors placed alongside the writings of women and minority authors whose importance is only now being recognized" (iii). And just as the anthologies measure the shift in the canon, the literary history compendiums reveal the changed census of those considered qualified to form it and comment on it. Of the contributors to *Literary History of the United States*, edited by Robert Spiller et al. (1946; rev. ed. 1953), all fifty-five were white men, while *The Columbia Literary History of the United States*, edited by Emory Elliot (1986), lists seventy-four contributors, sixteen of whom are women and at least four of whom are specialists in ethnic or minority American texts.

The simple rubric American Literature to the Civil War is thus deceptively constant in its continuing use in classroom texts, in course titles, and even in journal titles (*American Literature, Early American Literature, Studies in American Fiction, American Literary History*). A post-1960s generation of scholars and editors by no means invokes the term without awareness of its ideological complexities.

For the colonial period, New England Puritanism continues to be a scholarly force field. And though the issue of New England's exceptionalism will concern us momentarily, suffice it to say here that books beget books, and arguably the sheer quantity of studies of seventeenth-century New England (by one estimate, a book or article for every one hundred persons alive in New England in 1650) engenders vigorous continuing scholarship (Wood 26). A 1986 investigation, for instance, of John Cotton's rhetoric and the ways in which the spoken word was aural sculpture for the New England Puritans is indebted to Larzer Ziff's 1962 biography of John Cotton (Kibbey), while a 1990 study of identity formation in colonial New England acknowledges its paternity in Perry Miller's *New England Mind*: "My primary scholarly inspiration came from that prime inspirer of American Puritan studies, Perry Miller" (Canup vii).

Miller's position as founder of contemporary colonial studies continues secure (Wood). His two-volume *New England Mind* (*The Seventeenth Century*, 1939; *From Colony to Province*, 1953) had located in colonial Puritanism what he termed "the meaning of America," a heroic and individualistic mission. From a congeries of Puritan texts, Miller configured a paradigmatic univocal construct, the Puritan mind. His Puritans struggled with anxieties and fears and with their human scale as motes in the cosmos, but they were intellectual heroes in the New World wilderness, tough-minded, courageous, bold, robust, and central to Western civilization: "Puritanism was one of the major expressions of the Western intellect [and] achieved an organized synthesis of concepts which are fundamental to our culture." Committed to the idea of a Puritan "single intelligence," Miller was a self-identified cartographer and anatomist, "map[ping] the intellectual terrain of the seventeenth century" and "the anatomy of the Puritan mind" (*New England* 1: viii, vii).

Miller's drive, as he put it, to expound "the innermost propulsion of the nation" (*Errand* viii) rhetorically suited midcentury industrial America, and his insistence on a purely intellectual formulation for the founding psyche doubtless served the position of the United States as the democratically triumphant nation of World War II. The nation that twice used the atomic bomb needed vindication as democratic *and* rational, impervious to raging passions. According to Miller, the New England mind, struggling to exploit the triad of reason-will-understanding, the best of the postlapsarian mental components, strove not only to apprehend God's will but also to contain the unruly and wayward passions: "Reason, free and independent, is the king and ruler of the faculties, and its consort, the will, is queen and mistress. . . . [L]ogic was a corrective of sinful passions." Miller offered a heroically cerebral American paternity that put passion into the service of the intellect, where it was contained. Puritan "regeneration would take the form of a reinvigoration of rational discourse" (*New England* 1: 247, 263). There is no nuclear-age demonic Dr. Strangelove among Miller's rational, national founders.

Puritan passions, however, have been the unabated focus of subsequent scholarship, beginning in the early 1970s with the inversion of Miller's interpretation of the Puritan "errand into the wilderness," the phrase from a sermon by John Danforth and one centered on the lamentations of the Old Testament prophet Jeremiah. Miller considered the sermon to be testimony to the crisis of diminished piety and zeal on the part of the second-generation Puritans. Subsequent critics began to see eschatological affirmation where Miller read Puritan self-admission of decline. The newer scholarship, in a tradition initiated by Ernest Lee Tuveson, Aletha Joy Bourne Gilsdorf, and others but developed most fully by Sacvan Bercovitch, redirected colonial studies away from the previously dominant exegesis on the Puritan intellect. In a move that upended the heuristic subject position, it argued that the Puritan glass, or perhaps tankard, was not half empty but half full. Exegesis of Puritan millennialism enabled the formulation of the American self and its Christic mission in the New World (Bercovitch, *Puritan Origins*). This approach also located in Puritan lamentation a covert imperative for national renewal that, in literature, took the form of a recurrently inscribed sense of national mission extending from the seventeenth century into the presidential rhetoric of the television age (Bercovitch, *American Jeremiad* and "Horologicals"). "The New World ministers, already committed to a scheme which would not admit of failure, compensated for their thwarted errand by constructing a legendary past and prophetic future for the country. . . . The popular aspect of the legacy [of the Jeremiad] consists in the exuberant national eschatology embodied in the American Dream" ("Horologicals" 43, 75).

Identified as a middle-class culture, America in this configuration embodies a myth leading the country into the millennium prophesied in the New Testament book of Revelation. From the early 1970s into the later 1980s, colonial American literary study flourished via scholarly exegesis on eschatology, especially on the ways in which the Puritan American self and the United States are susceptible to recurrent renewable commitment to the national destiny. During those years, most of us working in the area of Puritan studies exploited the schema in our own scholarship, whether it focused on, say, biography or the American landscape (Middlekauff; Tichi, *New World*).

As presentism is invariably a part of scholarly findings, it is the case that just as the idea of the Puritan mind should find favor in a particular postwar climate, so should the millennialist arguments be enabled by the cultural moment of the 1960s (roughly 1965–75), the Vietnam War era, in which many in literary studies perceived the United States not as a global democratic benefactor but as a militaristic empire. Responding in the late 1970s to a question from the audience after a talk at the Boston Public Library, Bercovitch spoke for scholarly cohorts when he asserted that it is precisely the critic's situation in contemporary history that promotes scholarly insights, customarily by turning presumed truth into exposed myth. Because ideology discloses itself as a result of historical processes, he remarked, the eschatological literary discourses had become particularly accessible as the United States began to decline as a global imperial power.

The continuing diminution of United States imperial authority, together with its economic decline, is plausibly the historical basis for yet another change in colonialists' critical subject positions. Continuing the investigation of the literary history of the seventeenth-century emigrants' emotional lives, recent scholarship now concerns itself not with messianic passions but with those of anguish, grief, and mourning. Thus Anne Bradstreet, the Puritan poet who admitted that the sight of the New World made her nauseous, comes to the fore as a poet of feminist sensibilities at odds with patriarchal Puritanism (W. Martin 15–76). The discourses, moreover, of intellectual heroism and of imperial millennialism, other scholars argue, occlude another kind of discourse, that of the anguished Puritan as immigrant. Recent work emphasizes the dreadful ordeal of the errand, the psychological deracination of a people caught in a double bind, their native land in chaos, their alternative the upheaval of dislocation in the New World (Delbanco).

This newer position calls into question the kinds of Puritan colonial texts accorded privileged status over the past quarter-century. The premise of a paradigmatic masculine mind permits the scholar to construct a composite *Ur*-text from fragments of many kinds of writings, including sermons, diaries, and tracts. (Deconstructive theory, in fact, has come relatively late to colonial American literary studies, probably because one element necessary to its operation — the antecedent New Critical presumption of textual integrity — has always been a tenuous proposition in a field of study so dependent on the pastiche, or composite text.) Yet even the intact text, such as the Danforth sermon "Errand into the Wilderness," has been positioned as inclusively corporate, representative of a group of visible saints (as the Puritan church members were called). And the spiritual biography, such as Cotton Mather's "Nehemiah" on Governor John Winthrop (in the *Magnalia Christi Americana* [1702]), has been presented as representative of the univocal middle-class "American self" (Bercovitch, *Puritan Origins*). In all of these, the literary text is exclusively self-referential to one presumably homogeneous group, the Puritans, and is emphatically masculine even as it subsumes two genders. Reference to all others, whether Satanic Indians, heretics, or those outside the circle of church membership, essentially reinforces both Puritan centrality and the otherness — the alien status — of non-Puritans.

The poststructuralist moment, however, in colonial studies currently reveals itself in scholarly claims for a different kind of representative text. Such a text extends beyond the patriarchal male realm to bring into juxtaposition the newer categories of critical inquiry, gender and race and, implicitly, class. Gender was a salient issue in the 1637–38 antinomian controversy in which the Puritan wife and mother Anne Hutchinson, in her lay preaching, contested the spiritual authority of Puritan patriarchy and became a "disturber in Israel" with her female narrative of dissent (Lang, *Prophetic Woman*). Hutchinson left no written text (her voice recorded only in the transcript of her trial on charges of heresy), although her story, obsessively retold by others, was to ramify into, and to problematize, nineteenth-century American fiction and the essay (Lang).

Seventeenth-century studies have now identified the work that lends itself to considerations not only of gender but of the heuristics of race and class, resisting the totalizing tendencies indicated in such a term as *American self*. It is Mary White Rowlandson's *True History of the Captivity and Restoration of Mrs. Mary White Rowlandson* (see Lang, "Introduction"). The narrative describes the months during which Rowlandson, a mother and a Puritan minister's wife, was held captive by the Algonquians during King Philip's War (mid-1670s), as the colonists called it, when a confederation of Indian tribes led by their chief, Metacom ("King Philip"), fought the colonists because they feared loss of lands and tribal annihilation. Rowlandson's account began what has been called the first American literary genre, the captivity narrative. For the past three decades it has been, in excerpts, a staple of the classroom anthologies, in which interpretive headnotes customarily emphasized its importance in depicting Puritan trials and doctrinal orthodoxy on the colonial frontier.

Yet in the 1990s Rowlandson's text is being reread as an ethnographic juxtapositioning of two cultures, colonial whites and the indigenous Americans, and involving two genders, even as it presumes that the central experience of

New England Puritanism is that of mourning (Breitwieser; Lang, "Introduction"). The title of a 1990 critical study devolving from Rowlandson's narrative is indicative: *American Puritanism and the Defence of Mourning: Religion, Grief, and Ethnology in Mary White Rowlandson's Captivity Narrative* (Breitwieser). It argues that the fundamental Puritan experience is loss at every level (social, economic, personal) and that the most profound psychological impulse, accordingly, is grief and mourning. The mandate of the clerical leadership becomes, essentially, a valediction forbidding mourning, a channeling of thought and feeling away from grief into a spiritual utilitarianism. Loss is identified as the central ethos of Puritanism, though it is suppressed and repressed everywhere in the official culture. Loss becomes overwhelmingly present in its absence, and the Puritans become one ethnic group over and against another, the Algonquians. In this configuration, Rowlandson's text is dissonant, not only because its author was a woman whose intrinsic aggression was to write but because it is about mourning and because, as a captivity narrative of cross-cultural encounter, it becomes as well an ethnographic text of a kind dangerous to establishment Puritanism. Cultural relativity inadvertently comes into play: "If what seems white can turn out to be red . . . it is also the case that what has been thought red can turn out to be analogous to white. . . . Thus reversibility . . . reappears as a property of relative cultures" (Breitwieser 170–71). An understanding of what constitutes a rhetoric of dissonance in Puritan texts becomes the scholarly imperative. And the opening of ethnological rhetoric to discussion enables scholars to exploit ethnographers' and ethnographic historians' findings.

One critic asks, "What explains this remarkable scholarly attention [to New England Puritanism]?" and answers that it is "what" Puritanism seems to say about contemporary America, that there is "something" in it that still resonates in the late twentieth century, that in "some way or another" Puritanism has been, as Miller called it, an "ideal laboratory" for the study of America. The ineffable "what" and "something" both work ineffably, "some way or another" (Wood 26). Even though the Puritans themselves promulgated the myth of their exceptionalism (Gura 215–34), it may be surprising to find late-twentieth-century scholarly assent to the notion even by those historicizing the construction of New England Puritan studies: "The originating, generative power of the Puritan imagination continues to shape the way we tell the American literary story, indeed the way we explain the development of American culture" (D. Weber 101).

As some scholars recognize, the presumption of New England Puritan literary exceptionalism is, strictly speaking, neither a colonialist concern nor an antiquarian one, ramifying as it does directly into the nineteenth-century "classic" American literature, the canonical texts of Emerson and Thoreau, Hawthorne and Melville. The notion of a sui generis originating power is under challenge as research discloses the social construction of literary New England long represented as if it were a natural phenomenon (Baker, "Figurations" 148–49; Baym, "Early Histories," *Novels,* and *Women's Fiction;* Buell 193–250; Tompkins 3–39). Historically, one study finds, a kind of New

England academic interlocking directorate "made literary works and authors display the virtues and achievements of an Anglo-Saxon United States founded by New England Puritans." That New England's exceptionalism emerges in such research shows the extent to which the literature of the South was systematically excluded from schoolbooks on American literature, just as New England was systematically privileged as *the* literature of this nation. "When in the second decade of the twentieth century, academics defined . . . 'American literature,' they did so by appropriating and sophisticating a narrative already constructed in the plethora of American literary history textbooks" that "encouraged respect, veneration, and gratitude toward these men who had achieved American literature on behalf of the rest of us" (Baym, "Early Histories" 459–60).

The argument that New England is a regional literature (Buell) with a literary history of intraregional responses (Bell), and that its putative national scope is the result of its social construction by academic-publishing elites rooted in Boston (Baym, "Early Histories," *Novels,* and *Women's Fiction;* Tompkins) may renew scholarly efforts to historicize and to develop theoretical positions toward the literature of other regions. The South, despite prodigious scholarship (e.g., R. B. Davis's three-volume intellectual history of the colonial South), to date has not commanded such attention. Yet the articulation of the idea of the South as an Eden from which the inhabitants are dispossessed because of the inherently corruptive institution of slavery establishes the theoretical basis on which Southern colonial studies might proceed (see L. P. Simpson). Lewis Simpson's work points up the need for a multivalent theoretics of regional Americas. The recent conception, moreover, of four distinct sets of English folkways disseminated in North America (see Fischer) and persisting in the subcultures of the United States may renew interest in a moribund regional American literary studies.

As of now, the paradoxical centrality of the marginal text has become a fruitful approach to earlier American literature and marks a distinct change in scholarly direction. For the revolutionary and postrevolutionary–early national periods, for instance, traditional scholarship has focused on the texts that explicitly expound the problematics and potential of republican political principles — texts such as the Declaration of Independence, the *Federalist* papers, or the verse of the Connecticut Wits, Timothy Dwight, Joel Barlow, David Humphreys, Jonathan Trumball (e.g., L. Howard). Recently, however, critical theory has concentrated on other categories of texts, heretofore considered at most obliquely concerned with issues central to the formation of the Republic. These reveal their "cultural work . . . redefining the social order" (Tompkins xi). Early American fiction is one such textual category: "Because the novel as a form was marginalized by social authorities [including clergy, educators, political figures], because novelists could neither support themselves by their trade nor claim a respectable position within society because of it, the early American novel . . . was ideally suited to evaluate American society and to provide a critique of what was sorely missing in the exuberant postrevolutionary rhetoric of republicanism" (Davidson 218).

The Gothic novel, in this scheme, is particularly important as a social critique. Charles Brockden Brown's *Wieland,* for instance, in which an idyllic Philadelphia country-house life is disrupted by the arrival of a ventriloquist whose multiple voices are the catalyst for murder and mayhem — this text becomes engaging not for the solution of formal and thematic problems thought to be intrinsic to a "primitive" American fictional form nor for its psychoanalytical probings, but instead for the ways in which it pleads for the restoration of civic authority in a tumultuous postrevolutionary movement (Tompkins 40–61). Gothic novels can be seen, additionally, as criticisms of a hierarchical traditional society and of "the excesses of individualism" (Davidson 212–53).

Marxist and feminist approaches have also led to reconfigurations and revaluations of revolutionary and postrevolutionary–early national canonical and noncanonical texts — for instance, in work asserting the apposition between the narrative and the legal brief (R. A. Ferguson) and thus breaking the generic barrier between the belles lettres and documentary texts by insisting on the conceptual, structural, and argumentative enmeshment of letters and legal texts. And feminism has forced into unprecedented focus the patriarchal premises and presumptions of the canonical texts of the era, from Franklin's *Autobiography* to Jefferson's *Notes on the State of Virginia* (C. Jordan; Kerber). Feminist heuristics have so rigorously exposed patriarchy in the literature of this period and so thoroughly critiqued its arrogation of the power of social control by white males that the recent scholarly apologia for the revolutionary writers finds itself repudiating or redefining the nature and contingent status of patriarchy itself (Fliegelman).

Studies of the mid-nineteenth-century American Renaissance are also decentering the literary canon both by the reinterpretation of "major" texts and by the inclusion of those texts long thought to be marginal. Though the term was coined in 1829 by Samuel Knapp (see Gunn, "Kingdoms" 222), the rubric, as all Americanists know, was forcefully renewed by F. O. Matthiessen's *American Renaissance: Art and Expression in the Age of Emerson and Whitman,* itself a monumental act of canon formation, one that displaced the genteel "fireside" writers (Henry Wadsworth Longfellow, James Russell Lowell, John Greenleaf Whittier, Oliver Wendell Holmes) and instated a new constellation of major literary figures, among them Emerson, Thoreau, Hawthorne, Melville, and (as Emerson's designated poet-literatus) Whitman. In Matthiessen, the New England literary hegemony would remain intact, revivified — and also vivifying, as a vigorous post–World War II American literary criticism took flight from his scholarship (see Gunn, *Matthiessen;* Cain; Arac). As Charles Feidelson Jr., remarked at the outset of his own influential *Symbolism and American Literature,* "The first large-scale attempt to define the literary quality of American writing at its best was Matthiessen's *American Renaissance*" (3).

The central postwar critical texts — Henry Nash Smith's *Virgin Land: The American West as Symbol and Myth,* Feidelson's *Symbolism and American Literature,* R. W. B. Lewis's *American Adam,* Richard Chase's *American Novel and Its Tradition,* Daniel Hoffman's *Form and Fable in American Fiction,* Leo Marx's *Machine in the Garden,* and, towering above these, Matthiessen's *American Renaissance* — all emphasized the United States as a country of democratic values encoded in a "classic" mid-nineteenth-century literature centered in New England, itself implicitly a synecdoche of the nation. This generation of theorists, moreover, was the first to incorporate New Criticism in approaches to American literature. They brought the social dimensions of New Criticism into organicist reading of individual texts. "The theorists of American literature conceived the social structure of the literary work as a microcosm of collective psychology or myth and thus made New Criticism into a method of cultural analysis" (Graff, *Promise* 217). It is no coincidence that the myth-symbol school of American studies flourished at this time (H. N. Smith; L. Marx), based on the premise that patterns of symbol embedded in the literary text manifest the ethos of the nation. By precept and example, the work of these scholars has continued to influence the terms and the design of scholarship; for instance, one study presumes that "the problems of American politics and the problems of American literary genius may be said to belong to the same family of problems" (Marr 39; see also Porte).

The newer scholarly subject positions, however, reject as invalid any claims to the organicism implied in the term *family of problems.* Accordingly, they have approached antebellum American literature very differently. It may well be that the nickname *cold war criticism* will become the term by which post–World War II studies are known in retrospect. The "cold war consensus" (Pease, *Visionary Contacts*) is being defined as ideological in its very contention that the major American literary texts (those of indigenous "genius") transcend ideology. Recent scholarship finds that cold war consensus to be earmarked by its argument and its presumption that the "classic" texts enact democratic freedom in their structural openness and thus oppose (and repudiate) the closed systems denoting totalitarianism (Pease, *Visionary Contacts;* Bercovitch and Jehlen).

Such retrospect is possible, in fact inevitable, when critical subject positions change to the extent that both culture and text are seen as a field in which power is contested and in which the text inscribes the contention of competing and combative forces. From Roland Barthes's essay "The Death of the Author" and Michel Foucault's "What Is an Author?" the very conception of authorship has undergone the process of historicization that discloses how problematic is the term, how coordinate through the centuries with the unprecedented rise of individualization and private property. The *author* cannot now be presumed to stand outside a situated world of roiling forces — political, economic, ideological, cultural. The premise of transcendent democratic truths embodied in texts of aesthetic genius is thus reassessed as ideologically self-serving to certain groups, especially to white male elites, and enactive of its own historical moment, such as the cold war.

In New-Historicist terms, then, the criticism of the 1940s through 1960s becomes cold war criticism, an ideological construct, "a holistic master story of large-scale structural elements directing a whole society," when in actuality "selves and texts are defined by their relation to hostile others," such as "despised and feared Indians, Jews, Blacks" (Veeser xiii), and to disciplinary power represented in figures of institutional authority, such as Hawthorne's judge, Jaffrey Pyncheon, in *The House of the Seven Gables* or Melville's Captain Ahab. Previous criticism is seem to be flawed because of its evasion of these matters. Thus Matthiessen's treatment of mid-nineteenth-century American texts is condemned for its "most extravagant idealization: the diminishment of the Civil War. . . . Rather than facing up to divisions within the renaissance, Matthiessen divided the renaissance from the war. . . . His wish for wholeness led to disconnection" (Arac 97–98).

While American Renaissance has served for decades as a course title in countless colleges and universities, current scholarship is reconfiguring the terms of the rubric. Studies of antebellum American literature bring texts previously excluded or marginalized onto the field; they reread the "renaissance" texts in light of the proposition that the written text, the author, and his or her culture coexist in a dynamic interplay of contending forces — a point demonstrable in work on Hawthorne.

For decades, scholars demonstrated Hawthorne's indebtedness to *The Faerie Queene* as a source for the character Pearl in *The Scarlet Letter*, citing as one instance Hawthorne's naming his daughter, Una, after Spenser's allegorical character. Currently, however, Hawthorne, Una, and *The Scarlet Letter* are positioned as "interactive, contingent and interdependent participants in a collective process" (Herbert 287). *The Scarlet Letter* does not, in these terms, become the transmuted form of autobiographical or sociocultural and literary influences on Hawthorne, much less the work of art transcendent of these forces. Indeed, the presumption of such transcendence is discredited, downgraded into mere reification. "Instead of reifying Hawthorne's entangled brooding on Una's character into transcendent aesthetic terms, *The Scarlet Letter* extends that brooding and complicates the entanglement" (287).

Melville, to cite another canonical example, is similarly recontextualized, approached as a participant in a network of dynamic associations — familial, political, cultural, economic — in all of which he becomes a figure of historical contingency. The conception of Melville as author, recent critics assert, has been reified in scholarly emphasis on his separateness from his sociocultural contexts. To call Melville a genius or great author is emphatically to remove him from his cultural milieu. To enshrine him (or, for that matter, Emerson or Thoreau or Poe) in a fraternal pantheon of singular cohorts is to stress his separateness, his distinctness from the society he inhabited, which inscribes itself in his texts. Selfhood becomes not an index of singularity but a term referring to the historical process of which any individual, including the writer, is necessarily a part. The text, accordingly, is not seen to be an entity transcendent of its time but one inscriptive of it. In this sense, author, text, and context merge. And to approach Melville or any other canonical author in this way is not to be iconoclastic but to reclaim that figure and the texts from reification — and to rescue scholars from their roles as monument makers, agents of reification. Thus Melville is viewed as being involved in nineteenth-century

American imperialism even in his family relationships, those of "subversive genealogy," and *Moby-Dick* is revealed to enact the politics of imperialism, with Ahab exploiting Third World labor to plunder the globe's natural resources (Rogin; Dimock).

The "renaissance," not surprisingly, becomes a historical moment in which unexamined literary-cultural associations, in particular the economic, are investigated, as scholars draw from the work of Marx, Georg Lukács, and Raymond Williams to explore the ways in which the commodification of labor and the permeation of social relations by a market economy manifest themselves in literary texts previously thought impervious to such matters. The study of industrial capitalism in the United States reveals its development to be considerably earlier than once was thought, not a post–Civil War phenomenon but one occurring in the antebellum decades (Gilmore; Porter, *Seeing* and "Reification"; Shulman). According to the premises of New Historicism, the "classic" American writers are no longer simply oppositional critics of marketplace values but inevitably, if inadvertently, complicitous with them.

Their response to an insurgent corporate capitalism is shown to be formal, not only discursively resistant to the market system for its exploitation of workers' wage slavery but participating in — in fact, enacting — the presumptions of the new economic order. Although Melville's "Tartarus of Maids" has long seemed a trenchant critique of the evolving industrialism — testimony to his opposition to systematic murder by wage slavery — his acquiescence in the new order has lately come to light. For instance, the cetology chapters in *Moby-Dick*, in which Melville's sources on whales and whaling are printed verbatim, are read as the writer's raw materials that, when processed through the imagination, emerge as a finished product, a literary symbol, to be marketed as fiction for profit (Gilmore). The novel thus takes on the character of a factory. And the domestic novel, in which the sacrosanct home is customarily thought to be exempt from commercial values, instead reveals the infiltration of the market at its worst: *Uncle Tom's Cabin* "show[s] the involvement of the home and its keeper in the practice of slavery . . . slavery as itself a domestic institution [with] an intrusion of the marketplace into the home" (Lang, *Prophetic Woman* 197–98).

Even the most visionary of nineteenth-century literary symbols, Emerson's "transcendent eyeball," when examined in the context of industrial capitalism becomes the signifier of a society that alienates individuals from themselves and their work and insinuates itself within the social consciousness. Such a society "generates people who assume a passive and 'contemplative' stance in the face of objectified and rationalized reality — people who seem to themselves to stand outside that reality because their own participation in producing it is mystified" (Porter, "Reification" 189). Emerson and Thoreau, from this viewpoint, become figures whose contemplative stance and visionary attributes are products of nineteenth-century economic history. In fact, the visionary is redefined as the inevitable outcome of capitalist alienation, and transcendentalism thus takes its place as a phenomenon grounded in economic history.

With increasing aggressiveness, critics have repudiated the once-eulogized American individualism, its major exponent being the Emerson of "Self-Reliance." Of course, the postwar critics had drawn careful distinctions among writers with claims to individualism, especially juxtaposing Captain Ahab against the Thoreau of *Walden*. The two are individualist antitheses, with Ahab portrayed as the nemesis of the ideal, the very "embodiment of his author's most profound response to the problem of the individual free will *in extremis*. . . . He can see nothing but his own burning thoughts since he no longer shares in any normal fellow-feelings [and] refuses to be deflected from his pursuit by the stirring of any sympathy for others" (Matthiessen, *American Renaissance* 447–51). Ahab thus became a "fearful example of the self-enclosed individualism that . . . brings disaster both upon itself and upon the group of which it is a part" (459). In postwar critical terms, he is "a false culture-hero, pursuing a private grievance (rather than a divine behest) at the expense of the mankind in his crew . . . a Satan, a sorcerer, an Antichrist" (Hoffman 234). Investigators who take this approach read *Moby-Dick* as "a book about the alienation from life that results from an excessive or neurotic self-dependence," one in which Ahab is "guilty of or victimized by a distorted 'self-reliance'" (Lewis 105). The critic who celebrates *Moby-Dick* for embodying the "great cultural heritage" of the United States warns nonetheless that Melville must not be seen to approve Ahab's "intensity, power, and defiant spirit" because he represents the deformation of individualism and self-reliance (L. Howard, *Literature* 176–77). And if the cold war version of Captain Ahab echoes the horrors of Hitler and totalitarianism (and, retrospectively, in U.S. history, indicts the unchecked predations of the robber barons, as Matthiessen remarked), he also stands interpretively as an alienated anti-individualist.

Thoreau, on the contrary, was presented in the postwar era as the exemplar of the democratic common person, recommitting himself to American traditions of hard work and artisanship, his *Walden* also making a claim for "communal security and permanence," for "order and balance" (Matthiessen, *American Renaissance* 172–73). He was a "visionary hero" who "demonstrates his freedom in the liberation of others," thus working on behalf of other human beings to further the greatest cause of freedom (Lewis 21). Thoreau's "aggressiveness," though regrettably "excessive" for his time, is vindicated when his democratic "symbol of the hermitage" is exported to India for Mahatma Gandhi's successful struggle for independence (L. Howard, *Literature* 158–60). Thoreau, then, becomes the democratic heroic individualist precisely because he represents the dutiful and responsible postwar American working person committed to communal security and stability, and also to social order. In postwar criticism, then, the individualist must either be brought within the democratic fold, as was Thoreau, or, failing that, be consigned to un-American realms beyond — that is, to the alienationist domains of insanity, abnormality, deformity.

Beginning in the 1970s, however, a challenge to the ideal of American individualism as hostile to human interests and pernicious in its effects was undertaken. Narratives on American environmentalism were shown to endorse violence against the self and others; representations of life on the frontier were felt to be tributes not to personal and national independence and courage but to deracinative isolation and alienation. Regenerative energies were seen to be aroused precisely in violent, aggressive action (Kolodny, *Lay of the Land*; Slotkin).

Critics have continued to challenge individualist ideals. Studies of eighteenth-century commodity capitalism and the concomitant picaresque novel, both in England and America, reveal the imperative of incessant social upheaval that defines individualism as "change, difference, possibility, mobility, restlessness, flux," qualities that thwart stable cultural relationships and, when convergent, represent "the excesses of individualism" (Davidson 167, 219). And one recent study of individualism in the United States, *Habits of the Heart,* acknowledges in brief that "sometimes the flight from society is simply mad and ends in general disaster," offering Ahab as the consummate example of "asocial individualism" unredeemed by the postwar critics' solace of a democratically pervasive and enduring Ishmael (Bellah et al. 144–45). In this sense, Thoreau becomes not the exemplar of visionary democracy but the isolate in whom the potential to be an "inspiring friend replaces the need for any actual friendship" and who "etherealizes friendship to the point of mutual evanescence" (Pease, *Visionary Compacts* 263). "Thoreau did not want a friend of his own. . . . what he wanted in a friend was a confirmation of the self" (J. W. Warren 59). The masculine ethos of individualism in Thoreau, as well as in Cooper, Emerson, and Melville, is reidentified as egocentric narcissism: "The American myth of the individual has encouraged the development of narcissism, not only in the psychological sense of an individual's unsuccessful resolution of an early failure in identity but in a cultural sense. . . . The male individualist . . . sees himself as all-powerful and all-encompassing, and he sees only himself" (J. W. Warren 13).

If marketplace capitalism is one heuristic by which to critique the development of individualist ideology and its literary consequences, another is the inverted subject position focused on the founding of the New World. According to a line of argument that bypasses the colonial New England tradition, the dominant nineteenth-century canonical texts devolved from the European Enlightenment's projection of a mythic, pristine New World, the crucial concept being that of the *discovery* of America. This is not the nation understood to have developed through historical processes but instead perceived to be a world come upon intact, existing essentially outside of history. And the kinds of literary production emerging from that position were predetermined by it: the discovered, pristine America, existing primarily in a state of perfection, but its very definition admits of no change; literary representations of social or personal change in a fluid context were thus precluded. The literary opportunity is one of entitlement — and of tremendous constraint. It is chiefly one of ratification and celebration of the quotidian world whose representative American incarnates the continent itself (thus the scholarly title *American Incarnation,* with its pun on *nation*). "The American, and therefore the American artist, is identical with America and sufficient unto all of it. He incarnates America and encompasses its entire consciousness" (Jehlen, *American Incarnation* 132). Thus the novel — the genre central to historical process — is excluded because it is precluded, since nineteenth-century American genre and ideology must be inextricably connected in the dominant literary forms. What remains is nonfiction and the romance: the Emersonian or Thorovian essay and the likes of *The Scarlet Letter*. Literary efforts at the novel as a historical narrative (e.g., Hawthorne's *The Marble Faun* or Melville's *Pierre*) are doomed to fracture because they attempt the intervention of history into an America that is conceptually ahistorical.

Other reassessments of antebellum American literature resist the notion of dominant literary forms and inject the traditional rubrics — the Age of Emerson and Whitman, the American Renaissance — with irony as they redefine the period by widening its scope to include texts previously marginalized or excluded altogether, especially those categorized as belonging to popular culture or to sentimental (i.e., women's) fiction. While Matthiessen traced a trajectory "from Coleridge to Emerson" (*American Renaissance* 133), writers such as David S. Reynolds now argue that popular culture, particularly vernacular religious rhetoric, was at least as important a source for Emerson and his major-figure cohorts. Colloquial revivalism is now asserted to be an integral part of the formation of Emerson's discourse (as well as that of Whitman and Poe), and the "renaissance" shown to be so riddled with "subversive" works that "the major texts [become] artistic renderings of irrational or erotic themes predominant in a large body of overlooked sensational writings of the day" (169).

The sensational, mass-market press filled with ghoulish crimes, sex scandals, felonies, celebrity criminals, and the like becomes permeable with the previously sacralized literary productions of the canonical figures, and scholarly rubrics indicate this newer high culture–low culture inclusivity: Poe and Popular Irrationalism, Hawthorne and Crime Literature, *The Scarlet Letter* and Popular Sensationalism (Reynolds). Robert S. Levine argues that a pervasive cultural paranoia, much of it anti-Catholic and extending from the colonial era through the nineteenth century, recurrently engendered texts centered in anxiety about conspiratorial subversion. In this sense literary studies become cultural studies, diminishing the possibility of sensationalist, even prurient exposés of canonical figures. "Beneath" the American Renaissance, in Reynolds's phrase, may be an unfortunate and misleading preposition when criticism shows the more accurate term to be "within."

Locating diverse kinds of texts *within* the period, moreover, investigators looking at the sentimental tradition most closely identified with women writers and readers have taken a prominent position over the past decade. The *feminine*, a word disparaged in Hawthorne's dismissal of the "damned mob of scribbling women" (meaning his commercially successful women-author rivals), and sustained in the title of Fred Lewis Pattee's historical examination *The Feminine Fifties* (1940), had continued to be a term of opprobrium even in the scholarship that, in the 1970s, initiated the revaluation of the sentimental (see Ann Douglas, *Feminization*).

The long-forgotten body of popular texts written by and for nineteenth-century women has now come to the fore in analysis that earns the title "sentimental power" (Tompkins 122–201). Such examinations, begun originally as bibliographic study to determine authors, titles, sales figures, and audiences for nineteenth-century sentimental fiction (Baym), utilize that data to formulate arguments on the sociocultural power of these texts, whose authors include Susan Warner, E. D. E. N. Southworth, Elizabeth Stuart Phelps, Louisa May Alcott, and especially Harriet Beecher Stowe. If a positivist, materialist, and scientific-technological bent dominated later nineteenth- and twentieth-century American history, feminist criticism argues, that direction nonetheless must not conceal a mid-nineteenth-century ethos of evangelistic piety — much less prevent the study of it. The terms of the mid-nineteenth-century moral universe now demand exegesis, and the texts that represent that universe should be included in any configuration of American antebellum literature. No longer can these texts be dismissed as naive or ingenuous, such dismissal itself understood as having served a particular critical-political agenda in postwar literary criticism (Baker, "Figurations"; Tompkins).

Nor is sentimental, domestic American fiction divided along gender lines exclusively. The sentimental tradition is currently understood to include both the women writers and the canonical Hawthorne. Jane Tompkins (11) points out that Hawthorne was most valued in the mid-nineteenth century not for the ironic dark fiction the era of T. S. Eliot came to value but rather for the tales that moralize on domestic topics ("Sunday at Home," "A Rill from the Town Pump," "Little Annie's Ramble"). In interdisciplinary cultural studies, still best known as American studies, the study of sentimental fiction has been extended into cognate forms, especially into nineteenth-century American sculpture; for example, such objects as Hiram Powers's *Greek Slave* are only ostensibly classically derivative and, like the sentimental tradition itself, have been too long dismissed as vapid. Instead, as Joy S. Kasson shows, such sculpture enacts the tensions and political divisions of its antebellum era, including slavery, feminism, class divisions, the developing capitalist and marketplace economics.

The sentimental, moreover, is not solely a category for the scrutiny of domesticity and evangelistic piety. For instance, scholarship involving the "hard facts" of American literary culture, including the rhetoric of extirpation of the Indians in James Fenimore Cooper's fiction, includes an extended discussion of Stowe's *Uncle Tom's Cabin* under the heading "The Sentimental Novel and Slavery" (P. Fisher 87–127). And the legacy of Hutchinson, the "prophetic woman," is shown to be the narrative paradigm splaying into the texts of Emerson, Hawthorne, and Stowe (Lang). Beyond the issue of the social construction of gender and text lies the related but separate matter of sexuality and its construction over time. The seemingly "exaggeratedly male" Walt Whitman proclaiming his virility and phallic power becomes, in recent analysis of his poetic persona, a figure who is alternately female and transsexual, just as Poe is reread as a writer whose heroes are androgynous, embodied pleas for the human wholeness that must encompass the male and the female (Gilbert; C. Jordan 133–51). American literary studies, long dominated by an overarching presumption of masculinity in its primary and critical texts, may well continue to elicit kindred studies of sexuality and gender like that on Whitman (and like those currently appearing on Hemingway).

Another recent direction in American literary study involves the role(s) of the reader in the formulation of the text. The process of interpretation in which readers are thought to construct a text has also come in for particular attention as reader-response theory is applied to American literary study that asks, What are the cultural or political shapings of reading and what a priori literary conventions affect interpretation and assessment? Answers to such inquiry reveal that the reception of texts differentiates according to national-cultural patterns. *Moby-Dick,* for instance, was received differently in England and the United States. The British, preoccupied with literary conventions, evaluated the novel according to prescriptive rules for fiction and found it wanting because it defied taxonomic convention; American reviewers, less constrained by normative rules, were less exasperated by Melville's mix of genres (Mailloux 169–78). And the reader-response theorist now takes us through a Hawthorne story like "Rappaccini's Daughter" to disclose the process of the time flow of reading, its constraints and liberations, while the scholar of African American literature finds this methodology to be particularly useful for texts in which "the distinctions between telling and writing on the one hand, and hearing and reading on the other, are far more profound than they usually are determined to be in those interpretive groupings constituted by other types of fictive narrative" (Mailloux 80–92; Stepto, "Distrust" 306).

Those students of American literature conversant largely (or solely) with the traditions of Western civilization, moreover, are increasingly impaired, as scholars of ethnic and racial literary traditions explore the intratextual functioning of cultural-rhetorical patterns indigenous to non-Western groups. As one states, "It is well worth it to interpret America not narrowly as immigration but more broadly as ethnic diversity and include the pre-Columbian inhabitants of the continent, the kidnapped Africans and their descendents, and the Chicanos of the Southwest" (Sollors, *Beyond Ethnicity* 8). (It would be interesting to hear the postwar critics reevaluate their major studies in this light, as Henry Nash Smith did, acknowledging that *Virgin Land* ignored the populations of indigenous groups on the North American continent, whose very existence gives an ironic dimension to the term *Virgin* [see "Symbol and Idea"].)

The civil rights movement of the 1960s gave impetus to the study of African American literature, beginning with the examination of figures and images of the black in the literature and culture of the United States (Yellin; Boskin) and proceeding with an analysis of the ways in which American literary history excluded African American texts from "traditional, orthodox patterns of a spiritually evolving American literature" (Baker, "Figurations" 149). Studies of canonical texts have disclosed their criticism of racism — for instance, Melville's *Benito Cereno,* the story of the suppression of a slave mutiny, has been the focus of scholarship revealing Melville's scathing cri-

tique of the paternalistic white male, a type prominent in antebellum political life of the North and South, and his prescience in blasting the plantation
myth as politically and psychologically repressive (Sundquist; Rogin 210–15).

More recently, African American literature has been subjected to theoretical analysis of its rhetorical structures (Gates, *Signifying Monkey*).
Generations of Western writers have exploited their literary innovations to
surpass or to destroy the work of their predecessors, this argument says, but
the African American tradition operates very differently and needs to be
understood in its development from the sophisticated folk cultures of Africa.
(According to one scholar, the marginalization of those traditions in the hegemonic development of the West via classical Greece and the Hebrews had
profoundest impact in nineteenth-century concepts of race and therefore has
special bearing on the period under discussion here; see Appiah, "Race.")
"Black people," then, have embraced "a system of rhetorical strategies peculiar to their own vernacular tradition," in which "the Signifyin(g) Monkey is
the figure of a black rhetoric in the Afro-American speech community," existing to "embody the figures of speech in the black vernacular," and as the principle of self-consciousness in that vernacular, becoming "the meta-figure
itself" (Gates 53). The African American text, moreover, is not fixed in a deter-
minate sense but works by indeterminacy and uncertainty, so that simultaneous plurality of meanings is possible: "The ironic reversal of a received racist
image of the black as simianlike, the Signifying Monkey, [is] he who dwells at
the margins of discourse, ever punning, ever troping, ever embodying the
ambiguities of language." In African American texts he becomes the "trope
for repetition and revision, indeed [the] trope of chiasmus, repeating and
reversing simultaneously as he does in one deft discursive act" (52). (The
opening of ethnically and racially diverse traditions continued and was accel-
erated by the Columbian quincentennial year, 1992, in which academic conferences and scholarly publications focused on earlier Caribbean American
literature and the literature of New World cross-cultural encounter. This work
departs from the perspectives of the Mexican historian Edmundo O'Gorman,
who emphasizes the "invention" of America, as well as from Tzvetan
Todorov's argument on the Western European "conquest" of Mexico.)

The kinds of scholarship discussed in this essay have not come to the fore
without a degree of resistance and hostility on the part of a generation of
Americanists educated in the New Criticism, well trained in bibliographic
and research methods and plying these skills to excellent results in the college
classroom, in journal articles, and in books. One can point, moreover, to the
continuation of exemplary scholarship of a traditional design in this poststructuralist moment — for instance, in studies of national character in
Hawthorne and Melville, of democratic ideals pursued in the praxis of rhetoric, of Cooper's politics or of Thoreau's classical influences, or of the relation
of popular historical romance to Hawthorne's fiction (McWilliams, *Political
Justice*; Dauber; Richardson; Bell).

The controversy over the newer methodologies, however, is essentially
one of epistemology and of its political orientation as a struggle for the con-

trol of meaning. Professional, collegial, and scholarly endeavor are all seen at this point as overtly political. Editorial succession — for instance, for the journal *American Literature* — becomes a matter not only of the maintenance of scholarly scrupulousness but of ideological positioning, as groups of researchers perceive their interests to be potentially furthered or frustrated by a likely appointee. Disagreement about the openness of the long-established "flagship" journal to newer viewpoints has had the market-economy effect of the formation of a new, competing periodical, *American Literary History,* which is explicitly hospitable to articles on "theoretical problems" (perhaps implying lack of receptivity to such work in other, established journals).

At this juncture, as groups of Americanist scholars contend for interpretive legitimation and critical assent, those cognizant of both the postwar and post-1960s scholarship can point out certain as-yet unresolved (and even unacknowledged) problems in criticism. This is to say that the practitioners of the newer critical approaches can find themselves unwittingly in a vexed relation to the scholarship of their predecessors, the very scholarship they are challenging. Suppose one were to read Leo Marx's *Machine in the Garden,* for instance, as a cold war fable on a pastoral America threatened with the nuclear invasion figured in the machine and therefore to historicize that text as a critical act of the nuclear age mentality. To do so would require the elucidation of the American literary pastoralism so closely defined in *The Machine in the Garden.* Thus one historicizes the very texts whose data and argumentative shape are necessary for the foundations of one's own argument. The risk is one of simultaneous exploitation and reification, the latter an act that contemporary scholarship deplores.

The community most receptive to the new historicism, moreover, awaits the cogent theoretics who would justify and guide its assimilative practices. If the new historicist faults the New Critic predecessor for explaining away the irreconcilable and the contradictory in the sacralizing name of paradox and irony, for example, then the new historicist must bring to visibility — and account for — those lines of cultural and literary contention that pose challenge to — even threaten to subvert the plausibility of — the new historicist's own disclosures. As it is, new historicism implies a territorial comprehensiveness that functions to exclude realms fraught with oppositional possibility.

Those trained in traditional methods, at the same time, must be aware that literary study cannot be unaffected by historical process, that every literary critic belongs to an incessantly changing intellectual-cultural world, that no position, argument, stance can be impervious to change, as those scholars currently historicizing the discipline of literary studies have so well revealed. New Criticism was certain to have a limited shelf life, but so will any other "ism," though it remains to be seen whether poststructuralists will be any more prepared for what succeeds them — perhaps some neocanonicalism marshaled in arguments as yet unforeseen as the category of the aesthetic begins to reinsinuate itself in literary study. Any examination of changing patterns in American literary study ought to take notice of scholarship reflecting on the history of the profession, including Giles Gunn's *Culture of*

Criticism and the Criticism of Culture, Jonathan Culler's "Literary Criticism and the American University," and Gerald Graff's *Professing Literature: An Institutional History.*

Those who may feel that the insurgence of newer approaches represents certain professional betrayal might, in fact, find it useful to survey the social construction of an anthropological text considered especially congenial to literary study. Clifford Geertz's "Deep Play: Notes on the Balinese Cockfight" has been taken up virtually as a fable for critics, appearing as it did at the point in the history of New Criticism at which every possible interpretation of any given canonical text seemed already to have been published, ultimately with diminishing returns, and few could conceive of the usefulness of yet another interpretive refinement of a Hawthorne tale or Thorovian essay — in sum, when younger scholars could but feel themselves relegated to roles of acolytes to the preceding generations, producing secondhand versions of the arguments of their own scholarly parents.

At that point, enter Bali, in Geertz's term "the well-studied place" whose mythology, art, ritual, social organization, law, and child-rearing practices had all been "microscopically" examined by the authoritative master scholars (Gregory Bateson and Margaret Mead) but that now could suddenly yield itself anew as a text. Long overlooked as mere cultural minutiae, the Balinese cockfight, the heretofore marginal text, discloses previously unnoticed dimensions of intrapsychic struggle, social status, hierarchy, morality. The authorities had somehow missed these important dimensions, just as the master scholars of American and other literatures had undertaken massive studies but somehow overlooked crucial heuristics that would reopen the texts especially to the researchers of the succeeding generation. Though Geertz has recently been attacked for splitting language from reality (Bercovitch and Jehlen 12–13), the motives for literary scholars' affinity with his work are self-evident. The lesson of the cockfight is that the imprint of august scholars need not deter one, that "exhaustive" or "microscopic" examinations are only spuriously so, that the seemingly marginal text can yield insights of central importance, that the canonical text holds surprises if only one knows how to look for them. The lesson is cyclical and applicable to American literary study.

SELECTED BIBLIOGRAPHY

Baym, Nina. "Early Histories of American Literature: A Chapter in the Institution of New England." *American Literary History* 1 (1989): 459–88.
———. *Novels, Readers, and Reviewers: Responses to Fiction in Antebellum America.* Ithaca: Cornell UP, 1984.
  Two titles that survey the range of antebellum fiction, its market and audiences, and historicize the literary hegemony of New England.
Bercovitch, Sacvan. *The American Jeremiad.* Madison: U of Wisconsin P, 1978. A literary theory of nationalism rooted in Puritan eschatology.
———, ed. *Reconstructing American Literary History.* Cambridge: Harvard UP, 1986.
  Revaluative essays on the early republican era through the mid-nineteenth century and beyond.
Bercovitch, Sacvan, and Myra Jehlen, eds. *Ideology and Classic American Literature.* New York: Columbia UP, 1986.

Language and politics of mid-nineteenth-century texts examined by diverse groups of scholars.

Breitwieser, Mitchell. *American Puritanism and the Defence of Mourning: Religion, Grief, and Ethnology in Mary White Rowlandson's Captivity Narrative*. Madison: U of Wisconsin P, 1990.
A new theory of New England Puritanism based on a heuristics of race, gender, and, implicitly, class.

Buell, Lawrence. *New England Literary Culture: From Revolution through Renaissance*. New York: Cambridge UP, 1986.
A reconceptualization of New England literature.

Davidson, Cathy N. *Revolution and the Word: The Rise of the Novel in America*. New York: Oxford UP, 1986.
A study of the rise of the novel and its relation to political life of the early Republic.

Dimock, Wai-chee. *Empire for Liberty: Melville and the Poetics of Individualism*. Princeton: Princeton UP, 1989.
A new-historicist consideration of the Melville oeuvre.

Gates, Henry Louis, Jr. *The Signifying Monkey: A Theory of African-American Literary Criticism*. New York: Oxford UP, 1988.
A theory of language and signification in African American literature.

Gilmore, Michael T. *American Romanticism and the Marketplace*. Chicago: U of Chicago P, 1985.
An analysis of the insurgence of industrial capitalism in mid-nineteenth-century America and the response of Emerson, Hawthorne, and Thoreau.

Jehlen, Myra. *American Incarnation: The Individual, the Nation, and the Continent*. Cambridge: Harvard UP, 1986.
On the European projection of an America extrinsic to historical processes and the literary result of that conception of a nation whose citizens are its incarnation.

Jordan, Cynthia. *Second Stories: The Politics of Language, Form, and Gender in Early American Fictions*. Chapel Hill: U of North Carolina P, 1989.
Two generations of patriarchal texts and the permutations of language of gender.

Kasson, Joy S. *Marble Queens and Captives: Women in Nineteenth-Century American Sculpture*. New Haven: Yale UP, 1990.
Cultural study of sculpture, contemporary medicine, feminism, and social practices in the arts.

Lang, Amy Schrager. *Prophetic Woman: Anne Hutchinson and the Problem of Dissent in the Literature of New England*. Berkeley: U of California P, 1987.
The culturally obsessive narrative of the seventeenth-century Puritan woman as it reemerges in Emerson, Hawthorne, Stowe.

Mailloux, Steven. *Interpretive Conventions: The Reader in the Study of American Fiction*. Ithaca: Cornell UP, 1982.
Reader-response theory in the interrogation of American texts.

Michaels, Walter Benn, and Donald E. Pease, eds. *The American Renaissance Reconsidered: Selected Papers from the English Institute, 1982–83*. Baltimore: Johns Hopkins UP, 1985.
Revaluation of canonical texts and arguments for the inclusion of popular, sentimental, and ethnic texts.

Reynolds, David S. *Beneath the American Renaissance: The Subversive Imagination in the Age of Emerson and Melville*. New York: Knopf, 1988.
The permeability of popular and canonical texts in antebellum America.

Rogin, Michael Paul. *Subversive Genealogy: The Politics and Art of Herman Melville*. Berkeley: U of California P, 1979.
A New-Historicist and psychoanalytical study of Melville and his culture.

Shulman, Robert. *Social Criticism and Nineteenth-Century American Fictions*. Columbia: U of Missouri P, 1987.
A discussion of the impact of capitalism on canonical texts of the American Renaissance.

Tompkins, Jane. *Sensational Designs: The Cultural Work of American Fiction, 1790–1860*. New York: Oxford UP, 1985.
Examines the social power of the sentimental and the social construction of literary careers, principally that of Hawthorne.

Warren, Joyce W. *The American Narcissus: Individualism and Women in Nineteenth-Century American Fiction*. 1984. New Brunswick: Rutgers UP, 1989.
Argues that male narcissism in the guise of individualism precluded the participation of women in canonical texts.

WORKS CITED

Appiah, Kwame Anthony. "Race." *Critical Terms for Literary Study.* Ed. Frank Lentricchia and Thomas McLaughlin. Chicago: U of Chicago P, 1990. 274–87.
Arac, Jonathan. "F. O. Matthiessen: Authorizing an American Renaissance." Michaels and Pease 90–112.
Baker, Houston, Jr. "Figurations for a New American Literary History." Bercovitch and Jehlen 145–71.
Barthes, Roland. "The Death of the Author." *Image-Music-Text.* Trans. Stephen Heath. New York: Hill, 1977. 142–48.
Baym, Nina. *Women's Fiction: A Guide to Novels by and about Women in America, 1820–1870.* Ithaca: Cornell UP, 1978.
Bell, Michael Davitt. *The Development of American Romance: The Sacrifice of Relation.* Chicago: U of Chicago P, 1986.
Bellah, Robert N., Richard Madsen, William M. Sullivan, Ann Swidler, and Steven M. Tipton. *Habits of the Heart: Individualism and Commitment in American Life.* 1985. New York: Harper, 1986.
Bercovitch, Sacvan. "Horologicals to Chronometricals: The Rhetoric of the Jeremiad." *Literary Monographs.* Vol. 3. Ed. Eric Rothstein. Madison: U of Wisconsin P, 1970. 1–124.
———. *Puritan Origins of the American Self.* New Haven: Yale UP, 1975.
Boskin, Joseph. *Sambo: The Rise and Demise of an American Jester.* New York: Oxford UP, 1986.
Bradley, Scully, Richard Croom Beatty, and E. Hudson Long, eds. *The American Tradition in Literature.* 3rd ed. New York: Norton, 1967.
Cain, William E. *F. O. Matthiessen and the Politics of Criticism.* Madison: U of Wisconsin P, 1988.
Canup, John. *Out of the Wilderness: The Emergence of an American Identity in Colonial New England.* Middletown: Wesleyan UP, 1990.
Chase, Richard Volney. *The American Novel and Its Tradition.* Garden City: Doubleday, 1957.
Culler, Jonathan. "Literary Criticism and the American University." *Framing the Sign: Criticism and Its Institutions.* Norman: U of Oklahoma P, 1988. 3–40.
Dauber, Kenneth. *The Idea of Authorship in America.* Madison: U of Wisconsin P, 1990.
Davis, Richard Beale. *Intellectual Life in the Colonial South, 1585–1763.* 3 vols. Knoxville: U of Tennessee P, 1978.
Delbanco, Andrew. *The Puritan Ordeal.* Cambridge: Harvard UP, 1989.
Douglas, Ann. *The Feminization of American Culture.* New York: Knopf, 1977.
Elliot, Emory, ed. *The Columbia Literary History of the United States.* New York: Columbia UP, 1986.
Feidelson, Charles, Jr. *Symbolism and American Literature.* Chicago: U of Chicago P, 1953.
Ferguson, Robert A. *Law and Letters in American Culture.* Cambridge: Harvard UP, 1984.
Fisher, Philip. *Hard Facts: Setting and Form in the American Novel.* New York: Oxford UP, 1987.
Fliegelman, Jay. *Prodigals and Pilgrims: The American Revolution against Patriarchal Authority, 1750–1800.* New York: Cambridge UP, 1982.
Foucault, Michel. "What Is an Author?" Trans. Josué V. Harari. *Foucault Reader.* Ed. Paul Rabinow. New York: Pantheon, 1979. 101–20.
Geertz, Clifford. "Deep Play: Notes on the Balinese Cockfight." *Interpretation* 412–53.
Gilbert, Sandra M. "The American Sexual Poetics of Walt Whitman and Emily Dickinson." Bercovitch, *Reconstructing* 123–54.
Graff, Gerald. *Professing Literature: An Institutional History.* Chicago: U of Chicago P, 1987.
———. "The Promise of American Literature Studies." *Professing* 209–25.
Gunn, Giles. *The Culture of Criticism and the Criticism of Culture.* New York: Oxford UP, 1987.
———. *F. O. Matthiessen: The Critical Achievement.* Seattle: U of Washington P, 1975.
———. "The Kingdoms of Theory and the New Historicism in America." *Yale Review* 76 (1987): 207–36.
Gura, Philip F. *A Glimpse of Sion's Glory: Puritan Radicalism in New England, 1620–1660.* Middletown: Wesleyan UP, 1984.
Herbert, T. Walter, Jr. "Nathaniel Hawthorne, Una Hawthorne, and *The Scarlet Letter:* Interactive Selfhoods and the Cultural Construction of Gender." *PMLA* 103 (1988): 285–95.
Hoffman, Daniel. *Form and Fable in American Fiction.* 1961. New York: Oxford UP, 1965.
Howard, Leon. *The Connecticut Wits.* Chicago: U of Chicago P, 1943.
———. *Literature and the American Tradition.* Garden City: Doubleday, 1960.
Kerber, Linda. *Federalists in Dissent: Imagery and Ideology in Jeffersonian America.* Ithaca: Cornell UP, 1970.

Kibbey, Ann. *The Interpretation of Material Shapes in Puritanism: A Study of Rhetoric, Prejudice, and Violence.* New York: Cambridge UP, 1986.

Kolodny, Annette. *The Lay of the Land: Metaphor and Experience in American Life and Letters.* Chapel Hill: U of North Carolina P, 1975.

Lang, Amy Schrager. "Introduction to *The Captivity and Restoration of Mrs. Mary Rowlandson.*" *Journeys in New Worlds: Early American Women's Narratives.* Ed. Daniel B. Shea. Madison: U of Wisconsin P, 1990. 13–26.

Lauter, Paul, et al., eds. *The Heath Anthology of American Literature.* Lexington: Heath, 1990.

Lewis, R. W. B. *The American Adam: Innocence, Tragedy, and Tradition in the Nineteenth Century.* Chicago: U of Chicago P, 1955.

Marr, David. *American Worlds since Emerson.* Amherst: U of Massachusetts P, 1987.

Martin, Wendy. *An American Triptych: Anne Bradstreet, Emily Dickinson, Adrienne Rich.* Chapel Hill: U of North Carolina P, 1984.

Marx, Leo. *The Machine in the Garden: Technology and the Pastoral Ideal in America.* New York: Oxford UP, 1964.

Matthiessen, F. O. *American Renaissance: Art and Expression in the Age of Emerson and Whitman.* New York: Oxford UP, 1941.

McQuade, Donald, et al., eds. *The Harper American Literature.* New York: Harper, 1986.

McWilliams, John P. *Political Justice in a Republic.* Berkeley: U of California P, 1972.

Middlekauff, Robert. *The Mathers: Three Generations of Puritan Intellectuals, 1596–1728.* New York: Oxford UP, 1971.

Miller, Perry. *Errand into the Wilderness.* Cambridge: Harvard UP, 1956.

———. *The New England Mind.* 2 vols. Vol. 1: *The Seventeenth Century.* 1936. Vol. 2: *From Colony to Province.* 1953. Boston: Beacon, 1953.

O'Gorman, Edmundo. *The Invention of America: An Inquiry into the Historical Nature of the New World and the Meaning of Its History.* Westport: Greenwood, 1972.

Pease, Donald E. *Visionary Compacts: American Renaissance Writings in Cultural Context.* Madison: U of Wisconsin Press, 1987.

Porte, Joel, ed. *Emerson: Prospect and Retrospect.* Harvard English Studies 10. Cambridge: Harvard UP, 1982.

Porter, Carolyn. "Reification and American Literature." Bercovitch and Jehlen 188–217.

———. *Seeing and Being: The Plight of the Participant Observer in Emerson, James, Adams, and Faulkner.* Middletown: Wesleyan UP, 1981.

Richardson, Robert D. *Henry Thoreau: A Life of the Mind.* Berkeley: U of California P, 1986.

Simpson, Lewis P. *The Dispossessed Garden: Pastoral and History in Southern Literature.* Athens: U of Georgia P, 1975.

Slotkin, Richard. *Regeneration through Violence: The Mythology of the American Frontier.* Middletown: Wesleyan UP, 1973.

Smith, Henry Nash. "Symbol and Idea in *Virgin Land.*" Bercovitch and Jehlen 21–35.

———. *Virgin Land: The American West as Symbol and Myth.* Cambridge: Harvard UP, 1950.

Sollors, Werner. *Beyond Ethnicity: Consent and Descent in American Culture.* New York: Oxford UP, 1986.

Spiller, Robert, et al. *Literary History of the United States.* 1949. New York: Macmillan, 1953.

Stepto, Robert. "Distrust of the Reader in Afro-American Narratives." Bercovitch, *Reconstructing* 300–22.

Sundquist, Eric J. "*Benito Cereno* and New World Slavery." Bercovitch, *Reconstructing* 93–122.

Tichi, Cecelia. *New World, New Earth: Environmental Reform in American Literature from the Puritans through Whitman.* New Haven: Yale UP, 1979.

Veeser, H. Aram, ed. *The New Historicism.* New York: Routledge, 1989.

Weber, Donald. "Historicizing the Errand." *American Literary History* 2 (1990): 101–18.

Wood, Gordon S. "Struggle over the Puritans." *New York Review of Books* 9 Nov. 1989: 26+.

Yellin, Jean Fagan. *The Intricate Knot: Black Figures in American Literature, 1776–1863.* New York: New York UP, 1972.

American Literary and Cultural Studies since the Civil War

PHILIP FISHER

Fisher's essay is framed by recent changes in the field of American studies. In addressing the critical shifts within American studies, Fisher conceives of the new generation as moving from myth, *a singular, static story, to* rhetorics, *a plural, dynamic view of culture. Fisher begins by discussing of the development of American studies and its myth of American national identity. Despite the determination of Americanists to identify a grand unifying myth, reality fails to live up to the imagined, complicated by the pluralistic aspect of American culture. According to Fisher, diversity resists being subsumed by myth and thus often creates what he terms "episodes of regionalism in American cultural history" (p. 35). These regionalisms include geography, ethnicity, race, gender, and sexuality. Fisher describes American culture as a pendulum swinging between regionalisms and unifying projects.*

According to Fisher, the new American studies provides an alternative to regionalism by identifying a set of national facts, such as democratic culture and the culture of freedom, around which identities are formed. This allows for analysis within American studies to focus on sectors of a diverse culture rather than on a monopoly of power, recognizing rhetorics rather than ideology. Fisher's essay originally appeared as an introduction to his The New American Studies *(1991). The version here was adapted for inclusion in the collection* Redrawing the Boundaries *(1992), edited by Stephen Greenblatt and Giles Gunn.*

FROM MYTH TO RHETORICS

The essential books of the last fifteen years in the literary and cultural study of American life represent the work of a new generation within American studies, and they represent, at the same time, a new idea of what it might mean to do American studies and how one would go about doing it. In combination they also represent the rich diversity of explanations and materials

From *Redrawing the Boundaries: The Transformation of English and American Literary Studies,* ed. Stephen Greenblatt and Giles Gunn (New York: MLA, 1992) 232–50.

in the study of American culture. Films and photographs, Supreme Court decisions and industrial manuals, educational and domestic theory, the popular culture of Horatio Alger and the standard genres of domestic fiction: a culture in its full institutional and individual variety has been brought into play.

One way to characterize this newness would be to say that, in this generation of American studies, interest has passed from myth to rhetorics. *Myth* in this perhaps too simple formula is always singular, *rhetorics* always plural. Myth is a fixed, satisfying, and stable story that is used again and again to normalize our account of social life. By means of myth, novelty is tamed by being seen as the repetition or, at most, the variation of a known and valued pattern. Even where actual historical situations are found to fall short of myth or to lie in its aftermath, the myth tames the variety of historical experience, giving it familiarity while using it to reaffirm the culture's long-standing interpretation of itself.

Rhetoric, in contrast, is a tactic within the open questions of culture. It reveals interests and exclusions. To look at rhetorics is to look at the action potential of language and images, not just their power or contrivance to move an audience but the location of words, formulas, images, and units of meaning within politics. Rhetoric is the place where language is engaged in cultural work, and such work can be done on, with, or in spite of one or another group within society. Rhetorics are plural because they are part of what is uncertain or potential within culture. They are the servants of one or another politics of experience. Where there is nothing openly contested, no cultural work to be done, we do not find the simplification into one and only one rhetoric. Instead we find the absence of the particular inflammation and repetition that rhetoric always marks. We find no rhetoric at all, only the ceremonial contentment of myth. Rhetorics are also distinct from ideology. Within the term *ideology* we are right to hear a combination of calculation, cynicism about social truth, a schoolteacher's relation to the pupils, indoctrination, and propaganda. Whether as reality or hope, ideology implies that one part of the legitimacy of authority is a monopoly on representation, and this is exactly the condition in which rhetorics become irrelevant.

To understand what a move from myth to rhetorics might involve, it is useful to look at two things: first, how the claim of a unitary myth worked and was used during the period that we might call the transfer of literature to the American university; second, the counterelement to central myths within American studies — the force of regionalism.

MYTHS AND THE UNIVERSITY

The new field of American studies came to maturity in the years just before and after the Second World War. Its description of American experience had as its audience both Americans themselves and, even more important, a wider world in which American culture had begun to work as a kind of world culture. Both Europeans and Americans were asked to consider in mythic terms a prior state of American experience, one whose essence and importance lay in the fact that it no longer existed but had generated the cultural heart of American experience. But to this prior culture of Puritan mission, frontier, wilderness, garden, and innocence, contemporary Americans were just as much outsiders as Europeans and Asians were.

In this charged pre- and postwar atmosphere of cultural victory and cultural defeat, Americanists undertook the search for a central myth of America. Such key works as Henry Nash Smith's *Virgin Land,* Leo Marx's *Machine in the Garden,* R. W. B. Lewis's *American Adam,* and Richard Slotkin's *Regeneration through Violence* encouraged a study of literature, everyday culture, and history around a shared mythic content that captured American uniqueness and national identity. American studies as an academic field in its first generation took this myth of America to be its central topic and its method for linking the classics of American poetry, fiction, and painting to the culture of images, newspapers, sermons, political rhetoric, and, especially, popular fiction and verse. Here the western and the sermon met.

The first of these all-encompassing myths of America had, in fact, been defined half a century earlier. This was the frontier myth of Frederick Jackson Turner, a hypothesis as Turner called it, but ultimately a story rather than a scientific speculation, and a story whose appeal lay in the curious fact that it described just those social features that had been lost forever in the formal official closing of the American frontier noted in the census of 1890. Although Turner's great myth appeared before what we might call the capture of American culture by the universities, an event that took place in the 1930s and 1940s, his strategy of discovering one fundamental fact or myth that explained the identity of America as a nation set the stage for the mythic cast of the first generation of the academic study of American culture. After the frontier myth, the most important global explanation lay in the myth of the Puritans, their mission, the unique significance of intellectuals and ideology within the Puritan experience, the primacy of New England's religious forms for American political experience, and the residue of Puritan energy, now changed to commerce and self-cultivation, that remained as a permanent trace within the national character. If the frontier myth was a myth of the West, the Puritan myth was a myth of New England culture, asserting its right to a permanent steering function in national life. Where the western myth was democratic, based on the experience of immigration and self-reliance, the New England myth was ultimately a myth of the importance of intellectuals and, with them, of the crucial role played by writing and those who provide ideology, self-description, and history — the importance, finally, of preachers and their later descendants, the intellectuals of the nineteenth century and the university professors of the twentieth.

In spite of the built-in resistance of our literature and its awkward wildness, no cultural fact is more decisive over the past fifty years than the wholesale movement of every component of our literary life, past, present, and future, into the universities. American studies and American literature have everywhere arrived at legitimacy. American poets have been signed up as writers-in-residence. Our men and women of letters, following Philip Rahv and Irving Howe, have become professors, trading in their general audience of educated adults for a classroom full of students eighteen to twenty-five years old, and a secondary audience of their professional colleagues who have now become the main readers of their opinions. Our little magazines are now subsidized by colleges, where they too are now in residence, and they find their primary guaranteed sales to the periodical rooms of university libraries. The paperback revolution of the 1950s and 1960s that promised at first to democratize our culture by making inexpensive editions widely available, has ended up filling our bookstores with texts instead of books, texts designed for adoption as required reading in courses.

The high-level professional work on the new subject of American literature has been shaped to a remarkable degree by the residence of culture within the academic world. The university and the professor think, as they must, in terms of courses — that is, in terms of a coherent set of books or themes that fit into the fifteen-week semester. Such distinguished critical studies as F. O. Matthiessen's *American Renaissance,* Marx's *Machine in the Garden,* or Smith's *Virgin Land* represent our past as a set of model courses. The great interest in myths of the frontier, the machine, the Puritan errand into the wilderness (see P. Miller, *Errand*), American violence, or American individualism served to give shape to the academic year in an ordered, consecutive, schematic way with developments and oppositions. The problem of the American romance, as opposed to the novel, or the description of so arbitrary a period of our history as what is known as the Gilded Age, redesigned the past to fit the intellectual needs and temporal rhythms of the newly professionalized study of the past.

The most common thread of the first generation of the study of America has been what could be called the disappointment of myth by fact, the failure of reality to live up to the ways in which it has been imagined. America is first mythologized as the second Eden, its purpose linked to the Puritan mission, or pictured as a frontier or free space for the unbounded individual, but then, in each case, the myth is betrayed by fact. The promise is unkept. As the purity of what was imagined grew stained over time, American reality, by means of the apparatus of myth, took on the look of a fallen state. The frontier had been closed. The high moral purpose of the Puritans had given way to commerce and commercial purpose. The innocence had blood on its hands. What was there had the look of heavily discounted possibility; what might have been had been disappointed in the act of making. Significantly, one of the master texts of a whole generation of American study was Henry James's *The Ambassadors,* perhaps from an academic point of view the most perfect book ever written by an American. James's hero Strether creates a myth of Paris, a myth of his charge, Chad, a myth of Chad's relation to Mme. de Vionnet. Each myth is betrayed by fact, stained by the complexity of the real world. An entire academic generation saw its own love of criticism, observation, nuance, disappointment, myth, and defeat in James's novel.

As the great academic popularity of James's novel made clear, if there has been one history lovingly traced by intellectuals over the past fifty years, it has been the history of intellectuals themselves. From the work of Perry Miller in the late 1930s, the explanation of America as a long history of Puritan hope and decline resulted from the fact that, looking into the past to find not necessarily its chief actors but precisely those congenial figures whose analytic and critical stance most resembled their own, the academic intellectuals discovered in Puritan writing what was for them the most intelligible feature of the past, the one mirror most filled with familiar features. The Puritans too were intellectuals, engaged in holding up a mirror of admonition or exhortation to their society. In theocratic New England they embodied one of the most secret self-images of all intellectual cultures, a world in which the critics and intellectuals of society were not marginal but actually in power.

The Puritan intellectuals had their successors in the radical critics of society from the mid-nineteenth century to the 1950s and 1960s. Utopian intellectuals of the left in the 1930s found in the radical Puritans of three hundred years earlier their own model for the role and hoped-for importance of the intellectual within politics and society. However marginal intellectuals have been actually within American culture, the study of America has reclaimed them.

Useful as the history of intellectuals as written by their own aspiring descendants might be, it amounts only to a rather timid look into the most friendly and probably most unrepresentative district of the American past. The actors in exploration and settlement, in enterprise and invention, in the making of cities and the long history of money and speculation in America, in the tangled history of black and white, Native American and settler, political and personal rebellion, have been the primary characters of the American story, even if, unlike the intellectuals, they have seldom been their own best historians.

Myth creates a fault line between what ought to have taken place and what did. It permits ideas and facts to criticize each other. Like the rebellion of an individual or like the more collective movements of reform, myths embody what Henry Adams in his *Education* called the "spirit of resistance." The search for central myths — myths that were already closed off, as the frontier was at the moment of its first description as the most vital experience for the foundation of an American identity — was inseparable from the study of resistance within culture, whether in the Gothic style of *Pierre* or in the reflective émigré style of *The Ambassadors* or the self-ironic Adams of *Education*. The appetite for resistance led Lionel Trilling to propose that all culture in the modern period was basically adversarial, at war with the commonplace or everyday social energies and beliefs. In European society of the nineteenth century, this adversarial position reflected the failure of self-belief in the emerging middle classes that had at last arrived at political and cultural power equivalent to their economic importance. But in the United States the source was quite different. It lay in a utopian or even moral radicalism combined with or concealing the resentment of artists and intellectuals at their rather small voice in a national life dominated by business and politics.

The belief in spiritual radicalism led to a focus on those writers, like Melville, who said their "No! In thunder." Such oppositional figures as the hero of Melville's *Pierre* or of "Bartleby the Scrivener" or, in real life, Thoreau defiant of Concord and moving two miles away to Walden Pond or spending a night in jail, Henry James withdrawn to England because American reality was not thick enough, the protagonist of *The Scarlet Letter* stubborn and free: These defiant, adversarial figures, along with the challenging distance they created in standing out by standing against their world, are what the study of the tension between fact and all that resisted fact brought to the center. Within American studies the study of America had become the study of dissent. The rebels and dissidents came to the front as the leading patriots. It was the era of Thoreau, Henry Adams, and Bartleby, not of Emerson and Whitman.

By an accident of timing, American literature arrived in the university at a highly politicized moment. Its arrival coincided with the polarization between right and left or, in European terms, between fascism and communism in the period between the two world wars. The study of resistance was attractive, in part, because both the conservative right and the liberal left had rejected one key feature of what had been a synthesis in the most vital parts of nineteenth-century American culture. The right was hostile to democracy; the left to capitalism. They shared a distrust of the optimism, energy, confidence, and what might be called the surprisingly guiltless relation that figures like Emerson, Whitman, James Fenimore Cooper, or Francis Parkman had had to their own past. The lack of apology or contrition, the robust feeling of the right to be where and as they were in spite of slavery, Indian massacres, the failures of national politics to be dignified or even honest, the violence of the West, the polyglot hustle of the new cities — such guiltless self-regard seemed shallow to a left and to a right equally convinced, from different sides, of the nightmare of history. A whole new meaning of the term *innocence* had to be invented to make it seem that only some youthful unawareness of evil could explain the pride or health of Twain, Whitman, William James, or Emerson. That the greatest figures of our literature were not oppositional figures seemed almost beyond belief. But it was a fact. There is no margin of frictional energy that accounts for Emily Dickinson or Theodore Dreiser or William Faulkner. Whitman and Emerson continue to embarrass by their failure to have seen through democracy and capitalism or, rather, by their having imagined themselves to have seen into the philosophic and temperamental depths of those two systems and to have found them both profound and humane, exhilarating and enduring.

One key to the new ground claimed by critical work of the last few years has been the implicit rejection of this heroism of oppositional dissent and its replacement by collaborative and implicational relations between writer or speaker and culture. Emerson, Harriet Beecher Stowe, Twain, and William James are the masters of this new relation, not Melville and Thoreau. Richard Poirier's books on the tactics of Robert Frost within language (*Robert Frost: The Work of Knowing*) and the cultural meaning of Emerson (*The Renewal of Literature*) set out important accounts of the rich entanglement of writer and culture. In Poirier's account, the work always lives off and lives through the spaces open within the language and especially within the plural languages of culture.

The pressures of cultural life are plural and not a single hegemonic ideology that must be resisted, subverted, or surrendered to. Cultural life, in this formulation, is open to the activity of rebalancing and reconstruction that the literary work makes possible. Poirier's is an aesthetics of survival that represents at the same time a confident aesthetics of pleasure within the forces of culture and the possibility of mastery over them, what we might call the outwitting of the up-to-then apparently dead ends of language and feeling, the traps of rhetoric and commitment. In this respect, his work is remarkably similar to the claims of the major book within African American theory, *The Signifying Monkey*, by Henry Louis Gates Jr. For Gates, signifying is a way of taking over cultural formulas, living off and living within whatever is given because whatever is given can always be topped, reformulated, bent to build in whatever it was designed to place or to place out. In his theory of culture, the trickster once again displaces the victim as the essential subjectivity and actor within the cultural script. One major weakness of the theory of ideology and myth has always been its specification of subjectivity as either that of power, victim, or coopted dupe. What Gates celebrates in the trickster, Poirier had earlier called the "performing self," and the great model of this performance might be sketched out by combining the moves of Huck Finn and Whitman with those of Emerson and Frost. These tactics of freedom in the face of the givenness of reality are normative for Emersonian artists in the face of an already given set of forms, for adolescents discovering and differentiating themselves within a world of parents and parental society, and for African American culture and its practices within and yet above the surrounding culture into which they have been thrown.

A simple catalog of moves within collaboration would include boasts, lies, tricks, exaggeration, the mastery of language, even an entrepreneurial relation to language, the play with masks and roles, the caginess of Frost and Emerson, the folksy and the elusive. All are wrapped together as elements of a heightened self-consciousness and strategic style of thinking. They define the cultural location where the signifying monkey meets the performing self, when the ambiguity of Hawthorne and the glib half-serious language of Twain meet the canniness of Frost and the daring extravagance of Emerson's and Whitman's verbal bravado. Gates and Poirier have returned the study of moves within culture — the moves of the trickster — to their real importance over against the "No! In thunder" of opposition and the sentimental pathos of the many narratives of victims crushed by all-pervading scripts of power.

Sacvan Bercovitch's study of Hawthorne and what Bercovitch calls the "a-morality of compromise" interrogates and deflates the rhetoric of oppositional purity in favor of a remarkable and nuanced idea of politics, a term of extraordinary importance as an alternative to the purity of cultural dissent and protest. Politics and, along with it, the pragmatics of action and compromise within a given temporal horizon and in the face of specific counterforces that cannot be defeated but must be enlisted in a joint project define the essence of a stance beyond the merely gestural "No! In thunder" but equally beyond the various forms of radical purity — the expatriation of Henry James, the internal expatriation of Thoreau at Walden, the aloof aristocratic unemployment of Henry Adams, the utopian posture of Thoreau or the history of intellectual socialism and communism in the hundred years between the fall of the Paris Commune in 1870 and the collapse of that utopia in the face of the crisis in real-existing socialism at the end of the 1980s.

Like the texts by Poirier, Gates, and Bercovitch, but from an entirely different direction, Walter Benn Michaels's book on naturalism and the 1890s — *The Gold Standard and the Logic of Naturalism* — has demolished the oppositional simplicity in what had seemed the easiest period to locate the author automatically outside and over against the culture of capitalism. In my own book *Hard Facts*, the nineteenth-century models of cultural work are deliberately taken to be different from and more varied than the work of protest and negation or its opposite, pious complicity and conscious or unconscious propagation of a single leading ideology. In its literature a culture practices and memorizes its own self-relation, only one part of which involves its relation to what it takes to be its past, to what circumference of action and choice it holds itself accountable for in the present, and what future it takes to be its promise to itself, as opposed to the merely abstract or utopian bad infinity of possibilities. Cultural work is pragmatic, not Hegelian. Its plural objects are local, open matters, necessary cases, hard facts. One measure of cultural work is not realism but a certain decay within realism that announces that some local fact of culture has been altered or restabilized so that the work now done has made the earlier representation obsolete — that is, no longer realistic. For later periods the effectiveness of that work can be felt in what now seems like excess or exaggerated emphasis — what we sweep to the side as genre. What feels sentimental, in the bad meaning of the term, in Stowe or Wordsworth, Dickens or Dostoevsky, is exactly the marker of suffering now casually within the field of vision that once had to be forced into representation. What is now noticed as shrill in Whitman — once the work of Whitman to center the sexual and democratic self has succeeded — becomes obsolete, part of the genre or category of the egotistical sublime, the excess of Romanticism, the emotional fraud of mid-nineteenth-century boosterism, whether for land schemes, political candidates, or, in Whitman's case, self-description and construction of the role and stance of the democratic poet.

Cultural work is one concept of a cultural pragmatism, a concern with the effective strategies of culture that includes, at the level of individual psychology, such strategies as performing and signifying. Poirier's Emerson, in *The Renewal of Literature,* is a model of the tough-minded intellectual within American culture. One part of his model is that bravery of fools that Emerson shared with Whitman and Twain. Bercovitch's Hawthorne, with the notion of politics and the intriguing morality of compromise, is a second, equally important cultural model. Both are elements of the major recuperation of American philosophical pragmatism that has been a significant project of the new collaboration between American philosophy and American literary studies in the 1970s and 1980s.

The worldliness and local field of vision of pragmatism has always existed as the rough alternative both to dissent and to the spiritual purity of transcendentalism, utopianism, and Puritanism — those three overlapping radical energies within our culture. In the books of Stanley Cavell and Richard Rorty, the philosophical and literary tradition of American pragmatism has been returned to central interest in our cultural life. The easy combination of the literary and the philosophical is only one of the novelties of this recent examination of pragmatism. The contingency, irony, and solidarity that Rorty has brought together as key terms in one of his titles define a posture of liberal generosity and a dismissal of the vehemence and refusal of solidarity with one's own culture that are the classic tonal pitch of self-appointed radicalism. That Emerson and William James stand also for a genuinely popular and culturally central relation of the intellectual to society is no small part of their value and interest. They are, we might say, anti-Nietzschean models of the intellectual.

Cavell, Rorty, and Poirier have laid the basis in recent books for a profound and profoundly impure — that is, contingent and political — tradition of American intellectual culture. At the same time it is notable that Cavell and Poirier have created analyses of culture that broke the barrier between high culture and the innovative commercial and popular culture of our own time. Cavell has brought both philosophy and Hollywood into the register of literary vision. His work on film, especially on the Hollywood comedies of marriage and remarriage — *Pursuits of Happiness* — has set a new configuration in place of the older-style American studies negotiation between "major authors" and the "wider culture." Poirier's *The Performing Self* did similar decisive work in building analytic paths into the complex languages of popular music, political writing, and such authors as Frost and Norman Mailer. Gates's *The Signifying Monkey* is the key recent revision of our description of the text culture in its links to the strategies and range of everyday oral and written performance. An encyclopedic summary of what used to be called "our classic authors" in terms of this wider culture of possibilities was achieved by David Reynolds in his book *Beneath the American Renaissance.*

REGIONALISM AND CENTRAL CULTURE

Alongside the search for grand unifying myths, with their inevitable narrative of a fall into imperfection and disappointment, a second element shared the stage within American studies between the 1930s and the 1970s — the claim of pluralism within American culture. This diversity, which resists the single shelter of myth or ideology, has again and again risen to dominance in what we might call the episodes of regionalism in American cultural history.

Cultural life in American swings like a pendulum between a diversity of sectional voices and an ever-new project of unity, between the representation of the nation as made up of weakly joined districts and the depiction of a central national order. A hundred and fifty years ago our then strongly sectional culture was split along geographical lines: the New England mind, the southern way of life, the West of the pioneers, with their energy and violence. Each section had its own voices and themes, its own philosophies and religions, its unique spirit and humor. A common identity was rebuilt out of these regionalisms by the Civil War, by the mythic figure of Lincoln, by the railroads and telegraph, which conquered a geography grown too large for the earlier Federalist unity of Washington and Jefferson, and by the elaboration of an American way of life made up of Singer sewing machines, Coca-Cola, Remington rifles, and Ford Model T's — a way of life created around democratically available mass-produced goods rather than by the right to vote or to own property.

Each swing to regionalism has split the country along different fault lines, and each rewon unity involves not a return to a lost identity but a new plane of association. In early twentieth-century America a regionalism that was not geographic but ethnic appeared as a result of the massive immigration that had taken place between 1870 and 1914. The local color was not that of climates and regions but of what are called, metaphorically, hyphenated Americans: Jewish Americans, Italian Americans, Irish Americans, Wasps and Chinese Americans, Poles, Swedes, and Russians. It was a regionalism of languages, folk customs, humor, music, and beliefs set over against the pull of what came to be called Americanization.

In the case of ethnic regionalism it was not the railroads and the everyday objects of a thriving economy that created the unifying force, as they had done earlier. To this regionalism was opposed the core culture of public education and the pull of economic advancement, always purchased at the price of a surrendered culture, most obviously by the requirement within the schools and business world of the English language. A third unifying force was mobility itself. Only if immigrants remained in a ghetto, the ghetto of arrival, could the coherence of language, way of life, religion, and, most important, marriage within the ethnic group be preserved. To move even once was to enter the general American condition. And the two world wars and the democratic experience of the army worked, as the Civil War and the Revolutionary War had earlier, to fuse an identity that superseded the ethnic diversity of the late nineteenth and early twentieth centuries. Thus the pots in which the melting actually occurred were the schoolroom, the offices of the business world, the new suburbs out beyond the territorial inner city, and, finally, the fields of battle. Unity within American culture has always been a postwar unity, whether Federalist, after the Revolution, capitalist, after the Civil War, or contemporary American, after, and resulting from, the two world wars.

In recent years a further episode of regionalism, neither geographical nor ethnic, has begun. The regionalism of our own times, which comes on the heels of the generation that elaborated the myth of America within the shadow and aftermath of World War II, is one of gender and race. The civil rights movement after 1954 had, as its cultural side, the debate over black identity in America. The women's movement that followed, just as the nineteenth-century suffrage movement had followed and drawn its vocabulary from the abolitionist movement against slavery, set the model for the denial of what came to be called *essentialism*, the claim to an overriding common human identity. Later gay and lesbian movements, as well as ethnic identities that were now conceived not along the model of the earlier hyphenated identities but along the more radical model of black or female identity, reopened the full spectrum of regionalized culture. Native American, Chicano, gay, black, lesbian, female: Once again, an episode of regionalism set out its claims against, in this case, a central technological culture made up of the new media — television and film — but also against the older forces of education and mass representation. The model that black or female identity set in place for regionalism was refractory in a novel way because these regional — as opposed to universal — models for identity were the first within American experience that neither mobility nor the succession of generations would alter. Earlier geographic or ethnic identities had been episodic in that the mechanisms of the culture itself would erase them over time. California, with its new "identity," was obviously composed of people who had shed — by means of the simple act of driving across the country and choosing to settle there — their prior New England, midwestern, southern, or western identities. Jewish Americans who moved to the suburbs of New York City and watched their children marry Italian Americans, German Americans, or Wasps may have seen the fading and erasure of these regionalisms in the lives of the grandchildren who went off to school in Chicago or Los Angeles. Earlier American regionalisms had been temporary and easily bargained away once the alternatives were attractive enough. The weak hold of geography could be seen in the all-purpose category "Sun Belt," which encompassed not only the states from Florida through Texas to Southern California but also, in the case of Florida, the new security of retirement and the simple desire for a warm and convenient climate that would lead Americans to desert and shed their regional identities, homes, and friends, even late in life for a carefully calculated new start. By contrast, to be black or female was an unnegotiable identity, one that could not be dissolved by those American master plots: education, intermarriage, mobility. Insofar as other groups, including ethnic groups, took over the black model, they chose to see their own regional identity as final and began to argue for their own language, education, and culture.

    In American universities the departments of American studies, established in the 1930s, 1940s, and 1950s, found themselves in the 1960s and 1970s quickly regionalized into departments of black or African American studies, Jewish studies, women's studies, Native American studies, Chicano and Asian American studies, and, in some cases, gay studies. One consequence of these new identity claims was what the proponents viewed as an aggressive unmasking of the myths of the previous generation, among other things a series of overwhelmingly white male myths of America. The pastoral, the western, the Puritan mission, the frontier experience of individualism, self-reliance, and democratic values: all had, at their center, white male actors with various supporting casts. The self-appointed task of unmasking hegemony, essentialism, and the many disguised operations of power within the culture has defined what could be called the *fundamentalism* of this third and most recent swing of regionalism. We have lived for twenty years within a scholarship that could be more and more clearly identified as, in effect, the unnegotiable regional essentialism of gender, race, and ethnicity. This new regionalism demanded and made claims for a wider membership within the university on behalf of women, blacks, and others while supplying the new members with an automatic subject matter: themselves, their own history and rights within the national array of culture.

The new American studies has grown up alongside but also as an alternative or aftermath to this regionalism, which tore apart the previous unifying and singular myths of America. The key limitation to this new phase, as well as to all earlier regionalisms, was its need to define itself and thrive only within a highly politicized atmosphere. Regionalism is always, in America, part of a struggle within representation. It is seldom or never a matter of tolerance, the blooming of a thousand, or even of three, flowers. In the regionalism of the last two decades, identity is formed by opposition: black-white, female-male, Native American–settler, gay-heterosexual. Because of this opposition, identity is located above all in the sphere of politics — that is, in the sphere of felt opposition, of movement, laws, demands, negotiations over representation, and, in the university, in struggle over curriculum and requirements. The new American studies has stood outside this regionalism by locating a set of underlying but permanently open national facts around which all identities are shaped. It is with these permanently open cultural questions that the many rhetorics of our culture are engaged. Among these permanently open, that is, never won or lost, national facts are democratic culture and its demands; the culture of freedom that permits conditions of dominance, whether economic, sexual, or cultural, and has permitted even permutations of slavery as one aspect of the nature of freedom itself; the creation of a national life that is economic rather than religious or, in the anthropological sense, cultural. This troubled utopian core of enterprise, freedom, and democratic culture, baffled by preexisting social facts while never surrendering to them, is central to much of the best recent work in American studies.

THE CIVIL WAR WITHIN REPRESENTATION

One consequence of the new American studies has been to replace the traditional concept of the American Renaissance with the new category of a literature located within the Civil War and driven by the particular concepts of freedom and independence, politics and compromise that the war period, with its preparation and aftermath, froze into place. Recent European historical work, particularly Reinhart Koselleck's essays on the concept of revolution in his book *Future's Past,* has brought to the center of attention the part played by civil wars in the grounding and contesting of national identity in the three hundred years between the Thirty Years' War and the English Civil War of the seventeenth century and the end of the general European civil war of 1914–45. Like the American Civil War, or the French and Russian revolutions with their phases of civil war, all such conflicts put at risk the very existence of the society itself in the name of uncompromisable values. Periods of civil war are periods without ideology, because two or more rhetorics of self-representation, national purpose, and historical genealogy are in wide enough circulation to elicit complete support, even to the point of making people willing to die for them. Civil war is the alternative condition to what we call, following Foucault's relentless analysis, the power of the centralized state, the structured, all-pervading system for stabilizing and describing a fixed social reality.

In contrast to the condition of two or more contesting powers that we can, in a shorthand way, express by the notion of civil war, the very idea of a cultural period like that of Romanticism or the American Renaissance leads us to look for a unified set of ideas and aesthetic practices. We then come to think of such concepts as the ideology of the American Renaissance or some other period. Writers can be viewed as expressing or dissenting from that ideology. Ideology, dissent, a sense of identity and of an authoritative discourse within each period are all interdependent notions. Once the idea of civil war as a normative situation within representation replaces that of ideology, the entire array of concepts falls away together.

In literary studies of the last ten years what has been called the new historicism has, as a result of the strong influence of Foucault and modern experience of totalitarianism and its analysis by, among others, Hannah Arendt, Max Horkheimer, and Theodor Adorno, focused on the fate of representation within absolutist states or societies. The English Renaissance, taken as a glorious period of monarchy, along with its secondary pressures and exceptions, became the natural topic for new-historicist demonstrations.

The condition of civil war can be taken to be the fundamental alternative to that of monarchical power, self-display, uniform discourse, ideology, and controlled representation. American new historicism has its basis in the representational situation not of monarchy but of civil war. To see the central American historical episode as the civil war is to bring to the front the power of rhetorics, incomplete dominance of representation, and the borrowing or fusing of successful formulas of representation. The actual war of the 1860s stands in for the pervasive, continuously unsettled, open struggle within American culture. All cultural history in the United States is the history of civil wars.

The civil wars between contemporaries are only a local version of what, to use an Emersonian formulation, should be seen as the fundamental, permanent conflict in any society that is, as the United States is, an economy rather than a culture. That underlying civil war, as Emerson described it in his essay on Napoleon, is between the young and the old, between power that represents work done in the past and the effort of the young, who will displace all that is being defended in order to make room for themselves in the world. Railroads overthrew canals and water-based transportation, and no sooner had they succeeded than the automobile and long-distance truck overthrew the railroad. No sooner did Western Union have a monopoly on long-distance communication than the telephone industry emerged to make that monopoly worthless.

The representational topic of monarchy is the inheritance, diffusion, and protection of already-held power. The subject of civil war is the unstable contest for short-term control that is uninheritable and, in the end, undefendable. Power is not the topic of this historicism but its weak long-term expectations in a culture in which economic dominance is not located in land — that one genuinely scarce, readily transferable, and not easily variable basis of hegemony.

PRINT CULTURE WITHOUT THE STATE

The ordinary culture within which our classic authors and painters have worked has to be called a print culture, but now understood in a wider sense than the Gutenberg culture of the book. A photograph is also called a "print," as is the copy of a film. Newspapers and journals, advertisements and billboards are also, in this sense, prints, offprints, and reprints. In his book on the profession of the author in America, Michael Warner sets out the model of the printer Benjamin Franklin, with his new-made career within print culture, a culture replacing the oral culture of sermon, oratory, and statements linked to the personal presence of the speaker and the audience's identification with the spoken words. After Franklin all American authors, photographers, and filmmakers are printers.

In his important book on American photography, Alan Trachtenberg has defined the photographic print as a cultural text within the Civil War, the reform movements of the 1890s and 1930s, and the modernist aesthetic of the early twentieth century. In the photographic images of the war itself, Trachtenberg reads the rhetoric of representation as it appeared within the camera — which, like the machine gun, was one of the new instruments of this conflict. The very existence of photographs during wartime for the first time, alongside or combined with day-by-day newspaper reporting from the battlefield, set up a contest for the control and definition of this new visual genre. The photograph and newspaper did not define an ideology of the war experience and certainly not a myth. Instead, they embodied the rapidly shifting competitive rhetorics within the as-yet-unstabilized representation that would only later, with victory and time, become what we know as the "Civil" War.

Unlike myths that take on all possible historical circumstances as illustrations and by this means become universal explanations, rhetorical analysis is never universal. One important reason for the local nature of the analysis of rhetorics found in recent work is the lack of what might be called, in the European sense, the state in American experience and therefore an absence of any monopoly of either power or of violence on the part of the state. Centralization of power on the European model, and with it the centralization of the power of representation and self-conception as it has been described by Foucault, was never present in America. Unlike French schools, American education has always been local, variable, responsive, for good and ill, to local pressures and the demands of the moment. When, in the twentieth century, state control over, and funding of, culture became fundamental and deeply ideological in Europe and throughout much of the world, politicized between the radical cultural projects of the right and the left, American culture developed an almost singularly market- and consumer-based formula of funding, selection, and survival. American newspapers, music, film, radio, publishing, and television were all competitive, decentralized, and in the hands of ever-new players. Only the highly paradoxical analysis of European intellectuals, like those of the Frankfurt school, with their horror of popular or commercial culture, could have invented the claim that this unsponsored and competitive culture itself expressed an even more rigid and tricky ideology than the more obvious overt ideologies of twentieth-century European experience, the so-called ideology of capitalism (see Jay). But by 1945 no European intellectual could any longer imagine what it might mean to live in a society without a state that owned, sponsored, and used for its own purposes all the media of cultural life.

Even outside the arena of cultural conflict, or civil war per se, American culture provided the richest possible resources for escape, invisibility, and defiance. The right to "move on" or "head out west" was only one of the possibilities that limited the creation of a state. More important was the economic commitment to a rapidly changing culture of invention, with its dizzy cycles of the amassing, loss, and transfer of wealth and power. The economic commitment was far more decisive than the purely individual right to escape or move on, but even the apparently individual mobility was historically profound because it was the means of renewing the act of immigration — leaving behind and moving on — that was each individual's first drop of American identity. In fact, such an economic pressure — what has been called the "creative destruction" of the market economy — is a form of willed, collective instability, because it accepts the future as an already bankable asset that can be borrowed against to speed up the overthrow of the past. In a speculative culture, for instance, the profits of the railroads fall into an investment pool, where, since they are expected to yield the highest returns, they no longer are invested back into the railroad system itself but into the automobile industry, whose only purpose is to overthrow the railroads as the fundamental transportation system. By means of the speculative system, the past becomes the silent partner of a future that will abolish its own hold. A culture of speculation is opposite in its action to those of preservation, inheritance, and self-reproduction, which we tend to take anthropologically as the human norm. Pierre Bourdieu's *Outline of a Theory of Practice* — precisely because it is concerned with societies whose primary goal is reproduction in the widest sense of self-replication and continuation, as is, over time — can never describe an Emersonian or speculative society whose commitment to self-destruction in the name of its own next possibility is far more important than its interest in the transfer of the forms of the past to a future generation.

For these reasons analysis within American studies will always be of sectors of a diverse culture characterized by the absence of a monopoly of power. These studies will always be historical and not anthropological, because of the commitment of the culture itself to a rapid building up, wearing out, and replacement of systems of all kinds by new arrays of persons and forces. The updraft is strong, the door of immigration both to and within the country is open, the exhaustion of control is always imminent and control itself is porous. Because America had no experience of monarchy, it has a permanent democratic core working against not only the centralization of power but, more important, its inheritance or preservation over time.

In the absence of a state, we find ourselves freed of the intellectual component of the systematic state: ideology. We have rhetorics because we have no ideology, and we have no ideology because we lack the apparatus of ideology: a national religion, a unitary system of education under the control of the state, a cultural life and media monopolized by the state by means either of ownership or of subsidy. Ideology is a cultural mechanism of stabilization and transmission, neither of which is a primary topic of a culture of speculation. The study of rhetorics is our necessary alternative to the study of ideology. Rhetorics are the sign of the play of forces within cultural life, and at the same time of the power of invention and obsolescence within culture. Rhetoric is the mark of temporary location and justification. The nuances of provisional justification and defense, the opening up of newness within culture without escaping the grip of the master problems and resources of the culture: This is what is at issue within the newest writing on American literature and culture.[1]

NOTE

1. This essay has been adapted from the author's introduction to his volume *The New American Studies* (Berkeley: U of California P, 1991).

SELECTED BIBLIOGRAPHY

Bercovitch, Sacvan, ed. *Reconstructing American Literary History.* Harvard English Studies 13. Cambridge: Harvard UP, 1986.
    A particularly thoughtful group of essays, on literary issues and texts from the eighteenth century to the present, that reflect what the editor refers to as "the self-reflexiveness that characterizes this period of critical interregnum."
Cavell, Stanley. *In Quest of the Ordinary.* Chicago: U of Chicago P, 1988.
    One of Cavell's recent collections of essays that display his efforts to recuperate the writings of Emerson and Thoreau for serious philosophical reflection and show how their pragmatist absorption with the ordinary and the familiar constitutes a profound response to t-he modern problem of skepticism.
Fisher, Philip. *Hard Facts: Setting and Form in the American Novel.* New York: Oxford UP, 1987.
    A study of the way cultural forms like novels transform certain of the disagreeable facts at the center of social experience — in nineteenth-century America, the removal and destruction of Native American peoples, the enslavement of African Americans, and the later commercial objectification of all Americans — into something not only palatable but naturalized.

Gates, Henry Louis, Jr. *The Signifying Monkey: A Theory of African-American Literary Criticism.* New York: Oxford UP, 1988.
   An important work that focuses on the trickster in African American literary experience, a figure whose talents for signifying, for redescription, constitute a subjectivity that can elude the structures of rhetorical and ideological closure associated with the dominant society.
Gunn, Giles. *Thinking across the American Grain: Ideology, Intellect, and the New Pragmatism.* Chicago: U of Chicago P, 1992.
   A study of the renaissance of pragmatism in contemporary American intellectual culture and its application to a variety of literary and critical contexts.
Lewis, R. W. B. *The American Adam: Innocence, Tragedy, and Tradition in the Nineteenth Century.* Chicago: U of Chicago P, 1955.
   A definitive study of the myth of the American Adam in the nineteenth century and of some of the tragic collisions to which its moral and spiritual pretensions were exposed in the literature of the last two centuries.
Marx, Leo. *The Machine in the Garden: Technology and the Pastoral Ideal in America.* New York: Oxford UP, 1964.
   An examination of the development of nineteenth-century American literary pastoralism as a response to the social, political, and emotional threat of the rise of industrialization.
Matthiessen, F. O. *American Renaissance: Art and Expression in the Age of Emerson and Whitman.* New York: Oxford UP, 1941.
   A classic study of the American literature of the mid-nineteenth century that displaced the Fireside Poets as the preeminent authors of the period with a new canon that included Emerson, Thoreau, Whitman, Hawthorne, and Melville.
Michaels, Walter Benn. *The Gold Standard and the Logic of Naturalism.* Berkeley: U of California P, 1987.
   An exploration of the way literary and other cultural forms helped create value in the emergent environment of corporate capitalism at the end of the nineteenth century, as the literary romance mitigated the experience of alienation, trompe l'oeil painting served as a critique of money, and the contract became a device that eroticized slavery.
Miller, Perry. *Errand into the Wilderness.* Cambridge: Harvard UP, 1956.
   A work that summarizes some of the themes that circulated in Miller's numerous and often majesterial studies of the Puritan mind, from the role of the jeremiad in American culture to the place and function of millenarianism in the American psyche.
Poirier, Richard. *The Renewal of Literature: Emersonian Reflections.* New York: Random, 1987.
   A recuperation of a pragmatist tradition of American writing that runs from Emerson and the elder Henry James through William James, Gertrude Stein, Robert Frost, and Wallace Stevens to John Ashbery and, furthermore, shows how this body of writing, in addition to providing a countertradition to the high modernism of Ezra Pound and T. S. Eliot, may suggest a cultural alternative to postmodernism.
Reynolds, David. *Beneath the American Renaissance: The Subversive Imagination in the Age of Emerson and Melville.* New York: Knopf, 1988.
   A path-breaking study that rereads the work of what are here held to be the seven major writers of the middle years of the nineteenth century (in addition to Emerson, Thoreau, Hawthorne, Melville, and Whitman — Edgar Allan Poe and Emily Dickinson) against the background of a rich but little-known world of sensational and popular literature on which they drew for many of their themes, characters, settings, and even idioms.
Rorty, Richard. *Contingency, Irony, and Solidarity.* Cambridge: Cambridge UP, 1989.
   A more effective demonstration than any of his other books that Rorty has breathed new life into pragmatist motifs and concerns and resituated them at the center of contemporary cultural existence.
Ruland, Richard, and Malcolm Bradbury. *From Puritanism to Postmodernism.* London: Routledge, 1991.
   A literary history from the colonial era to the present that reflects the shift from ideological explorations of essential American myths to a pragmatic concern with the conversation between different American rhetorics and styles.
Trachtenberg, Alan. *Reading American Photographs: Images as History, Mathew Brady to Walker Evans.* New York: Hill, 1989.

An analysis of the translation of the history of American photographs into a social text. The approach not only affords a new way of reading that history but turns it into a theory of how American culture has itself been read.

WORKS CITED

Bourdieu, Pierre. *Outline of a Theory of Practice.* Trans. Richard Nice. Cambridge: Cambridge UP, 1977.

Jay, Martin. *The Dialectical Imagination: A History of the Frankfurt School and the Institute of Social Research.* Boston: Little, 1973.

Kosselleck, Reinhart. *Future's Past: On the Semantics of Historical Time.* Trans. Keith Tribe. Cambridge: MIT P, 1985.

Poirier, Richard. *The Performing Self: Compositions and Decompositions in the Languages of Contemporary Life.* New York: Oxford UP, 1971.

The End of "American" Literature: Toward a Multicultural Practice

GREGORY S. JAY

J*ay's essay originally appeared in an issue of* College English *(1991), but it sparked so much discussion that an essay collection,* The Canon in the Classroom *(1994), edited by John Alberti, was published presenting the essay with several responses to it. Jay begins with the radical notion that universities should no longer teach American literature. While he is pleased with recent progress in expanding the canon, he notes that these pluralistic revisions do not dismantle the "oppressive nationalist ideology" that has framed our study of American literature. Jay attempts to make visible the power dynamics and privilege that affect how cultural history and literature are reproduced and institutionalized. He believes a responsible pedagogy is multiculturalism at its best — one that seeks to foster dialogue with the Other. Jay is quick to distinguish his brand of multiculturalism from assimilationist "melting pot" rhetoric that attempts to erase difference.*

Rather than promoting a literary history based on fabricated consensus, Jay proposes replacing it with a history rooted in a geographical and historical paradigm, which allows us to see the borders between the United States, Canada, and Mexico as the products of our history rather than its origins. Similarly, the lines between cultural groups within the United States would be seen as permeable borders that allow for cultural exchange. The argument for dismantling American literature and replacing it with "Writing in the United States" pushes one to question the current approach to American literary studies. According to Jay, we must not merely expand the canon, but disrupt and problematize our notion of the field. This would entail addressing the way in which assimilation and translation inform American literature. American literature must be reconceived as a study of "how various cultural groups and their forms have interacted during the nation's ongoing construction" (p. 53) Jay concludes his essay with a practical discussion of what his revised Writing in the United States course might look like. For example, rather than organizing the syllabus by period or by theme, he proposes arranging the course along a list of problematics that would place texts from different cultural groups into dialogue with each

From *College English* 53.3 (1991): 264–81.

other. While noting that his list of possibilities is not exhaustive, Jay recommends origins, power, civilization, tradition, assimilation, translation, bodies, literacy, *and* borders. *Instructors interested in this approach may find it beneficial to arrange their syllabi according to a set of problematics and to make their reading selections based on representative responses to these issues.*

> The failure of the melting-pot, far from closing the great American democratic experiment, means that it has only just begun. Whatever American nationalism turns out to be, we see already that it will have a color richer and more exciting than our ideal has hitherto encompassed. In a world which has dreamed of internationalism, we find that we have all unawares been building up the first international nation.
>
> – RANDOLPH BOURNE

It is time to stop teaching "American" literature. The combined lessons of critical theory, classroom practice, and contemporary history dictate not only a revision of the curriculum and pedagogy of "American" literature courses, but a forceful uprooting of the conceptual model defining the field itself (Bercovitch; Elliot; Kolodny). On the one hand this means affirming the reforms that have taken hold at numerous institutions and in a number of new critical studies and anthologies, such as *Three American Literatures,* edited by Houston Baker, and the monumental achievement of Paul Lauter and his colleagues in *The Heath Anthology of American Literature.* On the other hand it means pointing out that many of these reforms have only been pluralist in character. (JanMohamed and Lloyd make the case against pluralism, while Ravitch upholds it.) They add a few new texts or authors without dismantling the prejudicial framework which has traditionally prescribed the kinds of works studied in "American" literature courses and the kinds of issues raised in "American" literary scholarship. That scholarship thus continues to depend upon, and reproduce, the oppressive nationalist ideology which is the nightmare side of the "American dream." Our goal should be rather to construct a multicultural and dialogical paradigm for the study of writing in the United States.

The recent work of Adrienne Rich exemplifies a literary and cultural criticism that neither colonizes nor excludes the Other, but tries to read, think, and feel the differences that our bodily locations — in history, in geography, in ethnicity, in gender, in sexual orientation — can make. Rich's "politics of location" would begin not with the continent or nation "but with the geography closest in — the body." She would

> pick up again the long struggle against lofty and privileged abstraction. . . . Even to begin with the body I have to say that from the outset that body had more than one identity [female, white, Jewish, middle-class, Southern, North American, lesbian, etc.]. . . . Two thoughts: there is no

liberation that only knows how to say "I"; there is no collective movement that speaks for each of us all the way through.

And so even ordinary pronouns become a political problem. . . . Once again, Who is *we*? (212–13, 215, 224, 231)

This mapping of the located body graphically resists the abstract liberal humanism which, for all its accomplishments, continued to force the Other to assimilate to the values and interests of an idiosyncratic though hegemonic Western self, and it attacks the complacency of that self in regarding its image as unitary, normative, and universal. Rich's argument closely resembles those made by postmodern anthropologists and ethnographers such as James Clifford, who writes that "once cultures are no longer prefigured visually — as objects, theaters, texts — it becomes possible to think of a cultural poetics that is an interplay of voices, of positioned utterances" (12). For Rich and Clifford multiculturalism is a dialogue among (and within) socially constructed bodies and subject positions. Students of writing in the United States will become like Clifford's "indigenous ethnographers," self-conscious both of the positions they write from and the positions they describe.

Thus I want to heed the warning of Guillermo Gómez-Peña not to "confuse true collaboration with political paternalism, cultural vampirism, voyeurism, economic opportunism, and demagogic multiculturalism" (133). I have to be self-conscious about the politics of the "we" in my own essay. In part it refers to a set of dominant groups I participate in — European-American, male, middle-class, heterosexual, US citizen, educated, institutionalized, and so on — and I speak to those groups about our need to deconstruct the basis of our own privileges. Danger (leading to "demagogic multiculturalism") lies in imagining that oppression is always someone else's responsibility. Before we get too busy celebrating our position at the forefront of the liberation of the culture, we must recognize that we are often the problem. It is our racism, our sexual prejudices, our class anxieties, our empowered desires that we must confront and resist. The unconscious character of these biases means that we cannot be complacent or comfortable even with the conscious avowal of our positions (as in this essay), for that can always be a defensive reassertion of our authority. Some who might read this essay do not belong to many of these privileged groups, so that their relation to the pronoun "we" will be different. In that case "I" and "you" and "we" may also operate performatively, in utopian fashion, as they do in the texts of Walt Whitman and of Rich — as invocations to the possibility of community. "What is it then between us?" asks Whitman: "What is the count of the scores or hundreds of years between us? . . . I too had received identity by my body" (130). In reference to our location in the United States, or the US, the problematic US indicates the specific heterogeneity of our cultural history and the difficulty of speaking for, or about, it in a univocal voice. Thus my decision to use the abbreviation for the remainder of the essay in order both to evoke and symbolically subvert the nation's identity. To play ungrammatically on Rich's question, the motto for American criticism should become: "Once again: Who is US?"

The history and literature of the US have been misrepresented so as to effectively underwrite the power and values of privileged classes and individuals. We should act on the now clichéd observation that literary judgments have always already been political; our responsibility for justice in cultural education requires more self-criticism than we have yet shown. We have to make explicit, and sometimes alter, the values at work in our schools and scholarship (see Giroux). We have to engage in struggles to change how the cultural history and writing of the US get institutionalized and reproduced. The movement toward multicultural literacy reflects more than a dedication to intellectual and historical accuracy; it expresses our sense that the legacy of nationalism must be reevaluated and that multicultural experience is our imperative reality. US multiculturalism is a living actuality we cannot escape and whose configurations we must begin to fathom, even as renascent nationalisms (here and elsewhere) pose serious political and theoretical questions. A commitment to multicultural education also belongs to our historical moment as we witness a renewed interest in democracy, and as we ask how a democratic culture might be fashioned. The contemporary failure of democracy in the US derives from oppressive social practices (material and ideological) that act against certain marked individuals, categorizing them as marginal to the interests of the nation. A responsible pedagogy requires a vigilant criticism of racism and discrimination in all their forms, aesthetic as well as political. It is the duty of educators to oppose the practices which today tolerate and even encourage cultural chauvinism and the violence of bigotry.

Aren't there dangers as well as values in multiculturalism? Diane Ravitch argues that a proper multiculturalism teaches respect for the diversity of America's "common culture" (and so is pluralistic), while a dangerous multiculturalism advocates conflicting ethnocentrisms and implies that "no common culture is possible or desirable" (and so is particularistic) (340). But the choice should not be posed as one between a common culture and chaotic ethnic rivalries. Any recourse to a notion of a national culture risks reimposing a biased set of principles or historical narratives, and Ravitch is conspicuously silent on what the content of that common culture may be. On the other hand, she is right to warn that replacing Eurocentrism with a series of ethnocentrisms would only multiply the original problem. With Elizabeth Meese I would urge that we avoid thinking of multicultural literacy as a process designed to foster or prop up an identity, whether of a person or a tradition or a nation or a school of criticism (31–32). Rather multicultural study should put people into a dialogue with the Other — with the subjects that have historically formed the boundaries of their cultural experiences. Essentialism does not have to be the result of affirmative action, especially if one understands the latter as affirmation of the Other and not of one's self. Our commonality is not a substance or essence (Americanness) but a process of social existence predicated on the espoused if not always realized principles of cultural democracy, political rights, community responsibility, social justice, equality of opportunity, and individual freedom. When these principles are subordinated to totalizing ideologies seeking to invent or impose a common culture, then the actual multicultural life of Americans suffers an oppression that is in no one's best interests.

A strong connection ties the historical development of a theory and institutional practice of American literary studies to the modern history of nationalism. The anxiety to invent an American nation and the anxiety to invent a uniquely American literature were historically coincident. As long as we use "American" as an adjective, we reinforce the illusion that there is a transcendental core of values and experiences that are essentially "American," and that literary or cultural studies may be properly shaped by selecting objects and authors according to how well they express this essence. This metaphysical approach has shaped American literary theory ever since the first attempts to invent a uniquely American literature in the 1820s, and has persisted throughout every theory that has used arguments for American exceptionalism. Current revisionary critiques show that the "American" of conventional histories of American literature has usually been white, male, middle- or upper-class, heterosexual, and a spokesman for a definable set of political and dual interests. Insofar as women, African and Asian and Native Americans, Hispanics, gays and lesbians, and others make an appearance in such histories, it is usually in terms of their also being made into spokesmen for traditional values and schemes. Their "assimilation" into American literature comes at the cost of their cultural heritage and obscures their real antagonism and historical difference in relation to the privileged classes.

The "melting pot" is a crock, as great and pernicious a myth in literary history as it is in social and political history. Today we are moving away from the myth of assimilation and into the struggle to create a just multicultural society that respects the values and practices of distinct if interdependent groups. Cultural education must aim to represent historically that ours always has been a multicultural society and that the repression of this heterogeneity (usually in the service of one group) ultimately threatens the cultural vitality and even survival of every group within it. In contrast, past histories of American literature have been active functionaries in reproducing the hegemony of culturally privileged groups. From 1882 to 1912 (and beyond), observes Nina Baym, "textbook writers made literary works and authors display the virtues and achievements of an Anglo-Saxon United States founded by New England Puritans" (459). This narrative served the purpose of "Americanizing" and assimilating the growing industrial and immigrant classes: "Paradoxically, the non-Anglo-Saxon could become American only to the extent of their agreement that only those of Anglo-Saxon lineage were really Americans" (463; see Bourne). At the level of class, the ambitions and disappointments of exploited workers could be mediated by an education in transcendentalism: "What more likely to deflect the (usually foreign-born) poor from their desire to have a substantial piece of the country's settled wealth than exposure to an idealism from whose lofty perspective the materialist struggle would seem unworthy?" (462). Literary history fabricated a symbolic consensus that papered over real social contradiction; as a social practice pedagogy manufactured compliant subject positions (see Graff, *Professing* 130–32, 209–25).

I propose that we replace the idealist paradigm with a geographical and historical one. Our focus of study ought to be "Writing in the United States." The objects of study will be acts of writing committed within and during the colonization, establishment, and ongoing production of the US as a physical, sociopolitical, and multicultural event, including those writings that resist and critique its identification with nationalism. Organizing courses on the bases of national entities inevitably reproduces certain biases and fallacies, and we need to protect against these by including specific theoretical questions and methodological devices in the curriculum. Or we could simply rename our discipline "Comparative American Literature," or establish courses and programs in North American Studies that would integrate the cultural history of the US with those of Canada, Mexico, the near Latin American countries, and the Caribbean, though this could end up repeating the history of colonial imperialism at the level of academic study. Still, the borders between these nations are less the origins of our history than the products of it.

Our peoples and writers have been flowing back and forth over the space these boundaries now delineate since before the colonial adventure began. These borders make little sense when one is studying the histories, say, of Native- or Hispanic- or African-American literature. This crossing of boundaries, as José Saldívar and others argue, becomes the paradoxical center of Mexican-American and Chicano literature, for example, which has been violating borders of nationality and of language since the 1500s (see Saldívar, Gómez-Peña; Rosaldo). How does one categorize a work like Rudolfo Anaya's *Bless Me, Ultima,* which crosses so many of these linguistic and cultural divides? What "Americanist" pedagogy could do justice to the traditions, historical representations, and contexts of utterance in *Black Elk Speaks* or James Welch's *Fools Crow*? Can the borders between Native-, Hispanic-, and Anglo-American literature be drawn without recalling the political treacheries that imposed a series of violated borders upon indigenous peoples and settlers from Mexico, borders that were shifted whenever white economic interest dictated, so that Hispanic- and Native-American cultures come to be an "outside" within the "inside" of "America"?

Within the boundaries of the US, the lines between cultural groups do not form impassable walls, though they often take oppressive shape. Historically these zones are an area of constant passage back and forth, as each culture borrows, imitates, exploits, subjugates, subverts, mimics, ignores, or celebrates the others. The myth of assimilation homogenizes this process by representing it as the progressive acquiescence of every other group to a dominant culture. Writers who analyze this myth often depict the experience instead under the metaphor of "passing" — as in to "pass" for white, for gentile, for straight, for American. The "object of oppression," writes Cherríe Moraga, "is not only someone outside of my skin, but the someone inside my skin" (30). Thus there are borders within, as well as between, our subject positions. This "divided consciousness" (to recall the phrasing of W. E. B. Du Bois) affects every group and individual with a specificity that must be understood and felt.

Language is a primary vehicle for passing, and literary critics should study the manner in which the formal development of genres and movements participates in its rituals and contradictions. As we highlight the politics of linguistic assimilation — of the consequences for non-English speaking people who must learn to speak and write the master's tongue — we can exploit the pun in the phrase "Writing in the United States." "Writing" here designates not simply a static set of objects, but the process of verbal or textual production in its historical and dynamic sense, and in the sense of what a speaker or writer experiences when she or he attempts to write within the boundaries of the US (see Baker, *Journey* 1–52; Gates, *Figures* 3–58). If we replace the term "literature" with "writing" we can resist the cultural biases built into the former term and institutionalized by departments that have built their curriculum around the privileged genres developed in modern Europe. Writing, or textuality if you prefer, names events of representations, and so includes previously marginalized forms and media as well as canonical forms produced by marginalized people.

Historically, "Writing in the United States" would begin with Native-American expressive traditions and include those narratives produced by the first European explorers and colonizers, Spanish and French as well as English. This would effectively decenter histories of American literature which have always placed their origins in the Anglo-Saxon culture of Puritan New England (see Reising 49–91). That culture was a culture of the Book — of the Bible — which confronted an oral culture among the Native Americans. The cultural and literary politics of this confrontation require consideration, as does the problematic of translation it dictates. The survival of Native-American discourse henceforth began to depend on its translation into written form, often through the mediation of whites, or on the translation of native experience into white expression in the public speeches and documents produced by Native Americans in defense of their lands and rights. The literary history of the US includes the story of how the destruction of Native-American culture was essential to the literary and political invention of "America," as the struggle for culture coincided with the struggle for land. The boundaries of "Writing in the United States" could thus be drawn geographically and historically, not linguistically, through attention to the demographics of cultural populations, as we witness the dialogical interaction of succeeding generations of natives and arrivals from Europe, Africa, Asia, and Latin America. "Writing in the United States" would then be placed within the history of colonialism and imperialism, as well as nationalism, better providing a foundation for comprehending the current political and social dilemmas facing the US as it reconceives itself as a multicultural society in a multicultural world.

The nationalist biases I have referred to are built into the organization of academic literary study. For about a century we have had departments of

English, French, German, Spanish, Portuguese, Italian, and so forth. These were originally conceived as the modern heirs to the tradition of classical philology, and centered on the study of language, with literature read as an illustration of the history of linguistic development. This philology, like the New Criticism that replaced it, was never entirely a formalism, for it inevitably reproduced the cultural values of the canonical texts it studied. Many language faculties advocated more cultural study in the curriculum, until a basic ambiguity haunted these departments: Were they designed to teach the history of a language or the history of a nation? (Graff, *Professing* 55–120). The question, as in the case of English, became vexing when languages crossed national borders and historical periods. When the *interpretation* of literary texts, as opposed to their philological description or use for historical documentation, became of significant institutional concern, the very rationale for language-based departments began to crumble, though we have not yet faced this fact or imagined real alternatives.

"English" is a misnomer for departments offering courses in psychoanalysis, Derrida, postcolonialism, film theory, feminism, Native-American autobiography, and Chicano poetry. "Indeed," says Annette Kolodny, "no longer can we hold to the linguistic insularity implied by the Americanist's presence in departments of *English*" (293). I would side with Kolodny against William Spengemann, who concludes that because "American" does not designate a language, we ought to abandon efforts to conceive an American literary history and instead return to the study of texts written in English, specifically those great texts that have markedly changed the language itself. Spengemann tumbles into tautology and circular reasoning when he advocates a canon based on the linguistic practices of modernism: Only those past texts that belong to modernism's history get into the canon, and modernism is the origin of the canon because past experiments in literary language lead to it.

In the study of US writing, the exclusion of texts not written in English or of authors drawing heavily on non-European sources limits the canon with pernicious results. One cannot even adequately interpret works in American English without some knowledge of the various cultures surrounding and informing them. Most writing produced here after the eighteenth century, moreover, borrows words, characters, events, forms, ideas, and concepts from the languages of African-, Hispanic-, Jewish-, Native-, and Asian-Americans. At the same time speakers and writers from these different cultures adapt the English language to create hybrid forms and texts. When analyzing writers such as Frederick Douglass, Isaac Singer, or Leslie Silko, a background in Chaucer or Restoration drama or imagist poetry may be less helpful than studying, say, the traditions of religious representation of the author's native people. The problematics of assimilation and translation inform writing in the US with a complexity that has scarcely been recognized or theorized. One could argue that the study of US writing cannot be adequately pursued within the boundaries of the English department, for this comparative project ultimately subverts the very premises of that academic organization.

✓ Though I believe in an historical approach to writing, it will suffer the same deconstruction of boundaries as any approach that tries to impose artificial limits on language or geography. US history cannot be represented a priori as a totality, a unity, or a grand story whose plot and hero we already know. A chief model for modern literary nationalism is that historiography which represents the nation as a collective self, a figurative mind or spirit which is realizing its great soul through the unfolding progress of the national community's history. Not surprisingly, this fiction has often been compared to the *bildungsroman,* and we are familiar with the claims it makes on us, from *The Autobiography of Benjamin Franklin* to the testimony of Oliver North. The metaphorical self used to figure such national histories, of course, turns out to wear the idealized face of a very real class or group of individuals — in the West, what we now handily call white patriarchy. The spiritual story of the nation's quest to realize its dream turns out to be a set of writing practices that participates in the manipulation, exploitation, repression, and even genocide of those subjects deemed peripheral to the tale.

Of course undoing the canon doesn't just mean adding on previously excluded figures; it requires a disturbance of the internal security of the classics themselves. In gay studies, for example, cultural revision extends beyond including avowedly same-sex oriented writers in the curriculum. Gay studies extends to questioning the sexual economies of ambiguous and (supposedly) straight texts — to the ways they police their desires. According to Eve Sedgwick one "could neither dismantle" the canon "insofar as it was seen to be quite genuinely unified by the maintenance of a particular tension of homo/heterosexual definitional panic" nor "ever permit it to be treated as the repository of 'traditional' truths that could be made matter for any true consolidation or congratulation." Since "the problematics of homo/heterosexual definition, in an intensely homophobic culture, are seem to be precisely internal to the central nexuses of that culture," teasing out these contradictions in classic texts reveals the subversiveness and repression integral to them, so that "this canon must always be treated as a loaded gun" (148). Because patriarchy reproduces itself through "the stimulation and glamorization of the energies of male-male desire," it must also incessantly deny, defer, or silence their satisfaction, forming the double-bind characteristic of much male writing; thus she remaps the territory of Leslie Fiedler by exposing the ties that bind homophobia and misogyny. The mask of identity worn by the straight man covers over a split subject, from Hawthorne and Melville to James, Eliot, Fitzgerald, Hemingway, Mailer, and beyond.

The literary history of the US ought to be represented not by "*the* American" and "*his* dream," but in terms of how various cultural groups and their forms have interacted during the nation's ongoing construction. As Meese explains, once we abandon notions of literature's intrinsic value and look instead at the contingencies of writing's use values, we may stop thinking in terms of canons altogether. The "history of literature," she writes, "if it seems necessary to create such a thing, might then be a description of the uses to which texts have been put" and of the value writings have had for their subjects (33; see Smith). Such a history would have many protagonists, wearing many faces, speaking many languages, recalling divergent histories, desiring different futures. Syllabi and critical studies could be focused around contestation rather than unity, putting to work in this area the principle Graff has dubbed "teaching the conflicts." Instead of selecting a set of books and authors that express a previously agreed-upon list of characteristics that are "uniquely American," we could assemble texts that openly conflict with each other's assumptions, terms, narratives, and metaphors. These conflicts, moreover, should settle national generalities by reference to the specific pedagogical locality — to the state, region, city, area, and social group of the students, the professor, and the institution.

My own involvement in African-American literature, for example, though precipitated by the Civil Rights movement of the 1960s, received its professional impetus from my being hired — fresh from an education in California and New York — to teach the American literature survey course at the University of Alabama in 1980. I felt strongly the responsibility to develop a multicultural curriculum, with specific attention to black writers. The politics of my pedagogical location would offer me a tough but simple lesson: these students knew a lot more about racism — consciously and unconsciously — than I did. Texts and authors that I thought I knew read differently in their eyes, and to me through them. I began to juxtapose Franklin's *Autobiography* with the *Narrative of the Life of Frederick Douglass*. (The semester ended with a paper contrasting William Faulkner and Alice Walker.) Franklin's optimistic assertion that the individual can rise from poverty and obscurity to fame and power appeared both denied and confirmed by Douglass's escape from slavery and rise to international celebrity. It was intriguing that both men saw the achievement of literacy as the key to freedom, and both made their careers through the material production of books and newspapers. Could both be assimilated to "the American Dream"?

The inescapable differences between them, however, could be found when one located their writings and careers in terms of their historical bodies, especially as regards the relation of the legal system and state power to myths of individual freedom and achievement. Franklin's rise came through his genius for manipulating the legal systems of discourse; Douglass's literacy was literally a crime, and his very claim to "manhood" a violation of the dictates of the state. The ideology of individual accomplishment that Franklin has been used to promote shows up as hollow in Douglass's case, betraying even Douglass's own complicity in it. Trained in that ideology, however, as well as in the discourse of racism, the majority of my white students wanted to read both Franklin and Douglass as presenting allegories of how the individual could triumph no matter the laws or powers of the state, since that belief is precisely what allows the law and the power of the state to go unchallenged and allows the individual to continue in the complacent myth of autonomy.

For many of my black students, who were attending a recently integrated bastion of white academic racism, these materials presented an uneasy situation. They did not desire to be drawn into open hostility with their white classmates and were sensitive to the bad effects of being located in one's historical body. Many were tired of being the token black or being asked to speak for their people on every occasion, rather than for themselves. Their pride in Douglass was muted by their puzzlement over just how to express their feelings in an oppressive context, which included me — a white instructor. Ultimately we had to make these and other local tensions that subject of classroom discussion, to teach these conflicts to each other by openly questioning the relation of reading to race and of race to individual achievement. Many students began to open up, telling personal stories of their experience of racial and class difference; at that point I had to undo my position as the liberal champion, always a dangerous delusion, and reinscribe myself as another white American, one who had grown up in Los Angeles but had never heard of Watts until he watched black rioters burn it down from the cool comfort of his backyard swimming pool. Racism to me had always been someone else's problem; now I began to feel my own participation in its history. I could criticize racism, but I would never be black (just as I could criticize sexism or homophobia, yet never know them quite as women or gays and lesbians did).

At that time I also began teaching a unit of Jewish-American literature. I had to spend hours in the library researching the history of American Judaism and the details of its culture, despite the fact that my own father was a Jew and my great-grandfather an Orthodox rabbi. I was myself, I realized, the split subject of assimilation. Jewish-American literature provides a useful vantage point for multicultural study, since the Jew both belongs to the hegemony of European cultural tradition and has been the excluded Other within the body of that culture. While Jewish-American writers, critics, and intellectuals have been very successful in securing recognition in the US, they have also made the pathos and incompleteness of their assimilation a constant subject of address. (Among literary critics the classic career of assimilation is that of Lionel Trilling, whose dissertation and first book enacted an identification with Matthew Arnold.) The complexity of these realities is captured brilliantly in Tillie Olsen's *Tell Me a Riddle*, where the contrast between Jewish-American and Mexican-American assimilation unfolds a multicultural fable of the politics of recollected identities.

The autobiographical basis of my illustration may seem gratuitous, but it isn't. By bringing the writing home in this way teachers and students begin to feel the friction between ideological myths and particular histories. Anyone who has tried to teach feminism, for example, will testify to how the personal becomes the pedagogical. The dialogue can be confusing, passionate, humiliating, and transformative, demanding that everyone learn better what Teresa de Lauretis calls "the semiotics of experience" (158–86). If we are to recapture the rich diversity of life in the US, we will have to stop masquerading behind assumed poses of abstraction and generality, even if we continue — with Whitman and Rich — to use the "we" pronoun for utopian purposes. As a teacher I cannot speak on behalf of a united cultural vision or tradition, and I don't want to borrow authority from an ideology that gives me power at the cost of truth.

Historically I belong to a class and generation raised in the knowledge of one tradition, and brought by theory, history, and experience to seek a knowledge of others. My bookshelves are filling with texts and authors never mentioned to me in school. It will take years to begin to absorb them or to know how to speak or write with confidence. Of course I could go on writing about Hawthorne or James or Eliot, but that, I think, would be irresponsible. It would also be less difficult and less interesting than meeting the ethical challenge to undertake what Kolodny describes as a "heroic rereading" of those uncanonized works "with which we are least familiar, and especially so when they challenge current notions of art and artifice." Armed with the criticism and scholarship of the past twenty years, revisionists should "immerse themselves in the texts that were never taught in graduate school — *to the exclusion of the works with which they had previously been taught to feel comfortable and competent*" (302).

What practical consequences can be drawn from such a reading lesson? We should probably abandon even a reconstructed version of the American literature survey course. No one- or two-semester course can possibly live up to the implied claim of historical or representative coverage; coherence is usually bought at the cost of reductive scenarios resting on dubious premises. At best one can construct courses that take the question "What is an American?" as their only assumption and then work through close readings of texts chosen for the radically different answers they provide (for curricular alternatives see Lauter, *Reconstructing*). The result is more of a rainbow coalition than a melting pot. Facile pluralism might be avoided through demonstrations of the real conflicts between texts and cultures. I advocate courses in which the materials are chosen for the ways in which they *actively interfere* with each other's experiences, languages, and values and for their power to expand the horizon of the student's cultural literacy to encompass peoples he or she has scarcely acknowledged as real.

The socially constructed ignorance of teachers and students will be a hard obstacle to multicultural literacy, for the knowledges it requires have been largely excluded from the mainstream classroom, dissertation, and published critical study. Teachers have enough trouble trying to supply their students with information on the literary forms, historical contexts, and cultural values shaping *The Scarlet Letter* or *The Red Badge of Courage* or *The Waste Land*. Think of the remedial work for everyone when we assign David Walker's *Appeal*, Catharine Sedgwick's *Hope Leslie*, Harriet Jacobs's *Incidents in the Life of a Slave Girl*, Judith Fetterley's anthology *Provisions: A Reader from 19th Century American Women*, William Wells Brown's *Clotel*, Whitman's *Calamus*, Charlotte Gilman's *Herland*, Jacob Riis's *How the Other Half Lives*, Agnes Smedley's *Daughter of Earth*, the poetry and prose of Langston Hughes, the *corridos* of the Southwest, Scott Momaday's *House Made of Dawn*, Audre Lorde's *Zami*, Maxine Hong Kingston's *The Woman Warrior*, or the stories of Bharati Mukherjee.

In terms of method, this reeducation sharpens our ability to discern the various ways a text can participate in (or even produce) its context; in terms of pedagogy, it makes the literature classroom part of a general project of historical recollection, analysis, and criticism; in terms of politics, it confronts the institution, the teacher, and the student with the imperative to appreciate the achievements of distinct cultural groups, which cannot be whitewashed with humanistic clichés about the universality of art, the eternal truths of the soul, or the human condition. In sum, a multicultural pedagogy initiates a cultural re-vision, so that everyone involved comes not only to understand another person's point of view, but to see her or his own culture from the outsider's perspective. This decentering of cultural chauvinism can only be healthy in the long run, especially if it leads each of us to stop thinking of ourselves as subjects of only one position or culture.

From the standpoint of literary theory, this approach treats written works as active agents in the socio-political process. This need not mean, as numerous critics have shown, abandoning attention to the formal properties of writing. On the contrary, it strengthens that focus by locating the historical and material specificity of those forms and by charting how they take effect, are appropriated or transformed in concrete contexts. This *does* mean that purely formalist generic categories such as "the novel" or "the elegy" or "tragedy" be called back from the hazy pedagogy of a naïve aestheticism. Theorists from Virginia Woolf and Kenneth Burke to Jameson and Baker and beyond have shown that forms of writing are socially symbolic actions. Styles are linguistic and material practices that negotiate between the binary illusions of documentation and fabrication, or history and fiction. In other words, a renovated rhetorical criticism can frame the written work as an historical utterance, as addressed both to the cultural traditions it draws upon and to the audiences it assumes or even transforms (see Mailloux). Such forms as the slave narrative (produced for abolitionists) or the Native-American autobiography (as told to an ethnographer) provide rich opportunities for deconstructing our categories and concepts of literary authorship and production.

Clearly a multicultural reconception of "Writing in the United States" will lead us to change drastically or eventually abandon the conventional historical narratives, period designations, and major themes and authors previously dominating "American literature." "Colonial" American writing, as I have already suggested, looks quite different from the standpoint of postcolonial politics and theory today, and that period will be utterly recast when Hispanic and Native-American and non-Puritan texts are allowed their just representation. What would be the effect of designating Columbus's *Journal*, the *Narrative of Alvar Nuñez Cabeza de Vaca*, or the creation myths of Native peoples as the origins of US literature, rather than Bradford's *Of Plymouth Plantation*? To take another example, the already shopworn idea of the "American Renaissance," probably the most famous and persistent of our period myths, ought to be replaced by one that does not reinforce the idea that all culture — even all Western culture — has its authorized origins in Greco-Roman civilization. The period of 1812–1865 would better be called that of "America during the Wars," since the final colonial war and the wars to take the property of the Native Americans and Mexican-Americans and to keep enslaved the bodies of African-Americans dominated the socio-political scene and heavily determined its literary output, including that of such canonical figures as Cooper, Hawthorne, Melville, Emerson, and Thoreau. This designation would bring back the historical context and along with it the verbal productions of those marginalized groups or cultures which were busy representing themselves in a rich array of spoken and written discourses. The transformation of this period has already begun through emphasis on Native- and African-American texts and on the writing of women in this period, many of whom were actively engaged in these political struggles. Likewise the era of "Modernism" as the period of Eliot, Pound, Stevens, Williams, Hemingway, and Faulkner has been shattered by questions about the gender and race limitations of this historical construct, prompting renewed attention to Stein, H. D., Moore, and Barnes and a reconsideration of the Harlem Renaissance.

Take finally the currently fashionable tag "postmodern," originally used in literary studies to categorize the self-reflexive fiction of white men (Barth, Coover, Barthelme, Vonnegut, Pynchon) who struggled with the legacy of their modernist fathers. In the popular formulation of Jean-Francois Lyotard, postmodernism names a period without "metanarratives," a sort of extended epistemological and semiotic version of what we used to call the death of God. From his locations in Paris and Irvine, however, Lyotard sees this as the crisis of peculiarly disembodied, abstract, and metaphysical concepts, whereas these metanarratives belong to the ideological apparatus of identifiable institutional and historical groups. As Edward Said points out in his critique of Lyotard, the (supposed) breakdown of the metanarratives of "emancipation" and "enlightenment" cannot be comprehended as solely an internal event of Western civilization. The collapse of Western metaphysical metanarratives, especially those of what is called "the Subject," is (and it's no coincidence) contemporary with the struggle of non-European populations and countries for historical self-determination — for the freedom to be agents rather than subjects.

According to Said, Lyotard "*separates* Western postmodernism from the non-European world, and from the consequences of European modernism — and modernization — in the colonized world." Moreover, the crisis of legitimacy characterizing Western modernism involved

> the disturbing appearance in Europe of various Others, whose provenance was the imperial domain. In the works of Eliot, Conrad, Mann, Proust, Woolf, Pound, Lawrence, Joyce, Forster, alterity and difference are systematically associated with strangers, who, whether women, natives, or sexual eccentrics, erupt into vision, there to challenge and resist settled metropolitan histories, forms, modes of thought. (222–23)

Once one puts the color back into postmodernism, if you will, then the period's inseparability from postcolonialism appears crucial. And this is not simply a matter of discerning the origins of modernism's traumatized consciousness in the West's confrontation with its Others or even of deconstructing the representations of those Others passed off by dominant discourses. Postcolonialism means recognizing, or at least trying to find a way to read, the texts produced by dominated peoples, and acknowledging their participation in narratives of resistance. The literary and cultural works of the marginalized during the nineteenth and twentieth centuries, then, suddenly appear as part of the ongoing development of a postmodern literature, insofar as they contradict the metanarratives of Western modernism. One could argue that, among "Americans" writing in English, a different canon of postmoderns could be compiled from the explosion of texts by contemporary African-, Asian-, and Native-American writers (see Vizenor).

Themes, like periods, derive from and are determined by a previously canonized set of texts and authors. The classic themes of American literature — the Virgin Land, the Frontier West, the Individual's conflict with Society, the City versus the Country, Innocence versus Experience, Europe versus America, Dream versus Reality, and so on — simply make no sense when applied to marginalized texts and traditions, including those produced by women. Thematic criticism can be especially discriminatory since these are by definition repeated elements of a totality or metanarrative centered in an historically limited point of view, though thematic criticism regularly universalizes that perspective and so transforms an angle of insight into an oppressive ideological fabrication. The cartoon simplicity of these themes serves as a mask for this ideological pretension: It presents a partial experience in the form of an eternal verity, thus at once obstructing any analysis of the historical construction of that perception or any analysis of viewpoints that don't conform to the theme or which lose their difference and cultural truth when they are made to conform to the theme.

To supplement or replace periods and themes as points for organizing classes and critical studies, I would offer rather a list of problematics whose analysis would put texts from different cultures within the US into dialogue with one another. Unlike a theme, a problematic does not designate a moment in the history of the consciousness of a privileged subject. A problematic rather indicates an event in culture made up simultaneously of material conditions and conceptual forms that direct the possibilities of representation. A problematic acts as one of the determinants of a representation, though it does not operate as an origin. A problematic indicates how and where the struggle for meaning *takes place*. Each of us could construct a list of problematics conditioning US writing, but for illustrative purposes I would argue for the following: (1) origins, (2) power, (3) civilization, (4) tradition, (5) assimilation, (6) translation, (7) bodies, (8) literacy, and (9) borders. While these problematics have indeed been addressed by some writers, and thus may appear to be themes, I want to resist reducing them to intentionalities or structures of consciousness. Having touched on most already, I want to end by saying something more about origins and power.

The deconstruction of metaphysical ideas about origins played a key role in the development of poststructuralist criticism and initially was resisted by advocates of marginalized groups, who rightly insisted on the need to affirm and recollect the difference of their beginnings (Gates, "The Master's Pieces"). I think we have a consensus today that no choice exists between essentialism and nihilism, as they are two sides of the same metaphysical coin. Because of the historic destruction of dominated (sub)cultures by privileged classes, much writing by women and persons of color tries to recover traditions rather then rebel against them. But as Michael Fischer argues, ethnicity is less an essence than a constantly traversed borderland of differences, "something reinvented and reinterpreted in each generation by each individual. . . . Ethnicity is not something that is simply passed on from generation to generation, taught and learned; it is something dynamic, often unsuccessfully repressed or avoided" (195). This process of recollection does not entail a simple nostalgia or the dream of recreating a lost world: more painfully and complexly it involves a risky translation of recovered fragments into imagined futures by way of often hostile presents.

"The constituency of 'the ethnic,'" writes R. Radhakrishnan, "occupies quite literally a 'pre-post'-erous space where it has to actualize, enfranchise, and empower its own 'identity' and coextensively engage in the deconstruction of the very logic of 'identity' and its binary and exclusionary politics" (199). What should be resisted are myths of origin that function in totalitarian fashion; what should be solicited are myths of beginning that delineate the historical and cultural specifics of a group's experiences and interactions (see Said's *Beginnings*). In multicultural studies we examine multiple sites of origin and multiple claims to foundational perspectives. Rather than adjudicate between these claims in a timeless philosophical tribunal, the student of culture ought to analyze the historical development of the conditions for these narratives and the consequences of their interactions. This would mean, for example, contrasting the disparate creation myths of Native and Puritan Americans and speculating upon how the values embodied in these myths shaped the outcome of the conflict between these groups.

Thus a deconstructive thinking about origins can work along with a politically charged criticism that affirms a dialogue with the Other, so that multicultural study need not lead to the metaphysical dead end of "identity politics." This point is made with exemplary tact by Meese in her chapter on Silko's *Ceremony* (29–49). The novel's choice of a "half-breed" protagonist and multiracial cast of characters and the plot turns that entangle them make it impossible, she argues, to interpret it as calling for a return to a fabled purity of Indian identity. Instead a more intricate process of "crossing cultures" gets represented and played out, one that analyzes the changing economy of values between acculturated subjects — and between that economy and the values of the reader.

Michel Foucault stressed the inseparability of knowledge and power, a problematic he revolutionized by using his experience as a gay man to rethink its traditional scenario. Multicultural studies cannot evade the question of power, since power is both a prime subject for analysis and a constitutive element of the situation of the analysis: the student and the professor are empowered in relation to the object of study, and this disciplinary power usually has its affiliations with distributions of power along lines of gender, region, class, age, ethnicity, and so on. While texts may be studied as expressions of struggles for power, and while we may reflect self-consciously on how scholarship participates in the institutions of power, we should not forget the cautions offered by poststructuralism regarding the fallacies of reference and mimesis. We cannot assume the veracity of a text's representations, and the powers of a text are certainly not confined to its correspondence to an objectively verifiable reality. We must discern how texts take power — how they gain power through the modes of their composition as well as through the modes of their (re)production.

The canonical status of a text is often justified by reference to its superior "power" and its endurance ascribed to the timeless claim it makes on readers. In response we need to question the aesthetics of power and the power of aesthetics. Once one demonstrates that the power of a text to move a reader is a culturally produced effect — that literary "taste" is not natural but taught, and taught in a way that reproduces values that go beyond aesthetics — then the issue of power becomes of vital pedagogical concern. Yet no teacher or text can ensure that the student will receive the letter as it is prescribed. No pedagogy or text, no matter the care of its address, can predetermine exactly the effect it has on everyone, for everyone's subjectivity is plural. Moreover texts are not clear messages or simple unities but occasions when a mediation of conflicts is symbolically enacted. Teachers have the responsibility to empower previously marginalized texts and readers, and to teach in a way that we risk surprising and painful changes in the interpretive habits, expectations, and values of our students — and of ourselves. If we acknowledge that the aesthetic power of a text is a function of the distribution of material and cultural power in society, our pedagogy cannot help but become politically embroiled. In teaching students to value other cultures and other world views we necessarily draw them with us into conflicts with the dominant culture that has produced and sustained our identities and which has the power to enforce its opinions as law. At the same time, we as readers and writers may become agents of change, not just subjects of discourse; we may draw or take power from the canon, from history, from the institution, and turn it in unexpected directions. "We" can fight the power.

WORKS CITED

Baker, Houston A., Jr. *The Journey Back: Issues in Black Literature and Criticism.* Chicago: U of Chicago P, 1980.

————, ed. *Three American Literatures.* NY: MLA, 1982.

Baym, Nina. "Early Histories of American Literature: A Chapter in the History of New England." *American Literary History* 1 (1989): 459–88.

Bercovitch, Sacvan. "America as Canon and Context: Literary History in a Time of Dissensus." *American Literature* 58 (1986): 99–108.

Bourne, Randolph. "Trans-National America." *Atlantic Monthly,* July 1916: 86–97.

Clifford, James. Introduction. "Partial Truths." Clifford and Marcus 1–26.

Clifford, James, and George E. Marcus, eds. *Writing Culture: The Poetics and Politics of Ethnography.* Berkeley: U of California P, 1986.

de Lauretis, Teresa. *Alice Doesn't: Feminism, Semiotics, Cinema.* Bloomington: Indiana UP, 1984.

Elliot, Emory. "New Literary History: Past and Present." *American Literature* 57 (1985): 611–25.

———. "The Politics of Literary History." *American Literature* 59 (1987): 268–76.

Fischer, Michael M. J. "Ethnicity and the Post-Modern Arts of Memory." Clifford and Marcus 194–233.

Foucault, Michel. Afterword. "The Subject and Power." *Michel Foucault: Beyond Structuralism and Hermeneutics.* Ed. Herbert L. Dreyfuss and Paul Rabinow. 2nd ed. Chicago: U of Chicago P, 1983.

Gates, Henry Louis, Jr. *Figures in Black: Words, Signs, and the "Racial" Self.* NY: Oxford UP, 1987.

———. "The Master's Pieces: On Canon Formation and the African American Tradition." *South Atlantic Quarterly* 89 (1990): 89–112.

Giroux, Henry A. "Liberal Arts Education and the Struggle for Public Life: Dreaming about Democracy." *South Atlantic Quarterly* 89 (1990): 113–38.

Gómez-Peña, Guillermo. "Documented/Undocumented." *The Graywolf Annual Five: Multicultural Literacy.* Ed. Rick Simonson and Scott Walker. Saint Paul: Graywolf, 1988.

Graff, Gerald. *Professing Literature: An Institutional History.* Chicago: U of Chicago P, 1987.

———. "Teach the Conflicts." *South Atlantic Quarterly* 89 (1990): 51–68.

JanMohamed, Abdul R., and David Lloyd. Introduction. Special issue on "The Nature and Context of Minority Discourse." Vol. 1. *Cultural Critique* 6 (1987): 5–12.

Kolodny, Annette. "The Integrity of Memory: Creating a New Literary History of the United States." *American Literature* 57 (1985): 291–307.

Lauter, Paul, ed. *The Heath Anthology of American Literature.* 2 vols. Boston: Heath, 1989.

———, ed. *Reconstructing American Literature: Courses, Syllabi, Issues.* Old Westbury, NY: Feminist P, 1983.

Lyotard, Jean-Francois. *The Postmodern Condition: A Report on Knowledge.* Trans. Geoff Bennington and Brian Massumi. Minneapolis: U of Minnesota P, 1984.

Mailloux, Steven. *Rhetorical Power.* Ithaca: Cornell UP, 1989.

Meese, Elizabeth. *(Ex)Tensions: Refiguring Feminist Criticism.* Urbana: U of Illinois P, 1990.

Moraga, Cherríe. "La Guera." *This Bridge Called My Back: Writings by Radical Women of Color.* Ed. Cherríe Moraga and Gloria Anzaldúa. NY: Kitchen Table P, 1983.

Radhakrishnan, R. "Ethnic Identity and Post-Structuralist Difference." *Cultural Critique* 6 (1987): 199–220.

Ravitch, Diane. "Multiculturalism: E Pluribus Plures." *American Scholar* (Summer 1990): 337–54.

Reising, Russell. *The Unusable Past: Theory and the Study of American Literature.* NY: Methuen, 1986.

Rich, Adrienne. *Blood, Bread, and Poetry: Selected Prose 1979–1985.* NY: Norton, 1986.

Rosaldo, Renato. "Politics, Patriarchs, and Laughter." *Cultural Critique* 6 (1987): 65–86.

Said, Edward W. *Beginnings: Intention and Method.* NY: Basic, 1975.

———. "Representing the Colonized: Anthropology's Interlocutors." *Critical Inquiry* 15 (1989): 205–25.

Saldívar, José David. "The Limits of Cultural Studies." *American Literary History* 2 (1990): 251–66.

Sedgwick, Eve Kosofsky. "Pedagogy in the Context of an Antihomophobic Project." *South Atlantic Quarterly* 89 (1990): 139–56.

Smith, Barbara Herrnstein. *Contingencies of Value: Alternative Perspectives for Critical Theory.* Cambridge: Harvard UP, 1988.

Spengemann, William. "American Things/Literary Things: The Problem of American Literary History." *American Literature* 57 (1985): 456–81.

Vizenor, Gerald. "A Postmodern Introduction." *Narrative Chance: Postmodern Discourse on Native American Indian Literatures.* Albuquerque: U of New Mexico P, 1989: 3–16.

Whitman, Walt. *Leaves of Grass and Selected Prose.* Ed. Lawrence Buell. NY: Random, 1981.

2   Considering Literary and Social Movements

$\mathbf{M}$any instructors struggle with how to make literature accessible to their students, particularly when the material seems so remote from the students' lives. While I often begin class discussions with student responses to the literature, I also want to make sure that we not only consider the text from our current vantage point but also attempt to approach the work from its own sociohistorical context. This gets harder and harder the further back in time we go. When I teach the literature of the Harlem Renaissance, it can be a stretch to get students to see the significance of race since so many of them think we are beyond racism, but it is much more of a stretch to provide the context for Thoreau's *Walden* or Jonathan Edwards's *Sinners in the Hands of an Angry God.* The nature of American culture and society continues to change, but an understanding of past literary and social movements helps to contextualize these changes.

The essays collected here address Puritanism, the American Renaissance, realism, naturalism, modernism, and the New Negro Movement. This is far from an exhaustive collection of movements, but it highlights earlier periods and complements the works frequently taught in American literature survey courses. Puritanism is often seen as a difficult topic to address; however, with the rise of the evangelical movement and students' increased investment in their religious views, the topic begins to seem less remote. Sacvan Bercovitch, in "The Puritan Vision of the New World," notes that Puritanism has its roots in Protestantism, which was conceived as a protest against Roman Catholicism, and of which Puritanism was a refinement. The Plymouth Pilgrims sought to perfect Puritanism, and "proclaimed their 'purified church-state' a model for all Christendom" (p. 69). Although Bercovitch does not comment explicitly about the complexities of defining Puritanism, he does note that there were at least three distinct brands of Puritanism and then focuses on the evolving doctrine of the Plymouth Pilgrims. Although Puritanism was initially a spiritual movement, it did not have a purely religious impact. According to Bercovitch, the Puritans had a lasting impact on the way the United States envisions itself.

Charlene Avallone's "What American Renaissance? The Gendered Genealogy of a Critical Discourse" reviews four main approaches to the American Renaissance as reflected in the works of literary critics: Charles Richardson's *American Literature, 1607–1885* (1886, 1888), Barret Wendell's *A Literary History of America* (1900), F. O. Matthiessen's *American Renaissance* (1941), and the current discussion reflected in the work of Ellen Moers, Jane Tompkins, Nina Baym, Lawrence Buell, Hazel Carby, Lora Romero, G. M. Goshgarian, Paul Lauter, and Joanne Dobson, among others. Scholars disagree about the time period covered by the American Renaissance, the canon of authors and texts, and the values of the literary tradition. Some critics have even suggested that the term exists primarily for scholarly convenience, and that it lacks a well-defined rationale. However, Avallone contends that the American Renaissance maintains currency despite the lack of scholarly consensus, and continues to validate literature in a manner that maintains male literary preeminence.

The difficulty associated with definitions seems to be inherent in social movements, which are considered to be composite rather than unified in nature. Thus it is fitting that the selection on realism and naturalism by Donald Pizer is subtitled "The Problem of Definition." Pizer notes that one difficulty in defining the terms is that both words carry both positive and negative connotations. On one hand, the terms suggest genuineness rather than pretension, but they are also associated with concrete experience and thus seen as lacking intellectual or spiritual qualities. Pizer then outlines the varying responses to realism and naturalism by different generations of critics before concluding that naturalism continues to attract writers and readers. Daniel Joseph Singal similarly notes the difficulty of characterizing modernism in his essay, "Towards a Definition of American Modernism." According to Singal, the modernist worldview conceives of the universe as unpredictable and moral absolutes thus impossible to sustain; one of the fundamental aspects of modernism is the idea that morality must fluctuate and adapt to changing circumstances. Singal's essay concludes by pointing toward the beginning of postmodernism.

The New Negro Movement, also known as the Harlem Renaissance, is clearly both a social and literary movement. The literature of the period reflects the self-assertive character of the New Negro, who would no longer be satisfied with second-class citizenship. The literary movement was an outgrowth of civil rights organizations, which sought to prove the humanity of African Americans by showcasing their creative abilities. *The Crisis* and *Opportunity*, publications of the National Association for the Advancement of Colored People and the National Urban League, respectively, sponsored literary contests and award programs to showcase the best and brightest and to forge connections between black writers and white publishers. These same publications as well as *The Messenger* and *The Nation* can also be excellent sources for contextual material that paints the scene of race relations of the period. For example, students might read W. E. B. Du Bois's "Returning Soldiers," Marcus Garvey's "The Future as I See It," George Samuel

Schuyler's "The Negro-Art Hokum," and Langston Hughes's "The Negro Artist and the Racial Mountain" to get a sense of black and white relations in general as well as an understanding of the specific concerns of African American writers.

Although the essays included here discuss very different movements, all of them point toward the difficulty of definition. The contours of these movements tend to be blurred and participants may have ideological differences; however, there is enough of a connection to allow these diverse individuals to coalesce and form a social movement. They form a collective identity in relation to their particular movement, an identity that can only be fully appreciated by addressing their particular sociohistoric context.

The Puritan Vision of the New World

SACVAN BERCOVITCH

*B*ercovitch traces the origins of the Puritan vision to the "discovery" of America and the rise of Protestantism. The Plymouth Pilgrims sought to perfect the Congregationalist and Separatist forms of Puritanism by forging a middle ground between these extreme positions. The second- and third-generation New World Puritans adapted European imagery of America to fit the notion of progress, and then recast the Protestant apocalypse in the New World. According to Bercovitch, the Puritans made three lasting contributions. First, they created a mythology of America in which they did not claim America by conquest, but reclaimed what was promised them as Canaan had been promised to the Israelites. The second, and closely related, legacy was the concept of the elect nation or "the American Israel." The third contribution was the idea of an alternative, visionary America that reflected how the disparate variations of the Puritan vision distinguished themselves from the commonplace set of American ideals. Bercovitch's discussion of the role of rhetoric in defining the Puritan vision, published in 1988, should provide an insightful approach to decoding the rhetoric of such figures as William Bradford, John Winthrop, Edward Taylor, and Jonathan Edwards.*

Looking back in the autumn of 1692, the bicentennial of Columbus's transatlantic passage, to the "antiquities" of colonial New England, Cotton Mather recognized that those "twin migrations" were the key to a great design. To begin with, the voyage of 1492 was one of three shaping events of the modern age, all of which occurred in rapid succession at the turn of the sixteenth century: the "resurrection of literature," which had been made possible by the invention of the printing press (1456) and which in turn made the Bible accessible for the first time to the entire community of believers; the discovery of America, which opened a New World, hitherto shrouded in "heathen darkness," to the light of the Gospel; and the Protestant Reformation, which signaled the dawn of a new era "after the long night of Catholic persecution." And in turn all three beginnings — textual, geographical, and spiritual —

From the *Columbia Literary History of the United States,* ed. Emory Elliott (New York: Columbia UP, 1988) 33–44.

pointed forward to something grander still: the imminent renovation of all things in "a new heaven and a new earth." A new beginning, then, and a newly urgent sense of an ending; and intermediate between these, at once linking them in time and confirming the overall design, like an apocalyptic play-within-a-play, was the story of New England. That, too, had its providential beginnings, culminating in 1630 when the fleet under the *Arbella* set sail for Massachusetts Bay. Mather describes the journey in language appropriate to its momentous spiritual-geographical-textual significance: "The *Church* of our Lord Jesus Christ, well compared unto a *Ship*, is now *victoriously* sailing round the Globe . . . [carrying] some thousands of *Reformers* into . . . an *American Desart*, on purpose that . . . He might there, *To* them first, and then *By* them, give a *Specimen* of many Good Things, which He would have His Churches elsewhere aspire and arise unto. . . . *Geography* must now find work for a *Christiano-graphy* in . . . the HISTORY OF A NEW-ENGLISH ISRAEL . . . to anticipate the state of the *New Jerusalem*."

By the 1690s all this was cultural commonplace. Mather's recognition is a summing up of local tradition, the re-cognition of a long-nurtured view of the colony's origin and mission. One reason for its persistence was the power of the vision itself. Another reason was that on some basic level it told the truth: not only the truth as rhetoric, the growth of New England as the Puritans perceived it, but historical truth, as the events bore out their perception, and specifically the three events of which Mather spoke. Of these, the invention of the printing press, along with the "resurrection of literature," is most obviously an example of the connection between rhetoric and fact. "Gutenberg's galaxy," as Marshall McLuhan termed it, marks a decisive turning point in Western culture. It has particular relevance to the New England Puritans because of their extraordinary reliance on texts. They were not only, like all Puritans, a self-declared people of the Book. They were a community that invented its identity *ex verbo*, by the word, and continued to assert that identity through the seventeenth century, expanding, modifying, and revising it in a procession of sermons, exhortations, and declarations, histories and hagiographies, covenants and controversies, statements and restatements of purpose — a stream of rhetorical self-definition unequaled by any other community of its kind (and proportionately, perhaps of any kind). The legacy of the Puritan vision, as the first-begotten corporate offspring of the printing press, was a rationale, a technique, and (in the material sense of the word) a process whereby a community could constitute itself by publication, declare itself a nation by verbal fiat, define its past, present, and future by proclamation, and justify its definition in histories like Mather's *Magnalia Christi Americana* (1693–1702) that in one form or another translated geography into Christiano-graphy.

The Puritan vision was also the offspring of the two other germinal events to which Mather referred: the discovery of America and the growth of Protestantism. It was an unlikely mixed marriage at the start. The discovery of America was preeminently a secular venture, a process of exploration and appropriation empowered by what scholars have come to call the forces of modernization: capitalist enterprise, state nationalism, the expansion of Western European forms of society and culture throughout the world. So considered, "America" meant the triumph of European imperialism. It was an act of naming that doubly certified the invaders' control of the continent: It meant control by brute power (land-grabbing, enslavement, genocide), and control by metaphor and trope. "America" denoted far more than the Italian entrepreneur Amerigo Vespucci, whose falsified sightings, once published, claimed the *terra incognita* for the Spanish throne. "America" entitled a carnival of European fantasies. It meant the fabled land of gold, the enchanted Isles of the West, springs of eternal youth, and "lubberlands" of ease and plenty. It verified theories of "natural man" and "the state of nature." It promised opportunities for realizing utopia, for unlimited riches and mass conversions, for the return to pastoral arcadia, for implementing schemes for moral and social perfection. Columbus thought that this new continent, providentially set between the cultured West and ancient East, had been the actual site of Eden. Later explorers and settlers, translating the myths of biblical geography into the landmarks of Renaissance geo-mythology, spoke of America as a second Eden, inhabited by pagan primitives (or perhaps the ten lost Hebrew tribes) awaiting the advent of civilization.

History and rhetoric: conquest by arms and conquest by the word — the "discovery of America" is the modern instance par excellence of how these two kinds of violence are entwined; how metaphor becomes fact, and fact, metaphor; how the realms of power and myth can be reciprocally sustaining; and how that reciprocity can encompass widely disparate outlooks. The same thing may be said about the rise of Protestantism, though from a wholly different perspective. Protestantism was from its origins a spiritual movement. It began as a protest against the worldliness of the Roman Catholic church — against the Catholic emphasis on temporal authority (as in the papacy), geographic locale (the Holy Roman Empire), and mercenary practices, from the selling of indulgences to political alliances. Above all, the early Reformers claimed, Christianity demanded an unmediated relation between the believer and Christ, the one true Mediator — which was to say, between the believer on the one hand, and on the other hand Christ as he manifested himself (through grace) in the believer's soul, and as he was manifest for all to see in the Bible (both the Old Testament, prophetically, and the New). *Sola fides* and *sola scriptura,* the primacy of personal faith and the supreme authority of Scripture: upon these twin principles Protestantism was established. But once established it, too, like every other venture in transcending human limitations, found itself entangled in the webs of history and rhetoric.

For in spite of their emphasis on the individual, the Protestants identified themselves, collectively, as a church or association of churches. And through their emphasis on the Bible, they identified themselves temporally, as part of the gradual progress of God's people, from the chosen Israelites to the New Christian Israel to the "latter-day" Israel that would usher in the millennium. The main text for that divine plan, the Book of Revelation, spoke in figures or types of an "elect nation" that in the "last days" would defeat "Antichrist," and so prepare the way for the Second Coming. That in any case was Martin Luther's view of Reformation history. For a time he identified Germany as the elect nation, and although he later abandoned that particular hope, he and the other founding Reformers retained the basic tenets of his historiography. Protestantism, they declared, was the true church; Catholicism, the Antichrist; and the conflict between these, the central action of this final period of time, attended by all the long-awaited "signs and wonders" (political and natural as well as ecclesiastical) of the apocalypse.

After its initial spiritual protest, then, Protestantism returned to history with a vengeance. But it was a special kind of history, sacred as distinct from secular. It was the story not of mankind but of God's "peculiar people," the covenanted saints who constituted the real subject of the unfolding drama of redemption. Basically, that is, Protestant rhetoric retained its traditional Christian roots — remained grounded in the belief that Christ's kingdom was not of this world — and so could break free, if necessary, of any local specificity. Still, the rhetoric of elect nationhood remained an intrinsic if not essential element of European Protestantism, and in the late sixteenth century it became entwined with the chauvinism of Elizabethan England.

By 1630 there were (broadly speaking) three groups of English Puritans. The largest, most eclectic group adopted the national or federal covenant as the basis for revolution and the establishment of a commonwealth under Oliver Cromwell (1649–60). The smallest of the three groups, the Separatists, took the opposite course. They purified their faith to the point where they refused allegiance to any institutional authority, including that of the English Protestant church, whether Anglican or Presbyterian. Instead, they hoped to join the progress of the "universal invisible church" in small congregations, modeled after the first Christian communities. Some remained in England, others fled persecution to Amsterdam, and then, in the case of the Plymouth Pilgrims, to the New World. The Massachusetts Bay immigrants of 1630 sought a "middle way" between these extremes. In doing so, they meant not to compromise but to perfect. They set out to combine what seemed to them in each case a partial gesture at reformation, in church and in state. Accordingly, they proclaimed their "purified church-state" a model for all Christendom. They were congregationalists in a "federal" or "national" covenant; a community of "visible saints" gathered for a venture in history; de facto Separatists who insisted not only on their vital connection to English Protestantism but (through this) on their central role in the worldwide struggle against Antichrist.

The Puritan immigrants do not seem to have had a distinct vision of the New World itself. Their focus was on the Reformation already under way: New England was to be a "model of Christian charity" for Protestants abroad, "a city set upon a hill" as a beacon to Europe. These phrases come from John Winthrop's justly famous lay sermon aboard the *Arbella* (1630), and when he added that "the eyes of all people are upon us" he was thinking mainly of the peoples of England, Germany, Holland, and other Protestant countries. The same may be said of virtually all other first-generation attempts at corporate self-definition: in promotional tracts (Edward Winslow), apologias for the church-state (Richard Mather), and evangelical treatises (John Norton), in sermons on "preparation" and conversion (Thomas Shepard, Thomas Hooker, John Eliot), in exegesis of scriptural prophecy (John Cotton, Ephraim Huit, Thomas Parker), in histories, "prognostics," and poetry (Edward Johnson, Thomas Aspinwall, Anne Bradstreet), and in polemics against sectarians at home (Anne Hutchinson, Roger Williams) and opponents abroad. In all cases, the Puritan vision was transatlantic, rather than American; it tended toward the universalist aspect of the immigrants' ambiguously universal-national outlook. By placing New England at the apex of history, the colonists were admitting their dependency on the Old World. So it was that after the failure of the English Puritan Commonwealth — and with it the waning of apocalyptic fervor throughout Protestant Europe — they found themselves trapped in an embarrassing paradox. They had declared themselves the advance guard of the Reformation, committed themselves to a worldwide mission, and invested their credentials of authority in scriptural prophecy. In 1660 the vision was intact, the community prospering, and their authority still dominant; but with Charles II now on the throne history seemed to have betrayed them. They were a beacon unheeded by the world, a city on a hill that no one noticed, or noticed only to scorn. In Perry Miller's words, they "were left alone with America."

Not entirely alone, however; for the rhetoric they carried with them offered a ready means of compensation. It allowed them by scriptural precedent and prophecy to *consecrate* their "outcast," "exiled," "wilderness condition." If they could not compel the Old World to yield to their vision, they could interpret the New in their own image. Having been left alone with America, the second- and third-generation Puritans felt free to incorporate Renaissance geo-mythology, as it suited their purposes, into their own vision. Explicitly and implicitly, they adapted the European images of America (land of gold, second paradise, utopia, "primitivism" as moral regeneration) to fit the Protestant view of progress. And having thus taken possession of the rhetoric of America, they proceeded one crucial step further. Recasting the relational aspect of their vision, from a transatlantic to a transcontinental direction, they situated the Protestant apocalypse — or what amounted to the same thing, the Protestant road to the apocalypse — in the New World.

We can hardly overestimate the importance of that astonishing westward leap of the imagination. It was an achievement comparable in its way to the two great rhetorical shifts on which it built: the Hebrews' redefinition (by verbal fiat) of Canaan — territory, name, "antiquities," and all — as *their* country; and the imperialism of the *figura* or type, whereby the Church Fathers declared that the Old Testament, the story of Israel in its entirety, from Adam through Abraham and David to the Messiah, heir of David, really belonged to Christ. Upon these foundations the Puritans built the rhetorical structures that once and for all resolved the paradox of vanguard isolation. Confronted with the uncertain meaning of their locale, they discovered the New World in Scripture — not literally (like Columbus) as the lost Eden, but figurally (in the manner of the Church Fathers discovering Noah in Moses and both in Jesus) as the second paradise foreseen by all the prophets. New Canaan was not a metaphor for them, as it was for other colonists. It was the continent before them, reserved from eternity for the latter-day elect nation that would be gathered, as choice grain from the chaff of Europe/Babylon/Egypt, so that God might "*To* them first, and then *By* them, give a *Specimen* of many Good Things" to come. In short, forced back by history upon the resources of rhetoric, the second- and third-generation New Englanders united geography, textuality, and the spirit in what amounted to a new symbology, centered on the vision of America.

The decisive decades in this development were the 1660s and 1670s, when a series of crises threatened to put an end to the enterprise: the restoration of Charles, an apparent decline of religion among the immigrants' children, and the Indian nations' alliance to reclaim their land. The literary result of these "Wars of the Lord" (as the Puritans termed all these events) was the first native flowering of New England mythology, through the first English-language genre developed in the New World, the American Puritan jeremiad. The immigrants had imported that jeremiad as an immemorial mode of lament over the corrupt ways of the world. They transformed it for their own purposes into a vehicle of social continuity. Here as nowhere else, the clergy explained, God's afflictions were like a "refining fire," intended to purify and strengthen, or like the punishment meted out by a loving father, the token of His special care. "God's controversy with New England," wrote the poet Michael Wigglesworth in 1662, *ensured* the colony's success. In the words of the Reverend Arthur Dimmesdale in *The Scarlet Letter,* it signaled "a high and glorious destiny for this newly chosen people of the Lord."

Dimmesdale is an immigrant minister, of course, here delivering the election-day sermon of 1649. This was not inaccurate on Hawthorne's part: there were ample first-generation foreshadowings of the American Puritan jeremiad; but as a distinctive genre the American jeremiad was essentially a ritual of continuity through generational rededication. It required a set of local precedents, a pride of tribal heroes to whom the community could look back in reverence, and from whom, therefore, it could inherit its mission. The immigrants had imported the rhetoric; their children and grandchildren supplied the antiquities needed to make the rhetoric American. They enshrined their forebears in scriptural tropes and types, re-cognized them as giants of a golden age, like Virgil's legendary Trojans entering upon the future site of Rome. Winthrop could compare himself to Moses only by implication. The next generations could entitle him the New England Moses — or, as Cotton Mather did, "the American Nehemiah" (after the prophet who "rebuilt the walls of Jerusalem") — and John Cotton the American Abraham, Joshua, and John the Divine combined. These and other immigrant leaders they canonized as founding fathers, translated their Atlantic crossing as the Great Migration, antitype of the Hebrew exodus, and consecrated their church-state as a venture that, because it fulfilled Old World prophecy, was wholly an event of this New World. It led by promise from New England *then* to New

England as it *would be,* when the *"American Desert"* would flower into the "Theopolis Americana." It was an errand into America, by the American Israel, for America first and then the world.

The Puritans made three lasting contributions to the American way. First, they invested America with a mythology of its own. Other colonists and explorers brought utopian dreams to the New World, but in doing so they claimed the land (New Spain, New France, Nova Scotia) as European Christians, by virtue of the superiority of Christian European culture. They justified their invasion of America through European concepts of progress. The Puritans denied the very fact of invasion by interpreting the newness of the New World as progress and then identifying *themselves* as the people peculiarly destined to bring that interpretation to life. "Other peoples," John Cotton pointed out in 1630, "have their land by providence; we have it by promise." The next generation of New Englanders drew out the full import of his distinction. They were not claiming America by conquest, they explained; they were reclaiming what by promise belonged to them, as the Israelites had once reclaimed Canaan, or (in spiritual terms) as the church had reclaimed the name of Israel. By that literal-prophetic act the Puritans raised America into the realm of *figura.* It was *"pulchèrrima inter mulieres,* the youngest and loveliest of Christ's brides" — the last, best hope of mankind, whether mankind knew it or not.

That vision of the New World was the harvest of the Renaissance rhetoric of discovery. It marked the Puritans' first contribution to American identity; and the second was inextricably bound up with it. I refer to the corporate ideal through which they resolved the ambiguities of their national-universalist venture. For as their opponents were quick to point out, this self-proclaimed Protestant Israel was unprecedented either in secular or in sacred history. On the one hand, the Puritans' national covenant differed in its Protestant emphasis (personal, voluntarist, and spiritual) from the nationalism of any other community, past or present. On the other hand, New England's Protestantism differed in its tribal, worldly emphasis (its insistence on locale, local origins, and territorial errand) from any other Christian community. The first generation tried to solve the problem through a rhetorical balancing act: "visible saints," "nonseparating congregationalism," "church-state." The second and third generations extended these ambiguities into a new, federal model of community. For as Cotton Mather might have put it, the concept of national election was heaven-sent for the Massachusetts Bay colonists. They were a community in search of an identity commensurate with their New World mission, and when they adopted the federal covenant as their "peculiar" social bond, the concept of elect nation became incarnate in the first wholly Protestant contribution to modern nationalism, the American Israel.

Thus it was that the colony came to signify a "Way," an "errand *into* the [indefinite American] wilderness." "New England" denoted a people that was neither merely national nor purely religious, but that nonetheless combined both these terms in a voluntary contract that merged the principles of *sola fides* and *sola scriptura,* the inward spiritual road to salvation and the communal road in time and space to the millennium. To recognize the meaning of New England, as Samuel Danforth explained in his great election-day address of 1670, was to re-cognize the colony in terms of its cause and end, in relation to its New World antiquities and to the New World Jerusalem, of which those antiquities were a specimen. Inevitably, this was to realize (through an inward sight of sin) "how far we have fallen" and at the same time to realize (through prophetic insight) "how far we must rise to make ourselves worthy of our errand." And that double sense of shortcoming implied its own remedy: an *act* both personal and public, through which the inward turning to the spirit issued in a social commitment to progress.

Danforth's *Brief Recognition of New England's Errand into the Wilderness* is characteristic in this regard. It echoes and is echoed in turn by a long procession of exhortations — among others, those of John Higginson (1663), William Stoughton (1669), Uriah Oakes (1673), Increase Mather (1674), William Adams (1679), Samuel Torrey (1683), John Whiting (1686), and James Allen (1689). These addresses constitute a triumph of the colonial Puritan imagination, and to some extent they persisted in their own right, as a literary genre, through intertextual connections from one ritual occasion to the next — on fast and thanksgiving days, days of humiliation, election days, and days of covenant-renewal. But above all they persisted for functional reasons, as an organic expression of the community. They were the *cultural* issue of a venture dedicated to the proposition that prophecy is history antedated, and history, postdated prophecy. They represented a community in crisis and therefore using crisis as a strategy of social revitalization; a plantation in peril and therefore drawing strength from adversity, transition, and flux; a company-in-covenant deprived by history of their identity and therefore using their self-declared newness to create a vision of America that re-cognized history at large (including that of the Old World) as hinging on their failure or success.

The legacy of this ritual mode may be traced through virtually every major event in the culture, from the Great Awakening through the Revolution and the westward movement to the Civil War, and from that "Armageddon of the Republic" to the Cold War and the Star Wars of *our* latter days. At every point, the rituals of generational rededication build on the distance between fact and promise; at every point they interpret that distance in terms of "errand" or its various equivalents ("manifest destiny," "continuing revolution," "new frontiers"); and at every point the errand is defined as the special obligation of the "Israel of our time," federally covenanted as "the nation of futurity" to be "the heir of the ages" and "the haven for God's outcasts and exiles" — "a new breed of humans called an American," destined "to begin the world over again" and "to build a land here that will be for all mankind a shining city on a hill."

These phrases come from a variety of Americans, as distant in time from each other, and as different in mind and imagination, as John Adams, Herman Melville, and Ronald Reagan. My purpose in running their words together is not to blur the differences, but, on the contrary, to highlight the disparate uses to which the Puritan vision lent itself. In particular, I want to call attention in this regard to our literary tradition: the internalized, adversarial, visionary "America" that inspired Emerson and his heirs; "the only true America," as Thoreau called it, which our major authors have recurrently drawn upon (or withdrawn into) as an alternative to the dominant American Way. That alternative America is the third aspect I referred to of the Puritan legacy, and it has its roots in the last phase of the New England Puritan vision. By 1693, when Cotton Mather started on his *Magnalia Christi Americana,* the church-state was defunct, and in his view New England had tragically abandoned its calling. The *Magnalia* self-consciously affirms the vision *in spite* of social continuities; it re-cognizes the entire errand, from its antiquities in the Great Migration to its fulfillment in the millennium, *as rhetoric.* "I write the wonders of the Christian religion, flying from the depravations of Europe to the American strand": With this double allusion to what he considered the main epics of classical and of Reformation history, Virgil's *Aeneid,* the myth of Rome's founding, and John Foxe's *Book of Martyrs,* the founding myth of England's national election, Mather began his would-be greater New World epic; and then he added, a little later in the General Introduction: "But whether *New-England* may *Live* any where else or no, it must *Live* in our *History!*"

This poignant-defiant transvaluation of fact into trope may be seen as the logical end of the Puritan vision. The second-generation colonists had turned to rhetoric to compensate for the betrayal of Europe. Mather took their strategy one step further: He transformed the rhetoric into compensation for the betrayal of history. For him, too, "New England" was a conjunction of geography, Scripture, and the spirit; he too created his symbology out of the rhetoric of discovery, the authority of the word, and the primacy of personal faith. But his aim in all this was not to clothe local history in myth. It was to preserve the myth from the course of history. This was the aim, too, of many of his later works as well as the works of other Old Guard visionaries — for example, Joshua Scottow (1694), Nicholas Noyes (1698), and Joseph Morgan (1715) — all of which might have been titled, like Samuel Sewall's tract of 1697, *Phaenomena quaedam Apocalyptica; or, A Description of the New Heavens as It Makes to Those Who Stand Upon the New Earth.* This anachronistic procession of cloud-capped Americas, passing largely unheeded into Yankee New England, would seem to be an apt *finale* to the apocalyptic play-within-a-play of "the history of New English Israel." "Elect nation," "New World," "*the* wilderness," "New Canaan," "latter-day Israel" — all the foundations of the New England Way were figures of speech. Conceived in rhetoric, they sprang to life for a season — a nation born *ex verbo* in a day — and then returned in due time to the realm of rhetoric.

There is a satisfying sense of closure in this view, and a certain poetic justice as well. But it happens to be historically inaccurate. The fact is that the Puritan vision survived the demise of the church-state. Like Hawthorne's anachronistic Grey Champion, it returned as an agent of social cohesion at every stage of cultural transition — including, ironically, the transition from Puritan colony to Yankee province. The fact is, too, that New England retained its mythic status as the origin of American identity (long after the region had lost its national importance), just as the telos it claimed to prefigure remained in one form or another (and quintessentially in scriptural form) inherent in the American dream. And the fact is, finally, that the strategy of Mather's *Magnalia*, his determination to make "history" of *his* Theopolis Americana — to bring interpretation to "life," whether it lived historically anywhere else or not — became a ritual mode of our literary tradition. Intrinsic to this process of ritual re-cognition, from the Romantic period onward, was the spiritual use of geography as *American* nature, the geographic specificity of consciousness as *American* self-realization, and the sustained use of Scripture as pre-text of *America's* promise. That symbology our classic writers never disavowed. However universalist their outlook, however fixed they were on transcendence and the self, they invested the meaning of those concepts in the same federal vision. In their optative moods, they spoke as unacknowledged representatives of America. In their despairing moods they interpreted the betrayal of the vision as the betrayal of all human aspirations — inverted millennium into doomsday, and mankind's best hope into its *last*.

Looking back now to the antiquities of "New England" — re-cognizing these through the interpretative modes of our time (our suspicion of language, our disagreements about the meaning of the dream, and our tendency to replace Puritan providence with a metaphysics of material causation) — it seems clear that in part the vision persisted because it facilitated the development of a new way of life, the nascent capitalist modes that Christopher Hill has shown to have been dominant in seventeenth-century English Puritanism, and that applied *in extremis* to the society established by the Massachusetts Bay Company, Incorporated. The literary legacy is more problematic. The New World vision that the Puritans bequeathed became in our major writers variously a symbolic battleground, an ideal to which they could aspire *because* it could never be realized in fact, and an alternative *cultural* authority through which they could denounce (or even renounce) the United States. But here, too, rhetoric and history are inextricable. The vision of New England was the child of Protestantism, Renaissance exploration, and the printing press. But "America," as the single most potent cultural symbol of the modern world, and also (in its various re-cognizable forms) as the symbolic center of our literary tradition, was the discovery of Puritan New England.

What American Renaissance?
The Gendered Genealogy
of a Critical Discourse

CHARLENE AVALLONE

Originally published in PMLA *in 1997, Avallone's essay begins by noting the lack of consensus about the term* American Renaissance *in spite of its wide usage. The American Renaissance was initially associated with Unitarian and transcendentalist writing, but has been expanded to encompass the 1790s to the 1890s, with particular attention devoted to the mid-nineteenth-century decades. Over the course of her essay, Avallone provides an excellent overview of the various critical approaches to the renaissance while also challenging the concept, particularly in reference to its gendered hierarchy. She argues that the construction of* American Renaissance *has silenced working-class and ethnic minorities, while disparaging the work of women writers. Avallone does not call for a redefinition of* American Renaissance, *but instead suggests that the term is antiquated and should be replaced by one that can better reflect the cultural contexts of men's and women's writing of the nineteenth century.*

The critical discourse of "renaissance" emerged over a century ago to become academic currency in recountings of nineteenth-century United States literary history.[1] In the past decade, this discourse has framed more than two dozen monographs and essays, even though there has been little consensus on the historical period, the canon of authors or texts, or the value this critical tradition figures. Initially identified with Unitarian and transcendentalist writing, the era of renaissance doubled to cover both extended periods from the 1790s to the 1890s and a decade or so of concentrated literary excellence usually located around mid-century. As a trope, renaissance lacks any stable referent, even by way of a resemblance to sixteenth- and seventeenth-century Europe; as a literary term, *renaissance* has increasingly figured valorization. The discourse's critical power comes from appeals to authority rather than from any well-defined paradigm of or rationale for what might constitute an American

From *PMLA* 112.5 (1997): 1102–20.

renaissance. Some critics acknowledge that the notion exists merely for scholarly convenience or authorization (see Matthiessen, *American Renaissance* xii; Wright 4; Leverenz 166; Colacurcio 478, 491). But these positions obscure the tradition's role in the negotiation of cultural values, the asymmetrical distribution of cultural capital, and the maintenance of a gender hierarchy. In the struggle to determine what counts in the American cultural field, who adjudicates that field, and what validations are given lasting and representative significance, the language of renaissance serves to maintain male preeminence. In those dynamic, "mutually defining relations among classification, function, and value" that, as Barbara Herrnstein Smith demonstrates, define evaluation, the discourse promotes the "cultural re-production of value," as well as men's ascendancy, through the aesthetics of renaissance excellence (47, 32). It enlists professional and institutional authority to consolidate value in a literary field largely reserved for male authors and academic critics while it lends the support of its cultural hierarchies to reinforce social ones.

The idea of a renaissance tradition surfaced in 1876 in opposition to progressive criteria that privileged transcendentalists among the previous generation of Massachusetts writers. Through the Harvard-trained Samuel Osgood, who had recently converted from Unitarian to Episcopalian orders and returned from Europe to lecture in German at Union College, the label became invested in valorizing Anglo men's writing and art by affiliation with British, Christian, and Greek traditions. Unlike other critical languages, that of renaissance was disseminated until the 1980s almost exclusively by men in English departments to assert male writers' "distinction in literary history" and was reciprocally legitimized by association with those it distinguished (Wendell 374).[2] Appropriated in 1886 by the Dartmouth professor Charles Richardson, who was among the first to make American literature a college subject, renaissance discourse helped demarcate a gendered field of literary value as the academy institutionalized nineteenth-century American letters. The discourse was endowed with "prestige" at Harvard (Myerson, *Transcendentalists* 13), where it was used by Barrett Wendell (the author of studies on the Renaissance men Cotton Mather and William Shakespeare) to underscore the merits of prominent New England men of letters and later by F. O. Matthiessen to identify certain men's work as aesthetic and nationally representative.

The multiplication of renaissances, defined by later literature, ethnicity, region, or ideology, and the conflicts between "New Americanists" and old (Crews) have solidified rather than undermined this notion's claims on national representation and aesthetic priority. While renaissance discourse may reconfigure periods, canons, and literary merit in response to social and academic change, it continues to assert the superior worth of androcentric culture and the lesser significance of women's work. Critics work to "redeem" the tradition's "possibilities for a new literary history in the practice of *American Renaissance*," which legitimates a field of research and pedagogy (Arac, *Critical Genealogies* 174, 171, 157).[3] Even after the development of feminist studies, the discourse continues to distinguish a tradition of male critical authority. Its system of classification forestalls the inclusion of women's writing in the annals of a cultural field women inhabited so widely and prominently as to provoke the reactionary discourse in the first place.[4] Indeed, apparent gains by American women in access to greater cultural, political, or economic power through their work have prompted scholars to revive in even fuller terms renaissance criticism as a means of containing women's claims to parity.

In contrast to silence on writers from working classes or ethnic minorities, which effectively preserved renaissance for the Anglo middle classes,[5] the discourse evolved a repertoire of active critical procedures to sustain opinions of women writers' lesser worth; the combination of these strategies of derogation and silencing has particularly disadvantaged African American women. The construction of American renaissance entailed intractable racist presumptions that survived redefinitions of race and literary merit. Opposed to second-wave immigration, Osgood encoded English heritage in the language of renaissance, which later scholars used to define Anglo-American men's cultural superiority to ethnic others: Native Americans, various European American groups, and "Africans," who were, in the view of one critic, if "not literally neolithic[,] . . . linger[ing] far behind," perhaps "unalterable aliens" in the United States (Wendell 342, 482; see also C. Richardson, *American Literature* 1: 1–62, 2: 410–11).[6] Alain Locke's effort to integrate a 1920s "New Negro renaissance" — what he characterized as the first "aesthetic" period in seven stages of American letters by black and white artists who represented "Negro life" and "idiom" — in the "general stream" of American culture foundered, Locke thought, on the "dilemma" of "applying race concepts to cultural productions" ("New Negro"; "American Literary Tradition" 433; "American Culture" 451; see also "Renaissance" 21). But racist concepts structured in the idea of renaissance would be mobilized along with nationalist rhetoric in Matthiessen's work to define nineteenth-century Anglo literature as "American" accomplishment and heritage. Although the discourse has recently broken its silence on African Americans' nineteenth-century writing, the presumption of Anglo men's superiority persists. Recognizing only Frederick Douglass's autobiographical "classic," Sacvan Bercovitch recommends an analysis that would foreground "excluded groups" in other periods and decenter "the American Renaissance." But his insistence that substantial "aesthetic power" distinguishes "major works of the American Renaissance" would forestall efforts to disrupt the mid-nineteenth-century primacy of Anglo men's writing and attendant determinations of period, genre, and value, and thus would continue to preclude discussion of black women's work of that era as literary "art" (*Rites* 370, 375–76, 368, 365; see also Buell 301; Romero 127–28). The discourse does not establish literary value for nineteenth-century black women's writing on alternative bases or extend to their mid-century production in the one assertion of their late-century intellectual renaissance (Carby); thus its operation as a figure of male aesthetic primacy remains unchallenged.[7] Generally, critics have begun to use the tradition's procedures to promote nineteenth-century black men to renaissance status by devaluing (black and white) women's achievement (Andrews; Leverenz 167, 131) or to demote black men through links with the lesser literary power attributed to (white) women relative to renaissance men (Railton 197–99).

This essay aims to show how critical procedures of derogation came to configure the notions of an American renaissance in the four academic revivals that most clearly elaborated the tradition's claims: the first began with Charles Richardson's *American Literature, 1607–1885* (1886, 1888); the second followed Barrett Wendell's *A Literary History of America* (1900); the third ensued from F. O. Matthiessen's *American Renaissance* (1941); the fourth is ongoing. In mapping the genealogy of this discourse I examine the consignment of women writers to a separate, subordinate sphere and the erasure of their writings' significance, rebirth metaphorics and body aesthetics, the institution of formalist reading strategies and of the modernist masterwork canon, and women's muted roles in current renaissance models. Such procedures are more consistent than other features of renaissance criticism, and they persist in new theories and methods. I trace interactions between criticism and women's history and between past and current criticism to show how the encoding of gender discrimination in renaissance aesthetics has made the discourse resistant to revisions that would comprehend the worth of women's writing or that would render a historically responsible account of American literature.

Many critics attribute the discourse of an American renaissance to F. O. Matthiessen, obscuring the extent to which *American Renaissance* is a palimpsest that transmits prior inscriptions of the notion. Others assume that early "innocent" inscriptions do not bear on modern thought (Colacurcio 459; see also 446) or presume that the tradition originates in antebellum writing.[8] Despite the commonplace early-nineteenth-century belief that the newly independent United States would give birth to a unique literature, no discourse of literary rebirth or renaissance emerged in the antebellum period. While some writers emphasized analogies to the European Renaissance, others challenged such ideas. Melville linked critics' "great mistake" in imagining an American literature "in the costume of Queen Elizabeth's day" with Americans' "Anglo Saxon superstitions" (245–46). Margaret Fuller argued that until American writings stopped performing as English cultural "colonists" and until they were informed by the "birth" of new ideas derived from material factors in the new country, including the "fusion of races," any "attempts to construct a national literature must end in abortions like the monster of Frankenstein" ("American Literature" 384–85), not the rebirth later critics envisioned.

Samuel Osgood appropriated the foundational term of renaissance criticism from European historians to oppose the idea that transcendentalism stemmed from radical German philosophy, especially from Frederick Jacobi and Johann Fichte, and manifested itself in such ideals as the emancipation of women and slaves (Frothingham 14–46, 175, 156). Threatened by emancipatory theory, Osgood in 1857 attacked "masculine . . . woman's rights reformers" for misleading women from their "true sphere." In 1851 he advocated assimilation as a means of maintaining Anglo-American men's "sway," which he believed was imperiled by German refugees contaminated by communist ideas and the "Bacchanalian poetry" that appeared in their press ("Our Daughters" 77; "German" 351, 355, 358–59). In the 1870s, when press coverage in New York featured nomination of a white female presidential candidate with a black male running mate, women's labor protests, deadly militia violence against immigrant women, and court actions against suffragists attempting to vote, Osgood's crafting of renaissance discourse to figure the primacy of an Anglo male elite paralleled the work of other male journalists, who, as Mary Ryan shows, tailored their representations of the public emergence of women to suit their own gender, class, and ethnic interests (158–64; see also Peterson 224–25).

In a review of Octavius Frothingham's *Transcendentalism in New England* (1876), Osgood argued, "[W]hat may be called the Renaissance in literature among the New England Puritans in the nineteenth century . . . is clearly a tendency to restoration" of sixteenth- and seventeenth-century British idealism ("Transcendentalism" 745). Apparently recalling the ironic admiration of British racial supremacy and Elizabethan idealism in Emerson's *English Traits,* Osgood grounded the value of the renaissance in "the great English race" and proclaimed William Ellery Channing's and Emerson's "great excellences," however deficient in originality or "eloquence" (754, 747, 751). Although Osgood valorized the renaissance revision of "manly thinking" by "both men and women," he belittled the writing and cultural leadership of Margaret Fuller, the only woman named in the review, in referring these achievements to domesticity: "Household life, too, has been the better by the infusion of the ideal element, and many Transcendental maidens who followed their sister superior, Margaret Fuller, into matrimony, have made good report of the light at their fireside, without her tragic end" (746, 751, 762).

Osgood maintained the conservatism of what he called the "American Renaissance" in eulogizing the antitranscendentalist New Yorker Evert Duyckinck. Osgood praised Duyckinck's "manly" criticism, which, Osgood wrote, preserved "old English standards of culture" in their "struggle for life" against both mid-century decline into "the new cosmopolitan era" of second-wave immigration and radical transcendentalist "invaders" of American culture, perhaps Germanic after all (*Duyckinck* 5, 2, 15, 7).

In the mid-1880s Charles Richardson wrote renaissance discourse into his *American Literature,* often recognized as the first comprehensive history of United States literature and, with Barrett Wendell's *Literary History of America,* as a "foundation" of the subject's academic study (Jones 99; see also Vanderbilt 105, 121–22, 146–47). During the previous decade, women's movement had claimed public power with territorial suffrage, labor organization, women's clubs, and participation in the academy. Racial inequities made change uneven and conflicted, but Helen Hunt Jackson, Sarah Winnemucca,

Elizabeth Peabody, Frances Harper, Mary Ann Shadd Cary, and Julia Ward Howe, among others, made public Native American and African American women's concerns. Women's clubs and the black press engaged in public discussion of national literature; one "Lady" wondered in *Lippincott's* "why should not the coming novelist be a woman as well as an African" and "make a new epoch in our literature?" (Gates, *Signifying Monkey* 174). The decade from the mid-1870s to the mid-1880s brought renewed attention to Margaret Fuller's writing: New issues of her books and biographies appeared; the first history of transcendentalism recognized her stature as "The Critic" (Frothingham 284–301, 358–59); several Fuller clubs were organized to promote women's cultural "improvement"; and *History of Woman Suffrage* commemorated her writings (Stanton, Anthony, and Gage).

In this context of women's expanding cultural participation, Richardson construed the renaissance in ways that constrained the influence of Fuller and other women, while reserving authority and stature for male critics and writers. Whereas Richardson's *Primer of American Literature,* written before he became a professor, appreciated women's work, even among "Masterpieces" (112), his *American Literature, 1607–1885* introduces renaissance discourse to affirm the value of national letters as the exclusive patrimony of a "prominent" male "aristocracy," whose "righteousness, intelligence, and goodbreeding, handed down from father to son," had existed since colonization (1: 55–56):

> American literature is the literature of a cultured and genuine Democracy, a sort of Saxon-Greek renaissance in the New World; a liberty that is as far removed from anarchy as it is from despotism. (1: 61–62)

Richardson translates race, class, and gender hierarchy into a system of literary status. This notion of renaissance marks off authentic culture (like classical democracy, excluding women, a serving class, and the foreign-born) against perceived threats to prerogatives long reserved to a male minority. Richardson's hierarchy persists in later versions of renaissance where writers' artistic excellence is partly defined by their opposition to more egalitarian democracy, including "political feminism" (D. Reynolds 394, 423).[9]

Richardson also invokes the idea of "Transcendental renaissance" in debating Fuller's "real place in American literature"; he concludes that her "notable" cultural "influence" is hardly worth notice in the "history of literature" (1: 427, 355, 431–32). To evaluate Fuller, Richardson sets aside his own stated standards, including influence and "intrinsic success," and substitutes Osgood's strategies: erasure of value and subordination to a separate sphere (1: x). Admitting that it cannot "be said that Miss Fuller's writing was of inferior merit, for some of it surpassed in value the essays and criticisms of her male peers (1: 432), Richardson nonetheless denies that Fuller wrote anything "of importance" and claims that "[f]ew nowadays, read the 'works' of Margaret Fuller. . . . [H]er personality and the memory of her influence [construed by Emerson and Hawthorne] are the things that interest us, not the present value of her printed pages" (1: 431, 432–33). Richardson thus dismisses the acknowledged value and influence of the woman writer's work in favor of what "interest[s] us" — male academics — more: the writing of Fuller's male compatriots (1: 433, 431, 433). Denied rank as an author in Richardson's system, Fuller only marks the anomalous space of the female author: her "name . . . is practically the first to show the position woman has already begun to take . . . in the literature of America . . . though we read not her books" (1: 433–34). In Richardson's view, perpetuated by generations of renaissance critics, women are extraneous to American literature — that is, the normative writing of men. Thus the "women who followed" Fuller constitute a series of exceptional individuals, not affiliated in literary traditions with one another or with men but, rather, assigned successively to a subordinate women's "position" (1: 434, 433).[10] Presuming that "the work of woman" does not "command a study as deep as that bestowed upon the work of men," Richardson judges even Helen Hunt Jackson, who he believed surpassed Fuller and "outranked . . . any other American woman" poet, "far enough below" Emerson, the male writer he cites as Jackson's peer (2: 240, 238, 239).

Separate-sphere devaluation and erasure of the significance of women's work endured in renaissance discourse even though critics assigned various men preeminent rank. For example, while Wendell concedes extraordinary "genius," "power," and "vitality" to Harriet Beecher Stowe, he nonetheless effaces her work's literary value and uses gender stereotypes to deny her "distinguished place" in his renaissance: the "best" of her work only "approaches excellence" because of domestic "distractions" (354–55). Wendell cites Fuller first among "most characteristic figures" of transcendentalism's "typically renascent" aspects, but he discusses neither her books nor the "surprisingly good" material that she wrote or edited for the early *Dial*, describes her as an "unsexed . . . Socrates" in her conversation classes, and gives her no rank in renaissance literature (300, 297, 302).

Although not academics, Thomas Wentworth Higginson and Henry Walcott Boynton borrow the period and value category "Professor Wendell suggestively calls 'The New England Renaissance'" and use it to deprecate and erase Fuller, Stowe, and Emily Dickinson, "perhaps the most remarkable" woman but still only "a woman of . . . less easily intelligible type" despite "lyrical power almost unequaled in her generation" (109, 130–31). Higginson and Boynton classify Catharine Sedgwick, Lydia Maria Child, Helen Hunt Jackson, and Louisa May Alcott as "women of that period" and ensure their "disappearance" notwithstanding "brilliant" literary achievement, "ranked" with the best work of male peers (126–27). Fred Lewis Pattee's renaissance includes twenty women, but Pattee depreciates them all as "feminine" writers who display an "element not 'classical'" in American literature, even though Stowe produced one of the "books that may be claimed as classics" (*First Century* 568, 565).

Although various nationalist and aesthetic discourses did valorize women writers,[11] academic renaissance criticism in the twentieth century continued to erase and displace women's achievement, as denials of women's work as literature gained sufficient authority to make demonstrations unnecessary. This strategic erasure persists in the subliterary status assigned to African American women's writing (D. Reynolds, 361, 419; see also Buell 301). Even recent studies that contain appreciative analyses of women's writing exclude it from consideration in rationales for the general significance and "artful" character of an American renaissance (L. Reynolds 174).[12] Fuller's writing remains peripheral to the renaissance, where she has "always hovered at the edges," or else she is part of the environment that "nourished the great writers" or of subliterary culture below true renaissance accomplishment (Colacurcio 453; Ziff xi; D. Reynolds; cf. Leverenz 179). Even the best critiques of gendered assumptions in renaissance scholarship presume that "the women's novel" is aesthetically deficient in comparison with men's "classics" (Romero 128–29).

Throughout the 1890s in Boston, antisuffrage organization and racial tensions mounted, as did the reactionary views of scholars like Wendell. Suffragists, reunited in a national movement despite ideological and racial conflicts, distanced their agenda from Elizabeth Cady Stanton's radicalism even as her syndicated essays and *Woman's Bible* (1895) were widely read (Griffith 212–13). Ethnic minorities struggled for agency in national women's organizations and set their own political and cultural agendas. Women entered universities in record numbers and challenged men's exclusive claim to high culture with writing then widely read and now admired as artistic and intellectual; Boston's *Atlantic Monthly,* the leading literary journal, attracted attention as "a field where women in particular . . . take high honors" and "make a permanent name in letters" (Kirk 199).[13] Anna Julia Cooper's criticism, praised in the Boston *Transcript* as evincing her race's "cultivation" (Gabel 31–32), offered a revisionary literary history that pointed to the cultural centrality of African Americans in oral and scholarly traditions; in literary treatments, such as *Uncle Tom's Cabin*; and in the writings of black authors (176–226). From homes in Beacon Hill, which neighbored Wendell's Back Bay, Julia Ward Howe and Josephine St. Pierre Ruffin worked together in multiple regional associations for reforms to benefit women and blacks while also leading national women's movements: Howe worked to reunite suffragists, Ruffin organized the National Association for Colored Women (1896), and both attempted racial integration of women's clubs (Flexner; Richards and Elliott; Carby 116–17; Arroyo). The indefatigable Howe protested restrictions on immigration, gave legislative testimony for suffrage, and spoke widely — for example, on behalf of the Tuskegee Institute with Booker T. Washington and W. E. B. Du Bois, and against lynching, with Ruffin's daughter (Richards and Elliot 225, 199–200, 261–62). She was so well known that hate mail arrived addressed to "Mrs. Howe, Negro Sympathizer, Boston" (266). Katharine Bates, a professor who invited Howe to give a poetry reading at Wellesley, wove into her literary history of "supreme achievements" by men bred in "privileges of race" suggestions for reading Douglass, Phillis Wheatley, and several other women (117, 328, 154, 346, 78). She also shifted her period label from "renascence" to a "national era" of literary "movement" whose "core" was the "moral enthusiasm" of abolition (117–18).

Wendell used his institutional eminence to revive the notion of a "New England renaissance" stretching from the Revolution to the twentieth century and encompassing more than two dozen men, as well as the muted figures of a half dozen women. He ascribed extraordinary value and representative national status to a professional "aristocracy" of an Anglo "native type" that had inherited patriarchal "traditions of New England manhood" and had best reinscribed those British renaissance traditions of moral, sociopolitical, and literary "authority" recorded in the King James Bible, common law, and English classics of "lasting literature" (242, 8). Tracing his renaissance's decline to emancipation and the subsequent weakening of this elite's dominance, he rationalized the lynching of African Americans by suggesting that like earlier opposition to abolitionist "Enthusiasm," it showed "thoughtful" concern about protecting white women from "the lust of brutal savages" (356, 339, 345–46). Wendell adapted social Darwinism in his cultural model of uneven evolutionary struggle between races and uneven physical, intellectual, and imaginative development of the sexes; he applied this model in writings that he boasted "sav[ed] Harvard from coeducation" and preserved the "pure virility of Harvard tradition" (Howe 87–88). His work guided "the first organized movement" to limit immigration (Solomon 47, 57–59) and advocated defending ideals of "imperial democracy" against foreign and domestic threats of an un-American "world-democracy" that favored equality (Wendell 526, 530; see also 8–9, 521–30).[14]

Wendell's professional authority and institutional status prompted a publisher's invitation to write the work that became *A Literary History of America*. In this study, Wendell claimed that the scholarly and literary "leaders [and] followers" of New England renaissance "were generally . . . Harvard men or men . . . closely allied" (261; see also 443–45). His "Boston renaissance" distinguished as "the nearest approach of America to lasting literature" the work of classically trained men who wrote for the *Atlantic* in the years 1857–64 — particularly the Harvard professors Henry Wadsworth Longfellow, Oliver Wendell Holmes, and James Russell Lowell; Emerson, a Harvard graduate; and Hawthorne, a member of this circle — but not women's writing in the periodical, though he mentioned the *Atlantic* writers Lucy Larcom, Mary Wilkins [Freeman], Sarah Orne Jewett, Stowe, and Alcott, in addition to Fuller, in describing regional renaissance (528, 370–77).[15] But Wendell found it hard to secure men's stature by European standards of classic letters. Anxiety over American men's "lasting potence," especially Emerson's, informs Wendell's renaissance aesthetics and development of the physiological analogy inherent in the discourse in his staging of male rebirth into transcendent culture (445–46; see also 316–17, 326).

Wendell ranked Emerson "most eminent," above writers of better art, thereby fitting him, in a social Darwinian model of canon, "to survive the rest much as Shakespeare" in "Classical immortality" (311, 335, 302, 315). Directives for reading Emerson "whatever his final value" show that renaissance stature is conferred through procedures that make a text "familiar"; literary deficiencies, "human circumstances," and "historical environment" thereby factor "less and less" in "vitality," which is attributed "to all phases of lasting literature" in a male line extending from Homer and Shakespeare (316, 315). Unlike analogies of "vigorous physical embodiment" (Arac, *Critical Genealogies* 162), this critical language presents the fantasy of male writers reborn as renaissance authors and of their works endowed with that "secret" of "vitality" that, as Matthiessen claims, gives them "immediate life of their own" (*American Renaissance* x, vii) — a "vitality" still presumed to be lacking in women's writing (Leverenz 278, 174–79).[16] Through this rebirth and intensified vitality, male genius embodies the enduring life and eternal value of literature and thus escapes history, while women's labor merely reproduces popular subculture.[17] The subtext of greater male aesthetic vitality persists in recent efforts at resituating women in renaissance and renaissance in history. Thus Stowe's "rebirth" is said to "reinvest" male renaissance work with particular power and "authority" (Pease, Introduction vii–viii). "[O]bsolescence," which a male renaissance "rival" of Stowe is said to have avoided through literary "techniques," is attributed to her work as a function of its value rather than as a consequence of critical ideology (Buell 280). And *Uncle Tom's Cabin*, the only woman's work one critic includes among "classic texts," is associated with the "sustaining vitality" of historical "forces." Discussed as "having a renaissance of its own," the novel is treated separately from works by male writers of an "old consensus" canon, who are associated with "irreducible" aesthetic power (Bercovitch, *Rites* 367, 370, 363, 360).

Metaphorics of male rebirth identify women writers with the material body and thus suggest that their work is less enduring, less cerebral. Wendell introduced the renaissance procedure of evaluating a woman writer by judging her body, especially its maternal or erotic aspects. Stowe's maternal body — genteelly coded as her "growing family" — is the evidence of the flaw that prevents her from becoming "a figure of lasting literary importance," despite the undeniable "vitality" of her creations; the body of "poor Margaret Fuller" ("nothing short of genius could connect her with the idea of sex") signals Hawthorne's superior creativity in fantasizing a "profoundly feminine" figure like Zenobia (354–55, 306). Matthiessen reiterated the contrast between Hawthorne's artistry, instanced in the "perfectly developed figure" of the naked Zenobia, and the "strained angularity" of "the living woman," Fuller (*American Renaissance* 296–97). And for Vernon Parrington, Fuller was the "embodiment" of renaissance aspects he most admired yet also a tragic "victim of sex" so "excessive" that she was unable to think or write as "an artist." Parrington cites as evidence of the lack of "beauty" and "art" in Stowe's work not textual shortcomings but her "ardent nature and multiplying domestic cares" (426, 420, 433, 370). Body aesthetics still serve to secure male authors' superior status. Recent criticism finds Caroline Kirkland's "realism" wanting because her work insufficiently foregrounds "mothering"; yet Stowe's polemic art is viewed as flawed because her work excessively valorizes "home and mother" (Leverenz 156; Railton 78, 85). Even efforts to appreciate

Fuller's work iterate that "[s]he lacked beauty, of course (L. Reynolds 79; cf. Ziff 149).

Wendell's notion of renaissance became "standard literary history" or a challenge "impossible to ignore" for many (Vanderbilt 146–47; Howells 50). Later critics traded on his idea and in so doing enhanced it. Only tenuously connected to the disciplinary establishment of historical literature, Alain Locke, a Howard University philosophy professor, and Van Wyck Brooks, an independent critic who had been a Stanford professor, strove to appropriate the discourse for contemporary writing. Locke, whose Harvard education "exposed" him to Wendell (Stewart 3), applied the discourse to describe a cultural movement stimulated by a call from W. E. B. Du Bois, a former student of Wendell's, for a "renaissance of American Negro literature" (299). Locke left Wendell's renaissance paradigm largely unchallenged, although he reevaluated African American folk traditions as a "national asset" and developed an ethnographic theory that insisted on organic interpretation and relativism to evaluate cultures ("American Art" 441; "Concept" 430–31). Locke's standards of "pure" art prevented him from valorizing African American writing before the 1880s, when "modern breaking-through of the Negro man of letters," with Dunbar and Chestnutt's "real success in the *Atlantic Monthly*," opened the way for aesthetic renaissance of the 1920s ("American Art" 444). By ignoring Charlotte Forten's *Atlantic* publications, shunting Frances Harper's dialect poetry into a lesser sphere of women's sentimental writing, and refusing to acknowledge the accomplishments of Jesse Fauset, Nella Larsen, and several female poets, Locke sustained the primacy of "men of letters" (Hull 7–10; Davis 158–61; see also Locke, "Harlem," Foreword, "Negro Youth"; Carby 163–75; duCille 66–148). Academic attention would not focus on African American writers until the 1960s (Gates, "Criticism" 303), while American studies, gathering critical mass by the 1920s, emphasized "proper ranking of American authors," which exalted white men (Hubbell 334–35; see also Lauter, *Canons* 24–31, 36). Parrington, also Wendell's student, at the University of Washington applied renaissance discourse to trace European influence on over fifty regional writers in Virginia, the deep South, and New York who preceded New England's renaissance. Although Parrington disavowed aesthetic concerns, he unsystematically invoked the renaissance phrasing to magnify the merits of certain men — such as William Gilmore Simms, the "most virile . . . figure of the old South," unsurpassed in the nation for "command of masculine English prose," that "muscular idiom of the old literature" of European Renaissance — while especially deprecating Wendell's "Boston renaissance" for Hawthorne's "intellectual poverty" and Lowell's "pottering" criticism (v, 121, 125, 439, 457). Stanley Williams at Yale defended the primacy of Boston's "genuine" renaissance, epitomized in Lowell (Williams 78, 108), and Pattee at Penn State endorsed New England's excellence, particularly in Longfellow, but reverted to the nationwide model of Richardson, his professor, to argue for a larger "mid-century renaissance" (*First Century* 535–36, v, 444). Van Wyck Brooks acknowledged Wendell, his professor, but narrowed Wendell's "whole New

England 'renaissance'" (*Flowering* 43, 107) and tried to shift the discourse to modern writers who "talked of a 'renaissance'" (*Indian Summer* 496). Brooks first located this renaissance in New York, then throughout the nation, and he relied on other critical languages to describe antebellum efflorescence (*Indian Summer* 499; *Confident Years* 485–86, 507–48, 554).[18] Brooks included some women without derogation, like Maria Brooks and Stowe, but academic reviewers, including Matthiessen, discredited his authority. Matthiessen's own work in progress was grounding renaissance aesthetics more in tastes for Anglican tradition cultivated by critics such as T. S. Eliot, another of Wendell's students. According to Matthiessen, Brooks's "method" of literary history lacked aesthetic "treatment of the few major artists" in "New England renaissance" and flattered Fuller excessively ("Flowering" 203, 199, 206; cf. *American Renaissance* xvii). The active discrediting of women's accomplishment persisted throughout the 1920s and 1930s, but it was Matthiessen who made the renaissance all male.

In the 1930s, as Matthiessen was writing *American Renaissance,* the reaction against the previous decade of women's activism amounted to a "crisis of masculinity" (McFadden 119). During the depression, legislation and public opinion impeded women's access to gainful employment, which was then scarce for men. Universities, including Harvard, set quotas limiting women's entry into professional programs, and a request that women be included in the leadership of the MLA's American Literature Group generated ridicule (Cott 223–24; Lauter, *Canons* 45–46n32). Mary Inman provoked censure from socialist circles, in which Matthiessen moved, when her feminist analysis of gender subservience and women's reproductive and domestic labor challenged theories of class oppression (Gluck 292–93). The gender hierarchy of the times informed Matthiessen's criticism, beginning with his biography of Jewett, which subordinates her "feminine contribution" to Whitman's and Melville's "deeper potency" (151–52). Symptomatically, Matthiessen's *American Renaissance* contains a critical fantasy of American literature as a "melodrama of beset manhood," as Nina Baym demonstrates ("Melodramas"), and an androcentric theory of symbolism, as Eric Cheyfitz shows (354–55).

Matthiessen wed the discourse to the modernist masterwork model of canon and to formalist reading methods and thus made renaissance a male preserve of national artistic achievement. The publication dates of seven "masterpieces" by five men defined 1850–55 as a period of superior value because of these works' exceptional originality and aesthetic "vitality" in appropriating European Renaissance sources and because of their conservative democratic politics (*American Renaissance* vii). These masterworks do not hold up well under the tension between the canon of classic authors that he took from Lewis Mumford (but attributed to "generations of common readers") and the reading method and aesthetic canons he pieced together from contemporary formalist critics and from Coleridge (Matthiessen, *American Renaissance* x). Even in his rationale of renaissance, Matthiessen concedes that

Emerson produced "no masterpiece" yet justifies labeling him a renaissance man nonetheless: "[Emerson] was the cow from which the rest drew their milk" (xviii, xii; cf. Mumford 94).[19] According to Matthiessen's reading, Hawthorne "never really succeeded" in unifying the characters or plot in *The House of the Seven Gables* (335). Appeal to the imitative fallacy defends the novel's stature despite its artistic failure: Hawthorne's "work [is] a mirror of its age by virtue . . . of its inevitable unconscious limitations" (336). Matthiessen's intense distaste for Hawthorne's "stiffness" of style, characterization, and Spenserian Renaissance allegory leads him to describe *The Scarlet Letter* as being "redeemed" by the critical tradition that emphasizes the "charm" of Hawthorne's moral psychology and that thereby discounts his aesthetic shortcomings (279, 295). Matthiessen also judges Melville's *Pierre* probably a "failure," too chaotic to embody the formal model of Renaissance tragedy or to meet New Critical standards for controlled ambiguity and sentiment (487, 474, 482). And despite the "complexity" of *Moby-Dick*'s ventriloquism of Renaissance models (its depictions of homoerotic desire and the fantastic male body — "Whitmanesque comradeship" and "the heroic phallus of the whale"), the novel was not a literary masterwork: "Melville did not achieve" the standards of "lucid . . . [and] universal" Renaissance masterpieces (431, 656). Even though the emblems of American renaissance excellence under Matthiessen's scrutiny turn out to be failures, the authors remain masters in Matthiessen's readings, which presume the inferiority of women's writing. The introduction to *American Renaissance* erases as "trash" the work of Fanny Fern, Maria Cummins, Susan Warner, and E. D. E. N. Southworth, dismissing these writers unread as "scribbling women" (x). Quoting Hawthorne to validate a possibly "arbitrary" selection of male authors, Matthiessen interprets those writers' lack of readership as evidence of their masterworks' extraordinary artistic value, which later "generations of common readers" have "taken from granted" (x–xi).[20] Thus Matthiessen lays the ground for the autonomous aesthetic value that modernism presumes of art and thereby makes the discrimination of that value in men's writing from women's "worthless scrabble" the foundation of modernist renaissance discourse.

American Renaissance offers neither analysis nor argument to sustain this differential valuing. Matthiessen does not read Stowe's and Fuller's work among renaissance masterpieces yet claims that he would include Stowe among "great authors" in another study and cites Fuller's essays to lend historical authority to his renaissance theses (viii; 103–04, 180). He never explains these contradictions. Instead he depreciates women to reinforce the renaissance stature of the masters. His description of Fuller's *Dial* work as merely expressing what "others were feeling" sets off Emerson's originality, just as the lack of beauty ascribed to Fuller counterpoints Hawthorne's artistry (296–97, 13).[21] Similarly, although Dickinson's poetry belongs "much more authentically in the metaphysical tradition" of Renaissance verse than Emerson's "ejaculatory" efforts do, Matthiessen makes Dickinson's theory of language "seem indistinguishable" from Emerson's and thereby bolsters

Emerson's status (115). Discounting Elizabeth Peabody's "radical" work helps valorize by antithesis Hawthorne's and Melville's aesthetic evasion of history, their "escape from mere contemporaneity . . . into possession of the primary attributes of man," the masculine humanism that makes them renaissance men (320–21).[22] Other contrasts with female inferiority help divert attention from male authors' inadequacies. Matthiessen presents Hawthorne's lapses of "moral perception" and Melville's sentimental style as characteristic of *Godey's Lady's Book,* and defends lack of "variety" in Melville's male casts of characters by arguing that "serious debate of ideas . . . tend[s] to leave [women] far in the background" (280, 486, 412).

Instead of challenging the gender biases or equivocations in Matthiessen's readings, later critics have relied on his "extended textual explications" or borrowed his method to demonstrate "the purely literary quality of the writings of the period" (Ziff xii), the "[l]iterariness" of these writings' formal features (D. Reynolds 7). Matthiessen's masterwork model of renaissance continues to be upheld as "seminal" in recent studies (L. Reynolds xi), even in those that revise his configurations of canon and period.

In the 1970s and 1980s, extended women's movement and reaction against it stimulated a revival of the largely dormant discourse of renaissance and thus of interest in Matthiessen's work. In the face of more women faculty members and administrators, women's studies programs, and feminist scholarship, renaissance discourse reemerged to reassert men's cultural superiority. Several studies followed Matthiessen in treating only male writers as representative of a renaissance.[23] The first study of "black . . . men of letters" in nineteenth-century renaissance affirms their artistry by contrast with the presumptive lack of artistry in black women's work (Andrews 38–39, 42–43).

However, women also began to engage renaissance criticism, generating feminist critique and increased attention to women writers, which opened the discussion enabling my argument. Challenging Matthiessen's canon and valuations, Ellen Moers reclaimed *Uncle Tom's Cabin* as "the 'female fiction' of the American Renaissance," thus anticipating Jane Tompkins's demonstration of an "other renaissance" of women's fiction (Moers 2, 4, 22; Tompkins, *Sensational Designs* 122–85; see also Tompkins, "Other American Renaissance"). Nina Baym demystified Matthiessen's (melo)dramatizing of American renaissance as a male "struggle for integrity and livelihood" against women, broadened periodization to the years 1820–70, endeavored to defer evaluation of women's work in favor of an ongoing process of recovery, and did not use the discourse in her work ("Melodramas" 10; Introduction xiv–xvii). Lawrence Buell sought to expand the discourse to comprehend New England women's writing. Hazel Carby challenged domination of black cultural history by critics' "invention" of the Harlem Renaissance with her conception of renaissance that valorizes African American women's organizational and intellectual movement of the 1890s (163–64). Lora Romero's appeal for including "the women's novel" in "the American Renaissance" canon (128) and G. M. Goshgarian's reading of the psychic underside of women writers' sentimental fiction worked to complicate understanding of mid-century novels' relation to domestic ideology. Paul Lauter and Joanne Dobson argued that literary assumptions must be radically reconsidered in the wake of Matthiessen's work. Moreover, Lauter proposed a way to include groups and regions excluded by "Matthiessen's definition of the American Renaissance." This proposal was intended to transform the period, literary history, and critical consciousness and ultimately to promote a cultural formation better suited to a democratic country entering the twenty-first century (*Canons* 110–11).

However, renaissance discourse proves inadequate to such a project, and thoroughgoing revision abandons that discourse. It does not organize discussion of the nineteenth century in Lauter's inclusive *Heath Anthology*, nor does the discourse appear in his arguments for "decentering . . . presumptively 'classic' texts from our structures of valuation" and for reevaluating nineteenth-century writing through new, dialectical combinations of literary and historical analysis (*Canons* 115). After Dobson delineates the deficiencies of renaissance conventions, her sketch for a more capacious literary history relies instead on the language of literary modes (167–75). Indeed, when white male primacy is displaced, renaissance phrasing ceases to have significance.

Implicitly, then, renaissance criticism remains inhospitable to women's cultural achievement. No body of women's writing serves canonical functions, such as defining the era's representative literary genres and aesthetics, analogous to those accorded to men's writing by American renaissance studies, nor does the discourse provide other grounds of equivalent valuation. Despite the theoretical sophistication and diversity of recent studies, the discourse continues to be characterized by separate-sphere derogation of women's writing, now figured through concepts of tokenism, subculture, and otherness. Tokenism defines an exceptional woman writer judged major (usually by modernist standards), such as Fuller, Dickinson, Stowe, or Kate Chopin, as a renaissance woman and values her above other women yet isolates her from her male peers.[24] Women writers may also be treated as a group that created a preliterary or subliterary subculture, worth consideration only in relation to renaissance men's superior work or as merely symptomatic of history (see Andrews; Hubbell; Leverenz; Railton; D. Reynolds; and Ziff). This model sustains presuppositions of inferiority with self-fulfilling predictions arguing that revisionary study need not destabilize literary standings or values, with invocations of self-evidence, with appeals to the authority of Matthiessen or of canonical male authors, or with (mis)readings that produce the very aspects of women's texts said to signify lesser art.[25] The most concerted efforts to integrate women with their male peers inevitably strain at the limits imposed by these gendered models of writing.[26] Even the notion of otherness, which defines an alternative renaissance for mid-century women, does not transform the discourse or avoid separate-sphere devaluation of women's achievements. Otherness confines appreciation of women's writing to a "woman's" genre of sentimental fiction, identifies *Uncle Tom's Cabin* as the genre's paradigmatic accomplishment, yet also as at least a partial exception to the genre (Goshgarian 79), and largely isolates the genre from the rest of nineteenth-century writing.[27] Consequently, revisionary renaissance discourse obscures the significance of other forms of women's writing, even such related forms as sentimental slave narratives, poetry, melodrama, and journalistic sketches. It thereby mutes women's participation in the thematics, the generic traditions, and the webs of influence that make up literary history. Likewise, the concept of an other renaissance of black women's writing of the 1890s reiterates the failure to recognize black women's mid-century work and fails to undermine the determination of aesthetic value as a "privilege reserved for only a few selected white men," as Barbara Christian points out (72).[28] Indeed, attempts to conscript the discourse to affirm women's writing do not extend to systemic criticism and forestall broadening the investigation of multiple grounds of cultural value that was initiated by the architects of women's renaissances.

As Annette Kolodny has observed, attempts to force women's writing and oral culture into conventional categories "result not in integration but in fundamental distortion" (296; see also Fetterley, *Provisions* 31; Peterson 5–6). The androcentrism, racism, and elitism of renaissance discourse, as well as the discourse's long dedication to maintaining cultural "hegemony" (Wendell 440), limit the possibility of oppositional uses.

As scholars redefine the European Renaissance as the more comprehensive early modern period, the notion of an American renaissance appears antiquated. Alternatives to that discourse can better avoid historical and critical distortions, better facilitate understanding of the relation of nineteenth-century women's and men's writings to each other and to our own cultural context, and better register the changing, multiple forms of value that may be produced by readings of nineteenth-century United States writing (see Smith 23–24; Lauter, *Canons* 128–30).[29] Literary studies need to move beyond American renaissance criticism if it is to help dismantle the apparatus that devalues women and their work. It needs to articulate values commensurate with America's hybrid culture and cross-cultural relations and with America's promise of democratic ideals.

NOTES

1. The term *renaissance* has no invariable referent in American studies. My applications of the term are contingent on its shifting usage in criticism.

2. The discourse remains discipline-bound, not intersecting the notion of renaissance in history or in art history except in the case of the Harlem Renaissance (see, e.g., Ritter's inventory of renaissance study [384–88]; Duffus). Women's early accounts of American literature either do not engage the discourse (Botta; Trimble; Cooper; Fisher) or skirt it (Bates 117–18).

3. Arac calls for a cultural studies attentive to gender, yet he continues the androcentric "practice of *American Renaissance*" in an international male historical and theoretical tradition (*Critical Genealogies* 307, 171). His book *Critical Genealogies* deletes credit given in an earlier essay to Tompkins's gender critique of renaissance (*Critical Genealogies* 161, "Matthiessen" 93).

4. On the dearth of history, see Fetterley, "Commentary" 602–05.

5. Scant references to working-class writers, usually women, maintain the assertion of renaissance authors' superiority (C. Richardson, *American Literature, 1607–1885* 1: 55–56; Matthiessen, *American Renaissance* 401; D. Reynolds 366–67).

6. Comments on the racism of early literary histories fail to note that it inheres in renaissance aesthetics (Jones 99–102; Vanderbilt 114–17, 120, 126–27, 142–43, 146).

7. See Christian 72; cf. Ammons, who does not use renaissance discourse (*Conflicting Stories* 3, 26, 84–85, 61–63).

8. Wendell (303), Williams (77), Matthiessen (*American Renaissance* vii), and Gunn (221–22) state this widespread assumption. Only Calhoun notes that the notion of renaissance has no origins in the antebellum American South (81).

9. Cf. Wendell's "world-democracy" (530; see also 471) and Matthiessen's "anarchy" (*American Renaissance* xv; cf. Wright 9). Even Parrington admired the southern renaissance as "humane and cultivated democracy, set free . . . to engage in the higher work of civilization" by slavery, like ancient Greece (94).

10. Showalter examines Fuller as a prototype of criticism's token female intellectual (22–29); Showalter's own commitment to modernist aesthetics entails depreciation of antebellum women's writing in sentimental modes.

11. See, e.g., Brown on Frances Watkins (Harper) and Charlotte Forten (Grimké); Pattee, *History* on Fuller; Trent on Fuller, Stowe, Sedgwick, Child, and Peabody. On Fuller, see also Kirk; West. On Stowe, see also Farmer, "Women in Literature" 184; Shoup 50; Warner 68–72.

12. Cf. Steele 172–85; Bercovitch, *Office* xxi–xxii; Railton 3, 10–11; Chai 1–14. Chai considers Fuller's criticism among "significant achievements of the period" (386), but the brevity of his remarks indicates that he assigns Fuller "*minor*" status (Colacurcio 475).

13. See Bernard on white women faculty members (31); Cooper on black women college graduates (74); and, on women writers, Ammons, *Conflicting Stories;* Foster; Carby; and duCille.

14. Wendell's school text *A History of Literature in America,* written with Chester Noyes Greenough, supported a new curriculum designed to promote social control of immigrant and working-class populations (Baym, "Early Histories" 81–83).

15. Hedrick notes that Stowe's *Atlantic* contributions helped establish a "cultural hierarchy" that later depreciated women's writing (288–91, 317–22). There were many other female contributors to the magazine: on Alcott, Harriet Spofford, Elizabeth Stuart Phelps (Ward), and Helen Hunt Jackson, see Coultrap-McQuin 2–7; on Alcott, see Elbert; On Lydia Maria Child, see Karcher; on Rebecca Harding Davis, see Olsen 86–129 and Yellin 287–96; on Charlotte Forten (Grimké), see Fetterley, *Provisions* 446–53, and Peterson 189–95, 216; on Julia Ward Howe, see Clifford; on Lucy Larcom, see Marchalonis; on Stowe, Jewett, Freeman, Rose Terry Cooke, Mary Murfree, and Celia Thaxter, see Fetterley and Pryse 641–46.

16. Cheyfitz's analysis of Matthiessen's conservative aesthetic "politics" shows that the "imperial male body," which is central to Matthiessen's theory of organic symbol, has to do less with physical embodiment than with idealizations of male power in elite art, in imperialism, and in the socioeconomic hierarchy (352, 354). *American Renaissance* fuses this symbolic body of romantic organicism with the male transcendent body of renaissance.

17. See Goshgarian on romance criticism (4–7).

18. Later, Brooks's modern renaissance included "Negroes" and the "alien" (*Confident Years* 508), but familiar procedures devalue women. For example, Brooks used the new masterwork model of canon to exclude all women from Locke's "Negro Renascence" (Brooks, *Confident Years* 539–45). And although his accounts of modern renaissance attributed its leadership to Amy Lowell before Ezra Pound, he erased the significance of her work: he described Lowell as only a "conventional child . . . [i]ndeed . . . never a poet" (*Indian Summer* 525, 536; contrast *Confident Years* 486).

19. Mumford's study *The Golden Day,* "a major event in [Matthiessen's] experience" (Matthiessen, *American Renaissance* xvii), modified Lawrence's "classic" canon and argued, in opposition to Lawrence's emphasis on Americans' deviation from the European tradition, that "Elizabethan dramatists and . . . Seventeenth Century preachers" fathered the "birth . . . of an imaginative New World" (Mumford 94, 91). Matthiessen adapted to Mumford's birth paradigm both renaissance discourse and André Malraux's agonistic model of originality, which held that each "civilization is like the Renaissance" in creating culture by conquest of the past (*American Renaissance* xv). The resultant contradictions led Matthiessen to equivocate that his renaissance both was and was not a "re-birth" (vii).

20. On women novelists as antagonists, as the demonized "other," and as the repressed of renaissance criticism after Matthiessen, see Tompkins, *Sensational Designs* 124–25; Romero 112–15, 128–29; Goshgarian.

21. Though Matthiessen denies Fuller's influence, his criticism reiterates her original arguments in promoting Emerson and Hawthorne and demoting Longfellow and Lowell (Fuller, "Emerson's Essays," "American Literature"). *American Renaissance* does not acknowledge Matthiessen's appreciation of Fuller's criticism of "her masters" (Matthiessen, "Best Critic").

22. Matthiessen linked Peabody's radicalism with the failure of her journal, *Aesthetic Papers*, which was based on the ideal that arts and aesthetic value are continuous with other aspects of life (Peabody), not on the modernist notion of autonomous art that Matthiessen found hard to reconcile with political radicalism. Renaissance criticism ignores Peabody despite Ronda's honorific.

23. See Bercovitch, *Puritan Origins*, "Ideological Context"; Gilmore; Irwin; essays in Carafiol and Garvin and in Michaels and Pease (except Tompkins); Pease, *Visionary Compacts*; R. Richardson, *Myth and Literature* (his "Margaret Fuller" does not invoke the language of renaissance). The *Emerson Society Quarterly* highlighted the discourse of renaissance when it became *ESQ: A Journal of the American Renaissance* in 1972. Like *ESQ*, reference works such as Myerson's *Studies in the American Renaissance* and *The American Renaissance in New England* mention nearly twenty women, but without explaining their participation in a renaissance and without reversing the criticism's devaluation of women's writing.

24. On Fuller, see Chai; Steele; and L. Reynolds. On Dickinson, see Buell; Arac, *Critical Genealogies;* and D. Reynolds. On Stowe, see Sundquist, who does not confer "classic" status on her work as he does on Douglass's (23), and Buell, who qualifies his inclusion of her. Loving extends renaissance to century's end, making Dickinson the token woman in part 1 and Chopin in part 2. L. Reynolds's notice of Fuller's influence on Whitman is a notable exception (137–39).

25. See, e.g., Buell 43–44; Bercovitch, *Rites* 137, 168, 174–79; Leverenz 137, 168, 174–79; and D. Reynolds 394, 419. D. Reynolds's misreadings of Fanny Fern's *Ruth Hall* and Rebecca Harding Davis's *Life in the Iron Mills* marry off characters left single by their authors, depriving these texts of narrative, psychological, and symbolic complexities (405, 411). Railton regards *Uncle Tom's Cabin* as "popular," unlike male writers' works of renaissance greatness, because despite extraordinary merit, the novel fails to interrogate gender conventions, a standard Railton does not use to evaluate male writers' works (3, 10–11, 15, 84–89).

26. Buell's readings (14–15, 280, 301, 354, 392–97) bestow regional renaissance significance on Dickinson, the exceptional woman, whose place with Emerson, Thoreau, and Hawthorne might be taken for granted, but the discourse's tropes reascribe "subliterary" status to the work of most women and qualify the "resuscitations" of other women writers (e.g., Elizabeth Stoddard, Fuller, and Alcott), often by constructing tensions between figuring significantly in renaissance and meeting the stated criteria of "major status." Romero's single-genre focus can make only a partial case for women's renaissance that maintains presumptions of aesthetic deficiency (127–28).

27. Moers; Tompkins ("Other American Renaissance" and *Sensational Designs*); and Bercovitch, *Rites* 370 and *Office* xxi–xxii, 86–89, 126. This model only "silently invoke[s]" men's work in studies of sentimentalism (Goshgarian xi; see also Dobson 169, 172). Bercovitch's recommitment of American studies to the "defense" of literature precludes other rationales for defining art and period (Afterword 426–27; *Rites* 360, 368).

28. Carby problematizes the Harlem Renaissance as a critical "invention" that dominates African American cultural history and diminishes women, yet her extension of the discourse to the 1890s does not escape similar effects (164). Her failure to intervene in the renaissance discourse of American studies prevents the disciplinary interrogation that is central to her practice of cultural studies (163–64, 178–79n24).

29. Since Smith, innumerable alternative discourses have emerged in American literary studies, but Lauter (*Canons,* 115–16) and Kolodny caution that reevaluation is only beginning.

WORKS CITED

Ammons, Elizabeth. *Conflicting Stories: American Women Writers at the Turn into the Twentieth Century.* New York: Oxford UP, 1992.
———, ed. *Critical Essays on Harriet Beecher Stowe.* Boston: Hall, 1980.
Andrews, William L. "The 1850s: The First Afro-American Literary Renaissance." *Literary Romanticism in America.* Ed. Andrews. Baton Rouge: Louisiana State UP, 1981. 38–60.
Arac, Jonathan. *Critical Genealogies: Historical Situations for Postmodern Literary Studies.* Social Foundations of Aesthetic Forms. Ed. Edward W. Said. New York: Columbia UP, 1987.
———. "F. O. Matthiessen: Authorizing an American Renaissance." Michaels and Pease 90–112.
Arroyo, Elizabeth Fortson. "Josephine St. Pierre Ruffin." *Black Women in America: An Historical Encyclopedia.* Ed. Darlene Clark Hine. Vol. 2. Brooklyn: Carlson, 1993. 994–97.
Bates, Katharine Lee. *American Literature.* New York: Chautauqua, 1897.
Baym, Nina. "Early Histories of American Literature: A Chapter in the Institution of New England." Baym, *Feminism* 81–101.
———. *Feminism and American Literary History: Essays.* New Brunswick: Rutgers UP, 1992.
———. Introduction. *Woman's Fiction: A Guide to Novels by and about Women in America, 1820–70.* 2nd ed. Urbana: U of Illinois P, 1993. ix–xlii.

———. "Melodramas of Beset Manhood: How Theories of American Fiction Exclude Women Authors." *American Quarterly* 33 (1981): 123–39. Rpt. in Baym, *Feminism* 3–18.

Bercovitch, Sacvan. Afterword. *Ideology and Classic American Literature.* Ed. Bercovitch and Myra Jehlen. Cambridge Studies in Amer. Lit. and Culture. Cambridge: Cambridge UP, 1986. 418–42.

———. "The Ideological Context of the American Renaissance." *Forms and Functions of History in American Literature: Essays in Honor of Ursula Brumm.* Ed. Winifred Fluck et al. Berlin: Schmidt, 1981. 1–20.

———. *The Office of the Scarlet Letter.* Baltimore: Johns Hopkins UP, 1991.

———. *The Puritan Origins of the American Self.* New Haven: Yale UP, 1975.

———. *Rites of Assent: Transformations in the Symbolic Construction of America.* New York: Routledge, 1993.

Bernard, Jesse. *Academic Women.* University Park: Penn State UP, 1964.

Botta, Anne C. Lynch. *Handbook of Universal Literature, from the Best and Latest Authorities.* 1860. Boston: Riverside-Houghton, 1896.

Brooks, Van Wyck. *The Confident Years: 1885–1915.* 1952. New York: Dutton, 1955.

———. *The Flowering of New England, 1815–1865.* 1936. Brooks, *Literature* 1–550.

———. *Literature in New England.* Garden City, NY: Garden City, 1944.

———. *New England: Indian Summer, 1865–1915.* 1940. Brooks, *Literature* 1–557.

Brown, William Wells. *The Black Man: His Antecedents, His Genius, and His Achievements.* 2nd ed. 1863. New York: Johnson Rpt., 1968.

Buell, Lawrence. *New England Literary Culture: From Revolution through Renaissance.* Cambridge Studies in Amer. Lit. and Culture. Ed. Albert Gelpi. Cambridge: Cambridge UP, 1986.

Calhoun, Richard James. "Literary Criticism in Southern Periodicals during the American Renaissance." *Critical Theory in the American Renaissance.* Ed. Darrel Abel. Hartford: Transcendental, 1969. 76–83.

Carafiol, Peter C., and Harry R. Garvin, eds. *The American Renaissance: New Dimensions.* Lewisburg: Bucknell UP, 1983.

Carby, Hazel V. *Reconstructing Womanhood: The Emergence of the Afro-American Woman Novelist.* New York: Oxford UP, 1987.

Chai, Leon. *The Romantic Foundations of the American Renaissance.* Ithaca: Cornell UP, 1987.

Cheyfitz, Eric. "Matthiessen's *American Renaissance:* Circumscribing the Revolution." *American Quarterly* 41 (1989): 341–61.

Christian, Barbara. "But What Do We Think We're Doing Anyway: The State of Black Feminist Criticism(s); or, My Version of a Little Bit of History." *Changing Our Own Words: Essays on Criticism, Theory, and Writing by Black Women.* Ed. Cheryl A. Wall. New Brunswick: Rutgers UP, 1989. 58–74.

Clifford, Deborah Pickman. *Mine Eyes Have Seen the Glory: A Biography of Julia Ward Howe.* Boston: Atlantic-Little, 1978.

Colacurcio, Michael J. "The American-Renaissance Renaissance." *New England Quarterly* 64 (1991): 445–93.

Cooper, Anna Julia. *A Voice from the South: By a Black Woman of the South.* 1892. New York: Negro Univ., 1969.

Cott, Nancy F. *The Grounding of Modern Feminism.* New Haven: Yale UP, 1987.

Coultrap-McQuin, Susan. *Doing Literary Business: American Women Writers in the Nineteenth Century.* Chapel Hill: U of North Carolina P, 1990.

Crews, Frederick. "Whose American Renaissance?" *New York Review of Books* 27 Oct. 1988: 68–81.

Davis, Thadious. *Nella Larsen, Novelist of the Harlem Renaissance: A Woman's Life Unveiled.* Baton Rouge: Louisiana State UP, 1994.

Dobson, Joanne. "The American Renaissance Reenvisioned." *The (Other) American Traditions: Nineteenth-Century Women Writers.* Ed. Joyce W. Warren. New Brunswick: Rutgers UP, 1993. 164–82.

[Du Bois, W. E. B.] "Negro Writers." *Crisis* 19 (1920): 298–99.

duCille, Ann. *The Coupling Convention: Sex, Text, and Tradition in Black Women's Fiction.* New York: Oxford UP, 1993.

Duffus, R. L. *The American Renaissance.* New York: Knopf, 1928.

Elbert, Sarah. *A Hunger for Home: Louisa May Alcott's Place in American Culture.* New Brunswick: Rutgers UP, 1987.

Farmer, Lydia Hoyt, ed. *What America Owes to Woman: The National Exposition Souvenir.* Introd. Julia Ward Howe. Buffalo: Moulton, 1893.

[Farmer, Lydia Hoyt]. "Women in Literature and Poetry." Farmer, *What America Owes* 181–93.

Fetterley, Judith. "Commentary: Nineteenth-Century American Women Writers and the Politics of Recovery." *American Literary History* 6 (1994): 600–11.

———. *Provisions: A Reader from Nineteenth-Century American Women.* Bloomington: Indiana UP, 1985.

Fetterley, Judith, and Marjorie Pryse, eds. *American Women Regionalists, 1850–1910.* New York: Norton, 1992.

Fisher, Mary. *A General Survey of American Literature.* Chicago: McClurg, 1899.

Flexner, Eleanor. *Century of Struggle: The Woman's Rights Movement in the United States.* 1959. New York: Atheneum, 1970.

Foster, Frances Smith. *Written by Herself: Literary Production by African-American Women, 1746–1892.* Bloomington: Indiana UP, 1993.

Frothingham, Octavius Brooks. *Transcendentalism in New England: A History.* New York: Putnam's, 1876.

Fuller, Margaret. "American Literature: Its Position in the Present Time, and Prospects for the Future." 1846. Myerson, *Margaret Fuller* 381–400.

———. "Emerson's *Essays.*" 1844. Myerson, *Margaret Fuller* 240–47.

Gabel, Leona C. *From Slavery to the Sorbonne and Beyond: The Life and Writings of Anna J. Cooper.* Introd. Sidney Kaplan. Smith Coll. Studies in History 49. Ed. Stanley Melkins et al. Northampton: Smith Coll. Dept. of History, 1982.

Gates, Henry Louis, Jr. "African American Criticism." *Redrawing the Boundaries: The Transformation of English and American Literary Studies.* Ed. Stephen Greenblatt and Giles Gunn. New York: MLA, 1992. 303–19.

———. *The Signifying Monkey: A Theory of African-American Literary Criticism.* New York: Oxford UP, 1988.

Gilmore, Michael T. *American Romanticism and the Marketplace.* Chicago: U of Chicago P, 1985.

Gluck, Scherna. "Socialist Feminism between the Two World Wars: Insights from Oral History." *Decades of Discontent: The Women's Movement, 1920–40.* Ed. Lois Scharf and Joan M. Jensen. Contributions in Women's Studies 28. Westport: Greenwood, 1983. 279–97.

Goshgarian, G. M. *To Kiss the Chastening Rod: Domestic Fiction and Sexual Ideology in the American Renaissance.* Ithaca: Cornell UP, 1992.

Griffith, Elisabeth. *In Her Own Right: The Life of Elizabeth Cady Stanton.* New York: Oxford UP, 1984.

Gunn, Giles B. "The Kingdoms of Theory and the New Historicism in America." *Yale Review* 77.2 (1988): 207–36.

Hedrick, Joan D. *Harriet Beecher Stowe: A Life.* New York: Oxford UP, 1994.

Higginson, Thomas Wentworth, and Henry Walcott Boynton. *A Reader's History of American Literature.* Boston: Houghton, 1903.

Howe, M. A. De Wolfe. *Barrett Wendell and His Letters.* Boston: *Atlantic Monthly,* 1924.

Howells, W[illiam] D[ean]. "Professor Barrett Wendell's Notions of American Literature." 1901. *Selected Literary Criticism.* Vol. 3. Gen. ed. David J. Nordloh. Introd. Ronald Gottesman. Bloomington: Indiana UP, 1993. 50–63.

Hubbell, Jay B. *Who Are the Major American Writers? A Study of the Changing Literary Canon.* Durham: Duke UP, 1972.

Hull, Gloria T. *Color, Sex, and Poetry: Three Women Writers of the Harlem Renaissance.* Bloomington: Indiana UP, 1987.

Irwin, John T. *American Hieroglyphics: The Symbol of the Egyptian Hieroglyphics in the American Renaissance.* New Haven: Yale UP, 1980.

Jones, Howard Mumford. *The Theory of American Literature.* 1948. Ithaca: Cornell UP, 1965.

Karcher, Carolyn L. *The First Woman in the Republic: A Cultural Biography of Lydia Maria Child.* New Americanists. Ed. Donald E. Pease. Durham: Duke UP, 1994.

Kirk, Ellen Olney. "Women Fiction Writers of America." Farmer, *What America Owes* 194–204.

Kolodny, Annette. "The Integrity of Memory: Creating a New Literary History of the United States." *American Literature* 57 (1985): 291–307.

Lauter, Paul. *Canons and Contexts.* New York: Oxford UP, 1991.

———, gen. ed. *The Heath Anthology of American Literature.* Vol. 1. Lexington: Heath, 1990.

Lawrence, D. H. *Studies in Classic American Literature.* 1923. New York: Viking, 1969.

Leverenz, David. *Manhood and the American Renaissance.* Ithaca: Cornell UP, 1989.

Locke, Alain. "American Literary Tradition and the Negro." *Modern Quarterly* 3 (1926): 215–22. Rpt. in Stewart 433–38.

———. "The Concept of Race as Applied to Social Culture." *Howard Review* 1 (1924): 290–99. Rpt. in Stewart 423–31.

———. Foreword. Locke, *New Negro* ix–xi.

———. "Harlem." *Graphic Survey* 53.11 (1925): 629–30. Rpt. in Stewart 5–6.

———. "The Negro's Contribution to American Art and Literature." *Annals of the American Academy of Political and Social Science* 140 (1928): 234–47. Rpt. in Stewart 439–50.

———. "The Negro's Contribution to American Culture." *Journal of Negro Education* 8 (1939): 521–29. Rpt. in Stewart 451–58.

———. "Negro Youth Speaks." Locke, *New Negro* 47–53.

———. "The New Negro." Locke, *New Negro* 3–16.

———, ed. *The New Negro: An Interpretation.* 1925. New York: Arno, 1968.

———. "Our Little Renaissance." 1927. Rpt. in Stewart 21–22.

Loving, Jerome. *Lost in the Customhouse: Authorship in the American Renaissance.* Iowa City: U of Iowa P, 1993.

Marchalonis, Shirley. *The Worlds of Lucy Larcom, 1824–93.* Athens: U of Georgia P, 1989.

Matthiessen, F. O. *American Renaissance: Art and Expression in the Age of Emerson and Whitman.* London: Oxford UP, 1941.

———. "The Best Critic of Her Day?" *New Republic* 8 Sept. 1941: 314.

———. "The Flowering of New England." *New England Quarterly* 9 (1936): 701–09. Rpt. in *The Responsibilities of the Critic: Essays and Reviews by F. O. Matthiessen.* Ed. John Rackliffe. New York: Oxford UP, 1952. 199–208.

———. *Sarah Orne Jewett.* Boston: Riverside-Houghton, 1929.

McFadden, Margaret T. "'America's Boy Friend Who Can't Get a Date': Gender, Race, and the Cultural Work of the Jack Benny Program, 1932–46." *Journal of American History* 80 (1993): 113–34.

Melville, Herman. "Hawthorne and His Mosses." 1850. *The Piazza Tales and Other Prose Pieces, 1839–1860.* Ed. Harrison Hayford et al. Evanston: Northwestern UP; Chicago: Newberry Lib., 1987. Vol. 9 of *The Writings of Herman Melville.* 239–53.

Michaels, Walter Benn, and Donald E. Pease, eds. *The American Renaissance Reconsidered.* Selected Papers from the English Inst. 1982–83 ns 9. Baltimore: Johns Hopkins UP, 1985.

Moers, Ellen. *Harriet Beecher Stowe and American Literature.* Hartford: Stowe-Day Foundation, 1978.

Mumford, Lewis. *The Golden Day: A Study in American Experience and Culture.* New York: Liveright, 1926.

Myerson, Joel, ed. *The American Renaissance in New England.* Detroit: Gale, 1978. Vol. 1 of *The Dictionary of Literary Biography.*

———. *Margaret Fuller: Essays on American Life and Letters.* New Haven: College and University, 1978.

———. *Studies in the American Renaissance.* Boston: Twayne, 1977–82. Charlottesville: UP of Virginia, 1983– .

———. *The Transcendentalists: A Review of Research and Criticism.* New York: MLA, 1984.

Olsen, Tillie. "A Biographical Interpretation." *"Life in the Iron Mills" and Other Stories.* By Rebecca Harding Davis. Rev. ed. New York: Feminist, 1985. 69–174.

Osgood, Samuel. *Evert Augustus Duyckinck, His Life, Writings, and Influence: A Memoir.* Boston: Clapp, 1879.

———. "The German in America." *Christian Examiner* Nov. 1851: 350–59.

———. "Our Daughters." *Harper's New Monthly Magazine* Dec. 1857: 72–77. Rpt. as "American Girls." *American Leaves: Familiar Notes of Thought and Life.* 1866. Essay Index Rpt. Series. Freeport: Books for Lib., 1972. 95–113.

———. "Transcendentalism in New England." *International Review* Nov. 1876: 742–63.

Parrington, Vernon L. *The Romantic Revolution in America, 1800–1860.* New York: Harcourt, 1927. New York: Harvest-Harcourt, 1954. Vol. 2 of *Main Currents in American Thought.*

Pattee, Fred Lewis. *The First Century of American Literature, 1770–1870.* New York: Appleton, 1935.

———. *A History of American Literature, with a View to the Fundamental Principles Underlying Its Development.* New York: Silver, 1896.

Peabody, Elizabeth P. "The Dorian Measure, with a Modern Application." *Aesthetic Papers.* Ed. Peabody. 1849. Facsimile ed. Ed. Joseph Jones. Gainesville: Scholars', 1957. 64–111.

Pease, Donald E. Introduction. Michaels and Pease vii–xi.

———. *Visionary Compacts: American Renaissance Writings in Cultural Context.* Madison: U of Wisconsin P, 1987.

Peterson, Carla L. *"Doers of the Word": African-American Women Speakers and Writers in the North (1830–1880).* Race and American Culture. Ed. Arnold Rampersad and Shelley Fisher Fishkin. New York: Oxford UP, 1995.

Railton, Stephen. *Authorship and Audience: Literary Performance in the American Renaissance.* Princeton: Princeton UP, 1991.

Reynolds, David S. *Beneath the American Renaissance: The Subversive Imagination in the Age of Emerson and Melville.* Cambridge: Harvard UP, 1989.

Reynolds, Larry J. *European Revolutions and the American Literary Renaissance.* New Haven: Yale UP, 1988.

Richards, Laura E., and Maud Howe Elliott. *Julia Ward Howe, 1819–1910.* Vol. 2. Boston: Houghton, 1915.

Richardson, Charles F. *American Literature, 1607–1885.* 2 vols. 1886, 1888. Popular Ed. New York: Putnam's, 1895.

———. *A Primer of American Literature.* Boston: Houghton, 1878.

Richardson, Robert D., Jr. "Margaret Fuller and Myth." *Prospects* 4 (1979): 169–84.

———. *Myth and Literature in the American Renaissance.* Bloomington: Indiana UP, 1978.

Ritter, Harry. *Dictionary of Concepts in History.* Westport: Greenwood, 1986.

Romero, Lora. "Domesticity and Fiction." *The Columbia History of the American Novel.* Ed. Emory Elliott. New York: Columbia UP, 1991. 110–29.

Ronda, Bruce A., ed. *Letters of Elizabeth Palmer Peabody: American Renaissance Woman.* Middletown: Wesleyan UP, 1984.

Ryan, Mary P. *Women in Public: Between Banners and Ballots, 1825–1880.* Baltimore: Johns Hopkins UP, 1990.

Shoup, Francis A. "*Uncle Tom's Cabin* Forty Years After." *Sewanee Review* 11 (1893): 88–104. Rpt. in Ammons, *Critical Essays* 49–59.

Showalter, Elaine. *Sister's Choice: Tradition and Change in American Women's Writing.* The Clarendon Lectures 1989. Oxford: Clarendon, 1991.

Smith, Barbara Herrnstein. *Contingencies of Value: Alternative Perspectives for Critical Theory.* Cambridge: Harvard UP, 1988.

Solomon, Barbara Miller. "The Intellectual Background of the Immigration Restriction Movement in New England." *New England Quarterly* 25.1 (1952): 47–59.

[Stanton, Elizabeth Cady]. *The Woman's Bible.* New York: European, 1895–98.

Stanton, Elizabeth Cady, Susan B. Anthony, and Matilda J. Gage, eds. *History of Woman Suffrage.* Vol. 1. New York: Fowler, 1881.

Steele, Jeffrey. *The Representation of the Self in the American Renaissance.* Chapel Hill: U of North Carolina P, 1987.

Stewart, Jeffrey C., ed. *The Critical Temper of Alain Locke: A Selection of His Essays on Art and Culture.* Critical Studies on Black Life and Culture 8. Ed. Henry Louis Gates. New York: Garland, 1983.

Sundquist, Eric J. "Slavery, Revolution, and the American Renaissance." Michaels and Pease 1–33.

Tompkins, Jane. "The Other American Renaissance." Michaels and Pease 34–57.

———. *Sensational Designs: The Cultural Work of American Fiction, 1790–1860.* Oxford: Oxford UP, 1985.

Trent, William P. *A History of American Literature, 1607–1865.* New York: Appleton, 1903.

Trimble, Esther J. *A Hand-book of English and American Literature.* Philadelphia: Eldredge, 1882.

Vanderbilt, Kermit. *American Literature and the Academy: The Roots, Growth, and Maturity of a Profession.* Philadelphia: U of Pennsylvania P, 1986.

Warner, Charles Dudley. "The Story of *Uncle Tom's Cabin.*" *Atlantic Monthly* July 1896: 311–21. Rpt. in Ammons, *Critical Essays* 60–72.

Wendell, Barrett. *A Literary History of America.* Lib. of Lit. History. New York: Scribner's, 1900.

Wendell, Barrett, and Chester Noyes Greenough. *A History of Literature in America.* New York: Scribner's, 1904.

West, Kenyon. "Margaret Fuller's Permanent Influence: The Measure of Her Footprint on Earth." *Poet-Lore* 7 (1895): 377–88.

Williams, Stanley T. *American Literature.* Philadelphia: Lippincott, 1933.

Wright, Louis B. "The Renaissance Tradition in America." *The American Writer and the European Tradition.* Ed. Margaret Denny and William H. Gilman. Minneapolis: U of Minnesota P, 1950. 3–15.

Yellin, Jean Fagan. Afterword. *Margaret Howth: A Story of Today.* By Rebecca Harding Davis. New York: Feminist, 1990. 271–302.

Ziff, Larzer. *Literary Democracy: The Declaration of Cultural Independence in America.* New York: Viking, 1981.

Realism and Naturalism: The Problem of Definition

DONALD PIZER

*T his selection is taken from the introduction of Pizer's essay col-
lection,* The Cambridge Companion to American Realism and Naturalism
(1995). *Pizer begins by discussing the problems associated with defining realism and
naturalism and provides a brief history of their definitions. This difficulty is in part
due to the fact that both terms have distinct definitions in philosophical discourse,
which at times cloud their meanings in literary studies. Attempts to define realism
and naturalism have also been complicated by their different use in European literary
history. Pizer observes that in the United States realism has been used to describe the
fiction of William Dean Howells and Henry James, (1870s and 1880s), while naturalism referred to the fiction of Frank Norris and Theodore Dreiser (1890s). After
reviewing the changing tides of critical reception of realism and naturalism, Pizer
concludes that despite an initial preference for realism, naturalism continues to
attract American writers and readers.*

Anyone seeking, as are the contributors to this volume, to write about
American literature between the Civil War and World War I in relation to the
literary movements known as realism and naturalism faces a twofold initial
difficulty. First, there exists a traditional suspicion, often arising from the very
attempt to write literary history, of large-scale classifying rubrics. Is there any
advantage, one might ask, in conceptualizing the richly diverse expression of
this period in terms of such inherent simplification as realism and naturalism? A second problem derives from the recent theorizing of literary study.
The attraction, for many theorists, of a deconstructive stance has bred skepticism toward interpretive enterprises that posit such communities of belief
and expression as those subsumed under the headings of realism and naturalism. And, from a somewhat different theoretical viewpoint, recent scholars
of a New Historicist bent have tended to discount traditional historical divisions in the study of American literature on the ground that they obscure

From *The Cambridge Companion to American Realism and Naturalism: Howells to London,*
ed. Donald Pizer (Cambridge: Cambridge UP, 1995) 3–14 and 16–18.

underlying ideological similarities present in all American writing since the Civil War.

Yet, as this volume testifies, the effort to describe and understand a historical phase of American writing in terms of major shared characteristics of that writing continues. At its deepest and probably most significant level of implication, this attempt derives from the same reservoir of humanistic faith which feeds the act of creative expression itself. The artist, putting pen to paper, is expressing a belief in the human capacity to overcome such obstacles to understanding as the existence in all communication acts of unconscious motive and value in both writer and reader, the inherent ambiguity of the symbolic expression which is language, and the heartbreaking distinction in human utterance between intent and effect. He or she does so, despite these difficulties, because of faith in the value of striving to create threads of shared experience and meaning out of the inchoate mix of life. The literary historian, in his or her own way, also functions within this charged field of doubt and faith. Indeed, the literary historian can profit from the increased appreciation in recent decades of the difficulties inherent in the effort to interpret. An awareness of the hazards and complexities of textual and historical analysis can lead, not to abandonment of the attempt to understand the past, but rather to a refining of that undertaking.

As a minor reflection of this awareness, I would like briefly to describe the assumptions that underlie the contents and organization of this collection of essays devoted to late-nineteenth- and early-twentieth-century American writing. The general notion of the volume is that of an exercise in literary history in which various conflicting impulses in the writing of literary history are paired off against each other — a method, in other words, that dramatizes some of the opposing pulls in the construction of history rather than one which assumes that they are somehow resolved within a single seamless narrative. One such opposition is social and intellectual history versus the close reading of texts. Another is the older modes of critical and historical analysis versus those currently in fashion. And a third is the traditional canon versus an emerging alternative canon. The first pair of tendencies is represented by the opening essays on American and European intellectual and social background and by the studies devoted to specific works of the period. The next is found in the review of earlier criticism of the period undertaken later in this introduction and in the essay on recent critical approaches. And the last is reflected in the traditional texts examined at length and in the essay on expanding the canon as well as in the final case studies on works by Johnson and Du Bois. The controlling strategy of this book, in brief, is that of dialectic. It is hoped that this approach suggests something of the dynamic nature of literary history, that it is an interpretive act in process, and (more specifically) that it will contribute to an understanding of some of the distinctive characteristics of late-nineteenth- and early-twentieth-century American literature.

Michael Anesko, in his essay "Recent Critical Approaches," will be discussing basic tendencies in the study of American realism and naturalism since approximately the early 1970s. It remains for me, therefore, to describe several areas of interest in earlier efforts to come to grips with the nature of late-nineteenth- and early-twentieth-century American fiction. One is the always troublesome issue of whether *realism* and *naturalism* are indeed satisfactory critical and historical terms in relation to the writing of the period. Another is the presence of distinctive phases in the critical interpretation of realism and naturalism since the emergence of the movements in the late nineteenth century. In addition, although this volume is devoted to discussions of fiction written between the Civil War and World War I, it may be useful to comment briefly on critical attempts to describe the existence of naturalistic strains in American literature since 1918.

A major problem inherent in the use of the terms realism and naturalism in discussions of literature is the fact that both words also have distinctive meanings in philosophical discourse that can spill over into literary analysis, with awkward consequences. For example, metaphysical and epistemological inquiries as to what is real, or the ethical implications of what is natural, can be used to undermine almost any act of literary historiography or criticism. This destabilization arises, not from the efforts of scholars who seek a meaningful engagement with the possible philosophical implications of a literary work, but rather from the attempts of various writers from the mid-nineteenth century onward to ridicule the pretensions of works purporting to be realistic or naturalistic by noting the emptiness, in relation to philosophical usage, of any such claims. As a result of this conventional stance of critics instinctively hostile to realistic or naturalistic expression, it has become common to preface serious discussions of the literary dimensions of realism or naturalism with statements disclaiming any relationship between the literary and philosophical usages of the terms.[1]

Another, somewhat related, problem is that the terms bear social and moral valences that are frequently attached to any work designated as realistic or naturalistic, whatever the specific character of that work. The real and natural, on the one hand, suggest the genuine and actual shorn of pretension and subterfuge. The real, especially in America, has therefore also had a positive political inflection, as is revealed by several generations of Howells scholars who have related his literary beliefs and practices to democratic values.[2] On the other hand, realism and naturalism imply, through their association with the concrete immediacies of experience, a literature unmediated by the intellect or spirit, and therefore lacking in those qualities necessary to sustain the mind or soul of man. Naturalism in particular is thus held to be morally culpable because it appears to concentrate on the physical in man's nature and experience.[3] (Theodore Dreiser's naturalism, Stuart P. Sherman stated in a famous pronouncement, derived from an animal theory of human conduct.)[4] Thus, it is assumed by critics seeking to exploit the negative associations conjured up by the terms *realism* and *naturalism* that any literature so designated proclaims the shallowness of mind and spirit of its creator.

Realism and *naturalism* have therefore often served as shibboleths in social and literary controversy — comparable to *liberal* and *reactionary* in present-day political affairs — at various moments in American cultural history. The terms played a central role during late-nineteenth-century debates on the value of the ideal versus the commonplace in experience, and they recurred in 1920s arguments about whether the writer should depict the rational or the irrational as central to human behavior. They reappeared in 1930s discussions about the need for literature to serve a social purpose rather than fulfill an aesthetic need, as well as in disputes during the 1960s and 1970s over whether or not the romance or novel is the distinctive form of American fiction.[5] Each of these controversies has usually cast more light on the polemical preoccupations of the moment than the literature under discussion. Of course, it can be maintained that the inseparability of subject from object, of the knower from what he wishes to know, is inherent in the act of seeking to know, and can therefore no more be avoided in the effort to "know" realism and naturalism than it can in any similar enterprise. The issue in this instance, however, is the blatant irrelevancy of much that has been imposed on *realism* and *naturalism* as terms by critics preoccupied with polemical ends. In other words, given this history in the use of the terms, can we have any faith in the possibility of a more "objective" use?

A final major problem in the use of *realism* and *naturalism* as key terms in American literary historiography arises from several significant differences in the way the terms have been used in European literary history. It has often been remarked that realism and naturalism occurred earlier in Europe than in America (from the late 1850s to the late 1880s in France); that they contained — in the pronouncements of Flaubert and Zola, for example — self-conscious and full-scale ideologies; and that they functioned within a coherent network of personal relationships for much of their existence. In America, on the other hand, it is noted that the boundaries of the period are the Civil War and World War I, which suggests a substitution of historical event for ideology as the significant basis for understanding literary production; that critical discussion, as characterized by Howells's definition of realism as "the truthful treatment of material,"[6] lacks depth; and that the movements also lacked a social base or center. For some critics, the inescapable conclusion to be drawn from these differences is that it is inappropriate and poor criticism to attempt to apply terms with a body of specific meaning derived from the specific characteristics of their European origin to a very different set of circumstances in American literary history.[7]

George J. Becker, who took the lead during the 1960s in this effort to dismiss the credibility of *realism* and *naturalism* as terms in American literary history, also noted another troublesome issue in their varying European and American usage. In Europe the terms were used interchangeably in the late nineteenth century and often still are, while in America they have served to distinguish between the fiction of the generation of Howells and James (the 1870s and 1880s) and that of Norris and Dreiser (the 1890s). To Becker, a reliance on this distinction is further evidence that both terms have been distorted in their application to American literary conditions and should therefore be discarded by American literary historians.[8]

Becker's objections, however, have not prevented the continued use of the terms *realism* and *naturalism* in American literary historiography. They are too deeply implanted to be dislodged, and their removal would leave unanswered the question of what would replace them. But Becker's attempt, as well as those made by such scholars as Harry Levin and René Wellek,[9] to describe Continental realism and naturalism as a body of belief and practice has clarified both the difference between the movements in Europe and America and what is distinctive in the American movements. In short, it is now generally held that American realism and naturalism are not similar to the European varieties, but that the differences between them should lead, not to a rejection of the use of the terms in America, but rather to studies that will exploit an understanding of these differences in order to help us interpret the American literary phenomena designated by the terms.

Thus, in the long debate on the advantages and disadvantages of using the terms *realism* and *naturalism,* a rough operative (rather than fully articulated) consensus has emerged. (Not to say that there are not vigorous dissenters to this consensus.) Efforts to dispose of the terms because of the various semantic confusions that have adhered to them over the last hundred years have been rejected. Whatever the philosophical, moral, and social baggage that encumbers them, they will have to do; including, indeed, this baggage itself as a profitable object of study. In addition, efforts to confine the meaning of the terms to normative definitions derived from European expression have also been rejected. Rather, it is now generally accepted that the terms can be used to historical and critical advantage to designate a body of writing produced during a distinctive phase of American expression. Or, to put it another way, that the historian can accept the premise that whatever was being produced in fiction during the 1870s and 1880s that was new, interesting, and roughly similar in a number of ways can be designated as *realism,* and that an equally new, interesting, and roughly similar body of writing produced at the turn of the century can be designated as *naturalism.* This is not, of course, an entirely satisfactory "solution" to the various problems inherent in the use of the terms *realism* and *naturalism* in American literary history. But when the evidence provided both by the texts themselves and by a complex cultural and intellectual history (as will be seen) cannot itself produce precise and uniform definitions, we must accept the fact that the definitions must be adapted to the evidence, and that an amorphous, flexible, and ultimately "undefinable" terminology is in itself a contribution to the understanding of what occurred.[10]

Literary historians of the 1920s and 1930s, following the lead of V. L. Parrington, tended to describe realism as a new phenomenon unleashed upon the American scene during the 1870s and 1880s by the rapid industrialization and urbanization of America in the post–Civil War period. But as Robert Falk and others have demonstrated, no such swift and complete rejection of earlier nineteenth-century literary beliefs and practices occurred. In particular, critical pronouncements during this period about the new writing were firmly Victorian in their basic assumptions about life and literature.[11]

One of the most important of these assumptions is closely identified with the critical views of W. D. Howells during the late 1880s, though it appears as well in the literary journalism of a number of other writers seeking to defend and promote the new fiction. Literature, Howells argued in his "Editor's Study" columns in *Harper's Monthly,* ought to reflect and play a major role in encouraging the social and political progress that characterized nineteenth-century life, progress that had received its fullest expression in the American effort to unite scientific inquiry and political democracy into a means for a better life for all men. Howells and such figures as Hamlin Garland, T. S. Perry, and H. H. Boyesen thus accepted wholeheartedly the central evolutionary premise of much nineteenth-century thought that loosely joined social, material, and intellectual life into a triumphant forward march.[12] The function of literature in this universal progress was to reject the outworn values of the past in favor of those of the present. Or, in more literary terms, the writer was to reject the romantic material and formulas of earlier fiction, as these derived from the limited beliefs and social life of their moment of origin, in favor of a realistic aesthetic which demanded that the subject matter of contemporary life be objectively depicted, no matter how "unliterary" the product of this aesthetic might seem to be. "Nothing is stable," Garland wrote in 1882, "nothing absolute, all changes, all is relative. Poetry, painting, the drama, these too are always being modified or left behind by the changes in society from which they spring."[13]

Garland's pronouncement, and many like it, appears to require a radical dismissal of traditional literary belief and practice. (The title of his 1894 collection of essays, *Crumbling Idols,* reflects a similar radical aura.) But in fact, when separated from its polemic posturing and examined for its specific proposals about fiction, criticism of this kind discloses a far less revolutionary cast than its rhetoric suggests. Howells's famous grasshopper analogy, in his 1891 collection of "Editor's Study" columns, *Criticism and Fiction,* is revealing in this context. All is to be true and honest in fiction, Howells states, within a realistic aesthetic in which the writer, like a scientist with democratic values, discards the old heroic and ideal, and therefore false, cardboard model of a grasshopper and depicts the commonplace activities of a commonplace grasshopper. This engaging plea, however, disguises the tameness, and indeed often the superficiality, of much fiction subsumed under the notion of the commonplace or realistic. For Howells and others, the "progressive realism of American fiction" (to use H. H. Boyesen's language) lay principally in portraying "the widely divergent phases of our American civilization,"[14] that is, a local-color literature. In addition, these "phases" were to be depicted normatively in the negative sense of omitting areas of human nature and social life that were "barbaric" in nature. The new literature, Garland announced in *Crumbling Idols,* "will not deal with crime and abnormalities, nor with diseased persons. It will deal . . . with the wholesome love of honest men for honest women, with the heroism of labor . . . , a drama of average types of character. . . ."[15]

In short, the underlying beliefs of this first generation of critics of realism were firmly middle-class. Literature had a job of work to do: to make us known to each other in our common political and social progress (and also, in Howells's later modification of his views, our defects). It was to serve social ends as these ends were defined by the socially responsible. It is therefore not surprising to find a disparity between the radical implications of the realists' ideal of change and the actual themes and forms of the literature proposed as meeting this ideal. We have a realistic fiction that "every year [grows] more virile, independent, and significant," announced Boyesen, who cited as examples of this expression the work of such thin and pastiche local colorists as Thomas Nelson Page, H. C. Bunner, and Edgar Fawcett.[16]

To put this distinction between critical pronouncement and literary production in somewhat different terms, Howells, Garland, Boyesen, and others appeared to have confused the proliferation and acceptance of local color, a literature expressive above all of middle-class taste and values, with their call for a fiction reflective of the radical changes occurring in American life. Something new and exciting was indeed happening in fiction, but it was happening principally in the work of the major novelists of the day, Henry James, Twain, and Howells, who, except for Howells, were writing outside the parameters of the commonplace, as well as in the largely neglected work of women and minority authors. In slighting these forms of expression in favor of the "positive" social work performed by a normative local color, Howells and others were misfiring in ways that had a permanent effect on the conception of American realism.

Realism, because of Howells's prominence as critic and novelist and because of its widespread public acceptance in the form of local color, attracted a considerable body of critical commentary during the late nineteenth century. But naturalism, as it emerged as a major new form of expression at the turn of the century, was often ignored, or, when not ignored, condemned out of hand. Socially and morally suspect because of its subject matter, and handicapped as well by the early deaths of Stephen Crane and Frank Norris and the long silence of Dreiser after the "suppression" of *Sister Carrie* in 1900, naturalism was for the most part slighted as a general topic except for Norris's miscellaneous comments in various essays and reviews. Less a profound thinker than a defender of his own work and a popularizer of "ideas in the air," Norris's conception of naturalism is nevertheless significant both for what it contains and what it omits. Naturalism, Norris declares, must abjure the "teacup tragedies"[17] of Howellsian realism and explore instead the irrational and primitive in human nature — "the unplumbed depths of the human heart, and the mystery of sex, and the problems of life, and the black, unsearched penetralia of the soul of man"[18] — and it should do so within the large canvas and allegorical framework that permit the expression of abstract ideas about the human condition.

So far so good. Norris is here describing not only *McTeague* and *The Octopus*, his best novels, as two poles of naturalistic inquiry (a chaotic inner life and a panoramic social world) but also suggestively revealing the appeal of this conception of literature for a large number of twentieth-century American writers ranging from Faulkner to Mailer. But Norris's idea of naturalism is also remarkably silent in a key area. For despite his close familiarity with the work of Zola and other French naturalists, nowhere in his criticism does he identify naturalism with a deterministic ideology. Naturalism, to Norris, is a method and a product, but it does not prescribe a specific philosophical base. Norris was thus identifying, in his criticism, the attraction of naturalism in its character as a sensationalistic novel of ideas flexible enough in ideology to absorb the specific ideas of individual writers — and this despite the efforts of several generations of later critics to attach an unyielding deterministic core to the movement.

A basic paradox characterizes much of the criticism of late-nineteenth-century realism produced between the two world wars. On the one hand, the writing of the period is often applauded for its depiction of the new actualities of post–Civil War America. This celebratory stance is revealed most obviously in the metaphors of progress and success present in the sectional titles of literary histories containing accounts of the period — "The Triumph of Realism" and the like.[19] On the other, critics also wished to register their disapproval of the restraints in choice of subject matter and manner of treatment imposed on writers by the literary and social conventions of late Victorian American life. In this connection, the terms *puritanism* and *genteel tradition* were heavily employed. Writers of the time, in short, were described as seeking to be free but as still largely bound.

This view is closely related, of course, to the prevailing winds of 1920s and 1930s social and literary discourse. During the twenties, when the act of rejection of American cultural codes and economic values (a rejection most clearly enacted by the expatriates' self-exile) was almost a requirement for serious consideration as an artist, it is no wonder that those late-nineteenth-century figures who sought to live out roles of personal and literary alienation — a Mark Twain at his bitterest or a Stephen Crane — were centers of attention,[20] while those who were seemingly willing to accept codes of gentility or cultural elitism, a Howells or a James, were relegated, in general accounts of the period, to the role of symbolic reflectors of these limitations. Thus, an entire generation of literary journalists, led by H. L. Mencken, but including such prominent and well-respected figures as John Macy, Van Wyck Brooks, Ludwig Lewisohn, Carl Van Doren, Randolph Bourne, Lewis Mumford, and Henry Seidel Canby, fed off the critical commonplace of a literature attempting to be free to depict American life fully and honestly but deeply flawed by the limitations placed upon this effort by its own time.

This broad-based attitude, because it served contemporary polemic purposes, tended toward the absolute dichotomy as a critical tool. One such polarization, as noted earlier, was that of distinguishing sharply between ante- and postbellum writing in order to dramatize the dramatic differences between a pre- and postindustrial America. Another, as in V. L. Parrington's *The Beginnings of Critical Realism in America* (1930), was to bifurcate American life into those forces contributing either to plutocracy or freedom. But despite the prevalence of these and a number of other widely shared beliefs and strategies, criticism of realism and naturalism during this period was neither monolithic nor static. A significant illustration of one of the shifting perspectives of the time is present in estimations of the work of Howells. To a Mencken, writing in the literary climate of the late teens and early twenties, Howellsian realism epitomized all that must be avoided by the writer seeking to be a meaningful critic of his own time and life.[21] Mencken thus did not so much attempt to understand Howells as to use him as a negative touchstone. But as economic issues became paramount in the minds of many literary historians and critics, beginning in the late 1920s, Howells's conversion to socialism served the very different role of dramatizing the response of a sensitive and thoughtful writer to the conditions of his day. For Parrington in 1930, and for Granville Hicks somewhat later, Howells assumed almost heroic stature. In Hicks's militant terminology, he was one of those who "marched out upon the field of battle" to struggle against the forces of economic oppression.[22]

Discussions of naturalism between the world wars, and especially of the work of Norris and the early Dreiser, were also deeply influenced by the polemic dynamics of the age. Initially, it was the naturalists' choice of material, in particular its more open sexuality, which led to their high standing as "trailblazers" of freedom. But gradually, with the greater prominence given economic and social issues in the 1930s, the naturalists of the 1890s became less valued as exemplars of freedom of expression than as reflectors of the closed and destructive mechanistic and Darwinian world of struggle in which it was assumed most Americans functioned.[23] It was during this stage in the criticism of naturalism that it became obligatory for the critic to spell out the relationship of American naturalism to Zolaesque determinism and firmly to equate the two. Since it was believed that American life at the turn of the century imprisoned the average American in a "moving box" of economic and social deprivation, naturalism (with its deterministic center) was a writer's appropriate, and indeed inevitable, response to this condition. Thus, while it might be acknowledged that Norris and Dreiser were often crude and formless and that their work appeared to be confined to the depiction of man as a victim, it was believed as well that naturalism of this kind was an apt expression of late-nineteenth-century American social reality.

From the end of World War II to the watershed years of the late 1960s and early 1970s, realism fared far better on the critical scene than did naturalism. Realistic fiction, whatever its degree of social criticism, was more readily reconcilable than naturalistic writing to the postwar emphasis on the role of American literary expression in affirming democratic values. In addition, with the exception of the work of Stephen Crane, naturalistic fiction, with its assumed defects of form and style, was largely ignored as a result of the New Criticism stress on close reading that dominated much criticism of the period.

Both the war and its Cold War aftermath generated a commitment on the part of most literary historians to demonstrate the vital presence of the American democratic tradition in all phases of American expression. Thus the work of Howells and his contemporaries was discovered to be deeply impregnated with such democratic beliefs as trust in the common vision and in pragmatic values. In addition, as Henry Nash Smith put it in his chapter on realism in the *Literary History of the United States,* by identifying and dramatizing the "problem areas" of American social life, realists were playing a role in the solution of those problems.[24] This point of view, with an emphasis on the importance of Howells's beliefs and practices, characterizes Everett Carter's *Howells and the Age of Realism* (1954) and E. H. Cady's work culminating in his *The Light of Common Day* (1971). Much criticism of the period, however, was also increasingly devoted to the fiction of Twain and James, finding in *Huckleberry Finn* and in James's major novels a rich source of formalistic analysis. Striking patterns of symbolic imagery and structure and suggestive currents of irony and ambiguity, it was discovered, could be found in these works as well as in those by Melville and Hawthorne.[25] These two strains — a stress on the functional value system underlying realistic portrayals and a revelation of the subtlety and complexity of realistic fictional aesthetics — joined triumphantly in Harold H. Kolb's *The Illusion of Life: American Realism as a Literary Form* (1969). Kolb accepted almost as proven the democratic underpinning of the three novels he concentrated on — *Huckleberry Finn, The Rise of Silas Lapham,* and *The Bostonians* — and devoted most of his attention to the ways in which such formal characteristics of the novels as point of view technique and imagery successfully express these foundations of belief.

Everett Carter's landmark study of Howells and his age, in addition to stressing Howells's democratic beliefs, is also noteworthy for its delineation of various stages in his ideas. So, for example, Carter locates the sources of Howells's concept of realism in Comte and Taine and then traces the permutations of the concept in Howells's career and in those of his major contemporaries. Realism, in short, was not a static entity but rather consisted of ideas in motion.[26] This appealing notion of the dynamic nature of the beliefs of the period — of writers responding to changing ideas and social life by rethinking their own beliefs — characterizes such major literary histories of the period as Robert Falk's essay in *Transitions in American Literary History* (1953) and (as is suggested by their titles) Warner Berthoff's *The Ferment of Realism* (1965) and Jay Martin's *Harvests of Change* (1967).[27]

These various threads of criticism — the celebratory democratic, the New Critical, and the dynamic — are related in their common affirmative view of realism as a significant moment in American literary history. No longer was the movement marginalized, as had been true of much criticism of the previous generation, because of its gentility or imperception. Its importance, centrality, and worth had, in the minds of most scholars, been firmly established.

Naturalism, however, suffered either dismissal or critical neglect for much of the postwar period. The assumed crudity and stylistic incompetence of Norris or Dreiser of course rendered their work suspect within a critical climate deeply affected by New Critical beliefs and methods. Also telling as a negative factor in the estimation of naturalism was the disillusionment, beginning in the mid-1930s, of American intellectuals with what they held to be the mindless authoritarianism of communist ideology. Many writers of the 1930s who had been identified with a resurgence of naturalism — Steinbeck, Dos Passos, and Farrell, for example — were also on the Left, an association confirmed above all by Dreiser's full endorsement of the Communist party and its goals from the early 1930s to his death in 1945. Discussions of naturalism, because of the movement's origins in Zola's beliefs and practice, had always contained a tendency toward considering it a foreign incursion with little relationship to American values and experience. This tendency, as well as other threads in the negative conception of naturalism, received full and influential expression in Oscar Cargill's *Intellectual America* (1941), in which Cargill disposed of naturalism as a crude and thinly derivative fiction with fascistic inclinations.[28] By the postwar years, with the revulsion against communism deepened by the Cold War, a powerful antinaturalism stance characterized the criticism of such major voices of the day as Lionel Trilling, Malcolm Cowley, and Philip Rahv.[29] As Irving Howe later noted, during the 1940s and 1950s Dreiser's work was "a symbol of everything a superior intelligence was supposed to avoid."[30]

Despite this hostile critical convention, a counterflow of more sympathetic inquiry into the nature of American naturalism also emerged during the 1950s and 1960s. Willard Thorp and Alfred Kazin, for example, asked the question begged by the rejection of naturalism: If naturalism is inept, intellectually impoverished, and foreign to American values, why has it persisted as a major element in all phases of twentieth-century American fiction?[31] A number of scholars accepted the challenge implicit in this question and began to examine the relationship between naturalism and American life on a deeper level than the obvious association between naturalistic factuality and American materialism. One influential effort was that by Richard Chase, who in his *The American Novel and Its Tradition* (1957) located naturalism within the American romance tradition because of its union of sensationalism and ideas. On the other hand, Charles C. Walcutt, in his *American Literary Naturalism, A Divided Stream* (1956), rejected the notion that the naturalistic novel had achieved formal coherence in favor of the concept of naturalism's unsuccessful search for an expressive form because of its divided roots in transcendental faith and scientific skepticism. And Donald Pizer, in his *Realism and Naturalism in Nineteenth-Century American Literature* (1966), as well as in later works,[32] sought not only to locate the American roots of naturalistic belief in a close reading of the works themselves (as had Walcutt) but also to establish the fictional complexity and worth of the naturalistic novel at its best. By the early 1970s, therefore, led by a number of major studies of Dreiser (Robert Penn Warren's *Homage to Theodore Dreiser* [1971] is symptomatic), it had become possible to discuss the movement outside of the a priori assumptions of inadequacy established by the New Critical and anticommunist critical contexts of the previous generation.

This more receptive critical climate for the study of naturalism has also contributed to the effort to describe its enduring presence in twentieth-century American fiction. While realism, as defined and practiced by Howells, has been confined in modern American fiction to a relatively minor role, naturalism, in its various interests and strategies, has continued to flourish. This is not to say that naturalism has been the principal force in American fiction since the turn of the century. Since the 1920s, the novel of social realism has had as a constant complement a fiction of the fantastic or fabulistic, whether as expressed by the sophisticated cleverness of a group of 1920s writers led by James Branch Cabell or by the more intellectualized allegories of such 1960s and 1970s figures as John Barth, Thomas Pynchon, and Donald Barthelme. Nor has American naturalism been static or monolithic in theme and form since its origin in the 1890s. Indeed, one of the striking characteristics of the movement has been its adaptability to fresh currents of idea and expression in each generation while maintaining a core of naturalistic preoccupations. The nature of this core is not easy to describe, given the dynamic flexibility and amorphousness of naturalism as a whole in America, but it appears to rest on the relationship between a restrictive social and intellectual environment and the consequent impoverishment both of social opportunity and of the inner life. This is the common theme of such major writers of the 1930s as John Steinbeck, John Dos Passos, and James T. Farrell, whether the theme is worked out in narratives of group defeat or of personal emptiness and collapse. It continues into the generation of the 1940s and 1950s in the early work of Saul Bellow, William Styron, and Norman Mailer, though now often combined with the existential theme of the need for a quest for meaning in the face of the inadequacy of social life and belief. And it persists in the partial recovery of the naturalistic themes of political constraint and urban blight in the work of such contemporary novelists as Robert Stone, Joyce Carol Oates (in her early novels), and William Kennedy. Naturalism thus seems to appeal to each generation of American writers as a means of dramatizing "hard times" in America — hard times in the sense both of economic decline and of spiritual malaise, with each generation also incorporating into this continuing impulse or tradition of naturalism the social and intellectual concerns of that age: Freudianism and Marxism in the 1930s, for example, or the Viet Nam War in more recent years.[33]

In addition to the writers already mentioned, it is also possible and useful to note the powerful naturalistic impulse in the fiction of such literary giants as Hemingway and Faulkner, as well as in that of a large number of relatively minor figures. Faulkner's major theme of the burden of the past as expressed through regional and family destiny strikes a firm naturalistic note, as does Hemingway's preoccupation with the behavioristic interplay between temperament and setting. Entire subgenres of modern American writing — the novel of urban decay, for example (Richard Wright and Nelson Algren), or the fiction of World War II (Norman Mailer and James Jones) — lend themselves to analysis in relation to naturalistic themes. Even a figure such as Edith Wharton is increasingly viewed in naturalistic terms, despite the upper-class milieu of much of her fiction, because of her central theme of the entrapment of women within social codes and taboos. Indeed, a great deal of fiction by women about women, from Wharton and Kate Chopin onward, can be said to reflect this naturalistic theme. Naturalism thus truly "refuses to die" in America. And it therefore especially behooves us, as students of American life, to reexamine its late-nineteenth-century roots.

NOTES

1. See, for example, René Wellek, "The Concept of Realism in Literary Scholarship," *Concepts of Criticism* (New Haven and London: Yale University Press, 1963), pp. 222–55, and George Levine, "Realism Reconsidered," *The Theory of the Novel: New Essays*, ed. John Halperin (New York: Oxford University Press, 1974), pp. 233–56.

2. See Everett Carter, *Howells and the Age of Realism* (Philadelphia: Lippincott, 1954), pp. 265–75, and Edwin H. Cady, *The Light of Common Day: Realism in American Fiction* (Bloomington: Indiana University Press, 1971), pp. 3–22.

3. Criticism reflecting this position is too plentiful to cite fully. For some blatant examples, however, see Paul Elmer More, "Modern Currents in American Fiction," *The Demon of the Absolute* (Princeton, N.J.: Princeton University Press, 1928); Floyd Stovall, *American Idealism* (Norman: University of Oklahoma Press, 1943); and Randall Stewart, *American Literature and Christian Doctrine* (Baton Rouge: Louisiana State University Press, 1958).

4. Stuart P. Sherman, "The Barbaric Naturalism of Mr. Dreiser," *On Contemporary Literature* (New York: Holt, 1917), pp. 93–4.

5. These various critical attitudes are discussed later in this introduction.

6. W. D. Howells, *Selected Literary Criticism, Vol. II: 1886–1897*, ed. Donald Pizer (Bloomington: Indiana University Press, 1993), p. 133.

7. This position is most fully expressed by George J. Becker in his "Introduction: Modern Realism as a Literary Movement," *Documents of Modern Literary Realism* (Princeton, N.J.: Princeton University Press, 1963), pp. 3–38, and *Realism in Modern Literature* (New York: Ungar, 1980), pp. 179–83. See also Lilian R. Furst and Peter N. Skrine, *Naturalism* (London: Methuen, 1971), pp. 33–6.

8. See Becker's "Introduction: Modern Realism as a Literary Movement," pp. 35–6, and his review of Donald Pizer's *Realism and Naturalism in Nineteenth-Century American Literature* (1966), in *Nineteenth-Century Fiction* 21 (1966): 196–9.

9. Harry Levin, *The Gates of Horn: A Study of Five French Realists* (New York: Oxford University Press, 1963), pp. 24–83, and René Wellek, "The Concept of Realism in Literary Scholarship."

10. Martin Kanes — in a review of Yves Chevrel's *Le Naturalisme* in *Comparative Literature* 36 (1984): 373 — notes Chevrel's effort to resolve this dilemma by assuming "that naturalism [in France] is that series of texts perceived by contemporary readers as being naturalistic."

11. See, in particular, Falk's *The Victorian Mode in American Fiction: 1865–1885* (East Lansing: Michigan State University Press, 1964). In his recent *The Problem of American Realism: Studies in the Cultural History of a Literary Idea* (Chicago: University of Chicago Press, 1993), Michael Davitt Bell recapitulates much of Falk's discussion of the Victorian character of American realism.

12. See Donald Pizer, "The Evolutionary Foundation of W. D. Howells's *Criticism and Fiction*" and "Evolutionary Ideas in Late Nineteenth-Century English and American Literary Criticism," *Realism and Naturalism in Nineteenth-Century American Literature*, 2d rev. ed. (Carbondale: Southern Illinois University Press, 1984), pp. 70–95.

13. Garland's unpublished essay "The Evolution of American Thought," quoted in Donald Pizer, *Hamlin Garland's Early Work and Career* (Berkeley and Los Angeles: University of California Press, 1960), pp. 17–18.

14. Boyesen, "The Progressive Realism of American Fiction," *Literary and Social Silhouettes* (New York: Harper's, 1894), p. 73.

15. Garland, *Crumbling Idols* (Chicago: Stone and Kimball, 1894), p. 28.

16. Boyesen, "Progressive Realism," p. 78.

17. Norris, "Zola as a Romantic Writer" (1896), *The Literary Criticism of Frank Norris*, ed. Donald Pizer (Austin: University of Texas Press, 1964), p. 72.

18. Norris, "A Plea for Romantic Fiction" (1901), in Pizer, *Literary Criticism of Frank Norris*, p. 78.

19. Russell Blankenship, "The Triumph of Realism," *American Literature as an Expression of the National Mind* (New York: Holt, 1931).

20. Two characteristic biographies of the 1920s that stress the theme of alienation in late-nineteenth-century writers are Van Wyck Brooks, *The Ordeal of Mark Twain* (1920) and Thomas Beer, *Stephen Crane* (1923).

21. Mencken, for example, tended to spice his attacks on American puritanism with offhand popshots at Howells, as in *A Book of Prefaces* (New York: Knopf, 1917), p. 218: "Of the great questions that agitated the minds of men in Howells' time one gets no more than a faint and far-away echo in his novels. His investigations, one may say, are carried out *in vacuo;* his discoveries are not expressed in terms of passion, but in terms of giggles."

22. Hicks, *The Great Tradition: An Interpretation of American Literature since the Civil War* (New York: Macmillan, 1933), p. 301. A frequent corollary of this emphasis was the dismissal of James's fiction as irrelevant to an understanding of American life, as in V. L. Parrington's brief comments on James in his *The Beginnings of Critical Realism in America* (New York: Harcourt, Brace, 1930), pp. 239–41, under the heading "Henry James and the Nostalgia of Culture."

23. V. L. Parrington states this position succinctly in notes for a lecture on naturalism (Parrington, *The Beginnings of Critical Realism,* p. 327): "Machine industrialism. The bigness of the economic machine dwarfs the individual and creates a sense of impotency."

24. Smith, "The Second Discovery of America," *Literary History of the United States,* ed. Robert E. Spiller et al. (New York: Macmillan, 1948), 2:790.

25. Also reflecting this shift in attitude is the fact that Jay Martin, in his *Harvests of Change: American Literature, 1865–1914* (Englewood Cliffs, N.J.: Prentice-Hall, 1967), devotes his longest chapter to the work of Henry James.

26. Carter, *Howells and the Age of Realism,* pp. 80–169.

27. Falk, "The Rise of Realism," *Transitions in American Literary History,* ed. Harry H. Clark (Durham: Duke University Press, 1953), pp. 379–442; Berthoff, *The Ferment of Realism: American Literature, 1884–1919* (New York: Free Press, 1965); Martin, *Harvests of Change* (1967).

28. Cargill remarks, for example (*Intellectual America: Ideas on the March* [New York: Macmillan, 1941] p. 175), that "The only possibility of Fascism in this country lies, not in the popularity of the doctrines of Fascism, but rather in the debility of the public will through wide acceptance of the philosophy of Naturalism."

29. The key documents are Trilling's "Reality in America," *The Liberal Imagination* (New York: Viking, 1950), pp. 3–21; Cowley's " 'Not Men': A Natural History of American Naturalism," *Kenyon Review* 9 (1947): 414–35; and Rahv's "Notes on the Decline of Naturalism," *Image and Idea* (Norfolk, Conn.: New Directions, 1949), pp. 128–38.

30. Howe, "The Stature of Theodore Dreiser," *New Republic,* July 25, 1964, p. 19.

31. Thorp, "The Persistence of Naturalism in the Novel," *American Writing in the Twentieth Century* (Cambridge, Mass.: Harvard University Press, 1960), pp. 143–95, and Kazin, "American Naturalism: Reflections from Another Era," *The American Writer and the European Tradition,* ed. Margaret Denny and William H. Gilman (Minneapolis: University of Minnesota Press, 1950), pp. 121–31.

32. See, in particular, the essays added to the second edition (1984) of this study and Pizer's *The Theory and Practice of American Literary Naturalism: Selected Essays and Reviews* (Carbondale: Southern Illinois University Press, 1993).

33. Summarized here is the central argument in Donald Pizer, *Twentieth-Century American Literary Naturalism: An Interpretation* (Carbondale: Southern Illinois University Press, 1982). Other significant attempts to describe twentieth-century American naturalism are the chapters on Anderson, Farrell, Steinbeck, Hemingway, and Dos Passos in Walcutt, *American Literary Naturalism, A Divided Stream* (1956); Thorp, "The Persistence of Naturalism in the Novel," *American Writing in the Twentieth Century* (1960); essays on Steinbeck, Wright, Farrell, and Algren in *American Literary Naturalism: A Reassessment,* ed. Yoshinobu Hakutani and Lewis Fried (Heidelberg: Carl Winter, 1975); and Don Graham, "Naturalism in American Fiction: A Status Report," *Studies in American Fiction* 10 (1982): 1–16.

Towards a Definition
of American Modernism

DANIEL JOSEPH SINGAL

In "Towards a Definition of American Modernism," Singal notes that although there is no consensus regarding what constitutes modernist culture, there is a growing agreement about what it is not. Singal distinguishes between modernization *and* modernism, *two related but distinct terms. According to Singal, modernization, a process of social and economic development, is characterized by the rise of industry, technology, and urbanization, while modernism is a culture with a set of related beliefs, ideas, and values. Singal associates modernism with efforts to order the human experience despite the chaos of the twentieth century, and puts it on par with such historical moments as Victorianism and the Enlightenment.*

Singal describes the development of American modernism by considering Victorianism, European Modernism, and cubism. According to Singal, the modernist worldview "begins with the premise of an unpredictable universe where nothing is ever stable, and where accordingly human beings must be satisfied with knowledge that is partial and transient at best" (p. 121). He concludes by addressing the beginning of the end of modernism in the 1960s and the move toward postmodernism. Singal's essay originally appeared in American Quarterly *in 1981.*

"On or about December 1910, human character changed." So declared Virginia Woolf in a statement that virtually all subsequent writers on Modernism have felt obliged to quote. Though historians tracing the origins of Modernist culture have quarreled with Woolf's exact choice of date, they have increasingly come to agree that sometime around the turn of the century the intelligentsia in Europe and America began to experience a profound shift in sensibility that would lead to an explosion of creativity in the arts, transform moral values, and in time reshape the conduct of life throughout Western society. Modernism, Peter Gay reports, "utterly changed painting, sculpture, and music; the dance, the novel, and the drama; architecture, poetry, and thought. And its ventures into unknown territory percolated from

From *American Quarterly* 39.1 (1981): 7–26.

the rarefied regions of high culture to general ways of thinking, feeling, and seeing." Indeed, notwithstanding the growing evidence that a new sensibility of "postmodernism" has recently made its appearance, many writers would contend that Modernism itself has served as the dominant culture of twentieth-century America from the period just after the First World War up to the present.[1]

Although there is assuredly no consensus on exactly what Modernist culture is, there does seem to be a growing accord on what it is not. Perhaps the commonest misconception is the practice of equating it with "modernization," a concept emanating from Max Weber and still fashionable among many social scientists. Put simply, Modernism should properly be seen as a *culture* — a constellation of related ideas, beliefs, values, and modes of perception — that came into existence during the mid to late nineteenth century, and that has had a powerful influence on art and thought on both sides of the Atlantic since roughly 1900. *Modernization,* by contrast, denotes a *process* of social and economic development, involving the rise of industry, technology, urbanization, and bureaucratic institutions, that can be traced back as far as the seventeenth century. The relationship between these two important historical phenomena is exceedingly complex, with Modernism arising in part as a counterresponse to the triumph of modernization, especially its norms of rationality and efficiency, in nineteenth-century Europe and America. Despite that initial hostility, however, the Modernist stance toward modernization has typically been marked by ambivalence, with Modernists simultaneously admiring the vitality and inventiveness of technological progress while decrying the dehumanization it appears to bring in its wake. Thus, despite the etymological similarity, Modernism and modernization must be sharply differentiated; nor should "modern" and "Modernist" ever be treated as synonyms.[2]

Another problematic view of Modernism equates it exclusively with the philosophy and style of life of the artistic avant-garde at the turn of the twentieth century. "Modernism" in this sense usually connotes radical experimentation in artistic style, a deliberate cultivation of the perverse and decadent, and the flaunting of outrageous behavior designed to shock the bourgeoisie. The entire movement, according to this definition, was comprised essentially of a small number of highly talented poets and painters based on the bohemian quarters of certain large cities, such as Paris, New York, Vienna, and Berlin, culminating around the time of the First World War in the work of such "canonical" masters as Picasso, Pound, and Joyce. A variation on this definition, put forth by literary critics like Irving Howe and Lionel Trilling, allows Modernism slightly more range by viewing it as an "adversary culture" originating in bohemia but later adopted by twentieth-century intellectuals in their growing estrangement from mass society, and ultimately reappearing as a virtual parody of its earlier self in the form of the 1960s counterculture. In either case, this perspective sees Modernist thought as essentially negative and rebellious in character, and far too amorphous ever to be susceptible to definition.[3]

As the present essay will attempt to show, however, there is a more recent and far more satisfactory approach to Modernism that takes issue with the "bohemian" interpretation, contending that those writing in the Trilling tradition confuse the tip for the whole iceberg by focusing on the more visible and spectacular manifestations of the culture during its period of ascendancy while missing its underlying structure. Far from being anarchic, Modernist thought in this view represents an attempt to restore a sense of order to human experience under the often chaotic conditions of twentieth-century existence, and it most assuredly does contain a unifying principle if one knows where to look. Not just the plaything of the avant-garde, it has assumed a commanding position in literature, music, painting, architecture, philosophy, and virtually every other realm of artistic or intellectual endeavor. Moreover, Modernism in this formulation has cast its influence well beyond the intellectual elite to encompass much of contemporary middle-class Western society. Its values, though somewhat diluted, are held by a majority of present-day Americans, and its style is manifested in such diverse contexts as suburban architecture, television advertising, and popular music. In short, the definition being proposed here suggests that Modernism deserves to be treated as a full-fledged historical culture much like Victorianism or the Enlightenment, and that it supplies nothing less than the basic contours of our current mode of thought.

To locate the inner dynamics of Modernism and to see how it came into being, it is necessary to return briefly to the culture against which the early Modernists rebelled. Victorianism, whose reign in America ran roughly from the 1830s to the early twentieth century, was closely associated with the rapidly expanding urban bourgeois class of that era. Its guiding ethos was centered upon the classic bourgeois values of thrift, diligence, and persistence, so important for success in a burgeoning capitalist economy, along with an immense optimism about the progress that industrialization seemed sure to bring. At the same time, Victorian culture, with its ideal vision of a stable, peaceful society free from sin and discord, proved immensely helpful in enabling the members of this new middle class to keep their balance in a world that was changing very fast, in ways they did not always expect or understand.[4]

At the core of this new culture stood a distinctive set of bedrock assumptions. These included a belief in a predictable universe presided over by a benevolent God and governed by immutable natural laws, a corresponding conviction that humankind was capable of arriving at a unified and fixed set of truths about all aspects of life, and an insistence on preserving absolute standards based on a radical dichotomy between that which was deemed "human" and that regarded as "animal." It was this moral dichotomy above all that constituted the deepest guiding principle of the Victorian outlook. On the "human" or "civilized" side of the dividing line fell everything that served to lift man above the beasts — education, refinement, manners, the arts, religion, and such domesticated emotions as loyalty and family love. The "animal" or "savage" realm, by contrast, contained those instincts and passions that constantly threatened self-control, and which therefore had to be repressed at all cost. Foremost among those threats was of course sexuality, which proper Victorians conceived of as a hidden geyser of animality existing within everyone and capable of erupting with little or no warning at the slightest stimulus. All erotic temptations were accordingly supposed to be rooted out, sexual pleasure even within marriage was to be kept to a minimum, and, as Nancy F. Cott has shown, the standard of respectable conduct, especially for women, shifted decisively "from modesty to passionlessness." A glorious future of material abundance and technological advance was possible, Victorians were convinced, but only if the animal component in human nature was effectively suppressed.[5]

Equally important was the way this moral dichotomy fostered a tendency to view the world in polar terms. "There is a value in possibilities," Masao Miyoshi observes, ". . . but the Victorians too often saw them in rigid pairs — all or nothing, white or black." Sharp distinctions were made in every aspect of existence: Victorians characterized societies as either civilized or savage, drew a firm line between what they considered superior and inferior classes, and divided races unambiguously into black and white. They likewise insisted on placing the sexes in "separate spheres," based on what Rosalind Rosenberg describes as "the Victorian faith in sexual polarity," which deemed women as "by nature emotional and passive," while men were "rational and assertive." Such dichotomies, it was believed, were permanently rooted in biology and in the general laws of nature. The "right" way, the moral way, was to keep these various categories distinct and segregated.[6]

Put in slightly different terms, what the Victorians aspired to was a radical standard of innocence. They were engaged in an attempt to wall themselves off as completely as possible from what they regarded as evil and corruption, and to create on their side of the barrier a brave new world suffused, in Matthew Arnold's words, with "harmonious perfection." Nineteenth-century thinkers, writes Donald H. Meyer, "longed for a universe that was not just intelligible, reassuring, and morally challenging, but symphonic as well." To be sure, actual behavior at times seemed to undercut this pursuit of innocence, but the point is that for the Victorian middle class innocence still remained a powerful and almost universal cultural ideal. Even when behavior diverged from it, as doubtless happened quite often, the ideal continued to be venerated. Nor was the Victorian ethos regarded as especially oppressive by the great majority of its nineteenth-century middle-class adherents. Rather, in the context of their experience it was both comforting and distinctly uplifting — a set of values that offered moral certainty, spiritual balm, and the hope that civilization might at last rid itself of the barbaric baggage remaining from humankind's dark, preindustrial past.[7]

Nevertheless, by the end of the century various individuals in Europe and the United States were beginning to chafe under the burden of Victorian repression and to challenge their inherited culture in different ways. A belief developed that modern bourgeois existence had become perilously artificial

and "over-civilized," and that the degree of self-control that Victorian morality required of each individual was stultifying the personality. "Many
yearned to smash the glass and breathe freely," writes T. J. Jackson Lears, "to
experience 'real life' in all its intensity." In most instances, though, these early
rebels should be seen as post-Victorians rather than incipient Modernists, for
they did not at bottom desire to overthrow nineteenth-century moralism, but
rather to temper or amend it in ways that would make it more bearable. Lears
skillfully documents the various exotic devices they resorted to in their futile
attempts to break with their conventional existence and regain contact with
"reality." But, as he also shows, identifying with medieval knights or taking
up Oriental religion were no more than safe substitutes for actual liberation
and could not resolve the cultural crisis these people were caught up in. The
overwhelming majority of post-Victorians were accordingly fated to dwell in
a kind of no-man's land. "Wandering between two worlds," Lears reports,
these victims of cultural transition typically "remained outsiders in both."[8]

The first true signs of Modernism appeared in Europe during the latter
half of the nineteenth century in the form of a succession of small movements,
each making its unique contribution to the new culture that was gradually
coming into being. Most conspicuous at the outset were the French symbolist
poets, beginning with Charles Baudelaire in the 1850s, who overturned the
traditional mimetic conventions of art by writing as much about what was
transpiring within their own minds as about events or objects in the "real"
world. "Paint not the thing, but the effect it produces," ran Stephane
Mallarmé's dictum. To that end, Symbolist verse employed highly allusive
language and imagery that described the subject of the poem only indirectly,
but conveyed as fully as possible the poet's emotional response to that subject. The Symbolists were soon joined by the Impressionist painters, who in
similar fashion devalued the ostensible subject matter and resolved to capture
on canvas their own subjective reactions. Both movements, in other words,
moved beyond the stable, rational, and seemingly objective world decreed by
nineteenth-century positivism in order to explore the far murkier and less
predictable operations of human perception and consciousness. In
Symbolism, Impressionism, and other allied movements, then, one sees
emerging one of the foremost tendencies of Modernism — the desire to
heighten, savor, and share all varieties of experience.[9]

At the same time developments taking place in more organized fields of
thought were providing a philosophical underpinning for this urge to seek
out experience. Writers as diverse as Henri Bergson, Friedrich Nietzsche, and
William James agreed in rejecting the prevailing theory that divided the mind
into separate compartments or "faculties," and in depicting experience as a
continuous flux of sensations and recollections — what James would term
"the stream of consciousness." That raw sensory flux, they concurred, was as
close as human beings could come to knowing reality. Abstract concepts,
along with all the other products of rationality that the Victorians had gloried
in as the highest achievements of civilization, were seen as inherently faulty
and misleading precisely because they represented an attempt to stop the

experiential flow and remove knowledge from its proper dynamic context. A perception imprisoned in an abstraction was as lifeless and imperfect a model of reality as a butterfly impaled in a specimen box. As James insisted: "When we conceptualize we cut and fix, and exclude anything but what we have fixed, whereas in the real concrete sensible flux of life experiences compenetrate each other." To be sure, most of these early Modernist thinkers regarded rational concepts, especially the truths of science, as useful fictions that helped to get the world's work done, so long as those concepts were not confused with permanent truths. Yet the main thrust of their writings involved the obligation to loosen formal and rational restraints, expand one's consciousness, open oneself to the world, and perfect one's ability to experience experience — exactly what the Victorians had most feared.[10]

Further momentum for this cultural sea-change came from new findings in the physical sciences. "In the twenty years between 1895 and 1915," notes Alan Bullock, "the whole picture of the physical universe, which had appeared not only the most impressive but also the most secure achievement of scientific thought, was brought into question." The certainties of Newtonian mechanics, and the Euclidian geometry on which it was based, gave way to a new physics in which everything depended on the relative position and motion of the observer and the object being observed. Non-Euclidian versions of geometry abounded, all equally verifiable, until Henri Poincaré was led to suggest in 1902 that "one geometry cannot be more true than another; it can only be more convenient." Radical theoretical shifts that served to demolish a host of familiar and distinct concepts were taking place at both the cosmic and microscopic levels: Space, far from being a void, was now seen as filled by fields of energy, while the atom, far from being solid, was itself made up of tiny particles that orbited each other at a distance. The discovery of radium, demonstrating that seemingly solid matter could turn into energy, was shocking enough, but it was soon followed by Albert Einstein's proof early in the century that space and time could no longer be construed as separate and distinct entities, but must be placed on a continuum. Clearly, the new science had little use for the rigid, dichotomous categories that the Victorians had relied upon to organize their world; it was as enamored of dynamic process and relativism as the new philosophy and art.[11]

By the early twentieth century the profusion of artistic and intellectual movements was striking, especially in Paris, which was fast becoming the international center of Modernist activity. Most important during the first two decades of the century were Post-Impressionism, Cubism, Imagism, Vorticism, and the Italian variant, Futurism, to be followed after the war by Expressionism (mainly based in the Germanic countries), Dadaism, Surrealism, and Russian Constructivism — and eventually by Existentialism and Structuralism. Modernist masters came to dominate in all the arts, from Picasso, Cézanne, Braque, and Klee in painting, to Joyce, Pound, Eliot, and Malraux in literature, Stravinsky and Webern in music, along with Mies van der Rohe and Frank Lloyd Wright in architecture. Moreover, the new theories and values being fashioned by the intellectual elite were increasingly paralleled by similar developments at the level of popular attitudes and behavior, becoming unmistakable in the rampant consumerism and youth culture of the 1920s. In both cases the motor source was the same: a response to the cultural malaise brought about by late Victorian repression.

What all these various manifestations of Modernism had in common was a passion not only for opening the self to new levels of experience, but also fusing together disparate elements of that experience into new and original "wholes," to the point where one can speak of an "integrative mode" as the basis of the new culture. Put simply, the quintessential aim of Modernists has been to reconnect all that the Victorian moral dichotomy tore asunder — to integrate once more the human and the animal, the civilized and savage, and to heal the sharp divisions that the nineteenth century had established in areas such as class, race, and gender. Only in this way, they have believed, would it be possible to combat the fundamentally dishonest conception of existence that the Victorians had propagated, free the natural human instincts and emotions that the nineteenth century had bottled up, and so restore vitality to modern life. In the blunt words of William Carlos Williams: "Man is an animal, and if he forgets that, denies that, he is living a big lie, and soon enough other lies get going." In short, Modernists were intent on nothing less than recovering an entire aspect of being that their predecessors had tried to banish.[12]

Again and again, from art to social policy, Modernists have attempted to bring together that which the previous culture tried to keep separate. Far from being "the mere rehabilitation of the irrational," Malcolm Bradbury and James McFarlane write, Modernism involves "the interpretation, the reconciliation, the coalescence, the fusion — of reason and unreason, intellect and emotion, subjective and objective." McFarlane in fact identifies three stages in the development of the culture: a first stage of early rebellion (in other words, the bohemian stage that is often mistaken for the culture as a whole) during which "the emphasis is on fragmentation, on the breaking up and the progressive disintegration of those meticulously constructed 'systems' and 'types' and 'absolutes'" that the Victorians had assiduously created; a second stage marked by "a re-structuring of parts, a re-relating of the fragmented concepts"; and a final, mature stage characterized by "a dissolving, a blending, a merging of things previously held to be forever mutually exclusive." Thus, he concludes, "the defining thing in the Modernist mode is not so much that things fall *apart* but that they fall *together*"; the true end result of Modernism "is not disintegration but (as it were) superintegration."[13]

The most graphic manifestation of this integrative mode was certainly Cubism, a movement that deliberately sought to revitalize the experience of perception by challenging artistic conventions that had stood since the Renaissance. Since there was no such thing as fixed reality or truth, Picasso and his colleagues maintained, all objects would have to be seen in shifting relation to each other. The painter's task was thus to break up forms into component parts and have those parts continuously overlap, conveying not so much a sense of fragmentation as of wholeness. Sharp outlines were always to be avoided; rather, colors and textures were to bleed from one object into another, with subdued colors usually employed to enhance the sense of unity. Whenever possible, both the interior and exterior of a form were to be rendered alongside each other; likewise, the background was to have the same value and prominence as the main subject of the painting, and the two were to interpenetrate. Finally, in Cubist collage "found" objects from the "real" world, such as scraps of metal or pieces of newspaper, were to be incorporated into the work to juxtapose the spheres of aesthetic creation and everyday life, emphasizing how the painting was both a collection of pleasing shapes and colors on a flat surface *and* simultaneously a statement about perceived reality. In this manner, as Eugene Lunn tells us, the Cubists mounted their "revolutionary assault on the seeming stability of objects, which are taken apart, brought into collision, and reassembled on the picture surface" into a series of "contingent syntheses by which human activity and perception remake the world."[14]

This ever-present drive for integration explains so much about the history of Modernism. It allows one to make sense, for example, of the predilection of twentieth-century thinkers and writers for such devices as paradox (which joins seeming opposites) and ambivalence (the fusing of contradictory emotions, such as love and hate), and for their tendency to place concepts and empirical observations along a continuum or spectrum rather than in tightly demarcated categories. It also helps account for the practice of cinematic montage, with its juxtaposition of events and experiences; the attempt to break down boundaries between stage and audience in twentieth-century theater; the resort to multiple overlapping harmonies and rhythms in contemporary music, especially jazz (which also blends the primitivism of its African origins with modern sophistication); and the concern for maximizing the simultaneity of experience in literature — perhaps most fully achieved in Joyce's *Ulysses,* a novel structured, as Stephen Kern points out, so that "traditional dividers of sequence and distance collapse into a unified whole which the reader must envision after several readings." In the realm of social action, it was this stress on breaking down barriers that created the necessary cultural preconditions for the twentieth century's concerted campaigns to eliminate a "separate sphere" for women, and to overthrow that most noxious by-product of Victorian dichotomizing, racial segregation.[15]

Underlying all these efforts at integration has been the Modernist reconstruction of human nature. If the Victorians sought to place a firm barrier between the "higher" mental functions, such as rational thought and spirituality, and those "lower" instincts and passions that Freud would in time ascribe to the "id," Modernists strove to unite these two levels of the psyche. Thus where the Victorians held "sincerity" to be their most prized character trait, with its injunction that a person's conscious self remain honest and consistent, Modernists have demanded nothing less than "authenticity," which requires a blending of the conscious and unconscious strata of the mind so that the self presented to the world is the "true" self in every respect. This, as Trilling observes, represents a far "more strenuous" standard than did the code of sincerity, and necessitates precisely the sort of intense self-knowledge that the Victorians sought to avoid. Hence the resort to stream-of-consciousness technique in Modernist novels in order to capture what D. H. Lawrence called the "real, vital, potential self" as opposed to "the old stable ego" of nineteenth-century character.[16]

Yet it is just at this point that a massive paradox arises within the culture, for with the universe characterized by incessant flux, and human beings unable to know its workings with anything approaching certainty, the goal of perfect integration must always remain unattainable, at least within the natural world. Thus, although the Modernist seeks integration and authenticity, he or she must also be aware that they will never fully arrive. Nor would complete integration really be desirable, for that would mean stasis. The coalescing of the varied fragments of our contemporary existence can never be consummated, but must constantly be sought. The sole exceptions to this rule are found in self-contained intellectual systems such as mathematics, language or logic, as the logical positivists affirmed, or in imaginary settings conjured up for the purposes of art (though Modernist practice typically demands that artifice of this sort be clearly identified as such). Otherwise, all that pertains to nature and life must be construed dynamically, as continuous process; the only lasting closure, in Modernist terms, come with death.

Here lies the reason why personal identity has often become problematic and tension-ridden for those living in the twentieth century. The Victorian expectation that a person be consistent and sincere rested on the assumption that character was defined largely by social role, which in turn was normally fixed by heredity, upbringing, and vocation. Accordingly, once an individual matured, any shift in his or her character was viewed with suspicion. By contrast, the Modernists, as Ronald Bush puts it, view human nature "in a state of continuous becoming." Neither the self, nor any work of art designed to portray the self, Bush explains, can achieve "completeness or closure"; such closure would automatically violate the criterion of authenticity. As a result, one must constantly create and re-create an identity based upon one's ongoing experience in the world. Difficult though this effort may be at times, nothing less will meet the Modernist standard.[17]

Finally, this paradoxical quest for and avoidance of integration accounts for the special role of the arts within Modernist culture. Precisely because they represent a realm where that quest can be pursued with relative safety through surrogate experience, the arts have become a medium for radical experimentation in new ways of amplifying perception, organizing the psyche, and extending culture. As Susan Sontag points out, art in this century "has come to be invested with an unprecedented stature" because of its mission of "making forays into and taking up positions on the frontiers of consciousness (often very dangerous to the artist as a person) and reporting back what's there." Art is aided in this task by its ready access to the devices of symbolism, metaphor, and myth, all of which, in Jerome Bruner's words, serve to connect "things that were previously separate in experience" and that cannot be joined through logic. Art in this way "bridges rationality and impulse" by fusing together metaphorically the objective and subjective, the empirical and the introspective — breaking apart conventional beliefs and rejoining the resulting fragments in a manner that creates relationships and meanings not suspected before. In short, where the Victorians saw art as didactic in purpose — as a vehicle for communicating and illustrating preordained moral truths — to Modernists it has become the principal means of creating whatever provisional order human beings can attain.[18]

Thus the Modernist worldview has taken shape. It begins with the premise of an unpredictable universe where nothing is ever stable, and where accordingly human beings must be satisfied with knowledge that is partial and transient at best. Nor is it possible in this situation to devise a fixed and absolute system of morality; moral values must remain in flux, adapting continuously to changing historical circumstances. To create those values and garner whatever knowledge is available, individuals must repeatedly subject themselves — both directly, and vicariously through art — to the trials of experience. Above all they must not attempt to shield themselves behind illusions or gentility, as so many did during the nineteenth century. To be sure, with passing time the Modernist worldview has, especially at the hands of the mass media, undergone the same tendencies toward corruption and routinization that have beset other major historical cultures. But in its ideal form at least, Modernism — in stark contrast to Victorianism — eschews innocence and demands instead to know "reality" in all its depth and complexity, no matter how incomplete and paradoxical that knowledge might be, and no matter how painful. It offers a demanding, and at times even heroic, vision of life that most of its adherents may in fact have fallen short of, but which they have used to guide themselves by nonetheless.

Although it has become common practice to identify the New York Armory Show of 1913, with its exhibition of Cubist and Postimpressionist painting, as the first shot fired in the battle to establish Modernism on this side of the Atlantic, significant skirmishes had in fact been underway for several decades. By the time the show opened, Gertrude Stein and Ezra Pound, the two principal intermediaries between the United States and European Modernism, were already firmly entrenched at their posts overseas, Greenwich Village was filling up with cultural and artistic rebels, and proponents of the major intellectual breakthroughs in fields such as physics, biology, philosophy, psychology, and the social sciences had long since established beachheads at American universities. Both the Armory Show and the opening of Alfred Stieglitz's famous gallery were important vehicles for communication with headquarters overseas, but in America the war had long since been started, and by the period just before the First World War its effects could be seen everywhere, from muckraking journalism to the irreverent history of Charles A. Beard to the calls for personal and political liberation in *The Masses*. There were of course some differences from Europe — in John Higham's neat formulation, "Americans rebelled by extending the breadth of experience, Europeans by plumbing its depths" — but the essential values and dynamics of the culture were the same. "What was happening," Richard Hofstadter sums up, ". . . was that a modern critical intelligentsia was emerging in the United States. Modernism, in thought as in art, was dawning upon the American mind."[19]

Surely the two key figures in the process of importing the new culture to this country and giving it American roots were William James and John Dewey. James, as conversant with the latest European thought as any American of his day, was won over early in his career to the Darwinian premise that human beings existed on a continuum with other animals, and that the human brain was no more or less than a biological organ designed to select from the environment those perceptions useful for survival. For James that meant that the Victorian practice of radically separating the "higher" rational faculties from the "lower" instinctual ones made no sense. Rather, the mind must be conceived of as functionally integrated: "Pretend what we may, the whole man within us is at work when we form our philosophical opinions. Intellect, will, taste, and passion co-operate just as they do in practical affairs. . . ." Once the mind, guided by its passions, had chosen which perceptions to bring to consciousness, it might proceed to formulate abstract concepts based on them, but in doing so, James insisted, it necessarily introduced further distortions. The initial raw sensory experience, he believed, was the closest we could come to knowing reality; each application of the intellect, however valuable it might be for practical purposes, took us further from the "truth."[20]

For this reason, James concluded, human beings were doomed forever to epistemological uncertainty. To the great majority of his contemporaries this was a horrible revelation, but to James it was infinitely exciting, precisely because it banished the closed, deterministic universe of nineteenth-century positivism in favor of an "open" universe governed by change and chance where the process of discovery would be continuous. Embracing pluralism as a positive good, and grounding his own system of thought on the experiential basis of "radical empiricism," James became the first important American Modernist intellectual.[21]

Dewey, although heavily influenced by James, was a more systematic thinker inclined to give greater recognition to the virtues of rationality and science. More explicitly, the central purpose of all of Dewey's thought was eradicating the dichotomy between intellect and experience, thought and action, that he and James had inherited. Sensory perceptions, he contended, must be filtered through intelligence to become meaningful, while at the same time scientific theorizing must always be controlled by testing in the real world. One might even say that Dewey, in keeping with the "integrative mode" of Modernist culture, devoted his career to combating dualisms of all kinds — including those dividing mind from body, science from art, the city from the countryside, and the elite from the common people — all the while, of course, resisting final closure. Everywhere one looks in his writings one finds this sensibility at work, as in his discussion of how the basic task of both art and science is to blend elements of perception into integrated "relation-ships" in such a way that the process can "recur" indefinitely:

> A well-conducted scientific inquiry discovers as it tests, and proves as it explores; it does so in virtue of a method which combines both functions. And conversation, drama, [the] novel, and architectural construction, if there is an ordered experience, reach a stage that at once records and sums up the value of what precedes, and evokes and prophesies what is to come. Every closure is an awakening, and every awakening settles something.

One can likewise see the Modernist ethos at work in Dewey's plan for "pro-gressive education," with its effort to connect the classroom with "real life" experience, its pluralistic stress on breaking down social barriers by encour-aging interaction among students from diverse class and ethnic backgrounds, and its imperative that teachers not deliver fixed truths, but rather impress upon children at the earliest age the tentative, pragmatic character of knowl-edge.[22]

Indeed, one might rightfully speak of two predominant "streams" of American Modernist culture, proceeding respectively from James and Dewey. The Jamesian stream centers its interest on the individual conscious-ness, celebrates spontaneity, authenticity, and the probing of new realms of personal experience, and flows mainly through the arts and humanities. The Deweyan stream, by contrast, tends to focus on society as a whole, empha-sizes the elimination of social barriers (geographic, economic, ethnic, racial, and gender), and tries to weld together reason and emotion in the service of programmatic social aims. With each passing decade of the twentieth centu-ry these two streams have increasingly diverged, ultimately creating an important internal tension within American Modernism, but that fact should not be allowed to obscure their many close resemblances, particularly at the beginning. James, after all, considered himself a professional scientist, while Dewey's educational program was always centered on the individual and designed to tap the child's natural spontaneity. Both strains, moreover, have reflected the frequent preoccupation of American Modernists with pragmat-ic empiricism and democratic pluralism, as opposed to the tendency of Modernists in war-ravaged Europe to focus on apocalyptic experience and a concomitant cult of the irrational.

By the latter part of the Progressive Era, as Henry May has shown, the cultural revolution that James and Dewey had helped to initiate in America was spreading everywhere. Muckraking journalists were setting aside Victorian codes of gentility and exposing corruption at the highest levels of American life, naming specific names when necessary. Scholars like Charles Beard and Thorstein Veblen were taking a new critical look at their society and its history, determined to shed their nineteenth-century innocence and ferret out "reality" no matter how sordid it might be. Social workers like Jane Addams were praising the earthy vitality of immigrant cultures and insisting that such Old World heritages be blended with rather than overwhelmed by the dominant national culture. In New York, the Young Intellectuals, including Max Eastman, John Reed, Floyd Dell, Margaret Sanger, Eugene O'Neill, Randolph Bourne, and Walter Lippmann, were meeting at Mabel Dodge Luhan's salon, discussing the latest European Modernist authors and calling noisily for sexual, artistic, and political liberation in their own country. At the same time Frank Lloyd Wright was busy reshaping American architecture along Modernist lines, stripping away "false" ornamentation and facades, employing "authentic" materials such as untreated wood, glass, and stone, and using an abundance of windows and doors to erase the demarcation between interior and exterior. "Wright's first objective," one historian notes, "was to reduce the number of . . . separate parts and make a unified space so that light, air, and vistas permeated the whole." His designs, though attenuated in quality as they were popularized, supplied the basic patterns for the mass suburban housing boom following World War II, ensuring that a majority of middle-class Americans in the second half of the century would live in Modernist-styled homes.[23]

Yet perhaps the most influential stirrings of the new culture in America could be found in the work of the anthropologist Franz Boas and the extraordinary group of disciples he trained at Columbia University. In *The Mind of Primitive Man,* published in 1911, Boas took direct aim at the bedrock Victorian dichotomy between civilization and savagery, contending that so-called savage peoples were fully capable of logic, abstraction, aesthetic discrimination, and the inhibition of biological impulses, while Europeans practiced any number of customs, taboos, and rituals that could only be construed as irrational. For Boas such attributes as "human" or "animalistic" were all a matter of cultural perspective, and there was no scientific reason for granting the European perspective superiority over another — the only permissible criterion for normative judgment was the Darwinian one of how successfully a culture allowed a particular society to adapt to its environment. These insights, spreading first within the ranks of social scientists and then through the general population, would in time transform American attitudes concerning race by undermining the reigning stereotype of black people, whom the old moral dichotomy had consigned to "savagery." Indeed, by knocking away the cultural and scientific props of racism and replacing them with a new cultural modality that favored pluralistic integration, this attitudinal change in turn provided the essential foundation upon which the various movements to secure black rights were able to build. As Marshall Hyatt concludes, "Boas's critical contribution . . . lay in providing a new way of thinking, without which America could not have traveled the long road from *Plessy v. Ferguson* to *Brown v. Board of Education.*"[24]

Finally, one should take note of how the Modernist sensibility invaded popular culture during the Progressive Era. That process is clearly visible in Lewis Erenberg's study of New York City nightlife, which charts the way members of the more prosperous classes overcame post-Victorian malaise by gradually throwing aside the restraints of gentility and seeking out more sensuous forms of entertainment. In the nineteenth century, he observes, each "sex, class, and race . . . was expected to occupy its exclusive sphere. Public life was increasingly divided, and the private realm of the home diverged from the values of public life." But the cabaret, the focal institution of the new nightlife, was notable precisely because it "relaxed boundaries between the sexes, between audiences and performers, between ethnic groups and Protestants, between black culture and whites." For example, traditional "barriers between the entertainer and his audience" fell with the elimination of the raised stage, curtain, and footlights; performers even went out into the audience during their acts. Moreover, the majority of the leading entertainers and songwriters came from immigrant backgrounds that fell outside the orbit of Victorian respectability and hence were valued in large measure for their ability to put well-to-do patrons in touch with the vitality and experiences of lower-class life — an attribute that became even more prized during the 1920s when cabaret-goers went "slumming" in Harlem in search of black performers thought to be especially "natural, uncivilized, [and] uninhibited." To be sure, patrons demanded an atmosphere of sumptuous elegance to provide a sense of order and guarantee that they would not be declassed themselves. But the basic thrust of this newly created and rapidly expanding popular culture remained the effort to erase the Victorian dividing line between human and animal and thus "to liberate some of the repressed wilder elements, the more natural elements, that had been contained by gentility."[25]

The most unmistakable evidence of this transformation in public sensibility was surely the dancing craze that swept the nation between 1912 and 1916, foreshadowing the youth rebellion of the 1920s. Victorian-era dances such as the waltz, Erenberg observes, had emphasized "control, regularity, and patterned movement," along with "a look but do not touch approach to one's partner." The scores of dances introduced after 1912, most of which had originated in black culture, featured "heightened bodily expression" and far more "intimacy" between partners. The very names of the dances — bunny hug, monkey glide, grizzly bear, and lame duck — suggested a delectable surrender to animality and "rebellion against the older sexual mores." Most notorious was the shimmy, "a black torso-shaking dance" that became the rage just after the war. It was accompanied by a new form of music called jazz, also of black origins, which featured still wilder rhythms, frequent improvisation, and recurrent attempts by early bands to make their instruments "duplicate animal sounds." Moral reformers, ministers, and members of the older generation were predictably aghast at this outbreak of impulse. "Jazz and modern dancing" in their eyes, writes Paula Fass, seemed to herald "the collapse of civilized life." It is clear in retrospect that, viewed from a Victorian perspective, such forebodings were not without justification, for the behavior of middle-class youth during the 1920s demonstrated just how widely Modernist values had spread within the nation and how quickly they were approaching dominance.[26]

To trace the course of Modernist culture in America in full detail would require far more space than is available here. Such a narrative would necessarily include 1920s novelists like Fitzgerald, Hemingway, Dos Passos, and Faulkner, who chronicled the disintegration of modern society and culture, but whose primary concern, Bradbury rightly observes, was somehow "to make the world re-cohere." It would also encompass the documentary-style writers of the 1930s who sought to immerse themselves in the consciousness of socially marginal groups like southern sharecroppers — most notably James Agee and Walker Evans, in their *Let Us Now Praise Famous Men,* with its impassioned effort to pare away the separation between the authors' consciousness and that of their impoverished, illiterate subjects (along with Agee's pained realization of the impossibility of breaking down those barriers). Other illustrations of the mature American Modernist sensibility would run the gamut of cultural and intellectual activity from the interwar period onward, including the "humanist existentialism" of postwar literature, the neo-orthodox theology of Reinhold Niebuhr and Paul Tillich, the pluralism of social science-oriented writers such as Richard Hofstadter and Daniel Bell, the pragmatic social reform initiatives of the New Deal and Great Society, the "International Style" in urban architecture, and the rise of modern advertising, where, as Bruce Robbins puts it, the "techniques of the modernist classics have been incorporated into modernist commercials." Finally, a complete account of the new culture's fortunes in America could not leave out the various countervailing movements that arose to challenge Modernist values, either seeking, like the Fundamentalists, Ku Klux Klan, and "New Right," to restore nineteenth-century certainties, or to proffer some new form of absolutism in the manner of scientism, orthodox Marxism, and the behaviorism of B. F. Skinner, or to provide refuge from the tensions accompanying Modernism through an emphasis on bureaucratic process, as have some varieties of corporate culture.[27]

It would appear that the culminating moment for American Modernism — and perhaps also the beginning of its end — came in the 1960s. The celebration of the animal component of human nature, the quest for spontaneity and authenticity, the desire to raze all dualisms and distinctions, the breaking down of social and cultural barriers, the quest for "wholeness," and the effort to expand consciousness and discover new modes of experience — all were given heightened realization. A new generation of rebels, ironically spoken of as a "counterculture" when they were in fact riding the crest of a cultural tidal wave, carried the Modernist embrace of natural instinct and primitivism to its seemingly inevitable conclusion by letting hair grow wild, experimenting with mind-altering drugs, overthrowing the last vestiges of conventional sexual mores, and creating in acid rock a music of pounding sensuality. The same forces could be found at work among the intellectual elite, where writers like Susan Sontag condemned a supposed "hypertrophy of the intellect at the expense of energy and sensual capability" in contemporary life and demanded that critics forego all attempts at describing or interpreting art. Contending that "our world" is "impoverished enough," she insisted that we abandon "all duplicates of it, until we again experience more immediately what we have." Numerous performing groups took this philosophy to heart, endeavoring to achieve authenticity by bridging life and art — most notably the

Living Theater, whose *Paradise Now* invited members of the audience to disrobe on stage and join the troupe in sexual high jinks. Viewed in retrospect, what seems most striking about such excesses is the way matters once vested with deep emotion and commitment by those engaged in the initial battle against Victorianism were now often reduced to a pointless game. One senses that the pendulum was again starting to swing, that Modernism, much like late Victorian culture in the 1890s, was at last becoming overripe and starting to caricature itself. If so, then the 1960s, instead of marking the dawn of an Aquarian age, might be more accurately viewed as the death-rattle of a fast aging culture.[28]

Since that decade, and partly in reaction to it, there has been increasing discussion of the possible arrival of "postmodernism." As one might expect, those attempting to describe this new sensibility have often disagreed with each other, but they do seem to concur that its presence first became unmistakable during the 1960s. It has manifested itself, according to most accounts, in the form of Pop and minimalist art, in an architecture that intentionally draws on cliches from popular culture ("learning from Las Vegas," as Robert Venturi puts it), and in the literary productions of Tom Wolfe, Donald Barthelme, and Joseph Heller, among others. What these various tendencies appear to have in common is what Richard Wolin calls "the valorization of mass culture" by the intellectual elite, "a pseudo-populist ethos which suggests that the gap between (high) art and life has been definitely bridged." To put this in slightly different terms, one might say that the democratic urge within Modernism to break down all division between the elite and the popular has at last overcome the long-standing practice of Modernist thinkers to dismiss mass culture on the grounds of inauthenticity. The result, Wolin argues, is a sensibility that is impatient with "complexity" and "wants instead works of literature . . . as absolute as the sun, as unarguable as orgasm, as delicious as a lollipop."[29]

Fredric Jameson likewise speaks of an "aesthetic populism" as the essence of postmodernism, and complains of a new superficiality, a "waning of content," in which "depth is replaced by surface, or multiple surfaces." "The postmoderns," he claims, "have in fact been fascinated precisely by this whole 'degraded' landscape of schlock and kitsch, of TV series and *Readers' Digest* culture, of advertising and motels . . . materials they no longer simply 'quote,' as a Joyce or Mahler might have done, but incorporate into their very substance." As he sees it, this new "cultural dominant" has resolved the Modernist crisis of personal identity by the simple expedient of eliminating the self as a subject of art or intellectual speculation. With no ego, there is conveniently no emotion, no troublesome conflict — just problems of "style," to the point where art becomes little more than a matter of "codes" and "pastiche," a "virtual grab-bag" of "random raw materials and impulses" reflecting the peculiar commodity fetishism of "late capitalism." What postmodernism seems to lack, in short, is the creative tension — the refusal to achieve closure — that had characterized Modernist art and thought at their best and provided their special resonance.[30]

If Jameson and Wolin are correct in their descriptions of postmodernism, what its advent may signal is a growing inability to tolerate the formidable demands made by Modernist culture, especially its abiding lack of resolution and certainty — just as post-Victorianism in the 1890s represented an effort to escape nineteenth-century moral constraints. Where Americans once sought an antidote to excessive repression, they may now be searching out a remedy for excessive liberation. The real underlying force beneath our present cultural activity may thus be the desire to find a stable point of reference, some firm rock upon which to rest our perceptions and values — though preferably without giving up the lessons about the relative nature of truth that Modernism itself provided. Thus we even find Jameson himself at the end of his critique calling almost plaintively for a new kind of cultural sextant and compass to fashion what he calls an "aesthetic of *cognitive mapping*."[31]

Some, including Jameson, seem to believe that the surest path to such regenerative intellectual cartography can be found in French poststructuralist theory, including the work of Derrida, Lacan, Foucault, and Althusser. One suspects, however, that, useful as some of its specific insights and techniques may be, poststructuralism in the long run will be viewed more as part of the postmodernist malady than as a cure. The prime characteristic of its grand systems, as Frederick Crews recently pointed out, has been "a growing apriorism — a willingness to settle issues by theoretical decree, without even a pretense of evidential appeal." In eschewing empiricism this way, he continues, the poststructuralists and their disciples have been proceeding from "an unarticulated feeling that one at least deserves the haven of an all-explanatory theory, a way of making the crazy world cohere." But in the midst of the cultural dilemma posed by late Modernism it does not seem likely that the world will agree to cohere that easily; the expedient of intellectual game-playing, for all its temptations, will not solve the problem.[32]

Moreover, it seems clear that the postmodernist initiative to date has taken place within an essentially Modernist framework. The democratic urge to close the gap between the intellectuals and the "people," the stipulation (in Pop art and architecture, for example) that all artifacts be clearly identified as artificial and inauthentic while at the same time being seen paradoxically as authentic artifacts, the poststructuralist resort to semiotic analysis — these and other postmodernist traits surely represent extrapolations from the basic Modernist methods. "Postmodernist anti-art was inherent in the logic of the modernist aesthetic," Gerald Graff observes astutely in support of his contention that a major cultural "breakthrough" has yet to occur in our time. Robert Martin Adams similarly finds that "where modernism has simply pushed ahead, it has exaggerated tendencies which were in it from the very beginning, by making symptomatic jokes out of them." In short, as was the case earlier with post-Victorianism, it would appear that those attempting to free themselves from inherited beliefs and values have thus far been unable to do so. Long-standing internal contradictions have surfaced, the old culture is wobbling, but its successor is still not here.[33]

Where then are we headed? If there is a lesson to be gleaned from the study of history, it is the necessity of expecting the unexpected. Few people at the turn of the twentieth century were able to discern the shape of the cultural era they were entering, and those few saw that shape only in its vaguest outline. There is no reason to think that prognostication will fare better this time. In the meanwhile, now that we are gaining a modicum of critical distance from it, perhaps the wisest course of action would be to occupy ourselves with improving our understanding of Modernism, as well as the more general process of cultural change in America, in order to gain as much perspective as possible on our recent historical experience. That seems the best answer available, though doubtless some will object that, with its relativism and contingency, it is indelibly a Modernist one.

NOTES

1. Virginia Woolf, *Mr. Bennett and Mrs. Brown* (London, 1924), 4; Malcolm Bradbury and James McFarlane, "The Name and Nature of Modernism," in Bradbury and McFarlane, eds., *Modernism, 1890–1930* (New York, 1976), 20, 28, 34–35; Peter Gay, *Freud, Jews and Other Germans: Masters and Victims in Modernist Culture* (New York, 1978), 21–22; Bruce Robbins, "Modernism in History, Modernism in Power," in Robert Kiely, ed., *Modernism Reconsidered* (Cambridge, Mass., 1983), 231–32, 234–39; Daniel Joseph Singal, *The War Within: From Victorian to Modernist Thought in the South, 1919–1945* (Chapel Hill, 1982), 3–4.

2. On modernization theory, see especially Cyril E. Black, *The Dynamics of Modernization: A Study in Comparative History* (New York, 1966), 7, 9–26, 46–49; and Alex Inkeles and David H. Smith, *Becoming Modern: Individual Change in Six Developing Countries* (Cambridge, Mass., 1974), 15–25; for its applicability within the context of American history, see Richard D. Brown, *Modernization: The Transformation of American Life, 1600–1865* (New York, 1976), especially 3–22. The dialectical linkage between Modernism and modernization is explored in Peter Berger et al., *The Homeless Mind: Modernization and Consciousness* (New York, 1973), though the authors use the term "demodernizing consciousness" in place of "Modernism." See also Eugene Lunn, *Marxism and Modernism: An Historical Study of Lukacs, Brecht, Benjamin and Adorno* (Berkeley, 1982), 40–42. For one among many examples of works that badly confuse Modernism and modernization, see Richard Wolin, "Modernism vs. Postmodernism," *Telos* 62 (Winter 1984–85): 9–11.

3. Gay, *Freud, Jews and Other Germans*, 22–26; Lionel Trilling, *Beyond Culture: Essays on Literature and Learning* (New York, 1968), xiii, 3, 30; Irving Howe, *The Decline of the New* (New York, 1968), 3–5, 9–10, 21–25; Mark Krupnick, *Lionel Trilling and the Fate of Cultural Criticism* (Evanston, 1986), 135–36, 143–45; Daniel Bell, *The Cultural Contradictions of Capitalism* (New York, 1976), 46–48.

4. Daniel Walker Howe, "American Victorianism as a Culture," *American Quarterly* 27 (December 1975); 508, 511–14, 521.

5. Walter E. Houghton, *The Victorian Frame of Mind, 1830–1870* (New Haven, 1957), 14, 144–45, 420; John S. Haller and Robin M. Haller, *The Physician and Sexuality in Victorian America* (New York, 1977), 126–28, 109; Nancy F. Cott, "Passionlessness: An Interpretation of Victorian Sexual Ideology, 1790–1850," in Nancy F. Cott and Elizabeth H. Pleck, eds., *A Heritage of Her Own: Toward a New Social History of American Women* (New York, 1979), 166–68.

6. Houghton, *Victorian Frame of Mind*, 162, 171, 144–45; Masao Miyoshi, *The Divided Self: A Perspective on the Literature of the Victorians* (New York, 1969), xv; Rosalind Rosenberg, *Beyond Separate Spheres: Intellectual Roots of Modern Feminism* (New York, 1982), xiv.

7. Houghton, *Victorian Frame of Mind*, 266, 297–300, 356; Matthew Arnold, *Culture and Anarchy*, ed. J. Dover Wilson (Cambridge, Eng., 1971), 11; Donald H. Meyer, "American Intellectuals and the Crisis of Faith," *American Quarterly* 27 (December 1975): 601; W. L. Burn, *The Age of Equipoise: A Study of the Mid-Victorian Generation* (New York, 1964), 41, 106.

8. T. J. Jackson Lears, *No Place of Grace: Antimodernism and the Transformation of American Culture, 1880–1920* (New York, 1981), 5–6, 13, 37, 48, 53, 57, 105–06, 166, 174; John Higham, "The Reorientation of American Culture in the 1890's," in Higham, *Writing American History: Essays on Modern Scholarship* (Bloomington, Ind.: 1970), 78–79, 99.

9. Bradbury and McFarlane, "Name and Nature of Modernism," 31; Lunn, *Marxism and Modernism*, 42–43, 45; Stephane Mallarmé, quoted in Stephen Kern, *The Culture of Time and Space,*

1880–1918 (Cambridge, Mass., 1983), 172; Clive Scott, "Symbolism, Decadence and Impressionism" in Bradbury and McFarlane, *Modernism*, 219; Gay, *Freud, Jews, and Other Germans*, 275. For a detailed account of the transition to Modernism in an American setting, see Singal, *The War Within*.

10. Kern, *Culture of Time and Space*, 204; James, quoted in ibid., 204; Sanford Schwartz, *The Matrix of Modernism: Pound, Eliot, and Early Twentieth-Century Thought* (Princeton, 1985), 5–6, 12, 17–19.

11. Alan Bullock, "The Double Image," in Bradbury and McFarlane, *Modernism*, 66–67; Robert W. Wald, *Space, Time, and Gravity: The Theory of the Big Bang and Black Holes* (Chicago, 1977), 10–11; Schwartz, *Matrix of Modernism*, 15–17; Henri Poincaré, quoted in ibid., 16; Kern, *Culture of Time and Space* 18–19, 132–36, 183–85; 153, 206; Albert Einstein, *Relativity: The Special and General Theory* (New York, 1961), 56–57, 94–96, 141–44; George Gamow, "The Declassification of Physics," in John Weiss, ed., *The Origins of Modern Consciousness* (Detroit, 1965), 167, 176–77, 188.

12. Singal, *The War Within*, 7–8; Peter Faulkner, *Modernism* (London, 1977), 19; Richard Hofstadter, *The Progressive Historians: Turner, Beard, Parrington* (New York, 1968), 185; William Carlos Williams, quoted in Robert Coles, "Instances of Modernist Anti-Intellectualism," in Kiely, *Modernism Reconsidered*, 217.

13. Bradbury and McFarlane, "Name and Nature of Modernism," 46, 48–49; James McFarlane, "The Mind of Modernism," in Bradbury and McFarlane, *Modernism*, 80–81, 83–84, 92.

14. Panthea Reid Broughton, "The Cubist Novel: Toward Defining a Genre," in Ann J. Abadie and Doreen Fowler, eds., *A Cosmos of My Own: Faulkner and Yoknapatawpha, 1980* (Jackson, Miss., 1981), 48–52; Eric Cahm, "Revolt, Conservatism and Reaction in Paris, 1905–25," in Bradbury and McFarlane, *Modernism*, 169; Kern, *Culture of Time and Space*, 143–45, 195, 7, 161–62; Lunn, *Marxism and Modernism*, 48–51.

15. McFarlane, "Mind of Modernism," 84–85; Kern, *Culture of Time and Space*, 219–20, 199–201, 75–79; Lunn, *Marxism and Modernism*, 35.

16. Singal, *The War Within*, 7–8; Lionel Trilling, *Sincerity and Authenticity* (Cambridge, Mass., 1972), 6, 11, 143–47; Gay, *Freud, Jews and Other Germans*, 72; Karen Halttunen, *Confidence Men and Painted Women: A Study of Middle Class Culture in America, 1830–1870* (New Haven, 1982), xvi–xvii, 51–54; D. H. Lawrence, quoted in Ronald Bush, "Modern/Postmodern: Eliot, Perse, Mallarme, and the Future of the Barbarians," in Kiely, *Modernism Reconsidered*, 197.

17. Jerome H. Buckley, "Towards Early-Modern Autobiography: The Role of Oscar Wilde, George Moore, Edmund Gosse, and Henry Adams," in Kiely, *Modernism Reconsidered*, 1–3; Bush, "Modern/Postmodern," 214, 196–201; McFarlane, "Mind of Modernism," 81; Singal, *The War Within*, 370; Trilling, *Sincerity and Authenticity*, 11; Erik H. Erikson, "The Problem of Ego Identity," in Erikson, *Identity and the Life Cycle* (New York, 1959), 118.

18. Bradbury and McFarlane, "Name and Nature of Modernism," 50; McFarlane, "Mind of Modernism," 82–89; Susan Sontag, "The Pornographic Imagination," in *The Susan Sontag Reader* (New York, 1982), 212; Jerome S. Bruner, *On Knowing: Essays for the Left Hand* (Cambridge, Mass., 1962), 62–63. McFarlane, in his otherwise excellent essay, makes the error of describing the "logic" of the dream as the guiding sensibility of Modernism. He notes, for example, how "a great many of the artists and writers of the first two decades of the twentieth century" found in the dream a "paradigm of the whole *Weltbild* in which reality and unreality, logic and fantasy, the banal and the sublime form an indissoluble and inexplicable unity." But surely this is an early and more extreme version of Modernism, and not necessarily a characteristic of the more mature culture. The latter involved not simply an attempt to assimilate the fiery processes of the unconscious, but also an effort to integrate them with those of rational thought. That is why metaphor provides a more accurate representation of the "logic" of Modernism than does dreamwork. See McFarlane, "Mind of Modernism," 86.

19. Higham, "Reorientation of American Culture," 101; Hofstadter, *Progressive Historians*, 184–85.

20. William James, "The Sentiment of Rationality," in James, *The Will to Believe and Other Essays* (New York, 1956), 92, 65–70; Elizabeth Flower and Murray G. Murphey, *A History of Philosophy in America*, 2 vols. (New York, 1977), 2: 643–44, 649–50, 669.

21. William James, *A Pluralistic Universe* (New York, 1909), 318–19; Flowers and Murphey, *History of Philosophy*, 2: 683.

22. John Dewey, *Art as Experience* (1934; New York, 1958), 169; idem, *The School and Society* (1900; Chicago, 1943), 11–14, 26–27. Dewey, with his Modernist animus against dichotomies of any sort, could even wax eloquent about integrating the various levels of education: "We want to bring all things educational together; to break down the barriers that divide the education of the little child from the instruction of the maturing youth; to identify the lower and the higher education,

so that it shall be demonstrated to the eye that there is no lower and higher, but simply education." Ibid., 92.

23. Henry F. May, *The End of American Innocence: A Study of the First Years of Our Own Time* (New York, 1959), 220, 280–84; Hofstadter, *Progressive Historians,* 184; John Higham, *Strangers in the Land: Patterns of American Nativism, 1860–1925* (New York, 1963), 251, 121; Kern, *Culture of Time and Space,* 186–87, 179; Frank Lloyd Wright, *The Natural House* (New York, 1954), 14–20, 38–40, 51–54, 62–65. The best treatment of the Greenwich Village movement is Leslie Fishbein, *Rebels in Bohemia: The Radicals of The Masses, 1911–1917* (Chapel Hill, 1982).

24. Franz Boas, *The Mind of Primitive Man* (1911; New York, 1965), 17, 29, 160–61, 154, 201, 205–10; Lewis Perry, *Intellectual Life in America: A History* (New York, 1984), 320–23; George W. Stocking, Jr., *Race, Culture, and Evolution: Essays in the History of Anthropology* (New York, 1968), 217–22, 226, 190–91; Marshall Hyatt, "Franz Boas and the Struggle for Black Equality: The Dynamics of Ethnicity," *Perspectives in American History* 2 (1985): 295, 269.

25. Lewis A. Erenberg, *Steppin' Out: New York Nightlife and the Transformation of American Culture, 1890–1930* (Westport, Conn., 1981), 5, 23, xii–xiv, 113, 125–26, 131, 187, 195, 255–56, 240–41, 154.

26. Ibid., 148, 150–51, 153–54, 249–51; Paula S. Fass, *The Damned and the Beautiful: American Youth in the 1920's* (New York, 1977), 301–03, 22.

27. Malcolm Bradbury, *The Modern American Novel* (New York, 1983), 61–62; James Agee and Walker Evans, *Let Us Now Praise Famous Men* (1941; New York, 1966), esp. 121, 129, 376–77; William Stott, *Documentary Expression and Thirties America* (New York, 1973), 302, 305–07, 310–11; Daniel Joseph Singal, "Beyond Consensus: Richard Hofstadter and American Historiography," *American Historical Review* 89 (October 1984): 978, 996; Howard Brick, *Daniel Bell and the Decline of Intellectual Radicalism: Social Theory and Political Reconciliation in the 1940s* (Madison, 1986), 20–21, 38–39, 165, 191–92, 208; Robbins, "Modernism in History," 234–35.

28. William L. O'Neill, *Coming Apart: An Informal History of America in the 1960s* (New York, 1971), 200–02, 204–08; Susan Sontag, "Against Interpretation," in *Sontag Reader,* 98–99, 104.

29. Fredric Jameson, "Postmodernism, or the Cultural Logic of Late Capitalism," *New Left Review* 146 (July–August 1984), 53–54; Wolin, "Modernism vs. Postmodernism," 18–20, 25, 26; Gerald Graff, "The Myth of the Postmodernist Breakthrough," *Triquarterly* 26 (Winter 1973): 392; Bradbury, *Modern American Novel,* 160–64; Robert Venturi et al., *Learning From Las Vegas: The Forgotten Symbolism of Architectural Form* (Cambridge, Mass., 1977), 6–9 and passim; Dell Upton and John Michael Vlach, eds., *Common Places: Readings in American Vernacular Architecture* (Athens, Ga., 1986). For an early view of literary postmodernism that now seems somewhat dated, see Ihab Hassan, "POSTmodernISM," *New Literary History* 3 (Autumn 1971): 5–30.

30. Jameson, "Postmodernism," 54–55, 59–62, 65, 72–73, 75.

31. Ibid., 87, 89–90.

32. Ibid., 71–72, 91–92; Frederick Crews, "In the Big House of Theory," *New York Review of Books,* 33 (May 29, 1986), 37, 39–42. On this debate, see also Jean Lyotard, *The Postmodern Condition,* trans. Geoff Bennington and Brian Masumi (Minneapolis, 1984).

33. Graff, "Myth of the Postmodernist Breakthrough," 387; Robert Martin Adams, "What Was Modernism?" *Hudson Review* 31 (Spring 1978): 29–30.

Revisioning the Harlem Renaissance

VENETRIA K. PATTON AND MAUREEN HONEY

This excerpt from Patton and Honey's introduction to Double Take: A Revisionist Harlem Renaissance Anthology *(2001) provides an overview of the Harlem Renaissance or New Negro Movement. The editors argue that a broader approach to the New Negro Movement allows for a better understanding of its recurring themes. Thus while a black folk tradition is celebrated and Africa is shown to be a source of pride, the works of the Harlem Renaissance also validate mothers and motherhood. The writers of the period consider the effect of migration and the role of nature as well as address issues of identity.*

In addition to discussing the various themes associated with the movement, Patton and Honey discuss the contested periodization of the Harlem Renaissance, arguing that 1916 and 1937 mark the beginning and end of the period. These dates are significant for the production of Angelina Weld Grimké's play, Rachel, *and the publication of Zora Neale Hurston's* Their Eyes Were Watching God. *The essay closes by addressing the relationship of literary works to developing civil rights organizations: National Association for the Advancement of Colored People, the National Urban League, and the Universal Negro Improvement Association.*

On March 21, 1924, almost all of the future stars of the Harlem Renaissance gathered at Manhattan's Civic Club to inaugurate what would become known as the New Negro Movement of the 1920s and 1930s. This event was a dinner arranged to honor Jessie Fauset for the publication of her first novel, *There Is Confusion,* just published by Boni and Liveright. Poet Gwendolyn Bennett wrote her poem "To Usward" especially for the occasion and recited it that evening. In the audience receiving a round of applause was the most famous black woman poet of her day, Georgia Douglas Johnson, author of two recent books of poetry: *The Heart of a Woman* (1918) and *Bronze* (1922).

Despite the reason for this gathering, Fauset's prominent role as literary editor of *The Crisis,* the leading African American periodical in the nation, and the spotlighted presence of Bennett and Johnson, the evening was dominated

From *Double Take: A Revisionist Harlem Renaissance Anthology* (New Brunswick: Rutgers UP, 2001) xix-xxxix.

by men. Most notably, the absent Jean Toomer, whose astonishing experimental novel *Cane* (1923) had also recently been published by Boni and Liveright, and Walter White, whose first novel, *The Fire in the Flint* (1924), would soon appear from Alfred A. Knopf, were praised effusively by the stream of male speakers who made up the program. Bennett's single poem was eclipsed by the evening's literary centerpiece, a poetry reading by rising star Countee Cullen. The most influential black power broker of the era, Alain Locke, was master of ceremonies — and known for his cultivation of male writers. . . .

Recurring Themes

Placing the texts of men and women, minor and major writers, lesser known and canonized selections, multiple genres, and homoerotic texts side by side, this anthology opens opportunities for new understandings of the Harlem Renaissance. The movement is traditionally viewed as one characterized by generational splits (rear guard vs. vanguard) or divides based on the debate over art versus propaganda; on the contrary, we have made selections that point to the connections shared by this diverse set of writers. Although women poets are associated with nature poetry, Langston Hughes wrote about nature too, for instance, and Georgia Douglas Johnson, like many male writers, used folk vernacular in her prose. A poem ignored by anthologies, such as Hughes's "Lullaby" (*The Crisis*, 1926), can suggest linkages to women who wrote about babies or motherhood. Similarly, Claude McKay's "Like a Strong Tree" (*Survey Graphic* and *The New Negro*, 1925) echoes Angelina Weld Grimké's often anthologized "The Black Finger" (*Opportunity*, 1923). An aesthetically flawed poem by gifted writer Zora Neale Hurston, "Passion" (*Negro World*, 1922), can illustrate the period's early focus on traditional love lyrics. By including the poetry, prose, or drama not often anthologized or associated with particular writers, we hope to illustrate the multidimensional commonalities that characterize the Harlem Renaissance.

Sterling Brown and others have identified certain themes that reappear despite the gender and generational differences so often commented upon: Africa is a source of race pride, black American heroes or heroines are apotheosized, racial political propaganda is considered essential, the black folk tradition is affirmed, and candid self-revelation is on display.[1] Nathan Huggins adds to this list an emphasis on the urbanity of the New Negro and joy of discovering both the variety and unity of black people. Much of the literature sought to define this "New Negro" or in some way addressed the issue of identity, according to Huggins: "What did Africa mean? What did the slave and peasant past mean? What could a folk tradition mean to the 'New Negro'? What was color, itself? Blackness, clearly, was not only a color, it was a state of mind. So, what of the mulatto, and what of 'passing'?"[2] Huggins and David Levering Lewis point to questions about the important role of art in the Renaissance. These questions are reflected in the debate about art and propaganda, but are also related to the issue of artistic integrity — could black artists avoid mimicking European forms and still produce great art? Other themes that critics have noted in relation to the movement are the prominent role of the Christian church in this very secular artistic movement, anger at racism, and an indictment of Western culture.

In addition to these themes, we have noticed recurring discussions across both genders of migration, domestic servitude, motherhood, children, nature, and passionate love. Because of the new urban identity of the New Negro, discussions of migration from the South or other rural areas are quite frequent. Washerwomen are another frequent subject for both genders, perhaps because they symbolized the exploitation of black labor as a whole and because white soap suds were an apt metaphor for white supremacy. Motherhood was a site of artistic production because it encompassed the past rape of black women by white masters during slavery and because black mothers represented the anticipated better future of the race. The validation of mothers present in the dominant culture had been denied African American women, whose representation as mammies caring for white people was a familiar stereotype. Writers of the Harlem Renaissance addressed this erasure by creating images of black women as maternal figures and centered their concept of artistic awakening on birth. Nature was a central source of imagery for both genders as well. Images of night, shadow, trees, dawn, dusk, earth stood for black pride, resilience, awakening, or protection. Finally, love and sensuality were important subjects for all of these writers. As Bernard Bell has noted, African Americans were dehumanized by a racist culture as incapable of romantic love, denied positive identities as sensual beings.[3] Participating in a larger cultural rebellion against Victorian prudery, writers of the Renaissance proclaimed themselves fully human followers of the heart, celebrants of the flesh.

There are key differences between male and female writers, however. As Cheryl Wall, Gloria Hull, Deborah McDowell, Claudia Tate, and others have pointed out, the system of patronage operating during the Harlem Renaissance privileged men.[4] As a result, it was harder for most women to get the financial and professional support they needed to get into print. While many of them had work published in the period's journals and anthologies, relatively few collections of poetry or short stories were published by women, and not as many of their plays were produced.

Critics also point to women's avoidance of the urban vernacular and "primitivism," particularly in their poetry (with the important exception of the blues singers). This vernacular and associations with "the primitive" of Africa resonated with sexuality, problematic terrain for black women at the time, who were burdened with a stereotype of themselves as prostitutes in the larger culture. To claim their humanity, intelligence, and artistic creativity, therefore, they tended to turn to middle-class subjects and traditional poetic forms even when celebrating their African roots. This tendency was fostered by the fact that most of them came from middle-class backgrounds, even though they were financially strapped. When women did dip into the vernacular, they tended to recuperate the folk dialect of the generation preceding them, a safer discourse in terms of its association with rural family life.

Women addressed gender oppression in their writing as well as racism. Essays by women frequently emphasized gender issues and the double burden of being female and black. Cheryl Wall notes that images of rooms, a symbol of confinement, reappear in women's texts, and allusions to journeys abound. Restricted in their ability to travel, they took imaginative flights instead. Women, like men, wrote about nature, but they infused these natural images with a feminist subtext. Pastoral settings dominated by female allusions are often contrasted with alien manmade urban spaces, for example, or nature is portrayed as a liberating force for women's spirits. Birds and flowers appear as representations of women's imprisonment or freedom. In these ways, women of the Harlem Renaissance responded to the feminist stirrings that resulted in gaining female suffrage in 1920, but they grappled uneasily with the sometimes conflicting imperatives of racial solidarity and feminist revolt.

CONTESTED PERIODIZATION

Another issue highlighted by gender awareness, as we will explicate later, is the contested nature of periodization. While there is general agreement about the significance of the Harlem Renaissance, there is less accord on when the movement begins and ends, since it is not marked by a consistent set of aesthetics or recognizable style. Literature from the period covered a wide range of forms from classic sonnets to modernist verse to blues and jazz aesthetics to folklore. The movement is associated with the 1920s, the Jazz Age, but just when it emerged and disappeared is a source of debate. In fact, Nathan Huggins refers to the Harlem Renaissance as a "convenient fiction,"[5] because there is no clear demarcation separating the old from the "New Negro." Despite this lack of clarity, writers and scholars have sought to impose order and meaning on this rather organic surge in artistic creativity; a brief review of this debate helps define this anthology's contribution.

In *The Harlem Renaissance Remembered,* Arna Bontemps divides the period into two phases: black propaganda (1921–1924) and connection of black writers to the white intelligentsia and publishing establishment (1924–1931), ending with the Depression of the 1930s. Nathan Huggins, in *Voices from the Harlem Renaissance,* follows Bontemps's lead by dating the era's beginnings to the end of World War I and its demise to the Depression. The editors of the more recent *Call and Response* echo these assessments in their preference for two distinct terms: *Harlem Renaissance* and the *Reformation,* the latter referring to the post-Renaissance aftermath of the thirties and forties.

However, for others, including ourselves, the 1930s are merely an extension of the Harlem Renaissance. For example, Alain Locke describes the thirties as the "second and truly sound phase of the cultural development of the Negro in American literature and art."[6] This extension of the movement into the 1930s is embraced by *The Norton Anthology of African American Literature,* edited by Henry Louis Gates Jr., and Nellie Y. McKay. According to its time line, 1919–1940, the years of the Harlem Renaissance traverse two full decades. David Levering Lewis also uses a more comprehensive time frame. In *The Portable Harlem Renaissance Reader,* he ascribes the years 1917–1935 to the movement, from the opening of American theater to black actors with the Broadway productions of Ridgely Torrence in 1917 to the Harlem Riot of 1935, and he places a great deal of importance on World War I and the race riots of 1919 as watershed events ushering in the concept of the New Negro.

Despite general agreement that the 1920s represent its zenith, then, periodization of the Harlem Renaissance is clearly an issue of some debate. Our anthology contributes to that conversation by heeding the observation of Cheryl Wall and Gloria Hull that narrower time and geographical parameters for the Harlem Renaissance work against women, most of whom published in a scattered way across a continuum of time and from regions outside Harlem. In that spirit, we are attaching the movement's parameters to two landmark works, neither of which was written in Harlem nor in the 1920s: the production of Angelina Weld Grimké's play *Rachel* (1916) and the publication of Zora Neale Hurston's novel *Their Eyes Were Watching God* (1937). Bracketing the Renaissance with these two texts not only opens up debates about gender and the movement's vast literary range, it pins the period to African American–authored creative literature rather than to political events, economic events, expository prose, or texts generated by whites: all areas dominated by men. Our parameters also underscore the importance of women to the movement, despite the handicaps of gender that limited their ability to get into print.

Although flawed aesthetically and outside the militant and vernacular discourse that has come to be identified with the Harlem Renaissance, there are sound reasons for tracing the period's beginnings to *Rachel* and for scrutinizing Grimké's play more carefully than we have done in the past. The play's groundbreaking nature is rooted in the fact that it was the first serious drama by an African American playwright to be performed on stage with an African American cast. It was performed in both Washington, D.C., and in New York. Subtitled "A Play of Protest," *Rachel* anticipated Du Bois's call to combine art with propaganda since the play centers on the evils of racism and lynching. It was seeing *Rachel* that persuaded the Renaissance's premier playwright, Willis Richardson, to devote his creative life to drama and directly led to his first play, *The Chip Woman's Fortune* (1923), the first serious African American–authored play to be produced on Broadway. We can see in *Rachel*'s foregrounding of racism's devastating impact on mothers and children glimpses of a major theme of women in the Harlem Renaissance: the equation of motherlessness with protest against racism. Finally, we see in this play some of the seeds about racism and family life sown for contemporary women writers, particularly Toni Morrison in her novels *The Bluest Eye* (1970) and *Beloved* (1991).

Hailed in its own day as the first drama to portray black people positively, a corrective to ubiquitous plantation stereotypes, *Rachel* was produced by the NAACP as a counter-narrative to D. W. Griffith's blockbuster film *The Birth of a Nation* (1915). Griffith's racist narrative glorified the Ku Klux Klan at a time when record numbers of black people were being lynched (by some estimates nearly two thousand in the century's first three decades alone). The propaganda function of *Rachel* was overtly theorized by Grimké, who aimed it at a white audience to gain support for anti-lynching legislation, although it was actually seen by mainly African American audiences. This was in part why it eschewed the folk vernacular that would become a hallmark of much Renaissance writing.

More importantly, *Rachel's* urban and middle-class characters constituted a dramatic change from the minstrel stereotypes to which American audiences were accustomed, and its language was a departure from the dialect art forms of Paul Laurence Dunbar, Joseph Cotter Sr., and Charles Chesnutt, who had dominated the first decades of the twentieth century. In this way Grimké's play was an important step toward expanding the limited forms in which black artists were trapped. It inaugurated the literature from Georgia Douglas Johnson, Countee Cullen, Jessie Fauset, Claude McKay, and others that would illustrate Du Bois's contention that African Americans should lay claim to the high art forms of the dominant culture in order to advance their acceptance as first-class American citizens and end segregation.

Ending the Harlem Renaissance with Hurston's *Their Eyes Were Watching God* (1937) conforms to critical consensus about the death of the movement, which is anywhere from 1935 to 1940. It also signals the devastating impact of the Depression on publishing opportunities for black writers and points to the coming ascendancy of urban realism and naturalism in African American letters with the publication of Richard Wright's *Black Boy* (1939) and *Native Son* (1940). Indeed, it was Wright's highly critical review of Hurston's novel in *New Masses* that helped bury the Renaissance. Wright's perspective sounded the death knell for rural folk vernacular as the basis of an authentic African American aesthetic and for women writers of the Harlem Renaissance — even the gifted Hurston, whose now-acclaimed novel went out of print for thirty years after its first run. . . .

THE ARTS AS CIVIL RIGHTS

Because of the large and growing black population and the city's history of African American excellence in the arts, New York was a natural center for the Harlem Renaissance. New York was America's cultural capital, and it was the center of publishing, drama, music, and painting. It was also the headquarters of the three biggest civil rights organizations: the NAACP (National Association for the Advancement of Colored People) founded by W. E. B. Du Bois (publisher of *The Crisis*) in 1909; the NUL (National Urban League) founded by Charles S. Johnson (publisher of *Opportunity*) in 1910; and the UNIA (Universal Negro Improvement Association) founded by Marcus Garvey (publisher of *Negro World*) in 1914.

These periodicals played a significant role in the development of the Harlem Renaissance because the organizations to which they were attached viewed support of the arts as the primary means to access civil rights. As

David Levering Lewis notes: "The Harlem Renaissance was a somewhat forced phenomenon, a cultural nationalism of the parlor, institutionally encouraged and directed by leaders of the national Civil Rights Establishment for the paramount purpose of improving race relations."[7] Leaders of the movement believed that whites would be persuaded to accept the humanity of African Americans if blacks could achieve artistic equality and that such equality would lead to the achievement of civil rights. The NAACP and the NUL sought to encourage interracial collaboration between liberal whites and Du Bois's "Talented Tenth," the best and brightest of African American artists and intellectuals. They worked actively to connect black writers with white publishers.

The relative paucity of African American literature produced before the launching of the Harlem Renaissance pointed to the lack of a cultural agenda for African Americans, in the view of civil rights leaders. According to David Levering Lewis, between 1908 and 1923 only a handful of significant literary works by black writers appeared: Sutton Griggs's *Pointing the Way* (1908), W. E. B. Du Bois's *The Quest of the Silver Fleece* (1911), James Weldon Johnson's *The Autobiography of an Ex-Colored Man* (1912), Du Bois's *Darkwater* (1920), McKay's *Harlem Shadows* (1922), and Jean Toomer's *Cane* (1923). We would add to that list Angelina Weld Grimké's *Rachel* (1916), Willis Richardson's *The Chip Woman's Fortune* (1923), Georgia Douglas Johnson's two books of poetry published in 1918 and 1922, and Joseph Cotter Jr.'s poetry collection, *The Band of Gideon* (1918). Leaders like Du Bois and Locke felt there was an opportunity to convince white America that African American writing was worthy of publication and that the race had the intellectual fortitude necessary to create such work. According to Du Bois, "until the art of black folk compels recognition they will not be regarded as human."[8] James Weldon Johnson also argued that the arts were a useful means for asserting the cultural dignity of African Americans: "No people that has produced great literature and art has ever been looked upon by the world as distinctly inferior. . . . And nothing will do more to change the mental attitude and raise his status than a demonstration of intellectual parity by the Negro through the production of literature and art."[9] These were the core beliefs that fueled the Harlem Renaissance.

The NAACP membership rolls included a number of scholarly writers who contributed frequently to *The Crisis*. Foremost among these were James Weldon Johnson, whose landmark anthology, *The Book of American Negro Poetry* (1922), brought many new writers to the fore; editor Du Bois; field organizer and novelist Walter White; and Jessie Redmon Fauset. In 1919 Du Bois appointed Fauset as literary editor because he wanted to nurture the best African American talent in the nation. Fauset was not only an excellent editor, but a talented writer in her own right, whose exceptional literary career flourished during the 1920s. Fauset has been frequently described as midwife to the Harlem Renaissance because she discovered and encouraged so many new writers: Gwendolyn Bennett, Countee Cullen, Langston Hughes, Georgia Douglas Johnson, Claude McKay, and Jean Toomer. Fauset mined this talent in such a way as to make *The Crisis* the premier African American magazine of the era. As early as 1919, its circulation had reach 104,000, whereas the circulation of *Opportunity*, the closest competitor, reached only 11,000 by 1928.

Although *Opportunity* did not enjoy the same level of success as *The Crisis*, its editor, Charles S. Johnson, was another key figure of the Harlem Renaissance. According to Langston Hughes, Johnson "did more to encourage and develop Negro writers during the 1920s than anyone else."[10] This point is affirmed by Zora Neale Hurston, who believed that the Renaissance was Johnson's doing, but "his hush-mouth nature has caused it to be attributed to many others."[11] Johnson was particularly frustrated by the lack of respect and visibility accorded to black writers who did not write in dialect, and he used *Opportunity* to break down the stereotypes that confined African American writers to that form. According to Robert Hemenway, Johnson "single-handedly made *Opportunity* an expression of 'New Negro' thought, and 'New Negroes' made it clear that they would not accept a subordinate role in American society."[12] However, Johnson needed the proper means of getting this point across; it was not sufficient merely to bring these great artists to a black audience.

This was the motivation behind Johnson's organization of the March 21, 1924, Civic Club dinner to celebrate Jessie Fauset's new novel, although it was Regina Anderson of the 134th Street Branch of the New York Public Library in Harlem and Georgia Douglas Johnson who had urged him to honor her. He wanted to bring white literary giants shoulder to shoulder with black writers. The dinner proved to be a tremendous success, with black artists securing financial support or the promise of future support. Among the carefully selected white editors, writers, and publishers whom Johnson invited was Paul Kellogg, editor of *Survey Graphic*. Kellogg was so impressed with what he saw that he decided to commission a special issue devoted to Harlem and selected as editor Alain Locke, whom Johnson hailed as "dean" of the New Negro movement. This special issue was later revised and expanded into Locke's landmark anthology, *The New Negro* (1925).

Shortly after this momentous dinner, *The Crisis* and *Opportunity* instituted award ceremonies to recognize black artists, which also helped solidify collaboration between them and the white publishing industry. In 1924 *The Crisis* announced the Amy Einstein Spingarn Prizes in Literature and Art. Amy Spingarn, wife of NAACP board member Joel Elias Spingarn, funded the program. She also served as a judge along with a racially integrated group of popular writers: Edward Bok, Witter Bynner, Charles Waddell Chesnutt, Sinclair Lewis, Robert Morss Lovett, Van Wyck Brooks, Carl Van Doren, Zona Gale, James Weldon Johnson, and Eugene O'Neill. The first *Opportunity* prizes were dispersed in May 1925 at an elaborate ceremony with approximately three hundred participants. The prizes were funded by the wife of National Urban League board chairman and Fisk University trustee L. Hollingsworth Wood. A week after the ceremony *The New York Herald Tribune* predicted that the country was "on the edge, if not already in the midst of, what might not improperly be called a Negro renaissance."[13] A second *Opportunity* awards banquet was followed by donations for future prizes and the establishment of other prizes related to African American arts and letters.

It is this interracial cooperation that sparked the influential anthology *The New Negro* in 1925 which grew out of the special issue of *Survey Graphic,* "Harlem: Mecca of the New Negro." Reaching a record number of 42,000 readers, the issue's sales persuaded Albert and Charles Boni to publish a revised and expanded collection of its poetry and prose, along with winners of the first *Opportunity* contest. In his foreword to the anthology, Locke set the terms that have come to be identified with the Harlem Renaissance: "There is a renewed race-spirit that consciously and proudly sets itself apart. Justifiably then, we speak of the offerings of this book embodying these ripening forces as culled from the first fruits of the Negro Renaissance." In the collection's first essay, his own "The New Negro," he sought to define this spirit: "[T]he younger generation is vibrant with a new psychology; the new spirit is awake in the masses."

Despite its limitations, *The New Negro* continues to hold a place of significance because it both alerted the world to the emergence of an international cultural revolution and attempted to define it. Although the text was held in high regard by its original audience, it is important to note the controversy surrounding it, strains of which run through the material here. Hailed as a definitive anthology, it was at the same time immediately critiqued by some contributors and even repudiated by others. These different responses appear to be rooted in Locke's attempts to smooth over important differences between the writers brought together in the collection, who differed in terms of ideology and aesthetics. For example, Jean Toomer would later write that Locke "tricked and misused" him because he did not consider himself a black writer despite his African American ancestry,[14] while Bruce Nugent was at least as concerned with his sexual identity as with his racial one. Langston Hughes and Countee Cullen were at opposite ends of the aesthetic spectrum, with Hughes preferring jazz- and blues-inspired poems over Cullen's lyrical verse. In fact, Cullen would later be the object of a veiled attack in Hughes's "The Negro Artist and the Racial Mountain" (1926) in which Hughes disparaged him for wishing to be known as a poet who "happened to be Negro," not as a "Negro poet" (see the essay section).

The New Negro did not address these important differences regarding aesthetics, politics, sexuality, and other pertinent issues dividing the younger and older generations of the movement. Indeed, Locke sought to glass over these tensions. He omitted some of socialist Claude McKay's most militant poems, such as "If We Must Die" (see the creative writing section) and "Mulatto," and toned down a McKay poem he did include, "The White House," by changing the title to "White Houses," something McKay bitterly denounced. Despite A. Philip Randolph and Chandler Owen's important contribution to the movement through their editing of *The Messenger,* they were not included. Locke also ignored Garveyism, which has been characterized as the most important mass movement in black America of the 1920s. Garvey's *Negro World,* with a circulation of 200,000 at its peak, made literature readily available to the black masses. However, Locke's exclusion of Garveyism was probably in deference to Du Bois, whose integrationist philosophy clashed with Garvey's more radical separatism. Locke's rather conservative and elitist view of culture seems to stem from what Lewis describes as his Eurocentric definition of culture, a limitation that has since come to be blamed for many of the Renaissance's failures.[15]

The ideological and artistic differences that Locke attempted to minimize in his anthology could not be contained. This is particularly true of the very public ongoing debate between Locke and Du Bois regarding the role of literature and whether black writing should be art or propaganda, a debate worth summarizing here. Locke had spent his career developing a particular theory of African American art, which he articulated and defended through the duration of the Harlem Renaissance. As literary critic for *Opportunity,* he urged black writers to make their work "universally" relevant. In an early essay, "The Colonial Literature of France" (1923), he argued that the black artist should embrace "art for its own sake, combined with that stark cult of veracity — the truth whether it hurts or not."[16] Thus, in editing *The New Negro,* he sought to show that the new Renaissance writers should create "art for art's sake," which distinguished them from the previous wave of African American writers, like Grimké and Fauset, who addressed social issues in their creative work, explicitly using it as a propaganda tool.

This distinction did not sit well with many members of the civil rights establishment, particularly Du Bois, who was not only a writer, but a sociologist and political leader. Although he and Locke both looked at literature as a way to advance the race, they differed sharply over what constituted propaganda: "Mr. Locke has newly been seized with the idea that Beauty rather than propaganda should be the object of Negro literature and art. His book proves the falseness of this thesis. . . . If Mr. Locke's thesis is insisted upon too much, it is going to turn the Negro Renaissance into decadence. It is the fight for Life and Liberty that is giving birth to Negro literature and art today and when turning from the fight or ignoring it, the young Negro tries to do pretty things or things that catch the passing fancy of the really unimportant critics and publishers about him, he will find that he has killed the soul of Beauty in art."[17] Locke responded by arguing that art as propaganda perpetuated notions of black inferiority.[18]

Although Du Bois and Locke were the primary figures in this debate, they were outdone by a group of young writers who took Locke's position much further than he had intended. Langston Hughes spoke for them in his 1926 essay, "The Negro Artist and the Racial Mountain" (see the essay section), which appeared in *The Nation:* "We younger Negro artists who create now intend to express our individual dark-skinned selves without fear or shame. If white people are pleased we are glad. If they are not, it doesn't matter. We know we are beautiful. And ugly too. The tom-tom cries and the tom-tom laughs. If colored people are pleased we are glad. If they are not, their displeasure doesn't matter either. We build our temples for tomorrow, strong as we know how, and we stand on top of the mountain, free within ourselves."

Following this manifesto of artistic freedom, Hughes and Richard Bruce Nugent envisioned a new magazine, which they named *Fire!!* They, along with Zora Neale Hurston, Gwendolyn Bennett, Aaron Douglas, and John Davis, selected the multitalented writer Wallace Thurman as editor. The editorial board members were determined to express their own sensibilities and to break free of the notion of art as politics to express instead the multiple dimensions of being African American. *Fire!!* promised "to burn up a lot of old, dead conventional Negro-white ideas of the past." The foreword to the first and only issue of November 1926 proclaimed to weave "vivid, hot designs upon an ebon bordered loom and . . . satisfy pagan thirst for beauty unadorned." In other words, this would be a daring and controversial journal. In fact, in order to underline its radical nature, Thurman decided that they needed to include at least one piece on homosexuality and another on prostitution. He and Nugent flipped a coin to determine who would write which story. Nugent's "Smoke, Lilies, and Jade!" about homoerotic attraction, and Thurman's "Cordelia the Crude," about a young prostitute, were the result (see the creative writing section).

Both pieces outraged middle-class African American sensibilities. Rean Graves of the *Baltimore Afro-American* was incensed by the magazine and wrote in his review, "I have just tossed the first issue of *Fire!!* into the fire." Benjamin Brawley went so far as to say that if the U.S. Post Office found out about Thurman's "Cordelia the Crude," the magazine might be barred from the mail.[19] Locke, although more balanced in his review, disapproved of the "effete echoes of contemporary decadence" he found throughout the issue.[20] For a time the writers associated with the project were ostracized by the black community. However, the real source of the magazine's demise was financial. The magazine was expensive to buy (one dollar), expensive to produce (one thousand dollars), lacked institutional support, and was poorly distributed. Ironically, hundreds of unsold copies burned in an actual apartment fire.

In many ways *Fire!!* was the antithesis of *The New Negro,* and it is telling that Alain Locke was not among its nine editors. Less than a year after appearing in his anthology, the younger writers had moved on without Locke. Symbolizing their upstart independence from the NAACP and NUL was Zora Neale Hurston's impudent dubbing of the influential whites that supported their contests and attended their parties as "Negrotarians," and her referral to prominent Harlem writers as the "Niggerati." In hopes of ironing out the differences between the younger and older generations, in late 1926 Du Bois organized a symposium entitled, "The Criteria of Negro Art" (see essay of the same name in the essay section). He feared that politics were disappearing from the Renaissance and that whites would point to the success of a handful of writers as evidence that there was no color line. However, the fissure remained, and the rebelling younger artists gained momentum, particularly with the publication of Claude McKay's *Home to Harlem* in 1928.

This first bestseller of the Renaissance embodied the values of the younger generation.

Whether major or minor, female- or male-authored, texts of the Harlem Renaissance enrich our understanding of African American history and culture. These texts served as inspiring, pathbreaking trails — away from silence, against all odds, toward futures their creators only dimly perceived.

NOTES

1. Steven Watson, *The Harlem Renaissance: Hub of African-American Culture, 1920–1930* (New York: Pantheon Books, 1995).

2. Nathan Huggins, *Voices from the Harlem Renaissance* (New York: Oxford University Press, 1976), 9. See also David Levering Lewis, ed., *The Portable Harlem Renaissance Reader* (New York: Viking, 1994).

3. Bernard Bell, *The Afro-American Novel and Its Tradition* (Amherst: University of Massachusetts Press, 1987).

4. Cheryl Wall, *Women of the Harlem Renaissance* (Bloomington: Indiana University Press, 1995); McDowell, *Changing Same;* and Claudia Tate, ed., *Georgia Douglas Johnson: The Selected Works* (New York: G.K. Hall, 1997).

5. Huggins, *Voices from the Harlem Renaissance,* 9.

6. Quoted in Patricia Liggins Hill et al., *Call and Response: The Riverside Anthology of the African American Literary Tradition* (Boston: Houghton Mifflin, 1998), 791.

7. Lewis, *Portable Harlem Renaissance Reader,* xv.

8. Quoted in Lewis, *Portable Harlem Renaissance Reader,* xvi.

9. James Weldon Johnson, ed., *The Book of American Negro Poetry* (New York: Harcourt, Brace & Company, 1922), vii.

10. Quoted in Arna Bontemps, ed., *The Harlem Renaissance Remembered* (New York: Dodd, Mead, 1972), 215.

11. Quoted in Bontemps, *Harlem Renaissance Remembered,* 215.

12. Robert E. Hemenway, *Zora Neale Hurston: A Literary Biography* (Champaign-Urbana: University of Illinois Press, 1977), 9.

13. Quoted in Lewis, *Portable Harlem Renaissance Reader,* xxviii. According to Lewis, this statement gave the movement its name.

14. Quoted in Arnold Rampersad, introduction to *The New Negro: Voices of the Harlem Renaissance,* ed. Alain Locke (New York: Athenaeum, 1992), xxii.

15. See Lewis, *When Harlem Was in Vogue.*

16. Quoted in Hill et al., *Call and Response,* 788.

17. Quoted in Hill et al., *Call and Response,* 789.

18. See Hill et al., *Call and Response,* 790.

19. Quoted in Trudier Harris and Thadious M. Davis, eds., *Afro-American Writers from the Harlem Renaissance to 1940,* vol. 51 of *Dictionary of Literary Biography* (Detroit: Gale, 1987), 263.

20. Quoted in Harris and Davis, *Afro-American Writers,* 220.

3   *Considering Identities*

What difference does identity play in our reading or teaching of literature? Does knowing that Paul Laurence Dunbar was African American impact our reading of the "we" in "We Wear the Mask"? Must this image of a two-faced existence be an African American existence? What effect does Amy Lowell's sexuality have on our reading of her poetry? Does it matter whether the beloved in "The Letter" is a man or a woman? What about the instructor's identity? Would an atheist be just as effective teaching Edward Taylor's "Upon a Spider Catching a Fly" as a Methodist? I think we have come to a point at which we recognize our ability to teach across identities while also realizing the continued significance of these social constructions.

The essays collected in this section explore some of the considerations related to identity that affect our reading and teaching of American literature, including identity construction, whiteness, ethnic literature, gender, class, and sexuality. Of course, this is not an exhaustive list of identities, but it does highlight some of the prevalent concerns of American literary studies. The opening essay, "Assumed Identities" by David Palumbo-Liu, addresses the belief of some social critics that we should move "beyond identity." He argues what we really need to do is to move beyond racial typing in order to actually reach individual identities. According to Palumbo-Liu, assumed identities do not rely on mutual recognition, but instead are based on indirect experience that shapes individual encounters. This indirect experience is related to dominant assumptions about racially marked people that are embedded within institutional practices. Thus, Palumbo-Liu makes an effective argument for the continued importance of considering identities.

AnnLouise Keating's "Interrogating 'Whiteness,' (De)Constructing 'Race'" addresses the importance of examining whiteness while avoiding the reinforcement of permanent racial categories. Keating explores the tricky balancing act of deconstructing race without losing sight of the fluidity of racial identities. To illustrate her own struggles with this balancing act, Keating provides several examples from her classes. She notes her successful practice of providing important contextual information to aid her students in identifying the influence of race in the writing of a Native American author, Scott

Momaday, and an African American writer, Nella Larsen. But when she asked students to discuss the impact of Ralph Waldo Emerson's whiteness, they could not respond. It was much easier for students to recognize racial subtexts in literature by nonwhites. Keating asserts that the invisible omnipresence of whiteness allows it to operate as an unacknowledged norm and thus makes it much more difficult to analyze. She also notes the temptation in class discussions to slip from discussions of whiteness to discussions of white people and thus reinforce the notion of permanent racial categories. In order to highlight the fluidity of race, Keating argues for an approach that addresses the artificial and fluctuating nature of race while also recognizing the material effects of racism. Her essay includes extended discussions of such writers as Zitkala-Sä (Gertrude Simmons Bonnin), Emerson, Frederick Douglass, and Henry Thoreau.

The essays by Keating and Palumbo-Liu address broader issues regarding racial identity, while the next four essays are each devoted to a particular ethnic literature. A. LaVonne Brown Ruoff's "Introduction to American Indian Literatures" focuses on worldviews and values shared by a diverse Native American population. Ruoff also provides a brief history of Native–Anglo American relations, including major events and key government policies. Native American oral and written literature is discussed in relation to Indian worldviews and within the context of Indian-white relations. Ada Savin's "Mexican-American Literature" addresses the development of Mexican American literature while also highlighting key moments of Mexican and Anglo contact. Savin also discusses la raza and the Chicana/o movement. Trudier Harris's "African-American Literature: A Survey" provides a brief overview of African American literature, while paying particular attention to the continued influence of the oral tradition and the slave narrative. Elaine H. Kim's "Asian American Literature" briefly defines Asian American literature and discusses major trends within the field. Because each of these essays takes a broad approach, they provide useful contextual information for instructors who are not trained in these literatures but would like to include ethnic literature in their American literature courses and provide a more representative slice of American literature.

The authors of the final set of essays all address gender, but from different perspectives. Lillian S. Robinson's "Treason Our Text: Feminist Challenges to the Literary Canon" addresses feminist criticism's two-pronged approach of reinterpreting women's literature and recovering lost and neglected women's literature. David Leverenz's "Manhood, Class, and the American Renaissance" is particularly useful in illustrating that discussions of gender should not be limited to discussions of women as he addresses the interconnection between manhood and middle-class consciousness in the literature of the American Renaissance. Michael Ryan's "Gender Studies, Queer Theory, Gay/Lesbian Studies" provides a brief overview of these fields and comments on the linkages between their approaches to literary studies.

Although the texts gathered here only scratch the surface of identity concerns, they do provide a good starting point for instructors delving into areas with which they are less familiar. An instructor armed with this material might create an American literature survey course organized by or informed by identity concerns. Students would address the implication of race not only in Phillis Wheatley's poetry, but also in Benjamin Franklin's autobiography. Discussions of gender would include Herman Melville as well as Harriet Jacobs. Conversations about sexuality might include commentary about Amy Lowell, Walt Whitman, and Richard Wright. These types of classroom discussions would break down notions that race equals nonwhite, gender means feminine, and sexuality refers to homosexuality.

Assumed Identities

DAVID PALUMBO-LIU

*P*alumbo-Liu *begins by noting that many think the topic of identity has been fully addressed and that we have moved beyond those concerns. This line of thought asserts that people should see themselves as part of "the Nation" rather than as members of particular groups. However, Palumbo-Liu suggests that the real need is to get at individual identity by moving beyond racial typing, the assumption that racially marked people are predisposed to actions that reveal their racial character. This assumption of identity is marked by a power differential in which dominant assumptions are reinforced by institutional practices, maintaining inequitable power distributions.*

Palumbo-Liu suggests that sociological discourse on identity tends to overlook "extrasituational experiences" in favor of the individual encounter. Yet indirect experience feeds into notions of social roles. Palumbo-Liu questions whether, when discussing ethnicity, gender, sexual orientation, etc., we are speaking of identity that relies on mutual recognition or on assumed identities. He concludes that the problem with the notion of postethnicity is that it supposes "extrasituational experiences" can be erased from memory and that identity is determined. This essay appeared in a special issue of New Literary History *(2000), "Is There Life After Identity Politics," which grew out of a two-day symposium of the same title, held at the University of Virginia in the spring of 1999.*

> We know of no people without names, no languages or cultures in which some manner of distinctions between self and other, we and they, are not made. . . . Self-knowledge—always a construction no matter how much it feels like a discovery—is never altogether separable from claims to be known in specific ways by others.
>
> – CRAIG CALHOUN, *SOCIAL THEORY AND THE POLITICS OF IDENTITY*[1]

One would think that the topic of identity (post-, or otherwise) would have been exhausted by now. When the word is mentioned these days, it tends not to meet with a straightening of the back and a defiant stare, nor even a wince and an evasive move, but rather a resigned sigh — "Oh, *that* again?" The constant probing, critiquing, stretching, shrinking of the term over the past two

---

From *New Literary History* 31 (2000): 765–801.

decades seems not to have resolved anything. At best it has marked off a set of common problems and positions to which one refers from time to time when the occasion calls for it. I shall not rehearse all those moves and arguments — they are well enough known. Suffice it to say that identity politics has acquired its own identity, which has made any inquiry into identity a suspect act that stands outside the decorum of polite academic talk. Identity politics has been reserved now to name a particular *bad* politics that intrudes upon what is taken to have been a polite consensus on how to seem not to do identity politics while all the while doing them.[2] It is minorities (sexual, racial, ethnic, class, and so on) whose articulation of identity is seen to be not only annoying, but impolite, for their voicing of these concerns forces others to engage in something they thought they had settled, and settled in their favor.

Besides this general aversion to speak any longer about identity, there is the specifically political move proposed by several social critics to move "beyond identity" and, in particular, into a "postethnic" era. These proposals do not necessarily come from the right; indeed, some of the more eloquent and persuasive advocates for this position identify themselves within a tradition of leftist (if not radical) thought. For these critics of "identity politics," the real issue of bettering the lives of people can only take place if we set aside the distinctions identity politics seems to fix upon, and work together on a common platform of economic rights. Those associated with this position include Todd Gitlin, Richard Rorty, David Hollinger, Michael Tomasky, and others. Each in his own way has argued that the progressive movement of the New Left was compromised by the emergence of identity politics. These critics argue that, whatever salutary value feminist, queer, or critical race and ethnic studies have had, they have caused the left to veer off track and into the minutiae of finer and finer distinctions of special interest groups, each claiming priority over the others. This blocks any effective coalition building.

I have elsewhere gone into some detail to outline the historical context for and rebut the basic assumptions of such arguments; here, suffice it to say that this argument has a stake in both downplaying the pervasive significance of racism, sexism, homophobia, and other violent manifestations of prejudice against those who are particularly *identified* (that is, those not just "claiming" identity, but having identities foisted on them), and overplaying the economic as an isolatable space outside the racial, gendered, and otherwise identified social and political spheres.[3] "The economic" is taken as the firm foundation on which all else rests — if economic life is improved for all, is that not all we can hope for? Others, such as myself, while certainly not disavowing the genuine virtue of coalition building around issues of economic justice, are less willing to accept at face value the subordinated position into which issues of race, ethnicity, gender, and sexual orientation are relegated.

In this essay I will argue that "postethnic" thinking subordinates group or collective rights to advocate as primary individual rights to economic justice. A corollary to this is the argument that individuals should set aside particular group identifications and see themselves as part of a larger, more encompassing whole, that is, the Nation. Nevertheless, I assert that foundational notions about identity production in sociological literature make a key and useful distinction between "identity" and "type" (that is, between individual and group identities) that alerts us to the way racial typing comes to stand in for individual identity. The real question thus is not how to get beyond identity, but rather how to *get to it* in the first place — how to make the transition from typecasting to a recognizing of, precisely, individual identity? The real difficulty in making this move is that "identity" is predicated upon a set of behaviors that, for racial and other minorities and women, is geared to a set of historical narratives about "them" precisely as groups, rather than as individuals, and these narratives form the perceptual grid that precedes them in the social discourse of identity.

Wahneema Lubiano provides a concise and astute way of opening this topic of what I will call "assumed identities":

> "Like being mugged by a metaphor" is a way to describe what it means to be at the mercy of racist, sexist, heterosexist, and global capitalist constructions of meaning of skin color on a daily basis. Like a mugging, this attack involves an exchange of assets: some aspect of the social order is enriched domestically and internationally by virtue of material inequities stabilized and narrativized by race oppression and I lose symbolically and monetarily. Further, I am physically traumatized and psychologically assaulted by an operation that is mystified. It goes on in the dark, so to speak — in the dark of a power that never admits its own existence.[4]

Lubiano's treatment nicely opens up this idea of stepping into a narrative-in-progress, of being cast in a role that has been worked out and placed into the realm of a naturalized assumption. In such cases, identity has been produced well in advance of the interpersonal encounter itself, and indeed this mystified operation counts on such preparation in advance, in the dark, in a set of assumptions which all have deep material origins and consequences.

Now what, exactly, do we mean by "identity"? The OED gives a partial answer. "Identity": "the sameness of a person or thing at all times or in all circumstances; the condition or fact that a person or thing is itself and not something else." In this definition, there is an overwhelming sense of determinateness and solidity attached to identity, which is transferable into all times and all circumstances — identity yields the same results no matter where or when it is called upon. But how do we know that this identity is identical to what was before, or elsewhere? Identity posits a certain set of actions and behaviors, a presumed set of characteristics and dispositions that are to be reiterated. Identity is manifest in its constancy, in the fact that the person or thing in itself always expresses the contents of its identity by acting in certain ways. My particular focus here is on the moment of intersubjective encounter, when identity is still virtual, comprised of a set of actions and behaviors assumed to inhere in a particular identity. The result of that encounter will reinforce identity, perhaps *not* because of any action taken by the object of identification, but rather by the sustaining of an assumed, *virtual* act. To put this more plainly, we expect certain types of behavior from certain people, and these expectations may well persist despite any evidence to the contrary. Indeed, evidence to the contrary may be dismissed as aberrational and kept from view by the predominance of those assumptions.

I am concerned here with the assumption that certain people marked by race are predisposed toward certain actions that in turn disclose their racial character. My contention is that in this case we are speaking not of identity, but of social roles, or types, which *pass* for identities (the collective passes for the individual), and that this confusion sometimes brings with it profoundly destructive outcomes. Most specifically, I want to address the situation wherein the interpretive act that assumes that certain behaviors accrue to certain identities moves along a set of put-in-place narratives that proleptically inscribe the outcome of acts which are themselves presupposed to be in the making. In these cases, there is a clear sense that it is the interpreter who has taken upon him- or herself the power to assign an identity to another. This assumption of power could not have been made without assuming as well the projectability of identity upon that Other.[5]

The definition of "assume" contains within it a powerful articulation of this complex phenomenon of taking on the mastery of positing identity on something or someone else. I will not run through the entire gamut of the definitions of "assume," but it is useful to trace a particular trajectory that will lead us directly into the issue at hand with my discussion of assumed identity. First, "to assume" is: "To take to be with one, to receive into association, to adopt into partnership, employment service, use; to adopt, take." That is, to assume is to enter into a particular relationship with the object of assumption. That relationship, I will argue, takes place against and within the backdrop of a history of narratives of similar encounters, real and imagined; the racial encounter — or, more broadly, the encounter with difference — manifests a story that has been told and silenced, repressed, left for dead even, and that story is the history of the production of racism. The encounter, and the assumptive act, at once requires and produces the articulation of both the raced and the racist, as an assumed identity is placed upon the other, an identity that has preceded that object already in a preexisting narration of race.

But even as this act of assuming is appropriative — in the sense that the racist has laid claim to the truth of the person he or she encounters, laid claim to the scene and made it, in short, a *pre-text* for the narrativizing of its own identity ("To take as being one's own, to arrogate, pretend to, claim, take for granted") — it may also be *in*appropriate: "To take to oneself as a right or possession; to lay claim to appropriate, arrogate, usurp." In my use of this definition, I argue that in the scene of identity production — in which the racist assumes the right to name the other as particularly raced, to invent the story which conveys the other — there is an area of indecidability, a gap that must be elided. For to name the scene, to create the other in the image of a character in one's own story, the racist must assume the consequence of a chain of events that he or she can *only* assume: "To take for granted as the basis of argument or action; to suppose: that a thing is, a thing to be."

The seemingly smooth transfer of narrative power from the extra-situational sphere to the encounter itself, from the historical narration of race to the specific moment of the discrete encounter, assumes that the movement from the universal to the particular is justified. How can we tell that racial identity is the same time and again, everywhere? In logic, the assumption is hidden: "The antecedent is assumed when the words of it are barely repeated in the second proposition, or assumption." It is here that we can draw together all these elements into an imputation not only of being, but of action, and identity. The action, in the case I am outlining, is *assumed* to be *going* to take place, about to reveal the name/identity of the actor in its acting out. The force of the assumption is in its ability to drive the narrative forward to its identificatory conclusion in the absence of any explicit voicing. It does not *need* to be said, its story does not need to be recalled, because it is so ingrained in the minds of the participants and reinforced by the historical persistence of institutionalized racism which repeats the story over and over again in its public policy, juridical decisions, and so on.

The elided term is exactly the composite of the narratives of the racial unconscious, the repertoire of stories about "those people" that are assumed to hold true. Crucially, these elided (yet functional) terms preclude the potential narrative for that person *not* to be *as such*. The thing that fortifies this elision, that erases evidence to the contrary and sets to work against the utopian hope of liberation, is precisely the material-historical reiteration of racism — its structural and institutional function: "The construction of identities uses building materials from history, from geography, from biology, from productive and reproductive institutions, from collective memory and from personal fantasies, from power apparatuses and religious revelations. . . . [T]he social construction of identity always takes place in a context marked by power relationships."[6] Here I will emphasize this issue of power, arguing that, as much as we might believe that assumptions of identity work both ways, to and fro between the dominant and the minority identity, we cannot ignore the way that one set of assumptions is embedded within a firm set of institutional practices that maintain an uneven distribution of power.

My essay follows a line of reasoning developed by sociological discourses on identity, namely the interactive model of identity production, and tries to show how the limitations of this model may produce important insights into not only the nature of social identities, but also into the way the imputation of identity through an assumed narrative of being and acting has important connections with both public actions and policy making, and the study of literature and society.

Since the 1930s, and especially in the 1970s, we find a vast sociological literature devoted to the study of identity that is focused on interactive encounters between the subject identified and other social agents. These studies build on early philosophical, and, later, psychological notions of the social production of the self. For instance, Locke has been noted for offering an early dialectical theory of socialization.[7] In 1890 we find William James giving a striking account of the production of "social selves" in relation to the interaction of self and other: "Properly speaking, *a man has as many social selves as there are individuals who recognize him* and carry an image of him in their mind. To wound any of these his images is to wound him. But as the individuals who carry the images fall naturally into classes, we may practically say that he as many different social selves as there are distinct *groups* of persons about whose opinion he cares."[8] Here we find a set of interests that will be central to later sociological treatments of identity: the notion of "recognition" as such, the *image* of that identity as something internalized by the viewer and mobilized situationally, and the shift from individual-to-individual encounters to individual-to-group judgments. The conception of identity as founded upon social contingency and conventions that may be ascertained through evidence, measured, and quantified, takes us squarely into the realm of sociology.

It was Erik Erikson who first took the study of social selves into the realm of identity and coined the term "identity crisis," describing identity as a product of interaction between an essential self and society. For him, the process of identity formation was "a process 'located' *in the core of the individual* and yet also *in the core of his communal culture,* a process which establishes, in fact, the identity of those two identities."[9] However, while Erikson retains some sense of an inner biological identity that withstands, ultimately, the forces of social interaction, sociologists place more emphasis on the latter.[10] It is this attitude that forms the core of sociological theories of identity formation. We find it encapsulated in Peter L. Berger's statement: "Looked at sociologically, the self is no longer a solid, given entity. . . . It is rather a process, continuously created and re-created in each social situation that one enters, held together by the slender thread of memory."[11] It is worth pausing here over this "slender thread." This thread, however slender, is seen as the very thing that ties together a history of precedents — each one contributes to the reformulation of identity, as new elements are added in.

Yet the primacy placed on the individual encounter downplays the considerable extrasituational experiences that also feed into that encounter. The prejudices formed from indirect experience may play just as much, or, indeed, *more* of a role in shaping the encounter itself, and we can include in this group narrative texts. That is to say, the running narrative of identity formation brings together a diverse set of narratives both of past encounters (and the reinterpretation of those encounters), and of other information-bearing stories that may have either a close or quite distant and indirect bearing on actual encounters. And their weight may be so strong as to lead the interpreter to distrust his or her own experience in favor of that evidence. For example, consider an anecdote from Korean-American cultural critic and filmmaker, Elaine Kim: a friend of Kim's was presented with a copy of *The Woman Warrior.* The presenter exclaimed that, having read the novel, she finally understood Kim's friend. Somehow Kingston's novel had the power to explain human beings in a way that direct personal contact could not. In its particular discourse the novel provided a mode of understanding that surpassed and even stood in for human relations.[12] What about that text allowed it to achieve such a potent reality effect? I would argue that it was the existence of a powerful discursive network of threads woven together from divergent sources that then rendered Kim's friend suddenly legible, believable, complete, in that she now was seen to fill in a role carved out of the novel, a legitimizing narrative.

The hermeneutic weight of extrasituational texts goes a long way to account for the interpretation of identity-forming encounters, which, as Thomas Scheff tells us, are predicated on sequences of actions that are expected from the individual, that is, what I have called assumed identities. Scheff sets up this idea of sequences and identity formation: "We have treated social relations and identity as merely different terms for referring to the same phenomena: the establishment of mutually recognized, expected sequences of behavior in a transaction. Identity refers to the individual's sequence of acts; relationship refers to the ensemble of acts made up by the sequences of all the parties involved."[13] That is, the very formation of identity is identical with social interaction, which is interactive to the degree that a sequence of actions emanating within and out of that encounter are assumed in advance. But we must note here the second crucial component of this transaction: the insistence on the ideas of reciprocity and symmetry, in other words, the emphasis placed on a *democratic transaction*. For identity to be formed according to this model, for a social relation to happen, there must be a *mutually* recognized sequence of actions that, implicitly, yields the same hermeneutic outcome for all parties involved. Scheff's theory of communicative action requires a social act that is assumed to be able to take place (indicating the parameters of reasonable behavior), emanating from social actors whose identities have given us those expectations about them.

The crucial importance of this mutual recognition is that it differentiates "identity" from "social role":

> We have taken social role to be a structural concept which differs in two ways from its complementary processual concept, identity. First, role is at a lesser level of complexity, since it is made up of a component part of the definition of identity; i.e., the expected sequence of acts in a transaction. Role, therefore, does *not* contain the added requirement of mutual recognition by the parties to the transaction. Secondly, role is treated to be part of a generalized pattern of expectations in the community, in contrast to a situational identity, which is the sequence of acts expected of a given participant in a transaction by all the parties to that specific transaction. (206)

The crucial issue here is whether, when discussing race, ethnicity, gender, class, sexual orientation, and so forth, we can speak of identity, which hinges upon *mutual* recognition, a *consensual* sense of the identities produced, and the sequence of actions and behaviors to be "expected," or whether we are not indeed speaking of social roles, posited not on individuals but upon "such people" without their consent. Furthermore, the question in Scheff is muted as to the likelihood that the "expectation" is, indeed, well founded (consensual or no). What kind of "assumptions" go into this encounter? It is here that Erving Goffmann productively revises Scheff's model by introducing both a more complicated temporal schematization and a real questioning of the agent of assumption:

> Typically, we do not become aware that we have made these demands or aware of what they are until an active question arises as to whether or not they will be fulfilled. It is then that we are likely to realize that all along we have been making certain assumptions as to what the individual before us ought to be. Thus, the demands we make might better be called demands made "in effect," and the character we impute to the individual might better be seen as an imputation made in potential retrospect — a characterization "in effect," a *virtual social identity*.[14]

In his study of social "stigma," Goffmann speaks of the ways stigmatized groups (cripples, disfigured people, people from the working class, racial and ethnic minorities, and so on) attempt to manage their stigmatization. Yet, importantly, once a stigma theory has been invented to account for both the justness of stigmatization and the behaviors and characteristics inherent in stigmatized groups, it is tremendously difficult for the stigmatized to respond without *confirming* his or her stigmatized identity: "We may perceive his defensive response to his situation as a direct expression of his defect, and then see both defect and response as just retribution for something he or his parents or his tribe did, and hence a justification of the way we treat him" (*S* 6). This produces an unsettling effect: "We normals will find these situations shaky too. We will feel that the stigmatized individual is either too aggressive or too shamefaced, and in either case too ready to read unintended meanings into our actions" (*S* 18). Isn't this precisely a description of what is called "political correctness"? Here we can come back to the notion that identity politics is an identity in itself, that calling attention to the undemocratic transactivity which undergirds the production of minoritarian identities reflects back on the protester to solidify his or her "difference," and that the narratives that serve to set up in advance "expected behaviors" of such individuals and groups are written under certain ideological and historical conditions. Thus, what Goffmann calls "cognitive recognition," "the perceptual act of 'placing' an individual," assumes a particular *mis*recognition because it assumes outcomes, behaviors, and so forth, that are based not on individuals, but on types that are fabricated in extrasituational texts (*S* 18).

The assumption of outcomes, the link between virtual identity and an assumed behavior that both manifests and confirms that identity, is deeply linked to social behavior and political and legal policy. It is precisely here that the slippage between social roles and individual identities is most pernicious: individual identities are subordinated to and confused with social types. One is not left wanting for examples of this issue. One has only to think of the 1986 Howard Beach incident commented upon forcefully by Patricia Williams, in which a group of young black men were beaten (and one died) on a public street because they were thought to be up to no good — what would blacks be doing in a white neighborhood in the middle of the night?[15] Or a 1997 case in Rohnert Park, California, an upscale bedroom community in which a young Asian man, Kuan Chung Kao, was shot to death by police in front of his house after neighbors called about a disturbance early in the morning. They claimed that he had posed a "martial arts threat" to the police officer who shot him. He had been playing with a broomstick over his head. He was very drunk and very doubtfully a real threat to life, yet the police officer felt that this Asian male could likely be a real threat because all Asians naturally know martial arts.[16]

Or the recent and deeply disturbing case of Amadou Diallo, a twenty-two-year-old West African immigrant who was shot forty-one times in February 1999, after being mistaken for a suspected serial rapist. The police officers were acquitted of all charges in March 2000. Reading the new accounts of the event, and the manner in which the body of Diallo is offered up to representation via an elaborate circuit of bureaucratic formulations and denials, Ebony Chatman brilliantly notes, "The corporeal body is subordinate to the textual circuit, if not locked out entirely. The text is entrusted with the two-dimensional task of representing a body that is *unacceptable* outside of the autobiographical fragments that are solicited. Under these terms and conditions, bureaucratic correspondence enacts its authority through a process of acceptance and denial that refuses to touch the actual body, but acts as if the document were that body — or the only body worth addressing."[17] Here again we find the mechanism whereby identity is recast as a statistical confirmation of a preexisting type, the narrative which conveys this identity at once presents identity and eclipses all other narratives. It is in this sense that Homi Bhabha's notion of forbearance comes into play.[18] And we can note that in all these examples, the state intervenes to be the ultimate arbiter, the final interpreter of the action and the reaction. I mention each of these cases to make the argument that none of them can be understood in isolation, although each has its own particular set of issues. Rather, I want to outline a pervasive history of institutional action that confirms and reconfirms, time and again, the logic of assumption and its deadly effect — there is no identity, only type.

Janet E. Halley's recent study of the "Don't Ask, Don't Tell" policy on gays in the military captures all these issues well and allows us a deeper insight into the production of legal discourses of identity, type, and behavior. She argues that the 1993 revision of the military's anti-gay policy by Department of Justice produced: "a new set of rules that allows homosexual conduct to be inferred from supposed homosexual status": "What actually emerged from the legislative process was a complex new set of regulations that discharge people on grounds that tie status to conduct and conduct to status in surprising, devious, ingenious, perverse, and frightening ways. . . . The most important innovation is a provision that all discharges for homosexuality will be grounded on the servicemember's commission of conduct that would manifest, to a reasonable person, a propensity to engage in homosexual acts. 'Telling' isn't speech in this formulation: it is an act that manifests a propensity."[19] This propensity is conveyed in what we may call the assumptive narrative of identity — it puts into place (as much as it may rehearse and reiterate) extrasituational narratives that are assumed to be the inherent dispositions and likely behaviors of those identified. In so doing, it erases the distinction between individual and group, between identity and social role. Once again, individual "essence" is made indistinguishable from social type; the behavior of the individual is assumed to be commensurate with the behavior of the group. For stigmatized people (to harken back to Goffmann's term), this institutes a "psychometric model of propensity. It attributes a pathological personal trait to each individual homosexual": "Presumptions are possibly the single easiest way to make sure that one party to a dispute steps up to the starting line with a heavy handicap. They are a classic way to achieve substantive outcomes under the guise of a merely technical change in procedure. . . . Most decisively, proponents of the 1993 revisions claim that giving the servicemember an 'opportunity' to rebut a presumption that he or she has a propensity to engage in homosexual conduct transforms a legal and actuarial prediction about a group into a *fact* about that *servicemember*" (D 64, 86). The construct used to measure both the normativeness of behavior and the reasonableness of the attribution of propensity is, precisely, that of a "reasonable person," which "makes the interpretive standpoint of heterosexual personhood an indispensable reference point for enforcement" (D 117). We should note that appeals to such a construct again make reference to the act of assumption — in this case, societies posit an ideal mental type to house and ventriloquize their own prejudgments; any fallabilities of a reasonable person will reflect "normal" errors, and are thus excused. And the very credentials of a reasonable person can only be ascertained to the degree that this person confirms or departs from expected behavior. Recourse to constructs like "reasonable person" or "common man" are last-ditch efforts to name an ideal type toward which we must all aspire, without interrogating the assumptions that undergird that construction. Indeed, the validity, or reasonableness of that attribution is often only gained in retrospect, after its judgment is rendered. Nevertheless, like all these cases of assumption, the conclusion to the narrative sequence that expresses and confirms the assumption of identity is often a foregone conclusion.

What better example than the 1922 case of *United States v. Thind*, in which a South Asian man petitioned for naturalization based on the fact that as a South Asian, he satisfied the "scientific" "Caucasian" criterion imposed by the court? When that was disputed, he argued that he also satisfied the "Aryan" criterion argued by the court. Finally, having used up its arsenal of weapons based on geography and biology to label the petitioner as ineligible, the court put forward the argument of the "common man": "We venture to think that the average well informed white American would learn with some degree of astonishment that the race to which he belongs is made up of such heterogeneous elements."[20] We may note how "common man" is itself a construct based on supposed behavior and judgment *that confirms and affirms his own race* at an encounter (need I point out that the "common man" designates maleness and whiteness, that this seemingly modest commonality does not hide the power that is there?). "He" is produced precisely as a narrated sub- ject — what "he would do" were he confronted with the idea that "white" could include South Asians, who are assumed to be variously "oriental" or "mongoloid," or "Asiatic," and therefore prohibited from being considered "white." But note too that this construct serves to ventriloquize power, that "common man" is a dubious and self-fulfilling identity, but this encounter and judgment is not mutually agreed upon, but the narrative construction of the "common man" gives it that illusion. The court chose to *narrate* an imag- inary scene of social intercourse that replicates the model of interaction: the common man is presented with a figure that astounds him, it breaches the assumptions he naturally held as to the notion of "white," that is, his notions of *himself*, the "race to which he belongs." In Halley's case, the "common man" is simply updated to be a "reasonable person," for whom the logic of "reason" confirms the heterosexual norms of interpreting its own centered- ness by rejecting the other. It is here that we can question Goffmann's claim that: "The stigmatized and the normal are part of each other; if one can prove vulnerable, it must be expected that the other can, too" (*S* 135). For Goffmann seems to suggest the democratic, evenly balanced model of identity forma- tion in which the subject and object of identifying agree on the appropriate- ness of the identity created in their encounter. I, on the contrary, have tried to draw attention to the unequal relations that obtain and that cancel out evi- dence to the contrary in favor of a preinscribed narrative of being. Yet Goffmann's democratic rendering offers a utopian moment: When will it be the case that identity is produced democratically?

Let me come back to the argument that we should move beyond identity (which certainly does not mean what it says — it is rather *particular* identities that are to be laid to rest). The urge to move beyond identity is first supported by the hypothesis that ethnic identification is already past us. As early as 1979, Herbert Gans argues that "ethnicity may be turning into symbolic ethnicity, an ethnicity of last resort."[21] Gans contends that, as more and more generations are born in the United States, ethnicity will be gradually loosened from formal organizations and even collective rituals — it will become more a matter of individual performance at discrete moments: "They may retain American forms of the religions their ancestors brought to America, but their secular cul- tures will be only a dim memory, and their identity will bear only the minut- est trace, if that, of their national origins" (449). This sort of wishfulness indeed informs most of the social-science literature on race and ethnicity in the United States since at least the 1920s — sheer exposure to American life will gradually but inevitably wear away ethnic identity, and with that will come accept- ance.[22] Yet, even as this view has persisted, there has also emerged a sense that the pace of change is much too gradual, and that Americans must take a more proactive role in erasing any facet of ethnic identity that might impede the full particulation of the ethnic subject in national life.

The most respected contemporary liberal view on the need to move beyond ethnicity comes in David Hollinger's *Postethnic America.* Hollinger pleads for us to set aside the insistence on ethnicity, and to focus rather on a common ground: "I have taken for granted that the economic, political, and cultural obstacles to a postethnic America are truly formidable, but I also take for granted that revulsion against ethno-racial prejudice is strong enough in the United States today to render the ideal of postethnicity worth developing."[23] It is interesting to note that Hollinger's argument here is nothing if not a pair of assumptions ("taking for granted"). The huge difference between the two assumptions is, of course, that while the "economic, political, and cultural obstacles to a postethnic America" are well documented historically and evinced in everyday life, as my examples above show, the faith Hollinger places in "revulsion against ethno-racial prejudice" is evinced only locally and discretely. While legislation against hate crimes can be pointed to as evidence to support Hollinger's faith, one can also point to an overwhelming body of evidence showing that prejudice is not only well and alive, but thriving (besides the widely documented cases of court-sanctioned violence against minorities and women, we can point to socioeconomic policies such as Clinton's "welfare reform," and so on). As worthy as Hollinger's plea for a "postethnic America" may be, it is important to note whom he is addressing — for he has in mind precisely those who argue in favor of multiculturalism. Hollinger asks us to drop our weapons and shake hands with a historical institutional situation that is armed to the teeth.[24]

Rather than to place the responsibility for moving beyond ethnicity on ethnic and racial minorities, it would be better to respect the dialectical engagement of race and ethnicity across multiple tableaux. Rather than to place faith in an assumption of psychological revulsion against racism and the historical efficacy of that revulsion, it would be better to see the production of inequality as taking place in specific institutional practices that are often as not shielded from sight, bureaucratically rationalized on the basis of assumed identities. Such cases require the *identification* of racism to bring them out from their assumed neutrality to their actual everyday historical life: "We can speak of identity only in terms of what Marx calls the 'ensemble' of social relations, a set of relations whose historicity is a fundamental aspect of identity's existence" (RI 115).

But the real problems with the argument for postethnicity, at least in terms of the sociological tradition that still deeply informs our sense of how identity is formed in the first place, are that, first, it imagines that the narratives which precede the social encounter can be erased from memory and made inactive. Rather, it is the case that the historical narratives of prejudice are carried forward in handed-down stories, and realized in present-day violence, as my several examples illustrate. Second, it assumes that the determination of identity is equally decided (that is, that we are dealing with a case of identity and not type). The pervasiveness of racism comes from the refusal to grant identity and the assumption that, for minorities, women, and other groups, behavior is that of the group identity, particularly arrived at. The question, again, is not how to get beyond identity in the classic sociological sense of "identity," but how to get to identity in the first place, that is, how to move beyond type to individuals whose identity formation is arrived at in democratic interaction. This move is necessary before we can go beyond ethnicity and see our way clear to a postethnic coalition (one which I would then heartily endorse). Yet this move will be far from easy, not because minorities and women obstinately cling to identity, but precisely because the narratives that have been put into place to deny them identity are deeply rooted, and the psychic form of racism is thoroughly entangled in institutional forms.

Cornelius Castoriadis's notion of the "imaginary" reveals a more precise and profound view into the murky terrain between institutional forms and psychic ones. For him, the imaginary is:

> the operative condition for every subsequent representation: the fundamental phantasy of the subject, his or her nuclear (and not "primitive") scene, where that which constitutes the subject in his or her singularity exists; the organizing-organized schema that provides its own image and exists not in symbolization but in the imaginary presentification that is already for the subject an embodied and operative signification, the initial grasp and the first, overall constitution of an articulated, relational system positing, separating and uniting the "inside" and the "outside," the sketch of gesture and the sketch of perception, the division into archtypal roles and the originary ascription of a role to the subject as such.[25]

More precisely, his comments on the particular gap between the social and the functional may be taken as approximating the area wherein what I have denoted as "assumption" takes place:

> [S]ocial significations do not exist strictly speaking in the mode of representation. . . . They can be grasped only indirectly and obliquely: as the gap, at once obvious and impossible to delimit precisely, between a first term — the life and actual organization of a society — and a second term, likewise impossible to define — this same life and organization conceived of in a strictly "functional-rational" manner; as a "coherent deformation" of the system of subjects, objects and their relations; as the curvature specific to every social space; as the invisible cement holding together this endless collection of real, rational and symbolic odds and ends that constitute every society. . . . (142–43)

It is in shifting between these spheres that we witness the performance of assumptions, the playing-out of elided terms, the surpassing of evidence to the contrary, the insistence on a particular way of rationalizing racism. It is here, too, that we find the possibility of intervention, but not, I would argue, solely in the private psychological adjustments of antiracism, but more importantly and significantly in the reformulation of institutional structures that underwrite the repetition of racism. For without this structural-functional change, the material histories that perpetuate these assumed identities will continue to populate in their specific phantasmatic manners the narration of identity.

NOTES

1. Craig Calhoun, *Social Theory and the Politics of Identity* (Oxford, 1994) pp. 9–10.

2. See, among others, George Lipsitz, *The Possessive Investment in Whiteness: How White People Profit from Identity Politics* (Philadelphia, 1998).

3. See my essay, "Awful Patriotism: Richard Rorty and the Politics of Knowing," *Diacritics*, 29.1 (1999), 37–56.

4. Wahneema Lubiano, "Like Being Mugged by a Metaphor: Multiculturalism and State Narratives," in *Mapping Multiculturalism*, ed. Avery F. Gordon and Christopher Newfield (Minneapolis, 1994), p. 64.

5. Here I should also say that I do not have in mind the notion of performance and assumption outlined by Judith Butler in *Bodies That Matter: On the Discursive Limits of "Sex"* (New York, 1993), especially pp. 93–120. It is not that I disagree with Butler, but rather that my interest will lie in a different dynamic.

6. Manuel Castells, *The Power of Identity* (Oxford, 1997), p. 7.

7. See, for instance, Stanley Aronowitz, "Reflections on Identity," in *The Identity in Question*, ed. John Rajchman (New York and London, 1995), pp. 111–46; hereafter cited in text as RI.

8. William James, *The Principles of Psychology*, Vol. 1 (New York, 1890), p. 294.

9. Erik Erikson, *Identity and the Life Cycle, Selected Papers* (New York, 1959), p. 22.

10. Philip Gleason, "Identifying Identity: A Semantic History," *The Journal of American History*, 69.4 (1983), 910–31.

11. Peter L. Berger, *Invitation to Sociology: A Humanistic Perspective* (New York, 1963), p. 106

12. Elaine Kim, *Asian American Literature: An Introduction to the Writings and Their Social Context* (Philadelphia, 1982), p. xix.

13. Thomas J. Scheff, "On the Concepts of Identity and Social Relationship," in *Human Nature and Collective Behavior: Papers in Honor of Herbert Blumer*, ed. Tamotsu Shibutani (Englewood Cliffs, N.J., 1970), p. 206; hereafter cited in text.

14. Erving Goffmann, *Stigma: Notes on the Management of Spoiled Identity* (New York, 1963), p. 2; hereafter cited in text as S.

15. Patricia Williams, *The Alchemy of Race and Rights: Diary of a Law Professor* (Cambridge, Mass., 1991), p. 58.

16. Michael Chang, "Asian American Public Interest Organizations in the Pursuit of Legal and Social Remedies to Anti-Asian Hate Crimes," *Asian Law Journal*, 7 (forthcoming, 2000). I thank him for providing the details on this case.

17. Ebony Chatman, "Deciding Mistakes: Rethinking the Death of Amadou Diallo" (Department of Modern Thought and Literature, Stanford University, 1999), 3.

18. Homi Bhabha, "The Art of Forbearance," Presidential Lecture in the Humanities presented at Stanford University, 6 March 2000.

19. Janet E. Halley, *Don't: A Reader's Guide to the Military's Anti-Gay Policy* (Durham, N.C., 1999), pp. 1–4; hereafter cited in text as D.

20. *United States v. Thind*, 261 US 204, 211 (1922), cited in Ian Haney Lopez, *White By Law: The Legal Construction of Race* (New York, 1996), p. 8. See also my *Asian/American: Historical Crossings of a Racial Frontier* (Stanford, 1999), p. 39, and Stanford M. Lyman's excellent study, "Marginalizing the Self: A Study of Citizenship, Color, and Ethnoracial Identity in American Society," *Symbolic Interaction*, 16.4 (1968), 16–22.

21. Herbert J. Gans, "Symbolic Ethnicity: The Future of Ethnic Groups and Cultures in America" in *On the Making of Americans: Essays in Honor of David Riesman*, ed. Herbert J. Gans, Nathan Glazer, Joseph R. Gusfield, Christopher Jenks (Philadelphia, 1979), p. 425

22. This was of course the hope of the Dillingham Commission, which was established by Congress in 1907 to investigate increased immigration from new and much more foreign shores.

23. David Hollinger, *Postethnic America: Beyond Multiculturalism* (New York, 1995), p. 170.

24. For a sharp critique of the discourse of postethnicity, see Tim Libretti, "Leaping Over the Color Line: Postethnic Ideology and the Evasion of Racial Oppression," *Working Papers Series* (Washington State University, 1999).

25. Cornelius Castoriadis, *The Imaginary Institution of Society* (Cambridge, Mass., 1987), pp. 142–43; hereafter cited in text.

Interrogating "Whiteness," (De)Constructing "Race"

ANNLOUISE KEATING

K*eating's essay originally appeared in a 1995 issue of* College English, *and was later reprinted in the collection* Teaching African American Literature, *edited by Maryemma Graham, Sharon Pineault-Burke, and Marianna White Davis (1998). Keating begins by acknowledging the importance of examining whiteness, but also expresses concern that "theorists who attempt to deconstruct 'race' often inadvertently reconstruct it by reinforcing the belief in permanent, separate racial categories" (p. 164). Keating worries that an emphasis on racialized identities may ignore the fluidity of racial designations. She argues that scholars should discuss the artificial and changing nature of race while also acknowledging the material effects of racism. One way that Keating approaches this is by looking at "passing" texts, which destabilize her students' notions of ahistorical, fixed races. She also uses the idea of cultural* mestizaje *to highlight the constant interaction and exchange of cultural identities. Thus she is able to emphasize the "mutually constituted and constantly changing nature of all racialized identities," and the importance of educating students about the sociohistorical forces that inform these changes.*

> Race is a text (an array of discursive practices), not an essence. It must be read with painstaking care and suspicion, not imbibed.
>
> – HENRY LOUIS GATES JR., *Loose Canons*

> Race has become metaphorical — a way of referring to and disguising forces, events, classes, and expressions of social decay and economic division far more threatening to the body politic than biological "race" ever was.
>
> – TONI MORRISON, *Playing in the Dark*

> Sticks and stones may break our bones, but words — words that evoke structures of oppression, exploitation, and brute physical threat — can break souls.
>
> – KWAME ANTHONY APPIAH, "THE CONSERVATION OF 'RACE'"

From *Teaching African American Literature: Theory and Practice*, ed. Maryemma Graham, Sharon Pineault-Burke, and Marianna White Davis (New York: Routledge, 1998) 186–209.

My title reflects several trends in contemporary cultural and literary studies. Because these trends involve exposing the hidden assumptions we make concerning racialized identities, they have far-reaching theoretical and pedagogical implications. The first phrase, "Interrogating 'Whiteness,'" refers to the recent demand for an analysis of "white" as a racialized category. Toni Morrison, for example, calls for an examination of "whiteness" in canonical U.S. literature. What, she asks, are the implications of "literary whiteness"? How does it function in the construction of an "American" identity? Arguing that a "criticism that needs to insist that literature is not only 'universal' but also 'race-free' risks lobotomizing that literature, and diminishes both the art and the artist," she urges scholars to examine the hidden racial discourse in U.S. literature.[1] Similarly, some educators have begun emphasizing the importance of developing critical pedagogies that examine how "whiteness" has (mis)shaped knowledge production in U.S. culture. According to Henry Giroux and Peter L. McLaren, the traditional Western view "of learning as a neutral or transparent process" is inaccurate and prevents us from recognizing the highly political, racialized nature of all pedagogical methods. They maintain that

> Teachers need critical categories that probe the factual status of white, Western, androcentric epistemologies that will enable schools to be interrogated as sites engaged in producing and transmitting social practices that produce the linear, profit-motivated imperatives of the dominant culture, with its attendant institutional dehumanization.[2]

bell hooks takes this demand for an interrogation of the relationship between "whiteness" and cultural dominance even further in her discussion of "white" theorists' exclusive analysis of the racial *Other*. According to hooks, "Many scholars, critics, and writers preface their work by stating that they are 'white,' as though mere acknowledgment of this fact were sufficient, as though it conveyed all we need to know of standpoint, motivation, [and] direction." Because she believes that this unquestioned acceptance of "whiteness" distorts contemporary cultural studies, she challenges "white" theorists to incorporate an analysis of their own racialized identities into their work:

> One change in direction that would be real cool would be the production of a discourse on race that interrogates whiteness. It would be just so interesting for all those white folks who are giving blacks their take on blackness to let them know what's going on with whiteness.[3]

These calls for an interrogation of "whiteness" cannot be dismissed as the latest scholarly fad in academia's publish-or-perish game. As Kobena Mercer and other contemporary theorists have argued, "whiteness" and its "violent denial of difference" serve a vital function in masking social and economic inequalities in contemporary Western cultures.[4] By negating these people — whatever the color of their skin — who do not measure up to "white" standards, "whiteness" has played a central role in maintaining and naturalizing a hierarchical social system and a dominant/subordinate world view.

However, as I began exploring recent definitions of "whiteness" and incorporating this analysis into my literature courses I encountered a number of unexpected difficulties, and this is where the second part of my title, "(De)Constructing 'Race,'" comes in. The word "(De)Constructing" — with the prefix in parentheses — reflects my assessment of the dangers in recent interrogations of "whiteness" and other racialized identities. More specifically, it refers to the way theorists who attempt to deconstruct "race" often inadvertently reconstruct it by reinforcing the belief in permanent, separate racial categories. Although they emphasize the artificial, politically and economically motivated nature of all racial classifications, their continual analysis of racialized identities undercuts their belief that "race" is a constantly changing sociohistorical concept, not a biological fact.

In what follows, I first summarize recent theorists' explorations of "whiteness" and discuss what I see as the difficulties that can occur when we attempt to incorporate these analyses into classroom lectures and discussions. I then offer tentative suggestions for alternative approaches that investigate "whiteness" while deconstructing "race." Before I begin, however, I want briefly to describe my own pedagogy. Whenever possible, I try to integrate my scholarship with my classroom instruction. I believe that both areas can be enriched by this interchange. The classroom functions as a laboratory where the theory I read and write takes on concrete form as I attempt to translate theoretical perspectives into accessible, practical terms. Students benefit from this process; they are introduced to a variety of theoretical perspectives and become critical readers, capable of recognizing how literary canons are shaped by personal and cultural issues.

This twofold approach has played an important role in shaping the ways I began incorporating analyses of "whiteness" into my U.S. literature and composition courses. For the past several years both my scholarship and my teaching had been informed by a critical analysis of how "race," gender, and sexuality are socially constructed, but until reading Morrison's call for an interrogation of "whiteness" I had never considered including an analysis of "white" in my explorations of racialized meanings in literary texts. Yet it only made sense to do so; after all, we examine "black," Chicano/a, Native American, and Asian American literary traditions. Should we not also look at "white" literary traditions? And so, shortly after reading Morrison and several other theorists, I began to include explorations of "whiteness" in the courses I teach, which have ranged from surveys of U.S. literature to introductory composition to an upper-level/graduate elective course on "Race," Gender, and Literature. While approximately three-fourths of the students in my classes identify as "white," the remaining fourth — some of whom can easily pass for "white" — identify as "Hispanic," "Native American," and "black." But however they identify, the majority are first-generation college students from working-class backgrounds. They are motivated by their own versions of the American Dream, the belief that hard work and education will enable *anyone* — regardless of "race," gender, or economic status — to succeed. My comments in the following pages are based on these students' reactions.

Although students are often startled by the notion that language is racialized and literature can be examined for its hidden and overt racial meanings, they find it much easier to explore the racialized subtexts in works by non-"white" writers than to explore the racialized meanings in writings by "whites." When I taught Leslie Marmom Silko, Scott Momaday, or Paula Gunn Allen, for example, I described their perspectives on contemporary Native American literary and cultural conventions and asked students to consider the ways in which their poetry and prose simultaneously reflected and shaped these conventions. After an initial period of questioning, they arrived at important observations. Similarly, when I taught Nella Larsen and Paul Dunbar, I discussed W. E. B. Du Bois's theory of the "color line," described the status of African Americans in the early 1900s, and asked students to consider how their "race" might have influenced their work. Again, they arrived at insightful comments.

However, when I suggested that "white" — like "Native American" or "African American" — is a *racialized* identity, continually reinforced and reinvented in literature, students were startled. People with pale skin are often referred to as "whites," and of course there are ethnic groups whose members have "white" skin — Italian Americans, Polish Americans, many U.S. Jews, and so on — but a white "*race*"? Although I discussed Morrison's call for and interrogation of literary "whiteness" at length, when I asked students to speculate on the contributions that Joanna Russ, John Updike, and other contemporary "white" writers have made to "white" literary tradition, they were troubled and unable to reply. Nor could they discuss Ralph Waldo Emerson's "whiteness," or analyze how Henry David Thoreau's "race" shaped *Walden.* Clearly, they had no idea what this "whiteness" entailed.

My students are not alone in their inability to comprehend "whiteness"; as Kobena Mercer states, "One of the signs of the times is that we really don't know what 'white' is." Thus he asserts that "the real challenge in the new cultural politics of difference is to make 'whiteness' visible for the first time, as a culturally constructed ethnic identity historically contingent upon the disavowal and violent denial of difference."[5] In short, "whiteness" has functioned as a pseudo-universal category that hides its specific values, epistemology, and other attributes under the guise of a nonracialized, supposedly colorless, "human nature."

Yet the hidden dimensions of this unmarked "white" culture are slowly becoming more visible as theorists in literature, cultural studies, and pedagogy embark on the first stages of an interrogation of "whiteness." Not surprisingly, though, the most commonly mentioned attribute of "whiteness" seems to be its nonpresence, its invisibility. A number of scholars associate this ubiquitous hidden "whiteness" with an unmarked superiority. As Richard Dyer suggests in his groundbreaking analysis of representations of "whiteness" in mainstream U.S. and British film, "white power secures its dominance by seeming not to be anything in particular."[6] Drawing on scientific studies of chromatics, he explains that whereas black — because it is always marked as a color — refers to particular objects and qualities, white does not: It "is not anything really, not an identity, not a particularizing quality, because it is everything — white is no color because it is all colors."[7] In literary and cultural studies this "colorless multicoloredness" gives "whiteness" an omnipresence quite difficult to analyze:

> It is the way that black people are marked as black (are not just "people") in representation that has made it relatively easy to analyze their representation, whereas white people — not there as a category and everywhere everything as a fact — are difficult, if not impossible, to analyze *qua* white.[8]

This invisible omnipresence gives "whiteness" a rarely acknowledged position of dominance and power. As Henry Giroux suggests, "whiteness," domination, and invisibility are intimately related. He asserts that although "'whiteness' functions as a historical and social construction," the dominant culture's inability or reluctance to see it as such is the source of its hidden authority; "whiteness" is an unrecognized and unacknowledged racial category "that secures its power by refusing to identify" itself.[9] Morrison makes a similar point in her analysis of canonical U.S. literature when she maintains that this unacknowledged "whiteness" has created a literary "language that can powerfully evoke and enforce hidden signs of racial superiority, cultural hegemony, and dismissive 'othering.'"[10]

By thus erasing its presence, "whiteness" operates as the unacknowledged standard or norm against which all so-called "minorities" are measured. Consider, for example, the implications of "minority and ethnic studies" in U.S. literature. Although scholars generally conceptualize the Harlem Renaissance as a *"black"* literary movement (I suppose because those identified as Harlem Renaissance writers were people of African descent), they do not conceptualize Transcendentalism as a *"white"* movement, even though — to the best of my knowledge — the transcendentalists were all people of European descent. In our "multicultural" era, we have studies of *"Chicano"* narrative, *"Asian American"* novels, *"Native American"* poetry, and so on. But imagine a course or a book devoted exclusively to white-skinned writers (as so many courses and books still are) that acknowledge this fact in its title: say, "Classics of the *White* Western World," "The *White* American Experience," or "*White* Regional Writers." In this schema, "minority" writings become deviations from the unmarked ("white") norm. As Dyer explains,

> Looking, with such passion and single-mindedness, at non-dominant groups has had the effect of reproducing the sense of oddness, differentness, exceptionality of these groups, the feeling that they are departures from the norm. Meanwhile the norm has carried on as if it is the natural, inevitable, ordinary way of being human.[11]

This invisible, omnipresent, naturalized "white" norm has lead to a highly paradoxical situation in literary and cultural studies: On the one hand, it is vital that we begin exploring the roles "whiteness" has played in shaping U.S. culture; on the other hand, its pervasive nonpresence makes it difficult

— if not impossible — to analyze "whiteness" as "whiteness." As Dyer asserts, "if the invisibility of whiteness colonizes the definition of other norms — class, gender, heterosexuality, nationality, and so on — it also masks whiteness as itself a category.[12] Consequently, theorists of all colors have been compelled to adopt a relational approach, where "whiteness" is examined in the context of "blackness" or other non-"white" racialized categories. In "White Woman Feminist," for example, Marilyn Frye draws on African Americans' discussions of "white" people to explore what she calls "whiteliness" — or "white" ways of thinking and acting.[13] Dyer centers his analysis of "whiteness" in mainstream cinema on instances where the narratives "are marked by the fact of ethnic difference."[14] Morrison takes a similar approach in *Playing in the Dark,* where she maintains that "blackness" — or what she terms "Africanisms" — are central to any investigation of literary "whiteness." She begins with the hypothesis that "it may be possible to discover, through a close look at literary 'blackness,' the nature — even the cause — of literary 'whiteness.'"[15] Like Dyer, she restricts her analysis to textual moments where "black" and "white" people interact, and throughout *Playing in the Dark* she explores literary "whiteness" by examining how "notions of racial hierarchy, racial exclusion, and racial vulnerability" influenced "white" writers "who held, resisted, explored, or altered these notions."[16] For instance, in her discussion of Willa Cather's *Sapphira and the Slave Girl* — which depicts the interactions between Sapphira, a "white" slave mistress, and her female slaves — Morrison examines the ways "white" womanhood acquires its identity, as well as its power, privilege, and prestige, at the expense of "black" womanhood. And in her examination of *Huckleberry Finn* she demonstrates that the notions of independence and freedom in this novel rely on the presence of the unfree Jim.

Similarly, Aldon Lynn Nielsen focuses his analysis of literary "whiteness" on the ways "white" writers depict "blackness." In *Reading Race: White American Poets and the Racial Discourse in the Twentieth Century,* he associates "whiteness" with a racist symbolic system deeply embedded in U.S. thinking and explores how "white" identity has been constructed through racist stereotyping of the "black" other. More specifically, he examines what he terms "frozen metaphors" or stereotypes of "blacks" that reinforce "an essentially racist mode of thought," privileging people of European descent while relegating people of African descent to an inferior position.[17] In the numerous racist stereotypes he describes, representations of "blackness" take a variety of sometimes contradictory forms yet have one thing in common: in each instance, they exist to affirm the validity of the power of "whiteness." By depicting people of African descent as lazy, carefree, unsophisticated, and primitive, he argues, Hart Crane, e. e. cummings, T. S. Eliot, and many other twentieth-century "white" writers locate "blackness" outside Western cultural traditions. He emphasizes that this racist stereotyping serves an important role by reinforcing already existing beliefs in the superiority of "white" aesthetics.

As Nielsen's investigation implies, this invisible, naturalized "white" norm also seems to encompass an authoritative, hierarchical, restrictive mode of thought. Frye, for example, associates "whiteliness" with the desire for personal and collective power by asserting that "Authority seems to be central to whiteliness, as you might expect from people who are raised to run things."[18] She describes "whitely" people as "judges" and "preachers" who — because they assume that their "ethics of forms, procedures, and due process" represent the only correct standard of conduct — attempt to impose their beliefs on all others.[19] Dyer makes a related point in his discussion of *Simba*, a colonial adventure film depicting the conflict between British colonizers and the Mau Mau in Kenya, in which "white" is coded as orderliness, rationality, and control, while "black" is coded as chaos, irrational violence, and total loss of control.[20] Morrison notes a similar pattern of restrictive "white" thinking which she associates with an insistence on purity, self-containment, and impenetrable borders. According to Morrison, "white" literary representations establish "fixed and major differences where the difference does not exist or is minimal." For instance, metaphoric references to "the purity of blood" have enabled writers to construct a rigid, inflexible division between "white" civilization and "black" savagery.[21] This division plays itself out in many works of U.S. literature, where false differences based on blood are used to empower "white" characters.

A number of theorists have associated "whiteness" with mystery, absence, and death. Morrison, for example, claims that although representations of "blackness" serve a variety of symbolic functions in U.S. literature, "Whiteness, alone, is mute, meaningless, unfathomable, pointless, frozen, veiled, curtained, dreaded, senseless, implacable."[22] Dyer, in his exploration of mainstream cinema, finds that on the infrequent occasions "when whiteness *qua* whiteness does come into focus, it is often revealed in emptiness, absence, denial, or even a kind of death."[23] In *Night of the Living Dead*, for instance, all "white" people are closely associated with death: "Living and dead are indistinguishable, and the zombies' sole *raison d'être*, to attack and eat the living, has resonance with the behavior of the living whites."[24] According to hooks, these literary and filmic representations of "whiteness" as mystery and death reflect a common belief in African American communities; during her own upbringing, she explains, "black folks associated whiteness with the terrible, the terrifying, the terrorizing. White people were regarded as terrorists."[25]

This shift from "whiteness" to "white *people*" concerns me, for it draws on false generalizations and implies that all human beings classified as "white" *automatically* exhibit the traits associated with "whiteness": They are, by *nature*, insidious, superior, empty, terrible, terrifying, and so on. Now, I know white folk who aren't like this, and while I would definitely agree that "white" skin and at least some of these "white" traits are often found together, I would argue that the relation between them is conditional. As Marilyn Frye suggests, "the connection between whiteliness and light-colored skin is a *contingent* connection: This character could be manifested by persons who are *not* white; it can be absent in persons who are."[26] In other words, the fact that the person is born with "white" skin does not necessarily mean that she will *not* think, act, and write in "white" ways. Leslie Marmon Silko beautifully illustrates this contingent nature of "whiteness" and skin color in *Ceremony*, where full-blood Native characters such as Emo, Harley, and Rocky think and act in "white" ways. Although she too demonizes "whiteness" — in *Ceremony* "whiteness" is associated with greed, restrictive boundaries, destruction, emptiness, absence, and death — Silko does not automatically associate "whiteness" with all "white" people. Indeed, it is the light-skinned mixed-blood protagonist, Tayo, who learns to recognize and resist this evil "whiteness."[27]

However, it's difficult not to equate the word "whiteness" — and, by extension, the negative qualities it seems to imply — with "white" people. In fact, when I first began reading about "whiteness," it became difficult for me not to make automatic assumptions about everyone who looked "white." I felt uncomfortable and distrustful around people I classified as "white"; and at this early stage in my own interrogation of "whiteness" I was tempted to draw on my African ancestry, disavow my "white" education, and entirely separate myself (intellectually, if not physically) from the so-called "white race." Interrogations of "whiteness" have had similar but far more extreme impact on my students. Despite my repeated attempts to distinguish between literary representations of "whiteness" and real-life people classified as "white," students of all colors found it extremely difficult (and at times impossible) not to blur the boundaries between them. Some became obsessed with highly negative explorations of "white" people.

Class discussion of "The School Days of an Indian Girl," an autobiographical narrative by early-twentieth-century mixed-blood writer Zitkala-Sä, illustrates this transition from "whiteness" to "white" people.[28] Although they could analyze the ways Zitkala-Sä depicted her early life in Sioux culture and her entrance into the "white" world of missionary school, students seem reluctant to take this analysis further by speculating on what these might tell us about representations of literary and cultural "whiteness." Instead, they focused their attention on the representations of "white" human beings, who, they believed, were portrayed in a highly negative light: "Whites" were emotionally and spiritually cold, overly concerned with rules and order, rude, and entirely dismissive of indigenous American cultures, peoples, and beliefs. Given the historical content of Zitkala-Sä's narrative — the U.S. government's repeated attempts to forcibly remove, assimilate, reeducate, sterilize, and Christianize Native peoples — my students' desire to demonize Zitkala-Sä's textual representations of "whiteness" is not surprising. Yet they made almost no distinction between literary "whiteness" and "white" people. Instead, they created a simplistic binary opposition between "good Indians" and "bad whites."

Classroom interrogations of "whiteness" can become even more confusing when analyzing texts by "white" writers, especially when these texts include no explicit reference to "race." Take, for example, an analysis of "whiteness" in Emerson's "Self-Reliance." Do we assume that, because Emerson was "white" his writings give insight into literary "whiteness" and should be placed in a canon of "white" U.S. literature? After all, this practice of categorizing literature according to the author's "race" has played a pivotal role in constructing African American, Native American, and other ethnic-specific canons. But this approach has problematic consequences. Should we code key themes in "Self-Reliance" — such as the desire for independence, a sense of self-confidence, a feeling of spiritual connection with nature and the divine, or a belief in the importance of creating one's own community — as "white"? To do so leads to additional problems when we encounter these "white" themes in texts by writers of color. If, for example, the quest for independence and self-trust is coded as "white," should we suggest that in his *Narrative* Frederick Douglass becomes or acts "white" when he asserts his intellectual independence from Covey, or when he resolves to "trust no one"? To my mind, such assumptions do not facilitate understanding of the literature we read.

These attempts to interrogate "whiteness" lead to other problems as well. How, for example, do we separate "whiteness" from masculinity and other forms of privilege? Is it "whiteness," masculinity, "white" masculinity, or some other combination that allows Emerson, Douglass, and Thoreau to attain remarkable levels of confidence and self-assertiveness in their prose? In class discussions of Emerson and Thoreau, several students assumed that both writers came from wealthy backgrounds and suggested that it was class privilege, rather than "whiteness," which enabled them to achieve self-reliance. Given the financial hardships both writers experienced at various points in their lives, this suggestion, while plausible, seems too simplistic.

My brief discussion of Zitkala-Sä, Emerson, Douglass, and Thoreau illustrates a few of the difficulties that can occur in classroom interrogation of "whiteness." To begin with, "whiteness" often becomes demonized and viewed as almost entirely evil and morally bankrupt, thus creating another binary between the good non-"whites" and the bad "whites." However, like all binary oppositions this dualism oversimplifies and conflates literary representations of "whiteness" and "white" people with real-life human beings classified as "white." Perhaps most importantly for my argument in the following pages, interrogations of "whiteness" and other racialized categories seem to confirm static concepts of identity which reinforce the already existing belief in entirely separate "races."

What I discovered from these classroom investigations of "whiteness" is that students' comments are generally based on the assumption that "race" is a permanent characteristic of U.S. life. In many ways, this perspective on "race" seems like common sense. After all, in the United States categorizing people by "race" has become an accepted way of comprehending and explaining ourselves and our world. Surveys, census forms, birth certificates, and job applications often ask us to identify ourselves according to our "race." Generally, we assume that physiological differences (in skin color, hair texture, and facial features, for instance) between the various so-called "races" indicate distinct underlying biological-genetic differences, differences implying permanent, "natural" divisions between disparate groups of people.

But, this commonly accepted view of "race" is far less accurate than most people realize. To begin with, the belief that each person belongs to only one "race" ignores many "biracial" and "multiracial" people living in this country. Indeed, the implicit belief in discrete, entirely separate "races" implies a false sense of racial purity, for we could all be described as multiracial. As Michael Thornton points out, "there are no such things as pure races."[29] Spaniards, for example, are a mixture of "Black Africans, Gypsies (from India), and Semites (Jews, Arabs, and Phoenicians), as well as Romans, Celts, Germans, Greeks, Berbers, Basques, and probably more."[30] Furthermore, the suggestion that we can automatically identify ourselves with others according to "race" assumes that we are fully cognizant of our ancestry. However, as one of the characters in Pauline Hopkins's *Contending Forces* asserts,

> It is an incontrovertible truth that there is no such thing as an unmixed black on the American continent. Just bear in mind that we cannot tell by a person's complexion whether he be dark or light in blood. . . . I will venture to say that out of a hundred apparently pure black men not one of them will be able to trace an unmixed flow of African blood since landing on these shores![31]

Similar comments can be made about people identified as "Latina," "Native American," or as members of any other so-called "race." Appearances can be extremely deceptive, and not one of us is "unmixed." Perhaps most importantly, this mythical perspective on discrete, biologically separate "races" relies on nineteenth-century pseudoscientific theories. As Kwame Anthony Appiah notes, "What most people in most cultures ordinarily believe about the significance of 'racial' difference" is not supported by scientific evidence. While biologists can interpret the data in various ways, they cannot demonstrate the existence of genetically distinct "races," for "human genetic variability between the populations of Africa or Europe or Asia is not that much greater than that within those populations."[32]

"Race" is an ambiguous, constantly changing concept that has little — if anything — to do with scientific descriptions; as Michael Omi and Howard Winant persuasively demonstrate, "The meaning of race is defined and contested throughout society, in both collective action and personal practice. In the process, racial categories themselves are formed, transformed, destroyed, and re-formed."[33] Yet we often proceed in our interrogations of "whiteness" and other racialized categories as if these "races" were permanent, unchanging categories of meaning. To return to the second half of my title, although the theorists of "whiteness" attempt to deconstruct "race," all too often they inadvertently reconstruct it by reinforcing fixed categories of racialized meanings. Theorists find it difficult not to conflate literary or cultural representations of "whiteness" with "white" people, and this perpetual reconstruction of separate "races" can be even more difficult to avoid in the classroom, where "whiteness" — generally played out in the context of racialized "black," "Indian," and other "colored" bodies — is associated only with "white" people.

Yet even a brief look at a few of the many ways racial groups have been redefined in this country illustrates how *unstable* and *artificial* racialized identities are. For instance, throughout the nineteenth century many U.S. state and federal agencies recognized only three "races," which they labeled "White," "Negro," and "Indian." Given the extremely diverse mixture of people living in the United States, this three-part classification was, to say the least, confusing. How were U.S. Americans of Mexican or Chinese descent to be described? Were they "White"? "Negro"? or "Indian"? The state of California handled this dilemma in a curious way: Rather than expand the number of "races," the government retained the existing categories and classified Mexican Americans as a "white" population and Chinese Americans as "Indian." According to Omi and Winant, this decision had little to do with outward appearance; it was motivated by socioeconomic and political concerns, for it allowed the state to deny the latter group the rights accorded to people classified as "white."[34]

Since then, both groups have been redefined numerous times. U.S. Americans of Chinese descent have been classified as "Orientals," "Asians," "Asian Americans," "Pan Asians," and "Asian Pacific Americans." Yet these terms are inadequate and erroneously imply a homogeneity unwarranted by the many nationalities, geographical origins, languages, dialects, and cultural traditions supposedly contained within these politically motivated categories. As Yehudi Webster notes, these monolithic labels indicate the U.S. government's attempt to group "heterogeneous populations into one category on the basis of apparent similarities in skin color, hair type, and eye shape."[35] Efforts to classify U.S. Americans of Mexican ancestry have been equally unsuccessful. Even in the last forty years, they have been redefined several times: In the 1950s and 1960s the government included them in an ethnic category labeled "Persons of Spanish Mother Tongue"; in the 1970s, they were redefined as "Persons of Both Spanish Surname and Spanish Mother Tongue"; and in the 1980s, the "Hispanic" category was created. This most recent government invention is especially confusing, for so many so-called "Hispanics" reject the term's association with Spanish ancestry and thus its "white" Eurocentric implications, as well as its erasure of their cultural specificity, and name themselves "Chicano/a," "Latino/a," "Cuban American," and so on. Indeed, in the 1990 census over 96 percent of the 9.8 million people who refused to identify themselves according to a particular race would have been classified by the government as "Hispanic."[36] As Omi and Winant observe, such changes "suggest the state's inability to 'racialize' a particular group — to institutionalize it in a politically organized racial system."[37]

The status of so-called "blacks" and "whites" is, perhaps, even more problematic. To begin with, the terms themselves are almost entirely inaccurate. "White" is the color of this paper, not the color of anyone's skin. And people referred to as "black" would be more accurately described as they are in Nella Larsen's *Quicksand*: as "taupe, mahogany, bronze, copper, gold, orange, yellow, peach, ivory, pinky white" or even "pastry white."[38] Furthermore, although many "Hispanics," "Native Americans," and "Asian Americans" have lighter skin than some so-called "whites," they are not classified as such unless they are passing.

Though we generally think of "white" and "black" as permanent, transhistorical racial markers indicating distinct groups of people, they are not. In fact, Puritans and other early European colonizers didn't consider themselves "white"; they identified as "Christian," "English," or "free," for at that time the word "white" didn't represent a racial category. Again, racialization was economically and politically motivated. It was not until around 1680, with the racialization of slavery, that the term was used to describe a specific group of people. As Yehudi Webster explains, "The idea of a homogeneous white race was adopted as a means of generating cohesion among explorers, migrants, and settlers in the eighteenth-century America. Its opposite was the black race, whose nature was said to be radically different from that of the white race."[39]

Significantly, then, the "white race" evolved in opposition to but simultaneously with the "black race." As peoples whose specific ethnic identities were Yoruban, Ashanti, Fon, and Dahomean were forcibly removed from their homes in Africa and taken to the North American colonies, the English adopted the terms "white" and "black" — with their already existing implications of purity and evil — and developed the concept of a superior "white race" and an inferior "black race" to justify slavery. It's important to note that the Europeans did not originally label the people who lived in Africa "black"; nor did they see them as evil savages. As Abdul JanMohamed explains, "Africans were perceived in a more or less neutral and benign manner before the slave trade developed; however, once the triangular trade became established, Africans were newly characterized as the epitome of evil and barbarity."[40]

The meanings of "black" and "white" are no more stable in the twentieth century than they were in the past. "Colored," "Negro," "black," "Afro-American," "African-American" (hyphenated), and "African American" (unhyphenated) all describe U.S. Americans of African descent. But these terms are not synonymous; each indicates a different racial identity with specific sociopolitical and cultural implications.[41] Although the term "white" — which has been used since the late seventeenth century to designate an elite group of people — seems more stable, its meaning has undergone equally significant changes. Many people today considered "white" — southern Europeans, light-skinned Jews, the Irish, and Catholics of European descent, for example — were most definitely *not* "white" in the eighteenth and nineteenth centuries. Since the late 1960s, with the rise of what Steven Steinberg calls "ethnic fever,"[42] the "white race" has undergone additional changes. Once again, the redefinition of "white" corresponded to shifts in the meaning of "black." As the Black Power movement developed an oppositional ideology to challenge existing definitions of "Negro," "white" ethnics began (re)claiming their European cultural "roots." Recently, conservative self-identified "whites" have attempted to redefine themselves as the new oppressed group. As Omi and Winant explain, the Far Right attempts "to develop a new white identity, to reassert the very meaning of *whiteness* which has been rendered unstable and unclear by the minority challenges of the 1960s."[43] This rearticulation of racialized identities continues today, in essays like hooks's "Loving Blackness as Political Resistance" (in her *Black Looks*) and in recent demands for an interrogation of "whiteness."

I have misgivings about this increased emphasis on "whiteness" and other racialized identities. Literary theorists who discuss representations of "race" rarely acknowledge the fluidity and the historical changes in the U.S. discourse on "race." Instead, they refer to "white," "black," "Indian," and other supposedly separate "races" as though these categories are permanent unchanging facts. What are the effects of continually reinforcing these fictionalized identities? Whose interests does this uphold? Whose does it harm? To be sure, increased racial discourse has served an extremely important purpose by enabling people of color to gain a sense of historical and sociopolitical agency. Thus Houston Baker describes a "race" as "a recently emergent, unifying, and forceful sign of difference *in the service* of the 'Other.'" He explains that for people of color, racial identities function as "an inverse discourse — talk designed to take a bad joke of 'race' . . . and turn it into a unifying discourse."[44] Although Baker acknowledges the destructive, fictionalized aspects of "race" (it is, after all, a "bad joke"), he maintains that African Americans and other so-called "minority" groups can reverse its negative implications and use racial discourse in affirmative ways. For example, by aligning themselves with other people of African descent, self-identified African Americans attempt to challenge oppressive definitions of the so-called "black race."

Yet such oppositional tactics are problematic, for they cannot challenge the assumptions underlying *all* references to "race." Even the highly affirmative talk of a black, or Chicano/a, or Native American racial identity reinforces already existing conceptions of "race," conceptions that have functioned historically to create hierarchical divisions based on false generalizations concerning physical appearance and other arbitrary characteristics. By thus reinforcing fictionalized identities, contemporary racialized discourse creates further divisions between people. As Henry Louis Gates Jr. points out,

> The sense of difference defined in popular usage of the term "race" has both described and *inscribed* difference of language, belief system, artistic tradition, and gene pool, as well as all sorts of supposedly natural attributes such as rhythm, athletic ability, cerebration, usury, fidelity, and so forth. The relation between "racial character" and these sorts of characteristics has been inscribed through tropes of race, lending the sanction of God, biology, or the natural order to even presumably biased descriptions of cultural tendencies and differences.[45]

This naturalized use of "race" is especially insidious, for it reifies the destructive stereotypes already circulating in U.S. culture. Despite the many historic and contemporary changes in racial categories, people generally treat "race" as an unchanging biological fact. Often, they make simplistic judgments and gross overgeneralizations based primarily on appearance. You know the stereotypes: "Blacks are more athletic, and boy can they dance"; "All whites are bigots"; "All Hispanics are hot-blooded." Indeed, even social scientists (who should know better) acknowledge the politically, economically motivated nature of racial formation yet discuss the "black race," "the Hispanic race," "the white race," and so on as if these supposed "races" were God-given facts. In so doing, they reinforce oppressive social systems and erect permanent barriers between supposedly separate groups of people. One of the most striking examples I've encountered can be found in the 1992 bestseller *Two Nations: Black and White, Separate, Hostile, and Unequal.* In his introduction Andrew Hacker describes "race" as a "human creation," not a fixed biological fact, and acknowledges that because people use the word in numerous ways, clear-cut definitions are impossible.[46] Yet throughout the book he continuously refers to the "black race" and the "white race" without complicating the terms. Indeed, I would argue that by downplaying the economic, cultural, and ethnic diversity found within each of these two "races," Hacker heightens and reifies the tension between them. Moreover, by focusing almost entirely on the "black/white" binary, Hacker reinforces the myth of racial purity and ignores the incredible diversity found in this country.

This simplistic binary between fixed definitions of "blackness" and "whiteness" occurs in literary interrogations of "whiteness" as well. Take, for example, Nielsen's exploration of "whiteness" in *Reading Race.* Unlike Morrison — who begins blurring the artificial boundaries between "blackness" and "whiteness" by exploring what "white" representations of "blackness" tell us about literary "whiteness" — Nielsen focuses almost entirely on "white" poets' racist stereotypes of "blacks." Although he acknowledges the fictional, contradictory nature of these "white" representations of "blackness," his constant focus on the stereotypes themselves inadvertently reifies the racist imagery he tries to undercut. This approach seems especially dangerous in the classroom where, as Sharon Stockton points out, "students tend to think in terms of stereotyped binary oppositions."[47] In classroom interrogations of "whiteness," Nielsen's method leads to overly generalized discussions of racist, bigoted "whites" and lazy, ignorant, inferior blacks. Moreover, by continually emphasizing racism, we risk giving students the pessimistic belief that racism is inevitable and racialized barriers will never be overcome. As Omi and Winant argue in their discussion of 1960s theories of institutionalized racism, "An overly comprehensive view of racism . . . potentially served as a self-fulfilling prophecy."[48]

Let me emphasize: I am not saying that we should adopt a "color-blind" approach and ignore the roles racist thinking has played in constructing "whiteness." To do so simply reinforces the increasingly popular but very false belief that "race" no longer matters in twentieth-century U.S. culture.

Racism is deeply embedded in U.S. society, and students of all colors must be aware of its systemic nature. Nor can we analyze racialized dimensions of texts by writers of color without also explaining "whiteness," for this partial analysis reinforces the long-standing belief in "white" invisibility. However, instructors must be aware of the impact interrogations of "whiteness" can have on our students. Although self-identified students of color find it satisfying to see the "white" gaze which has marked them as "Other" turned back on itself, I question the long-term effectiveness of this reversal. As I have argued, such reversals inadvertently support existing stereotypes. Moreover, these reversals trigger a variety of unwelcome reactions in self-identified "white" students, reactions ranging from guilt to anger to withdrawal and despair. Instructors must be prepared to deal with these responses. The point is not to encourage feelings of personal responsibility for the slavery, decimation of indigenous peoples, land theft, and so on that occurred in the past. It is, rather, to enable students of all colors more fully to comprehend how these oppressive systems that began in the historical past continue misshaping contemporary conditions. Guilt-tripping plays no role in this process. Indeed, guilt functions as a useless, debilitating state of consciousness that reinforces the boundaries between apparently separate "races." When self-identified "white" students feel guilty, they become paralyzed, deny any sense of agency, and assume that their privileged positions in contemporary U.S. culture automatically compel them to act as "the oppressor."

The compromise I've arrived at — admittedly temporary and always open to further revision — entails a twofold approach where we explore the artificial, constantly changing nature of "black," "white," and other racialized identities without ignoring their concrete material effects. I select texts by Nella Larsen, Zora Neale Hurston, and Langston Hughes, where students can clearly see these racialized identities as transitional states. In the stories collected in Hughes's *The Ways of White Folks,* for instance, we see "black" people reconstructing themselves as "white," self-identified "blacks" who act exactly like "whites," and "white" people who act just like "blacks."[49] These stories, as well as other textual representations of passing, destabilize students' "common-sense" beliefs in racial purity and ahistorical, fixed "races." Another topic I've employed is the concept of cultural *mestizaje.* I borrow this term from Cuban literary and political movements where its usage indicates a profound challenge to existing racial categories. As Nancy Morejón explains, *mestizaje* transculturation defies static notions of cultural purity by emphasizing

> the constant interaction, the transmutation between two or more cultural components with the unconscious goal of creating a third cultural identity . . . that is new and independent even though rooted in the preceding elements. Reciprocal influence is the determining factor here, for no single element superimposes itself on another; on the contrary, each one changes into the other so that both can be transformed into a third. Nothing seems immutable. [qtd. Lionnett 15–16][50]

This idea of constant transformation and change provides an important alternative to the well-known stereotype of the "American" melting pot. Unlike the melting pot, which works to assimilate culturally specific groups with distinct traditions into indistinguishable "whites," *mestizaje* emphasizes the mutually constituted and constantly changing nature of all racialized identities.

Yet these tactics are only temporary measures. I'm still searching for more effective ways of incorporating interrogations of "whiteness" into classroom discussions. Ironically, what began as an interrogation of "whiteness" has turned into an interrogation of "race," and I have even *more* questions than I had when I began. On the one hand, I agree with Mercer and others who call for an examination of the ways "whiteness" has been socially constructed. Because "whiteness" — *whatever* it is, and I would argue that at this point no one really knows — has functioned as an oppressive, mythical norm that negates people (whatever their skin color) who do not conform to its standard — we need to understand and deconstruct it. On the other hand, I worry that this analysis simply reifies already existing hegemonic conceptions of "race." As Gates explains, "we carelessly use language in such a way as to *will* this sense of *natural* difference into our formulations. To do so is to engage in a pernicious act of language, one which exacerbates the complex problem of cultural or ethnic difference, rather than to assuage or redress it."[51]

As I see it, the problems with discussing "whiteness" and other racial categories without historicizing the terms and demonstrating the relational nature of all racialized identities include (but aren't limited to) the following. First, our conceptions of "race" are scientifically and historically inaccurate; they transform arbitrary distinctions between people into immutable, "natural," God-given facts. Second, constant references to "race" perpetuate the belief in separate peoples, monolithic identities, and stereotypes. Third, in this country racial discourse quickly degenerates into a "black"/"white" polarization that overlooks other so-called "races" and ignores the incredible diversity among people. And fourth, racial categories are not — and never have been — benign. Racial divisions were developed to create a hierarchy that grants privilege and power to specific groups of people while simultaneously oppressing and excluding others. If, as Gates implies in the first epigraph to my paper, "race" is a text that everyone in this country unthinkingly "reads," I want to suggest that we need to begin reading — and rewriting — this text in new ways. At the very least, we should complicate existing conceptions of "race" — both by exploring the many changes that have occurred in all apparently fixed racial categories and by informing students of the political, economic, and historical facts shaping the continual reinvention of "race."

NOTES

1. Toni Morrison, *Playing in the Dark: Whiteness and the American Literary Imagination* (Cambridge: Harvard University Press, 1992), p. 12.

2. Henry Giroux and Peter McLaren, "Radical Pedagogy as Cultural Politica: Beyond the Discourse of Critique and Anti-Utopianism," in *Texts for Change Theory/Pedagogy/Politics,* ed. Donald Morton and Mas'ud Zavarzadeh (Urbana: University of Illinois Press, 1991), p. 160.

3. bell hooks, *Yearning: Race, Gender, and Cultural Politics* (Boston: South End Press, 1990), p. 54.

4. Kobena Mercer, "Skin Head Sex Thing: Racial Difference and the Homoerotic Imaginary," in How Do I Look? *Queer Film and Video,* ed. Bad Object-Choices (Seattle: Bay Press, 1991), p. 206.

5. Ibid., pp. 205–06.

6. Richard Dyer, "White," in *The Matter of Images: Essays on Representations* (New York: Routledge, 1993), p. 44.

7. Ibid., p. 142.

8. Ibid., p. 143.

9. Henry Giroux, "Post-Colonial Ruptures and Democratic Possibilities: Multiculturalism as Anti-Racist Pedagogy," *Cultural Critique* 21 (1992): 15.

10. Morrison, *Playing in the Dark,* pp. x–xi.

11. Dyer, "White," p. 141.

12. Ibid., p. 143.

13. Marilyn Frye, "White Woman Feminist," in *Willful Virgin: Essays in Feminism, 1976–1992* (Freedom, CA: Crossing, 1992), pp. 147–69.

14. Dyer, "White," p. 144.

15. Morrison, *Playing in the Dark,* p. 9.

16. Ibid., p. 11.

17. Aldon Lynn Nielsen, *Reading Race: White American Poets and the Racial Discourse in the Twentieth Century* (Athens: University of Georgia Press, 1988), p. 3.

18. Frye, "White Woman Feminist," p. 156.

19. Ibid., p. 155.

20. Dyer, "White," pp. 146–48.

21. Morrison, *Playing in the Dark,* p. 68.

22. Ibid., p. 59.

23. Dyer, "White," p. 141.

24. Ibid., p. 157.

25. bell hooks, *Black Looks: Race and Representation* (Boston: South End Press, 1992), p. 170.

26. Frye, "White Woman Feminist," pp. 151–52, her emphasis.

27. Leslie Marmon Silko, *Ceremony* (New York: Penguin, 1977).

28. Zitkala-Sä [Gertrude Simmons Bonnin], "The School Days of an Indian Girl," *Atlantic Monthly* 85 (1900): 37–45.

29. Michael C. Thornton, "Is Multiracial Status Unique? The Personal and Social Experience," in *Racially Mixed People in America,* ed. Maria P. Root (Newbury Park, CA: Sage, 1992), p. 322.

30. Carlos A. Fernandez, "La Ràza and the Melting Pot: A Comparative Look at Multiethnicity," in *Racially Mixed People,* ed. Maria P. Root (Newbury Park, CA: Sage, 1992), p. 143.

31. Pauline E. Hopkins, *Contending Forces: A Romance Illustrative of Negro Life North and South* (1900; reprint, New York: Oxford University Press, 1988), p. 151.

32. Kwame Anthony Appiah, "The Uncompleted Argument: Du Bois and the Illusion of Race," in *"Race," Writing, and Difference,* ed. Henry Louis Gates Jr. (Chicago: University of Chicago Press, 1986), p. 21.

33. Michael Omi and Howard Winant, *Racial Formation in the United States from the 1960s to the 1980s* (Rev. ed., New York: Routledge, 1993), p. 61.

34. Ibid., p. 82.

35. Yehudi O. Webster, *The Racialization of America* (New York: St. Martin's Press, 1992), pp. 132–33.

36. Ibid., p. 143.

37. Omi and Winant, *Racial Formation,* p. 82.

38. Nella Larsen, *Quicksand and Passing* (1928; edited with an introduction by Deborah McDowell; reprint, New Brunswick: Rutgers University Press, 1986), p. 59.

39. Webster, *The Racialization of America,* p. 9.

40. Abdul R. JanMohamed, "The Economy of Manichean Allegory: The Function of Racial Difference in Colonialist Literature," in Gates, *"Race," Writing, and Difference,* pp. 78–106, 80.

41. Henry Louis Gates Jr., *Loose Canons: Notes on the Culture Wars* (New York: Oxford University Press, 1982), pp. 131–51.

42. Stephen Steinberg, *The Ethnic Myth: Race, Ethnicity, and Class in America* (1982; reprint with epilogue, Boston: Beacon, 1989), p. 3.

43. Omi and Winant, *Racial Formation,* p. 120.

44. Houston Baker, "Caliban's Triple Play," in Gates, *"Race," Writing, and Difference,* pp. 381–95, 386; his emphasis.

45. Gates, *"Race," Writing, and Difference,* p. 5.

46. Andrew Hacker, *Two Nations: Black and White, Separate, Hostile, and Unequal* (New York: Ballantine, 1992), p. 4.

47. Sharon Stockton, "'Blacks vs. Browns': Questioning the White Ground," *College English* 57 (1995): 70.

48. Omi and Winant, *Racial Formation,* p. 70.

49. Langston Hughes, *The Ways of White Folks* (1933; reprint, New York: Vintage, 1971).

50. Francoise Lionnett, *Autobiographical Voices: Race, Gender, Self-Portraiture* (Ithaca, NY: Cornell University Press, 1989), pp. 15–16.

51. Gates, op. cit., his emphasis.

Introduction to American Indian Literatures

A. LAVONNE BROWN RUOFF

*R*uoff *begins this essay by noting that the literature of the United States originated with American Indians, not Western Europeans. She presents basic background information regarding the American Indian population and languages. While noting the diversity among individual Indians, Ruoff maintains that they share certain worldviews and values, such as "an emphasis on the importance of living in harmony with the physical and spiritual universe, the power of thought and word to maintain this balance, a deep reverence for the land, and a strong sense of community" (p. 181). Ruoff observes that American Indian literature also reflects Indian-white relations, and she provides a brief overview of major events and government policies. Ruoff then moves into a discussion of Indian oral literatures, noting that due to the diversity of lifestyles and languages, these materials should be analyzed within their social and historical contexts. Using specific examples, she illustrates how Indian worldviews and values are represented in their literature, pointing to a Yokuts prayer to illustrate the power of the word and a Keres song to exemplify oneness with the community. Other examples are drawn from contemporary Indian writers such as Leslie Marmon Silko and N. Scott Momaday. Ruoff concludes with a discussion of the transmission of oral literature and the effect of translation and transcription. This selection is taken from the introduction to Ruoff's* American Indian Literatures *(1990).*

> They carried dreams in their voices;
> They were the elders, the old ones.
> They told us the old stories,
> And they sang the spirit songs.
> — Big Tree (Kiowa)

> American literature begins with the first human perception of the American landscape expressed and preserved in language.
> — N. Scott Momaday (Kiowa)

From *American Indian Literatures: An Introduction, Bibliographic Review, and Selected Bibliography* (New York: MLA, 1990) 1–19.

BACKGROUNDS

The literature of this nation originated with the native peoples who migrated to North America over twenty-eight thousand years ago, not with the Western Europeans who began to immigrate in the late sixteenth and early seventeenth centuries. When Western Europeans arrived, 18 million people inhabited North America and 5 million lived in what is now the United States. After contact, the population of the native peoples of North America greatly diminished — primarily as a result of diseases brought by whites. According to the United States Census Bureau, there were only 210,000 left in this country by 1910. In the twentieth century, however, the Indian population in the United States has greatly increased. The 1980 census, which Indians feel gives a very low count, indicated that the native population of the United States (including Alaska) was 1,418,195. Of these, 681,213 lived on reservations and 736,982 lived off reservations. Thus over half of the Indian population now lives in towns or cities rather than on reservations.

At the time of contact, the native peoples of North America were divided into more than three hundred cultural groups and spoke two hundred different languages, plus many dialects, derived from seven basic language families. By 1940, 149 of these languages were still in use (Spencer, Jennings, et al. 38–39). Divided into numerous cultural and language groups, native North Americans practiced many different religions and customs. However, there are some perspectives on their place in the universe that many native American groups shared and continue to share. Among these are an emphasis on the importance of living in harmony with the physical and spiritual universe, the power of thought and word to maintain this balance, a deep reverence for the land, and a strong sense of community. Although individual Indians today vary in the extent to which they follow tribal traditions, their worldviews and values continue to reflect those of their ancestors.

The history of American Indian literature reflects not only tribal cultures and the experience and imagination of its authors but Indian-white relations as well. Although a detailed discussion of Indian-white relations is beyond the scope of this volume, a brief overview of some of the major events is important to understanding the interrelationship between Indian history and literature. Whites' settlement in Indian territory was inevitably followed by attempts to expand their land holdings and Indians' determined efforts to retain their ancestral land. During the seventeenth century, Indians rose up against white domination in the Pequot War in New England (1637), King Philip's War (1672–76) against the British, and the Pueblo Revolt of 1680 against the Spanish. As the fur trade expanded into Indian territories, Indians became increasingly dependent on whites for firearms, metal traps, and other trade goods. So important did trade become to Indians that from the late seventeenth century through the War of 1812, tribal relations were frequently dictated by trapping and trade opportunities. For example, between 1644 and 1680, the Iroquois, whose lands were depleted of fur-bearing game, defeated Indian tribes from the Hudson to Illinois in their westward invasion to gain new trapping territory in order to meet whites' demands for fur. Before the end of the War of 1812, the British, Americans, and French enlisted Indian tribes to help secure their claims to various territories or to defeat their enemies, Indian and non-Indian. Controversies over trade and Indian land helped precipitate the American Revolution. After the conclusion of the Revolutionary War, there was considerable racial animosity against Indians because of accusations about their wartime atrocities, the allegiance of most of the Iroquois to the British, and the demand by whites for Indian land. Settlers' westward migration into the Ohio Valley brought new conflicts. After the defeat of England in the War of 1812 essentially ended that nation's threat to American interests on the continent, the United States no longer felt it necessary to placate Indians to ensure that they would fight the British. Increasingly, legislators and settlers advocated the relocation of the Indians. During the debate on removal, the federal government negotiated numerous treaties between 1815 and 1830 arranging for immediate or ultimate resettlement. The death knell of Indian hopes for retaining tribal lands east of the Mississippi free from white encroachment was sounded in 1830, when Congress passed the Indian Removal Bill, which authorized the federal government to move Indians from these areas to Indian Territory, now Oklahoma, and other locations deemed suitable. Some tribes were forced to move several times. No sooner had the Removal Bill been implemented than whites violated it by migrating westward into Indian territories.

In 1848, the Treaty of Guadalupe Hidalgo with Mexico brought new territory and numerous tribes under the jurisdiction of the United States. The discovery of gold in California in 1849 stimulated new encroachments on Indian land as hordes of emigrants passed through Indian land on their way to the California gold fields, Idaho ore deposits, or Oregon timber. What began as a stream of settlers in the 1830s became a flood by the 1850s.

The 1862 rebellion of the Santee Sioux in Minnesota and the allegiance of the Five Civilized Tribes in Oklahoma (Cherokee, Chickasaw, Creek, Choctaw, Seminole) to the Confederacy during the Civil War provided new excuses for removal of the Santee and drastic reductions in land holdings of the Five Civilized Tribes after the Civil War. In the Southwest, the withdrawal of federal troops led to attacks by Navajos and Apaches, who were then rounded up onto reservations by Kit Carson and others. Conflicts between Colorado Indians and whites resulted in the Sand Creek Massacre of 1864, in which Colonel J. M. Chivington and his men brutally murdered Cheyennes, primarily old men, women, and children. The opening of the Bozeman Trail through Indian land during the Civil War resulted in fierce retaliations by the Teton Sioux. Western migration, slowed during the Civil War, greatly increased when the end of the war brought renewed demand for land. As a result, the government was determined to pacify the Indians once and for all. To do so, they forced Indians onto reservations by destroying their food supplies — the buffalo and stored winter food. Public outrage over the Indians' victory over General George A. Custer and his men in 1876 brought swift retribution to defiant tribes. By the end of the 1880s, the buffalo had been exterminated from the Plains and the last of the tribes had been forced onto reservations.

As part of its policy of assimilationism, the government passed the General Allotment Act of 1887, which had been sponsored by Senator Henry L. Dawes. Popularly called the Dawes Act, it allotted in severalty land previously owned by tribes. This bill was supported by liberals, who felt the Indians could survive only by becoming independent farmers, and by land grabbers, who plotted to gain Indian territory by legal and illegal means. It was also supported by Indians like Sarah Winnemucca (Paiute) and Charles A. Eastman (Sioux), who felt it offered Indians independence and citizenship. The Allotment Act resulted in enormous losses of Indian land, however. Wilcomb E. Washburn estimates that by 1934, Indians had lost over sixty percent of the land they owned in 1887 (*The Indian in America* 242–43).

The last gasp of Indian resistance was the Ghost Dance religion, a messianic movement that swept across the Plains in the late 1880s and 1890. Its leader was Wovoka, or Jack Wilson (Paiute), who predicted that the Plains would again support millions of buffalo and that whites would disappear. By 1890, his words roused the Plains tribes and frightened whites before it died out. One tragic result was the massacre at Wounded Knee, South Dakota, in 1890, when Big Foot's band of Sioux Ghost Dancers was slaughtered after a dispute about turning in their weapons. This incident ended the Indian wars.

One dimension of the government's assimilationist policy was the education of Indian children in English and in Western European traditions. Many Indian children were shipped off to boarding schools in such faraway places as Carlisle, Pennsylvania, and Riverside, California, where they were separated for years from their families and forbidden to speak their native languages or practice their tribal customs and religions. The isolation of Indian children eroded strong family bonds and ancient tribal traditions.

Although official policy was to assimilate Indians into the dominant society, the government did not grant Indians citizenship until 1924. Because Indians volunteered, were wounded, and died in World War I far out of proportion to their numbers in the society, Congress awarded them citizenship out of gratitude for their service. Another major gain for Indians in the first half of the twentieth century was the passage of the Wheeler-Howard Indian Reorganization Act in 1934, which its advocates called the Indian Magna Carta. The act ended allotment in severalty, continued the trust period indefinitely, confirmed cultural pluralism, and reestablished tribal government. After World War II such policies came under increasing criticism, as politicians sought ways to end the "Indian problem." In 1953, House Concurrent Resolution 108 was passed, which began the campaign to terminate the federal government's role in Indian affairs. Under this policy, tribes such as the Klamath and Menominee lost their reservation status and the government actively encouraged Indians to move to cities. As a result, urban Indian populations greatly increased during this period, but termination was disastrous for the tribes. After fighting for years to regain reservation status for their land, the Menominee finally won their battle in 1973, when they again became wards of the government.

The battle for justice for Indians has increasingly been fought in Congress, state legislatures, and courts. Many Indian organizations — such as the Indian Rights Association, National Association of Indian Affairs, National Indian Education Association, and National Congress of American Indians — emerged to serve as effective advocates for Indian causes. Indian activism was stimulated by the American Indian Chicago Conference of 1961, after which many young Indian activists formed the National Indian Youth Council to mobilize "Red Power." Other groups that developed during the 1960s include the American Indian Civil Rights Council, National Tribal Chairmen's Association, the American Indian Movement, and the National Council of Indian Opportunity. The revitalism of Indian identity during the 1960s led to renewed interest in tribal languages, customs, and religions. Increased Indian militancy resulted in the occupation of Alcatraz Island (1969); the Bureau of Indian Affairs office in Washington, D.C. (1972); and Wounded Knee, South Dakota (1973).

Strong Indian advocacy resulted in the passage of several bills that ensured Indian rights. The Indian Civil Rights Act (1968) provides for free exercise of religion, speech, press, and right of assembly; protection against the taking of property without just compensation; and tribal consent before the state can assume civil and criminal jurisdiction over Indian reservations within its borders. In 1971 the Alaska Native Claims Settlement Act was passed. The Indian Self-Determination and Education Assistance Act, which became law in 1974, allows tribes to contract with the government to provide educational and other services to tribal members. Two measures passed in 1978 were the American Indian Religious Freedom Act and Indian Child Welfare Act, which guarantee the exercise of native religion and ensure a tribal role in the adoption of Indian children.

Indian tribes continue to fight many crucial battles over such issues as control over their water, mineral, and wildlife resources; retention of rights guaranteed by treaties; just compensation for land; self-determination; and tribal legal jurisdiction over crimes committed on Indian land. The history of the native peoples of America is one of endurance despite adversity. Through the diversity of their cultures, significant achievements as tribes and individuals, and the richness of their literatures, American Indians remind us of their important contributions to the mosaic of American culture.

ORAL LITERATURES

Indian oral literatures are a vibrant force that tribal peoples continue to create and perform and that strongly influence the written works of Indian authors, as Simon Ortiz (Acoma) makes clear:

> The oral tradition is not just speaking and listening, because what it means to me and other people who have grown up in that tradition is that whole process, . . . of that society in terms of its history, its culture, its language, its values, and subsequently, its literature. So it's not merely a simple matter of speaking and listening, but living that process. ("Interview" 104)

Because the oral literatures of Native Americans reflect the diversity of their religious beliefs, social structures, customs, languages, and lifestyles, these literatures should be studied within the contexts of both the cultural groups that produced them and the influences on these groups resulting from their interactions with other tribes and with non-Indians.

Central to American Indians' traditional way of life is the belief that human beings must live in harmony with the physical and spiritual universe, a state of balance vital to an individual and communal sense of wholeness or beauty; this theme pervades American Indian oral and written literatures as well. In traditional Indian societies, all aspects of life are conducted according to the religious beliefs and rituals deemed essential to the survival and well-being of the group. Breath, speech, and verbal art are so closely linked to each other that in many oral cultures they are often signified by the same word. The reverence for the power of thought and the word that is an integral part of American Indian religions is exemplified in Navajo culture. In *Language and Art in the Navajo Universe*, Gary Witherspoon points out that the Navajo world was brought into being by the gods, who entered the sweathouse and thought the world into existence. The thoughts of the gods were realized through human speech, song, and prayer (16). The following excerpt from Witherspoon's translation of the "Beginning of the World Song" illustrates the interrelation among knowledge, thought, and speech in Navajo culture:

> The earth will be, from ancient
> times with me there is knowledge of it.
> The mountains will be, from ancient
> times with me there is knowledge of it.
> [and so on, mentioning other things to be]
>
> The earth will be, from the very
> beginning I have thought it.
> The mountains will be, from the very
> beginning I have thought it.
> [and so on]
>
> The earth will be, from ancient times
> I speak it.
> The mountains will be, from ancient times
> I speak it.
> [And so on] (16)

According to Witherspoon, the language of the Navajo emergence myth indicates "that in the beginning were the word and the thing, the symbol, and the object." For the Navajos, the awareness of symbol is knowledge. "Symbol is word, and word is the means by which substance is organized and transformed" (46).

Such emphasis on word as symbol and the power of symbols to structure the universe is common among American Indian societies. Jack Frederick Kilpatrick and Anna Gritts Kilpatrick (Cherokee) stress in *Run toward the Nightland* that in "any magical ritual all generative power resides in thought" and that the songs which focus and direct the thought are alone inviolate. The singer or medicine man merely augments the authority of thoughts, applies or disseminates it more effectively (6). Lame Deer emphasizes that the Sioux live "in a world of symbols and images where the spiritual and the commonplace are one":

> To us they are part of nature, part of ourselves — the earth, the sun, the wind and the rain, stones, trees, animals, even little insects like ants and grasshoppers. We try to understand them not with the head but with the heart, and we need no more than a hint to give us the meaning. (*Lame Deer: Seeker of Visions* 109)

The power of thought and word to create and the continuum of the oral tradition from the mythic past of the Lagunas to the present are beautifully demonstrated by Leslie Marmon Silko (Laguna) in her introduction to her novel *Ceremony*. In the following passage, Silko describes how the Laguna creator thought the universe into existence:

> Ts'its'tsi'nako, Thought-Woman
> is sitting in her room
> and whatever she thinks about
> appears.
>
> ──────
>
> Thought-Woman, the spider,
> named things and
> as she named them
> they appeared.
>
> She is sitting in her room
> thinking of a story now
> I am telling you the story
> she is thinking. (1)

American Indians hold thought and word in great reverence because of their symbolic power to alter the universe for good and evil. The power of thought and word enables native people to achieve harmony with the physical and spiritual universe: to bring rain, enrich the harvest, provide good hunting, heal physical and mental sickness, maintain good relations within the group, bring victory against an enemy, win a loved one, or ward off evil spirits. Thought and word can also be used for evil against one's enemies. Because of their power and because words spoken can turn back on the speaker, for good or evil, thought and word should be used with great care. The power of the word to help the individual fit into the universe is exemplified in the Yokuts prayer below:

> My words are tied in one
> With the great mountains,
> With the great rocks,
> With the great trees,
> In one with my body

And my heart.
Do you all help me
With supernatural power,
And you, Day
And you, Night!
All of you see me
One with this world!
– Kroeber, *Handbook of Indians of California* 511

Coupled with the power of the word is the power of silence. Momaday, in "The Native Voice," calls silence "the dimension in which ordinary and extraordinary events take their proper places." In the American Indian oral tradition, "silence is the sanctuary of sound. Words are wholly alive in the hold of silence; there they are sacred" (7). The Mescalero Apache express this reverence for the power of silence. In "Singing for Life," Clare R. Farrer indicates that the Apache believe that the Creator God communicates through the power of thought in dream. People can utilize this channel through "communicating without words." To think a thought during this state is often all that is necessary for action to occur (151). Keith H. Basso concludes in "'To Give Up on Words'" that the critical factor in a Western Apache's decision to speak or keep silent was the nature of his or her relationships to other people. Apaches "give up on words" in such diverse situations as a meeting with strangers, the initial stages of courting, verbal attack, and the presence of someone for whom they sing a ceremony (153–58). Although attitudes toward silence vary from tribe to tribe, those outlined by Basso emphasize the importance of understanding the social customs governing the use of silence in individual Indian communities.

American Indians' desire for harmony is also reflected in their deep reverence for the land, another recurrent theme in their oral and written literatures. Because the earth nurtured them and because their tribal origins and histories are associated with specific places, Native North Americans have a strong sense of the sacredness of these places. In "Native Oral Traditions," Larry Evers and Paul Pavich say this sense of place is made possible by the "cultural landscape," which is created "whenever communities of people join words to place" (11). The words of a Havasupai Medicine Song, sung by Dan Hanna, illustrate tribal identification with the land:

The land we were given
The land we were given

It is right here
It is right here

Red rock
Red rock

Streaked with brown
Streaked with brown

Shooting up high
Shooting up high

All around our home
All around our home
– Hinton and Watahomigie, *Spirit Mountain* 108–09

American Indian authors continue to emphasize in their writings the importance of place, as Momaday movingly does in *The Way to Rainy Mountain:*

> Once in his life a man ought to concentrate his mind upon the remembered earth, I believe. He ought to give himself up to a particular landscape in his experience, to look at it from as many angles as he can, to wonder about it, to dwell upon it. He ought to imagine that he touches it with his hands at every season and listens to the sounds that are made upon it. He ought to imagine the creatures that are there and all the faintest motions of the wind. He ought to recollect the glare of noon and all the colors of the dawn and dusk. (83)

In an interview, Silko reveals the importance of cultural landscape when she describes how the river that runs through Laguna pueblo influenced tribal stories and her own work. Though muddy and shallow, the river was "the one place where things can happen that can't in the middle of the village." It was a special place where all sorts of things could go on. As an adolescent, Silko realized that the river was a place to meet boyfriends and lovers: "I used to wander around down there and try to imagine walking around the bend and just happening to stumble upon some beautiful man." Later she understood that these fantasies were exactly the kind of thing that happened in the Laguna Yellow Woman stories, a series of abduction/seduction myths, as well as in the pueblo's stories about those who used the river as a meeting place:

> These stories about goings-on, about what people are up to, give identity to a place. There's things about the river you can see with your own eyes, of course, but the feeling of the place, the whole identity of it was established for me by the stories I'd hear, all the stories. . . . (Evers and Carr, "A Conversation with Silko" 29)

Linked to reverence for the land is the emphasis on directionality and circularity that occurs frequently in American Indian oral and written literatures. Following the natural order of the universe, humankind moves in a circle from east to south to west to north to east. For many tribes, the numeral four, representing the cardinal directions, seasons, and stages of human life, is a sacred number often incorporated into the content and form of their literatures. Multiples of four and the number six, representing the cardinal directions plus the directions above and below the earth, are also common.

The circle symbolizes the sun and its circuit. It also represents the cycle and continuum of human life as it passes through infancy, childhood, adulthood, old age. Black Elk explains the significance of the circle to the Sioux:

You have noticed that everything an Indian does is in a circle, and that is because the Power of the World always works in circles, and everything tries to be round. In the old days when we were a strong and happy people, all our power came to us from the sacred hoop of the nation, and so long as the hoop was unbroken, the people flourished. The flowering tree was the living center of the hoop, and the circle of the four quarters nourished it. The east gave peace and light, the south gave warmth, the west gave rain, and the north with its cold and mighty wind gave strength and endurance. This knowledge came to us from the outer world with our religion. Everything the Power of the World does is done in a circle. The sky is round, and I have heard that the earth is round like a ball, and so are the stars. The wind, in its greatest power, whirls. Birds make their nests in circles, for theirs is the same religion as ours. The sun comes forth and goes down again in a circle. The moon does the same, and both are round. Even the seasons form a great circle in their changing, and always come back again to where they were. The life of a man is a circle from childhood to childhood, and so it is in everything where power moves. Our tepees were round like the nests of birds, and these were always set in a circle, the nation's hoop, a nest of many nests, where the Great Spirit meant for us to hatch our children. (*Black Elk Speaks* 198–200)

The circle is also reflected in many American Indian ceremonies and dances. Among the Mescalero Apache, for example, the girls performing the puberty ceremony provide a visual reminder of the circularity of time and the cycles of life by running around a basket four times (Farrer 150). In addition, circularity and cycles are often incorporated into the structure of narratives. For instance, mythic culture heroes or heroines may leave the community only to return after many trials and adventures.

A strong sense of communality and cooperativeness, reflecting Native Americans' belief in the importance of harmony, is another recurrent theme in American Indian literatures. Tribes often stress cooperation and good relations within the group, demonstrated in communal rituals, work and play, and decision making. Among many tribes, generosity, helpfulness to others, and respect for age and experience are highly valued virtues that enabled them to survive. Ella C. Deloria comments in *Speaking of Indians* (1944) that her people, "the Dakotas, understand the meaning of self-sacrifice, perhaps because their legends taught them that the buffalo, on which their very life depended, gave itself voluntarily that they might live" (14). In *The Life, Letters and Speeches of Kah-ge-ga-gah-bowh* (1850), George Copway describes how his Ojibwa father taught him the importance of generosity to the aged:

> If you reverence the aged, many will be glad to hear of your name. . . . The poor man will say to his children, "my children, let us go to him, for he is a great hunter, and is kind to the poor, he will not turn us away empty." The Great Spirit, who has given the aged a long life, will bless you. (24)

The following Keres song, which Paula Gunn Allen learned from her cousin, exemplifies this sense of oneness with the community and with the land:

I add my breath to your breath
That our days may be long on the Earth
That the days of our people may be long
That we may be one person
That we may finish our roads together
May our mother bless you with life
May our Life Paths be fulfilled.
    – Qtd. in *The Sacred Hoop* 56

Some themes are more culturally specific. For example, the narratives of the pueblo-dwelling Hopis tend to stress hard work, while those of the nomadic Navajos tend to emphasize movement (Courlander, *Hopi Voices* xxvii–xxix; Astrov, "Concept of Motion as the Psychological Leitmotif of Navaho Life and Literature").

American Indian oral literatures were most often transmitted aurally. However, some groups did record portions of their literatures. The Ojibwa, for example, used pictographic symbols to preserve their Midé (Grand Medicine) rituals on birchbark scrolls and other materials; other tribes, such as those on the Plains and Northwest Coast, also kept pictographic accounts. One of the few tribes to record their literature in books was the Quiche Maya of the Guatemala highlands, who preserved the stories of the origin of their culture in a work called the *Popol Vuh,* or *Council Book.* Their scribes continued to create books before the arrival of Western Europeans, who subsequently burned hundreds of hieroglyphic volumes. According to Dennis Tedlock, only four have survived, three in Europe and one recently discovered in Guatemala (*Popol Vuh* 23–27).

Native American oral literatures include both the works performed by American Indians within the communities that produced them and performances preserved in written transcriptions. These literatures reflect the mythology and history of the past as well as the experiences of the present. Although traditional ceremonies, myths, and songs follow general patterns established within the group over time, ceremonialists, storytellers, and singers create their own performances within those patterns. So long as the interpretations are accepted by the group as true to the spirit and content of the original, are performed appropriately, and achieve the desired result, many tribes may consider each performer's version as valid. The Iroquois follow this approach in their ceremonies, according to Michael K. Foster. After studying four Iroquois Longhouse speech events performed by seven speakers, Foster concludes in *From the Earth to Beyond the Sky* that their rituals are not memorized verbatim but are composed, or "literally built anew," each time a performer rises to speak:

What speakers share, and what gives continuity to the tradition across longhouse and reserve lines, is a set of composition rules for each ritual type (rules governing the statement, development and resolution of themes) and a common repertoire of conventionalized formulas. (vi)

Foster emphasizes that flexibility is the key resource for the speaker, who uses what works at the moment.

However, the degree to which improvisation is permissible may vary from one form of literature to another within the tribe. Discussing the magical rituals of the Cherokee in *Run toward the Nightland,* Kilpatrick and Kilpatrick state that master singers of rituals are "at perfect liberty to improvise a text if the spirit moves" them to do so. While the singers will not knowingly alter a text that has descended to them through tradition, they may occasionally elect to use only part of it (7). In *Singing for Power,* Ruth Murray Underhill comments that among the Papago, the storytellers work years to memorize the complicated mass of prose and verse that constitutes that tribe's bible. When the sun stands still, the storytellers recite this bible over four winter nights to those gathered in the ceremonial house. Although the storytellers may elaborate the prose with their own illustrations and explanations, they cannot do so with the verse. The words and tune of every song and the point at which they enter the story were given by Elder Brother, their culture hero. Nevertheless, as Underhill notes, some variations have crept in (12).

In *Kinaaldá,* Charlotte Johnson Frisbie indicates that improvisation is restricted in this Navajo girl's puberty rite and that an essential core exists in both myth and ceremony. Songs can be lengthened or shortened and verses within them ordered differently or even omitted, although the details of ceremonial songs per se may not be changed. Characters must retain their original names, costumes, and habitats; they must pursue their established journeys and perform determined acts. However, Frisbie also states that the timing and performances of the ceremony can vary not only for reasons inherent in Navajo customs and religion but also for more immediate, observable causes — available material, economic welfare, personal preference, environmental conditions, death of relatives, school restrictions, and regional customs and beliefs (82–84, 91–92). While tribal custom determines the degree to which improvisation is acceptable in communal rites as well as in traditional songs and narratives, American Indian artists also create oral literature that reflects their personal experience and imagination.

Even if verbatim memorization is not essential, the performance of oral literatures can sometimes demand great feats of recall. For example, the Navajo Night Chant, or Nightway, a healing ceremony, begins at sunset and ends eight and a half days later at sunrise. Because each ceremony, story, and song survived through time immemorial only in tribal memory, every generation faced the danger of losing its ancestral oral traditions if tribal members did not preserve them in their memories and encourage their performance. In *Indian Boyhood* Charles Eastman describes how his people, the Sioux, trained their young boys from an early age to assume the task of preserving and transmitting tribal and ancestral legends:

> Almost every evening a myth, or a true story of some deed done in the past, was narrated by one of the parents or grandparents, while the boy listened with parted lips and glistening eyes. On the following evening, he was usually required to repeat it. If he was not an apt scholar, he struggled long with his task; but, as a rule, the Indian boy was a good lis-

tener and has a good memory, so that the stories were tolerably well mastered. The household became his audience, by which he was alternately criticized and applauded. (42–43)

Many American Indians consider religious ceremonies, myths, and songs as too sacred to be discussed or collected for study by those outside the tribe. In an interview with Joseph Bruchac, Ray A. Young Bear (Mesquakie) describes his family's opposition to collecting the tribe's oral narratives:

> I have been consulting my Grandmother as well as other people, and I am afraid that it is simply impossible. The first and only stories we could have picked from Mesquakie people were published by William Jones, who was a protégé of Franz Boaz [sic], in the early 1900s. I tried to tell my relatives that there had been previously published material on Mesquakie people by our forefathers. I thought it would still be possible to, at least, try and share some stories now before they are forgotten. But this idea of trying to keep a culture free of what would be called cultural contamination is still very prevalent among the Mesquakie. It would be easier just to forget the stories and not publish them at all. If one attempts to do that, they are risking their lives. As my grandmother [sic] told me, "I used to hear stories about William Jones being here on the Settlement when I was young. He must have gone around with a bag over his shoulder, collecting these stories. But what happened to him? He went overseas and was killed by the Philip[p]ines or some tribe in those islands in the Pacific." She uses that as a reference and I think it is reference that must be heeded. (*Survival This Way* 348)

Some Indians and non-Indians believe that printing oral literature dooms it as oral performance; others feel that because stories and songs are fast-vanishing relics, performed only for anthropologists and folklorists, they must be captured in books in order to survive. In *Yaqui Deer Songs*, Larry Evers and Felipe S. Molina emphasize that their experience suggests the contrary: "that Yaqui deer songs and the traditions which surround them are very much alive and that more than sixty years of recording and printing versions of them has complemented and reinforced more traditional oral modes of continuance, rather than contributing to their disappearance" (14).

Because the verbal arts are performed arts, the recordings and transcriptions of them should incorporate as much of the performance as possible. Elizabeth C. Fine comments in *The Folklore Text* that although the literary model of the text is the most widespread format for folklore publications, it ignores recording performance context and style. As Fine makes clear, the ethnolinguistic text, developed by early anthropologists and continued by modern linguistic anthropologists, is primarily an accurate verbatim transcript of "connected discourse to aid linguistic analysis and to preserve vanishing cultural traditions." Early ethnolinguistic texts preserved little, if any, information about "the informant, setting, or cultural significance of the tale." Many of the published folklore texts may be reports or summaries rather than records of authentic performances (55, 61).

In addition, many of those who recorded oral literatures sometimes abbreviated or revised the texts to suit the tastes of the time. Aspects of style and performance that are part of the total verbal art of a given work include choice of ritual or ordinary language, repetition, structure of the work, revisions of the text to incorporate relevant allusions to the present, appeals to the audience, and use of the voice and body to dramatize the content. As Andrew O. Wiget emphasizes in "Telling the Tale," performance theory sees stories as "storytelling events." Performance is simply one of many ways of providing a "frame" for communication, which Barbara Babcock-Abrahams defines in "The Story in the Story" as "an interpretative context or alternative point of view within which the content of the story is to be understood and judged" (66). According to Wiget, "a frame signals to the receiver, through a variety of verbal and nonverbal markers, that a particular kind of message is being sent" that must be interpreted in a specific way to be intelligible (314).

In "The Poetics of Verisimilitude," Dennis Tedlock notes that Zuni narrators use a variety of the techniques of style and performance described above to create the appearance of reality. According to Tedlock, a few gestures seem to be standard usages in tale telling:

> A sweeping motion of a partially outstretched arm and hand may indicate the horizontal or vertical motion of a tale actor; a completely outstretched arm and hand, accompanied by the words, 'It was at this time,' may indicate the height of the sun at a particular point in the stories; the forefingers or palms may be held a certain distance apart to indicate the size of an object; and so forth. (166)

In keeping with the fact that tales take place "long ago," the Zuni narrators exclude modernisms from quotations and insert archaisms (167). Tedlock states that the narrators break the story out of its frame set in the "long ago" by alluding to the present, by such phrases as "It was about this time of year," centering the story action in the narrator's own house or alluding to members of the audience or their actions (168–69).

Whereas Tedlock bases his analysis of the storyteller's art on performances he attended and tape-recorded, Wiget bases his, in "Telling the Tale," on a videotaped performance by Helen Sekaquaptewa. Using photographs to illustrate his discussion, Wiget examines Sekaquaptewa's skill as a storyteller through her choice of words, the way she expresses the words, and the way she augments her tale with gestures and facial expressions. Discussing the kinesthetic features of her performance, Wiget notes, for example, that Sekaquaptewa basically sits in a neutral body position, erect and a bit forward on her sofa, hands in her lap and eyes slightly lowered. Though she varies this position, she always returns to it. Her most engrossing movements are those that reach into what is exclusively audience space, including actually touching the audience. Wiget concludes that gestures create suspense and climax (320–25).

The audience also plays a role in the performance of American Indian verbal arts. In *Verbal Art as Performance* Richard Bauman suggests that there is a "heightened intensity of communicative interaction which binds the audience to the performer in a way that is specific to performance as a mode of communication." The performers elicit the participative attention and energy of their audience. To the extent that audience members value the performance, "they will allow themselves to be caught up in it" (43).

Proper etiquette in many Indian cultures requires the audience to give the storyteller a gift, usually tobacco. Often the audience is expected to give a ritual response during the course of the story, to encourage the storyteller either to begin or to continue. If such encouragement is not forthcoming, the storyteller may stop. Audience participation becomes part of some ceremonies. Foster notes in *From the Earth to Beyond the Sky* that in the Iroquois Longhouse, the speaker for the men of the leading side begins the day's events with the Thanksgiving Address. At the end of each section, the men of the opposite moiety utter a term of assent. The speaker for the nonleading side then takes the floor (28–29). In *Yaqui Deer Songs,* Evers and Molina point out that in the Yaqui ceremonies the old men serve as ceremonial hosts and clowns. They are always interacting with the audience, which is drawn to them. "During their joking and repartee, they constantly play to their audience and expect laughter and verbal response." Even when the eldest member delivers the opening and closing sermons, he expects the audience to respond with the formulaic affirmative "*heewi*" (78). Another example of audience participation in ritual is described by Joann W. Kealiinohomoku in "The Drama of the Hopi Ogres." Kealiinohomoku indicates that the "ogre" ritual is unique because it is one of the few Hopi ceremonies totally performed in public and because its dramatis personae include members of the audience — Hopi children and some of their adult relatives. Those depicting ogres interact with audience members by incorporating them into highly structured, improvised scenes (38).

Accurate and appropriate translation is crucial to the preservation in English of American Indian verbal arts. Unfortunately, all too often translations have not been true to the original texts. In the past, translations were rendered in the Victorian or pseudo-biblical styles considered by non-Indians to be appropriate for literature and incorporated elements common to Western European literature but not present in the literature of native North America. In "On the Translation of Style in Oral Narrative," Tedlock reveals how Frank Cushing, whose translations of Zuni literature were widely praised in the past, interjected such oaths as "Souls of my ancestors" and "By the bones of the dead" into his translations. According to Tedlock, the Zunis themselves have no such oaths and never make profane use of words denoting death, souls, ancestors, corpses, "Powers," and gods (35). He also points out that Cushing incorporated devices, lines, and whole passages of his own invention. At the opposite extreme were the highly literal and often graceless translations of Zuni literature made by the followers of the great anthropologist Franz Boas, whose work and disciples dominated the field of American Indian anthropology early in the twentieth century (36–37).

Other translations molded individual songs to fit the translators' or retranslators' interpretations of what the texts were about. Recently, poets and critics have reworked some of the early translations to produce their own versions. Evers and Molina illustrate in *Yaqui Deer Songs* what can happen to the beauty of the original Yaqui text. Working in 1982 from Juan Ariware's original performance of a Yaqui song recorded on phonographic cylinder by Frances Densmore in 1922, Molina transcribed the following song:

Sikili . . .
  kaita va vemu weamakasu
    hakun kukupopoti hiusakai

Sikili . . .
  kaita va vemu weamakasu
    hakun kukupopoti hiusakai

Iyiminsu seyewailo
  huya nainsasukuni
    kaita va vemu weamakasu
      hakun kukupopoti hiusaka

Sikili . . .
  kaita va vemu weamakasu
    hakun kukupopoti hiusaki. (26)

Densmore, one of the earliest and most prolific recorders and translators of American Indian music, translates this simply as "The quail in the bush is making his sound (whirring)" (song 84, *Yuman and Yaqui Music* 157). Molina's translation demonstrates how much is lost in Densmore's paraphrase.

Little red [quail],
  walking afar where there is no water,
    where do they make the kukupopoti sound?
Little red [quail],
  walking afar where there is no water,
    where do they make the kukupopoti sound?

Over here, in the center
  of the flower-covered wilderness,
    walking afar where there is no water,
      where do they make the kukupopoti sound?
Little red [quail],
  walking afar where there is no water,
    where do they make the kukupopoti sound? (26)

As Evers and Molina make clear, Densmore's paraphrase omits the line, stanza structure, rhetorical structure, action, onomatopoeic representation of the sound of the quail, and other features that contribute to the song's aesthetic effect in Yaqui (26–27). They also demonstrate the dangers of generalizing about American Indian songs on the basis of faulty translations. This danger is exemplified by Kenneth Rexroth's comments in "American Indian

Songs." Using Densmore's abbreviated translations, Rexroth erroneously concludes not only that "the texts of almost all these songs are . . . extremely simple, but that most of them are pure poems of sensibility resembling nothing so much as classical Japanese poetry or Mallarmé and certain other modern French and American poets" (282). Although Densmore may sometimes provide paraphrases rather than translations, she nevertheless made invaluable contributions to the history of American Indian song. Indefatigable, she moved from tribe to tribe recording, transcribing, and translating or paraphrasing a voluminous collection of songs.

The history of the collection of oral literatures of native America begins in Mesoamerica in the books of the Maya. After contact, some of the Spanish priests helped to preserve the literature. In his *General History of the Things of New Spain*, Fray Bernardino de Sahagun included considerable native literature, which he translated into Spanish. His example was followed by other priests, who encouraged their Indian converts to record their cultural heritage. Tedlock notes in *Popol Vuh* that although the priests' primary concern was to prepare grammars and dictionaries, their interest encouraged their pupils to preserve their Indian literary legacy (28). In North America, some myths were incorporated into the accounts of Jesuits and other early explorers of the continent. However, the systematic collection of the oral literature of what is now the United States was stimulated by the publication of Henry Rowe Schoolcraft's *Algic Researches* (1839), which focused on Ojibwa culture and literature. Presses responded to the public's subsequent interest in the culture of the supposedly vanished "noble savages" and in their literature by publishing a number of life histories and autobiographies, most of which included selected examples of oral literature.

The scholarly collection of oral literatures did not flourish until the development of the anthropological and linguistic study of American Indian cultures in the late nineteenth and early twentieth centuries. In *The Folklore Text*, Fine credits John Wesley Powell, founding director of the Bureau of American Ethnology from 1879–1902, and Boas with establishing the ethnolinguistic approach that dominated the collection of American Indian verbal arts during this period. One of Powell's main reasons for collecting oral literatures was to provide samples of connected discourse to aid in learning the structure of Indian languages. The verbal arts also provided insights into Indian culture. Boas had a deeper interest in the literature itself. Fine concludes that his rejection of cultural evolutionism, respect for American Indian culture, and appreciation of the aesthetic values and important cultural functions of Indian folklore strongly influenced other anthropologists and linguists (19–22).

Tribes and individual scholars vary considerably in their categorization of oral literatures. Native Americans have their own distinctive terms to identify particular genres, which often do not correspond to Euroamerican genres. Dan Ben-Amos's history of the attempts to categorize oral literatures, in the introduction to *Folklore Genres*, demonstrates the complexity of the task. Ben-Amos stresses that ethnic-particular and cross-cultural systems may use different concepts of genre. Forms of oral tradition are not merely analytical constructs but "distinct modes of communication which exist in the lore of peoples" (xxv, xxi).

WORKS CITED

Allen, Paula Gunn (Laguna/Sioux). *The Sacred Hoop: Recovering the Feminine in American Indian Traditions.* Boston: Beacon, 1986.

Astrov, Margot. "The Concept of Motion as the Psychological Leitmotif of Navaho Life and Literature." *JAF* 63 (1950): 45–56.

Babcock-Abrahams, Barbara. "The Story in the Story: Metanarration in Folk Narrative." Bauman, *Verbal Art* 61–79.

Basso, Keith H. "'To Give Up on Words': Silence in Western Apache Culture." *Southwestern Journal of Anthropology* 26 (1970): 312–30. Rpt. in *Apachean Culture History and Ethnology.* Ed. Basso and Morris E. Opler. Anthropological Papers of the Univ. of Arizona 21. Tucson: U of Arizona P, 1971. 151–61.

Bauman, Richard. *Verbal Art as Performance.* 1977. Prospect Heights: Waveland, 1984.

Ben-Amos, Dan, ed. *Folklore Genres.* Austin: U of Texas P, 1976.

*Black Elk (Sioux). John G. Neihardt. *Black Elk Speaks.* 1932. Introd. Vine Deloria, Jr. Lincoln: U of Nebraska P, 1979. New York: Washington Square, 1972. Autobiography.

Bruchac, Joseph (Abenaki), ed. *Survival This Way: Interviews with American Indian Poets.* Sun Tracks 15. Tucson: U of Arizona P, 1987. Interviews with Paula Gunn Allen (Laguna/Sioux), Peter Blue Cloud (Mohawk), Diane Burns (Ojibwa/Chemehuevi), Elizabeth Cook-Lynn (Sioux), Louise Erdrich (Ojibwa), Joy Harjo (Creek), Lance Henson (Cheyenne), Linda Hogan (Chickasaw), Karoniaktatie (Mohawk), Maurice Kenny (Mohawk), Harold Littlebird (Laguna/Santo Domingo), N. Scott Momaday (Kiowa), Duane Niatum (Klallam), Simon Ortiz (Acoma), Carter Revard (Osage), Wendy Rose (Hopi/Miwok), Luci Tapahonso (Navajo), Gerald Vizenor (Ojibwa), James Welch (Blackfeet/Gros Ventre), Roberta Hill Whiteman (Oneida), and Ray A. Young Bear (Mesquakie).

Chapman, Abraham, ed. *Literature of the American Indians: Views and Interpretations.* New York: NAL, 1975.

Coltelli, Laura, ed. *Winged Words: American Indian Writers Speak.* American Indian Lives. Lincoln: U of Nebraska P, 1990. Interviews with Paula Gunn Allen (Laguna/Sioux), Michael Dorris (Modoc), Louise Erdrich (Ojibwa), Joy Harjo (Creek), Linda Hogan (Chickasaw), N. Scott Momaday (Kiowa), Simon Ortiz (Acoma), Wendy Rose (Hopi/Miwok), Gerald Vizenor (Ojibwa), and James Welch (Blackfeet/Gros Ventre).

Copway, George (Ojibwa). *The Life, History, and Travels of Kah-ge-ga-gah-bowh (George Copway). . . .* Albany: Weed and Parsons, 1847. Rev. ed. *The Life, Letters and Speeches of Kah-ge-ga-gah-bowh, or G. Copway. . . .* New York: Benedict, 1850. Autobiography.

Courlander, Harold, ed. *Hopi Voices: Recollections, Traditions, and Narratives of the Hopi Indians.* Albuquerque: U of New Mexico P, 1982.

Deloria, Ella C. (Sioux). *Speaking of Indians.* Ed. Agnes Picotte (Sioux) and Paul N. Pavich. 1944. Vermillion: Dakota P, 1979.

Densmore, Frances, ed. *Yuman and Yaqui Music.* BBAE 110 (1932). Music Reprint Ser. New York: Da Capo, 1972.

Eastman, Charles A. [Ohiyesa] (Sioux). *Indian Boyhood.* 1902. New York: Dover, 1971. Autobiography.

Evers, Larry, and Denny Carr. "A Conversation with Leslie Marmon Silko." *Sun Tracks* 3 (1976): 28–33.

———, and Felipe S. Molina (Yaqui). *Yaqui Deer Songs/Maso Bwikam: A Native American Poetry.* Sun Tracks 14. Tucson: U of Arizona P, 1987.

———, and Paul Pavich. "Native Oral Traditions." Lyon and Taylor, *A Literary History of the American West* 11–28.

Farrer, Clare R. "Singing for Life: The Mescalero Apache Girls' Puberty Ceremony." Frisbie, *Southwestern Indian Ritual Drama* 125–59.

Fine, Elizabeth C. *The Folklore Text: From Performance to Print.* Bloomington: Indiana UP, 1984.

Foster, Michael K. *From the Earth to beyond the Sky: An Ethnographic Approach to Four Longhouse Iroquois Speech Events.* National Museum of Man, Mercury Ser., Canadian Ethnology Service Paper 20. Ottawa: National Museums of Canada, 1974.

Frisbie, Charlotte Johnson. *Kinaaldá: A Study of the Navaho Girl's Puberty Ceremony*. Middletown: Wesleyan UP, 1967.

———, ed. *Southwestern Indian Ritual Drama*. Albuquerque: U of New Mexico P, 1980.

Hinton, Leanne, and Lucille J. Watahomigie (Hualapai), eds. *Spirit Mountain: An Anthology of Yuman Story and Song*. Sun Tracks 10. Tucson: U of Arizona P, 1984.

Kealiinohomoku, Joann W. "The Drama of the Hopi Ogres." Frisbie, *Southwestern Indian Ritual Drama* 37– 69.

Kilpatrick, Jack Frederick, and Anna Gritts Kilpatrick (Cherokee), eds. *Run toward the Nightland: Magic of the Oklahoma Cherokees*. Dallas: Southern Methodist UP, 1967.

Kroeber, A. L., comp. *The Handbook of Indians of California*. ARBAE 78 (1925). Berkeley: California Book Co., 1953.

*Lame Deer [John Fire] (Sioux). Richard Erdoes. *Lame Deer: Seeker of Visions*. New York: Simon, 1972. Autobiography.

Momaday, N. Scott (Kiowa). "The Native Voice." *The Columbia Literary History of the United States*. Ed. Emory Elliott. New York: Columbia UP, 1988. 5–15.

———. *The Way to Rainy Mountain*. Albuquerque: U of New Mexico P, 1969. Autobiography, myth, history.

Ortiz, Simon J. (Acoma). "Interview." Coltelli, *Winged Words* 103–19.

Rexroth, Kenneth. "American Indian Songs." Chapman, *Literature of the American Indians* 278–91.

Sahagun, Bernardino de. *General History of the Things of New Spain: Florentine Codex*. Monographs of the School of American Research 14. 13 vols. in 12. Salt Lake City: U of Utah P, 1950–82.

Schoolcraft, Henry Rowe. *Algic Researches, Comprising Inquiries Respecting the Mental Characteristics of the North American Indians*. 2 vols. 1839. New York: Garland, 1979.

Silko, Leslie Marmon (Laguna). *Ceremony*. New York: Viking, 1977. New York: Penguin, 1986. Fiction.

Spencer, Robert F., Jesse D. Jennings, et al. *The Native Americans: Ethnology and Backgrounds of the North American Indians*. 2nd ed. New York: Harper, 1977.

Tedlock, Dennis. "The Poetics of Verisimilitude." Orig. pub. as "Pueblo Literature: Style and Verisimilitude." *New Perspectives on the Pueblos*. Ed. Alfonso Ortiz. Albuquerque: U of New Mexico P, 1972. 219–42. Rev. *The Spoken Word* 159–77.

———. "On the Translation of Style in Oral Narrative." *JAF* 84 (1971): 114–33. Rev. *The Spoken Word* 31–61.

———, trans. *Popol Vuh: The Mayan Book of the Dawn of Life*. New York: Simon, 1985.

Underhill, Ruth Murray. *Singing for Power: The Song Magic of the Papago Indians of Southern Arizona*. 1938. Berkeley: U of California P, 1976.

Washburn, Wilcomb E. *The Indian in America*. The New American Nation. New York: Harper, 1975.

Wiget, Andrew O. "Telling the Tale: A Performance Analysis of a Hopi Coyote Story." Swann and Krupat, *Recovering the Word* 297–336.

Witherspoon, Gary. *Language and Art in the Navajo Universe*. Ann Arbor: U of Michigan P, 1977.

Mexican-American Literature

ADA SAVIN

In discussing the complicated history of Mexican Americans, Ada Savin begins by noting that they "have been here for 450 years and for 45 seconds." Mexican Americans claim both a centuries-long (im)migration and a presence prior to Anglo-Americans. Savin traces the origins of Mexican American literature while also providing a brief history of Mexican and Anglo contact. She devotes a good deal of attention to the development of the Chicano movement of the 1970s and discusses some of its major authors. Savin also briefly addresses la raza, a reference to the Indo-Hispanic heritage of Mexican Americans, and continues with a discussion of the rise of Chicana writers in the 1980s. Many of these Chicana writers began by rethinking prefeminist icons: la Malinche, the Virgin of Guadalupe, Sor Juana, and La Llorona. Savin notes that more recent Chicano writing tends to be autobiographical. She concludes that Chicano literature, along with other ethnic literature, continues to revise and challenge the literary canon. This essay originally appeared in New Immigrant Literatures in the United States *(1996), edited by Alpana Sharma Knippling.*

INTRODUCTION

Presenting Mexican-American literature as *one* of the immigrant literatures produced in the United States calls for a prompt caveat. Unlike any other group of immigrants, Mexican Americans "have been here for 450 years and for 45 seconds"; hence, some of them do not consider themselves immigrants, claiming that not they, but rather the border, has migrated. As a community they locate themselves somewhere between the native and the colonial experience, recognizing a centuries-long process of (im)migration while simultaneously claiming a presence prior to Anglo-Americans. Indeed, whether directly or indirectly, today's Mexican-American community traces its physical and spiritual presence in the North American Southwest to pre-Anglo-American times. One can claim, for that matter, that a writer like Rudolfo Anaya, whose roots in New Mexico go very deep, may well be a remote descendant of the union between a Spanish conquistador heading toward the

From *New Immigrant Literatures in the United States: A Sourcebook to Our Multicultural Literary Heritage,* ed. Alpana Sharma Knippling (Westport: Greenwood P, 1996) 341–65.

seven cities of Cibola and an Indian woman from the northern provinces of New Spain.

Given the historical precedence of Spaniards, Indians, and Mexicans in the American Southwest, the question that arises is, When did Mexican-American literature begin? For one thing, the *Relaciones* or *Narracion de los naufragios* (1542) by Cabeza de Vaca — arguably, the "father" of Mexican-American literature — preceded by almost a century John Smith's *Generall Historie of Virginia, New England, and the Summer Isles* (1624). One can argue that the sixteenth-century Spaniard's encounter with the American Indians prefigured the leitmotif of cultural ambivalence that has been the hallmark of Mexican-American literature to this day.

The Spanish exploration narratives can also be regarded as the beginnings of a distinct Mexican-American autobiographical discourse, much like their English counterparts — William Bradford's *Of Plymouth Plantation* (1630–1651) or John Winthrop's *Journal* (1630–1649). "Both Spanish and British narratives constitute the beginnings of American literature since they express a literary response to the New World and were shaped by the experience in the Americas" (Padilla, "Recovery" 47).

The annexation of northern Mexico, sealed by the Guadalupe Hidalgo Treaty (1848), brought the local population under the political domination and cultural influence of the United States, thereby signing the birth certificate of the first generation of Mexican Americans. In retrospect, the nineteenth-century confrontation between Mexico and the United States was the source of the first significant encounter between the two main cultural traditions facing each other in the New World — the Anglo-American and the Latin-American.

The origin of the deep fracture between North and South America is to be found in the particular circumstances of their colonization by the Old World. Europe projected two diverse images of itself onto the Americas, which, to this day, account for the underlying difference between the Anglo-American and the Latin-American post-colonial experience and their respective literary representations:

> The eccentricity of the English is insular and is characterized by isolation: an eccentricity that excludes. Hispanic eccentricity is peninsular and consists of the co-existence of different civilizations and different pasts: an inclusive eccentricity. (Paz, *Nobel Lecture* 3)

The distinction highlighted by Paz is particularly relevant in the perspective of this chapter, which argues that Mexican-American literature functions as a bridge between these two traditions while, at the same time, it is in the process of significantly expanding — spatially, temporally, and formally — the cultural boundaries of U.S. literature.

As Octavio Paz aptly pointed out, though diverse in their origins, both Latin-American and Anglo-American literature began as projections of Europe; they are written in "transplanted languages." English and Spanish "were rooted out from their native soil and their own tradition, and then planted in an unknown and unnamed world: they took root in the new lands and, as they grew within the societies of America, they were transformed" (Paz, *Nobel Lecture* 2). Historically the first literary works to feature a "double cultural and linguistic transplant" (through the use of the two languages, Spanish and English), Mexican-American writings thus seem "manifestly destined" to play a unique, crucial role within the cultural landscape of the Americas.

The adverse circumstances of the conflictual encounter between the United States and Mexico, followed by the political and ideological domination exercised by the former, did not manage to erase the artistic and literary heritage of the Mexican tradition. Issued from the *mestizaje*[1] of Indian and Spanish blood, the Mexican people are inheritors of a twofold tradition, one European, with a long-standing literate culture, the other indigenous, based on the orally transmitted wisdom of the Indian ancestors.

Actually, the intercultural contact following the 1848 annexation unwittingly created a new literary space within which cultural differences as well as potential compatibilities could be confronted and dialogized. Through its use of Hispanic and Indian motifs and traditions and, most strikingly, by bringing another language into play — Spanish — Mexican-American literature was to add new dimensions to the U.S. literary space. Over a century ago, in a letter to the city fathers of Santa Fe, Walt Whitman had foreseen the new vistas that could open if the Hispano-Indo-Anglo cultural contact were renewed:

> We Americans have yet to really learn from our antecedents, and sort them, to unify them. They will be found ampler than has been supposed, and in widely different sources. To that composite American identity of the future, Spanish character will supply some of the most needed parts. (quoted in Moquin 224–225)

This chapter intends to highlight the potential contribution of Mexican-American literature to the creation of a Pan-American literary paradigm in which the multiple cultural layers making up the New World imagination would co-exist. From this point of view, Chicano literary works (and, more generally, Hispanic writings in the United States) can be regarded as attempts at dialogizing the Indo-Afro-Ibero-Américan (Carlos Fuentes's term) and the Anglo-American traditions.[2] After a closer examination of the Mexican Americans' literary-cultural history, the chapter focuses on the dominant concerns and specific features of the literature produced after World War II.

LITERARY-CULTURAL HISTORY

> I find three levels of time-space, within which anybody lives and functions. The historical time-space, which is the collective time-space, one that describes reality as accorded by a consensus of people. There is a personal time-space that is very individual, psychological. It belongs to the individual and not to the collective

> group. And a third level, the mythological time-space that unifies
> the personal and historical time-spaces.
>
> – ALURISTA, INTERVIEW WITH JUAN BRUCE-NOVOA,
> *Chicano Authors: Inquiry by Interview,* 279

The Pre-Columbian Heritage

Rediscovered, sometimes reinvented during the Chicano movement years, Aztec religion, symbols, and mythology underlie much of present-day Mexican-American literature. The nationalist movement's myth of origin, Aztlan — a symbolic place on the map of the American Southwest, a counterpart to Plymouth, as it were — provided the Chicano writers with a necessary rallying symbol, thereby also opening up the vast repertoire of their ancestors' mythology to modern literary use. As the Chicano poet Alurista observed, Aztlan subsequently became a "state of mind," the rekindling of the old myth resulting in a new faith, in a new, assertive self-concept for the Mexican Americans.

The Spanish Colonial Heritage

Stricto sensu, Mexican-American literature dates back to 1848, the year Mexico ceded the large territory known today as the Southwest of the United States. However, as Luis Leal and Juan Bruce-Novoa, among others, have pointed out, there is a strong case for considering the writings of the sixteenth–eighteenth-century *cronistas* (chroniclers) as the literary predecessors of Chicano literature and, more generally, as forming part of the rubric of American colonial literature.

The colonization of New Spain's northern provinces has left behind an impressive number of *cronicas, historias, relaciones,* and *diarios* that provide the first descriptions of the region's countryside and inhabitants. Cabeza de Vaca's *Relaciones* (1542) or Pérez de Villagra's *Historia de la Nueva Mexico* (1610) are among the first written accounts of the cultural encounter between Spaniards and Indians in the present territories of Texas and New Mexico — the very site of the mythical Aztlan, which the Mexican Indians had crossed during their migration north to south on their way to Tenochtitlan (today's Mexico City) in the twelfth century. Four centuries later the Spanish colonizers began to explore, settle, and name the remote northern provinces of New Spain, a process that lasted well into the eighteenth century.

The "I"/"eye" of the Spanish explorers thus recorded and attempted to describe the realities of a world unknown to the Europeans: Cabeza de Vaca delights in the buffalo's meat, Pérez de Villagra writes about the helpful Indian vaqueros (the future cowboys) or names the mighty river that today separates Mexico and the United States, Rio Bravo.

The explorers' and missionaries' narratives — of Coronado, Onate, De Anza, and Serra, among others — testify to the gradual emergence of an identity that is somewhat distinct from that of the rest of New Spain. This difference can be ascribed, on one hand, to geographical distance from the center (Mexico), leading to isolation, and, on the other hand, to the frequent contacts, conflicts, and clashes with other populations — native Indians, French, Anglo-Americans. As Juan Bruce-Novoa has argued, Cabeza de Vaca's intercultural experience was to change both his and the others' perception of his identity: If in Spain he felt more like an Indian, in Mexico he was considered a Spaniard.

Mutatis mutandis, the Mexican Americans are facing a similar existential quandary: Not entirely American in the United States, they are not regarded as Mexicans south of the Rio Grande, either. The very essence of Chicanismo, according to some critics, this ambiguity accounts for the obsessive search for identity in Mexican-American literature, often in the form of (fictionalized) autobiographies.

The Mexican-Indian Heritage

No sooner had the Spanish-speaking population in the Southwest been reduced to the status of a foreign minority than the Spanish component of Mexican culture became a cult, especially in California (cf. Pitt). On the other hand, the native Mexican-Indian oral tradition has long been regarded with contempt, if not utterly ignored. Américo Paredes's pioneer study *With His Pistol in His Hand* (1958) focused scholarly attention on the folk base of Chicano literature. Paredes considers the *border corrido* as a peculiar Mexican-American expression of the cultural conflict between Mexico and the United States. Thus, Gregorio Cortez, the hero of the most famous *border corrido*, has become a Pan-Hispanic symbol of Latino resistance, popularized more recently through a television video. The *corrido* has accompanied the Mexican Americans' trials and tribulations north of the Rio Grande to this day, whether to express protest against social injustice or participation in events affecting the entire nation, like the assassination of the Kennedys or of Martin Luther King.

Many Mexican-American legends, myths, and folk beliefs trace their ancestry to Aztec and Mayan sources or to events linked with the 1519 conquest of Mexico. Having long been denied expression of their Indian heritage, the Chicano militant writers of the 1960s revived and sometimes reinvented this mythological legacy in their quest for cultural self-definition. More recently, contemporary Chicano writers have been using the legendary figures of La Llorona, La Malinche, or La Virgen de Guadalupe in a more personal, at times subversive, way (e.g., Bernice Zamora, Sandra Cisneros, Ana Castillo).

Folk beliefs in the existence of witches (*brujas*), *curanderos/as* (folk healers), ghosts, and evil spirits — some of which are part of a common Indian heritage of the Americas — have also proved to be a rich source of inspiration for Mexican-American writers from Rudolfo Anaya to Ana Castillo.

"Strangers in Their Own Country"

One of the few Californios to maintain a seat in the state Senate after 1848, Pablo de la Guerra was painfully aware of the changing power relationship that would silence his countrymen's political and cultural voice. Under the new circumstances, the first-generation Mexican Americans, who, in his words, had become overnight "strangers in their own country," felt the need to express their concerns about, and general attitude toward, the political, socioeconomic, and cultural upheaval. They did it mainly through the Spanish-language newspapers, of which about 132 were published in the Southwest between 1848 and 1900.

Among these, *El Clamor Publico* stands out due to the outspoken articles of its editor, Francisco Ramirez, whom Luis Leal considers a forerunner of the Chicano movement. While arguing the necessity for Mexican Americans to learn English, Ramirez nevertheless insisted on the need for a bicultural education as well as the publication of California state laws in English and in Spanish; thus, he defended outlaws like Joaquin Murrieta on the ground that they were ignorant of the criminal code because it had not been translated into Spanish.

Another important mode of expression was undoubtedly the autobiographical narrative, which has only recently received due attention. According to Genaro Padilla, the shock waves set off by the 1848 annexation may have generated an autobiographic impulse in the Mexican-American community:

> Social rupture led to a decontextualization of individual and communal life that required a form of verbal restoration of that community with which the individual had identified his or her very locus of meaning. Before relocating life in the new regime, the life of the past had somehow to be accorded purpose, dignity, integrity. Autobiographic social history served this re-integrative, psycho-social process. ("Recovery" 47)

The "autobiographic impulse" in Mexican-American writings has clearly persisted to this day. However, it has undergone momentous shifts in perspective matching the writers' collective or individual quest for identity in their old/new land; the relative emphasis placed on one or the other of the two cultural poles — Mexico and the United States — functions as the litmus test of Mexican-American cultural identity. This does not preclude the attempt to forge a "borderlands" identity, which is manifest in certain recent writings, like Gloria Anzaldúa's *Borderlands — La Frontera: The New Mestiza.*

The late nineteenth-century *memorias, historias, reminiscencias,* and *vidas* from archives in Texas, New Mexico, and California have brought to light the manifold contradictions of the Mexicano self shaped in the turmoil of both intra- and intercultural conflicts. The recent reexamination of these narratives has, by the same token, considerably altered the rigid, somewhat monolithic construction of the Chicano self proposed by the ideologues of the Chicano movement.

From Immigrant to Ethnic — Mexican-American Identity in the Making

The Mexican Revolution can be considered a "distant degree zero" of contemporary Chicano fiction insofar as, in most works written since the 1950s, it indirectly represents the starting point for the evolution of the Chicano literary hero in the United States. Actually, the only historical novel set during the 1910 revolution is José Antonio Villareal's *The Fifth Horseman* (1974), which can be read as an exploration of the Chicanos' Mexican past, while its mythic revolutionary hero stands as a counterexample to the negative image of Mexican refugees in American and Mexican literature.

In the first two decades of the twentieth century, the Mexican-American community and its culture got a new lease on life with the arrival of numerous political refugees and thousands of Mexican farmworkers and laborers. While the first generation of Mexican Americans had clung to their traditions against all odds, this second *entrada*, not of hidalgos in search of gold and silver but of peons in search of bread and job, ensured the revival of Mexican culture north of the Rio Grande (cf. McWilliams).

The early twentieth century witnessed the gradual crystallization of a Mexican-American identity distinct from that of the Mexicans'. The latter actually started evincing negative opinions on the Mexican-American *pochos*, who, in José Vasconcelos's opinion, had become "mexicano-yankee hybrids" through the betrayal of their culture of origin and the adoption of what he called "North-American primitivism." The author of *La Raza Cosmica* could not conceive of, let alone foresee, the gradual emergence of an intercultural borderlands identity that would bring together the Anglo-American and the Hispano-American worlds. Yet in the barrios of California and Texas this process was taking place, eventually turning this "invisible and inaudible minority" into a highly visible and articulate ethnic group.

DOMINANT CONCERNS AND MAJOR AUTHORS

The decades leading up to the Chicano movement saw the Mexican-American community engaged in a daily struggle for survival, which hardly left it time or opportunity for literary pursuits. Yet some of the most significant contemporary Mexican-American writers drew their inspiration from those very years when, as children, they had accompanied their parents on their journey north in search for a place of their own in the land of the gringos. The two landmark novels preceding the Chicano literary renaissance of the 1960s and 1970s — José Antonio Villareal's *Pocho* (1959) and John Rechy's *City of Night* (1963) — both draw their material from those years.

In *Pocho*, Villareal introduces the fictionalized autobiographic hero — the writer's adolescent alter ego — in the process of "transition from the culture of the old world to that of the new" (135). By presenting, in bildungsroman fashion, the Rubio family's difficulty in maintaining the old traditions under the day-to-day pressure of American society, Villareal is the first Mexican-

American contemporary writer to use the genre and to pose the cultural identity theme. With numerous variations, Chicano writers would explore, in their turn, the effects of assimilation on the collective identity of their community or on the private self.

John Rechy's first novel had an altogether different reception and legacy. Excluded for many years from the literary "canon" established by the nationalist standards of the Chicano movement, only recently have Chicano critics started reappraising his work, in which "ethnicity ceases to be an explicit subject, becoming one alluded to through the metonymy of the author's background" (Bruce-Novoa, *Retrospace* 101). As gay and lesbian topics have become increasingly present in recent Chicano literature, Rechy's work no longer appears marginal and isolated. Moreover, ethnicity itself is being treated in less blatant terms than in the 1960s and 1970s.

The political and social effervescence of the mid-1960s signaled the first conscious attempts within the Mexican-American community to break with over a century of Anglo economic and cultural domination, which had turned it into an "invisible minority." The Chicano movement's ideological agenda crystallized the claims springing from two fronts: the farmworkers led by Cesar Chavez and the students from the barrios, whose spokesman became Rodolfo "Corky" Gonzalez.

Some of the landmark literary works of the community were rooted in direct contact with the movement's commitment to affirmation of cultural pride, the struggle for civil and human rights and, most important, the ferment instilled by the Chicano student activists. In the early phase of what has been termed the "Chicano cultural renaissance," this contact was quasi-symbiotic, as in the case of the *Teatro Campesino* (1965), brought forth out of the farmworkers' struggle. Luis Valdez's *Actos* (e.g., "Las dos caras del patroncito" (1965) or "Los Vendidos" (1967)), brief sketches initially performed by Chicano farmworkers, were designed to primarily educate and entertain Chicano audiences through a Manichean satirical portrayal of Anglo and Chicano stereotypes in a specific social reality and use of the interlingual idiom of the people. Forever restless, Valdez would jump outside the defined boundaries of Chicano literature.

The other landmark work of the first stage of Chicano nationalism, Rodolfo "Corky" Gonzalez's epic poem *I Am Joaquin* (1967), was, according to its author, "a journey back through history, a painful self-evaluation, a wandering search for my peoples and, most of all, for my own identity" (1). Written first and foremost for the Chicano movement, *I Am Joaquin* prefigures its nationalist ideology, its search for a past ethnocultural unity as a springboard for the awakening of a collective Mexican-American identity. The poem "swept through the Chicano Movement like a popular manifesto, and it is still considered the best crystallization of the early Movement rhetoric in its stage of cultural nationalism" (Bruce-Novoa, *Retrospace* 77).

While the Chicano movement's role in the boosting of original literary creation was undoubtedly instrumental, in retrospect, one must also acknowledge its excessive ideological impact on most of the works written at the time. The monologic nationalist stance of the militant 1970s was probably an inevitable stage in the community's long history of cultural obliteration. But literature and the arts tend to resist ideological imposition if they are to be authentic. The desire to rekindle the community's collective memory and the need to reinvent a Chicano ethnocultural past or to write about one's own life in the barrio in the language of the barrio were certainly legitimate; but when the programmatic intention took over, it often yielded a literature of self-imposed ethnic stereotypes couched in linguistic clichés. As Juan Bruce-Novoa put it, "[T]he standard formula for a successful Chicano piece calls for five or six *carnales,* a dozen *eses* and *batos,* a sprinkle of Spanish and a well-placed '*Chinga tu madre*'" (*Retrospace* 16). Much of the didactic, overtly political writing of the period has long been forgotten.

However, the 1970s were crucial years for the subsequent evolution of Mexican-American literature, and the credit for putting the Mexican Americans on the contemporary U.S. literary map goes to the Chicano movement. Undoubtedly a watershed year for Mexican-American literature, 1971 saw the publication of major literary works in the three genres: poetry, prose (the novel, the autobiographical narrative), and drama. *Actos,* a compilation of *actos* written by Luis Valdez between 1965 and 1971, was published that year, as was Alurista's *Floricanto en Aztlan,* which remains to this day the best expression of the Chicanos' quintessential search for a collective identity.

One of the authors of *El Plan Espiritual de Aztlan* (1969), Alurista was the spokesman of *la raza,* a term abundantly used in the 1970s to highlight the Mexican-Americans' Indo-Hispanic heritage and to raise the community's awareness of the past and present domination, as well as the necessary affirmation of its identity (cf. the poem "When Raza?"). In consonance with the Chicano movement's ideology, Alurista's poetic universe is dominated by a dichotomous vision that pits the traditional virtues of *la raza* against the inhumanity of Anglo-America. From this point of view, his poetry, which rules out any possible dialogue with the Other, has become outdated; the monologic, didactic, and prophetic vision has given way to a more open, dialogic poetic mode in the past decade. Alurista's literary reputation and lasting influence lie more in the pioneering role he played in innovating a modern interlingual *ars poetica.* Defying the laws of the market, he resorted to frequent code switching not only between English and Spanish but also including black English, Nahuatl, or Maya, "the full range of colors, the full rainbow," as he said himself. In a way, Alurista's multilingual code-switching contradicts the dichotomous ideology that underlies his poetry (cf. "El sarape de mi personalidad").

Twenty-five years after its publication, Tomas Rivera's . . . *Y no se lo trago la tierra* (1971, translated as . . . And the Earth Did Not Devour Him) remains one of the few masterpieces of Mexican-American literature. The author's untimely death has probably deprived the Mexican-American literary community of one of its most gifted writers. Written in the third person, the book is a series of fourteen short stories and thirteen vignettes in which the narrator encapsulates a year in his adolescent life as the son of Mexican migrant workers. Taking his distance from the dogmatic precepts of the Chicano movement, Rivera was the first writer to create the Chicano as a complete figure in contemporary Mexican-American literature, which he considered part of the "whole American scene." The narrator-protagonist, clearly the writer's young alter ego, writes a bildungsroman of sorts, drawing both on the American tradition of the autobiographical narrative of a would-be writer and on the writer's knowledge and experience of Mexican migrant life in the United States. To this day, the novel strikes the reader by the astonishing skill with which Rivera used the stream-of-consciousness technique to give coherence to the apparently disjointed, embedded episodes that make up the book. An admirer of the quest for mental and intellectual liberation that has been so important for the Americas, Rivera was a searcher himself who succeeded in finding his particular idiom, which blends folkloric and (post)modernist techniques. Rivera's book received the first Quinto Sol National Award, sponsored by the publisher of the renowned journal *El Grito*. A whole generation of Chicano novelists, known as the Quinto Sol Generation, came to occupy central stage in the early 1970s, rendering substance and credence to the Chicanos' presence within Anglo-American culture.

Before turning to their works, brief mention has to be made of Ernesto Galarza's autobiography, *Barrio Boy* (1971), in which the author narrates the story of his assimilation to American life in Sacramento, California, during the 1920s. Although Galarza accurately renders the geographical segregation of the barrio, he draws a somewhat idyllic portrait of his smooth cultural and linguistic assimilation, which, however, did not prevent him from retaining the link to his Mexican roots. (Eleven years later, another autobiographical narrative that favored assimilation to the American society, Richard Rodriguez's *Hunger of Memory* [1982], was going to create a scandal in the Chicano literary community, which largely perceived the author as a *vendido* [a sell-out] to white Anglo-America.)

Galarza's book fits only marginally into the Chicano literary scene of the early 1970s. If Mexican-American cultural identity was a central issue with most writers, the emphasis was rather on re(capturing) a sense of the community's collective identity than on one specific, individual experience. Thus, authors like Rudolfo Anaya and Rolando Hinojosa, who have become the classics of Mexican-American literature, expanded the Chicano literary space beyond the here and now by turning to ancient myths and folk motifs (Anaya's *Bless Me, Ultima*, 1972; Second Quinto Sol Prize) and to regional traditions along a border area (Hinojosa's *Estampas del Valle*, 1973). Set, respectively, in New Mexico and Texas, the two novels dwell on the endurance and sense of determination of Mexican Americans who were not only recent immigrants to Anglo-America but also inhabitants whose roots date back many generations. While, in his subsequent works, Anaya remained very anchored in his native soil, somehow impervious to the influences of the outside world, Hinojosa's historical novels about south Texas are an example of "*mestizaje*, a cross-breeding of traditional and non-traditional North American and Latin American literary and cultural traditions" (Saldivar,

Dialectics 63). In 1976, Hinojosa's second novel, *Klail City y sus alrededores,* was awarded the prestigious Casa de las Américas Prize in Cuba.

Oscar Zeta Acosta's two autobiographical novels, *The Autobiography of a Brown Buffalo* (1972) and its sequel, *The Revolt of the Cockroach People* (1973), are both frenzied existential musings of an adrift Chicano lawyer in quest of his identity. Alienated from everyone, Acosta is caught up in the political move-ment of the late 1960s, when he becomes the lawyer of militant Chicanos in East Los Angeles. Although the *Autobiography* ends up with the protagonist's being crushed by those he had set out to help, Acosta has nevertheless come to an awareness of his ethnic identity:

> Ladies and gentlemen . . . my name is Oscar Acosta. My father is an Indian from Durango. Although I cannot speak his language . . . you see, Spanish is the language of our conquerors. English is the language of our conquerors. . . . No one ever asked me or my brother if we wanted to be American citizens. We are citizens by default. They stole our land and made us half-slaves. . . . Now what we need is, first to give ourselves a new name. We need a new identity. A name and a language all our own. (198)

Through its ties and orientation, Miguel Méndez's *Peregrinos de Aztlan* (1974) represents the transition from the Quinto Sol Generation to the post-1975 Isolated Generation of novelists. At the same time, *Peregrinos* signaled the Chicano writers' affiliation with the experimental Latin American New Novel. Within the United States–Mexico border problematics central to migrant Chicanos and would-be Chicanos, Méndez fuses myth and history with linguistic variants to create an alternative interlingual aesthetics.

The early and mid-1970s witnessed an unprecedented flourishing of Chicano poetry whose content generally gravitated around life in the barrio or in the prison (the so-called *pinto* poetry). As Francisco Lomeli has pointed out, "[P]erhaps the most refined poetic encapsulation of a marginalized Chicano character is José Montoya's 'El Louie' (1970), an eloquent eulogy to a dead *pachuco*" (*Handbook* 94).[3] The poem brings back to life the image of the dead *pachuco*:

> Kind of slim and drawn,
> there toward the end,
> aging fast from too much
> booze y la vida dura. But
> class to the end.

Montoya symbolically restores to the Mexican-American community an essential cultural signifier. Starting with the famous line "Hoy enterraron al Louie" ("Today they buried Louie"), the poem remains to this day the epit-ome of a Chicano poetics whose salient feature is interlingualism, the blend-ing of languages, mainly Spanish and English, into what Tino Villanueva has called a "bisensitive poetry," which goes beyond the binary phenomenon of bilingualism. According to Juan Bruce-Novoa, "Chicano speech (and poetry) expands both the connotative and the denotative range of words in both languages, creating not a binary phenomenon, but a new phenomenon unfamiliar to the bilingual" (*Chicano Authors* 29). This type of interlingual poetry was characteristic of the early 1970s, when poets like Abelardo Delgado with *Chicano: 25 Pieces of a Chicano Mind,* Raul Salinas with *The Trip through the Mind Jail,* or Ricardo Sanchez with *Canto y grito mi liberacion* tried to capture in a narrative mode the quintessential features of the Chicano — humane, in harmony with nature, a victim of the Anglo — the callous conqueror living in a dehumanized, sterile society. This essentially dichotomous stance, often accompanied by a didactic tone, actually went against the interlingual mode, which attempted to achieve a synthesis of the two languages, English and Spanish, into a third.

The publication of Tino Villanueva's *Hay Otra Voz: Poems* (1974) signaled the emergence of a distinct, powerful poetic voice; he considerably widened the range of Chicano poetry by composing intimate poems in which the poet drew his inspiration from writers like Dylan Thomas, Anne Sexton, Octavio Paz, or D. H. Lawrence, to whom he refers in "Love Taste." Villanueva also wrote interlingual poems about Chicano farmworkers, *pachucos* or *la raza.* Most remarkable was, and still remains, his "ability to slide along the spectrum of interlingual mixture from standard English to standard Spanish" (Martinez and Lomeli 169).

While, by the mid-1970s, poets like Alurista, Abelardo Delgado, and Ricardo Sanchez were still active, issuing, respectively, *Timespace Huracan, It's Cold: 52 Cold-Thought Poems of Abelando,* and *HechizoSpells,* two new poetic voices came to the fore with the publication of *Restless Serpents* (1976) by a Chicana poet, Bernice Zamora, and *The Elements of San Joaquin* (1977) by Gary Soto. The latter's vision of a sterile society from which God has disappeared, his windswept images suggesting a barren landscape, prompted Juan Bruce-Novoa to compare Soto's collection of poems to T. S. Eliot's *The Waste Land;* however, the persona's grandmother's migration from Mexico and the hovering, mistrusted figure of La Malinche turn *The Elements of San Joaquin* into a Chicanized wasteland.

Before Bernice Zamora, only one Chicana writer, Estela Portillo Trambley, had achieved public attention, with her play *The Day of the Swallows* (1971), followed in 1975 by a volume of short stories, *Rain of Scorpions.* However, Bernice Zamora's *Restless Serpents* poems prefigured the powerful emergence on the literary scene of the Chicana writers, whose voice had practically remained silent during the male-dominated Chicano movement. Deeply anchored in the traditions of her New Mexico ancestors, such as the religious rites of the Penitentes, Zamora's poetry is concerned with the spiritual condition of modern society and, to a large extent, with the condition of women in a culture of male-chauvinists traditions. Zamora's originality lies in her expanding the Chicano poetic discourse through poems of intertextual reference (to Shakespeare, Robinson Jeffers, or Hesse). In one of her most quoted poems, "So Not to Be Mottled," she masterfully conveys the complexity of Chicana identity, whose "divisions are infinite" — a definition to which many of her followers would subscribe, like Ana Castillo, Sandra Cisneros, and others.

In 1975 occurred another turning point in the evolution of contemporary Chicano fiction. While the Quinto Sol Generation writers continued to publish works conveying a macrocosmic, existential view of Mexicans/Chicanos meant to underscore their full humanity in somehow ahistorical terms, the writers of the Isolated Generation — Alejandro Morales, Ron Arias, and Isabella Rios — emerged independently onto the Chicano literary scene with novels that obviously modified the previously established paradigms. As Francisco Lomeli aptly put it:

> If the Quinto Sol Generation presents a horizontal view of experience, the Isolated Generation of 1975 advances a vertical conceptualization of marginalized social sectors. The former sought to legitimize what Chicano meant and the latter proceeds to probe into the meaning of Chicanismo with a magnifying glass. ("State of Siege" 186)

Thus, Alejandro Morales's *Old Faces and New Wine* (originally published in Spanish as *Caras viejas y vino nuevo*) signals a radical departure from other Chicano novels in its crude, microscopic focus on life in a hard-core, nameless barrio during the civil rights decade of the 1960s. Morales's characters are caught in a vicious circle of rampant violence and self-victimization that belie any moralistic, academic categorization, since dichotomies like oppressed-oppressor paradoxically coexist within a deconstructed world of perverted alienation.

Ron Arias's *The Road to Tamazunchale* (1975) displays a different kind of narrative experimentation; an admirer of García Márquez and Borges, Arias artfully mixes reality and fantasy in the protagonist's (the old bookseller Fausto) imaginary construct of his last days as if it were a novel. With Morales and Arias, just as with Zamora or Soto, Chicano literature showed the first signs of a shift away from the community-oriented sociopolitical writing of the previous decade to a more individualistic, personal vision of reality. The thematic and ideological criteria that defined a literary work as Chicano (the yardstick being the author's loyalty to the political goals of the community) seemed increasingly anachronistic in view of the aesthetic and formal evolution in the cultural production that the writers wanted and achieved.

Toward the end of the 1970s, it appeared that Chicano literature was losing its focus. The ethnocultural clichés of the 1960s seemed exhausted, while researchers brought to light Mexican-American literary writings of the past, and some, like Juan Bruce-Novoa, tried to open up fresh perspectives for a more diversified cultural production. Indeed, as of 1977, with Nash Candelaria's *Memories of the Alhambra*, writers started contesting the validity of the movement's ideals and Chicanismo itself, a move that grew in the early 1980s.

The late 1970s brought one momentous literary event: Luis Valdez wrote and directed the immensely successful play *Zoot Suit*, later turned into a movie by Universal Studios. The protean playwright, who had already been criticized by "mainstream Chicano circles" for his *Mitos*'s lyricism and escapism, now came under attack for selling out to the American mainstream

and its commercial theater. Valdez had creatively blended a historical
episode, the 1942 Sleepy Lagoon incident, with the *pachuco* literary tradition,
giving his musical docu-drama a Brechtian touch.

The Chicano literary space was definitely expanding, yet, as Juan Bruce-
Novoa has pointed out, in the late 1970s

> [t]he most significant change was not generic, thematic nor stylistic, but
> much more fundamental and radical: it was sexual. . . . The questions
> that Zamora, Portillo and other Chicanas raised about the oppression
> women suffered at the hands of men within traditional Chicano culture
> brought cries of protest from Chicanos. (*Retrospace* 86)

Chicanas responded with more or less overt feminist works, proclaiming
their solidarity with the Chicano movement's ideals of liberation but, by the
same token, unmasking the traditional male-chauvinist attitudes that persisted in its ranks. In some of her poems written in the mid-1970s, Lorna Dee
Cervantes, one of the most gifted Chicana poets, founder of the literary magazine *Mango* (1976), seemed to prefigure the creative potential soon to be
released by so many Chicana writers.

THE 1980s — THE DECADE OF THE CHICANAS

If the Chicano renaissance works had foregrounded the issue of Mexican-
American cultural identity (traditions, language, ethnic pride) in opposition
with the Anglo world, on the whole, these writings, largely written by male
writers, at best ascribed traditional roles to the feminine characters (cf.
Anaya's *curandera* [woman healer] Ultima). More often they saw the woman
as *la chingada* or altogether omitted her both from their works and from their
political and ideological preoccupations. The monological stance of Chicano
militantness allowed for no dialogue with the dominant Anglo-American
society, let alone with the Chicanas, who started venting their frustration at
being left out of the political debates of their *carnales* (brothers).

The official, static, and closed version of ethnicity proposed by the literature of the Chicano movement was bound to come under attack from other
voices in the community that had been silenced for too long; first and foremost among them were the women writers who gave Chicano literature a
new lease on life by opening it up to a dialogue both with itself and with the
American mainstream and other ethnic writings. At first reluctant, Chicano
critics are in the process of reconsidering Mexican-American literature, its
past and present, which involves an acceptance of the dialogic nature of
Chicano literature, whose textuality is characterized by an interplay of voices
and perspectives.

Chicana writers themselves started out by reconsiderations of "four prefeminist icons of *herstory* and female identity — La Malinche, the Virgin of
Guadalupe, Sor Juana and La Llorona — for each embodies important images
of *la mujer* that have helped define and circumscribe the roles of Latin
American women for at least five centuries" (Candelaria 143). This recupera-

tion basically consists in seeking the Otherness of the figures, which the male tradition has not recognized. Thus, La Malinche, the Indian woman who became Cortéz's lover and interpreter, long denigrated for having betrayed her people, is being revised by Chicana writers (Lucha Corpi, Naomi Quinonez, Sandra Cisneros, and others) who see her as a distant alter ego, an ambivalent figure caught in the difficult but rewarding enterprise of mediating between cultures. Likewise, the emblematic figures of La Llorona and La Virgen are given multiple identities, again in contrast with the closed, binary vision of gender in male Chicano writing.

While Bernice Zamora (particularly with "So Not to Be Mottled") and Lucha Corpi (*Palabras de mediodia — Noon Words: Poems* 1977) had paved the way for a feminist liberating discourse, during the early 1980s, Chicana writers made their forceful appearance on the literary scene. The year 1981 saw the publication of two very different books that were to become works of reference, as it were, for future Chicana writing: Lorna Dee Cervantes's collection of poems *Emplumada* and *This Bridge Called My Back: Writings by Radical Women of Color,* edited by Cherrie Moraga and Gloria Anzaldua.

Cervantes's *Emplumada* signaled the presence of a complex poetic persona whose intersecting voices made up a multifaceted identity blending the motifs of the Chicana, attached to her family's feminine lineage ("Beneath the Shadow of the Freeway"), revolted by the racial injustice in her land ("Poem for the Young White Man"), and intent on acting as a mediator between Mexico's oral tradition and the U.S. literate world in which she was brought up. Likewise, in her more intimate poems, Cervantes transcends the apparent cultural dichotomy that defines her by blending her two linguistic consciousnesses into one utterance through a process of hybridization, as in "Astro-no-mia":

> But all I could remember was that man
> Orion, helplessly shooting his shaft
> into my lit house from the bow.
> Y Yo? Hay bow. Y ya voy. (*Americas Review* 15.3–4 [1987]: 44)

Cervantes's second collection of poems, *From the Cables of Genocide: Poems on Love and Hunger* (1991), dedicated to Sylvia Plath, Frida Kahlo, and Violeta Parra, confirmed the penetrating feminist and human vision of her poetic universe, which she now opened up to intertextual references beyond the Americas (Neruda, Kundera, Duras, Lorca).

During the 1980s, poets like Ana Castillo (*Women Are Not Roses,* 1984), Angela de Hoyos (*Woman, Woman,* 1985), Evangelina Vigil (*Thirty an' Seen a Lot,* 1982), Pat Mora (*Chants,* 1984; *Borders,* 1986), Sandra Cisneros (*My Wicked, Wicked Ways,* 1987) and others confirmed the literary breakthrough of Chicana poets as well as their crucial role in deconstructing the monologic character of the 1960s and 1970s Chicano literature.

By addressing the interrelated issues of ethnicity, gender, and class from a depolarized perspective, the new Chicana poetic discourse was beginning to undermine the ideological strategies of exclusion both within the ethnic group and in relation to the mainstream. Moreover, as Wilson Dominic Neate has suggested, "the articulation of the subject in Chicana poetry may be appropriated by the practice of Chicano literature which must define itself in such a way as to undermine the ideological strategies of exclusion of the national group." (61). In other words, the example of Chicana writing should carry over to, and benefit, Mexican-American literature as a whole.

This Bridge Called My Back, a collection of essays, poems, tales, and testimonials whose editors, Cherrie Moraga and Gloria Anzaldúa, adhered to the ideology of Third World feminism, broke new ground in Chicano literature in that it viewed the woman of color's subjectivity as the locus of multiple, conflicting voicings in resistance to competing notions for self-identification. Gloria Anzaldúa quips, "What am I? *A third world lesbian feminist with Marxist and mystic leanings.* They would chop me up into little fragments and tag each piece with a label" (*Bridge* 205).

In 1983 Cherrie Moraga published *Loving in the War Years: lo que nunca paso por sus labios,* an innovative autobiographical work made up of essays, poems, and stories that are meant, in Moraga's words, "to create a kind of emotional/political chronology" of the author's multivoiced consciousness; with remarkable honesty and insight, Moraga probes her Chicana lesbian self to reveal the instrumental role of Mexicano culture's view of the woman, originating in the myth of *la chingada, La Malinche.*

In *Borderlands — La Frontera: The New Mestiza* (1987), Gloria Anzaldúa takes the race, class, and gender issues one step further by addressing their multiple intersections as well as the interrelations of post-colonialism, nationalism, and ethnicity. Her focus is on the exploration of Chicana identity within a specific localization, the United States/Mexico borderlands, a place of hybridity, struggle, and transgression. Through the uncanny mixture of genres (autobiography, historical document, political manifesto, poems) matched by the constant switching of languages (English, Spanish, Nahuatl), the literary text becomes itself a graphic expression of post-modernist *mestizaje.* The most original aspect of the book lies in the conceptualizing of the borderlands as an interstitial space, a painful but exhilarating collective experiment, possibly leading to the emergence of multiple, shifting, cross-cultural identities.

In the past few years, several Chicano writers have also focused their attention on the increasingly complex reality of the border(lands): Guillermo Gomez-Pena in his essay "Documented/Undocumented" (1988), Richard Rodriguez in *Days of Obligation* (1992), and Rubén Martinez in *The Other Side* (1993). In Chicana fiction two names have eventually made a breakthrough into major American publishing houses: Sandra Cisneros and Ana Castillo. In *The House on Mango Street* (1985), Cisneros's compelling series of vignettes makes up a kind of bildungsroman in which Esperanza Cordero, the author's alter ego, evokes her coming-of-age in a Chicago neighborhood and her gradual realization that she is meant to be a writer. The book has been compared to Galarza's *Barrio Boy* and to Rivera's . . . *Y no se lo trago la tierra,* although Cisneros's world is a heterogeneous one, devoid of the *pureza* ethic of her male predecessors. Renato Rosaldo's comment on *Mango Street* also holds true for Cisneros's second collection of short stories, *Woman Hollering Creek* (1991):

> What culture is losing in coherence and in "pureza" it is gaining in range and engagement. The politics of culture found in these short story cycles moves toward terrain of borders, spaces that readily include African-Americans, Anglos, schools, workplaces, and heterogeneous changing neighborhoods. (93)

Neither Mexican nor American, the hybrid persona of the narrator (a *Merican*), this modern Malinche, taboo-free, open-minded, and resilient like her famous ancestor, is negotiating a modus vivendi between her deep-rooted affinity to her own people (Mexicans and Mexican Americans) and the everyday reality of the Anglo-American world in which she was born and is living.

In her epistolary novel *The Mixquiahuala Letters* (1986), dedicated to the memory of the Argentinean writer Julio Cortázar, Ana Castillo also crosses physical, spiritual, and sexual borders, observing and recording the limitations inherent to both the Anglo-American and the Mexican cultures. Combining the subjective and the objective narratives in a quasi-ethnographic manner, the writer keeps a certain aloofness from each of the two societies, as well as from the Chicano community, for that matter. More recently, Castillo published *So Far from God* (1993), a novel set in contemporary New Mexico that daringly combines the world of magical realism with the cruel reality of today's wars, environmental issues, and diseases. Both Cisneros and Castillo have received the Before Columbus American Book Award for *The House on Mango Street* and *The Mixquiahuala Letters*, respectively.

The unprecedented flourishing of Chicana literary production has prompted many a literary critic to test new approaches to their works. Besides authors like Castillo, Moraga, Cisneros, and Anzaldúa, who are also engaged in literary criticism, a growing number of female scholars have published articles and/or edited magazines (e.g., Norma Alarcon and *Third Woman*), thus keeping up the dialogue within the Chicano/a literary community.

CONCLUSION

If the 1980s were primarily the decade of Chicana feminist writing, some Chicano writers of the previous generation continued to publish (Anaya, Hinojosa, Morales, Méndez), while a few new male voices emerged on the Chicano literary scene. One of the most promising was that of Arturo Islas, whose untimely death in 1991 left only two works, *The Rain God* (1984) and *Migrant Souls* (1990). In both books the narrator is, in many ways, the author's alter ego — a homosexual, physically handicapped academic — who writes a fictionalized autobiography that becomes "an act of exorcism, a ritual within which the writer is both confessor and collective sinner" (Sanchez, "Ideological Discourses" 119). Thus Islas, not unlike many a Chicana writer, resents the patriarchy of both Mexican and American society, with its gender roles, power relations, and values.

Richard Rodriguez's *Hunger of Memory: The Education of Richard Rodriguez* (1982) has triggered heated ideological debates that continue to send ripples in Chicano academic circles. The author's condemnation of bilingual education and affirmative action programs precluded an unbiased reading of this autobiography, whose main thrust, clearly stated in the title, was to portray the anguish of the immigrants' son, confronted with the passage from his native language and culture to those of the host country and his deep-felt need to retrieve what was so painfully lost in the process — the link to his family, to his Mexican roots. In many ways *Days of Obligation: An Argument with My Mexican Father* (1992) is an attempt by the estranged author to renew the dialogue with his parents, with their Mexican culture whose traditions and values seem to outweigh those of the pragmatic United States. It would seem that the tension between the self-made and the ancestral components of Rodriguez's identity is, if not resolved, at least relieved by the descent into past, into memory. Here's his confession in the closing chapter of his 1992 spiritual autobiography:

> As me what it was like to have grown up a Mexican kid in Sacramento and I will think of my father's smile, its sweetness, its introspection, its weight of sobriety. Mexico was most powerfully my father's smile, and not, as you might otherwise imagine, not language, not pigment. My father's smile seemed older than anything around me. Older than Sutter's Fort. (220)

Rodriguez's *Days of Obligation* features an important element that can also be found in other recent Chicano/a writings: the numerous cross-ethnic references in his book — to blacks, Japanese, Irish, Chinese, Italians, and others — seem to indicate their relevance in the construction of a composite Mexican-American identity within an increasingly multiethnic nation.

Thus, recent Chicano writing shows a marked inclination for the autobiographical mode (Gary Soto's *Lesser Evils: Ten Quartets*, Victor Villasenor's *Rain of Gold*, Floyd Salas's *Buffalo Nickel*, or Luis Rodriguez's *Always Running*), often with a focus on the United States/Mexican border or on Los Angeles as sites of encounter between the First World and the Third World (John Rechy's latest novel, *The Miraculous Day of Amalia Gomez*). In *Days of Obligation*, Rodriguez commutes between Tijuana and San Diego, where past and present seem to have exchanged roles. An autobiographical narrative of a different kind, *Diary of an Undocumented Immigrant* by Ramon "Tianguis" Pérez (1991) is unique in that it reveals a highly perceptive, intelligent, and witty observer of American life in the person of an undocumented immigrant who eventually prefers to cross the border again, this time legally, and return to Mexico. Guillermo Gomez-Pena, the performance artist and writer, clearly states his option for "borderness" as a state of mind and a way of life. More recently, with *The Other Side: Fault Lines, Guerrilla Saints, and the True Heart of Rock 'n Roll* (1993), Rubén Martinez has brought an internationalist, effervescent vision to the area.

Almost three decades after its renaissance, Mexican-American literature is certainly alive, probably in a more challenging way than ever. Echoing a heterogeneous community that lives in an increasingly complex society, the writers' response has been one of opening up to, acknowledging, the Other — be it the Anglo, the Mexican, or the Italian — and they have thus reached a truer knowledge of themselves. Together with other ethnic literatures— Native American, African-American, Asian-American — Chicano literature has successfully challenged and is revising the mainstream literary canon. *The Heath Anthology of American Literature* displays a multiethnic perspective that acknowledges the Hispanic contribution to American literature from Cabeza de Vaca's *Relaciones* to contemporary writers like Tomas Rivera or Sandra Cisneros. In the past ten years Chicano literature has also made a considerable breakthrough overseas. Universities in Germany, France, Spain, and Austria have been organizing lectures and international conferences on Chicano and, more generally, on Hispanic literature in the United States.

If, according to Octavio Paz, the great Latin American writers have actually transgressed the Castillan idiom, it would seem that the best Mexican-American writings are the result of a double transgression — that of English and Spanish. By explicitly and implicitly using each or both languages, the Chicano author does more than invent: He or she uncovers the latent, virtual possibilities of an interlingual-intercultural idiom. The most valuable Mexican-American writings — and the best is yet to come — actually invalidate binary oppositions. Rather, their existential, cultural, and formal raison d'être lies in a search for inter-American complementary differences and areas of confluence.

NOTES

1. A cultural term that favorably describes the process of miscegenation, the mixture of different racial backgrounds. Chicanos in the 1960s started using the term with pride to refer to their mixed-blood heritage, European and Indian.

2. Following the *Harvard Encyclopedia of American Ethnic Groups,* the terms "Mexican-American" and "Chicano" will be used interchangeably without the nationalist connotation the latter acquired during the Chicano movement of the 1960s and 1970s.

3. Originally zoot-suited Chicano youths in Los Angeles during the 1940s, *pachucos* came to refer more generally to Chicano "dudes" from the barrios as characterized by their dress, invented language (*calo*), and socially marginal behavior.

SELECTED PRIMARY BIBLIOGRAPHY

Acosta, Oscar Zeta. *The Autobiography of a Brown Buffalo.* San Francisco: Straight Arrow Books, 1972.
———. *The Revolt of the Cockroach People.* San Francisco: Straight Arrow Books, 1973.
Alarcon, Norma, A. Castillo, and Charles Moraga, eds. *Third Woman: The Sexuality of Latinas.* Vol. 4. Berkeley: Third Woman Press, 1989.
Alurista (Alberto Urista). *Floricanto en Aztlan.* Los Angeles: Chicano Cultural Center, 1971.
———. *Nationchild Plumaroja.* San Diego: Toltecas on Aztlan, 1972.
———. *Return: Poems Collected and New.* Ypsilanti: Bilingual Review, 1982.
Anaya, Rudolfo. *Bless me, Ultima.* Berkeley: Quinto Sol, 1972.
———. *Albuquerque.* Albuquerque: University of New Mexico Press, 1992.
Anzaldúa, Gloria. *Borderlands — La Frontera: The New Mestiza.* San Francisco: Spinsters/Aunt Lute, 1987.

————, ed. *Making Face, Making Soul. Haciendo Caras*. Creative and Critical Perspectives by Woman of Color. San Francisco: Spinsters/Aunt Lute, 1990.

Arias, Ron. *The Road to Tamazunchale*. 1975. Tempe, AZ: Bilingual Press, 1987.

Arteaga, Alfred. *Cantos*. Los Angeles: Chusma House, 1991.

Barrio, Raymond. *The Plum Plum Pickers*. Sunnyvale, CA: Ventura Press, 1976.

Brito, Aristeo. *El diablo en Texas*. Tucson: Peregrinos, 1976.

Bruce-Novoa, Juan. *Inocencia Perversa*. Phoenix: Baleen Press, 1977.

Bus, Heiner, and Ana Castillo, eds. *Recent Chicano Poetry*. Bamberg: Universitäts Bibliothek. 1994.

Cabeza de Vaca, Alvar Nunez. *Adventures in the Unknown Interior of America*. Trans. Cyclone Covey. Albuquerque: University of New Mexico Press, 1983.

Candelaria, Nash. *Memories of the Alhambra*. Palo Alto, CA: Cibola, 1977.

Castillo, Ana. *Women Are Not Roses*. Houston: Arte Público Press, 1984.

————. *The Mixquiahuala Letters*. Binghamton, NY: Bilingual Press, 1986.

————. *So Far from God*. New York: Norton, 1993.

Cervantes, Lorna Dee. *Emplumada*. Pittsburgh: University of Pittsburgh Press, 1981.

————. *From the Cables of Genocide: Poems on Love and Hunger*. Houston: Arte Público Press, 1991.

Chavez, Denise. *The Last of the Menu Girls*. Houston: Arte Público Press, 1986.

Cisneros, Sandra. *The House on Mango Street*. Houston: Arte Público Press, 1985.

————. *My Wicked, Wicked Ways*. Berkeley: Third Woman Press, 1987.

————. *Woman Hollering Creek*. New York: Random House, 1991.

————. *Loose Woman. Poems*. New York: Norton, 1994.

Corpi, Lucha. *Palabras de mediodia — Noon Words: Poems*. Berkeley: El Fuego de Aztlan, 1977.

de Hoyos, Angela. *Woman, Woman*. Houston: Arte Público Press, 1985.

Delgado, Abelardo. *Chicano: 25 Pieces of a Chicano Mind*. Denver: Barrio, 1969.

————. *It's Cold: 52 Cold-Thought Poems of Abelardo*. Salt Lake City: Barrio, 1977.

Fernandez, Roberta, ed. *In Other Words: Literature by Latinas of the United States*. Houston: Arte Público Press, 1994.

Galarza, Ernesto. *Barrio Boy: The Story of a Boy's Acculturation*. Notre Dame, IN: University of Notre Dame Press, 1971.

Gomez-Pena, Guillermo. "Documented/Undocumented." *Multi-Cultural Literacy*. Saint Paul: Graywolf Press, 1988.

Gonzales, Rodolfo "Corky." *Yo soy Joaquin*. Denver: Crusade for Justice, 1967.

Hinojosa, Rolando. *Estampas del Valle y otras obras*. Berkeley: Quinto Sol, 1973.

————. *Klail City y sus alrededores*. Havana: Casa de las Americas, 1975.

Islas, Arturo. *The Rain God*. Palo Alto, CA: Alexandrian Press, 1984.

————. *Migrant Souls*. New York: Morrow, 1990.

Martinez, Rubén. *The Other Side: Fault Lines, Guerrilla Saints, and the True Heart of Rock 'n Roll*. New York: Random House, 1993.

Méndez, Miguel. *Peregrinos de Aztlan*. Tucson: Editorial Peregrinos, 1974.

Montoya, José. "El Louie." *Rascatripas* 2 (1970): n.p.

Mora, Pat. *Chants*. Houston: Arte Público Press, 1984.

————. *Borders*. Houston: Arte Público Press, 1986.

————. *Communion*. Houston: Arte Público Press, 1991.

Moraga, Cherrie. *Loving in the War Years: Lo gue nunca paso pos sus Labios*. Boston: South End Press, 1983.

Moraga, Cherrie, and Gloria Anzaldua, eds. *This Bridge Called My Back: Writings by Radical Women of Color*. Watertown, MA: Persephone Press, 1981.

Morales, Alejandro. *Caras viejas y vino nuevo/Old Faces and New Wine*. 1975. Trans. Max Martinez. San Diego: Maize Press, 1981.

————. *Reto en el paraiso*. Ypsilanti, MI: Bilingual Press, 1983.

————. *Rag Doll Plagues*. Houston: Arte Público, 1992.

Pérez, Ramon "Tianguis." *Diary of an Undocumented Immigrant*. Houston: Arte Público Press, 1991.

Pineda, Cecile. *Face*. New York: Penguin, 1985.

Portillo Trambley, Estela. *Rain of Scorpions and Other Writings*. Berkeley: Tonatiuh International, 1975.

Quinonez, Naomi. *Sueno de colibri/Hummingbird Dream*. Albuquerque: West End Press, 1986.

Rechy, John. *City of Night*. New York: Grove Press, 1963.

————. *The Miraculous Day of Amalia Gomez*. New York: Little, Brown, 1991.

Rios, Isabella. *Victuum*. Ventura, CA: Diana-Etna, 1976.

Rivera, Tomas. . . . *Y no se lo trago la tierra*. Berkeley: Editorial Justa, 1971.

————. *The Harvest*. Houston: Arte Público Press, 1989.

Rodriguez, Luis. *Always Running — La Vida Loca: Gang Days in L.A.* New York: Simon and Schuster, 1993.

Rodriguez, Richard. *Hunger of Memory: The Education of Richard Rodriguez.* 1982. New York: Bantam Books, 1983.

———. "An American Writer." *The Invention of Ethnicity.* Ed. W. Sollors. New York: Oxford University Press, 1989. 3–13.

———. *Days of Obligation: An Argument with My Mexican Father.* New York: Viking, 1992.

Salas, Floyd. *Buffalo Nickel.* Houston: Arte Público Press, 1992.

Salinas, Raul. *Un Trip through the Mind Jail y Otras Excursions.* San Francisco: Editorial Pocho-Che, 1980.

Sanchez, Ricardo. *Canto y grito mi liberacion.* El Paso: Mictla, 1971.

———. *HechizoSpells.* Los Angeles: Chicano Studies Center, 1976.

Soto, Gary. *The Elements of San Joaquin.* Pittsburgh: University of Pittsburgh Press, 1977.

———. *Lesser Evils: Ten Quartets.* Houston: Arte Público Press, 1988.

Valdez, Luis, and El Teatro Campesino. *Actos.* San Juan Bautista: Cucaracha Press, 1971.

Valdez, Luis, and Stan Steiner, eds. *Aztlan — An Anthology of Mexican American Literature.* New York: Vintage Books, 1972.

Vigil, Evangelina. *Thirty an' Seen a Lot.* Houston: Arte Público Press, 1982.

Villanueva, Alma. *Bloodroot.* Austin: Place of Herons Press, 1982.

Villanueva, Tino. *Hay Otra Voz: Poems.* Madrid and New York: Mensaje, 1974.

———. *Shaking Off the Dark.* Houston: Arte Público Press, 1984.

Villarreal, José Antonio. *Pocho.* New York: Doubleday, 1959.

———. *The Fifth Horseman.* New York: Doubleday, 1974.

Villasenor, Victor. *Rain of Gold.* Houston: Arte Público Press, 1991.

Viramontes, Helena Maria. *The Moths and Other Stories.* Houston: Arte Público Press, 1985.

Zamora, Bernice. *Restless Serpents.* Berkeley: Disenos Literarios, 1976.

SELECTED SECONDARY BIBLIOGRAPHY

Alarcon, Norma. "The Theoretical Subject(s) of *This Bridge Called My Back* and Anglo-American Feminism." *Criticism in the Borderlands: Studies in Chicano Literature, Culture and Ideology.* Ed. Hector Calderon and Jose D. Saldivar. Durham, NC: Duke University Press, 1991. 28–43.

Anaya, Rudolfo, and F. Lomeli, eds. *Aztlan: Essays on the Chicano Homeland.* Albuquerque, NM: Academia/El Norte Publications, 1989.

Bruce-Novoa, Juan. "The Space of Chicano Literature." *De Colores* 1.4 (1974): 22–42.

———. *Chicano Authors: Inquiry by Interview.* Austin: University of Texas Press, 1980.

———. *Chicano Poetry: A Response to Chaos.* Austin: University of Texas Press, 1982.

———. *Retrospace: Collected Essays on Chicano Literature.* Houston: Arte Público Press, 1990.

Bus, Heiner. "Gender Roles and the Emergence of a Writer in Denise Chavez's *The Last of the Menu Girls.*" *Missions in Conflict: Essays on U.S.–Mexican Relations and Chicano Culture.* Ed. Renate von Bardeleben. Tubingen: Gunter Narr Verlag, 1986. 277–287.

———. "The Establishment of Community in Zora Neale Hurston's *The Eatonville Anthology* (1926) and Rolando Hinojosa's *Estampas del Valle* (1973)." *European Perspectives on Hispanic Literature of the United States.* Ed. Geneviève Fabre. Houston: Arte Público Press, 1988. 66–81.

———. "Homosexuality and the Chicano Novel." *European Perspectives on Hispanic Literature in the U.S.* Ed. Geneviève Fabre. Houston: Arte Público Press, 1988. 98–106.

Buxo Rey, Maria Jesus, and T. Calvo Buezas, eds. *Culturas Hispanas de los Estados Unidos.* Madrid: Ediciones de Cultura Hispanica, 1990.

Calderon, Hector, and José D. Saldivar. *Criticism in the Borderlands: Studies in Chicano Literature, Culture, and Ideology.* Durham, NC: Duke University Press, 1991.

Candelaria, Cordelia. *Chicano Poetry: A Critical Introduction.* Westport, CT: Greenwood Press, 1986.

Fabre, Geneviève. "Dialectics of the Masks in El Teatro Campesino: From Images to Ritualized Events." *Missions in Conflict: Essays on U.S.–Mexican Relations and Chicano Culture.* Ed. Renate von Bardeleben. Tubingen: Gunter Narr Verlag, 1986. 93–101.

———, ed. *European Perspectives on Hispanic Literature of the United States.* Houston: Arte Público Press, 1988.

Fitz, Earl. *Rediscovering the New World: Inter-American Literature in a Comparative Context.* Iowa City: University of Iowa Press, 1991.

Fuentes, Carlos. *Myself with Others: Selected Essays.* London: Picador, 1989.

Grandjeat, Yves-Charles. "Doxy and Heterodoxy in the Emerging Chicano Critical Discourse: Metacritical Notes on Criticism in the Borderlands." *Annales du C.R.A.A.* 18 (1993): 313–23.

Gutierrez, Ramon, and Genaro Padilla, eds. *Recovering the U.S. Hispanic Heritage.* Houston: Arte Público Press, 1993.

Herrera-Sobek, Maria, ed. *Beyond Stereotypes: The Critical Analysis of Chicana Literature.* New York: Bilingual Press, 1985.

Huerta, Jorge. *Chicano Theater: Themes and Forms.* Ypsilanti: Bilingual Press, 1982.

Jiménez, Francisco, ed. *The Identification and Analysis of Chicano Literature.* New York: Bilingual Press, 1979.

Kanellos, Nicolas. *Hispanic Theater.* Austin: University of Texas Press, 1989.

Lattin, Vernon, ed. *Contemporary Chicano Fiction: A Critical Survey.* Binghamton, NY: Bilingual Press, 1986.

Leal, Luis, et al. *A Decade of Chicano Literature. 1970–1979: Critical Essays and Bibliography.* Santa Barbara: Editorial La Causa, 1982.

Lomeli, Francisco. "State of Siege in Alejandro Morales' *Old Faces and New Wine.*" *Missions in Conflict: Essays on U.S.–Mexican Relations and Chicano Culture.* Ed. Renate von Bardeleben. Tubingen: Gunter Narr Verlag, 1986. 185–95.

———, ed. *Handbook of Hispanic Cultures in the U.S.: Literature and Art.* Houston: Arte Público Press, 1993.

Lomeli, Francisco, and Carl Shirley. *Dictionary of Literary Biography Volume 82: Chicano Writers First Series.* Detroit: Gale Research, 1989.

Lomeli, Francisco, and D. Urioste. *Chicano Perspectives in Literature: A Critical and Annotated Bibliography.* Albuquerque: Pajarito, 1976.

Martinez, Julio, and F. Lomeli, eds. *Chicano Literature: A Reference Guide.* Westport, CT: Greenwood Press, 1985.

McWilliams, Carey. *North from Mexico: The Spanish-Speaking People of the United States.* New York: Greenwood Press, 1948.

Moncada, Alberto Lorenzo, et al. eds. *El Poder Hispano. Actas del V Congreso de Culturas Hispanas en los Estados Unidos.* Madrid: Universidad de Alcala, 1994.

Moquin, Walter, ed. *A Documentary History of the Mexican-Americans.* New York: Bantam Books, 1972.

Neate, Wilson Dominic. "Re-Writing/Re-Reading Ethnicity: The Lesson of Chicana Poetry." *Missions in Conflict: Essays on U.S.–Mexican Relations and Chicano Culture.* Ed. Renate von Bardeleben. Tubingen: Gunter Narr Verlag, 1986. 53–73.

Olivares, Julian, ed. *International Studies in Honor of Tomas Rivera.* Houston: Arte Público Press, 1986.

Padilla, Genaro. "The Recovery of Nineteenth-Century Chicano Autobiography." *European Perspectives* (1988): 44–54.

———. *My History, Not Yours: The Formation of Mexican American Autobiography.* Madison: University of Wisconsin Press, 1993.

Paredes, Américo. *With His Pistol in His Hand: A Border Ballad and Its Hero.* Austin: University of Texas Press, 1958.

Paz, Octavio. *The Labyrinth of Solitude: Life and Thought in Mexico.* New York: Grove Press, 1961.

———. *Nobel Lecture 1990.* The Nobel Foundation, 1990.

Pitt, Leonard. *The Decline of the Californios.* Berkeley: University of California Press, 1966.

Rocard, Marcienne. *Les fils du soleil: la minorité mexicaine à travers la littérature des Etats-Unis.* Paris: Maisonneuve et Larose, 1980. Trans. E. Brown, Jr. *The Children of the Sun: Mexican Americans in the Literature of the United States.* Tucson: University of Arizona Press, 1989.

Rosaldo, Renato. "Fables of the Fallen Guy." *Criticism in the Borderlands: Studies in Chicano Literature, Culture and Ideology.* Ed. Hector Calderon and Jose D. Saldivar. Durham, NC: Duke University Press, 1991. 84–97.

Saldivar, José David. *The Dialectics of Our America: Genealogy, Cultural Critique, and Literary History.* Durham, NC: Duke University Press, 1991.

Saldivar, Ramon. *Chicano Narrative: The Dialectics of Difference.* Madison: University of Wisconsin Press, 1990.

Sanchez, Martha. *Contemporary Chicana Poetry.* Berkeley: University of California Press, 1985.

Sanchez, Rosaura. "Ideological Discourses in Arturo Islas's *The Rain God.*" *Criticism in the Borderlands: Studies in Chicano Literature, Culture and Ideology.* Ed. Hector Calderon and Jose D. Saldivar. Durham, NC: Duke University Press, 1991. 114–27.

Savin, Ada. "Lorna Dee Cervantes: Portrait of the Woman as an Artist." *Missions in Conflict: Essays on U.S.–Mexican Relations and Chicano Culture.* Ed. Renate von Bardeleben. Tubingen: Gunter Narr Verlag, 1986. 123–31.

———. "Langue, identité et altérité dans *Hunger of Memory* de R. Rodriguez." *L'altérité dans la littérature et la culture du monde anglophone.* Le Mans: Presses Universitaires du Maine, 1991.

——. "Bilingualism and Dialogism: Another Reading of Lorna Dee Cervantes's Poetry." *An Other Tongue: Nation and Ethnicity in the Linguistic Borderlands.* Ed. A. Arteaga. Durham, NC: Duke University Press, 1994.

——. "Course and Discourse in G. Anzaldua's *Borderlands — La Frontera.*" *Parcours identitaires.* Ed. G. Fabre. Paris: Presses de la Sorbonne Nouvelle, 1994. 110–20.

——. "Mexican-American Literature: A Bridge over the Americas." Binghamton, NY: Bilingual Press, forthcoming.

Sommers, Joseph. "From the Critical Premise to the Product: Critical Modes and Their Applications to a Chicano Literary Text." *New Directions in Chicano Scholarship.* Ed. R. Romo and R. Paredes. Santa Barbara: Center for Chicano Studies, 1984. 51–80.

Sommers, Joseph, and Tomas Ybarra-Frausto, eds. *Modern Chicano Writers: A Collection of Critical Essays.* Englewood Cliffs, NJ: Prentice-Hall, 1979.

Tatum, Charles. *Mexican-American Literature.* Orlando: Harcourt Brace Jovanovich, 1990.

Todorov, Tzvetan. *La conquête de l'Amérique.* Trans. *The Conquest of the Americas.* New York: Harper and Row, 1984.

Villanueva, Tino. *Chicanos: Antologia historica y literaria.* México City: Fondo de Cultura Economica, 1980.

——. Introduction. *Imagine* 1.1 (1984): vii–xxxvii.

von Bardeleben, Renate, ed. *Missions in Conflict: Essays on U.S.–Mexican Relations and Chicano Culture.* Tubingen: Gunter Narr Verlag, 1986.

——. "Gender, Self, and Society." Proceedings of the Fourth International Conference on the Hispanic Cultures of the U.S. Frankfurt: Peter Lang, 1993.

Ybarra-Frausto, Tomas. "The Chicano Movement and the Emergence of a Chicano Poetic Consciousness." *New Directions in Chicano Scholarship.* Ed. Joseph Somers. Santa Barbara: Center for Chicano Studies, 1984. 81–110.

African-American Literature: A Survey

TRUDIER HARRIS

*O*riginally *appearing in* Africana Studies: A Survey of Africa and the African Diaspora *(1998), edited by Mario Azevedo, Harris's essay surveys the field of African American literature. She begins with a discussion of oral tradition and slave narrative and connects these to the development of poetry, fiction, and drama. Her comments on poetry range from the eighteenth to twentieth centuries, with particular attention to Phillis Wheatley, Paul Laurence Dunbar, James Weldon Johnson, Langston Hughes, Robert Hayden, Gwendolyn Brooks, Michael Harper, and Rita Dove. Attention is also paid to the New Black Aesthetic or Black Arts movement and the role of jazz and blues. Harris's discussion of fiction and drama notes the influence of the slave narrative upon the novel form. She also comments on the less realistic novels of the Harlem Renaissance, which tended to stress positive images. According to Harris, African American fiction became more realistic in the 1930s with Zora Neale Hurston and Richard Wright, both of whom are discussed in greater detail. Finally, Harris provides a brief overview of drama, beginning with William Wells Brown and ending with August Wilson. She concludes by stressing the continued significance of oral tradition and the slave narrative in contemporary African American literature.*

INTRODUCTION

In order to understand African-American literature, it is first necessary to understand the roles that the oral culture and the slave narrative had in its formation. This chapter examines those traditions in relation to the written literature and surveys the development of each genre (poetry, fiction, drama). Issues central to the literature begin with the role of the African-American writer in relation to his or her community. Should a literate black individual devote a career to trying to improve the condition of the group, or should that person feel free to write out of individual desires and wishes?

From *Africana Studies: A Survey of Africa and the African Diaspora,* 2nd ed., ed. Mario Azevedo (Durham: Carolina Academic P, 1998) 329–40.

This intersection of politics and art dominated discussions of African-American literature well into the twentieth century. Issues include the representation of black characters: Should they always be complimentary or should they be realistic, even when they run the risk of damaging the group socially? In what language should literature be composed — black English or standard English? What of nationalism (the Black Aesthetic)? Who should teach the literature? African-Americans? White Americans? Others? Where should it be taught? English Departments? Black Studies Departments? Others? To whom should black writers address their works? The problem of ghettoizing the African-American creative effort was also raised in the twentieth century; black writers complained that critics discussed them only in connection with other black writers, not with the larger traditions of literary creativity. And today, the issue of the relevance of current critical theories to discussions of African-American literature dominate the energies of many scholars.

Major terms and concepts: The role of writers in their communities, influences on literary creativity, racism, slavery, slave narratives, folklore, oral tradition, Harlem Renaissance, protest literature, Black Aesthetic, Black Arts Movement.

ORAL TRADITION AND SLAVE NARRATIVE

A study of African-American literature naturally begins with the African-American oral tradition and with the slave narrative. Africans brought to the United States and enslaved were obviously not brought here to produce poems, plays, short stories, and novels. Nor were they here with any consideration of perpetuating their own cultural traditions. Thus thrown into circumstances where their bodies were emphasized over their minds, and where the usual bonds of language were absent, enslaved Africans adapted the English language and used it to communicate as best they could. Through this hybrid, they passed on what they remembered of their own cultures, combined it with what they witnessed on new soil, or created something totally new. What they communicated in the patterned forms known as folklore reflected the best of the values they wished to pass on.

Their narratives, legends, jokes, songs, rhymes, and sayings recorded a world in which they reacted to their circumstances as an enslaved group and in which they passed on imaginative ways of interacting within that world. Early tales reveal, for example, the discrepancies in the economic conditions of slaves and masters. In 1853 in *Clotel; or, The President's Daughter*, the first novel by an African-American, William Wells Brown recorded one of the earliest documented folk rhymes:

> The big bee flies high,
> The little bee make the honey;
> The black folks makes the cotton
> And the white folks gets the money.

It captures the thematic essence of the protest tradition that Richard Wright and other writers of the twentieth century would advocate so fervently. In a land so rich in resources and which professed to believe so strongly in democracy, it was unconscionable, these folk artists and literary writers would argue, for an entire group of people to be excluded from those resources, especially when those individuals had played a key role in the building of the country.

The song tradition, whether in spirituals, blues, or Gospel, similarly portrayed a people on the lower echelon of the social stratum who hoped for resolution of their plight in the afterlife if not in this world. Spirituals frequently suggested being done with "de troubles of the world" and going home to live with Jesus. While writers may not have advocated a literal interpretation of that tradition, the general tenet of the need for rectification of social conditions became a common theme in the literature. Music as an expression of the ability to deal with the troubles of the world similarly informs the literature, whether it is a Richard Wright character soothing her worries by singing in a short story like "Bright and Morning Star" (1938) or a character in James Baldwin's "Sonny's Blues" (1964) similarly singing to ease the burden of bearing her troubles. Music captured the general *weltschmerz* (pessimism at the state of the world; literally, "world pain") of being African and American in a country where simply being American was preferable.

Not only were the themes common to the written literature passed on in the oral tradition, but the structures as well. In the 1920s, Langston Hughes, in addition to adapting the themes of the blues, would adapt the AAB rhyme scheme of the genre as one of his primary literary structures. Thus compositions such as the following one from his "Miss Blues'es Child" became common:

> If the blues would let me,
> Lord knows I would smile.
> If the blues would let me,
> I would smile, smile, smile.
> Instead of that I'm cryin' —
> I must be Miss Blues'es child.

In addition to the blues, folk narratives also provided the shaping force for literary creativity. The structure of Ralph Ellison's *Invisible Man* (1952) is based on an African-American folktale.

Numerous writers drew upon the African-American folk tradition for characters and concepts. "Badman" heroes, for example, pervade the literature from Charles W. Chesnutt's Josh Green in *The Marrow of Tradition* (1901) to Appalachee Red in Raymond Andrews's *Appalachee Red* (1978). Conjure women and other healers modeled on characters from the folk tradition make their debut in Brown's *Clotel*, continue through Chesnutt's *The Conjure Woman* (1899), get transformed in Alice Walker's "The Revenge of Hannah Kemhuff" (1970), and emerge with true supernatural powers in Toni Morrison's *Beloved* (1987) as well as in Gloria Naylor's *Mama Day* (1988). Other writers and works that draw upon this tradition of characterization include Charles R. Johnson, *Faith and the Good Thing* (1974); Toni Cade Bambara, *The Salt Eaters* (1980); and Tina McElroy Ansa, *Baby of the Family* (1989). Traveling bluesmen are the subject of Langston Hughes's *Not Without Laughter* (1930) and Albert Murray's *Train Whistle Guitar* (1974). The man-of-words tradition, as exemplified in Muhammad Ali's rhymes such as "Float like a butterfly/sting like a bee/That's why they call me/Muhammad Ali," joins the preaching tradition as the focus of such works as Ellison's *Invisible Man* (1952), where mastery of language is the measure of reputation and effectiveness in the society. Other writers simply saturate their works with an aura of the folk tradition; these include Zora Neale Hurston, *Their Eyes Were Watching God* (1937), Ernest Gaines, *The Autobiography of Miss Jane Pittman* (1974), and Charles R. Johnson, *Middle Passage* (1990).

The slave narrative tradition, in which the protagonist documents (in the first person) his or her movement from slavery to freedom and from South to North, defines the autobiographical tradition that so informs the literature as well as the archetypal pattern of movement for literary characters, that is, from the South to the North. Perhaps the most exemplary of the slave narratives is Frederick Douglass's *Narrative of the Life of Frederick Douglass: An American Slave, Written by Himself* (1845), though Harriet Wilson's *Our Nig* (1859) and Harriet Jacobs's *Incidents in the Life of A Slave Girl* (1860) have gained prominence in recent years. Although it is technically classified as the first novel written by an African-American woman, Wilson's *Our Nig* nonetheless documents the atrocities of enslavement; since the action is set in the Boston area, the book is especially interesting for providing a look at bondage on other than southern soil.

Douglass and Jacobs fit the tradition of documenting atrocities during slavery, the process by which they learned to read and write, how they became dissatisfied with their dehumanizing conditions, the aid they enlisted in planning and executing escapes, and the free existences that awaited them on northern soil. Douglass's work is as much literary as it is historical, for he is an effective storyteller who molds characters and circumstances to best advantage in making his points about slavery. He is also a master of figurative language usually identified with poetry and other consciously created imaginative works. Jacobs's narrative is particularly important for documenting the creation of a female self against the backdrop of sexual abuses during slavery. It, like Douglass's narrative, also recounts the process of literary creation, the assistance these early writers received in structuring their works and in getting them published.

The major theme of slave narratives, therefore, found a counterpart in the consciously created literary works. The progression from slavery or restriction (the South) to freedom and opportunity (the North) provides a prevailing pattern in the literature. The Great Migration that led to the tripling and quadrupling of African-American populations in various northern cities between 1900 and 1930 illustrates the historical pattern as well. Writers who have their characters leave the South for presumed opportunities in the North include Wright in "Big Boy Leaves Home" (1938); Ellison in *Invisible Man* (1952); John Oliver Killens in *Youngblood* (1954), and a host of others.

Folklore and slave narratives, therefore, addressed the basic condition of black existence in the United States, of the discrepancy between a theoretical democracy and the reality of the failure of democratic principles. As the genres of the written tradition developed, they in turn were conceptualized, especially in the early years of development, with the larger issues of black life and culture in mind. Brown's *Clotel,* for example, is as much a treatise against slavery as it is a novel; it includes advertisements for runaways, accounts of dogs chasing slaves, abolitionist discussions, and characters who espouse one side of the slavery issue or the other. When Brown completed *The Escape; or, A Leap for Freedom* in 1858, that first drama by an African-American also found its subject in slavery. Frances Ellen Watkins Harper, who published *Poems on Miscellaneous Subjects* in 1854, became a popular abolitionist lecturer, as did Brown. Her poems, such as "Bury Me in a Free Land" and "The Mother," depict the consequences of slavery on the family life of African-Americans.

AFRICAN-AMERICAN POETRY

Although the poetry in the latter part of the nineteenth century would be engaged with political issues, that was less true of the first verses composed by African-Americans. Lucy Terry, who is credited with composing the first poem by an African-American in 1746, centered her composition upon an Indian raid in Deerfield, Massachusetts. As a slave in a Deerfield home, she naturally identified more with the whites than with the "savage" Indians; the poem, "Bars Fight," reflects her identification. It was not published, however, until 1895. The first African-American poet to publish a work in the United States was Jupiter Hammon, whose broadside entitled *An Evening Thought: Salvation by Christ, with Penitential Cries,* appeared on Christmas day in 1760. Phillis Wheatley, perhaps the best known of the early poets, published her *Poems on Various Subjects, Religious and Moral* in 1773. Brought as a child to the United States, Phillis grew up learning English and being encouraged to compose poetry in the Wheatley house in Boston. Her poems treat subjects as diverse as Africans being brought to America, the antics of students at Harvard, the military successes of George Washington, and the reception she received from the Countess of Huntington when she traveled to England. George Moses Horton, a slave poet in the country near Chapel Hill, North Carolina, put his talents to use in the service of the students at the University of North Carolina. He composed love poems and other sentiments at their requests. His first volume, *The Hope of Liberty,* appeared in 1829; a second volume, *The Poetical Works of George M. Horton, The Colored Bard of North Carolina,* appeared in 1845, the same year as Douglass's narrative.

It was Frances Harper, however, who retained the reputation as America's best-known African-American poet until Paul Laurence Dunbar's reputation overshadowed hers in the last few years of the nineteenth century.

Dunbar, born in Dayton, Ohio, in 1872, began publishing poems in 1893, when his *Oak and Ivy* appeared. A combination of standard English and dialect poems, the volume was well received and was followed thereafter by *Majors and Minors* (1896), *Lyrics of Lowly Life* (1896), and a host of others. He also wrote novels, the most famous of which is *The Sport of the Gods* (1902), which appeared just four years before his death in 1906.

African-American poetry in the twentieth century has varied widely. It began with the dialect tradition that Dunbar institutionalized, the remnants of which were around well into the Harlem Renaissance of the 1920s. James Weldon Johnson, whom Dunbar knew well, included dialect poems such as "Sence You Went Away" in his first compositions at the turn of the century, yet he recognized the limitations of the medium. James David Corrothers and James Whitfield Campbell also wrote dialect poetry. The tradition finally led Johnson to complain in the introduction to *The Book of American Negro Poetry* (1922), which he edited, that dialect had "but two full stops, humor and pathos." He longed for the day when African-American poets would be able to represent the complexity of black life and experience without resorting to "the mere mutilation of English spelling and pronunciation."

Certainly Langston Hughes's blues poetry in the 1920s was a move in a new direction, as was the folk poetry of Sterling Brown in the 1930s. Although Brown resorted to folk patterns of speech in *Southern Road* (1932), he did not rely on caricature and phonetic distortion. His characters, like those of Hughes in poems such as "Mother to Son," were able to retain a certain dignity and garner the respect of readers. Brown's successes in being more expansive in capturing the nuances of black language and life led Johnson to write a brief introduction to *Southern Road*. Another trend in poetry during the Harlem Renaissance was reflected in the works of Claude McKay, perhaps one of the most militant voices of the era. McKay's militancy derives not only from the sentiments he expresses but from his transformation of the traditional forms in which he writes. Using the Shakespearean sonnet, a form usually reserved for lofty sentiments of love, McKay documented the failures of democracy, painted the violence of societally sanctioned crimes such as lynching, and called upon African-Americans to take up arms against all who would seek to destroy them. In his signature poem, "If We Must Die," he urges oppressed people to "meet the common foe" and to "deal one death-blow!" for the thousand blows of the enemy. He concludes the poem with this couplet: "Like men we'll face the murderous, cowardly pack,/Pressed to the wall, dying, but fighting back!" His poetry certainly did not distort African-American experience in the way that Johnson believed dialect poetry did.

Perhaps Johnson's call for a different kind of poetry was more fully realized in the academic verses of Robert Hayden and Gwendolyn Brooks in the 1940s. These poets, steeped in the western traditions of verse, structure, composition, and density of language, were judged to be successful by the more literary poetic establishments in the country. Hayden published *Heart-Shape in the Dust* in 1940, which picks up some of the themes of the writers of the Harlem Renaissance, especially questions of identity. By 1948 and his publication of *The Lion and the Archer,* however, he had dramatically altered his style to reflect the influence of such poets as Gerald Manley Hopkins, Stephen Spender, C. Day Lewis, and Rainer Maria Rilke; the result was six poems generally judged to be "baroque" in structure and execution. These include "A Ballad of Remembrance" and "Homage to the Empress of the Blues" (Bessie Smith). A later poem, "Middle Passage," which describes the transportation of Africans to the West Indies and other parts of the New World for purposes of enslavement, is one of the most anthologized of Hayden's works. Like Hayden, Brooks preferred the density and structure of poetry that reflected white western influences upon her. Her subjects are certainly those of African-American life and experience, but they are shrouded in styles that appear at times to be antithetical to the very experiences she records. Her first volume, *A Street in Bronzeville* (1945), focuses on black people on the South side of Chicago and recounts occurrences in their everyday lives; narrative is the major technique she employs. She won the Pulitzer Prize for *Annie Allen* (1949), which is loosely based on the *Aeneid;* it follows a young girl growing up in a Chicago tenement. Although the volume was judged to be difficult and self-conscious, it nonetheless received more praise than not.

The New Black Aesthetic movement of the 1960s brought a poetic revolution in its wake. It introduced a group of poets who are still publishing today. Nikki Giovanni, Haki Madhubuti (formerly Don L. Lee), Amiri Baraka (formerly LeRoi Jones), Sonia Sanchez, and others fashioned the poets' response to social change during this period. Advocating a nationalistic approach to literature, they called upon black people to take an active role in freeing themselves from a racist, undemocratic society. They also provided the path by which blacks were to arrive at being a nation of African-Americans. They were to change their hair and clothing styles, their patterns of behavior, and even their names; it became the age of dashikis and afros. The nationalistic bent was reflected in the language of the poetry itself; it attempted to imitate speech patterns and colloquialisms of common black folk, and it consciously sought to dissociate itself with the conventions of western poetry. New words were created ("blkpoets," "nationbuilding," "u," "bes"), and structures were designed to resemble African-American cultural forms such as jazz, not traditional sonnets or free verse.

There were still poets during this period who continued in the more traditional veins, including Robert Hayden and Michael Harper. Like Madhubuti and others, however, Harper did give attention to African-American themes and structures, including adapting stanzaic forms based on compositions by jazz great John Coltrane. The difference is that Harper did not alter his poetry as radically as did some of the younger poets; nor was he as consciously militant. Brooks joined the younger poets in reevaluating her role in relation to the black community as well as in modifying her stanzaic forms. She published several small volumes for children in the 1960s and 1970s and wrote a poem on the occasion of Harold Washington being elected mayor of Chicago, a first for a black politician.

Brooks's success in winning the Pulitzer Prize in 1950 for *Annie Allen* (1949) was matched in the mid-1980s when newcomer Rita Dove won the Pulitzer Prize for her volume, *Thomas and Beulah* (1986). Focusing on the relationship between a man and his wife over an extended period of time, the volume alternates voices between Thomas and Beulah, allowing them to recount and record their own perceptions. The collection illustrated that less self-conscious structures and themes in poetry could be equally appealing to a panel of judges for one of the most prestigious literary prizes currently available.

African-American Fiction and Drama

Fiction moved from its dual function as slave narrative and literature in the mid-nineteenth century, to romance and imitation of white writers in the late nineteenth century, to the autobiographical mode and more consciously designed protest novels in the twentieth century. Chesnutt explored the color problem in *The House Behind the Cedars* (1900), a novel focusing on a light-skinned black woman whose brief attempt to pass for white ends in disaster. He also reflects social concerns in *The Marrow of Tradition* (1901), a novel about the Wilmington, North Carolina, riot of 1898. On that occasion, black people who tried to vote were attacked and many of them killed by the whites who were intent upon preserving white supremacy.

The influence of the slave narrative upon the novel form can be seen in the autobiographical mode of *The Autobiography of An Ex-Colored Man* (1912), which James Weldon Johnson published anonymously. Johnson executed the first-person narrative device so well that readers believed the novel was indeed the historical life story of its author. The novels follows the life of a talented mulatto musician who is caught between the opportunities his talent offers and the limitations his classification as a Negro ultimately brings. He finally opts to deny his black ancestry and "pass" for white. It was only when Johnson acknowledged authorship of the book in 1927 that tales of its authenticity abated. Indeed, Johnson recounted attending a party prior to 1927 in which one of the guests "confided" to the gathering that he was the author of *The Autobiography of An Ex-Colored Man.*

Fiction published by writers of the Harlem Renaissance ranged from Jean Toomer's *Cane* (1923), which (to a degree) romanticizes black life in Georgia, to Claude McKay's *Home to Harlem* (1929), an account of the adventures of a fun-loving world traveler. It also included the genteel tradition of fiction writing represented by Nella Larsen's *Quicksand* (1928) and *Passing* (1929), and Jessie Fauset's *Plum Bun* (1924). Fauset, who assisted W. E. B. Du Bois in editing the *Crisis* magazine in which many of the Renaissance writers were published, held *salons* at her Harlem apartment at which invited guests were expected to hold conversations in French about the latest developments in literature or world affairs.

One problem with these early novels was that very seldom were African-Americans represented realistically in them. Indeed, there was a general movement in the first three decades of the twentieth century that might be referred to as "the best foot forward" tradition; writers were encouraged to portray complimentary images of African-Americans. Characters should be engaged in pursuits that were in keeping with the objectives of the larger society. Therefore, general principles of democracy were to be upheld and education was a goal to be valued, as were habits of morality and cleanliness. "Bad niggers," whether male or female, were best left out of the literature. The belief that such positive images were important led in 1926 to a forum in *Crisis* magazine. It was entitled "The Negro in Art: How Shall He Be Portrayed? A Symposium." The forum received responses from Sherwood Anderson, Benjamin Brawley, Charles W. Chesnutt, Countee Cullen, W. E. B. Du Bois, Jessie Fauset, Langston Hughes, Georgia Douglas Johnson, Alfred A. Knopf, Sinclair Lewis, Vachel Lindsay, H. L. Mencken, Joel Spingarn, and Walter White.

Fictional portraits of African-Americans began to be more realistic in the decade of the 1930s. Zora Neale Hurston depicted a black preacher in *Jonah's Gourd Vine* (1934) that any reader would recognize. Her portrait of Janie Crawford Logan Starks Killicks in *Their Eyes Were Watching God* (1937) brought a new dimension in realism to portraits of African-American female characters. Janie is a working-class woman who prefers spiritual fulfillment to gentility. After two disastrous marriages, she finally finds happiness with an itinerant laborer who takes her to pick beans in the Florida muck. The novel does not raise large political issues, although the social issues of woman's place in the society and what sacrifices she must make to find personal happiness are certainly important ones.

Hurston's more individually focused issues gave way to the politics of Richard Wright, who dismissed her work because she did not write as consciously in the protest tradition as he would have expected. For Wright, any black author should use his or her pen to point out the hypocrisies in American democracy, how black people were ground under the heels of white privilege and prejudice. He began such depictions in his first collection of short stories, *Uncle Tom's Children*, which was published in 1938. Almost all the stories are violent, and at least two of them embrace the communist philosophy to which Wright was becoming attracted at this time; he believed that African-Americans had a better chance of obtaining democracy in America through that philosophy. His stories document black people being lynched and shot, denied medical services or the sympathy that should attend them, beaten by mobs, and burned alive. The few who decide to fight back, such as Silas in "Long Black Song," only end up being killed more dramatically. However, in "Fire and Cloud," one of the stories that embraces communist philosophy, Reverend Taylor is able to gather white and black working-class people together to put pressure on a city government to provide food during the Depression. Before that possible hope, though, characters such as Big Boy in "Big Boy Leaves Home" and Mann in "Down by the Riverside" are simply buffeted by the misfortunes of the societies in which they live. They must either escape to the North or die in the attempt.

Wright's hard-hitting approach to fiction continued in 1940 with the publication of *Native Son,* his most famous work in the protest tradition. It posits that black men in America are so confined physically and psychologically that the fear they sometimes experience can drive them to kill almost instinctively. Bigger Thomas does just that when he is found in the bedroom of his white employer's daughter, whom he has helped there because she was in a drunken stupor. Smothering Mary Dalton to death gives him a feeling of horror, but also one of exhilaration, for it is the first time in his life that he has acted against the wishes of the white power structure.

Other novels from the forties that fit into the protest tradition include Chester Himes's *If He Hollers Let Him Go* (1945), about a black man forced to join the military or be sent to prison because he was accused of raping a white woman, and Ann Petry's *The Street* (1946), about a black woman who suffers the stings of poverty and sexual politics when she tries to rear her son alone in Harlem. Such literary voices did not portend a particularly inviting future for African-Americans. It would be the next decade before writers could assert with authority that the promise of American democracy did indeed apply to African-Americans.

That authoritative voice belonged to Ralph Ellison, who asserted in *Invisible Man* (1952) that blacks should "affirm the principles on which the country was founded" — even when the day-to-day execution of those principles seemed to leave them out of the great American experiment. His optimistic voice for the larger nationalist agenda led into the cultural nationalism that would inform the fiction of the 1960s, such as John A. Williams's *The Man Who Cried I Am* (1967), which asserts that blacks must fight as best they can against the forces of repression.

More focus on the black community tended to occupy fiction writers in the 1970s, which began with Toni Morrison's publication of *The Bluest Eye.* That novel indicts the entire society for judging little black girls by standards of beauty that are culturally antithetical to them, but it especially places the blame on unthinking, unfeeling members of the black middle class. The pattern of focusing on black communities continued in the 1980s with Toni Cade Bambara's *The Salt Eaters* (1980), Alice Walker's *The Color Purple* (1982), Terry McMillan's *Mama* (1987) and *Disappearing Acts* (1989), and Tina McElroy Ansa's *Baby of the Family* (1989).

The last couple of decades have also witnessed an outpouring of dramas by African-Americans. The dramatic scene is a far cry from where it started in 1858 with Brown's *The Escape; or, A Leap for Freedom.* Brown's play was written to be read rather than produced; it was not until the musical comedy era of the 1880s and 1890s that black playwrights saw their works on the stage. One of the earliest such achievements was a collaboration between James Weldon Johnson and Paul Laurence Dunbar. They wrote music and lyrics for *Clorindy, or the Origin of the Cakewalk* (1898). In 1900 Dunbar collaborated with black composer Will Marion Cook in the production of *Uncle Eph's Christmas.*

The first three decades of the twentieth century did not see much development in traditional dramas by black Americans, although the musical comedy tradition was popular until well into the 1920s. The year 1920 saw the publication of Angelina Weld Grimké's *Rachel: A Play in Three Acts* (produced in 1916), but it would be well into the 1930s before a black writer completed a drama that would have a successful run on Broadway. That distinction belonged to Langston Hughes, whose *Mulatto,* a dramatic rewrite of his short story, "Father and Son," ran on Broadway from 1935 to 1936, as well as for an additional two years on tour.

In the 1930s and 1940s, several black theatre companies were formed; most of their productions, however, were reworkings of plays by continental and white American playwrights. Alice Childress, whose *Trouble in Mind* was optioned for Broadway in the mid-1950s, worked closely with one of these companies. Other plays by African-Americans that were produced during this period include *St. Louis Woman* (1946), a collaboration by Arna Bontemps and Countee Cullen in which Bontemps's novel, *God Sends Sunday* (1931), was adapted for stage; Louis Peterson's *Take a Giant Step* (1953); and Hughes's *Simply Heavenly* (1957).

Perhaps the most dramatic event in the history of the production of plays by black Americans occurred in 1959, when Lorraine Hansberry's *A Raisin in the Sun* opened in Philadelphia. It was the first time, James Baldwin asserts, that black people truly recognized themselves on the American stage. Blacks flocked to see the play because they saw accurate reflections of themselves, and they recognized Hansberry as a witness to their blackness and their aspirations in American society. That event was followed in 1964 by LeRoi Jones's *Dutchman,* which, in its depiction of the sexual tempting of a black man by a white woman and her eventual killing of him, had an equally profound effect on the American theatre as well as on black viewing audiences. Playwrights such as Ossie Davis (*Purlie Victorius,* 1961), James Baldwin (*The Amen Corner,* 1965), Ed Bullins (*In the Wine Time,* 1968), and Charles Gordone all had plays produced in the very successful decade of the 1960s. Gordone became the first black playwright to win the Pulitzer Prize for drama, for his *No Place to Be Somebody* (1969).

The shocker for the next decade would be Ntozake Shange's *For Colored Girls Who Have Considered Suicide When the Rainbow is Enuf* (1976), which focused critical attention on the problematic relationships between black males and black females. In 1981, Charles Fuller's *A Soldier's Play* opened on Broadway; the next year it followed the path of *No Place to Be Somebody* by winning the Pulitzer Prize for drama. The most publicized dramatic successes of the 1980s belonged to August Wilson, whose *Fences,* the story of an embittered player from the Negro Baseball League, won the Pulitzer Prize for drama in 1987. His other works include *Ma Rainey's Black Bottom* (1986), *The Piano Lesson* (1987), and *Joe Turner's Come and Gone* (1988).

SUMMARY

In recent years, there has been a reevaluation of what southern territory means in African-American literature, and writers have set their works on that soil and allowed their characters to define themselves and their world in that previously restricting territory. Such writers and works include Toni Morrison's *Song of Solomon* (1977), in which a spoiled middle-class black Michiganer returns to Virginia to uncover the meaning of personal history and ancestry; Alice Walker's *The Color Purple* (1982), in which a black woman who has been abused physically and psychologically overcomes these debilitations to become an entrepreneur in Memphis; and Gloria Naylor's *Mama Day* (1988), in which a descendant of slaves controls not only her family's destiny but the very elements of the universe. For these writers, the South is no longer forbidden territory, no longer a place of death, but a place where African-Americans can choose reasonably well under what circumstances they will live in the world.

Its roots in the oral tradition and in the African-American slave narrative have enabled African-American literature to come of age in the twentieth century. From a literature that made obeisances to white reading audiences, as was the case with Charles W. Chesnutt, it has grown to insist, as Toni Morrison does, that readers come to meet it wherever it starts and agree to go wherever it takes them. Forms that were initially rooted in politics, such as Frances Harper's lyrics, gave way to the mythologically sophisticated verses of poets such as Jay Wright. And dramas that were initially intended for living room consumption serve as the origins of works that have won several Pulitzer Prizes.

The publishing industry has kept pace with audiences for African-American literature, and today novels, poems, and plays by black writers are available for use in courses in American Studies, African-American Studies, Religious Studies, History, and Sociology, as well as in the traditional English Department classes. Readership has transcended languages and national boundaries; Morrison's works, for example, are available in German and Japanese, among other languages, and she won Italy's highest prize for a creative writer in 1990. Doctoral students in India, Spain, Germany, Japan, and the Netherlands routinely come to the United States to study with specialists in African-American literature, and they regularly write dissertations on African-American writers. From a creative effort with a purpose, African-American literature has grown to be recognized internationally as a complex area of study that will sustain many generations of students, teachers, and scholars.

STUDY QUESTIONS AND ACTIVITIES

1. How has the portrayal of African-American characters changed in literary works from the nineteenth to the twentieth centuries?
2. What are some of the influences of the African-American oral tradition upon the literature?
3. What would have been the consequences for an African-American writer who ignored the fact of his or her race during the nineteenth century?

4.   What are the social, cultural, and political implications of writing in a language you grew up speaking as opposed to one you have been taught?
5.   In what ways was the New Black Aesthetic movement purely literary? In what ways was it political?

REFERENCES

William L. Andrews. *To Tell A Free Story: The First Century of Afro-American Autobiography, 1760–1865*. Urbana, IL: University of Illinois Press, 1986.

Houston A. Baker, Jr. *Blues, Ideology, and Afro-American Literature, A Vernacular Theory*. Chicago: University of Chicago Press, 1984.

Bernard Bell. *The Afro-American Novel and Its Tradition*. Amherst, MA: University of Massachusetts Press, 1987.

Hazel V. Carby. *Reconstructing Womanhood: The Emergence of the Afro-American Woman Novelist*. New York: Oxford University Press, 1987.

Barbara Christian. *Black Women Novelists: The Development of a Tradition, 1892–1976*. Westport, CT: Greenwood Press, 1980.

Henry Louis Gates Jr. *The Signifying Monkey: A Theory of Afro-American Literary Criticism*. New York: Oxford University Press, 1988.

Stephen Henderson. *Understanding the New Black Poetry: Black Speech and Black Music as Poetic References*. New York: William Morrow & Company, 1973.

James Weldon Johnson (ed.). *The Book of American Negro Poetry*. New York: Harcourt, Brace and World, 1922.

Lawrence Levine. *Black Culture and Black Consciousness: Afro-American Folk Thought From Slavery to Freedom*. New York: Oxford University Press, 1977.

Loften Mitchell. *Black Drama: The Story of the American Negro in the Theatre*. New York: Hawthorn Books, 1967.

Joan R. Sherman. *Invisible Poets: Afro-Americans of the Nineteenth Century*. Urbana, IL: University of Illinois Press, 1974.

Jean Wagner. *Black Poets of the United States: From Paul Laurence Dunbar to Langston Hughes*. Urbana, IL: University of Illinois Press, 1973.

Asian American Literature

ELAINE H. KIM

Kim defines Asian American literature as "published creative writings in English by Americans of Chinese, Filipino, Japanese, Korean, and Southeast Asian (for now, Burmese and Vietnamese) descent about their American experiences" (p. 244n). While acknowledging the important role that autobiography has played in Asian American literature, particularly during earlier years, she notes that in more recent years Asian American literature has diversified in response to changes in immigration and naturalization laws, increased social integration, and greater ethnic awareness. Contemporary Asian American writers are finding a broader range of publishing opportunities and are more likely to experiment with genre and form. In this essay from the Columbia Literary History of the United States (1988), Kim traces the development of Asian American literature while commenting on recurring themes and highlighting major writers.

As writers of all ethnic and racial minority groups in the United States have noted, it is difficult to publish from a perspective that is American but not white, English, and even Protestant. This difficulty has been especially intense for Asian American writers — in part because a great ocean separates the United States from Asia, and even more because a great cultural gap separates Asian American writers from readers who lack solid information about Asian cultures and their peoples. One of the big problems facing Asian American writers has been the tendency of readers to view their works as sociological or anthropological documents rather than as literary ones. Too often Asian American works are taken to be representations of entire groups rather than expressions of individual artists. Given the large role that political and military issues have played in relations between Asian peoples and the United States, most critical assessments of Asian American literature have been influenced by political concerns.[1]

Only in the last decade has criticism begun to place social and literary issues at the center of interpretations of Asian American literature, exposing its texture, topography, tensions, and beauty. What has been revealed is that, from a historical perspective, Asian American writing mirrors the evolving

From the Columbia Literary History of the United States, ed. Emory Elliott (New York: Columbia UP, 1988) 811–21.

self-image and consciousness of an often misunderstood and increasingly significant racial minority group, not only by documenting the experiences of Asians in the United States, but also by giving powerful expression to individual experiences and perceptions through the particular voices of Asian American artists.

Autobiography has been a popular genre among Asian American writers, largely because it has been the most marketable. Given the popular image of Asian Americans as perpetual foreigners, some publishers preferred writings with anthropological appeal over fiction. Others encouraged Asian American writers to present their work as autobiographical even when it was not. Carlos Bulosan was persuaded to write *America Is in the Heart* (1946) as personal history because it seemed likely to sell best that way. Although Maxine Hong Kingston's *The Woman Warrior* (1975) is fiction, it has been classified and sold as autobiography, or more broadly as nonfiction.

During the latter part of the nineteenth century, scholars and diplomats, who had been exempted from exclusionary legislation, published a number of "life stories" intended to counter negative views of Asia and Asians. For the most part, these writers used charming superficialities of food and dress, or ceremonies and customs, to appeal to the benign curiosity of Western readers. The first published works of this kind were Lee Yan Phou's *When I Was a Boy in China* (1887) and New Il-Han's *When I Was a Boy in Korea* (1928), narratives about upper-class childhood in China and Korea respectively.

Perhaps the best-known interpreter of Asia to the West is Lin Yutang, a self-styled cultural envoy who during four decades published a score of books on subjects ranging from "the importance of living" to tracts against communism to the feel of American life from a "Chinese" point of view. Lin's best-known work, *My Country and My People* (1937), enjoyed enormous popularity in Europe and the United States, although Chinese critics have pointed out that Lin ignored the everyday life-and-death struggles of the Chinese people under foreign domination. In contrast, Younghill Kang's quasi-autobiographical *East Goes West* (1937) marks a transition from the viewpoint of a visitor acting as a "cultural bridge" to that of an immigrant searching for a permanent place in American life. *East Goes West* is a vivid portrait of the life of Korean exiles — their work, their aspirations, and their exclusion from American social and intellectual life.

These early autobiographical works disclose a marked dissociation between their authors and the common people of both Asia and the West. Even their tentative apologetic pleas for racial tolerance are made primarily for members of the authors' own privileged class. Publishers and readers accepted them as representing all Asian Americans, but with few exceptions these works ignored the large numbers of laborers recruited for agricultural and construction work in Hawaii and the American West between 1840 and 1924.

One exception is Carlos Bulosan's quasi-autobiographical *America Is in the Heart*. A self-educated Filipino migrant worker, Bulosan wrote in order "to give literate voice to the voiceless one hundred thousand Filipinos in the

United States, Hawaii, and Alaska." Bulosan's work comes to us almost by accident: He was able to study and write while recuperating from tuberculosis in a California charity hospital. *America Is in the Heart* describes the lives of the Filipino migrant workers who followed the harvest, laboring in the fields and canneries from Alaska to the Mexican border during the 1920s and 1930s. The book, which emphasizes the promise of democracy against fascism, has been translated into several European languages and was hailed by *Look* magazine as one of the fifty most important American books ever published.

Among the first published works by American-born Asians are two Chinese American autobiographies, Pardee Lowe's *Father and Glorious Descendant* (1942) and Jade Snow Wong's *Fifth Chinese Daughter* (1945). These appeared in print at a time when Chinese, like Filipinos, were viewed as American allies and enjoyed unprecedented popularity. Both Lowe and Wong attempt to claim America as their own country, Lowe because he is so very American and Wong because she is uniquely yet acceptably Chinese. In *Father and Glorious Descendant*, Lowe describes Chinese objects as "alien" and "strange," Chinese customs as "old junk," and Chinese people as "emotionless automatons." America, on the other hand, with its schools, libraries, bathtubs, toilets, and railroad trains, Lowe presents as "God's own country." In *Fifth Chinese Daughter*, Wong introduces the reader to exotic and harmlessly interesting aspects of Chinese American family and community life. Assuming the role of an anthropological guide, she takes the reader on a tour of San Francisco Chinatown, even offering recipes for tomato beef and egg foo yung, complete with exact measurements and instructions. Both books are presented as evidence of how America's racial minorities can "succeed" through accommodation, hard work, and perseverance; and both more or less blame Chinese Americans — their families, their communities, their race — for whatever difficulties they face or failures they suffer.

While publishers encouraged writers like Lowe and Wong, they discouraged or even suppressed writers who insisted on going in other directions. Toshio Mori's *Yokohama, California*, which indirectly challenged the views of writers like Lowe and Wong, was scheduled for publication in 1941 but did not appear until 1949, after World War II had ended. By 1953, when Monica Sone's *Nisei Daughter* was published, the Japanese had long since been released from wartime detention camps and were no longer concentrated in ethnic enclaves as they had been before the war. At first glance *Nisei Daughter* appears to be a cheerful Japanese version of *Fifth Chinese Daughter* — a reassuring picture of the appealing qualities of a recently maligned group. On closer reading, however, it becomes a story of the enormous price exacted from second-generation Japanese Americans by politics and racism. In *Nisei Daughter*, the warmth and harmony of Japanese American family and community life are totally disrupted by the relocation experience.

In spite of such protests, however, during the 1970s, when the effects of the civil rights movement were being felt all across America, Japanese American "success" stories were widely publicized as evidence that racial minorities should blame themselves rather than external factors, such as racial discrimination, for social inequality. In particular, Japanese American "success" stories came to be regarded as examples that blacks and other minorities should follow. In this climate, major American publishers welcomed Japanese American autobiographies, and among those published were Daniel Inouye and Lawrence Elliott's *Journey to Washington* (1967), Daniel Okimoto's *American in Disguise* (1971), Jim Yoshida and Bill Hosokawa's *The Two Worlds of Jim Yoshida* (1972), and Jeanne Wakatsuki Houston and James D. Houston's *Farewell to Manzanar* (1973).

When it was first published, John Okada's *No-No Boy* (1957) was not favorably received. *Fifth Chinese Daughter* had been read by a quarter of a million people and was still being used in junior high and high school literature classes in 1975 as the best example of Chinese American literature. The first edition of *No-No Boy* had still not sold out when Okada died in 1971. Far from being another "success" story, *No-No Boy* explores the devastating effects of racism on the Japanese American community of Seattle just after the end of the war. Depicting a people incapacitated by uncertainty and self-hatred, Okada refuses to celebrate Japanese Americans as merely patient, hardworking, law-abiding, and long-suffering. To the contrary, he presents them as disfigured by the experience of relocation and racial hatred. In the *nisei* world of *No-No Boy*, no sacrifice is too great for the prize of social acceptance: The people in the community envy the war veteran who has lost his leg because his "patriotism" is evident at a glance. In Okada's confused and torn world, no one is complete: Brothers betray brothers, children turn against their parents, parents turn to alcohol or suicide, husbands desert their wives, and wives commit adultery with their husbands' friends.

In many stories that portray Asian American community life, there are no white characters at all simply because segregated existence excluded them. As a result, issues of racism and race relations are submerged. In *Yokohama, California* and *The Chauvinist and Other Stories* (1979), Toshio Mori presents Japanese American community life — featuring new immigrants and American-born characters of both sexes and all ages, farmers, laborers, small business owners, housewives, and students — in vignettes that bring out what he sees as deeply human joys and sorrows.

In half a dozen remarkable short stories published between 1949 and 1961, Hisaye Yamamoto offers a vivid picture of prewar family and community life among Japanese Americans on the West Coast, with a particular focus on women's perspectives. Yamamoto's stories concentrate on the relationships between immigrant husbands and wives and those between immigrant parents and their American-born children. Marked by subtle irony and understatement, Yamamoto's style juxtaposes two currents that reflect one of the quintessential qualities of Japanese American life. Beneath an apparently placid surface, often represented by a wholesome young *nisei* narrator, there are hints of hidden tragedy, usually tinged with death and violence. Sometimes, as in *Seventeen Syllables* (1949), Yamamoto accomplishes this by presenting fleeting glimpses into the mother's dark past and repressed desires through the half-uncomprehending eyes of the narrator daughter.

Milton Murayama's *All I Asking For Is My Body* (1975) is a powerful critique of authoritarianism and tyranny among Japanese Americans in Hawaii during the years immediately preceding World War II. Unquestioning acceptance of hierarchical authority thwarts the human freedom of dutiful sons who obey their fathers and of plantation workers who accept exploitation. The fictional company town of Pepelau is structured exactly like a pyramid: The plantation boss's house is built on top of the hill, followed by the houses of the Portuguese, Spanish, and *nisei* lunas (plantation foremen). Below these are the identical wood frame houses of the Japanese laborers, and at the bottom of the hill, where the toilet pipes and outhouse drainage ditches empty downhill, are the run-down shacks of the Filipino workers.

Both Lin Yutang's *Chinatown Family* (1948) and Chin Yang Lee's *Flower Drum Song* (1957) present euphemistic portraits of Chinatown, and both quickly earned popular and financial success. By contrast, Louis Chu's *Eat a Bowl of Tea* (1961) offers a more realistic insider's view of the daily life, manners, attitudes, and problems of the Chinese American community — and it failed to gain readers or make money. Focusing on the hypocrisy and self-deception that governs Chinese American life, Chu, like Murayama, presents the picture "with love, with all the warts showing." The vital quality of Chu's portrayal results in part from his ability to appreciate the spoken language of a people who regarded verbal skill and witty exchanges as a social art.

In recent decades, the Asian population in the United States has grown and diversified primarily as a result of changes in immigration and naturalization laws. Contemporary Asian American literature reflects this increasing diversity. Both greater social integration and new ethnic awareness have stimulated Asian American writing, in part by giving today's writers new confidence, and in part by creating markets that are less circumscribed by mainstream expectations. Some contemporary Asian American works are privately published; others appear in Asian American or minority journals and anthologies; still others are published by small presses interested in ethnic literature. But major publishing houses have also begun to express interest in the literature emerging from the Asian American community. Having first been performed for Asian American audiences, David Henry Hwang's plays became successful in New York theaters. In 1983, four of Hwang's works appeared together under the title *Broken Promises,* making him one of the first Asian American playwrights to be published.

In a growing spirit of self-determination, contemporary Asian American writers are experimenting with genre, form, and language to express sensibilities that are uniquely their own. Poetry presentations and dramatic readings with music and dance are flourishing in community forums. Recent writers blend drama with prose and poetry, fiction with nonfiction, and literature with history. Maxine Hong Kingston combines history, folk legends, and fictional interpretations, no one form dominating her work. Janice Mirikitani writes short stories that blend prose with poetry and poetry that is written to be accompanied by *koto* music and dance interpretations. Bienvenido N. Santos's *You Lovely People* (1965) combines the short-story and novel forms in a collection of self-contained short episodes that come together like a novel through the counterpointing of two narrative voices representing different aspects of Filipino American identity. The prose and poetry in the late Theresa Hak Kyung Cha's *Dictee* (1982) is presented in English and French and is illustrated with graphics derived from old photographs of Korea. Many writers, especially poets, are experimenting with Asian American colloquialisms. In *Yellow Light* (1982), Garrett Kaoru Hongo combines Japanese words with colloquialisms used in Japanese American communities in Hawaii and Gardena, California. The novelist Milton Murayama presents dialogue that combines direct translations of formal Japanese with both standard English and the pidgin spoken in Hawaii. *Sansei* poet Ronald Tanaka mixes traditional Japanese poetic forms with Japanese American expressions in the *Shino Suite* (1981).

Since the 1970s, Asian American writers have been concerned with filling in spaces, mending rifts, and building bridges across generations. Self-determination means telling the Asian American story from an Asian American perspective, "restoring the foundations" of a culture that has been damaged or denied by racism. Such efforts, especially the search for historical foundations, have involved not only searching for works by little-known Asian American writers but also locating and translating works written by immigrants in their native languages. *Island: Poetry and History of Chinese Immigrants on Angel Island* (1980) consists of poetry discovered on the walls of the Angel Island Detention Center barracks. The editors present this poetry as "a vivid fragment of Chinese American history and a mirror capturing the image of the past." In *Island* we hear the voices of thousands of immigrants that might otherwise have been forever lost.

Chinese American writer Laurence Yep helps repair the foundations of the Asian American heritage in *Dragonwings* (1975) — a historical novel based on a newspaper account of the Chinese Fung Joe Guey, who invented and flew a biplane in 1901. Lacking information about Guey, Yep fashions a complex character, filled with apprehensions and motivated by dreams and longing, who proves to be capable of intense love and loyalty.

Rewriting Asian American history in literature from an Asian American perspective has given life to new heroes and heroines. Playwright David Henry Hwang's *The Dance and the Railroad* (1982) is about the 1867 Chinese railroad workers' strike, and the two main characters are railroad laborers. A number of contemporary Japanese American writers have re-created the World War II era in their works to show the effects of internment on individual lives. Lawson Inada's poetry anthology is titled *Before the War* (1971), reminding us that many Japanese Americans were marked for life by the relocation experience. In *kibei* Edward Miyakawa's *Tule Lake* (1979) and Jeanne Wakatsuki Houston's *Farewell to Manzanar,* contemporary Japanese American writers probe the effects of the camp experience, as does the Japanese Canadian poet and novelist Joy Kogawa in *Obasan* (1981).

Attempts to reconstruct the lost past have also involved exploring the half-buried mysteries of parents' and grandparents' experiences. Today's

Asian American writer is often forced to seek the meaning of the past in shreds of stories heard in childhood. In Wing Tek Lum's "A Picture of My Mother's Family" (1974), a poet searches for the significance of each detail in an old photograph of his family, hoping to piece together a relevant story about his half-forgotten ancestors. Similarly, Filipino poets Al Robles and Presco Tabios have devoted years to collecting the life stories and oral histories of the Filipino elderly of San Francisco — men who, like Carlos Bulosan, immigrated to America as youths and then spent their lives laboring in fields and canneries. Bienvenido N. Santos, a Filipino expatriate who has lived in the United States since 1982, says that he has tried to write about the recent immigrant community but that his attention returns continually to "old-timers among our countrymen who sat out the evening of their lives before television sets in condemned buildings." Santos continues to write about the old exiles (*You Lovely People* [1965]; *The Day the Dancers Came* [1967]; *Scent of Apples* [1979]) because "now I realize that perhaps I have also been writing about myself."

The paucity of female characters in early writings by Asian American men reflects the harsh realities of the bachelor life created by American exclusion and antimiscegenation laws. Aside from Toshio Mori, few Asian American male writers have attempted multidimensional portrayals of Asian American women, focusing instead on defining themselves as men and on exploring their status as members of a minority. With the exception of the mother in the Philippines, most of Carlos Bulosan's women are either non-Asian prostitutes or idealized white women who represent the America that the narrator seeks to enter. The Chinese woman named Mei Oi in Louis Chu's *Eat a Bowl of Tea* is part seductress and part child, which makes her intrusion into the confines of the male-dominated Chinatown ghetto of the late 1940s profoundly disruptive. But the novel is about the men. Although Mei Oi reminds us that the men have failed as husbands and fathers, she lacks their dimensions as a character: She fails to understand, let alone consciously influence, the forces that shape both her life and theirs. The female characters in John Okada's *No-No Boy* are also stick figures. In the early 1970s, Frank Chin and Jeffery Paul Chan argued that Asian American men in particular were victims of "racist love" in American society. Citing the popular image of Asian men as asexual and the popular image of Asian women as wholly sexual, imbued with an innate understanding of how to please and serve men, they noted that both images served to bolster the notion of the white man's virility. But even when female characters play significant roles, as they do in the works of Frank Chin and Jeffery Paul Chan, they usually emerge either as domineering wives or mothers or as empty-headed girl friends who provide little more than an ironic audience for the metaphysical angst of male protagonists.

Although men are sometimes portrayed compassionately and convincingly in the writings of Asian American women, they generally remain in the shadows. Hisaye Yamamoto's men are conventional and colorless compared with the spirited women who must be subdued by husbands and fathers who resemble jailers. Unable to protect, inspire, or even understand women, many male characters in Asian American women's writing tend to seek emotional or physical escape rather than confront the things that limit them. The would-be lover in Eleanor Wong Telamaque's *It's Crazy to Stay Chinese in Minnesota* (1978) departs for China, leaving the heroine to battle her problems alone. Sometimes there are striking contrasts between female characters who are triumphant boundry breakers and male characters who are too narrow and inflexible to flourish in American society. The brother in Wendy Law Yone's *The Coffin Tree* (1983) had been the strong one in Burma, but it is the sister who survives in America. The brother dies insane, leaving his sister in an alien world as the family's sole survivor.

Among both men and women writers today, intense longing for reconciliation persist. The narrator in Wakako Yamauchi's "That Was All" (1980) is haunted by her vision of the slim brown body and mocking eyes of the man whom she sees, as an aging woman, in a fleeting dream. In "The Boatmen on River Toneh" (1974), the female narrator is "swept against the smooth brown cheeks of a black-haired youth . . . and into his billowing shirt" only in death. Yet a mending of the rift may be at hand. The narrator in Shawn Hsu Wong's *Homebase* dreams of the woman he loves, while in David Henry Hwang's play *FOB* (1979), the gap between the immigrant and the American-born Chinese is bridged. During the play, the legendary woman warrior Fa Mu Lan teaches Gwan Kung, god of warriors and writers, how to survive in America; and at the end of the play Gwan Kung goes off with Steve, the immigrant. Perhaps Hwang, who says he was inspired by both Maxine Hong Kingston and Frank Chin, is consciously attempting to bridge the gap between Kingston and Chin, who have often been characterized respectively as writers for women or men.

In Asian American writing, gender has many dimensions. The "failure" of fathers is a favorite theme in Frank Chin's plays and short fiction and in Jeffery Paul Chan's short stories. Deprived of a masculine image and marked by their experience in a racist culture, male writers have struggled to destroy the myths that threaten their identities as men. The identity crises of the young stems in part from the complicity of older generations of Chinese Americans, who cling to "mildewed memories" of China or cater to tourists' exotic fantasies. Chinatown is a place of death, a "human zoo," an "elephant graveyard," and its people are like mechanical wind-up toys. Both the self and the family disintegrate, making flight the only possible means of surviving a suffocating environment. The young protagonists find establishing a new identity almost impossible, in part because the older men refuse to relinquish illusions that have limited their lives, preventing them from becoming real men. Both Chin's *Chickencoop Chinaman* (1974) and Chan's "Jackrabbit" (1974) focus on failed father-son relationships. One variation on this theme occurs in Shawn Hsu Wong's lyrical short novel, *Homebase* (1979), where the narrator seeks and finds his true American identity through the reconciliation of a father and son who share American roots as well as a Chinese American heritage. By claiming America as his own while reaffirming the love that connects his life to the lives of his father and forefathers, the narrator affirms his American identity. Wong's Chinese American is like a wild plant commonly "condemned as a weed" that survives to bear flowers, creating beauty and shade in the most difficult conditions.

The quest for a place in American life is a recurrent theme in Asian American literature. Contemporary writers, however, focus not on accommodation or racial self-negation but on the ideal that Carlos Bulosan articulated in the 1940s, of an America of the heart, where it is possible to be both American and nonwhite. Indeed, several contemporary Asian American writers express kinship with other nonwhite Americans, especially blacks and Native Americans, who frequently appear in their works. It is a Native American who tells the narrator in *Homebase* that he must find out where his people have been and see the California town he is named for before he can claim his home, his history, and the legacy of his forefathers in America. "Soon the white snow will melt," writes poet Al Robles, and "the brown, black, yellow earth will come to life."

During the late 1960s and early 1970s, many Asian American writers began to reject assimilation into what they view as a sterile and spiritually bankrupt white American mainstream that demands nothing less than denial of one's ancestry and heritage. The war in Vietnam strengthened such attitudes, as we see in "Japs" (1978), by Janice Mirikitani, a third-generation Japanese American:

> if you're too dark
> they will kill you
> if you're too swift
> they will buy you
> if you're too beautiful
> they will rape you
> Watch with eyes open
> speak darkly
> turn your head like the owl
> behind you

Young Asian American writers have also been moved to portray the recent immigrant experience. In "Song for My Father" (1975), a poem by Jessica Tarahata Hagedorn, the narrator is caught between America, "the loneliest of countries," and the land of her father, islands of music and tropical fruits. In a satirical story titled "The Blossoming of Bongbong" (1975), Hagedorn, who emigrated from the Philippines at an early age, traces the experiences of a young Filipino immigrant in a hostile America.

Consciousness of cultural conflict is also a major theme in the work of the Korean immigrant writer Kichung Kim, whose short story, "A Homecoming" (1972), depicts the confusion of a young Korean who returns to his homeland after ten years in the United States. In Ty Park's *Guilt Payment* (1983), many of the Korean immigrant characters fail to escape the haunting memories of the life they left behind. Of the few works of fiction in English by refugees from Southeast Asia, most focus on Asia. The protagonist of Tran Van Dinh's

Blue Dragon White Tiger (1983) is a Vietnamese who has lived in America, but the novel itself is set largely in Vietnam. *The Coffin Tree*, an important novel by Burmese immigrant writer Wendy Law Yone, tells the story of a female protagonist who moves from Burma to America, only to face a contrast so severe that she almost loses her mind.

Although familiar themes still dominate it, Asian American writing has followed Asian American experience in accommodating an ever-widening range of perspectives. The poetry of Mei Mei Berssenbrugge (*Random Possession* [1979]), Alan Chong Lau (*Songs for Jadina* [1980]), James Mitsui (*Crossing the Phantom River* [1978]), and John Yau (*Crossing Canal Street* [1976] and others) demonstrates that Asian American writers cannot be confined by "Asian American" themes or by narrow definitions of "Asian American" identity. Their writings are all the more "Asian American" because they contribute to the broadening of what that term means. The most effective poems in Cathy Song's *Picture Bride* (1983) are not the ones replete with images of jade sour plums; they are those that explore the relationship between the persona and her family, from whom she ventures forth and with whom she is eventually reconciled.

Asian American writers are stronger today than ever before, and they deserve greater recognition and support, particularly as they strive to explore aspects of Asian American experience that remain misunderstood and unappreciated. Meanwhile, as they continue to celebrate the complexity and diversity of Asian American experience, they will also contribute to the emerging mosaic of American literature and culture.

NOTE

1. Asian American literature is defined here as published creative writings in English by Americans of Chinese, Filipino, Japanese, Korean, and Southeast Asian (for now, Burmese and Vietnamese) descent about their American experiences.

Treason Our Text: Feminist Challenges to the Literary Canon

LILLIAN S. ROBINSON

*I*n an essay that originally appeared in Tulsa Studies in Women's Literature (1983), Robinson discusses the feminist challenge to the literary canon, which critiques the neglect of many women writers and the distortion and misreading of the few recognized women writers. According to Robinson, feminist criticism can either emphasize alternative readings that reinterpret women's character and actions and thus challenge sexist ideology, or it can focus on expanding the canon to include more women writers. In fact, the origins of feminist literary study are associated with "discovery, republication, and reappraisal of 'lost' or undervalued writers and their work." The next step is to determine if the recovered works meet existing aesthetic quality criteria or if the criteria intrinsically excludes women and thus need to be revised. In addition to the creation of a "feminist countercanon," feminist critics have sought to establish a female literary tradition. During the course of her discussion, Robinson notes the different concerns raised by black and lesbian feminist scholars and addresses the issue of inclusion within feminist criticism.

> Successful plots have often had gunpowder in them. Feminist critics have gone so far as to take treason to the canon as our text.[1]
>
> – JANE MARCUS

THE LOFTY SEAT OF CANONIZED BARDS (POLLOK, 1827)

As with many other restrictive institutions, we are hardly aware of it until we come into conflict with it; the elements of the literary canon are simply absorbed by the apprentice scholar and critic in the normal course of graduate education, without anyone's ever seeming to inculcate or defend them. Appeal, were any necessary, would be to the other meaning of "canon," that is, to established standards of judgment and of taste. Not that either definition is presented as rigid and immutable — far from it, for lectures in literary history are full of wry references to a benighted though hardly distant past

From *Tulsa Studies in Women's Literature* 2.1 (1983): 83–98.

when, say, the metaphysical poets were insufficiently appreciated or Vachel Lindsay was the most modern poet recognized in American literature. Whence the acknowledgment of a subjective dimension, sometimes generalized as "sensibility," to the category of taste. Sweeping modifications in the canon are said to occur because of changes in collective sensibility, but individual admissions and elevations from "minor" to "major" status tend to be achieved by successful critical promotion, which is to say, demonstration that a particular author does meet generally accepted criteria of excellence.

The results, moreover, are nowhere codified: they are neither set down in a single place, nor are they absolutely uniform. In the visual arts and in music, the cold realities of patronage, purchase, presentation in private and public collections, or performance on concert programs create the conditions for a work's canonical status or lack of it. No equivalent set of institutional arrangements exists for literature, however. The fact of publication and even the feat of remaining in print for generations, which are at least analogous to the ways in which pictures and music are displayed, are not the same sort of indicators; they represent less of an investment and hence less general acceptance of their canonicity. In the circumstances, it may seem somewhat of an exaggeration to speak of "the" literary canon, almost paranoid to call it an institution, downright hysterical to characterize that institution as restrictive. The whole business is so much more informal, after all, than any of these terms implies, the concomitant processes so much more gentlemanly. Surely, it is more like a gentlemen's agreement than a repressive instrument — isn't it?

But a gentleman is inescapably — that is, by definition — a member of a privileged class and of the male sex. From this perspective, it is probably quite accurate to think of the canon as an entirely gentlemanly artifact, considering how few works by nonmembers of that class and sex make it into the informal agglomeration of course syllabi, anthologies, and widely commented-upon "standard authors" that constitutes the canon as it is generally understood. For, beyond their availability on bookshelves, it is through the teaching and study — one might even say the habitual teaching and study — of certain works that they become institutionalized as canonical literature. Within that broad canon, moreover, those admitted but read only in advanced courses, commented upon only by more or less narrow specialists, are subjected to the further tyranny of "major" versus "minor."

For more than a decade now, feminist scholars have been protesting the apparently systematic neglect of women's experience in the literary canon, neglect that takes the form of distorting and misreading the few recognized female writers and excluding the others. Moreover, the argument runs, the predominantly male authors in the canon show us the female character and relations between the sexes in a way that both reflects and contributes to sexist ideology — an aspect of these classic works about which the critical tradition remained silent for generations. The feminist challenge, although intrinsically (and, to my mind, refreshingly) polemical, has not been simply a reiterated attack, but a series of suggested alternatives to the male-dominated membership and attitudes of the accepted canon. In this essay, I propose to examine these feminist alternatives, assess their impact on the standard canon, and propose some directions for further work. Although my emphasis in each section is on the substance of the challenge, the underlying polemic is, I believe, abundantly clear.

THE PRESENCE OF CANONIZED FOREFATHERS (BURKE, 1790)

Start with the Great Books, the traditional desert-island ones, the foundation of courses in the Western humanistic tradition. No women authors, of course, at all, but within the works thus canonized, certain monumental female images: Helen, Penelope, and Clytemnestra, Beatrice and the Dark Lady of the Sonnets, Bérénice, Cunégonde, and Margarete. The list of interesting female characters is enlarged if we shift to the Survey of English Literature and its classic texts; here, moreover, there is the possible inclusion of a female author or even several, at least as the course's implicit "historical background" ticks through and past the Industrial Revolution. It is a possibility that is not always honored in the observance. "*Beowulf* to Virginia Woolf" is a pleasant enough joke, but though lots of surveys begin with the Anglo-Saxon epic, not all that many conclude with *Mrs. Dalloway.* Even in the nineteenth century, the pace and the necessity of mass omissions may mean leaving out Austen, one of the Brontës, or Eliot. The analogous overview of American literary masterpieces, despite the relative brevity and modernity of the period considered, is likely to yield a similarly all-male pantheon; Emily Dickinson may be admitted — but not necessarily — and no one else even comes close.[2] Here again, the male-authored canon contributes to the body of information, stereotype, inference, and surmise about the female sex that is generally in the culture.

Once this state of affairs has been exposed, there are two possible approaches for feminist criticism. It can emphasize alternative readings of the tradition, readings that reinterpret women's character, motivations, and actions and that identify and challenge sexist ideology. Or it can concentrate on gaining admission to the canon for literature by women writers. Both sorts of work are being pursued, although, to the extent that feminist criticism has defined itself as a subfield of literary studies — as distinguished from an approach or method — it has tended to concentrate on writing by women.

In fact, however, the current wave of feminist theory began as criticism of certain key texts, both literary and paraliterary, in the dominant culture. Kate Millett, Eva Figes, Elizabeth Janeway, Germaine Greer, and Carolyn Heilbrun all use the techniques of essentially literary analysis on the social forms and forces surrounding those texts.[3] The texts themselves may be regarded as "canonical" in the sense that all have had significant impact on the culture as a whole, although the target being addressed is not literature or its canon.

In criticism that is more strictly literary in its scope, much attention has been concentrated on male writers in the American tradition. Books like Annette Kolodny's *The Lay of the Land* and Judith Fetterley's *The Resisting*

Reader have no systematic, comprehensive equivalent in the criticism of British or European literature.[4] Both of these studies identify masculine values and imagery in a wide range of writings, as well as the alienation that is their consequence for women, men, and society as a whole. In a similar vein, Mary Ellmann's *Thinking About Women* examines ramifications of the tradition of "phallic criticism" as applied to writers of both sexes.[5] These books have in common with one another and with overarching theoretical manifestos like *Sexual Politics* a sense of having been betrayed by a culture that was supposed to be elevating, liberating, and one's own.

By contrast, feminist work devoted to that part of the Western tradition which is neither American nor contemporary is likelier to be more even-handed. "Feminist critics," declare Lenz, Greene, and Neely in introducing their collection of essays on Shakespeare, "recognize that the greatest artists do not necessarily duplicate in their art the orthodoxies of their culture; they may exploit them to create character or intensify conflict, they may struggle with, criticize, or transcend them."[6] From this perspective, Milton may come in for some censure, Shakespeare and Chaucer for both praise and blame, but the clear intention of a feminist approach to these classic authors is to enrich our understanding of what is going on in the texts, as well as how — for better, for worse, or for both — they have shaped our own literary and social ideas.[7] At its angriest, none of this reinterpretation offers a fundamental challenge to the canon *as canon;* although it posits new values, it never suggests that, in the light of those values, we ought to reconsider whether the great monuments are really so great, after all.

Suche as all the worlde hathe confirmed and agreed upon, that it is authentique and canonical. (T. Wilson, 1553)

In an evolutionary model of feminist studies in literature, work on male authors is often characterized as "early," implicitly primitive, whereas scholarship on female authors is the later development, enabling us to see women — the writers themselves and the women they write about — as active agents rather than passive images or victims. This implicit characterization of studies addressed to male writers is as inaccurate as the notion of an inexorable evolution. In fact, as the very definition of feminist criticism has come increasingly to mean scholarship and criticism devoted to women writers, work on the male tradition has continued. By this point, there has been a study of the female characters or the views on the woman question of every major — perhaps every known — author in Anglo-American, French, Russian, Spanish, Italian, German, and Scandinavian literature.[8]

Nonetheless, it is an undeniable fact that most feminist criticism focuses on women writers, so that the feminist efforts to humanize the canon have usually meant bringing a woman's point of view to bear by incorporating works by women into the established canon. The least threatening way to do so is to follow the accustomed pattern of making the case for individual writers one by one. The case here consists in showing that an already recognized woman author has been denied her rightful place, presumably because of the general devaluation of female efforts and subjects. More often than not, such work involves showing that a woman already securely established in the canon belongs in the first rather than the second rank. The biographical and critical efforts of R. W. B. Lewis and Cynthia Griffin Wolff, for example, have attempted to enhance Edith Wharton's reputation in this way.[9] Obviously, no challenge is presented to the particular notions of literary quality, timeless-ness, universality, and other qualities that constitute the rationale for canon-icity. The underlying argument, rather, is that consistency, fidelity to those values, requires recognition of at least the few best and best-known women writers. Equally obviously, this approach does not call the notion of the canon itself into question.

WE ACKNOWLEDGE IT CANONLIKE, BUT NOT CANONICALL. (BISHOP BARLOW, 1601)

Many feminist critics reject the method of case-by-case demonstration. The wholesale consignment of women's concerns and productions to a grim area bounded by triviality and obscurity cannot be compensated for by tokenism. True equity can be attained, they argue, only by opening up the canon to a much larger number of female voices. This is an endeavor that eventually brings basic aesthetic questions to the fore.

Initially, however, the demand for wider representation of female authors is substantiated by an extraordinary effort of intellectual reappropri-ation. The emergence of feminist literary study has been characterized, at the base, by scholarship devoted to the discovery, republication, and reappraisal of "lost" or undervalued writers and their work. From Rebecca Harding Davis and Kate Chopin through Zora Neale Hurston and Mina Loy to Meridel LeSueur and Rebecca West, reputations have been reborn or remade and a female countercanon has come into being, out of components that were largely unavailable even a dozen years ago.[10]

In addition to constituting a feminist alternative to the male-dominated tradition, these authors also have a claim to representation in "the" canon. From this perspective, the work of recovery itself makes one sort of prima facie case, giving the lie to the assumption, where it has existed, that aside from a few names that are household words — differentially appreciated, but certainly well known — there simply has not been much serious literature by women. Before any aesthetic arguments have been advanced either for or against the admission of such works to the general canon, the new literary scholarship on women has demonstrated that the pool of potential applicants is far larger than anyone has hitherto suspected.

Would Augustine, if he held all the books to have an equal right to canonicity . . . have preferred some to others? (W. Fitzgerald, trans. Whitaker, 1849)

But the aesthetic issues cannot be forestalled for very long. We need to understand whether the claim is being made that many of the newly recovered or validated texts by women meet existing criteria or, on the other hand, that those criteria themselves intrinsically exclude or tend to exclude women and hence should be modified or replaced. If this polarity is not, in fact, applicable to the process, what are the grounds for presenting a large number of new female candidates for (as it were) canonization?

The problem is epitomized in Nina Baym's introduction to her study of American women's fiction between 1820 and 1870:

> Reexamination of this fiction may well show it to lack the esthetic, intellectual, and moral complexity and artistry that we demand of great literature. I confess frankly that, although I have found much to interest me in these books, I have not unearthed a forgotten Jane Austen or George Eliot or hit upon the one novel that I would propose to set alongside *The Scarlet Letter*. Yet I cannot avoid the belief that "purely" literary criteria, as they have been employed to identify the best American works, have inevitably had a bias in favor of things male — in favor of, say, a whaling ship, rather than a sewing circle as a symbol of the human community. . . . While not claiming any literary greatness for any of the novels . . . in this study, I would like at least to begin to correct such a bias by taking their content seriously. And it is time, perhaps — though this task lies outside my scope here — to reexamine the grounds upon which certain hallowed American classics have been called great.[11]

Now, if students of literature may be allowed to confess to one Great Unreadable among the Great Books, my own *bête noire* has always been the white whale; I have always felt I was missing something in *Moby-Dick* that is clearly there for many readers and that is there for me when I read, say, Aeschylus or Austen. So I find Baym's strictures congenial, at first reading. Yet the contradictory nature of the position is also evident on the face of it. Am I or am I not being invited to construct a (feminist) aesthetic rationale for my impatience with *Moby-Dick*? Do Baym and the current of thought she represents accept "esthetic, intellectual, and moral complexity and artistry" as the grounds of greatness, or are they challenging those values as well?

As Myra Jehlen points out most lucidly, this attractive position will not bear close analysis: "[Baym] is having it both ways, admitting the artistic limitations of the women's fiction . . . and at the same time denying the validity of the rulers that measure these limitations, disdaining any ambition to reorder the literary canon and, on second thought, challenging the canon after all, or rather challenging not the canon itself but the grounds for its selection."[12] Jehlen understates the case, however, in calling the duality a paradox, which is, after all, an intentionally created and essentially rhetorical phenomenon. What is involved here is more like the *agony* of feminist criticism, for it is the champions of women's literature who are torn between defending the quality of their discoveries and radically redefining literary quality itself.

Those who are concerned with the canon as a pragmatic instrument rather than a powerful abstraction — the compilers of more equitable anthologies or course syllabi, for example — have opted for an uneasy compromise. The literature by women that they seek — as well as that by members of excluded racial and ethnic groups and by working people in general — conforms as closely as possible to the traditional canons of taste and judgment. Not that it reads like such literature as far as content and viewpoint are concerned, but the same words about artistic intent and achievement may be applied without absurdity. At the same time, the rationale for a new syllabus or anthology relies on a very different criterion: that of truth to the culture being represented, the *whole* culture and not the creation of an almost entirely male white elite. Again, no one seems to be proposing — aloud — the elimination of *Moby-Dick* or *The Scarlet Letter,* just squeezing them over somewhat to make room for another literary reality, which, joined with the existing canon, will come closer to telling the (poetic) truth.

The effect is pluralist, at best, and the epistemological assumptions underlying the search for a more fully representative literature are strictly empiricist: By including the perspective of women (who are, after all, half-the-population), we will know more about the culture as it actually was. No one suggests that there might be something in this literature itself that challenges the values and even the validity of the previously all-male tradition. There is no reason why the canon need speak with one voice or as one man on the fundamental questions of human experience. Indeed, even as an elite white male voice, it can hardly be said to do so. Yet a commentator like Baym has only to say "it is time, perhaps . . . to reexamine the grounds," *while not proceeding to do so,* for feminists to be accused of wishing to throw out the entire received culture. The argument could be more usefully joined, perhaps, if there *were* a current within feminist criticism that went beyond insistence on representation to consideration of precisely how inclusion of women's writing alters our view of the tradition. Or even one that suggested some radical surgery on the list of male authors usually represented.

After all, when we turn from the construction of pantheons, which have no *prescribed* number of places, to the construction of course syllabi, then something does have to be eliminated each time something else is added, and here ideologies, aesthetic and extra-aesthetic, do necessarily come into play. Is the canon and hence the syllabus based on it to be regarded as the compendium of excellence or as the record of cultural history? For there comes a point when the proponent of making the canon recognize the achievement of both sexes has to put up or shut up; either a given woman writer is good enough to replace some male writer on the prescribed reading list or she is not. If she is not, then either she should replace him anyway, in the name of telling the truth about the culture, or she should not, in the (unexamined) name of excellence. This is the debate that will have to be engaged and that has so far been broached only in the most "inclusionary" of terms. It is ironic that in American literature, where attacks on the male tradition have been most bitter and the reclamation of women writers so spectacular, the appeal has still been only to pluralism, generosity, and guilt. It is populism without the politics of populism.

To canonize your owne writers (Polimanteria, 1595)

Although I referred earlier to a feminist countercanon, it is only in certain rather restricted contexts that literature by women has in fact been explicitly placed "counter" to the dominant canon. Generally speaking, feminist scholars have been more concerned with establishing the existence, power, and significance of a specifically female tradition. Such a possibility is adumbrated in the title of Patricia Meyer Spacks's *The Female Imagination;* however, this book's overview of selected themes and stages in the female life-cycle as treated by some women writers neither broaches nor (obviously) suggests an answer to the question whether there is a female imagination and what characterizes it.[13]

Somewhat earlier, in her anthology of British and American women poets, Louise Bernikow had made a more positive assertion of a continuity and connection subsisting among them.[14] She leaves it to the poems, however, to forge their own links, and, in a collection that boldly and incisively crosses boundaries between published and unpublished writing, literary and anonymous authorship, "high" art, folk art, and music, it is not easy for the reader to identify what the editor believes it is that makes women's poetry specifically *"women's."*

Ellen Moers centers her argument for a (transhistorical) female tradition upon the concept of "heroinism," a quality shared by women writers over time with the female characters they created.[15] Moers also points out another kind of continuity, documenting the way that women writers have read, commented on, and been influenced by the writings of other women who were their predecessors or contemporaries. There is also an unacknowledged continuity between the writer and her female reader. Elaine Showalter conceives the female tradition, embodied particularly in the domestic and sensational fiction of the nineteenth century, as being carried out through a kind of subversive conspiracy between author and audience.[16] Showalter is at her best in discussing this minor "women's fiction." Indeed, without ever making a case for popular genres as serious literature, she bases her arguments about a tradition more solidly on them than on acknowledged major figures like Virginia Woolf. By contrast, Sandra Gilbert and Susan Gubar focus almost exclusively on key literary figures, bringing women writers and their subjects together through the theme of perceived female aberration — in the act of literary creation itself, as well as in the behavior of the created persons or personae.[17]

Moers's vision of a continuity based on "heroinism" finds an echo in later feminist criticism that posits a discrete, perhaps even autonomous "women's culture." The idea of such a culture has been developed by social historians studying the "homosocial" world of nineteenth-century women.[18] It is a view that underlies, for example, Nina Auerbach's study of relationships among women in selected novels, where strong, supportive ties among mothers, daughters, sisters, and female friends not only constitute the real history in which certain women are conceived as living but function as a normative element as well.[19] That is, fiction in which positive relations subsist to nourish the heroine comes off much better, from Auerbach's point of view, than fiction in which such relations do not exist.

In contrast, Judith Lowder Newton sees the heroines of women's fiction as active, rather than passive, precisely because they do live in a man's world, not an autonomous female one.[20] Defining their power as "ability" rather than "control," she perceives "both a preoccupation with power and subtle power strategies" being exercised by the women in novels by Fanny Burney, Jane Austen, Charlotte Brontë, and George Eliot. Understood in this way, the female tradition, whether or not it in fact reflects and fosters a "culture" of its own, provides an alternative complex of possibilities for women, to be set beside the pits and pedestals offered by all too much of the Great Tradition.

CANONIZE SUCH A MULTIFARIOUS GENEALOGIE OF COMMENTS. (NASHE, 1593)

Historians like Smith-Rosenberg and Cott are careful to specify that their generalizations extend only to white middle- and upper-class women of the nineteenth century. Although literary scholars are equally scrupulous about the national and temporal boundaries of their subject, they tend to use the gender term comprehensively. In this way, conclusions about "women's fiction" or "female consciousness" have been drawn or jumped to from considering a body of work whose authors are all white and comparatively privileged. Of the critical studies I have mentioned, only Bernikow's anthology, *The World Split Open*, brings labor songs, black women's blues lyrics, and anonymous ballads into conjunction with poems that were written for publication by professional writers, both black and white. The other books, which build an extensive case for a female tradition that Bernikow only suggests, delineate their subject in such a way as to exclude not only black and working-class authors but any notion that race and class might be relevant categories in the definition and apprehension of "women's literature." Similarly, even for discussions of writers who were known to be lesbians, this aspect of the female tradition often remains unacknowledged; worse yet, some of the books that develop the idea of a female tradition are openly homophobic, employing he word "lesbian" only pejoratively.[21]

Black and lesbian scholars, however, have directed much less energy to polemics against the feminist "mainstream" than to concrete, positive work on the literature itself. Recovery and reinterpretation of a wealth of unknown or undervalued texts has suggested the existence of both a black women's tradition and a lesbian tradition. In a clear parallel with the relationship between women's literature in general and the male-dominated tradition, both are by definition part of women's literature, but they are also distinct from and independent of it.

There are important differences, however, between these two traditions and the critical effort surrounding them. Black feminist criticism has the task of demonstrating that, in the face of all the obstacles a racist and sexist society has been able to erect, there is a continuity of black women who have written and written well. It is a matter of gaining recognition for the quality of the writing itself and respect for its principal subject, the lives and consciousness of black women. Black women's literature is also an element of black literature as a whole, where the recognized voices have usually been male. A triple imperative is therefore at work: establishing a discrete and significant black female tradition, then situating it within black literature and (along with the rest of that literature) within the common American literary heritage.[22] So far, unfortunately, each step toward integration has met with continuing exclusion. A black women's tradition has been recovered and revaluated chiefly through the efforts of black feminist scholars. Only some of that work has been accepted as part of either a racially mixed women's literature or a two-sex black literature. As for the gatekeepers of American literature in general, how many of them are willing to swing open the portals even for Zora Neale Hurston or Paule Marshall? How many have heard of them?

The issue of "inclusion," moreover, brings up the questions that echo those raised by opening the male-dominated canon to women. How do generalizations about women's literature "as a whole" change when the work of black women is not merely added to but fully incorporated into that tradition? How does our sense of black literary history change? And what implications do these changes have for reconsideration of the American canon?

Whereas many white literary scholars continue to behave as if there were no major black women writers, most are prepared to admit that certain well-known white writers were lesbians for all or part of their lives. The problem is getting beyond a position that says either "so *that's* what was wrong with her!" or, alternatively, "it doesn't matter who she slept with — we're talking about literature." Much lesbian feminist criticism has addressed theoretical questions about *which* literature is actually part of the lesbian tradition, all writing by lesbians, for example, or all writing by women about women's relations with one another. Questions of class and race enter here as well, both in their own guise and in the by now familiar form of "aesthetic standards." Who speaks for the lesbian community: the highly educated experimentalist with an unearned income or the naturalistic working-class autobiographer? Or are both the *same kind* of foremother, reflecting the community's range of cultural identities and resistance?[23]

A CHEAPER WAY OF CANON-MAKING IN A CORNER
(BAXTER, 1639)

It is not only members of included social groups, however, who have challenged the fundamentally elite nature of the existing canon. "Elite" is a literary as well as a social category. It is possible to argue for taking all texts seriously as texts without arguments based on social oppression or cultural exclusion, and popular genres have therefore been studied as part of the female literary tradition. Feminists are not in agreement as to whether domestic and sentimental fiction, the female Gothic, the women's sensational novel functioned as instruments of expression, repression, or subversion, but they have successfully revived interest in the question as a legitimate cultural issue.[24] It is no longer automatically assumed that literature addressed to the mass female audience is necessarily bad because it is sentimental, or for that matter, sentimental because it is addressed to that audience. Feminist criticism has examined without embarrassment an entire literature that was previously dismissed solely because it was popular with women and affirmed standards and values associated with femininity. And proponents of the "continuous tradition" and "women's culture" positions have insisted that this material be placed beside women's "high" art as part of the articulated and organic female tradition.

This point of view remains controversial within the orbit of women's studies, but the real problems start when it comes into contact with the universe of canon formation. Permission may have been given the contemporary critic to approach a wide range of texts, transcending and even ignoring the traditional canon. But in a context where the ground of struggle — highly contested, moreover — concerns Edith Wharton's advancement to somewhat more major status, fundamental assumptions have changed very little. Can Hawthorne's "d——d mob of scribbling women" *really* be invading the realms so long sanctified by Hawthorne himself and his brother geniuses? Is this what feminist criticism or even feminist cultural history means? Is it — to apply some outmoded and deceptively simple categories — a good development or a bad one? If these questions have not been raised, it is because women's literature and the female tradition tend to be evoked as an autonomous cultural experience, not impinging on the rest of literary history.

WISDOME UNDER A RAGGED COATE IS SELDOME CANONICALL. (CROSSE, 1603)

Whether dealing with popular genres or high art, commentary on the female tradition usually has been based on work that was published at some time and was produced by professional writers. But feminist scholarship has also pushed back the boundaries of literature in other directions, considering a wide range of forms and styles in which women's writing — especially that of women who did not perceive themselves as writers — appears. In this way, women's letters, diaries, journals, autobiographies, oral histories, and private poetry have come under critical scrutiny as evidence of women's consciousness *and expression*.

Generally speaking, feminist criticism has been quite open to such material, recognizing that the very conditions that gave many women the impetus to write made it impossible for their culture to define them as writers. This acceptance has expanded our sense of possible forms and voices, but it has not challenged our received sense of appropriate style. What it amounts to is that if a woman writing in isolation and with no public audience in view nonetheless has "good" — that is, canonical — models, we are impressed with the strength of her text when she applies what she has assimilated about writing to her own experiences as a woman. If, however, her literary models were chosen from the same popular literature that some critics are now beginning to recognize as part of the female tradition, then she has not got hold of an expressive instrument that empowers her.

At the Modern Language Association meeting in 1976, I included in my paper the entire two-page autobiography of a participant in the Summer Schools for Women Workers held at Bryn Mawr in the first decades of the century. It is a circumstantial narrative in which events from the melancholy to the melodramatic are accumulated in a serviceable, somewhat hackneyed style. The anonymous "Seamer on Men's Underwear" had a unique sense of herself both as an individual and as a member of the working class. But was she a writer? Part of the audience was as moved as I was by the narrative, but the majority was outraged at the piece's failure to meet the criteria — particularly, the "complexity" criteria — of good art.

When I developed my remarks for publication, I wrote about the problems of dealing with an author who is trying too hard to write elegantly, and attempted to make the case that clichés or sentimentality need not be signals of meretricious prose and that ultimately it is honest writing for which criticism should be looking.[25] Nowadays, I would also address the question of the female tradition, the role of popular fiction within it, and the influence of that fiction on its audience. It seems to me that, if we accept the work of the professional "scribbling woman," we have also to accept its literary consequences, not drawing the line at the place where that literature may have been the force that enabled an otherwise inarticulate segment of the population to grasp a means of expression and communication.

Once again, the arena is the female tradition itself. If we are thinking in terms of canon formation, it is the alternative canon. Until the aesthetic arguments can be fully worked out in the feminist context, it will be impossible to argue, in the general marketplace of literary ideas, that the novels of Henry James ought to give place — a *little* place, even — to the diaries of his sister Alice. At this point, I suspect most of our male colleagues would consider such a request, even in the name of Alice James, much less the Seamer on Men's Underwear, little more than a form of "reverse discrimination" — a concept to which some of them are already overly attached. It is up to feminist scholars, when we determine that this is indeed the right course to pursue, to demonstrate that such an inclusion would constitute a genuinely affirmative action for all of us.

The development of feminist literary criticism and scholarship has already proceeded through a number of identifiable stages. Its pace is more reminiscent of the survey course than of the slow processes of canon formation and revision, and it has been more successful in defining and sticking to its own intellectual turf, the female countercanon, than in gaining general canonical recognition for Edith Wharton, Fanny Fern, or the female diarists of the Westward Expansion. In one sense, the more coherent our sense of the female tradition is, the stronger will be our eventual case. Yet the longer we wait, the more comfortable the women's literature ghetto — separate, apparently autonomous, and far from equal — may begin to feel.

At the same time, I believe the challenge cannot come only by means of the patent value of the work of women. We must pursue the questions certain of us have raised and retreated from as to the eternal verity of the received standards of greatness or even goodness. And, while not abandoning our newfound female tradition, we have to return to confrontation with "the" canon, examining it as a source of ideas, themes, motifs, and myths about the two sexes. The point in so doing is not to label and hence dismiss even the most sexist literary classics, but to enable all of us to apprehend them, finally, in all their human dimensions.

NOTES

1. Jane Marcus, "Gunpowder Treason and Plot," talk delivered at the School of Criticism and Theory, Northwestern University, colloquium "The Challenge of Feminist Criticism," November 1981. Seeking authority for the sort of creature a literary canon might be, I turned, like many another, to the *Oxford English Dictionary*. The tags that head up the several sections of this essay are a by-product of that effort rather than of any more exact and laborious scholarship.

2. In a survey of 50 introductory courses in American literature offered at 25 U.S. colleges and universities, Emily Dickinson's name appeared more often than that of any other woman writer: 20 times. This frequency puts her in a fairly respectable twelfth place. Among the 61 most frequently taught authors, only 7 others are women; Edith Wharton and Kate Chopin are each mentioned 8 times, Sarah Orne Jewett and Anne Bradstreet 6 each, Flannery O'Connor 4 times, Willa Cather and Mary Wilkins Freeman each 3 times. The same list includes 5 black authors, all of them male. Responses from other institutions received too late for compilation only confirmed these findings. See Paul Lauter, "A Small Survey of Introductory Courses in American Literature," *Women's Studies Quarterly* 9 (Winter 1981): 12. In another study, 99 professors of English responded to a survey asking which works of American literature published since 1941 they thought should be considered classics and which books should be taught to college students. The work mentioned by the most respondents (59 citations) was Ralph Ellison's *Invisible Man*. No other work by a black appears among the top 20 that constitute the published list of results. Number 19, *The Complete Stories of Flannery O'Connor*, is the only work on this list by a woman. (*Chronicle of Higher Education*, September 29, 1982.) For British literature, the feminist claim is not that Austen, the Brontës, Eliot, and Woolf are habitually omitted, but rather that they are by no means always included in courses that, like the survey I taught at Columbia some years ago, had room for a single nineteenth-century novel. I know, however, of no systematic study of course offerings in this area more recent than Elaine Showalter's "Women in the Literary Curriculum," *College English* 32 (May 1971): 855–62.

3. Kate Millett, *Sexual Politics* (Garden City, N.Y.: Doubleday, 1970): Eva Figes, *Patriarchal Attitudes* (New York: Stein & Day, 1970); Elizabeth Janeway, *Man's World, Woman's Place: A Study in Social Mythology* (New York: William Morrow, 1971); Germaine Greer, *The Female Eunuch* (New York: McGraw-Hill, 1971); Carolyn G. Heilbrun, *Toward a Recognition of Androgyny* (New York: Harper & Row, 1974). The phenomenon these studies represent is discussed at greater length in a study of which I am a co-author; see Ellen Carol DuBois, Gail Paradise Kelly, Elizabeth Lapovsky Kennedy, Carolyn W. Korsmeyer, and Lillian S. Robinson, *Feminist Scholarship: Kindling in the Groves of Academe* (Urbana: University of Illinois Press, 1985).

4. Annette Kolodny, *The Lay of the Land: Metaphor as Experience and History in American Life and Letters* (Chapel Hill: University of North Carolina Press, 1975); Judith Fetterley, *The Resisting Reader: A Feminist Approach to American Fiction* (Bloomington: Indiana University Press, 1978).

5. Mary Ellmann, *Thinking About Women* (New York: Harcourt, Brace & World, 1968).

6. Carolyn Ruth Swift Lenz, Gayle Greene, and Carol Thomas Neely, eds. *The Woman's Part: Feminist Criticism of Shakespeare* (Urbana: University of Illinois Press, 1980), p. 4. In this vein, see also Juliet Dusinberre, *Shakespeare and the Nature of Women* (London: Macmillan, 1975); Irene G. Dash, *Wooing, Wedding, and Power: Women in Shakespeare's Plays* (New York: Columbia University Press, 1981).

7. Sandra M. Gilbert, "Patriarchal Poetics and the Woman Reader: Reflections on Milton's Bogey." *PMLA* 93 (May 1978): 368–82. The articles on Chaucer and Shakespeare in *The Authority of Experience: Essays in Feminist Criticism*, ed. Arlyn Diamond and Lee R. Edwards (Amherst: University of Massachusetts Press, 1977), reflect the complementary tendency.

8. As I learned when surveying fifteen years' worth of *Dissertation Abstracts* and MLA programs, much of this work has taken the form of theses or conference papers rather than books and journal articles.

9. See R. W. B. Lewis, *Edith Wharton: A Biography* (New York: Harper & Row, 1975); Cynthia Griffin Wolff, *A Feast of Words: The Triumph of Edith Wharton* (New York: Oxford University Press, 1977); see also Marlene Springer, *Edith Wharton and Kate Chopin: A Reference Guide* (Boston: G. K. Hall, 1976).

10. See, for instance, Rebecca Harding Davis, *Life in the Iron Mills* (Old Westbury, N.Y.: Feminist Press, 1972), with a biographical and critical Afterword by Tillie Olsen; Kate Chopin, *The Complete Works*, ed. Per Seyersted (Baton Rouge: Louisiana State University Press, 1969); Alice Walker, "In Search of Zora Neale Hurston," *Ms.*, March 1975, pp. 74–75; Robert Hemenway, *Zora Neale Hurston* (Urbana: University of Illinois Press, 1978): Zora Neale Hurston, *I Love Myself When I Am Laughing and Also When I Am Looking Mean and Impressive* (Old Westbury: Feminist Press, 1979), with introductory material by Alice Walker and Mary Helen Washington; Carolyn G. Burke, "Becoming Mina Loy," *Women's Studies* 7 (1979): 136–50; Meridel LeSueur, *Ripening* (Old Westbury: Feminist Press, 1981); on LeSueur, see also Mary McAnally, ed., *We Sing Our Struggle: A Tribute to Us All* (Tulsa, Okla.: Cardinal Press, 1982); *The Young Rebecca: Writings of Rebecca West, 1911–1917*, selected and introduced by Jane Marcus (New York: Viking Press, 1982).

The examples cited are all from the nineteenth and twentieth centuries. Valuable work has also been done on women writers before the Industrial Revolution. See Joan Goulianos, ed., *By a Woman Writ: Literature from Six Centuries by and about Women* (Indianapolis: Bobbs-Merrill, 1973); Mary R. Mahl and Helene Koon, eds., *The Female Spectator: English Women Writers before 1800* (Bloomington: Indiana University Press, 1977).

11. Nina Baym, *Women's Fiction: A Guide to Novels by and about Women in America, 1820–70* (Ithaca: Cornell University Press, 1978), pp. 14–15.

12. Myra Jehlen, "Archimedes and the Paradox of Feminist Criticism," *Signs* 6 (Summer 1981): 592.

13. Patricia Meyer Spacks, *The Female Imagination* (New York: Alfred A. Knopf, 1975).

14. *The World Split Open: Four Centuries of Women Poets in England and America, 1552–1950*, ed. and intro. Louise Bernikow (New York: Vintage Books, 1974).

15. Ellen Moers, *Literary Women: The Great Writers* (Garden City, N.Y.: Doubleday, 1976).

16. Elaine Showalter, *A Literature of Their Own: British Women Novelists from Brontë to Lessing* (Princeton, N.J.: Princeton University Press, 1977).

17. Sandra M. Gilbert and Susan Gubar, *The Madwoman in the Attic: The Woman Writer and the Nineteenth-Century Literary Imagination* (New Haven, Conn.: Yale University Press, 1979).

18. Carroll Smith-Rosenberg, "The Female World of Love and Ritual: Relations Between Women in Nineteenth-Century America," *Signs* 1 (Fall 1975): 1–30; Nancy F. Cott, *The Bonds of Womanhood: "Woman's Sphere" in New England, 1780–1830* (New Haven, Conn.: Yale University Press, 1977).

19. Nina Auerbach, *Communities of Women: An Idea in Fiction* (Cambridge, Mass.: Harvard University Press, 1979). See also Janet M. Todd, *Women's Friendship in Literature* (New York: Columbia University Press, 1980); Louise Bernikow, *Among Women* (New York: Crown, 1980).

20. Judith Lowder Newton, *Women, Power, and Subversion: Social Strategies in British Fiction* (Athens: University of Georgia Press, 1981).

21. On the failings of feminist criticism with respect to black and/or lesbian writers, see Barbara Smith, "Toward a Black Feminist Criticism," *Conditions*, 2 (1977); Mary Helen Washington, "New Lives and New Letters: Black Women Writers at the End of the Seventies," *College English*, 43 (1981); Bonnie Zimmerman, "What Has Never Been: An Overview of Lesbian Feminist Literary Criticism," *Feminist Studies* 7 (1981).

22. See, e.g., Smith, "Toward a Black Feminist Criticism"; Barbara Christian, *Black Women Novelists: The Development of a Tradition, 1892–1976* (Westport, Conn.: Greenwood Press, 1980); Erlene Stetson, ed., *Black Sister: Poetry by Black American Women, 1764–1980* (Bloomington: Indiana

University Press, 1981) and its forthcoming sequel; Gloria Hull, "Black Women Poets from Wheatley to Walker," in *Sturdy Black Bridges: Visions of Black Women in Literature,* ed. Roseann P. Bell et al. (Garden City, N.Y.: Anchor Books, 1979); Mary Helen Washington, "Introduction: In Pursuit of Our Own History," *Midnight Birds: Stories of Contemporary Black Women Writers* (Garden City, N.Y.: Anchor Books, 1980); the essays and bibliographies in *But Some of Us Are Brave: Black Women's Studies,* ed. Gloria Hull, Patricia Bell Scott, and Barbara Smith (Old Westbury: Feminist Press, 1982).

23. See Zimmerman, "What Has Never Been"; Adrienne Rich, "Jane Eyre: Trials of a Motherless Girl," *Lies, Secrets, and Silence: Selected Prose, 1966–1978* (New York: W. W. Norton, 1979); Lillian Faderman, *Surpassing the Love of Men: Romantic Friendship and Love Between Women from the Renaissance to the Present* (New York: William Morrow, 1981); the literary essays in *Lesbian Studies,* ed. Margaret Cruikshank (Old Westbury, N.Y.: Feminist Press, 1982).

24. Some examples on different sides of the question are: Ann Douglas, *The Feminization of American Culture* (New York: Alfred A. Knopf, 1976); Elaine Showalter, *A Literature of Their Own* and her article "Dinah Mulock Craik and the Tactics of Sentiment: A Case Study in Victorian Female Authorship," *Feminist Studies* 2 (May 1975): 5–23; Katherine Ellis, "Paradise Lost: The Limits of Domesticity in the Nineteenth-Century Novel," *Feminist Studies* 2 (May 1975): 55–65.

25. Lillian S. Robinson, "Working/Women/Writing," *Sex, Class, and Culture* (Bloomington: Indiana University Press, 1978), p. 252.

Manhood, Class, and the American Renaissance

DAVID LEVERENZ

Leverenz brings together a discussion of manhood and class as identity markers, arguing that class lines have been blurred in the United States because of the overwhelming triumph of the middle class. Thus, according to Leverenz, an emphasis was placed on manhood rather than class. Leverenz identifies three types of American manhood: patrician manhood based on "property, patriarchy, and citizenship," artisan manhood based on self-sufficiency, and the new manhood based on capitalist competition. Leverenz points to social historians and writers to support his contention that class tensions shaped notions of manhood and suggests that while patriarchy may reflect women's experience of men, it does not reflect men's relations with each other. In making his argument, Leverenz discusses texts such as Herman Melville's "Bartleby, the Scrivener" and Moby-Dick, *Nathaniel Hawthorne's* House of the Seven Gables *and* The Blithedale Romance, *and makes passing reference to Benjamin Franklin, Ralph Waldo Emerson, and Walt Whitman among others. This essay appears in* American Literature, Culture, and Ideology, *edited by Beverly R. Voloshin (1990), but a fuller discussion may be found in Leverenz's book,* Manhood and the American Renaissance *(1989).*

One of the most basic themes in American history has been the widely shared belief that the possibilities for individual upward mobility effectively blur class lines. Benjamin Franklin first gave mythic status to the rags-to-riches dream in his *Autobiography.* Elsewhere he emphasized the "happy mediocrity" of the American situation, so relatively free from class hierarchy and tyrannical aristocratic institutions. In the decades before the Civil War, especially in the Northeast, the idea of being self-reliant or a "self-made man" — a phrase apparently coined by Henry Clay in 1832 — amounted to an obsession. Appropriately, Clay associates the phrase with the dominant values of American individualism. As he says during a lengthy speech defending tariffs, "In Kentucky, almost every manufactory known to me, is in the

From *American Literature, Culture, and Ideology: Essays in Memory of Henry Nash Smith,* ed. Beverly R. Voloshin (New York: Peter Lang, 1990) 79–92.

hands of enterprising and self-made men, who acquired whatever wealth they possess by patient and diligent labor."

In the last few years, various studies have suggested a middle-class frame for the paradoxes of American individualism. Its ethic of hard work, self-control, and material rewards rested on the presumption that everyone could be successful. The very term "middle class" came into use in the 1830s, replacing "the middling orders" or "the middling sort," to emphasize the paradoxical possibility of upward mobility for everyone.[1] Part of the reason class lines have been so blurred in America, I think, is that the triumph of middle class values and the economic system fostering them has been so overwhelming.

The triumph of the "new men" over the mercantile elite brought a preoccupation with manhood rather than class among men of the Northeast. The conflict was not a class war in conventional European terms, but an ideological tension felt in terms of gender. What did it mean to be manly? Did it mean a craftsman's independence and self-respect, or an entrepreneur's ability to best his competitors and exploit resources, human as well as material? Did a man's self-respect depend on a sense of being free and equal to any other man, or on a struggle to be dominant?

Here I will sketch three paradigms of American manhood. I think of them as akin to Max Weber's ideal types: conceptual categories never fully existing in the world, yet useful for studying more complicated social stresses. Their usefulness also extends to literary study, partly because writers such as Hawthorne and Melville employ similar stereotypes in their characterizations.

The patrician paradigm defined manhood through property, patriarchy, and citizenship. It was the ideology of a narrow elite: merchants, gentry, large landowners, lawyers — in old English as well as old Marxist perspective, the upper bourgeoisie. Its manly ideal of character and paternalism had much in common with older British aristocratic ideals of honor, a code which survived much longer in the South. So long as mercantile capitalism dominated economic production in the Northeast, this ideal of manhood held relatively comfortable sway.

The artisan paradigm defined manhood in Jeffersonian terms, as autonomous self-sufficiency. A man worked his land or his craft with integrity and freedom. Longfellow's "The Village Blacksmith" catches the myth:

> His brow is wet with honest sweat,
>   He earns whate'er he can,
> And looks the whole world in the face,
>   For he owes not any man.

As one can tell from the patrician paternalism of Jefferson and Longfellow, this ideal of manhood worked well with mercantile capitalism, which depended for its raw materials on independent yeoman farmers, and whose characteristic mode of production was the small patriarchal village shop. The relationship between Colonel Henry "Manly" and his servant Jonathan in Royall Tyler's popular drawing-room comedy, *The Contrast* (1787), celebrates the triumph of true American manhood over quasi-British aristocratic manners, and presumes the harmony of master and servant.

In practice, many artisans shared the patriarchal emphasis on citizenship and the good of the whole. The result was what Nick Salvatore has called, in a different context, "deferential democracy." In the world that Eugene V. Debs grew up in, an artisan's sense of manhood was based primarily upon his work, and to a somewhat lesser extent on his role as father and husband. A man must provide for his family, and he must be "a model of industry and honesty." This code of manhood "also required an active political participation and the fulfillment of one's duty as a citizen." Such an ideal of work could deny existing class interests and stress a common purpose in part because it was such a small-town world. Ostensibly based on pride of craft, the "skilled worker's vision of manhood" also depended on what Salvatore calls "a fundamental cohesion within their society and culture."[2] In a larger, more amorphous marketplace world, where a man felt more and more like a hand, the already romanticized ideal of community could no longer be presumed as a frame for manly freedom and pride of craftsmanship. Skilled labor now seemed more like exploitation and oppression.

Faith in a patriarchal elite had its intimate counterpart in the patriarchy of the home. Though Jay Fliegelman's *Prodigals and Pilgrims* argues for a basic change from stern to benign fathering from 1750 to 1800, the assumption of father's primacy as father remains unquestioned.[3] Considerable psychological conflict roils under the surface of both paradigms, especially in the artisan model, where independence is uneasily yoked to filial deference. The classic text for the transition from artisan to patrician patriarchy is Franklin's *Autobiography*.

The real class tension came from the undeferential, ambitious entrepreneurs and speculators who challenged patrician modes of power. Mary Kelley calls the victory of the new men the greatest social transformation in American history.[4] While that judgement may seem excessive, it catches some of the stress of the time, as men struggled to redefine for themselves what it meant to work. Lemuel Shaw, Melville's father-in-law, played a crucial role as Chief Justice of the Massachusetts Supreme Court in redefining the gentry ideal of property rights from an absolute end in itself to an instrumental means, thus allowing for corporate expansion. Traditional artisan ideals of manliness as independence, hard work, and pride in one's labor, the backbone of American rhetoric then and now, were also being challenged in a marketplace emphasizing competition, risk, and calculation, with all the instability attending the economic change to industrial capitalism. Instability itself, the sense of not knowing one's place, was another prime source for obsessive competitiveness.

Franklin himself was a ruthless entrepreneurial competitor, mixing wiles and pugnacity to dominate his rival printers, one of whom he drove to Barbados. He fell back on Deborah Read for a wife only after he failed to gain one with a £100 dowry. While he clothes the reality of his entrepreneurial success in the appearance of retrospective patrician mellowness, a newer generation would seek the main chance with less attentiveness either to self-image or civic usefulness.

The greatest paradox in the triumph of the capitalist middle class is that its collective success depended upon maximizing individual competition, which thrives on the zest for dominance and the fear of failure. What Mary Ryan has called the "ebullience of artisan culture" depended on a relatively stable village world with strong kinship ties. That world was giving way to a much more rivalrous, alienated, and uncertain market, with visions of greater gain and precipitous falls on every hand. As Melville puts it at the beginning of *Pierre,* the greatest of patriarchal families now "rise and burst like bubbles in a vat."

Mary Ryan's *Cradle of the Middle Class,* foremost among the recent social histories arguing for the growth of a new middle class during this period, finds a decisive change in the social expectations for adult men. As the role of father became more peripheral, or intermittent, the complementary myths of the self-made man and the cult of true American womanhood fostered a narrow intensity of will, work, and self-reliance in the man, while the family became the domestic cradle for nurturing little republicans of the future. Sons became strangers to their mothers at an early age. Joseph Kett's study of American adolescence also finds a striking change, in the 1840s, toward heightened expectations for boys to be hard working and self-disciplined.

Ryan also argues for a complementary paradox. If the intensified individualism of the new middle-class male was a response to heightened competition, it was also a response by families to protect their children. While "the fragmentation of the patriarchal household economy" led to much greater gender separation, the family remained as the basic survival unit. The goal of the family, according to Ryan, was not to be upwardly mobile so much as to maintain its middle-class status. Along with the fear of individual failure came the fear that their children might fall into the emerging working class. The legacy of such families to their children became education, not property, to give them the skills necessary for commercial or professional careers.[5]

There is a vitality and zest as well as risk and fear in the entrepreneurial spirit, to be sure. This was the age of "Go ahead!," of try, fail, land on your feet and try again. In particular, and here I differ from Ryan, the norm-setting entrepreneurs relished the struggle to gain some measure of dominance in the marketplace. Money was a means, a tangible yardstick of prowess. They experienced themselves much as George Stigler, a Nobel Prize–winning economist, so appreciatively describes them, as "men of force":

> The competitive industry is not one for lazy or confused or inefficient men: they will watch their customers vanish, their best employees migrate, their assets dissipate. It is a splendid place for men of force: it rewards both hard work and genius, and it rewards on a fine and generous scale.

Or as Vince Lombardi put it, in a phrase that has been widely misquoted, these are men for whom "Winning isn't everything, but wanting to win is."[6] Appropriating an artisan rhetoric of freedom, the entrepreneurial ideology of manhood veils a drive for competitive dominance in the language of equality.

Probably the first literary record of the self-made entrepreneur in the New World is Cotton Mather's fulsome praise of Governor William Phips, by all accounts except Mather's an Ahab of the second order. Kenneth Silverman calls him just a "choleric adventurer" who cursed up a storm, regularly knocked people down, and occasionally threw things at governors before he became one himself. Mather relishes stories of how Phips quelled mutinies on his ships and how he dominated people on ship and shore. The bookish clergyman, filled with a good measure of choleric feelings himself, had various reasons for making his celebration of Phips the lengthy coda to *Magnalia Christi Americana* (1702), including political gratitude. Beyond his political and psychological pleasure in depicting Phips's rise from obscure sheepherder to great power, Mather presents Phips as the kind of man who can thrive in America: the exploitive, even brawling entrepreneur who seizes his chances and makes the most of them. The will to dominate is as fundamental to Mather's portrait as is the claim, almost a coinage of "self-made man," that Phips was "*A Son to his own Labours!*"[7]

A trickle of such men in the 1690s had become a torrent by the 1830s. True, these men of force, who gathered such great rewards from the economy they spurred, were not the ordinary men Ryan focuses on. As she argues, problematically, I think, middle-class boys were socialized not to become aggressive entrepreneurs but to aim for achievement and respectability.[8] Nonetheless, the bully-boys now set the pace and the norms for manhood in the market place. The social structure no longer restrained them. The artisan ideal now jostled with a new ideal of manhood, one previously accessible only to kings, court politicians, and great military leaders. Faced with a middle-class man of force, anyone on the other side of his dominance must have felt a little more fearful, a little less free. Sean Wilentz quotes an Irish artisan speaking at a New York labor rally in 1850: "'Even in this liberal country, the middle class stands above the workingmen, and every one of them is a little tyrant in himself, as Voltaire said.'"[9]

Emerson explicitly describes the new middle-class man in terms of ruthless power. In *Representative Men* (1850), he personifies the new middle class as Napoleon, the ultimate man of force. Napoleon, he says, represents "the class of business men . . . the class of industry and skill." He has all the virtues and vices of "the middle class of modern society; of the throng who fill the markets, shops, counting-houses, manufactories, ships, of the modern world, aiming to be rich." Utterly lacking in civilized generosity, "never weak and literary," "egotistic and monopolizing," "a boundless liar," Napoleon is always on stage to be seen and to manipulate his audience. He is "a monopolizer and usurper of other minds," to the end of exercising power and making "a great noise." Emerson's patrician disdain is clear. His admiration for

Napoleon's force is also abundantly present. Many members of the elite had portrayed Andrew Jackson in much the same way.

It seems at least plausible, then, to see class tensions shaping the issue, What did it mean to be a man. Not only social historians but writers themselves, at least the best ones, sometimes dramatize social change with class-linked characterizations of manhood. Part of the dark comedy of Melville's "Bartleby, the Scrivener" is Bartleby's refusal to be categorized in the class niches assigned by the genteel narrator to Turkey, the down-at-the-heels deferential gentleman, and to Nippers, the young and ambitious if mechanical "new man" preoccupied with ward politics. If the narrator defines himself quite comfortably as an appendage of the old elite, prudent, unaggressive, safe and snug amid his legal briefs and Christian civilities, the story exposes him as a false self, unable to deal with anger and moral equality. The narrator starts to feel "unmanned," he says twice, at being dictated to by an underling. "'What earthly right have you to stay here?'" he finds himself expostulating. "'Do you pay any rent? Do you pay my taxes? Or is this property yours?'" He relies on traditional patrician conventions of self-controlled benevolence to evade his implicit connection to Bartleby's equally unexpressed anger. By the end he unwittingly becomes linked with Monroe Edwards, the "gentleman forger."[10] In Hawthorne's *Blithedale Romance,* too, the dispossessed elite become personified in Coverdale and Old Moodie, both narcissistic and shallow "men of show." They are ineffectual if meddling bystanders for the exploitive new Napoleons of power, Hollingsworth and Westervelt, or "western world."

Hawthorne's *House of the Seven Gables* also emphasizes class tensions. It begins with a lengthy, patronizing narration of Hepzibah's fall from leisured gentility into the prosaic necessity of running a shop. If the narrator makes fun of her at ponderous, ostensibly sympathetic length, he more unequivocally takes the side of hapless patrician Clifford against the apotheosis of the new man of power, Jaffrey Pyncheon. The real climax comes as the narrator circles slowly and vindictively around Jaffrey's ominous, threatening body, sitting motionless in a chair. The narrator's controlled glee at Jaffrey's death complements the out-of-control giddiness of Clifford's wild train ride. Yet Clifford's superficial release only exposes his permanent incapacity to be a man. The happy ending is left to Holgrave, the benign "new man" whose residual craftsman's integrity and patrician's chivalry rescue him from his Jaffrey-like inclinations toward heartless exploitation and dominance.

Despite path-breaking studies by Carolyn Porter, Myra Jehlen, and especially William Charvat, no analysis of classic American writing has come close to the brilliant Marxist synthesis that Raymond Williams's *Culture and Society* achieves for English literature.[11] The reason, I think, has to do with the relative prominence of gender issues over class consciousness in American self-perceptions. Perhaps that in turn has something to do with the relative absence of an empowered and leisured aristocracy. As Michel Chevalier concludes his *Society, Manners, and Politics in the United States* (trans. 1839), "The higher classes in the United States, taken as a whole and with only some exceptions, have the air and attitude of the vanquished; they bear the mark of defeat on their front."[12]

Partly because the middle class has come to be so diffusely triumphant, American men tend to define their self-respect much more stringently through their work than through any other aspect of their lives. Accordingly, the contradictions and intensities of gender ideology refract implicit class tensions subsumed in the workplace and the work ethic. Feminist descriptions of manhood as patriarchy quite rightly reflect women's experience of men at home, during this period. But patriarchy does not reflect men's experience of each other at work. Rather, it is associated with mercantile and artisan norms of manhood now being displaced by the new norm of capitalist competition.

The other side of a man's drive for dominance is his fear of humiliation. Melville's Ahab represents the extreme of both ends. He is at once the supreme entrepreneurial man of force and, toward the end of *Moby-Dick*, especially in "The Candles," a man who begs to be beaten by a stronger, even more heartless competitor. His drive for dominance stems neither from patriarchy nor from testosterone but from having been grossly humiliated, as he conceives of it, by a faceless competitor acting through the whale. *Moby-Dick* is really a gigantic suicide trip, as Ahab becomes possessed by the new ideology of manhood, which for Melville is equivalent to the destruction of any kind of self.

"I hate to be ruled by my own sex," Miles Coverdale says to Zenobia in *The Blithedale Romance* (ch. 14, "Eliot's Pulpit"); "it excites my jealousy, and wounds my pride. It is the iron sway of bodily force which abases us, in our compelled submission." Despite such feelings, Coverdale seems on the verge of falling in love with Hollingsworth. Unlike Westervelt, this man of force also has a woman's capacity for tenderness. He makes the self-conscious narrator feel befriended and cared for rather than challenged in rivalry. "Hollingsworth's more than brotherly attendance gave me inexpressible comfort," Coverdale muses in chapter 6 ("Coverdale's Sick-chamber"). Most men, he continues, "have a natural indifference, if not an absolutely hostile feeling," toward the sick, the injured, and the weak, "amid the rude jostle of our selfish existence." This "ugly characteristic of our sex . . . has likewise its analogy in the practice of our brute brethren, who hunt the sick or disabled member of the herd from among them, as an enemy." Coverdale is astonished that Hollingsworth doesn't similarly turn on him, as any normal man would do.

However, when Hollingsworth appeals to Coverdale to join his cause, Coverdale reports his sensations as if he were being raped. It was "as if Hollingsworth had caught hold of my own heart, and were pulling it towards him with an almost irresistible force. . . . Had I but touched his extended hand, Hollingsworth's magnetism would perhaps have penetrated me with his own conception of all these matters." Coverdale's language eerily foreshadows Zenobia's fate, as Hollingsworth pokes a pole into her dead body.

The implicit rivalry between the two men is an allegory of class conflict as well as a psychodrama of homosexual fear. It ends with an ambiguous mixture of dominance and humiliation. Hollingsworth marries Priscilla, whom Coverdale suddenly announces he loves, yet Hollingsworth is deflated and defeated by his guilt for Zenobia. The man of force becomes a limp little boy, while the scared and skittish Coverdale can now smugly portray Hollingsworth's defeat and announce his love for the woman who tends his rival's humiliation.

Anyone preoccupied with manhood, in whatever time or culture, harbors fears of being humiliated, usually by other men. The sources for humiliation may be diverse, in parents or the loss of class position, in marketplace competition or other fears of being dominated. A preoccupation with manhood becomes a compensatory response. To adapt a term from John von Neumann's game theory, manhood becomes a way not of dominating, though that may be a by-product, but of minimizing maximum loss.[13] While the loss may be symbolized as castration, for instance in *Moby-Dick*, its roots lie not in the body but in a man's fear that other men will see him as weak, and therefore vulnerable to attack.

The new middle-class ideology of manhood intensifies fears of humiliation. Earlier ideologies of manhood link self-esteem to institutionalized social structures: class and patriarchy. The ideology of manhood emerging with entrepreneurial capitalism makes competition and power dynamics in the workplace the only source for valuing oneself. Manhood therefore becomes much more fundamental to a man's unconscious self-image.[14]

Seen in this context, classic male writers appear exceptionally self-conscious about their deviance from emerging business norms of manhood. The appendix to Lawrence Buell's fine recent study, *New England Literary Culture*, makes clear both the overwhelmingly elite origins of male writers and their search for careers other than in business. As covert acts of fight and flight, American Renaissance texts have received a very good press from twentieth- century academic critics, most of whom share these writers' alienation from business norms of manhood. The classic paradigms for canonized American texts presume victimization by bourgeois society as the inception of the writer's alienated imagination. We have the American Adam, a World Elsewhere of style, the Imperial Self, the prophetic and redemptive American Self, the Romance as a sacrifice of relation, the chaste marriage of wilderness males. Nina Baym has perceptively labelled these paradigms, all established by male critics, as "Melodramas of Beset Manhood."[15] The word "Melodramas," however, too easily dismisses the centrality of beset manhood to the texts these paradigms describe.

Male writers developed pre-modernist styles to explore their sense of being deviant from male norms emphasizing rivalry and exalting men of force. Women writers developed evangelical or more broadly moral narrations of domesticity to articulate the needs of a largely female reading public. As Alfred Habegger emphasizes, later writers such as Howells and James might accept with more equanimity the "sissy" role given to male writers in an industrializing middle-class society.[16] But from the 1820s through the 1850s, the writer's role and the male writer's audience were more uncertain.

American Renaissance self-refashioning — of reader as well as writer — develops as a rhetorical strategy responsive to these social conditions.

Most strikingly, in ways I don't have space to show here, a common rhetorical pattern appears at the start of the diverse masterpieces of Thoreau, Melville, and Whitman. In *Walden, Moby-Dick,* and "Song of Myself," a "you" is accused and appealed to, as double and conventional man but also as potential convert and comrade for the self-refashioned "I." Male rivalry looms under the promise of fraternity, and the rivalry returns in the rhetoric of self-refashioning, along with fears of humiliation. My argument is the reverse, really the underside, of Leslie Fiedler's well-known claim that classic American literature expresses a mythic male bonding in the wilderness. Fiedler is certainly right to emphasize the myth.[17] Where he explains it as a fantasized flight from heterosexual anxiety, however, I see it as the wishful surface of fears about male rivalry and male deviance.

To focus on this literature as social rhetoric brings out issues of manhood, especially male rivalry and fears of humiliation. Such preoccupations both express and mystify class conflicts, while also voicing and veiling more personal fears. Ultimately the effect of reading major texts this way, at least for me, is to demystify an enduring reverence for them as centerpieces of liberal and democratic values. As compensation, we can come to appreciate the writers' sensitivities to class and gender conflicts, in themselves as well as in their time.

NOTES

1. Karen Halttunen, *Confidence Men and Painted Women: A Study of Middle-Class Culture in America, 1830–1870* (New Haven: Yale University Press, 1982), p. 29.

2. Nick Salvatore, *Eugene V. Debs: Citizen and Socialist* (Urbana: University of Illinois Press, 1982), pp. 10, 23–24. On the complexities of artisan culture, see Eric Foner's *Tom Paine and Revolutionary America* (New York: Oxford University Press, 1976), Charles G. Steffen, *The Mechanics of Baltimore: Workers and Politics in the Age of Revolution 1763–1812* (Urbana: University of Illinois Press, 1984), and Sean Wilentz, *Chants Democratic: New York City & the Rise of the American Working Class, 1788–1850* (New York: Oxford University Press, 1984). All of these studies stress the connections between artisan culture and the American rhetoric of social radicalism.

3. Jay Fliegelman, *Prodigals and Pilgrims: The American Revolution Against Patriarchal Authority, 1750–1800* (Cambridge: Cambridge University Press, 1982). On tensions between independence and filial deference, see Philip Greven's *Four Generations: Population, Land, and Family in Colonial Andover, Massachusetts* (Ithaca: Cornell University Press, 1970), and Robert Blair St. George, "Fathers, Sons, and Identity: Woodworking Artisans in South-East New England, 1620–1700," in *The Craftsman in Early America,* ed. Ian M. G. Quimby (New York: Norton, 1984), pp. 89–125.

4. Mary Kelley, *Private Woman, Public Stage: Literary Domesticity in Nineteenth-Century America* (New York: Oxford University Press, 1984), pp. 297, 392. Kelley is drawing on the work of Gordon Wood and Stowe Persons.

5. Mary P. Ryan, *Cradle of the Middle Class: The Family in Oneida County, New York, 1790–1865* (Cambridge: Cambridge University Press, 1981), pp. 236 (ebullience), 155 (roles), 220 (sons), 210 (fragmentation), 184 and 238 (fear of falling into lower class), 169–171 (education); Joseph F. Kett, *Rites of Passage: Adolescence in America 1790 to the Present* (New York: Basic Books, 1977). On the new middle class, see a fine review essay by Stuart M. Blumin, "The Hypothesis of Middle-Class Formation in Nineteenth-Century America: A Critique and Some Proposals," *American Historical Review,* 90 (April 1985), pp. 299–338.

6. Stigler is quoted, with relish, by Gary Hart, *A New Democracy* (New York: Quill, 1983), p. 46. On Lombardi, see a letter from Jerry James to *The New York Times* (Sunday, September 28, 1986, section E), p. 24. "It's the only thing" was said by John Wayne, playing a football coach in "Trouble Along the Way."

7. Cotton Mather, *Magnalia Christi Americana,* ed. Kenneth B. Murdock (Cambridge, Mass.: Harvard University Press, 1977), pp. 273–359, quotation p. 279; Kenneth Silverman, *The Life and Times of Cotton Mather* (New York: Harper & Row, 1984), pp. 162–65.

8. Ryan, *Cradle of the Middle Class,* argues that mothers tried to socialize their children to reproduce petit-bourgeois traits and become cautious, prudent small-businessmen, not entrepreneurs. This argument confuses what mothers wanted with how their sons turned out. It also presumes strong maternal socialization, despite Ryan's demonstration that sons were removed quite early from maternal influence. See pp. 161 and 153 on the new imperative "of maximizing individual gain in a competitive market."

9. Wilentz, *Chants Democratic,* p. 380.

10. For a superb account of the story in its Wall Street setting, see Stephen Zelnick, "Melville's 'Bartleby': History, Ideology, & Literature," *Marxist Perspectives,* 2 (Winter 1979/80), pp. 74–92.

11. Raymond Williams, *Culture and Society 1780–1950* (Garden City: Anchor Books, 1960, 1st pub. 1958); Carolyn Porter, *Seeing and Being: The Plight of the Participant-Observer in Emerson, James, Adams, Faulkner* (Middletown, Ct.: Wesleyan University Press, 1981); Myra Jehlen, "New World Epics: The Novel and the Middle-class in America," *Salmagundi* (Winter 1977), 49–68, and also her *American Incarnation: The Individual, the Nation, and the Continent* (Cambridge, Mass.: Harvard University Press, 1986), which explores how rhetorical uses of the land incarnate a middle-class ideology of liberal individualism; William Charvat, *The Profession of Authorship in America, 1800–1870,* ed. Matthew J. Bruccoli (Columbus: Ohio State University Press, 1968), esp. pp. 61–64.

12. Michel Chevalier, *Society, Manners, and Politics in the United States: Letters on North America,* trans. T. G. Bradford, ed. John William Ward (Ithaca: Cornell University Press, 1961), pp. 418–19.

13. John von Neumann's "min-max" or minimax theory comes from his mathematical analysis of game strategy. It was popularized by others, who derived from it the idea that corporations function not to maximize profit but to minimize maximum loss. John von Neumann and Oskar Morgenstern, *Theory of Games and Economic Behavior* (Princeton: Princeton University Press, 1953), pp. 153–55.

14. My recent book, *Manhood and the American Renaissance* (Ithaca: Cornell University Press, 1989), explores all these issues at much greater length. For a more informal and personal exploration, see my essay, "Manhood, Humiliation, and Public Life: Some Stories," *Southwest Review,* 71 (Autumn 1986), 442–62.

15. Lawrence Buell, *New England Literary Culture from the Revolution to the Civil War* (Cambridge: Cambridge University Press, 1986); Nina Baym, "Melodramas of Beset Manhood: How Theories of American Fiction Exclude Women Authors," *American Quarterly,* 33 (1981), 123–39.

16. Alfred Habegger, *Gender, Fantasy, and Realism in American Literature* (New York: Columbia University Press, 1982).

17. Leslie Fiedler, *Love and Death in the American Novel,* rev. ed. (New York: Stein and Day, 1966).

Gender Studies, Queer Theory, Gay/Lesbian Studies

MICHAEL RYAN

In this excerpt from Ryan's Literary Theory, *he addresses the linkages between gender studies, queer theory, and gay/lesbian studies. Ryan notes that gay and lesbian critics seek to identify a tradition of homosexual writing while also questioning the notion of sexual identity and the logic of gender categorization. Similarly, gender studies has led to analyses of "compulsory heterosexuality and normative masculinity." Ryan identifies Queer Theory as "a more activist intellectual and political movement," developed out of gay/lesbian and gender theory, which suggests that everyone is potentially gay, but that heterosexuality is manufactured as the dominant form of sexuality. Ryan closes with suggestions for a gender reading of Elizabeth Bishop's "In the Waiting Room."*

INTRODUCTION

In the late 1960s, closets opened, and gay and lesbian scholars who had up till then remained silent regarding their sexuality or the presence of homosexual themes in literature began to speak. Their work, along with feminism, helped bring into being a new school of gender theory in the 1980s. Gender critics, inspired especially by Foucault's work on the history of sexuality, began to study gender and sexuality as discursive and historical institutions. Gender Theory and Gay/Lesbian Studies were soon joined by a more activist intellectual and political movement — Queer Theory — which linked gay/lesbian scholarship to such public concerns as HIV/AIDS.

Gender and gay/lesbian theorists are concerned with unearthing a hidden tradition of homosexual writing and with examining the gender dynamics of canonical literature. The building of a counter-tradition is made difficult by the fact that, while there have been many gay writers — from Sappho to Tennessee Williams — few of them wrote openly about their lives and experiences. Heterosexual culture was intolerant of gay perspectives either on the streets or in books, and while women might have been put in

From *Literary Theory: A Practical Introduction* (Malden: Blackwell Publishers, 1999) 115–27.

the attic for being "mad," gays were put in jail for being "perverse." Wilde is the most famous example, but writers like Elizabeth Bishop and Henry James, who remained "in the closet" for much of their lives, were more common.

While much gay/lesbian work is concerned with tradition building, gay critics also interrogate the very notion of sexual identity and question the logic of gender categorization. They question the relation of gender categories to sexuality and physiology. The relation of such categories as masculine and feminine to such supposedly stable bodily and psychological identities as male and female or man and woman is, they contend, contingent and historical. Not only do traits like masculine and feminine circulate quite freely in combination with biological appearances and sexual choices, but also the meaning of each of the terms is highly variable and changes both culturally and historically. Layer in the axes of class and race, and the meanings proliferate further. There is no guarantee consequently that what one is identified as being (either biologically or culturally male or female) will line up in a predictable and necessary way with a particular set of sexual behaviors or psychological dispositions or social practices. The normative alignment of male and female with heterosexual masculinity or femininity in the dominant gender culture must therefore be seen as a political rather than a biological fact.

In a similar vein, these theorists question the opposition between heterosexual and homosexual, interrogating the identity of each and the hierarchical relation (mainstream and margin) between the two. Rather than opposed and exclusive quantities, they are differentially connected moments of a continuum that includes numerous other possible variations. Heterosexuality contains a moment of homosexuality, when the child identifies with the parent of the same sex, or when heterosexual men relate to each other while competing over women, and homosexuality comprises both masculinity and femininity, supposedly heterosexual qualities, in highly mixed and variable amounts.

Such possible variations are quelled by the dominant, normative discourses regarding gender and sexuality, which enforce what they describe. The dominant discourses assume that there are stable identities such as masculine and feminine or man and woman or heterosexual and homosexual that give rise to the discourses that describe them. But such identities are produced by discourse and by cultural representation. The apparent alignment of dominant discourse with seemingly stable identities — as in the long reign of compulsory heterosexuality — is the result of a politically enforced naturalization of a particular contingent style or form of sexuality that comes to be mistaken for an originating ground through constant repetition and rote learning. Normatively heterosexual men are masculine and normatively heterosexual women feminine because the reigning cultural discourses instruct them in behavior appropriate to the dominant gender representations and norms, while stigmatizing nonnormative behavior. Alternative sexual practices to heterosexual genital contact, for example, are in certain places strictly

enjoined. The supposed identities of male or female and the norms of reproductive sexuality are thus effects of enforcement procedures that operate
through cultural and legal discourse, privileging certain object choices or psychological dispositions while denigrating (and jailing) others. Such gender
identities as "woman" are not pre-discursive foundations but rather normal-
izing injunctions produced by discursive performances.

In a similar fashion, the continuities between a variety of sexual practices
across a variety of possible gender formulations (masculine lesbian, masculine heterosexual woman, feminine gay man, feminine heterosexual man,
etc.) are erased and subsumed to enforced norms of oppositional identity
(either masculine heterosexual or feminine heterosexual, either heterosexual
or homosexual). Contiguously connected, differentially related terms are displaced in favor of essential, total identities. They substitute an entire representation — lesbian — for a plurality of connected gender and sexual
possibilities that might include lesbian as one moment but that are not fully
reducible to such categorical singularity. Lesbian is internally differentiated
into a plurality of possibilities (varieties of feminine, varieties of masculine,
etc.) and externally differentiated through its connection to or disconnection
from a plurality of other possibilities. It is not a singular totality that stands
opposed to another singular totality — the normative heterosexual woman,
for example, who in any event generally engages in relations that contain
homosexual components, as do men with men.

Gender Studies also examines the structures of male heterosexual
oppression, both cultural and social, that have contributed to the marginalization and exclusion of homosexuality. Critics have particularly noted the
way the more rigorous forms of heterosexual masculinity originate in sexual
panic, a fear or anxiety in heterosexual men regarding their sexual identities.
The cultural and social violence exercised against homosexuals originates in
part from the instability of heterosexual identity, a fear that such identity may
be a contingent construct that serves as a defensive bulwark against a potentially overwhelming reality of diverse, ethically neutral sexual choices and
identity possibilities that exist simultaneously in the self and in society.
Gender Studies has thus given rise to analyses of the repressed "homosocial"
strains that motivate the heterosexual tradition's construction of compulsory
heterosexuality and normative masculinity.

One of the most interesting and subversive approaches to develop out of
gay/lesbian and gender theory — Queer Theory — pushes this point even further. One argument it makes is that homosexuality is not an identity apart from
another identity called heterosexuality. Rather, everyone is potentially gay, and
it is only the laborious imprinting of heterosexual norms that cuts away those
potentials and manufactures heterosexuality as the dominant sexual format.
Yet latent and suppressed homosexuality is queered into being in the various
kinds of homophilia central to heterosexual culture, from football to film star
identification. Sexual transitivity is stilled for the sake of the labor of large-scale
species reproduction, but in the realms of cultural play, the excess of desire and
identification over norm and rule testify to more plural potentials. . . .

Suggestions for a Gender Reading of Elizabeth Bishop's "In the Waiting Room"

Elizabeth Bishop was a lesbian, although she rarely alluded to this in her printed poetry. When she did — very obliquely — in "The Shampoo," *The New Yorker,* her usual publishing venue, balked at printing it, and the one poem in which she playfully discusses the topic of gay identity, "Exchanging Hats," remained unpublished. "In the Waiting Room" might be read from a gender perspective as being about a young lesbian girl's awakening to her sexual difference. As the poem begins, she is "in the waiting room" in regard to sexual identity, and the poem tracks the emergence of her first sense of being different, of being "unlike" others. It is important that the waiting room is in a dentist's office and that she is literally waiting while her aunt has an appointment with the doctor. A dentist at the time (1918) would have been male, and dentists, of course, are notorious for inflicting pain on patients. The pain the dentist inflicts on her aunt might be a metaphor for the masochistic position assigned women in patriarchal heterosexuality. They must deny themselves and submit to men. The waiting room might thus be read as a metaphor for a lesbian girl's condition as she confronts a normative hetero-sexual identity that she might think of as painful and alien. A lesbian girl who has begun to be aware of her difference from the heterosexual paradigm just might think of an aunt who submits to it as a "timid, foolish old woman."

Elizabeth's awakening is clearly not without anxiety, and the way place and placelessness work in the poem are important in this regard. So also are her reactions to the pictures in the *National Geographic,* a magazine that was an early popular form of erotica for young people, since there they could see nakedness enjoined in the rest of the culture. Note how the pictures are emblematic of Elizabeth's awakening identity.

Pay attention as well to how like and unlike work in the poem. What does it mean to feel unlike others? What might it mean for Elizabeth to real-ize that she is not like other women but that she likes them? Note how the issue of identity gets played out as a distinction between inside and outside and how anxiety is remedied by boundaries and exactness.

4

Considering the Geopolitical

In the age of New Historicism, it has become common practice to discuss texts within their sociohistoric contexts; however, it is also becoming more apparent that fully addressing American literature often necessitates crossing boundaries and enlarging our perspective. Thus more and more critics and instructors are asserting the need to consider the intersection of politics, geography, demography, and economics. At the most basic level, considering the geopolitical entails addressing geographic and political factors influencing a region. One common way to approach this task is to consider borders and border crossings and their impact on literature. Another popular avenue is to analyze the commonalities and differences between national literatures. An increasingly fashionable line of research involves the study of diasporas and linkages between the literature of an originally homogenous population that has been dispersed through forced or voluntary migration. The essays that follow provide a brief sampling of some of the very different avenues that a concern with the geopolitical might take.

John Carlos Rowe's essay, "Nineteenth-Century United States Literary Culture and Transnationality," addresses the impact of transnationalism on American literary studies. Noting that the United States pursued colonial policies despite its own anticolonial revolution, Rowe asserts the necessity of addressing transnational experience within the contexts of nationalism, decolonization, and postnationalism. Using several literary examples, Rowe argues that the postrevolutionary nationhood of the United States was in many ways a consequence of its colonial imaginary. Instructors may find Rowe's discussion particularly helpful in their teaching of transcendentalism, Nathaniel Hawthorne's *The Scarlet Letter,* Harriet Beecher Stowe's *Uncle Tom's Cabin,* and Harriet Jacobs's *Incidents in the Life of a Slave Girl,* among others.

Amy Kaplan's "Manifest Domesticity" takes the geopolitical notion of manifest destiny into the realm of gender. Kaplan complicates notions of separate spheres of private and public by associating them on a national scale with the domestic and the foreign. Kaplan begins by asserting that foreign policy as a concept relies on a sense of the nation as a domestic space, while the idea of the foreign requires boundaries to distinguish the nation as home. Thus, Kaplan places women squarely in the middle of concerns regarding nationalism and foreign policy. She describes a mobile domesticity that both expands and contracts boundaries of home and nation, while producing variable notions of the foreign. Kaplan discusses such figures as Catherine Beecher, Sarah Josepha Hale, E.D.E.N. Southworth, and Harriet Beecher Stowe as she concludes that manifest domesticity turned "an imperial nation into a home."

In his essay, "American Literary Emergence as a Postcolonial Phenomenon," Lawrence Buell argues for the value of viewing the American Renaissance through the lens of postcolonialism. Noting the colonial influence of Britain, Buell invites readers to imagine the American Renaissance as an emergence from Britain's cultural authority. For example, Buell argues that Walt Whitman's 1855 preface to *Leaves of Grass* and Ralph Waldo Emerson's "The American Scholar" are at opposite ends of a continuum of the American Renaissance's literary nationalism, with Whitman envisioning a very different American voice, one that has repressed its international precedents, and Emerson presenting a vision of international tendencies within American Renaissance high culture. Although these are very different approaches, both continue a dialogue with Europe. Buell contends that American Renaissance writers wrote for both an American and a transatlantic audience. He concludes his essay by addressing various marks of postcolonialism in American Renaissance literature. In addition to Emerson and Whitman, Buell discusses James Fenimore Cooper, Herman Melville, Nathaniel Hawthorne, William Cullen Bryant, and Henry Thoreau in some detail.

The essays collected here lay the groundwork for discussions regarding what constitutes American literature. A unit on the American Renaissance might be prefaced with texts on American identity, such as excerpts from Hector St. John de Crevecoeur's *Letters from an American Farmer*, Thomas Paine's *Common Sense*, and Thomas Jefferson's *Notes on the State of Virginia*, as well as Absalom Jones's "Petition of the People of Colour, free men . . . of Philadelphia," Tecumseh's *Speech of Tecumseh to Governor Harrison*, Margaret Fuller's *Woman in the Nineteenth Century*, and Sojourner Truth's "Speech to a Women's Rights Convention." Readings relevant to the development of an American literature include Edward Tyrell Channing's "On Models in Literature" and an excerpt from Cooper's *Notions on the Americans*. Readings from the American Renaissance can then be read and discussed in terms of how well they respond to the call for a national literature. Some texts that would be particularly well suited for this discussion include Emerson's "The American Scholar," an excerpt from Stowe's *Uncle Tom's Cabin*, Thoreau's "Resistance to Civil Government," Frederick Douglass's *Narrative of the Life*, Hawthorne's *The Scarlet Letter*, Melville's "Bartleby the Scrivener," excerpts from Whitman's *Leaves of Grass*, and a selection of Emily Dickinson's poetry.

Nineteenth-Century United States Literary Culture and Transnationality

JOHN CARLOS ROWE

*I*nitially appearing in a special issue of PMLA devoted to "America: The Idea, the Literature" (2003), Rowe's essay explores the impact of transnationalism on American literary studies. Rowe begins by rehearsing some of the different definitions associated with transnationalism, postcolonialism, and postnationalism. He cautions against identifying transnationalism only with postmodern globalization or its opponents and against the use of transnational to avoid the paradoxes posed by "post-" terminology. Rowe takes issue with scholars such as Lawrence Buell, whose essay is also included in this chapter, for describing the United States as a postcolonial state because it emerged from its own anticolonial struggle in the eighteenth century. According to Rowe, the United States also pursued colonial policies despite its own anticolonial revolution. He traces the paradoxical use of transnationalism in American literature, such as transcendentalists' use of transnationality to further imperialist aims. He also addresses Native American and African American responses to transnationalism, concluding that a reinterpretation of United States culture from a transnational perspective reveals the depth of U.S. subordination of other societies.

The term *transnationalism* is used frequently in reference to the rapid circulation of "capital, labor, technology, and media images" in the global economy governed by postindustrial capitalism (Sharpe 110). When incorporated into such phrases as *transnational capitalism,* the term implies a critical view of historically specific late modern or postmodern practices of globalizing production, marketing, distribution, and consumption for neocolonial ends. By the same token, *transnationalism* is often used to suggest counterhegemonic practices prompted by or accompanying the migrations and diasporas occasioned by these new economic processes of globalization. Thus, Homi Bhabha's privileging of "cultural hybridity" as a way to resist global homogenization is often traceable to his emphasis on "migrant workers," who are "part of the massive economic and political diaspora of the modern world" and thus

From *PMLA* 118.1 (2003): 78–89.

"*embody* [. . .] that moment blasted out of the continuum of history" (8). If these new, exploited cosmopolitans experience every day their dislocation from the familiar boundaries of nation, first language, and citizenship, they may also be particularly able to comprehend how to negotiate transnational situations, even in some cases turning such circumstances to their advantage. Pheng Cheah has argued that "the hybrid revival of cosmopolitanism" depends on two questionable claims: "an antilocalist/antinationalist argument, and an argument that new radical cosmopolitanisms already exist" ("Given Culture" 167). But Bhabha's notion of migratory and thus hybrid cosmopolitanism need not be derived exclusively from literally displaced peoples; traditional imperialisms did effective jobs of dislocating people who stayed at home. By the same token, subalterns of the many different global empires have done far more than simply "write back." Drawing on a wide variety of material and semiotic resources, postcolonial states and their subjects, at home and on the road, have variously, albeit unevenly, appropriated and transcoded the apparently monologic practice of First World globalization.

Transnationalism also suggests a weakening over the past fifty years of national sovereignties and geopolitical borders. In many contexts, *trans* is used instead of *post* to avoid the often vexing questions provoked by the term *postnational.* In some contexts, *transnational* is employed to cross national borders intellectually and abstractly without disturbing them. In this sense, the tourist is as transnational as the migrant worker, political refugee, or invading army; academic life, as in "traveling theory," can also be a transnational phenomenon. From the outset, I want to reject this overly cautious use of *transnational,* especially as it is invoked as a way of avoiding the practical and theoretical paradoxes deliberately posed by *postcolonial* and *postnational.* Each of the latter terms calls attention to the negative heritage of colonial or national practices, suggesting that the critical study of these discourses can best be accomplished from a utopian postcolonial or postnationalist perspective. Neither approach assumes that colonialism or nationalism has disappeared (or will shortly do so); each works on the assumption that critical studies of colonialism and nationalism have as their aim the political as well as intellectual transformation of inherently exclusive and repressive systems.

All this suggests that we can and should push such critical study back into the eighteenth and nineteenth centuries, when the nation and its sustaining, often generative imperialisms were the dominant forms of state organization. Paul Giles has argued that "transnationalism has a specific history, often connected to developments in communications technology and the various metaphorical displacements associated with them, and that canonical American authors often appear in quite a different light if they are examined through [this] matrix" (16). If we identify transnationalism only with postmodern forces of globalization or with resistances to them, such as creolization and hybridization, then we are likely to forget the roots of these postmodern economic and cultural practices in modernization. Much as I disagree with many of the criticisms leveled against the "presentness" of cultural and postcolonial studies, I admit that there is a tendency in these related approaches to alienate new global phenomena from their complex histories (Rowe, *New American Studies* 65–79). Yet as we return to these crucial histories to understand better what we mean by postcolonial, postmodern, and transnational phenomena, we should also be cautious not to project such terms — framed in the current crises occasioned by the exploitative reach of transnational capitalism and by new modes of production and commodification — too unilaterally onto the related but different histories that have given rise to such circumstances.

By the same token, postcolonial studies of eighteenth- and nineteenth-century nationalisms and their processes of expansion — that is, modernization — should not lead us to conclude hastily that because the United States emerged from the eighteenth-century anticolonial struggle, it qualifies as a postcolonial state (Buell 411–15). We should be precise in defining the postcolonial perspective as thoroughly anti-imperialist and thus be as critical of the colonialism practiced by the decolonized as we are of that practiced by the original colonizers. If we maintain this high standard for the use of the term, we may find it impossible to speak of a postcolonial condition or achieved postcoloniality, insofar as most decolonized societies have practiced their own versions of territorial, human, and symbolic domination in the interests of consolidating national or other forms of state identity. As a consequence, most postcolonial studies focus critically on the colonial, national, and other state formations that have prevented the attainment of a postcolonial, postnationalist ideal. The historical fact that the United States pursued colonial policies in conjunction with its anticolonial revolution is an interesting subject of study for postcolonial scholars, and it gives further evidence that postnational and transnational phenomena deserve to be understood in the historical contexts of nationalism, including colonial expansions and anticolonial struggles, decolonization, re- and neocolonizations, and neo- and postnationalisms of various sorts. Such historical genealogies are complex and have only recently been the objects of intense scholarly inquiry. Yet even as we encourage such research and the theoretical models on which it depends, we must be careful not to confuse our methods, models, and terminology with geopolitical realities. Desirable as certain postcolonial and postnationalist states ought to be for those conducting postcolonial inquiries — as the utopian horizons of such historical interpretations — we would be hard-pressed to identify a successful example of such states, even if we took "state" as a philosophical or psychological condition rather than as a geopolitical reality.

The postrevolutionary United States emerged as a coherent nation in many respects as a consequence of its colonial imaginary and the latter's deployment of a wide range of symbolic instruments. Culture was from the outset fantastically conceived as unified, in order to legitimate the indisputable fiction of a union of states previously held together primarily by means of British colonial foreign policies and laws, many of which varied drastically to regulate different regions and economies in British North

America. It is possible to speak of early United States nationalism as itself a colonial project, insofar as the formations of the nation depended crucially on the transformation of British colonialism into national institutions and practices in a rapid, defensive manner. The urgency, even hysteria, of this nationalism is evident in the Alien and Sedition Acts, anti-Jacobin sentiments in the widely rumored Illuminati conspiracy, and general anti-European sentiments prompted by the feared anarchy of the French Revolution (Levine 17, 26). The transnational imaginary of the early United States republic is significantly shaped by free-floating paranoia regarding wandering anarchists, dangerous foreigners, and murderous "savages." Charles Brockden Brown's novels are symptomatic of such cultural hysteria, and the remedy in both literary and geopolitical fictions seems to be the imposition of artificial borders to control such threatening foreignness. It is especially interesting that Brown's weird literary works should have been considered for so long the origins of the American novel.

Well before it was declared a national purpose, manifest destiny begins in the social psychology of such defensive nationalism, so that the expansion of the national border functions as one means of controlling threats within an unstable, new, and contrived nation by projecting them outside or beyond that nation. From the journals of the Lewis and Clark expedition to Washington Irving's fictionalized travel narratives and Edgar Allan Poe's plagiarisms of fact-based narratives for his poetic fantasies, such as *Narrative of Arthur Gordon Pym* (1838) and *The Journal of Julius Rodman* (1840), the borderlands of the United States are narratively imagined as requiring national incorporation for their realization as civilized or even natural. Whether the territory west of the Mississippi is contaminated by the disease of Native Americans, as Poe represents it in *Julius Rodman,* or by the mongrelization of racial inbreeding brought by French trappers (and thus a flawed colonial enterprise), as Irving represents it in *Astoria* (1836), the wilderness must be purified by United States expansion (Rowe, *Literary Culture* 53–76).

Although it seems incredible today that nineteenth-century manifest destiny could be distinguished from other European imperial projects in the Western Hemisphere — virtually all of which were being contested in various ways by native people and colonial emigrés — the United States transnational imaginary was rationalized by such philosophical rhetorics as American transcendentalism. However critical Ralph Waldo Emerson, Henry David Thoreau, Margaret Fuller, Walt Whitman, and other transcendentalists may have been of specific United States imperial projects, like the Mexican-American War and slavery, transcendentalism relied on a rhetoric of transcendental expansion, internalization (and thus appropriation), and psychic progress and development well suited to the politics of Jacksonian America. The transcendentalist was intrinsically cosmopolitan and transnational, so much so that John Aldrich Christie could write an entire book on the paradox, *Thoreau as World Traveler,* arguing that Thoreau's lack of travel (his only foreign travel was to Montreal in 1844; his only other travels outside New England were to Fire Island, New York, in 1850 and to Minnesota in 1861) was more than compensated for by his careful reading and citation of travel writers. Indeed, the maps Christie includes in his study of Thoreau's global "travels" and local trips are designed to suggest some impossible homology between microcosm and macrocosm.[1]

It is difficult to find examples of transnationality in the writings of the transcendentalists that do not serve imperialist aims and purposes. In one of his most impassioned essays for abolition, "An Address on the Emancipation of the Negroes in the British West Indies" (1844), Emerson invokes the British abolitionist Thomas Clarkson's argument to Prime Minister William Pitt that an end to the British slave trade would have the advantage of opening Africa to British commercial and political colonization, likely to be of far greater profit to Britain than the slave trade.[2] The transcendentalists were particularly good in developing analogies between the physical frontier and the psychic and metaphysical boundaries to be overcome by the contemplative, educated man. Thus, Thoreau insists on the mystery of "*fronting* IT," a phrase used repeatedly in *A Week on the Concord and Merrimack Rivers* (e.g., 401), and Whitman more famously equates poetic authority with that of the colonial conqueror, as when he identifies with Columbus in "A Passage to India" (1871) and "Prayer of Columbus" (1874).[3] Critical of the missionaries' vain attempts "by once or twice holding up the cross, to turn deer and tigers into lambs," Fuller nonetheless accepts the myth of the vanishing American and rejects the alternative of "amalgamation" as "the only true and profound means of civilization," on the grounds that "those of mixed blood fade early, and are not generally a fine race" (95–96). Even as she condemns the violence of United States colonialism toward Native Americans, Fuller maintains the distinction between "savagism" and "civilization" so crucial to transcendentalism. While endorsing the rights of Indian self-government over "a [United States] patriarchal government," she despairs of saving any more from Native American culture than what might be housed in "a national institute, containing all the remains of the Indians." In her final analysis, "man has two natures, — one, like that of the plants and animals, adapted to the uses and enjoyments of this planet, another which presages and demands a higher sphere, — he is constantly breaking bounds, in proportion as the mental gets the better of the mere instinctive existence" (100–01).

Writing back and otherwise resisting such imperial uses of transnationality, many Native American intellectuals and political activists recognized the need to employ the rhetoric of nationalism if they were to gain any sort of voice in United States society. Cheryl Walker has demonstrated the political variety of Native Americans' nationalist discourse in the late eighteenth and nineteenth centuries. She argues that different Native American narratives about United States nationalism still lead to the same political conclusion — "Indian nations would be better off if they achieved a stable political arrangement with the U.S. government" — and that "most therefore advocate American citizenship for Native Americans" (185). Despite taking what might appear a generally accommodationist position, nineteenth-century Native American leaders nonetheless managed to use nationalist discourse to challenge the natural right of manifest destiny its related idea of Euroamericans as chosen people or Puritan elect, the prevailing notion that United States militarism always conducted just wars in the defense of the nation, and above all the myth of the inevitable disappearance of Native Americans unable to adapt to civilized life (Walker 185–205). In short, even as Native Americans employed the discourse of nationalism, they collectively refigured it by calling attention to those people still aspiring to national inclusion of various sorts and living within the actual or ideal geopolitical boundaries of the nation. In such cases, we have national discourse that enunciates the concerns of transnationality and postcolonial study, reminding us that the latter approaches cannot dispense with the study of such nationalism and its associated rationalizations and resistances.

Much as I admire the general argument of Walker's *Indian Nation,* I think we must complicate the transnational implications of the Native American uses of nationalist ideology. One of Walker's central examples is *The Life and Adventures of Joaquín Murieta,* by John Rollin Ridge (Yellow Bird), a popular novel of 1854 that fictionalizes the exploits of the legendary California bandit. What interests me about Ridge's sensational melodrama is the way it stages the conflict between two colonialisms — those of Spanish Mexico and the United States in the Southwest, especially California — and presents the primarily negative consequences for two groups marginal to both colonial states: *Californios* (before and after the Mexican-American War) and Native Americans, who suffered under both Mexican and United States rule. Ridge's political opinions — including his proslavery views — in *Joaquín Murieta* are in keeping with the accommodationist values of the Cherokee faction, led by his father and cousin Elias Boudinot, that had signed the New Echota Treaty with the United States government in 1835. Indeed, Ridge's popular novel anticipates in many respects his anti-Lincoln, Copperhead journalism during the Civil War and expresses clearly his lofty contempt for California Indians (Rowe, *Literary Culture* 97–119). The novel also expresses virulent racism toward Chinese workers in California, singling them out for especially gratuitous displays of frontier violence at the hands of Murieta's gang and its Yankee enemies.

As a minority subject, clearly defined as subaltern within the legal and political realities of the nineteenth-century United States, Ridge does not simply choose one of the two options available: uncritical identification with national ideology or violent resistance to the colonial force of United States nationalism. Instead, he imaginatively recodes United States ideology to make himself (and his fictional alter ego) acceptable. Yet in doing so, he reaffirms social hierarchies as racial distinctions, including those that distinguish between "noble" (e.g., Cherokee and Iroquois) and "degraded" (the Tejon and other California tribes) Indians, between "heroic" hybrids, like Joaquín (who is of mixed Sonoran Indian and Hidalgo ancestry), and "criminal" Yankees. Postcolonial studies are properly interested in how postrevolutionary and postliberation nationalisms often end up imitating, however obliquely, the nationalist ideology of the departing colonial power. Such neonationalisms may well have their historical roots in the way subaltern peoples appropriated nationalist discourse in response to the pressures of colonial domination and in the interests of assimilation. And such neonationalisms should be distinguished from postcolonial nationalisms that may be crucial stages, even final goals, of the sociopolitical reorganizations of decolonized states.[4] Nationalism need not in itself be taken as a corrupt or defective social organization; what matters is how the nation imagines itself in relation to other states.

Religion is one of the commonest examples of transnationality in nineteenth-century United States culture. The influence of religions across geopolitical borders and often in direct conflict with national authority is enormous and frequently neglected in postcolonial and cultural studies.[5] One reason for this neglect may be that religions, especially Christianity, have been deeply involved in most imperialisms, so that decolonization often tacitly involves a certain anticlericalism, if unevenly a politics of secularism. Indeed, many anticolonial, revolutionary struggles have succeeded in large part because of the moral, political, and economic support provided by organized religion.

Of the numerous varieties of religious transnationalism in late-eighteenth- and nineteenth-century United States culture, I will mention only a few interesting examples. Nathaniel Hawthorne's *The Scarlet Letter* (1850) and Susan Warner's *The Wide, Wide World* (1850) both conclude their fundamentally religious educations with significant efforts to reconnect Europe and America. The "land" from which Pearl's letters are sent to Hester, "with armorial seals upon them, though of bearings unknown to English heraldry," and Pearl's child, for whom Hester presumably is "embroidering a baby-garment, with such a lavish richness of golden fancy as would have raised a public tumult" in "our sober-hued community," suggest some utopian transcendence of the conflict between Old and New World, aristocratic privilege and democratic equality, New England Puritanism and European Catholicism (Hawthorne 309–10). In Warner's romance, Ellen Montgomery's patient endurance of her trials in New York City and upstate New York earns her not only her future husband, John, and his godlike authority over her but also her reunion with her aristocratic and devoutly Protestant relations in Edinburgh, where she and John are symbolically (albeit not yet maritally) united at the end of the narrative. Both works suggest some allegorical recuperation of the aristocratic privilege associated with Europe, if their protagonists learn the religious lesson of their transatlantic *felix culpa*. What links these protagonists to their European origins is not primarily language, nation, or class but Christian obedience to divine authority that expresses itself symbolically in family relationships, especially that of parent and child. Indeed, even though Warner's narrative concludes with the promise John will marry Ellen when she is ready — she is, after all, little more than fourteen years old at the end of the romance — his relationship to her is certainly that of a father to a chid. In Hawthorne and Warner, religion suggests a genuinely transnational utopia, but the political values of such Christian transnationalism are decidedly reactionary, especially as far as women's rights are concerned. Just as not all nationalisms are evil, so too not all transnationalisms are emancipatory.

Jane Tompkins situates Warner's romance in the "ideology of the evangelical reform movement that had molded the consciousness of the nation in the years before the Civil War" (593). Religious reform movements often went beyond the nation when they discovered such common causes as the abolition of slavery. Yet the transnationalism of religiously motivated antislavery arguments often ended up reinforcing nationalist ideologies and justifying colonialism as a way of avoiding the racial conflicts many expected would follow emancipation. In this review of Harriet Beecher Stowe's *Uncle Tom's Cabin* (1852), William Lloyd Garrison concluded that the work "contains some objectionable sentiments respecting African colonization, which we regret to see" (131). In the conclusion to the novel, Stowe defends the antebellum colonization societies that sent freeborn and emancipated African Americans primarily to Liberia and that educated potential emigrés "to the [. . .] advantages of Christian republican society and schools, until they have attained to somewhat of a moral and intellectual maturity," before aiding "their passage to those shores, where they may put in practice the lessons they have learned in America" (626). Stowe was attempting to distinguish between northern and southern antislavery societies, the latter intent on achieving the racist ends of deporting free African Americans who challenged slavery as an institution and white supremacy as the dominant ideology. Yet whether subjected to colonization in Liberia or mere adaptation to entrepreneurial capitalism in the North, Stowe's emancipated African American required Christian reeducation, fueled by the moral righteousness and international cause of abolition.

Garrison found a different transnational warrant for the abolition of slavery, challenging Stowe's appeal to universal Christianity and its colonial subtext by aligning the African American right to overthrow slavery with modern rebellions by "the Greeks, the Poles, the Hungarians, our Revolutionary sires." Rejecting what he took to be Stowe's Christian pacifism and forbearance, typified for him by Uncle Tom's "Christian nonresistance," Garrison seeks to align the African American cause with the righteousness of other "insurrectionary movements" prompted by the simple need of "self-defense." Only "because the VICTIMS ARE BLACK," Garrison contends, Stowe's characters "cannot be animated by a Christian spirit and yet return blow for blow, or conspire for the destruction of their oppressors" (129).

Garrison's appeal for political coalitions across racial and national boundaries added considerable strength to forces building in the United States for the immediate overthrow of slavery, but some abolitionists warned of the dangers of an uncritical alignment of African Americans and other peoples of color with European peasants, English workers, and other exploited peoples. In *Incidents in the Life of a Slave Girl* (1861), Harriet Jacobs contrasts the plight of African Americans in the antebellum South with Irish victims of the potato famine: "I would ten thousand times rather that my children should be the half-starved paupers of Ireland than to be the most pampered among the slaves of America" (31). Apparently rejecting an opportunity for political solidarity with another colonized people and refusing the recognition that both peoples' labor was stolen by their oppressors, Jacobs makes a more important political point: the rights of international workers should not appropriate and thus diminish the urgent and particular demands of the legally enslaved. For Jacobs, the "half-starved" Irish peasant is still considerably richer than the North Carolina slave. Victorian labor activists and literary authors appropriated the racialized terms of slavery, blackness, and savagery to call attention to the deplorable working conditions of white English workers, but they did so often at the cost of trivializing the particular rights of peoples of color and thereby reinscribing racial hierarchies and stereotypes. Interesting as the racialization of the Irish in the modern English imaginary may be, Jacobs warns us not to equate it with the United States construction of the African American as racially subordinate. Transnational affinities can often mislead us into reductive equations that ignore specific historical, cultural, political, and ideological differences.

A transnational perspective also helps call attention to the several ways African American and white abolitionist writers imagined slaves as symbolic heirs of the biblical diaspora — the "exiles of Israel," in a repeated phrase — who found themselves colonized in a foreign land. Such rhetoric is often used to suggest that the United States is a nation divided effectively into two nations, which briefly during the Civil War it was. Perhaps even more important is the anticipation of twentieth-century African American nationalism in abolitionists' various formulations of African American diasporic and resistant communities. A basic convention of the fugitive slave narrative is the dangerous border crossing between southern slavery and northern freedom. In Frederick Douglass's 1845 *Narrative,* Stowe's *Uncle Tom's Cabin,* William Craft and Ellen Craft's *Running a Thousand Miles to Freedom* (1860), and numerous other factual and imaginary narratives of the perilous escape from slavery, readers are reminded of the political and racial borders in the United States.

The Underground Railroad ran north to Canada, as many fugitive slave narratives remind us, in part because freedom did not always lie just beyond the Mason-Dixon line for African Americans. To be sure, Canada's significance in nineteenth-century United States political and social struggles may be understood as an anticipation of the cultural colonialism the United States still exercises over Canada, epitomized by how peripheral Canadian studies have been to mainstream American studies and even in recent discussions of how to organize global literatures (Weissman). Too often in nineteenth-century United States culture, Canada figures primarily as an imagined place of ultimate freedom and its border a sort of psychic double for the internal border dividing South from North. Such an imagined Canada signifies well into twentieth-century United States literature, as the example of William Faulkner's Canadian Shrevlin McCannon in *Absalom, Absalom!* (1936) suggests. Shreve is both Faulkner's ultimate northerner and ideal reader, who can cross the regional, racial, psychic, and cultural borders separating him from the sins of the South to understand, help narrate, and finally even take partial responsibility for that heritage. In fact, of course, Shreve McCannon is no more Canadian than Quentin Compson or his creator, Faulkner, despite the latter's tour of duty in the British Royal Air Force in Canada.

The new comparative American studies must include Canada as a crucial and distinct multiculture, whose complex history includes not only the struggle between British and French imperialisms (and their consequences for revolution and nation building in the United States) but also the diaspora and subordination of native peoples ("First Peoples" in Canada), many of whom refused to recognize the national boundaries dividing Canada from the United States. Twentieth-century Native American writers, like Louise Erdrich in *Love Medicine* (1984; 1993) and *Tracks* (1988) and Thomas King in *Green Grass, Running Water* (1993), draw on the contemporary implications of their nineteenth-century ancestors' refusal to respect national boundaries. Frequent border crossings in their fiction are symbolic reminders of how the artificiality of national boundaries has had real consequences in Indian suffering. What such contemporary work teaches us is that the study of nineteenth-century transnationality must include not only the Canadian border but also the different and shifting borders imposed on native peoples by the systematic violence of enclosure we know as imperialism.

Nineteenth-century African American and abolitionist culture should also call our attention to alternative, often resistant communities in the antebellum South and to their self-conscious ties with Afro-Caribbean and West African communities. In *To Wake the Nations*, Eric Sundquist discusses many of the African retentions that shape nineteenth-century African American and Euroamerican literature and culture. From Gabriel Prosser's frustrated insurrection in 1800 in Richmond, Virginia, to Denmark Vesey's plan to revolt in 1822 in Charleston, South Carolina, and Nat Turner's Southampton insurrection of 1831, African American efforts to revolt against slavery drew on what Sundquist terms "the trope of San Domingo," the mythic status of its leader, Touissaint L'Ouverture, and the historical reality of the Haitian revolution as *the* successful slave rebellion in the Western Hemisphere (32). Sundquist points out that the study of African American rebellions should not be restricted to the celebrated but finally unsuccessful efforts to Prosser, Vesey, and Turner. Maroon communities of fugitive slaves, often forming hybrid communities with local or displaced Native Americans, successfully resisted slavery by refusing its legal and martial authority. Judie Newman notes that "many runaway slaves had built free or 'maroon' communities in the swamps and mountains of the South, thus offering a continual threat to white authority. Guerrilla-type raids on plantations were common" (22–23). As Zora Neale Hurston explains in *Tell My Horse*, such maroon communities originated in the Caribbean and thus provide further links between Afro-Caribbean and African American political resistance and social organization (22).[6]

Martin Delany's *Blake; or, The Huts of America* (1859–62) is one of Sundquist's central examples of how nineteenth-century African American writing drew on the inspiration of the Haitian revolution, the Caribbean anti-colonial struggle in general, and the transnational community of diasporic Africans in the Western Hemisphere (Sundquist 183–221). Delany's novel reminds us that the consideration of transnationality from the perspective of slave insurrections in the Western Hemisphere requires a more central treatment of Spanish imperialism and cultural influences in their relations with the nineteenth-century United States, as well as in Spanish territories. As the locus of action in the second half of the novel, Cuba suggests yet another complex transnational site for the nineteenth-century United States cultural imaginary. With the "longest-standing slave trade in the Americas" and as the principal port of entry for slaves "destined for illegal landing in the United States," Cuba was understandably a site of proposed United States expansion, especially by proslavery interests, well before the Spanish-American War (Sundquist 200). For Delany's Henry Blake, Cuba is the staging ground for a revolution against slavery in Cuba and ultimately in the United States, the seeds of which uprising Blake spreads in the South before fleeing to Canada and finds already present in maroon communities in the South, legacies of Prosser, Vesey, and Turner.

Delany's vision is revolutionary, vigorously critical of United States nationalism's racism, and nationalist, insofar as he "espoused a nationalist philosophy of emigration [. . .] to Canada [. . .] to Latin America or Africa" (Sundquist 192). Delany distinguishes clearly his plans for colonies outside the United States in the Western Hemisphere and in Africa, from the American Colonization Society's Liberia, which he characterizes as "a pitiful dependency on the American Colonizationists," but his own projects follow the prevailing nineteenth-century equation of colonialism with the progress of civilization (*Condition* 169). Delany's plans for colonies in the American tropics and then in Africa, prompting his exploration of the Niger Valley in 1859, were designed to serve the political goal of hastening an end to United States slavery by demonstrating the potential economic self-sufficiency of African Americans and reconnecting them with their cultural roots (*Official Report*). But Delany also "expected that these enclaves of Americans" in Africa, small though they would be, "would influence the people of Africa to accept [the Americans'] way of life" (Bell 16). In other words, nineteenth-century African American notions of transnationality were inevitably related to colonial and imperial ideology, despite the political purposes of African American colonial projects to contribute to the work of decolonizing United States slavery. Nineteenth-century discussions of different expatriation and emigration projects make it clear that there were good and bad (and many degrees in between) versions of colonialism all but forgotten today.

Stowe's *Dred: A Tale of the Great Dismal Swamp* (1856) uses the idea of the maroon community as an alternative to the violence and hypocrisy of the white slavocracy. The African American protagonist, Dred, employs a powerful millenarian rhetoric that inspires the African American and white members of his exiled community, and he displays romantic affinities with nature that suggest a utopian transcendence of slavery's sins against natural law.

What is most interesting about this neglected work, especially because its writer had recently endorsed Liberian colonization, is its insistence on some overt rebellion against an intractable economic, political, and immoral system. Stowe does not offer Dred's maroon community as an alternative nation or other kind of postcolonial state. In keeping with the horizons of nineteenth-century United States abolitionist thought, she uses the maroon community as one stage in the Underground Railroad, whose escape route will take the fugitives to the northern states and finally to Canada. Nevertheless, Stowe's maroon community in *Dred* suggests how white abolitionist narratives drew on Afro-Caribbean sources and found alternatives to the corruptions of a slave-holding nation in the history of the African American diaspora.

No reconsideration of nineteenth-century United States culture from a transnational perspective should ignore the importance of the Pacific islands and Asia in the formation of national identity. Herman Melville's criticism in *Typee* (1846), *Omoo* (1847), and *Mardi* (1849) of imperialism in the South Pacific, especially fledgling United States colonial ventures in the Marquesas and Hawai'i, implicates his own ethnographic curiosity (and thus that of his reader) in such exoticism as Taipi "cannibalism" and liberal sexual mores. But Melville also uses cultures in the South Seas to discuss United States racial, gender, labor, and class issues in ways that subordinate a comparative transnationalism to a nationalist allegory. In distinguishing between postmodern economic practices of globalization that we consider exploitative and postcolonial ideas of transnational mutuality and understanding, we can learn a great deal from such liberal discourses as Melville's Polynesian romances, which struggle to respect the integrity of the foreign cultures they represent while using such settings to investigate urgent United States social problems, such as slavery and women's rights (Rowe, *Literary Culture* 77–96).

Comparative transnationalism should also encourage us to think more broadly about how we interpret cultural relations among China, Japan, and the United States in the nineteenth century. United States trade with Asia, the development of Pacific trade routes, and competition with European colonial powers for Asian spheres of influence certainly played crucial roles in the development of the United States as a free-trade imperialist power and helped pave the way for our twentieth-century ventures in the Korean and Vietnam wars. Literary and cultural historians focus on the relatively isolated examples of nineteenth-century "life-stories" written by Asian "scholars and diplomats" to "counter negative views of Asia and Asians," such as Lee Yan Phou's *When I Was a Boy in China* (1887) or the letters, personal diaries, songs, and occasional verse produced by Chinese workers in the United States, a large number of whom were deported back to China under the Chinese exclusion laws (Kim 812).[7] For many scholars, Asian American literary culture begins much later, usually in the 1940s, when Asian-born Americans, especially as the exclusion laws were revised and finally removed in 1943, began to publish accounts of their identification with United States nationalism.[8] From the arrival of Chinese as miners during the California Gold Rush and as workers on the transcontinental railroad, there was a significant Chinese American culture throughout the period of legal exclusion that needs to be considered in relation to nineteenth-century nation formation and the development of foreign policies toward Asian states and their immigrants to the United States.[9] Transnational Asian and early Asian American perspectives on nineteenth-century United States society should help us understand better the cultural, economic, and political forces motivating John Hay's open door policy and more general attitudes toward the Pacific Rim that contributed centrally to the emergence of the United States as a global, neoimperial power in the 1890s (Rowe, *Literary Culture* 165–94).

Reinterpreting late-eighteenth- and nineteenth-century United States culture from postcolonial and transnational perspectives certainly reveals how pervasively other societies, nations, and states were subordinated to the triumphalism of United States nationalism. The few alternatives to this model I have considered tend to appropriate the prevailing nationalist rhetoric of the period, even if they include American Indian or African American "nations" as better versions of the violent and exclusive nationalism they criticize in the United States. In certain qualified ways, such nineteenth-century alternative nationalisms as we find in Delany, Stowe, Ridge, and Melville anticipate the postcolonial nationalisms judged by many postcolonial critics as indispensable means of resisting one-way globalization.[10] The advantages of this historical perspective are considerable, and they include our recognition that postcolonial approaches and even postnationalist political ambitions do not mean the relegation of the nation to the dustbin of history. Even if such historical study teaches us merely that imagining communities other than the nation is difficult, in part because of the powerful grip of nationalist rhetoric on our theoretical models, intellectual methods, and educational institutions, then extending transnationality to the heyday of United States nationalism is a valuable enterprise. The national form is indeed compelling, perhaps even compulsive, not because it is inherent or natural to human beings — it is of recent invention — but because its history is so much a part of us.

But I want to conclude more positively that postnationalist and postcolonial ideals become clearer as we study the limitations of the nationalist imaginings of transnational states, peoples, and histories. In this essay, I have tried to distinguish between a genuinely comparatist understanding of political, cultural, and historical otherness or foreignness and the cultural imperialism that finds itself replicated everywhere either as instances of its civilized superiority or in the sympathetic identification whereby the national subject substitutes its own image to silence and repress other peoples. Effective postcolonial studies will build on the important methodological leads and concrete historical work of the new historicism developed in the 1980s; postcolonial studies should add new emphases on historical instances of resistance to, even rare cases of the transformation of, the dominant ideology. For some the task of decolonization has hardly begun, and we are still trapped in those national imaginaries designed to invent new modes of domination. For others the task of decolonization has a long, complex history, whose interpretation and understanding are part of the ultimate project of defining new kinds of social organization that will dispense with the hierarchies, exclusions, and fears of the past.

NOTES

1. Christie includes these maps in the front endpapers of the book, where the New England travels are a kind of early picture-in-picture of the global map of Thoreau's travel references.
2. Emerson 29. See my discussion of Emerson's essay in *At Emerson's Tomb* 25–29.
3. See my discussion of the spiritual frontier in transcendentalism in *Through the Custom-House* 35–36. On Whitman and nineteenth-century United States imperialism, see Grünzweig.
4. Cheah argues that postcolonial nationalism has been crucial in defending certain Third World nations against the overpowering forces of transnational capitalism and globalization and thus urges us not to dispense too easily with the nation form ("Spectral Nationality").
5. On the importance of religion in the new American studies, see Mechling.
6. See my discussion of *Tell My Horse* in *Literary Culture* 270–91.
7. For one example of Chinese American folk and literary culture from this period, see Chi-shan Ko Chi.
8. Kim 813. The Burlingame Treaty with China of 1868 guaranteed Chinese immigration but did not guarantee the rights of Chinese immigrants to United States naturalization. In response to anti-Chinese riots and xenophobia, especially in California, Chinese exclusion laws were adopted from 1877 to 1943. In 1943 these acts were repealed and replaced by a law setting the annual quota for Chinese immigrants at a mere 105 a year, but it importantly granted naturalization to the Chinese admitted.
9. See Choy, Dong, and Hom; Kingston; and Yong Chen.
10. Cheah suggests that postcolonial studies must be careful not to make easy distinctions between good and bad nationalisms, especially in the ongoing histories of decolonization and of the social reorganization of previously colonized states: "Any analytical separation between an oppressive, hierarchical nationalism and a good, demotic nationalism needs to account for the common element or continuity between these two forms. It is this continuity that allows nationalism as such to modulate between its good and bad faces without any sharp transition" ("Spectral Nationality" 238). That transition or modulation is not as ambiguous or indeterminate as Cheah implies here and elsewhere in his essay; it can be understood by careful historical interpretation and understanding.

WORKS CITED

Bell, Howard H. Introduction. *Search for a Place: Black Separatism and Africa, 1860.* By M. R. Delany and Robert Campbell. Ed. Bell. Ann Arbor: U of Michigan P, 1969. 1–22.
Bhabha, Homi. *The Location of Culture.* New York: Routledge, 1994.
Buell, Lawrence. "American Literary Emergence as a Postcolonial Phenomenon." *American Literary History* 4 (1992): 411–42.
Cheah, Pheng. "Given Culture: Rethinking Cosmopolitical Freedom in Transnationalism." *Boundary 2* 24.2 (1997): 157–97.
———. "Spectral Nationality: The Living On [*Sur-vie*] of the Postcolonial Nation in Neocolonial Globalization." *Boundary 2* 26.3 (1999): 223–52.
Chi-shan Ko Chi. *Songs of Gold Mountain: Cantonese Rhymes from San Francisco Chinatown.* Selected and trans. Marlon K. Hom. Berkeley: U of California P, 1987.
Choy, Philip P., Lorraine Dong, and Marlon K. Hom, eds. *Coming Man: Nineteenth-Century American Perceptions of the Chinese.* Seattle: U of Washington P, 1995.
Christie, John Aldrich. *Thoreau as World Traveler.* New York: Columbia UP, 1965.
Delany, Martin Robinson. *The Condition, Elevation, Emigration, and Destiny of the Colored People of the United States.* 1852. Salem: Ayer, 1988.
———. *Official Report of the Niger Valley Exploring Party. Search for a Place: Black Separatism and Africa, 1860.* By Delany and Robert Campbell. Ed. Howard H. Bell. Ann Arbor: U of Michigan P, 1969. 23–148.
Emerson, Ralph Waldo. "An Address . . . on . . . the Emancipation of the Negroes in the British West Indies." *Emerson's Anti-slavery Writings.* Ed. Len Gougeon and Joel Myerson. New Haven: Yale UP, 1995. 7–33.

Fuller, Margaret. *Summer on the Lakes.* Ed. Arthur B. Fuller. 1844. New York: Haskell, 1970.

Garrison, William Lloyd. "Review of Harriet Beecher Stowe's Novel *Uncle Tom's Cabin.*" 26 Mar. 1852. *William Lloyd Garrison and the Fight against Slavery: Selections from* The Liberator. Ed. William E. Cain. Boston: Bedford/St. Martin's, 1995. 127–31.

Giles, Paul. *Virtual Americas: Transnational Fictions and the Transatlantic Imaginary.* Durham: Duke UP, 2002.

Grünzweig, Walter. "Noble Ethics and Loving Aggressiveness: The Imperialist Walt Whitman." *An American Empire: Expansionist Cultures and Policies, 1881–1917.* Ed. Serge Ricard. Aix-en-Provence: L'Université de Provence, 1990. 151–65.

Hawthorne, Nathaniel. *The Scarlet Letter.* Boston: Houghton, 1883. Vol. 5 of *The Complete Works of Nathaniel Hawthorne.* Riverside Ed. 14 vols.

Hurston, Zora Neale. *Tell My Horse: Voodoo and Life in Haiti and Jamaica.* New York: Harper, 1938.

Jacobs, Harriet. *Incidents in the Life of a Slave Girl.* Ed. Jean Fagan Yellin. Cambridge: Harvard UP, 1987.

Kim, Elaine. "Asian American Literature." *Columbia Literary History of the United States.* Ed. Emory Elliott. New York: Columbia UP, 1988. 811–21.

Kingston, Maxine Hong. *China Men.* New York: Knopf, 1980.

Levine, Robert S. *Conspiracy and Romance: Studies in Brockden Brown, Cooper, Hawthorne, and Melville.* New York: Cambridge UP, 1989.

Mechling, Jay. "Rethinking (and Reteaching) the Civil Religion in Post-nationalist American Studies." *Postnationalist American Studies.* Ed. John Carlos Rowe. Berkeley: U of California P, 2000. 63–80.

Newman, Judie. Introduction. *Dred: A Tale of the Great Dismal Swamp.* By Harriet Beecher Stowe. Halifax, Eng.: Ryburn, 1992. 9–25.

Rowe, John Carlos. *At Emerson's Tomb: The Politics of Classic American Literature.* New York: Columbia UP, 1997.

———. *Literary Culture and U.S. Imperialism: From the Revolution to World War II.* New York: Oxford UP, 2000.

———. *The New American Studies.* Minneapolis: U of Minnesota P, 2002.

———. *Through the Custom-House: Nineteenth-Century American Fiction and Modern Theory.* Baltimore: Johns Hopkins UP, 1982.

Sharpe, Jenny. "Is the United States Postcolonial?" *Postcolonial America.* Ed. C. Richard King. Urbana: U of Illinois P, 2000. 103–21.

Stowe, Harriet Beecher. *Uncle Tom's Cabin; or, Life among the Lowly.* New York: Viking-Penguin, 1981.

Sundquist, Eric. *To Wake the Nations: Race in the Making of American Literature.* Cambridge: Harvard UP, 1993.

Thoreau, Henry David. *A Week on the Concord and Merrimack Rivers.* Boston: Houghton, 1893. Vol. 1 of *The Writings of Henry David Thoreau.* New Riverside ed. 11 vols.

Tompkins, Jane. Afterword. *The Wide, Wide World.* By Susan Warner. New York: Feminist, 1987. 584–608.

Walker, Cheryl. *Indian Nation: Native American Literature and Nineteenth-Century Nationalisms.* Durham: Duke UP, 1997.

Weissman, Adam. "Reading Multiculturalism in the United States and Canada: The Anthological vs. the Cognitive." *University of Toronto Quarterly* 69 (2000): 689–715.

Yong Chen. *Chinese San Francisco, 1850–1943.* Stanford: Stanford UP, 2000.

Manifest Domesticity

AMY KAPLAN

K*aplan argues for a rethinking of domesticity that would "shift the cognitive geography of nineteenth-century separate spheres." Typically, when the domestic is considered a private realm, men and women are seen as inhabiting different domains. However, when domesticity is viewed in relation to the foreign, men and women share the same space, and people are divided not by gender, but by race. Kaplan further complicates the notion of the domestic by noting that domesticity is not only a static condition but also a process. Domestication in this sense would be related to "the imperial project of civilizing"; thus, according to Kaplan, it both polices the borders between civilization and savagery and regulates the savage within. Noting the contemporaneous development of domestic discourse and* Manifest Destiny, *Kaplan suggests that these spatial configurations are linked in complex ways. In fact, Kaplan concludes that women's domestic narratives are inseparable from narratives of empire and nation. Kaplan's essay originally appeared in* American Literature *in 1998.*

The "cult of domesticity," the ideology of "separate spheres," and the "culture of sentiment" have together provided a productive paradigm for understanding the work of white women writers in creating a middle-class American culture in the nineteenth century. Most studies of this paradigm have revealed the permeability of the border that separates the spheres, demonstrating that the private feminized space of the home both infused and bolstered the public male arena of the market, and that the sentimental values attached to maternal influence were used to sanction women's entry into the wider civic realm from which those same values theoretically excluded them. More recently, scholars have argued that the extension of female sympathy across social divides could violently reinforce the very racial and class hierarchies that sentimentality claims to dissolve.[1]

This deconstruction of separate spheres, however, leaves another structural opposition intact: the domestic in intimate opposition to the foreign. In this context *domestic* has a double meaning that not only links the familial

From *American Literature* 70.3 (1998): 581–606.

household to the nation but also imagines both in opposition to everything outside the geographic and conceptual border of the home. The earliest meaning of *foreign,* according to the *OED,* is "out of doors" or "at a distance from home." Contemporary English speakers refer to national concerns as domestic in explicit or implicit contrast with the foreign. The notion of domestic policy makes sense only in opposition to foreign policy, and uncoupled from the foreign, national issues are never labeled domestic. The idea of foreign policy depends on the sense of the nation as a domestic space imbued with a sense of at-homeness, in contrast to an external world perceived as alien and threatening. Reciprocally, a sense of the foreign is necessary to erect the boundaries that enclose the nation as home.

Reconceptualizing domesticity in this way might shift the cognitive geography of nineteenth-century separate spheres. When we contrast the domestic sphere with the market or political realm, men and women inhabit a divided social terrain, but when we oppose the domestic to the foreign, men and women become national allies against the alien, and the determining division is not gender but racial demarcations of otherness. Thus another part of the cultural work of domesticity might be to unite men and women in a national domain and to generate notions of the foreign against which the nation can be imagined as home. The border between the domestic and foreign, however, also deconstructs when we think of domesticity not as a static condition but as the process of domestication, which entails conquering and taming the wild, the natural, and the alien. Domestic in this sense is related to the imperial project of civilizing, and the conditions of domesticity often become markers that distinguish civilization from savagery. Through the process of domestication, the home contains within itself those wild or foreign elements that must be tamed; domesticity not only monitors the borders between the civilized and the savage but also regulates traces of the savage within itself.[2]

If domesticity plays a key role in imagining the nation as home, then women, positioned at the center of the home, play a major role in defining the contours of the nation and its shifting borders with the foreign. Those feminist critics and historians whose work has been fundamental in charting the paradigm of separate spheres, however, have for the most part overlooked the relationship of domesticity to nationalism and imperialism. Their work is worth revisiting here because their language, echoing that of their sources, inadvertently exposes these connections, which scholars have just recently begun to pursue. Jane Tompkins, for example, lauds Catherine Beecher's *Treatise on Domestic Economy* as "the prerequisite of world conquest" and claims of a later version that "the imperialistic drive behind the encyclopedism and determined practicality of this household manual . . . is a blueprint for colonizing the world in the name of the 'family state' under the leadership of Christian women."[3] As her title indicates, Mary P. Ryan's *Empire of the Mother: American Writing about Domesticity, 1830–1860* employs empire as a metaphor framing her analysis; yet she never links this pervasive imperial metaphor to the contemporaneous geopolitical movement of imperial expansion or to the discourse of Manifest Destiny. This blind spot, I believe, stems from the way that the ideology of separate spheres has shaped scholarship; until recently it has been assumed that nationalism and foreign policy lay outside the concern and participation of women. Isolating the empire of the mother from other imperial endeavors, however, runs two risks: First, it may reproduce in women's studies the insularity of an American studies that imagines the nation as a fixed, monolithic, and self-enclosed geographic and cultural whole; second, the legacy of separate spheres that sees women as morally superior to men can lead to the current moralistic strain in feminist criticism, which has shifted from celebrating the liberatory qualities of white women's writing to condemning their racism. In this essay I try instead to understand the vexed and contradictory relations between race and domesticity as an issue not solely of individual morality nor simply internal to the nation but as structural to the institutional and discursive processes of national expansion and empire building.[4]

My essay poses the question of how the ideology of separate spheres in antebellum America contributed to creating an American empire by imagining the nation as a home at a time when its geopolitical borders were expanding rapidly through violent confrontations with Indians, Mexicans, and European empires. Scholars have overlooked the fact that the development of domestic discourse in America is contemporaneous with the discourse of Manifest Destiny. If we juxtapose the spatial representations of these discourses, they seem to embody the most extreme form of separate spheres: the home as a bounded and rigidly ordered interior space is opposed to the boundless and undifferentiated space of an infinitely expanding nation. Yet these spatial and gendered configurations are linked in complex ways that are dependent upon racialized notions of the foreign. According to the ideology of separate spheres, domesticity can be viewed as an anchor, a feminine counterforce to the male activity of territorial conquest. I argue, to the contrary, that domesticity is more mobile and less stabilizing; it travels in contradictory circuits both to expand and contract the boundaries of home and nation and to produce shifting conceptions of the foreign. This form of traveling domesticity can be analyzed in the writings of Catherine Beecher and Sarah Josepha Hale, whose work, despite their ideological differences as public figures, reveals how the internal logic of domesticity relies on, abets, and reproduces the contradictions of nationalist expansion in the 1840s and 1850s. An analysis of Beecher's *A Treatise on Domestic Economy* demonstrates that the language of empire both suffuses and destabilizes the rhetoric of separate spheres, while an analysis of Hale's work uncovers the shared racial underpinnings of domestic and imperialist discourse through which the separateness of gendered spheres reinforces the effort to separate the races by turning blacks into foreigners. The essay concludes with suggestions about how understanding the imperial reach of domestic discourse might remap the way we read women's novels of the 1850s by interpreting their narratives of domesticity and female subjectivity as inseparable from narratives of empire and nation building.

Domesticity dominated middle-class women's writing and culture from the 1830s through the 1850s, a time when national boundaries were in violent flux; during this period the United States doubled its national territory, completed a campaign of Indian removal, fought its first prolonged foreign war, wrested the Spanish borderlands from Mexico, and annexed Texas, Oregon, and California. As Thomas Hietala has shown, this convulsive expansion was less a confident celebration of Manifest Destiny than a response to crises of confidence about national unity, the expansion of slavery, and the racial identity of citizenship — crises that territorial expansion exacerbated.[5] Furthermore, these movements evoked profound questions about the conceptual border between the domestic and the foreign. In the 1831 Supreme Court decision, *Cherokee Nation v. the State of Georgia,* for example, Indians were declared members of "domestic dependent nations," neither foreign nationals nor United States citizens.[6] This designation makes the domestic an ambiguous third realm between the national and the foreign, as it places the foreign inside the geographic boundaries of the nation. The uneasy relation between the domestic and the foreign can also be seen in the debates over the annexation of new territory. In the middle of the Mexican War President Polk insisted that slavery was "purely a domestic question" and not a "foreign question" at all, but the expansion he advocated undermined that distinction and threatened domestic unity by raising the question of slavery's extension into previously foreign lands.[7] In debates about the annexation of Texas and later Mexico, both sides represented the new territories as women to be married to the U.S.; Sam Houston, for example, wrote of Texas presenting itself "to the United States as a bride adorned for her espousals"; and President Taylor accused annexationists after the Mexican War of trying to "drag California into the Union before her wedding garment has yet been cast about her person."[8] These visions of imperial expansion as marital union carried within them the specter of marriage as racial amalgamation. While popular fiction about the Mexican War portrayed brave American men rescuing and marrying Mexican women of Spanish descent, political debate over the annexation of Mexico hinged on what was agreed to be the impossibility of incorporating a foreign people marked by their racial intermixing into a domestic nation imagined as Anglo-Saxon.[9] One of the major contradictions of imperialist expansion was that while it strove to nationalize and domesticate foreign territories and peoples, annexation incorporated nonwhite foreign subjects in a way perceived to undermine the nation as a domestic space.

My point here is not to survey foreign policy but to suggest how deeply the language of domesticity suffused the debates about national expansion. Rather than stabilizing the representation of the nation a home, this rhetoric heightened the fraught and contingent nature of the boundary between the domestic and the foreign, a boundary that breaks down around questions of the racial identity of the nation as home. If we begin to rethink woman's sphere in this context, we have to ask how the discourse of domesticity negotiates the borders of an increasingly expanding empire and a divided nation. Domestic discourse both redresses and reenacts the contradictions of empire through its own double movement to expand female influence beyond the home and the nation while simultaneously contracting woman's sphere to police domestic boundaries against the threat of foreignness both within and without.

At this time of heightened national expansion, proponents of a "woman's sphere" applied the language of empire to both the home and women's emotional lives. "Hers is the empire of the affections," wrote Sarah Josepha Hale, influential editor of *Godey's Lady's Book*, who opposed the women's rights movement as "the attempt to take woman away from her empire of home."[10] To educational reformer Horace Mann, "the empire of the Home" was "the most important of all empires, the pivot of all empires and emperors."[11] Writers who counseled women to renounce politics and economics, "to leave the rude commerce of camps and the soul hardening struggling of political power to the harsher spirit of men," urged them in highly political rhetoric to take up a more spiritual calling, "the domain of the moral affections and the empire of the heart."[12] Catherine Beecher gives this calling a nationalist cast in *A Treatise on Domestic Economy* when, for example, she uses Queen Victoria as a foil to elevate the American "mother and housekeeper in a large family," who is "the sovereign of an empire demanding as varied cares, and involving more difficult duties, than are exacted of her, who wears the crown and professedly regulates the interests of the greatest nation on earth, [yet] finds abundant leisure for theaters, balls, horse races, and every gay leisure."[13] This imperial trope might be interpreted as a compensatory and defensive effort to glorify the shrunken realm of female agency, in a paradox of what Mary Ryan calls "imperial isolation," whereby the mother gains her symbolic sovereignty at the cost of withdrawal from the outside world.[14] For these writers, however, metaphor has a material efficacy in the world. The representation of the home as an empire exists in tension with the notion of woman's sphere as a contracted space because it is in the nature of empires to extend their rule over new domains while fortifying their borders against external invasion and internal insurrection. If, on the one hand, domesticity draws strict boundaries between the home and the world of men, on the other, it becomes the engine of national expansion, the site from which the nation reaches beyond itself through the emanation of woman's moral influence.

The paradox of what might be called "imperial domesticity" is that by withdrawing from direct agency in the male arena of commerce and politics, woman's sphere can be represented by both women and men as a more potent agent for national expansion. The outward reach of domesticity in turn enables the interior functioning of the home. In her introduction to *A Treatise on Domestic Economy*, Beecher inextricably links women's work at home to the unfolding of America's global mission of "exhibiting to the world the beneficent influences of Christianity, when carried into every social, civil, and political institution" (12). Women's maternal responsibility for molding the character of men and children has global repercussions: "To American women, more than to any others on earth, is committed the exalted privilege of extending over the world those blessed influences, that are to renovate degraded man, and 'clothe all climes with beauty'" (14). Beecher ends her introduction with an extended architectural metaphor in which women's agency at home is predicated on the global expansion of the nation:

> The builders of a temple are of equal importance, whether they labor on the foundations, or toil upon the dome. Thus also with those labors that are to be made effectual in the regeneration of the Earth. The woman who is rearing a family of children; the woman who labors in the school-room, the woman who, in her retired chamber, earns with her needle, the mite to contribute for the intellectual and moral elevation of her country; even the humble domestic, whose example and influence may be molding and forming young minds, while her faithful services sustain a prosperous domestic state; — each and all may be cheered by the consciousness that they are agents in accomplishing the greatest work that ever was committed to human responsibility. It is the building of a glorious temple, whose base shall be coextensive with the bounds of the earth, whose summit shall pierce the skies, whose splendor shall beam on all lands, and those who hew the lowliest stone, as much as those who carve the highest capital, will be equally honored when its top-stone shall be laid, with new rejoicing of the morning stars, and shoutings of the sons of God. (14)

One political effect of this metaphor is to unify women of different social classes in a shared project of construction while sustaining class hierarchy among women.[15] This image of social unity both depends upon and underwrites a vision of national expansion, as women's varied labors come together to embrace the entire world. As the passage moves down the social scale, from mother to teacher to spinster, the geographic reach extends outward from home to schoolroom to country, until the "humble domestic" returns back to the "prosperous domestic state," a phrase that casts the nation in familial terms. Women's work at home here performs two interdependent forms of national labor; it forges the bonds of internal unity while impelling the nation outward to encompass the globe. This outward expansion in turn enables the internal cohesiveness of woman's separate sphere by making women agents in constructing an infinitely expanding edifice.

Beecher thus introduces her detailed manual on the regulation of the home as a highly ordered space by fusing the boundedness of the home with the boundlessness of the nation. Her 1841 introduction bears a remarkable resemblance to the rhetoric of Manifest Destiny, particularly to this passage by one of its foremost proponents, John L. O'Sullivan:

> The far-reaching, the boundless future will be the era of American greatness. In its magnificent domain of space and time, the nation of many nations is destined to manifest to mankind the excellence of divine principles; to establish on earth the noblest temple ever dedicated to the worship of the most high — the Sacred and the True. Its floor shall be a hemisphere — its roof the firmament of the star-studded heavens, and

its congregation an Union of many Republics, comprising hundreds of happy millions, calling, owning no man master, but governed by God's natural and moral law of equality.[16]

While these passages exemplify the stereotype of separate spheres (one describes work in the home and the other work of nation building), both use a common architectural metaphor from the Bible to build a temple coextensive with the globe. O'Sullivan's grammatical subject is the American nation, which is the implied medium in Beecher's text for channeling women's work at home to a Christianized world. The construction of an edifice ordinarily entails walling off the inside from the outside, but in both these cases there is a paradoxical effect whereby the distinction between inside and outside is obliterated by the expansion of the home/nation/temple to encompass the globe. The rhetorics of Manifest Destiny and domesticity share a vocabulary that turns imperial conquest into spiritual regeneration in order to efface internal conflict or external resistance in visions of geopolitical domination as global harmony.

Although imperial domesticity ultimately imagines a home coextensive with the entire world, it also continually projects a map of unregenerate outlying foreign terrain that both gives coherence to its boundaries and justifies its domesticating mission. When in 1869 Catherine Beecher revised her *Treatise* with her sister, Harriet Beecher Stowe, as *The American Woman's Home*, they downplayed the earlier role of domesticity in harmonizing class differences while enhancing domesticity's outward reach. The book ends by advocating the establishment of Christian neighborhoods settled primarily by women as a way of putting into practice domesticity's expansive potential to Christianize and Americanize immigrants both in Northeastern cities and "all over the West and South, while along the Pacific coast, China and Japan are sending their pagan millions to share our favored soil, climate, and government." No longer a leveling factor among classes within America, domesticity could be extended to those conceived of as foreign both within and beyond American national borders: "Ere long colonies from these prosperous and Christian communities would go forth to shine as 'lights of the world' in all the now darkened nations. Thus the Christian family and Christian neighborhood would become the grand ministry as they were designed to be, in training our whole race for heaven."[17] While Beecher and Stowe emphasize domesticity's service to "darkened nations," the existence of "pagans" as potential converts performs a reciprocal service in the extension of domesticity to single American women. Such Christian neighborhoods would allow unmarried women without children to leave their work in "factories, offices and shops" or their idleness in "refined leisure" to live domestic lives on their own, in some cases by adopting native children. Domesticity's imperial reach posits a way of extending woman's sphere to include not only the heathen but also the unmarried Euro-American woman who can be freed from biological reproduction to rule her own empire of the mother.

If writers about domesticity encouraged the extension of female influence outward to domesticate the foreign, their writings also evoked anxiety about the opposing trajectory that brings foreignness into the home. Analyzing the widespread colonial trope that compares colonized people to children, Ann Stoler and Karen Sánchez-Eppler have both shown how this metaphor can work not only to infantilize the colonized but also to portray white children as young savages in need of civilizing.[18] This metaphor at once extends domesticity outward to the tutelage of heathens while focusing it inward to regulate the threat of foreignness within the boundaries of the home. For Beecher, this internal savagery appears to threaten the physical health of the mother. Throughout the *Treatise,* the vision of the sovereign mother with imperial responsibilities is countered by descriptions of the ailing invalid mother. This contrast can be seen in the titles of the first two chapters, "Peculiar Responsibilities of American Women" and "Difficulties Peculiar to American Women." The latter focuses on the pervasive invalidism that makes American women physically and emotionally unequal to their global responsibilities. In contrast to the ebullient temple building of the first chapter, Beecher ends the second with a quotation from Tocqueville describing a fragile frontier home centered on a lethargic and vulnerable mother whose

> children cluster about her, full of health, turbulence and energy; they are true children of the wilderness; their mother watches them from time to time, with mingled melancholy and joy. To look at their strength, and her languor one might imagine that the life she had given them exhausted her own; and still she regrets not what they cost her. The house, inhabited by these emigrants, has no internal partition or loft. In the one chamber of which it consists, the whole family is gathered for the night. The dwelling itself is a little world; an ark of civilization amid an ocean of foliage. A hundred steps beyond it, the primeval forest spreads its shade and solitude resumes its sway. (24)

The mother's health appears drained not by the external hardships inflicted by the environment but by her intimate tie to her own "children of the wilderness," who violate the border between home and primeval forest. This boundary is partially reinforced by the image of the home as an "ark of civilization" whose internal order should protect its inhabitants from the sea of chaos that surrounds them. Yet the undifferentiated inner space, which lacks "internal partition," replicates rather than defends against the boundlessness of the wilderness. The rest of the treatise, with its detailed attention to the systematic organization of the household, works to "partition" the home in a way that distinguishes it from the external wilderness.[19]

The infirmity of American mothers is a pervasive concern throughout the *Treatise,* yet its physical cause is difficult to locate in Beecher's text. Poor health afflicts middle-class women in Northeastern cities as much as women on the frontier, according to Beecher, and she sees both cases resulting from a geographic and social mobility in which "everything is moving and changing" (16). This movement affects women's health most directly, claims Beecher, by depriving them of reliable domestic servants. With "trained" servants constantly moving up and out, middle-class women must resort to hiring "ignorant" and "poverty-stricken foreigners," with whom they are said in *American Woman's Home* to have a "missionary" relationship (332). Though Beecher does not label these foreigners as the direct cause of illness, their presence disrupts the orderly "system and regularity" of housekeeping, leading American women to be "disheartened, discouraged, and ruined in health" (18). Throughout her *Treatise* Beecher turns the absence of good servants — at first a cause of infirmity — into a remedy; their lack gives middle-class women the opportunity to perform regular domestic labor that will revive their health. By implication, their self-regulated work will also keep "poverty-stricken foreigners" out of their homes. Curiously, then, the mother's ill health stems from the unruly subjects of her domestic empire — children and servants — who bring uncivilized wilderness and undomesticated foreignness into the home. The fear of disease and of the invalidism that characterizes the American woman also serves as a metaphor for anxiety about foreignness within. The mother's domestic empire is at risk of contagion from the very subjects she must domesticate and civilize, her wilderness children and foreign servants, who ultimately infect both the home and the body of the mother.[20]

This reading of Beecher suggests new ways of understanding the intricate means by which domestic discourse generates and relies on images of the foreign. On the one hand, domesticity's "habits of system and order" appear to anchor the home as a stable center in a fluctuating social world with expanding national borders; on the other, domesticity must be spatially and conceptually mobile to travel to the nation's far-flung frontiers. Beecher's use of Tocqueville's ark metaphor suggests both the rootlessness and the self-enclosed mobility necessary for middle-class domesticity to redefine the meaning of habitation to make Euro-Americans feel at home in terrain in which *they* are initially the foreigners. Domesticity inverts this relationship to create a home by rendering prior inhabitants alien and undomesticated and by implicitly nativizing newcomers. The empire of the mother thus shares the logic of the American empire; both follow a double compulsion to conquer and domesticate the foreign, thus incorporating and controlling a threatening foreignness within the borders of the home and the nation.

The imperial scope of domesticity was central to the work of Sarah Josepha Hale throughout her half-century editorship of the influential *Godey's Lady's Book,* as well as to her fiction and history writing. Hale has been viewed by some scholars as advocating a woman's sphere more thoroughly separate from male political concerns than Beecher did.[21] This withdrawal seems confirmed by the refusal of *Godey's* even to mention the Civil War throughout its duration, much less take sides. Yet when Hale conflates the progress of women with the nation's Manifest Destiny in her history writing, other scholars have judged her as inconsistently moving out of woman's sphere into the male political realm.[22] Hale's conception of separate spheres, I will argue, is predicated on the imperial expansion of the nation. Although her writing as editor, essayist, and novelist focused on the interior spaces of the home, with ample advice on housekeeping, clothing, manners, and emotions, she gave equal and related attention to the expansion of female influence through her advocacy of female medical missionaries abroad and the colonization of Africa by former black slaves. Even though Hale seems to avoid the issue of slavery and race relations in her silence about the Civil War, in the 1850s her conception of domesticity takes on a decidedly racial cast, exposing the intimate link between the separateness of gendered spheres and the effort to keep the races apart in separate national spheres.

In 1846, at the beginning of the Mexican War, Hale launched a campaign on the pages of *Godey's Lady's Book* to declare Thanksgiving Day a national holiday, a campaign she avidly pursued until Lincoln made the holiday official in 1863.[23] This effort typified the way in which Hale's map of woman's sphere overlaid national and domestic spaces; *Godey's* published detailed instructions and recipes for preparing the Thanksgiving feast, while it encouraged women readers to agitate for a nationwide holiday as a ritual of national expansion and unification. The power of Thanksgiving Day stemmed from its center in the domestic sphere; Hale imagined millions of families seated around the holiday table at the same time, thereby unifying the vast and shifting space of the national domain through simultaneity in time. This domestic ritual, she wrote in 1852, would unite "our great nation, by its states and families from the St. John to the Rio Grande, from the Atlantic to the Pacific."[24] If the celebration of Thanksgiving unites individual families across regions and brings them together in an imagined collective space, Thanksgiving's continental scope endows each individual family gathering with national meaning. Furthermore, the Thanksgiving story commemorating the founding of New England — which in Hale's version makes no mention of Indians — could create a common history by nationalizing a regional myth of origins and imposing it on the territories most recently wrested from Indians and Mexicans. Hale's campaign to transform Thanksgiving from a regional to a national holiday grew even fiercer with the approach of the Civil War. In 1859 she wrote, "If every state would join in Union Thanksgiving on the 24th of this month, would it not be a renewed pledge of love and loyalty to the Constitution of the United States?"[25] Thanksgiving Day, she hoped, could avert civil war. As a national holiday celebrated primarily in the home, Thanksgiving traverses broad geographic circuits to write a national history of origins, to colonize the western territories, and to unite North and South.

The domestic ritual of Thanksgiving could expand and unify national borders only by also fortifying those borders against foreignness; for Hale, the nation's borders not only defined its geographical limits but also set apart nonwhites within the national domain. In Hale's fiction of the 1850s, Thanksgiving polices the domestic sphere by making black people, both free and enslaved, foreign to the domestic nation and denying them a home within America's expanding borders. In 1852 Hale reissued her novel *Northwood,* which had launched her career in 1827, with a highly publicized chapter about a New Hampshire Thanksgiving dinner showcasing the values of the American republic to a skeptical British visitor. For the 1852 version Hale changed the subtitle from "A Tale of New England" to "Life North and South" to highlight the new material on slavery she had added.[26] Pro-union yet against abolition, Hale advocated African colonization as the only means of preserving domestic unity by sending all blacks to settle in Africa and Christianize its inhabitants. Colonization in the 1850s had a two-pronged ideology, both to expel blacks to a separate national sphere and to expand U.S. power through the civilizing process; black Christian settlers would thereby become both outcasts from and agents for the American empire.[27]

Hale's 1852 *Northwood* ends with an appeal to use Thanksgiving Day as an occasion to collect money at all American churches "for the purpose of educating and colonizing free people of color and emancipated slaves" (408). This annual collection would contribute to "peaceful emancipation" as "every obstacle to the real freedom of America would be melted before the gushing streams of sympathy and charity" (408). While "sympathy," a sentiment associated with woman's sphere, seems to extend to black slaves, the goal of sympathy in this passage is not to free them but to emancipate white America from their presence. Thanksgiving for Hale thus celebrates national coherence around the domestic sphere while simultaneously rendering blacks within America foreign to the nation.

For Hale, colonization would not simply expel black people from American nationality but would also transform American slavery into a civilizing and domesticating mission. One of her Northern characters explains to the British visitor that "the destiny of America is to instruct the world, which we shall do, with the aid of our Anglo-Saxon brothers over the water. . . . Great Britain has enough to do at home and in the East Indies to last her another century. We have this country and Africa to settle and civilize" (167). When his listener is puzzled by the reference to Africa, he explains, "That is the greatest mission of our Republic, to train here the black man for his duties as a Christian, then free him and send him to Africa, there to plant Free States and organize Christian civilization" (168). The colonization of Africa becomes the goal of slavery by making it part of the civilizing mission of global imperialism. Colonization thus not only banishes blacks from the domestic union, but, as the final sentence of *Northwood* proclaims, it proves that "the mission of American slavery is to Christianize Africa" (408).

In 1852 Hale published the novel *Liberia,* which begins where *Northwood* ends, with the settlement of Liberia by freed black slaves.[28] Seen by scholars as a retort to *Uncle Tom's Cabin, Liberia* can also be read as the untold story of Stowe's novel, beginning where she ends, with former black slaves immigrating to Africa.[29] Although the subtitle, "Mr. Peyton's Experiment," places colonization under the aegis of white males, the narrative turns colonization into a project emanating from woman's sphere in at least two directions. In its outward trajectory, the settlement of Liberia appears as an expansion of feminized domestic values. Yet domesticity is not only exported to civilize native Africans; the framing of the novel also makes African colonization necessary to the establishment of domesticity within America as exclusively white.

While Hale writes that the purpose of the novel is to "show the advantages Liberia offers to the African," in so doing it construes all black people as foreign to American nationality by asserting that they must remain homeless within the United States. At the same time, Hale paints a picture of American imperialism as the embodiment of the feminine values of domesticity: "What other nation can point to a colony planted from such pure motives of charity; nurtured by the counsels and exertions of its most noble and self-denying statesmen and philanthropists; and sustained, from its feeble commencement up to a period of self-reliance and independence, from pure love of justice and humanity" (iv). In this passage America is figured as a mother raising her baby, Africa, to maturity; the vocabulary of "purity," "charity," "self-denial," and "love" represents colonization as an expansion of the values of woman's separate sphere.

The narrative opens with a threat to American domesticity on two fronts. The last male of a distinguished Virginia family is on his death bed, helpless to defend his plantation from a rumored slave insurrection; the women of the family, led by his wife, "Virginia," rally with the loyal slaves to defend their home from an insurrection that never occurs. Thus the novel opens with separate spheres gone awry, with the man of the family abed at home and white women and black slaves acting as protectors and soldiers. While the ensuing plot to settle Liberia overtly rewards those slaves for their loyalty by giving them freedom and a homeland, it also serves to reinstate separate spheres and reestablish American domesticity as white.

When the narrative shifts to Africa, colonization has the effect not only of driving black slaves out of American nationhood but also of Americanizing Africa through domesticity. A key figure in the settlement is the slave Keziah, who has nursed the white plantation owners. She is the most responsive to Peyton's proposal for colonization because of her desire both to be free and to Christianize the natives. Her future husband, Polydore, more recently arrived from Africa and thus less "civilized," is afraid to return there because of his memory of native brutality and superstition. This couple represents two faces of enslaved Africans central to the white imagination of colonization: the degenerate heathen represented by the man and the redeemed Christian represented by the woman. Keziah, however, can only become a fully domesticated woman at a geographic remove from American domesticity. When Keziah protects the plantation in Virginia, her maternal impulse is described as that of a wild animal — a "fierce lioness." Only in Africa can she become the domestic center of the new settlement, where she establishes a home that resembles Beecher's Christian neighborhood. Keziah builds a private home with fence and garden, and civilizes her husband while expanding her domestic sphere to adopt native children and open a Christian school.

Keziah's domestication of herself and her surroundings in Africa can be seen as part of the movement in the novel noted by Susan Ryan, in which the freed black characters are represented as recognizably American only at the safe distance of Africa.[30] Once banished from the domestic sphere of the American nation, they can reproduce themselves for readers as Americans in a foreign terrain. The novel not only narrates the founding of Liberia as a story of colonization, but Hale's storytelling also colonizes Liberia as an imitation of America, replete with images of an open frontier, the Mayflower, and the planting of the American flag. A double narrative movement at once contracts American borders to exclude blacks from domestic space and simultaneously expands U.S. borders by recreating that domestic space in Africa. The novel thus ends with a quotation that compares the Liberian settlers to the Pilgrims and represents them as part of a global expansion of the American nation:

> I do not doubt but that the whole continent of Africa will be regenerated, and I believe the Republic of Liberia will be the great instrument, in the hands of God, in working out this regeneration. The colony of Liberia has succeeded better than the colony of Plymouth did for the same period of time. And yet, in that little company which was wafted across the mighty ocean in the *May Flower*, we see the germs of this already colossal nation, whose feet are in the tropics, while her head reposes upon the snows of Canada. Her right hand she stretches over the Atlantic, feeding the millions of the Old World, and beckoning them to her shores, as a refuge from famine and oppression; and, at the same time, she stretches forth her left hand to the islands of the Pacific, and to the old empires of the East. (303)

African slaves are brought to America to become Christianized and domesticated, but they cannot complete this potential transformation until they return to Africa.

Hale's writing makes race central to woman's sphere not only by excluding nonwhites from domestic nationalism but also by seeing the capacity for domesticity as an innate, defining characteristic of the Anglo-Saxon race. Reginald Horsman has shown how by the 1840s the meaning of Anglo-Saxonism in political thought had shifted from a historical understanding of the development of republican institutions to an essentialist definition of a single race that possesses an innate and unique capacity for self-government.[31] His analysis, however, limits this racial formation to the male sphere of politics. Hale's *Woman's Record* (1853), a massive compendium of the history of women from Eve to the present, establishes woman's sphere as central to the racial discourse of Anglo-Saxonism; to her, the empire of the mother spawns the Anglo-Saxon nation and propels its natural inclination toward global power.[32] In her introduction to the fourth part of her volume on the present era, Hale represents America as manifesting the universal progress of women that culminates in the Anglo-Saxon race. To explain the Anglo-Saxon "mastery of the mind over Europe and Asia," she argues that

> if we trace out the causes of this superiority, they would center in the moral influence, which true religion confers on the female sex. . . . There is still a more wonderful example of this uplifting power of the educated female mind. It is only seventy-five years since the Anglo-Saxons in the New World became a nation, then numbering about three million souls. Now this people form the great American republic, with a population of

twenty three millions; and the destiny of the world will soon be in their keeping! Religion is free; and the soul which woman always influences where God is worshipped in spirit and truth, is untrammeled by code, or creed, or caste. . . . The result before the world — a miracle of advancement, American mothers train their sons to be men. (564)

Hale here articulates the imperial logic of what has been called "republican motherhood," which ultimately posits the expansion of maternal influence beyond the nation's borders.[33] The Manifest Destiny of the nation unfolds logically from the imperial reach of woman's influence emanating from her separate domestic sphere. Domesticity makes manifest the destiny of the Anglo-Saxon race, while Manifest Destiny becomes in turn the condition for Anglo-Saxon domesticity. For Hale domesticity has two effects on national expansion: It imagines the nation as a home delimited by race and propels the nation outward through the imperial reach of female influence.

Advocating domesticity's expansive mode, *Woman's Record* includes only those nonwhite women whom Hale understood to be contributing to the spread of Christianity to colonized peoples. In the third volume, Hale designates as the most distinguished woman from 1500 to 1830 an American missionary to Burma, Ann Judson, a white American (152). The Fourth Era of *Woman's Record* focuses predominantly on American women as the apex of historical development. In contrast to the aristocratic accomplishments of English women, "in all that contributes to popular education and pure religious sentiment among the masses, the women of America are in advance of all others on the globe. To prove this we need only examine the list of American female missionaries, teachers, editors and authors of works instructive and educational, contained in this 'Record'" (564). While Anglo-Saxon men marched outward to conquer new lands, women had a complementary outward reach from within the domestic sphere.

For Hale, African colonization can be seen as part of the broader global expansion of woman's sphere. In 1853 Hale printed in *Godey's Lady's Book* "An Appeal to the American Christians on Behalf of the Ladies' Medical Missionary Society," in which she argued for the special need for women physicians abroad because they would have unique access to foreign women's bodies and souls.[34] Her argument for the training of female medical missionaries both enlarges the field of white women's agency and feminizes the force of imperial power. She sees female medical missionaries as not only curing disease but also raising the status of women abroad: "All heathen people have a high reverence for medical knowledge. Should they find Christian ladies accomplished in this science, would it not greatly raise the sex in the estimation of those nations, where one of the most serious impediments to moral improvement is the degradation and ignorance to which their females have been for centuries consigned?" (185). Though superior to heathen women in status, American women would accomplish their goal by imagining gender as a common ground, which would give them special access to women abroad. As women they could be more effective imperialists, penetrating those interior feminine colonial spaces, symbolized by the harem, that remain inaccessible to male missionaries:

> Vaccination is difficult of introduction among the people of the east, though suffering dreadfully from the ravages of small-pox. The American mission at Siam writes that thousands of children were, last year, swept away by this disease in the country around them. Female physicians could win their way among these poor children much easier than doctors of the other sex. Surely the ability of American women to learn and practice vaccination will not be questioned, when the more difficult art of inoculation was discovered by the women of Turkey, and introduced into Europe by an English woman! Inoculation is one of the greatest triumphs of remedial skill over a sure loathsome and deadly disease which the annals of Medical Art record. Its discovery belongs to women. I name it here to show that they are gifted with genius for the profession, and only need to be educated to excel in the preventive department.
>
> Let pious, intelligent women be fitly prepared, and what a mission-field for doing good would be opened! In India, China, Turkey, and all over the heathen world, they would, in their character of physicians, find access to the homes and harems where women dwell, and where the good seed sown would bear an hundredfold, because it would take root in the bosom of the sufferer, and in the heart of childhood. (185)

In this passage the connections among women circulate in many directions, but Hale charts a kind of evolutionary narrative that places American women at the apex of development. Though inoculation was discovered by Turkish women, it can only return to Turkey to save Turkish children through the agency of English women transporting knowledge to Americans, who can then go to Turkey as missionaries and save women who cannot save themselves or their children. While Hale is advocating that unmarried women be trained as missionaries, the needs of heathen women allow female missionaries to conquer their own domestic empire without reproducing biologically. Instead, American women are metaphorically cast as men in a cross-racial union, as they sow seeds in the bosom of heathen women who will bear Christian children. Through the sentiment of female influence, women physicians will transform heathen harems into Christian homes.

My reading of Hale suggests that the concept of female influence so central to domestic discourse and at the heart of the sentimental ethos is underwritten by and abets the imperial expansion of the nation. While the empire of the mother advocated retreat from the world-conquering enterprises of men, this renunciation promised a more thorough kind of world conquest. The empire of the mother shared with the American empire a logical structure and a key contradiction: Both sought to encompass the world outside their borders; yet this same outward movement contributed to and relied on the contraction of the domestic sphere to exclude persons conceived of as racially foreign within those expanding national boundaries.

Understanding the imperial reach of domesticity and its relation to the foreign should help remap the critical terrain upon which women's domestic fiction has been constructed. We can chart the broader international and national contexts in which unfold narratives of female development that at first glance seem anchored in local domestic spaces. We can see how such narratives imagine domestic locations in complex negotiation with the foreign. To take a few well-known examples from the 1850s, Susan Warner's *The Wide Wide World* sends its heroine to Scotland, while the world of Maria Cummins's *The Lamplighter* encompasses India, Cuba, the American West, and Brazil. In E. D. E. N. Southworth's *The Hidden Hand*, the resolution of multiple domestic plots in Virginia relies on the participation of the male characters in the Mexican War, while the geographic coordinates of *Uncle Tom's Cabin* extend not only to Africa at the end but also to Haiti and Canada throughout.[35] Such a remapping would involve more than just seeing the geographic settings anew; it would turn inward to the privileged space of the domestic novel — the interiority of the female subject — to find traces of foreignness that must be domesticated or expunged. How does this struggle with foreignness within "woman's sphere" shape the interiority of female subjectivity, the empire of the affections and the heart? While critics such as Gillian Brown, Richard Brodhead, and Nancy Armstrong have taught us how domestic novels represent women as model bourgeois subjects,[36] my remapping would explore how domestic novels produce the racialized national subjectivity of the white middle-class woman in contested international spaces.

Many domestic novels open at physical thresholds, such as windows or doorways, that problematize the relation between interior and exterior; the home and the female self appear fragile and threatened from within and without by foreign forces. These novels then explore the breakdown of the boundaries between internal and external spaces, between the domestic and the foreign, as they struggle to renegotiate and stabilize these domains. This negotiation often takes place not only within the home but also within the heroine. The narrative of female self-discipline that is so central to the domestic novel might be viewed as a kind of civilizing process in which the woman plays the role of both civilizer and savage. Gerty in *The Lamplighter,* for example, like Capitola in *The Hidden Hand,* first appears as an uncivilized street urchin, a heathen unaware of Christianity whose anger is viewed as a "dark infirmity" and whose unruly nature is in need of domesticating. We later learn that she was born in Brazil to the daughter of a ship captain, who was killed by malaria, the "inhospitable southern disease, which takes the stranger for its victim."[37] To become the sovereign mother of her own domestic empire, Gerty must become her own first colonial subject and purge herself of both her origin in a diseased uncivilized terrain and the female anger identified with that "dark" realm. This split between the colonizer and the colonized, seen here within one female character, appears in *Uncle Tom's Cabin* racially externalized onto Eva and Topsy.[38]

My point is that where the domestic novel appears most turned inward to the private sphere of female interiority, we often find subjectivity scripted by narratives of nation and empire. Even at the heart of *The Wide, Wide World*, a novel usually understood as thoroughly closeted in interior space, where the heroine disciplines herself through reading and prayer, her favorite book is the popular biography of George Washington, the father of the nation. Her own journal to live with her Scottish relatives can be seen as a feminized reenactment of the American revolution against the British empire. Similarly, in *The Hidden Hand*, the most inner recess of woman's sphere is conjoined with the male sphere of imperial conquest. While the American men in the novel are invading Mexico, in Virginia, a bandit, significantly named "Black Donald," invades the heroine's chamber and threatens to rape her. To protect the sanctity of her home and her own chastity, Capitola performs a founding national narrative of conquest. She drops the rapist through a trap door in her bedroom into a deep pit dug by the original owner in order to trick the Indian inhabitants into selling their land. The domestic heroine thus reenacts the originating gesture of imperial appropriation to protect the borders of her domestic empire and the inviolability of the female self.

Feminist criticism of *Uncle Tom's Cabin* has firmly established that the empire of the mother in Stowe's novel extends beyond the home to the national arena of antislavery politics. This expansive movement of female influence, I have been arguing, has an international dimension that helps separate gendered spheres coalesce in the imperial expansion of the nation by redrawing domestic borders against the foreign. In light of my reading of Hale's *Liberia*, we might remap the critical terrain of Stowe's novel to ask how its delineation of domestic space, as both familial and national, relies upon and propels the colonization of Africa by the novel's free black characters. Rather than just focusing on their expulsion at the end of the novel, we might locate, in Toni Morrison's terms, "the Africanist presence" throughout the text.[39] Africa appears as both an imperial outpost and a natural embodiment of woman's sphere, a kind of feminized utopia, that is strategically posed as an alternative to Haiti, which hovers as a menacing image of black revolutionary agency. The idea of African colonization does not simply emerge at the end as a racist failure of Stowe's political imagination; rather, colonization underwrites the racial politics of the domestic imagination. The "Africanist presence" throughout *Uncle Tom's Cabin* is intimately bound to the expansionist logic of domesticity itself. In the writing of Stowe and her contemporary proponents of woman's sphere, "Manifest Domesticity" turns an imperial nation into a home by producing and colonizing specters of the foreign that lurk inside and outside its ever shifting borders.

NOTES

I wish to thank the organizers of the conference "Nineteenth-Century American Women Writers in the Twenty-First Century" (Hartford, May 1996) for inviting me to present my first formulation of the ideas in this essay. Special thanks to Susan Gillman, Carla Kaplan, Dana D. Nelson, and Priscilla Wald for their helpful and encouraging readings at crucial stages.

1. Influential studies of this paradigm by historians and literary critics include Barbara Welter, "The Cult of True Womanhood," *American Quarterly* 18 (summer 1966): 151–74; Kathryn Kish Sklar, *Catherine Beecher: A Study in American Domesticity* (New Haven: Yale Univ. Press, 1973); Nancy Cott, *The Bonds of Womanhood: "Woman's Sphere" in New England, 1780–1835* (New Haven: Yale Univ. Press, 1977); Ann Douglas, *The Feminization of American Culture* (New York: Knopf, 1977); Nina Baym, *Woman's Fiction: A Guide to Novels by and about Women in America, 1820–1870* (Ithaca, N.Y.: Cornell Univ. Press, 1978); Mary P. Ryan, *Cradle of the Middle Class: The Family in Oneida County, New York, 1790–1865* (Cambridge, Eng.: Cambridge Univ. Press, 1981), and *Empire of the Mother: American Writing about Domesticity, 1830–1860* (New York: Institute for Research in History and Haworth Press, 1982); Mary Kelley, *Private Woman, Public Stage: Literary Domesticity in Nineteenth-Century America* (New York: Oxford Univ. Press, 1984); Jane Tompkins, *Sensational Designs: The Cultural Work of American Fiction, 1790–1860* (New York: Oxford Univ. Press, 1985); Gillian Brown, *Domestic Individualism: Imagining Self in Nineteenth-Century America* (Berkeley and Los Angeles: Univ. of California Press, 1990); and the essays in *The Culture of Sentiment: Race, Gender, and Sentimentality in Nineteenth-Century America*, ed. Shirley Samuels (New York: Oxford Univ. Press, 1992). See also the useful review essay by Linda K. Kerber, "Separate Spheres, Female Worlds, Woman's Place: The Rhetoric of Women's History," *The Journal of American History* (June 1988): 9–39.

2. On the etymology of the word *domestic* and its relation to colonialism, see Karen Hansen, ed., *African Encounters with Domesticity* (New Brunswick, N.J.: Rutgers Univ. Press, 1992), 2–23; and Anne McClintock, *Imperial Leather: Race, Gender, and Sexuality in the Colonial Contest* (New York: Routledge, 1995), 31–36. On the uses of domesticity in the colonial context, see Vicente L. Rafael, "Colonial Domesticity: White Women and United States Rule in the Philippines." *American Literature* 67 (December 1995): 639–66.

3. Tompkins, *Sensational Designs*, 143, 144. Despite Tompkins's well-known debate with Ann Douglas, both critics rely on imperial rhetoric. While Tompkins applauds the imperialist impulse of sentimentalism, Douglas derides sentimental writers for a rapacious reach that extends as far as the "colonization of heaven" and the "domestication of death" (240–72).

4. Even recent revisionist studies that situate woman's sphere in relation to racial and class hierarchies often overlook the international context in which these divisions evolve. In the important essays in *Culture of Sentiment*, for example, many of the racialized configurations of domesticity under discussion rely on a foreign or imperial dimension that remains unanalyzed. To take a few examples, Laura Wexler's analysis of Hampton Institute makes no mention of its founding by influential missionaries to Hawaii ("Tender Violence: Literary Eavesdropping, Domestic Fiction, and Educational Reform," 9–38); Karen Halttunen's analysis of a murder trial revolves around the uncertain identity of a white woman's foreign Spanish or Cuban lover ("'Domestic Differences': Competing Narratives of Womanhood in the Murder Trial of Lucretia Chapman," 39–57); Lynn Wardley ties domesticity's obsession with detail to West African fetishism ("Relic, Fetish, Femmage: The Aesthetics of Sentiment in the Work of Stowe," 203–20). Several essays note comparisons of slavery to the oriental harem, including Carolyn Karcher on Lydia Maria Child's antislavery fiction ("Rape, Murder, and Revenge in Slavery's Pleasant Homes: Lydia Maria Child's Antislavery Fiction and the Limits of Genre," 58–72) and Joy Kasson's analysis of Hirams's *The Greek Slave* ("Narratives of the Female Body: *The Greek Slave*," 172–90). The only essay to treat the imperial dimensions of domesticity is Lora Romero's "Vanishing Americans: Gender, Empire, and New Historicism" (115–27).

5. Thomas R. Hietala, *Manifest Design: Anxious Aggrandizement in Late Jacksonian America* (Ithaca, N.Y.: Cornell Univ. Press, 1985).

6. *Cherokee Nation v. the State of Georgia*, in *Major Problems in American Foreign Policy: Documents and Essays*, ed. Thomas G. Paterson, 2 vols. (Lexington, Mass.: Heath, 1989), 1:202.

7. Quoted in Walter La Feber, *The American Age: United States Foreign Policy at Home and Abroad* (New York: Norton, 1989), 112.

8. Quoted in George B. Forgie, *Patricide in the House Divided: A Psychological Interpretation of Lincoln and His Age* (New York: Norton, 1979), 107–8.

9. On popular fiction of the Mexican War, see Robert W. Johannsen, *To the Halls of the Montezumas: The Mexican War in the American Imagination* (New York: Oxford Univ. Press, 1984), 175–204.

10. Sarah Josepha Hale, "Editor's Table," *Godey's Lady's Book*, January 1852, 88.

11. Quoted in Ryan, *Empire of the Mother*, 112.

12. From "The Social Condition of Woman," *North American Review*, April 1836, 513; quoted in Annette Kolodny, *The Land Before Her: Fantasy and Experience of the American Frontiers, 1630–1860* (Chapel Hill: Univ. of North Carolina Press, 1984), 166.

13. Catherine Beecher, *A Treatise on Domestic Economy* (Boston: Marsh, Capen, Lyon, and Webb, 1841), 144. Subsequent references to this work are cited parenthetically in the text.

14. Ryan, *Empire of the Mother*, 97–114.

15. Kathryn Kish Sklar is one of the few scholars to consider Beecher's domestic ideology in relation to nation building. She analyzes the *Treatise* as appealing to gender as a common national denominator, and as using domesticity as a means to promote national unity to counterbalance mobility and conflicts based on class and region. Sklar fails to see, however, that this vision of gender as a tool for national unity is predicated upon the nation's imperial role (*Catherine Beecher*). Jenine Abboushi Dallal analyzes the imperial dimensions of Beecher's domestic ideology by contrasting it with the domestic rhetoric of Melville's imperial adventure narratives in "The Beauty of Imperialism: Emerson, Melville, Flaubert, and Al-Shidyac" (Ph.D. diss., Harvard University, 1996), chap. 2.

16. John L. O'Sullivan, "The Great Nation of Futurity," in *Major Problems in American Foreign Policy*, ed. Paterson, 1:241.

17. Catherine Beecher and Harriet Beecher Stowe, *The American Woman's Home* (Hartford, Conn.: J. B. Ford, 1869), 458–59.

18. Karen Sánchez-Eppler, "Raising Empires like Children: Race, Nation, and Religious Education," *American Literary History* 8 (Fall 1996): 399–425; Ann Stoler, *Race and the Education of Desire: Foucault's "History of Sexuality" and the Colonial Order of Things* (Durham, N.C.: Duke Univ. Press, 1995), 137–64.

19. Although the cleanliness and orderliness of the home promises to make American women healthier, Beecher also blames a lack of outdoor exercise for American women's frailty, suggesting that the problematic space outside the home — the foreign — can both cause and cure those "difficulties peculiar to American women."

20. This generalized anxiety about contamination of the domestic sphere by children may stem from the circulation of stories by missionaries who expressed fear of their children being raised by native servants or too closely identifying with native culture. Such stories circulated both in popular mission tracts and in middle-class women's magazines such as *Godey's* and *Mother's Magazine*; see, for example, Stoler, *Race and the Education of Desire*; and Patricia Grimshaw, *Paths of Duty: American Missionary Wives in Nineteenth-Century Hawaii* (Honolulu: Univ. of Hawaii Press, 1989), 154–78. The licentiousness of men was also seen as a threat to women's health within the home. For example, in "Life on the Rio Grande" (*Godey's Lady's Book*, April 1847), a piece celebrating the opening of public schools in Galveston, Texas, Sarah Josepha Hale quotes a military officer who warns that "liberty is ever degenerating into license, and man is prone to abandon his sentiments and follow his passions. It is woman's high mission, her prerogative and duty, to counsel, to sustain — as to control him" (177). On the borderlands, women have the role of civilizing savagery in their own homes, where men's passions appear as the foreign force to be colonized. In general, domesticity is seen as an ideology that develops in middle-class urban centers, (and, as Sklar shows, in contrast to European values) and is then exported to the frontier and empire, where it meets challenges and must adapt. It remains to be studied how domestic discourse might develop out of the confrontation with foreign cultures in what has been called the "contact zone" of frontier and empire.

21. Sklar, *Catherine Beecher*, 163; Douglas, *Feminization of American Culture*, 51–54.

22. Nina Baym, "Onward Christian Women: Sarah J. Hale's History of the World," *New England Quarterly* 63 (June 1990): 249–70.

23. Sarah J. Hale, "Editor's Table," *Godey's Lady's Book*, January 1847, 53.

24. Sarah J. Hale, *Godey's Lady's Book*, November 1852, 303.

25. Ruth E. Finley, *The Lady of Godey's, Sarah Josepha Hale* (Philadelphia: Lippincott, 1931), 199.

26. Sarah J. Hale, *Northwood; or, Life North and South: Showing the True Character of Both* (New York: H. Long and Brother, 1852). See Hale's 1852 preface, "A Word with the Reader," on revisions of the 1827 edition. Further references to *Northwood* will be cited parenthetically in the text.

27. On the white ideological framework of African colonization, see George Fredrickson, *The Black Image in the White Mind: The Debate on Afro-American Character and Destiny, 1817–1914* (New York: Harper and Row, 1971), 6–22, 110–17; Susan M. Ryan, "Errand into Africa: Colonization and Nation Building in Sarah J. Hale's *Liberia*," *New England Quarterly* 68 (December 1995): 558–83.

28. Sarah J. Hale, *Liberia; or Mr. Peyton's Experiment* (1853; reprint, Upper Saddle River, N.J.: Gregg Press, 1968).

29. On *Liberia* as a conservative rebuff to Stowe, see Thomas F. Gossett, *"Uncle Tom's Cabin" and American Culture* (Dallas, Tex.: Southern Methodist Univ. Press, 1985), 235–36.

30. Susan Ryan, "Errand into Africa," 572.

31. Reginald Horsman, *Race and Manifest Destiny: The Origins of American Racial Anglo-Saxonism* (Cambridge: Harvard Univ. Press, 1981), 62–81.

32. Sarah J. Hale, *Woman's Record* (New York: Harper & Brothers, 1853).

33. Linda K. Kerber, *Women of the Republic: Intellect and Ideology in Revolutionary America* (Chapel Hill: Univ. of North Carolina Press, 1980).

34. Sarah J. Hale, "An Appeal to the American Christians on Behalf of the Ladies' Medical Missionary Society," *Godey's Lady's Book,* March 1852, 185–88.

35. Susan Warner, *The Wide Wide World* (1850; reprint, New York: Feminist Press, 1987); Maria Susanna Cummins, *The Lamplighter* (1854; reprint, New Brunswick, N.J.: Rutgers Univ. Press, 1988); E. D. E. N. Southworth, *The Hidden Hand; or, Capitola The Madcap* (1859; reprint, New Brunswick, N.J.: Rutgers Univ. Press, 1988); Harriet Beecher Stowe, *Uncle Tom's Cabin* (1852; reprint, New York: Viking Penguin, 1981).

36. Nancy Armstrong, *Desire and Domestic Fiction: A Political History of the Novel* (New York: Oxford Univ. Press, 1987); Brown, *Domestic Individualism;* Richard Brodhead, "Sparing the Rod: Discipline and Fiction in Antebellum America," in *The New American Studies: Essays from "Representations,"* ed. Philip Fisher (Berkeley and Los Angeles: Univ. of California Press, 1991).

37. Cummins, *The Lamplighter,* 63, 321. On the male characters' involvement in imperial enterprises in India in *The Lamplighter,* see Susan Castellanos, "Masculine Sentimentalism and the Project of Nation-Building" (paper presented at the conference "Nineteenth-Century Women Writers in the Twenty-First Century," Hartford, May 1996).

38. On this split, see Elizabeth Young, "Topsy-Turvy: Civil War and *Uncle Tom's Cabin,*" chap. 1 of *A Wound of One's Own: Gender and Nation in American Women's Civil War Writing* (forthcoming).

39. Toni Morrison, *Playing in the Dark: Whiteness and the Literary Imagination* (Cambridge: Harvard Univ. Press, 1992), 6.

American Literary Emergence as a Postcolonial Phenomenon

LAWRENCE BUELL

Initially published in American Literary History *(1992), Buell's essay attempts to use the lens of postcolonial literatures to perform a retrospective reading of the American Renaissance of the mid-nineteenth century. Buell seeks to examine American literary emergence in light of the cultural colonization of the thirteen American colonies by Britain. One aspect of his argument is a consideration of the non-American implied reader of American Renaissance texts; he suggests that American writers imagined a transatlantic audience in addition to an American one. Buell also points to several marks of postcolonialism in the writing of the American Renaissance such as semi-Americanization of the language, cultural hybridization, the belief that artists are agents of national liberation, the confrontation of neocolonialism, the issue of "alien genres," and pastoralism. You might refer to John Carlos Rowe's essay, earlier in this chapter, for a different response to the application of postcolonialism to American literature.*

1

As the first colony to win independence, America has a history that Americans have liked to offer as a prototype for other new nations, yet which by the same token might profitably be studied by Americans themselves in light of later cases. In the field of American literary history, however, such a retrospective rereading has rarely been tried. This essay attempts precisely that: to imagine the extent to which the emergence of a flourishing national literature during the so-called Renaissance period of the mid-nineteenth century can be brought into focus through the lens of more recent postcolonial literatures. This is a project I have come to as an Americanist by training who has since turned to studying Anglophone writing on a more global scale. Although this body of writing and the critical commentary that has arisen to frame it interest me mainly for their own sake, as an Americanist I have also found that they have caused me to rethink what I thought I already knew.

From *American Literary History* 4.3 (1992): 411–42.

If my approach seems strange, as I hope it will, the reasons should be clear. Some formidable barriers inhibit Americanists from analogizing between this country's literary emergence and even that of Canada or Australia, let alone West India or West Africa — barriers both of ignorance and of principle. Most Americanists know little about those other literatures, nor am I much beyond my novitiate. As to the barrier of principle, even mildly liberal academics will suspect the possible hypocrisy of an exercise in imagining America of the expansionist years as a postcolonial rather than proto-imperial power, as if to mystify modern America's increasingly interventionist role in world affairs. All the more so is my study subject to such suspicions given the ease with which it is possible to slide from thinking about America as the first new nation to thinking about America as the model for other new nations. And all the *more* so if the analogizing also risks, as mine will, blurring the distinction between the European settler as colonial and the indigene as colonial. I shall return to these issues at the end of my essay but shall bracket them for now.

A more discipline-specific barrier is that American literary study has tended to focus so overwhelmingly on American texts as to reduce the internationalist (usually European) quotient within its field of vision. This foreshortening of vision can happen as easily to scholars of cosmopolitan erudition as to Americanists who in fact know little more than American literary history. In Harold Bloom's theory of American poetic succession, for example, no foreign power disrupts the symposium once Emerson enters it; British and American literary histories are kept rigorously distinct, though presumably Bloom is quite aware that until well into the twentieth century the "strong" American poets read Anglo-European masters more attentively than they read each other. Of course, American literary scholarship always has and probably always will recognize the legitimacy of monographs on Emerson and Carlyle, Fuller and Goethe, and so forth, but such influence studies implicitly occupy a minor niche in the larger scheme of things, the equivalent of the prefatory section on the zeitgeist or background influences in a large-scale thematic study.

Up to a point, there is certainly nothing strange or amiss about focusing the study of American letters on America. Studies of all national literary histories commit the same reductionism. A problem more particular to American literary studies arises, however, when the restriction of focus to the national field is regulated in terms of notions of American cultural distinctiveness used to sort authors and texts in or out according to a criterion of emerging indigenousness that fails to take account of such factors as the interpenetration of the "indigenous" and the "foreign," the extent to which the former is constructed by the latter, and consequently the extent to which the sorting of individual authors in or out of the American canon by this criterion (Hawthorne in, Longfellow out) is arbitrary and quixotic. But precisely this has been the tendency since the establishment of American literature as a scholarly subfield in the 1920s, which also (by no coincidence) marked the point at which literary historiography began to be practiced in the climate of major thesis books about the coherence of the American literary tradition, for example, in the pioneering work of D. H. Lawrence, William Carlos Williams, Lewis Mumford, and Vernon L. Parrington. One of the reasons F. O. Matthiessen's *American Renaissance* continues to endure as a landmark study is that it was the last major precontemporary book on the era to be informed by a profound appreciation for Anglo-American intertexts: how his five figures saturated themselves in the rhetorics of Shakespeare, Milton, metaphysical poetry and prose, neoclassicism, and Romanticism. Since Matthiessen, however, the study of American literary emergence has evolved around assumptions about the coherence of the American canon formed in the image of such myths of American distinctiveness as Puritan inheritance or Adamic innocence, generic patterns like the jeremiad or the captivity or the romance considered as national artifacts, as well as particular lineal succession stories like from Edwards to Emerson, Emerson to Whitman, Whitman to Stevens, and so on. Through these devices the unity, the density, and (of course) the respectability of the specialization gets consolidated. These are indeed important reference points; the problem lies not so much in the scholarship that has established them as in its unintended consequence of prompting ever-more-intensive refinements of the map of American letters.

Thus we find ourselves practicing de facto a kind of cisatlantic hermeticism. This starts with our experience as students in American literature courses, when we are socialized (for instance) into forgetting that except for Thoreau's debt to Emerson no American Renaissance writer can confidently be said to have formed his or her style chiefly from native influences, nor with the exception of Melville's essay on Hawthorne is there a clear case on record of one canonical American Renaissance writer insisting that another ranks with the great world authors. We form the habit of picturing Hawthorne as leading to Melville rather than to, say, George Eliot, even though nothing in the Melville canon follows a Hawthornian pretext more faithfully than *Adam Bede* follows *The Scarlet Letter* (see Mills 52–71). We then find ourselves perpetuating the same aesthetic order in American Renaissance courses.

Today, we are better able than in the recent past to combat such parochialisms. Feminist and African-Americanist critiques of the American canon as it crystallized between the 1920s and the 1960s have begun to inspire a pervasive reflexivity about all our instruments of classification, including our conception of literary genealogy, and have in some instances prodded us into thinking transatlantically, as with Henry Louis Gates's exposition of the permutations of Eshu in *The Signifying Monkey* or the image of a Euro-American community of nineteenth-century women writers implicit in feminist criticism of Emily Dickinson since Gilbert and Gubar's *The Madwoman in the Attic*.[1] A small but growing number of Americanists have even taken Anglo-American or Euro-American literary interrelations as their main subject: for example, Jonathan Arac (*Commissioned Spirits*), Leon Chai (*The Romantic Foundations of the American Renaissance*), Nicolaus Mills (*American and English Fiction in the Nineteenth Century*), Larry Reynolds (*European Revolutions and the American Literary Renaissance*), Robert Weisbuch (*Atlantic

Double-Cross), and William Spengemann (*A Mirror for Americanists*), not to mention monographs on single figures like George Dekker's *James Fenimore Cooper: The American Scott* and Jeffrey Rubin-Dorsky's study of Irving, *Adrift in the Old World*.[2]

This work, however, has not yet seriously affected the way Americanists conduct business as usual. The pedagogy and criticism if not the personal conviction of literary Americanists still for the most part give the appearance of being driven, as Spengemann put it, by "the idea that an appreciation of American writing depends upon our keeping it separate from the rest of the world" (141). Spengemann seems to believe this holds for all eras of American literary historiography. Maybe so; but I confine myself here to the period of literary emergence, not only because I know it best but also because the compartmentalizing seems more customary than in the study of, say, literary modernism or the early colonial period. We continue to think much more about how he might have read Scott, more about how Whitman's prosodic experimentalism might have been encouraged by Emerson or Poe than by Keats or Tennyson. We know much more about how American writers of woman's fiction relate to each other than how they related to Dickens or other popular British sentimentalists of either sex. The average article or monograph therefore projects a vision of nineteenth-century American literary history far more autotelic than that of the writers themselves except in their wildest cultural nationalist dreams. This is probably not so much because American literary scholarship continues to be passionately attached to the idea of American distinctiveness at this late date, as because the familiar procedure of grouping American writers together is so ingrained. The effect is to perpetuate at the level of literary commentary the utopian fantasy of American literary autonomy cherished during the early national period, and to abet, in consequence, an American exceptionalist mentality that may without our fully realizing it reinforce in us — or in those who listen unwarily to us — an insularity of perspective that is hazardously inaccurate. It is striking, for example, that for all its critical sophistication, the New Historicist critique of the ideological duplicity of classic American Renaissance texts (their ostensible radicalism versus their actual centrism) has not seriously challenged the assumption that these texts can be adequately understood as an internally coherent and nationally distinctive series.

My own approach to resisting Americanist centripetalism, for which I hold myself as accountable as anyone, will be to reexamine the notion of American literary emergence itself. I do not intend to argue that the American Renaissance never happened, but rather that its achievement, and by extension the "native" literary traditions it helped to create or sustain, cannot be understood without taking into account the degree to which those traditions arose out of "a culture in which the ruled were constantly tempted to fight their rulers within the psychological limits set by the latter," to appropriate Ashis Nandy's diagnosis of the intellectual climate of colonial India (3). To transpose from the colonial to the postcolonial stage of the first half of the American nineteenth century, we need only substitute cultural authority for political/military authority as the object of resistance. Although the thirteen American colonies never experienced anything like the political/military domination colonial India did, the extent of cultural colonization by the mother country, from epistemology to aesthetics to dietetics, was on the whole much more comprehensive — and partly because of the selfsame comparative benignity of the imperial regime.

2

For most students of the American Renaissance, the phenomenon of American writers' cultural dependence has come increasingly to look like a side issue and, after about 1830, a virtual nonissue. Especially since the intensification of Puritan legacy studies, the seeds of an indigenous culture have come to seem so early planted and so deeply rooted as to assure its full flowering eventually if not immediately, so as to make America's continuing imbrication in old-world culture seem uninterestingly epiphenomenal. This mentality has conduced to the view that postcolonial dependency was merely a virus that infected the juvenilia of the great canonical writers of the antebellum era. I daresay many of us who teach nineteenth-century American literature have set up our courses by using British reviewer Sydney Smith ("In the four quarters of the globe, who reads an American book?") as a straw man for our syllabi to refute rather than as an ever-present anxiety and constituent shaping force.

If so, consider the case of Henry T. Tuckerman, whose *America and Her Commentators* (1864), a self-consciously monumental and monumentally self-conscious synopsis of the history of transatlantic views of America, is still a useful sourcebook. Tuckerman asserts that Smith's dictum is "irrelevant and impertinent to-day" (286): "In history, poetry, science, criticism, biography, political and ethical discussions, the records of travels, of taste, and of romance, universally recognized and standard exemplars, of American origin, now illustrate the genius and culture of the nation" (285–86); but his project refutes him, preoccupied as it is with expounding upon how America has been anatomized as literary object rather than reborn as literary force. The idea of America's emerging culture elicits Tuckerman's patriotism, but what commands his awe is the conviction that "never was there a populous land whose inhabitants were so uniformly judged *en masse*" (444). Tuckerman's argument that Americans are no longer mere culture consumers is quixotic and halfhearted. "The statistics of the book trade and the facts of individual culture prove that the master minds of British literature more directly and universally train and nurture the American than the English mind," argues Tuckerman ingeniously (287–88). This glosses over the statistics themselves (as late as 1876, the ratio of American book imports to exports stood at 10 to 1) and the consumer mentality that Tuckerman gamely tries to make the best of: namely that from the "distance that lends enchantment" as well as the diffusion of general education, "Shakespeare and Milton, Bacon and Wordsworth, Byron and Scott have been and are more generally known, appreciated, and loved. and have entered more deeply into the average intellectual life, on this than on the other side of the Atlantic" (288). In short, American cultural autonomy is proven by the fact that more copies of the English classics are bought and avidly read in America than in Britain. Tuckerman's book is itself a kind of vade mecum for the discriminating book importer.

Tuckerman does not draw a connection between how British classics "enchant" American readers and his efforts throughout his assiduous compendium to resist the enchantment of foreign travelers' representations of America. Yet his book, by its mere existence, dramatizes that the authority of European letters was felt to extend itself to the form of an extensive discourse of America that the American writer had to reckon with. Although scholars have been studying this body of travelers' reports for more than half a century, and some of its most distinguished examples are well known (notably Alexis de Tocqueville's *Democracy in America*), the significance of this "occidentalist" writing emerges more fully in light of recent studies of colonial discourse.[3] During what is now called our literary renaissance, America remained for many foreign commentators (especially the British), albeit diminishingly, the unvoiced "other" — with the predictable connotations of exoticism, barbarism, and unstructuredness. This notwithstanding America's legislative innovations and growing economic potency, notwithstanding that no racial barrier separated most travelers from the dominant American racial group, and notwithstanding that European travelers were very well aware that *these* natives had the will and the technology to answer them back publicly in a European language. Indeed, American sensitiveness to foreign opinion was proverbial, and several travelers commented that this severely diminished the frankness with which they could write or speak. Still, it is clear that many nineteenth-century Americans considered themselves to be treated as a minor power by foreign visitors, like the politician who complained to British geologist Charles Lyell that "you class us with the South American republics; your embassadors [sic] to us come from Brazil and Mexico to Washington, and consider it a step in their advancement to go from the United States to . . . some second-rate German court" (1: 226).

For this there was much evidence. Foreign visitors denied America refinement (the want of which was, for Frances Trollope in *Domestic Manners of the Americans*, the greatest American defect). Nineteenth-century travelers on the notorious American practice of tobacco chewing and spitting, for instance, sound like V. S. Naipaul on Indian shitting.[4] European travelers acknowledged American skill at practical calculation (deprecating it as part of the apparatus of American materialism) but tended to depict Americans as more irrational than rational, as an unphilosophical culture whatever its legislative genius, as hasty and slapdash nation builders. They regularly denied America a voice in a culturally substantial sense à la mode Sydney Smith. ("If the national mind of America be judged of by its legislation, it is of a very high order. . . . If the American nation be judged by its literature, it may be pronounced to have no mind at all" [Martineau 2: 200–01].) They even denied the Americans language in the spirit of Rudyard Kipling's remark that "the American has no language," only "dialect, slang, provincialism, accent, and so forth" (24).[5]

It was common for foreign travelers to frame their accounts as narratives of disillusionment, to stress that they started with hopeful, even utopian, expectations of finding a model nation-in-the-making only to discover a cultural backwater. Dickens is a notable case in point, since his *American Notes* avoids stating his disillusionment overtly but proceeds to narrativize it more dramatically than most, as if this were a spontaneous deposition. Starting exuberantly with a stimulating visit to Boston, Dickens gradually sours amid New York slums, Washington rowdiness, and an arduous trip to the interior that reaches a positively Conradian moment during a steamboat voyage down the Ohio River. Dickens luridly evokes the dreary solitude ("For miles, and miles, and miles . . . unbroken by any human footstep"), the sudden ugly rent in the forest for a primitive cabin and straggling field ("full of great unsightly stumps, like earthy butchers'-blocks"), and the malevolent tangle of fallen trees in the current ("their bleached arms start out . . . and seem to try to grasp the boat, and drag it under water") (*American Notes* 159–60). This is merely the travel-book version, the equivalent of Conrad's Congo diaries. For purposes of Martin Chuzzlewit's ill-fated venture to "Eden," the *Heart of Darkness* equivalent, the phantasmagoria is heightened:

> On they toiled through great solitudes, where the trees upon the banks grew thick and close; and floated in the stream; and held up shrivelled arms from out the river's depths; and slid down from the margin of the land, half growing, half decaying, in the miry water. On through the weary day and melancholy night: beneath the burning sun, and in the mist and vapour of the evening: on, until return appeared impossible, and restoration to their home a miserable dream. (375)

Both Dickens and Tocqueville, in their separate ways, reckoned America a country of the future; but Tocqueville's estimate (that America represented the vanguard of the inevitable democratization of modern society that was afoot, willy-nilly, in Europe also) was less typical than Dickens's estimate of America as a crudely vigorous young country still a long way from maturity. Not surprisingly, Tuckerman lauded Tocqueville and deplored Dickens's "superficial and sneering" manner (130–31, 221). Yet Tocqueville himself exhibits perhaps the single most condescending occidentalist gesture, also a hallmark of Orientalism: the overbearing confidence with which occidental traits are generalized. "Americans of all ages, all conditions, and dispositions constantly form associations"; "the Americans are much more addicted to the use of general ideas than the English and entertain a much greater relish for them"; "the love of wealth is . . . to be traced, as either a principal or an accessory motive, at the bottom of all that the Americans do" (2: 114, 15, 240). Tocqueville's many shrewd hits should not blind us to the arrogance of this rhetoric of the imperial generalization. One wonders, as when reading Foucault, whether Tocqueville felt a need to make magisterialism compensate for his theory of individual powerlessness at the level of his sociohistorical vision. The imperial generalization, in any case, is a time-honored device for formulating natives, as Albert Memmi and others have pointed out.[6]

3

The Americans encapsulated in nineteenth-century European travelers' reports were thus by no means wholly like Africans or Asians: They were, after all, mostly Anglo-Saxon, as well as being energetic entrepreneurs of burgeoning economic and military potency, impressive for their efforts at general education if not for their high culture. But as a civilization, America was still comparatively barbarous, the frontier hinterland its dominant reality and its gentry (as Francis Grund stressed in *Aristocracy in America*) pathetic cardboard Europhiles. A thriving oral culture existed, but with exceptions most travelers could count on the fingers of one hand, literary culture did not, and the most visible approximation to a literary class were American journalists, a disreputable lot. Though an American businessman would not have found this composite portrait especially daunting, an aspiring writer would have felt almost as marginalized by it qua writer as Caliban contemplated by Prospero.

With this as our backdrop, we can better understand the terms under which Whitman sought to give voice to American poetry in *Leaves of Grass*. The 1855 Preface starts with the magisterial image of America as the calm witness to the corpse of European tradition being "slowly borne from the eating and sleeping rooms of the house" (709). Because Whitman craftily adopts a pose of impassivity here, and because we are taught to classify this document firmly within the success story of American literary independence, it takes an effort of will to realize that what he has actually done is to make grotesque a trope from the traditional repertoire of Eurocentrism, the *translatio studii* — the transfer of art and learning from the Old World to the New — a trope that had been invoked to underwrite colonization efforts and subsequently the hegemony of the late colonial gentry. It is a figure Whitman uses not just once but repeatedly, for example, in the 1871 "Song of the Exposition," which noisily summons the Muse to "migrate from Greece and Ionia," to "Placard 'Removed' and 'To Let' on the rocks of your snowy Parnassus," and envisions her wafting her way amid the "thud of machinery and shrill steam-whistle undismay'd," "Bluff'd not . . . by drain-pipe, gasometers, artificial fertilizers, / Smiling and pleas'd with palpable intent to stay, / . . . install'd amid the kitchen ware!" (196, 198). The calculated tackiness that subverts old-world decorums while nominally observing them seems more pointed if we see it as akin to, for example, modern West Indian inversions of the Prospero-Caliban trope, as in George Lamming's autobiographical essays *The Pleasures of Exile* and Aimé Cesaire's dramatic redaction *A Tempest*, or (analogously) the Crusoe-Friday inversion in Derek Walcott's play *Pantomime*. For what Whitman has done in these passages I have cited is in effect to Calibanize *translatio studii*, to render it hairy and gross and thereby to reveal America's ongoing struggle to extricate its forms of thought from old-world categories, meaning not just rhetorical figures but also social figurations like the Americans-as-barbarians stereotype. To see this, however, one needs to know what the prototypes of struggle have been. Even if we know something about the history of *translatio studii,* we Americanists tend not to think this far, because we think of *translatio studii* as a motif that America left behind soon after the turn of the nineteenth century; and we have lately grown accustomed to thinking of Caliban as a figure elevated to hero status by third-world, particularly Caribbean, intellectuals, over against a Eurocentrism that includes America as well as the earlier imperial powers. Yet as the most articulate West Indian proponent of Caliban as "our symbol" sheepishly admits, Caliban appears to have been associated with Yankeedom before Latin Americans thought to canonize him (Fernández Retamar 10). Whitman himself, in fact, was likened in one British review to "Caliban flinging down his logs, and setting himself to write a poem" — the reviewer's proof text being the "barbaric yawp" passage (qtd. in Murphy 60). Whitman proceeded to select this among the other excerpts to append as promotional material for the 1856 edition of *Leaves of Grass.*

As the Caliban analogy suggests, Whitman's rewriting of *translatio studii* anticipates one of the major modern postcolonial strategies. Indeed, *Leaves of Grass* as a whole makes the same move on a much vaster scale, with its bending and breaking epic tradition (McWilliams 218–37). This rewriting process reflects a resistance-deference syndrome that artists and scholars alike have found it hard to talk about without hypocrisy. Whitman by turns sought to eradicate old-world myth and to reinstate it ("Old Brahm I, and I Saturnius am" [443]). The critic for whom the narrative of national differentiation is primary is tempted to identify the former posture as more "authentic" or "progressive" than the latter, when in fact it was the creative irritant of their interaction that produced their unique result, an interaction in which the "imperial" epic model figures as part of the empowerment as well as an object of resistance.

Another case that will help to clinch this point is James Fenimore Cooper's Leatherstocking. No vernacular hero has been more influential in all of American literary history, with the possible exception of Huckleberry Finn, for whom Natty Bumppo probably helped to prepare the way. Yet Bumppo was not, strictly speaking, an indigenous figure, though he can be traced to "real-life" frontiersman prototypes, so much as the result of a rewriting of the trope of the genteel protagonist cum vernacular comic sidekick in Scott's Waverley novels (e.g., Henry Morton and Cuddie Headrigg in *Old Mortality*), a characterological pattern that indeed dates from the very beginnings of the "modern" novel (in *Don Quixote*). Cooper's inversion of this pattern was of landmark significance, providing American literature's first compelling model of the common unlettered person as hero. Yet this breakthrough did not come easily to Cooper; he seems to have discovered his desire to upend the Scottian hierarchy only during the process of composing *The Pioneers,* which begins squarely focused upon the Oliver Edwards–Judge

Temple melodrama and only gradually discovers that Bumppo is a much more interesting character than either. Even at that, Cooper continues to require a Waverley figure as a concomitant and to labor over the proper mimetic level at which to peg Bumppo, whose speech, as Richard Bridgman remarks, "wobbles from one realm of usage to another," from racy slang to grand-manner cliché (67). As if to hold his incipient populism in check, Cooper sees to it that Bumppo retains his vassal status through the first four Leatherstocking tales; only after Cooper has reinvented him at his most decorous, in *The Deerslayer*, does Bumppo finally cease playing the factotum.

The imperfectness of Cooper's break from Scott might be seen as a mark of the "colonized mind." Natty's genteel charges, like Oliver Edwards and Duncan Uncas Middleton of *The Prairie*, are indeed pathetic residues of Cooper's classism, as is the savagist machinery that motors Chingachgook, Bumppo's Indian companion. But why expect a clean break in the first place, and why indeed should one even long to find one when the hierarchicalized genteel hero/folk companion pattern proved to be so productive of innovation? Cooper's achievement looks more substantial when considered as a hard-won new-world adjustment of a transcontinental intertext than either as a homespun invention compromised by the pollution of foreign mannerisms, or (see Green 129–50) as another avatar of old-world conquest narrative.[7]

A third exhibit to set beside Whitman and Cooper is Emerson's "The American Scholar," "our intellectual declaration of independence," as twentieth-century American scholars (following Oliver Wendell Holmes) still like to call it. Its exordium contains Emerson's most famous literary nationalist aperçu: "Our day of dependence, our long apprenticeship to the learning of other lands, draws to a close" (52). But when we examine the two specific signs of this, deferred until the end of the discourse, we find them presented as European-instigated trends only now on the verge of coming to fruition in the New World: the valorization of the humble and the familiar ("This idea has inspired the genius of Goldsmith, Burns, Cowper, and, in a newer time, of Goethe, Wordsworth, and Carlyle" [68]) and the renewed respect accorded the individual person — which Emerson makes a point of emphasizing has not yet trickled over to America ("We have listened too long to the courtly muses of Europe. The spirit of the American freeman is already suspected to be timid, imitative, tame" [69]). Emerson seeks, paradoxically, to shame his nation into celebrating common life and self-sufficiency by reminding his countrymen that they are living in "the age of Revolution" (67). Unlike Tocqueville, Emerson makes no claim that America is already in the vanguard of this international movement, although nothing would have been easier given the nature of the occasion than for him to do so; it is as if he has chosen to create his national history in the image of his own belated intellectual emergence, for which Coleridge helped much more than any American thinker to provide the scaffolding. Perhaps this helps explain why the whole literary nationalist theme, as "The American Scholar" handles it, is so comparatively muted and so belated. The bulk of the discourse is taken up with expounding the scholar's triad of resources — nature, books, and action —

which in principle can be seen as a distinctly "new-world" recipe (the argument being to devalue classical education, indeed formal study in general, and to aggrandize direct noncosmopolitan experience and pragmatic application) yet which does not explicitly define this regimen as a cultural nationalist program. One further lesson that might be drawn from this silence, a lesson that much of Whitman's poetry teaches also, is that the whole issue of cultural distinctiveness versus internationalism is not equally pressing throughout a writer's canon, or even throughout the space of an individual work. Perhaps because he was addressing one of the most Anglophile audiences in America, but more likely because he himself was too cosmopolitan (and too honest) to restrict the scholar solely to American influences or to exerting a solely American influence, Emerson kept his cultural nationalist rhetoric to a minimum: a few mandatory flourishes at start and close. Self-reliance clearly interested Emerson far more than national self-sufficiency.

Altogether, "The American Scholar" and Whitman's 1855 Preface might be taken as the two poles between which the literary nationalism of American Renaissance high culture tends to oscillate: On the one hand, Emerson's vision of cultural emergence catalyzed by auspicious international tendencies that emergence might be expected to develop further; on the other hand, Whitman's vision of a scandalously different American voice whose international precedents have been repressed, although by no means deleted, out of self-mystification and dramatic effect. In either case, "Europe" plays a weighty, conflict-producing role, measured by citation or elision, as the case may be.

4

Intimately related to the question of the models underlying literary practice is the question of the audience to which writing is implicitly directed. This has been a major subject of debate in the study of so-called newer English literatures, which appear, in some interpretations, to represent national culture with international audiences in mind. For a sense of what is at stake, consider this short passage toward the start of Chinua Achebe's *Things Fall Apart*, the first third-world novel accepted into the Anglophone canon. "Okoye said the next half a dozen sentences in proverbs. Among the Ibo the art of conversation is regarded very highly, and proverbs are the palm-oil with which words are eaten" (10). Such expository rhetoric, common in African Anglophone writing, immediately raises such questions as: For whom is this passage written? Do Ibos need to hear it? Do even Yoruba and Hausa readers need to hear it? Is Achebe mainly addressing a Euro-American audience, then? (Achebe denies this but also declares that "my audience is not limited to Nigeria. Anybody who is interested in the ideas I am expounding is my audience" [Egejuru 17].)[8] The rhetoric of this passage, anyhow, carefully negotiates the insider-outsider dualism by explicating ethnic custom with anthropological lucidity while casting the explanation in Ibo form, as a proverb.

A comparable instance from classic American literature might be this passage from an early chapter in Herman Melville's *White-Jacket:* "Owing to certain vague, republican scruples, about creating great officers of the navy, America has thus far had no admirals; though, as her ships of war increase, they may become indispensable. This will assuredly be the case should she ever have occasion to employ large fleets; when she must adopt something like the English plan . . ." (20).

Americanists do not usually read American Renaissance texts as if the implied reader were other than American; yet on reflection we know that is nonsense: Actually, American writers keenly desired to be read abroad. Melville himself voyaged to England in order to market *White-Jacket* and sometimes made (or consented to) substantive revisions in the interest of British readers. Indeed, the very first words of Melville's first book (the preface to *Typee*) were got up with British readership in mind, and that narrative is strategically sprinkled with familiarizing English place references (Cheltenham, Stonehenge, Westminster Abbey, etc. [96, 154, 161]).[9] In the passage from *White-Jacket*, the expository elaborateness and the obliquity with which it edges toward the narrator's outspoken antiauthoritarianism become more understandable if we take them as studiously devious in anticipation of being read by both patriotic insiders and Tory outsiders, whether literal foreigners or Yankee Anglophiles. We know from Melville's letters and criticism that he was acutely aware of the problem of negotiating between ideologically disparate readerships, but no one thinks much about the possibility that his doctrine that the great writer communicates to his ideal reader through double meanings which philistine readers are intended to miss might have been brought into focus partly by his position as a postcolonial writer.

The textual consequences of anticipating transcontinental readership are admittedly harder to establish than the impact of foreign literary influences. Open-and-shut cases like the diplomatically vacillating chapter on European travelers' accounts of America in Irving's *The Sketch Book* are rare. Direct evidence is usually limited to textual variants for which the responsibility is unclear (Did the author devise? advise? consent? reluctantly agree to delegate?), or to ex cathedra statements (like Cooper's to a British publisher that *The Prairie* "contains nothing to offend an English reader" [1: 166]) which do not in themselves prove that the work would have been written differently had the author designed it for an American readership alone. What we can assert more positively is this. First, that some of the most provincially embedded American Renaissance texts bear at least passing direct witness to anticipating foreign readers, like Thoreau's *Walden*, which (in keeping with its first "publication" before the Concord lyceum) begins by addressing fellow townspeople but ends by musing as to whether "John or Jonathan will realize all this" (333). And second, that the hypothesis of Americans imagining foreign as well as native opinion, whatever their conscious expectation of literal readership, makes luminous some otherwise puzzling moments in American Renaissance literature. One such moment is Whitman's abrupt reconception of his persona between 1855 and 1856 as coextensive not simply with America but with the world (e.g., in "Salut au Monde!"). Another is the oddly extended sequence in *Moby-Dick* reporting the gam between the *Pequod* and the *Samuel Enderby,* and its aftermath (chs. 100–01).

James Snead remarks that Achebe's novels "provide an unexpectedly tricky reading experience for their western audience, using wily narrative stratagems to undermine national and racial illusions," such as "the almost casual manner in which they present African norms" to international readers: glossary apparatus that seems deliberately incomplete, interjection of reminders of the Western reader's outsidership in the course of a cozily familiar-seeming, European-style realist narrative (241). For example, the guidebook dimension of the passage quoted above creates a deceptive degree of transparency for the Western reader, inasmuch as its "we have a saying" formula is a common introductory formula in Ibo proverbial statement not remarked upon as such; the passage, then, maintains a certain covertness despite, indeed because of, its forthrightness. Melville uses narrative geniality and cross-culturalism somewhat similarly in the sequence under view so as to sustain the young-America-style jauntiness with which *Moby-Dick* customarily treats old-world cultures, but without the kind of bluntness used against "the Yarman," for instance (Melville, *Moby-Dick* 351–60).

The gam with the *Samuel Enderby* reworks a cross-cultural comparison repeatedly made by British travelers to America: that Americans were grim workaholic zealots with no time for small talk. The chapter is obviously framed with national stereotypes in mind. Melville initially sketches the encounter between Ahab and Captain Boomer, or rather the interruptive byplay between Boomer and the ship's surgeon, so as to make the Englishmen seem like patronizing boobies. Yet it is Ahab's truculence that finally comes off as more disturbing and that makes English joviality (itself an American stereotype) seem healthy by comparison. The last emotion to be expressed is the good-humored British captain's honest astonishment. In the ensuing chapter ("The Decanter") Ishmael aligns himself with that same spirit of comic banter (long since identified as an Ishmaelite trait) and pays a mock-heroic homage to the whole firm of Enderby, which in fact turns out to have dispatched the first ships ever to hunt the sperm whale in the Pacific, the waters the *Pequod* is about to enter. Ishmael then proceeds, in what first looks like a complete digression, to report a later, more convivial and rousing gam with the *Samuel Enderby* in which he partook, a drunken feast "at midnight somewhere off the Patagonian coast" (444).

Ishmael's reinstitution of good fellowship with his English counterparts "atones" ex post facto for Ahab's bad manners and "validates" the English captain's good-humored bewilderment at Ahab's stormy departure. Yet through this dexterous maneuver, Melville is given license to laugh at the cliché version of British thickheadedness not once but twice — first apropos Ahab's tragedy, then apropos the farce of sailorly roistering — thereby propitiating American cultural nationalism without offending British readers. It is testimony both to Melville's wiliness and to his deference that the vigorous in-house censorship upon which his British publishers insisted, of religiously and culturally offensive matter in the manuscript of *The Whale* (resulting in the deletion of chapter 25 on British coronation procedures, for instance), left chapters 100–01 untouched (Melville, *Moby-Dick* 681–83).[10]

5

The marks of postcolonialism in American Renaissance writing are far more numerous than a short article can hope to discuss. Here is a brief checklist of some of the most salient.

1. *The semi-Americanization of the English language.* What language shall we speak? American settlers did not face this question in its most radical form, as put by Ngugi wa Thiong'o in *Decolonizing the Mind,* which argues that African literature should be written in the indigenous languages. But the weaker version of the argument (namely how to creolize and neologize American English so that it spoke a voice of the culture distinct from the standardizing mother tongue) does certainly link Cooper and Emerson and Whitman and Twain with Amos Tutuola, Gabriel Okara, and Raja Rao, whose work sheds light on such subissues as the inextricability of "naturalness" and "artifice" in Whitman's diction and the inextricability of idealization and caricature in Cooper's vernacular heroes like Natty Bumppo. Bill Ashcroft, Gareth Griffiths, and Helen Tiffin remark that postcolonial literatures are "always written out of the tension between the abrogation of the received English which speaks from the center, and the act of appropriation which brings it under the influence of a vernacular tongue" (39). That is a duality crucial to American literary emergence as well. In the early national period, we see it especially in texts that counterpoint characters who speak dialect (who are always comic) with characters who speak Standard English, for example, Colonel Manly versus his servant Jonathan in Royall Tyler's *The Contrast* and Captain Farrago versus his servant Teague O'Reagan in Hugh Henry Brackenridge's *Modern Chivalry.* At this stage, the vernacular is still clearly a national embarrassment to be indulged only obliquely, through satire. "Vulgarity," as Bridgman puts it, "had to be fenced in with quotation marks" (7). This is the American equivalent of, say, the colloquial dramatic monologues of Indo-Anglian poet Nissim Ezekiel:

> I am standing for peace and non-violence
> Why world is fighting fighting
> Why all people of world
> Are not following Mahatma Gandhi
> I am simply not understanding. (22)

By the time of Thoreau and Whitman, the American inventiveness with language, through individual neologizing and provincial variant usages, that Tocqueville (and others) considered one of the most "deplorable" consequences of democratization had become positive aesthetic values (Tocqueville 2: 71). Thus without any hint of parody, in section 5 of "Song of Myself," Whitman could allow the sublime vision following from the persona's possession by his soul to come to rest on "the mossy scabs of the worm-fence" (33) — the latter an American coinage never used in poetry before, referring to a characteristic motif of American agricultural construction that foreign visitors often singled out as particularly wasteful and ugly (Mesick 161–62). The "mossy scabs" metaphor makes it absolutely clear, if further proof be needed, that Whitman seeks to fashion the sublime from the positively vulgar. Not that he was prepared to forgo literary English. His position — almost quintessentially postcolonial in this respect — was to justify an Americanization of English expression as the poetic way of the future on the ground that English itself was remarkable for its engraftment of other linguistic strains (Warren 5–69).

2. *The issue of cultural hybridization.* Another recurring motif in American Renaissance texts is their fondness for cross-cultural collages: Whitman's composite persona; Thoreau's balancing between the claims of post-Puritan, Greco-Roman, Native American, and Oriental mythographies in *A Week* and *Walden*; Melville's multimythic elaboration of the whale symbol in tandem with the *Pequod* as a global village; Cooper's heteroglossic tapestry of six or seven different nationalities in *The Pioneers*. David Simpson argues, respecting Cooper, that Templeton's polyglot character, each resident speaking his or her own peculiar dialect (except for the Temple family, of course), registers the social fissures of still-experimental nationhood (149–201); and I think we might further understand this phenomenon by thinking of it in reference to (for example) composite national-symbol characters like Salman Rushdie's Saleem Sinai (in *Midnight's Children*) and G. V. Desani's Mr. Hatterr, or the syncretism of Wole Soyinka's interweave between Yoruba and Greek mythology. What Lewis Nkosi says of modern African Anglophone poetry's quest to define its path applies beautifully to the world of Cooper's *Pioneers*: "[T]he first requirement . . . was precisely to articulate the socio-cultural conditions in which the modern African writer had to function, the heterogeneity of cultural experiences among which the poet had to pick his or her way" (151).[11]

3. *The expectation that artists be responsible agents for achieving national liberation,* which in turn bespeaks a nonspecialized conception of art and an ambivalence toward aestheticism that threatens to produce schizophrenia. Soyinka calls attention to the pressure upon the postcolonial African writer to "postpone that unique reflection on experience and events which is what makes a writer — and constitute himself into a part of that machinery that will actually shape events" (16). Emerson wrestles with a very similar looking public/private dilemma in "The American Scholar" and later attempts at political interventions like the first Fugitive Slave Law address. Anozie's statement that "[t]here seemed to exist a genetic struggle between a romantic pursuit of art for its own sake and a constantly intensive awareness of the social relevance of art" could apply equally well to Soyinka and Emerson, though in fact it refers to Nigerian poet Christopher Okigbo (175), the closest approximation to a "pure aesthete" among the major figures of the illustrious first contemporary generation of Nigeria's Anglophone literati but later killed as a soldier in the Biafran war.

4. *The problem of confronting neocolonialism,* the disillusionment of revolutionary hopes, which threatens to turn the artist against the audience that was prepared to celebrate him or her as symptomatic of cultural emergence. Postcolonial Africa, for instance, has inspired an oppositional literature that both helps to explain American Renaissance oppositionalism as a predictable postrevolutionary symptom and to define its limits. Thoreau as individualistic civil disobedient both is and is not the counterpart of Ngugi's revolutionary socialism.

5. *The problem of "alien genres":* Eurocentric genres that carry authority but seem not to be imitable without sacrifice of cultural authenticity. There is a striking semicorrespondence here between the critique of the protagonist-centered realist novel by third-world intellectuals and complaints by nineteenth-century American fictionists from Cooper to Hawthorne to James that the novel was not transplantable to American soil. Conversely, some genres have seemed not only transplantable with great ease but precisely tailored for American and other new-world contexts. A prime example is my next and last rubric, which I should like to unfold at somewhat greater length than the others.

6. *New-world pastoral.* "Pastoralism" in the broadest sense of a recurring fascination with physical nature as subject, symbol, and theater in which to act out rituals of maturity and purification has long been seen as a distinctive American preoccupation, but without it being grasped how this can be generalized. Mutatis mutandis the same can be said of Canadian and Australian writing, although their versions of nature are (and for more complicated reasons than just geography) less benign than ours; and a version of the same can be said of third-world writing as well, despite manifest differences between white-settler pastoral and nonwhite indigene pastoral. Here the obvious analogue is negritude, as well as other forms of cultural nationalism that hold up a precolonial ideal order as a salvific badge of distinctiveness. Retrospective pastoralization of ancient tribal structures occurs in the American Renaissance as well: particularly in the more sentimental treatments of Puritan heritage and the old plantation order, not to mention the even more vicarious sort of nostalgia represented by Anglo-American savagist fantasies like Longfellow's *Song of Hiawatha.* Perhaps this explains why Thoreau became simultaneously addicted to nature and to New England antiquities. *Walden* and *The Scarlet Letter* are predictable complements in their mutual preoccupation with cultural origins.

But to stay with pastoral at the level of physical nature, what Americanists tend to miss, and what recent postcolonial critiques have been helpful in pointing out (e.g., Amuta 49), is the extent to which the conception of naturism as a mark of cultural independence needs to be countered by the conception of naturism as a neocolonial residue. Thomas Jefferson's *Notes on the State of Virginia,* which contains the classical statement of the American pastoral ideal, shows this clearly. Jefferson recommends that the new country follow the agrarian way in the explicit awareness that that will mean dependence on European manufactures. The preservation of national virtue, which he associates with rurality, he considers worth the cost. Some, even today, would argue that it is. But my point here is the lacuna in Jefferson's earlier thinking: his belief that moral self-sufficiency can coexist with economic dependence. Some years later, as Leo Marx shows in *The Machine in the Garden* (139), Jefferson changed his mind about America industrializing. What Marx does *not* diagnose is the status of Jefferson's original position as the intellectual artifact of a late-colonial intellectual. Marx shows, of course, that the conception of America as a pastoral utopia originates in Europe, but he ceases to think of European antecedence as important once pastoral thinking becomes naturalized in America by the mid-eighteenth century, and this in turn keeps him from beginning to approach figures like Jefferson and Thoreau in the light of being driven against their conscious intent by an ideological mechanism set in place to appropriate the New World in the interest of the Old — the antithesis of the state both men saw themselves as promoting.

Nothing could have been more natural than for the American Romantics to valorize physical nature as a central literary subject (whether benign, as in Transcendentalism, or ominous, as in *Moby-Dick* or the forest sequence in *The Scarlet Letter*), for this was an obvious way of turning what had often been deemed a cultural disadvantage into a cultural asset. But this same move, which capitalized upon an aesthetic value of international Romanticism as well as an established old-world image of the New World, was not without its risks. A text that illustrates these is the well-known sonnet addressed by William Cullen Bryant in farewell to his friend the painter Thomas Cole, bound for Europe.

> Thine eyes shall see the light of distant skies:
>   Yet, Cole! thy heart shall bear to Europe's strand
>   A living image of thy native land,
> Such as on thy own glorious canvass lies;
> Lone lakes — savannahs where the bison roves —
>   Rocks rich with summer garlands — solemn streams —
>   Skies, where the desert eagle wheels and screams —
> Spring bloom and autumn blaze of boundless groves.
> Fair scenes shall greet thee where thou goest — fair,
>   But different — every where the trace of men,
>   Paths, homes, graves, ruins, from the lowest glen
> To where life shrinks from the fierce Alpine air.
>   Gaze on them, till the tears shall dim thy sight,
>   But keep that earlier, wilder image bright!

Bryant's valedictory tribute affirms a nationalist vision of America as nature's nation (lakes, savannahs, rocks, skies), over against a European scene that everywhere bears "the trace of men." Bryant rightly credits Cole's American landscape paintings with having registered this sense of the American difference. Like Whitman, Bryant revises *translatio studii*, charging Cole to bear an American aesthetic gospel to Europe, but the poem's cautionary ending betrays a postcolonial anxiety as to whether Cole will keep the faith. That very significant and well-warranted anxiety is, however, a telling moment, the only moment that the poem begins to acknowledge the extent to which Bryant and Cole have in fact always already been affected by the European gravitational field whether consciously or not. Cole, like other self-consciously American landscape painters of his day, had been deeply influenced by the tropes of European Romantic landscape (and in his case also history) painting (Novak 226–73). As for Bryant, although his poem is replete with distinctively American references (such as bison, eagle, and the fall colors that regularly amazed European travelers), what strikes a modern reader much more strongly is its bondage to old-world language and form: "savannahs" as a cosmopolitan synonym for "prairies"; the placement of the eagle in a generic, symbolic "desert"; "Alpine" as a surrogate for the sublimity of American mountains; and above all, Bryant's unconsciously ironic choice of sonnet — a hypercivilized form if ever there was one — as the vehicle for enjoining his gospel of the "wilder image." In short, the authentic insider's view of America Bryant/Cole have to offer Europe as new-world cultural evangelists is at most a slightly nuanced version of the view that their position as Euro-American settlers has prepared them for.

In an excellent recent study of American landscape representation in the Revolutionary era, Robert Lawson-Peebles discusses this effect under the heading of "the hallucination of the displaced terrain."[12] Lawson-Peebles points out that cultural nationalist visions of a pastoralized America pulled "towards Europe and away from the facts of the American continent. Even the writers who attended closely to those facts shaped them so that they answered European criticisms, and in doing so they collaborated in a dream-world" (57). Bryant is a clear case in point: it is almost as if "the American Wordsworth" had set out with the intention of playing back to Coleridge an image of America just slightly (but not alarmingly) more feral than Coleridge had entertained thirty years before in *his* sonnet on "Pantisocracy," which envisions a rural valley purified of nightmare and neurosis, where "Virtue" dances "to the moonlight roundelay" and "the rising Sun" darts "new rays of pleasaunce trembling to the heart" (68–69).

In stressing the postcolonial basis of American pastoral visions like Bryant's, I do not mean to discredit them; on the contrary, I am convinced they potentially have great power even today as mimetic and ideological instruments. No doubt, for example, the American pastoral tradition helps account for the high degree of public environmental concern that now obtains in America, despite notorious slippages between doctrine and daily practice, between law and implementation. But in order to understand the potentially formidable continuing power of pastoral as a cultural instrument, we need also to understand the element of mimetic desire that has historically driven the pastoralizing impulse.

In Naipaul's autobiographical narrative, *The Enigma of Arrival,* he remembers how

> as a child in Trinidad I had projected everything I read onto the Trinidad landscape, the Trinidad countryside, the Port of Spain streets. (Even

Dickens and London I incorporated into the streets of Port of Spain. Were the characters English, white people, or were they transformed into people I knew? A question like that is a little like asking whether one dreams in color or in black and white. But I think I transferred the Dickens characters to people I knew. Though with a half or a quarter of my mind I knew that Dickens was all English, yet my Dickens cast, the cast in my head, was multiracial.) (169–70)

The resemblance to Thoreau's projective creation of Walden is quite close. During the first summer's Walden journal, Thoreau sustains his high excitement by repeatedly imagining his experience in epic and pastoral terms, ancient Greece connoting for him, as for other Romantics, the morning of Western culture: the pastoral moment of the race. This carries over into the book itself, especially the "Visitors" and the "Reading" chapters. In the encounter with the woodchopper, particularly, Thoreau plays the kind of game Naipaul describes: loving and believing in the magnification that he halfway allows himself to realize is a game. This awareness is manifested elsewhere too in "The Ponds" chapter in his reference to his locale as "my lake country." His first descriptive encapsulation of the pond environment stresses that "for the first week, whenever I looked out on the pond it impressed me like a tarn high up on the side of a mountain" (86): Walden as Alpine lake. In order for Thoreau's spirit to accompany his body to the literal spot, or rather in order for the Thoreauvian persona to re-present the pond in a serious work of American literature, he must approach this bit of Yankee real estate as the image of some more resonantly romantic elsewhere.

For both Naipaul and Thoreau, the game of animating the provincial quotidian with imagery from the repertoire of metropolitan culture is of course class-specific (the elegant recreation of the cultivated person for whom Euroculture is the touchstone for local knowledge), but in either case this type of consciousness entails not simply a limitation of vision but an access of vision also, vision indeed of two types (both of the ordinary object, now seen luminously, and of oneself, of one's own imagination's tricks and needs). Their visions should not, then, be seen as nothing more than false consciousness. But they invite that interpretation (in Thoreau's case, for example) if we begin from the premise that his pastoralizing ought to be read as American Adamism deployed against Euroculture, rather than simply a development within the latter camp.

6

The case of Thoreau, whose art is patently more homegrown than Bryant's, raises the question of when, if at all, the postcolonial moment in American literary history ended or at what point "postcolonialism" ceases to become a meaningful category of analysis. To settle the point with respect to this, the first postcolonial literature, might be especially helpful in orienting discussion of later instances as well as the American one. The beginning of an answer is to recognize that no clear answer can be given. On the one hand, "postcolonial" is from the start an objectionably reductive term since it coerces us to look at everything within the indigenous cultural field as old-world driven. On the other hand, American culture can be said to remain at least vestigially postcolonial as long as Americans are impressed by the sound of an educated British accent — or (to take a more pertinent example) as long as D. H. Lawrence's *Studies in Classic American Literature* remains an iconic text for American literary studies. American scholarship has, ironically, absorbed Lawrence's wilderness-romance–oriented paradigm of American literature as obsessed with rebellion against civilized structures while largely deleting the Lawrentian premise that gave rise to it, that is, the vision of America as a postcolonial society caught in a state of cultural adolescence because still caught in the same escapist impulse that originated in the desire to flee from the motherland.[13] This diagnosis reflects, of course, the uses to which Lawrence himself put aboriginal America (Cowan 1–12, 124–28) — Lawrence being a Coleridgean dreamer who really acted out his dreams.

In could be argued that once "civilization" becomes imaginatively localized within America instead of placed across the Atlantic as in Bryant's sonnet, then American pastoral becomes for all practical purposes fully Americanized — although of course this happened for different writers at different times, and for some nineteenth-century American writers, like Henry James, it never happened at all. Another criterion might be the rise in the nineteenth century of what is now called American imperialism. One might argue that by the time Mark Twain, in *The Connecticut Yankee*, could imagine an American state of military and political superiority to an archaized Britain (reversing the British traveler's report of a generation earlier), or when Melville could imagine a Yankee entrepreneurialism roughly homologous to a decadent Spanish imperialism in "Benito Cereno," the American postcolonial moment was over, or at least evanescent. This however, raises another fundamental question as to the link between American postcolonialism and American imperialism. Such a link there seems indeed to be. Captain Frederick Marryat, who as naval officer and as author of juvenile fiction helped to underwrite British expansionism, was told during his visit to America that Britain need not exult over its continuing superiority as an imperial power because America would soon pick up some colonies for itself (*A Diary in America*).

In the literary sphere, Cooper and Whitman are interesting test cases. The anxious patriotic hubris that generated the Whitmanesque "I" can never rest until it circles the globe in massive retaliatory overcompensation. Cooper played the postcolonial to the extent that he deferred to Scott's plot forms, but he played the imperialist to the extent that his own narratives reflected and perpetuated the romance of American expansionism. It begins to appear, then, that the old-world tropes whose ingestion by the new-world citizen marks his or her cultural subordination can in turn become reactivated, whether on the frontier within one's own borders or on the frontiers beyond (e.g., bwana Hemingway in East Africa), to reproduce new versions of cultural subordination. This again, is not the sole or inevitable consequence of postcolonialism, only the most disturbing, but it is by the same token the most dramatic reminder of the quixotism of positing a firm boundary between a postcolonial era and what follows it.

NOTES

Preliminary versions of this essay were delivered as lectures at Texas A & M University, Columbia University, Brown University, and the American Antiquarian Society. I am most grateful for comments and suggestions received on all four occasions.

1. Gilbert and Gubar may be credited with establishing "I think I was enchanted" (593) — a reflection upon the influence of Elizabeth Barrett Browning — as central to the Dickinson canon (647–48; Gilbert 33–37). An interesting test case of the larger consequences of this placement of Dickinson among a Euro-American sisterhood, as opposed to the Edwards-Emerson tradition, is the shifting interpretation of "He fumbles at your soul" (315). Before 1980, the generally preferred approach — still sometimes espoused (e.g., Phillips 179–80) — was to read the "He" as bullying preacher or perhaps deity (Duchac 149–51). Feminist revisionism ensured the currency of a more specifically gendered reading of the "he" as "the pure energy of the *idea* of the masculine" (Dobson 81). The two readings can of course be conflated (e.g., Rich 56–57), but in practice a critical emphasis on gender tends to run counter to a "New England mind"–oriented reading. This may also be the place to comment on my almost total concentration in the balance of this essay, seemingly ironic in light of my honorific citation of feminist and African-Americanist revisionism, upon white male writers. My choice reflects these two hypotheses: that the main symptom of "colonization" in antebellum African-American discourse arises from the pressure on black writers to write in "white" genres and rhetorical forms, and, secondly, that women writers of the period were less troubled about extricating themselves from the shadow cast by Europe than were their male counterparts, partially though not exclusively for the reason advanced by Gilbert and Gubar (i.e., that pre-modern women writers were not mutually competitive, anxious for rather than repressed by their female precursors). These concerns, which require further research, I intend to pursue on another occasion.

2. I have profited from all of these works. Spengemann presents the most outspoken theoretical/historical argument for considering Anglo-American writing as part of English literature generally. Arac, Chai, Reynolds, and Mills provide more specific, less polemical case studies: Arac, of literature as social prophecy in the nineteenth century; Chai, of tendencies in international Romanticism; Reynolds, of American responses to 1848. Mills undertakes specific book-to-book comparisons of American and English authors. All these writers focus on intertextual and intercultural influences or connections with minimal attention to American cultural dependence as a (post)colonial event. Weisbuch comes closest to my approach in a series of somewhat Bloomian studies of American writers reacting against British precursors, set in the context of a defensive-antagonistic model of Anglo-American literary relations. This leads to results that are very illuminating and provocative, although I think the variability of American attitudes toward European culture (including extreme deference and total insouciance, as well as rivalry and antagonism, sometimes all of these commingling in the same person or text) needs to be taken more greatly into account. In addition to the studies of broad scope just mentioned, a growing number of significant monographs on individual authors address issues of postcolonialism without necessarily conceptualizing them as such: e.g., Rubin-Dorsky and Dekker.

3. My term "occidentalism" designedly echoes Said's use of "Orientalism." Some differences between the two discourses are noted below. My lowercase "o" registers another: "occidentalism" is my neologism, not a term of European usage, much less of the long-established field of academic research Said's *Orientalism* was written to critique. (The academic field of American studies is of course the obverse of Orientalism in having been constituted in the US and still largely dominated by American scholars.) Yet Said's larger argument, that Europeans formulated a condescending discourse of the "other" region as a fascinating but inferior civilization, also applies to antebellum travel narratives, and even more exactly to American perceptions of how they were viewed by these. "*Orientalism*," writes Said, "is premised upon exteriority, that is, on the fact that the Orientalist, poet or scholar, makes the Orient speak, describes the Orient, renders its mysteries plain for and to the West. . . . What he says and writes, by virtue of the fact that it is said or written, is meant to indicate that the Orientalist is outside the Orient, both as an existential and as a moral fact" (20–21). This is largely true for what I am calling "occidentalism" as well. In focusing on America as the object of "occidentalist" discourse, it should, of course, not be forgotten that (Euro-)Americans were at the same time themselves "Orientalists"; see, for example, Baird 3–80.

4. Naipaul: "Indians defecate everywhere. They defecate, mostly, beside the railroad tracks. But they also defecate on the beaches; they defecate on the river banks; they defecate on the streets; they never look for cover" (*Area* 74). Dickens: "In the courts of law, the judge has his spittoon, the crier his, the witness his, and the prisoner his; while the jurymen and spectators are provided for, as so many men who in the course of nature must desire to spit incessantly" (*American Notes* 112–13). In this way both writers, with nervous/sardonic intensity, put the former colony under the sign of filth.

5. The pervasiveness of these and other motifs of commentary are conveniently summarized by Tuckerman; Mesick; and Berger.

6. See Memmi: "Another sign of the colonized's depersonalization is what one might call the mark of the plural. The colonized is never characterized in an individual manner; he is entitled only to drown in an anonymous collectivity ('They are this.' 'They are all the same.')" (85). Of course it would be rash to say that Tocqueville and other generalizers thought they actually knew America thoroughly, to the core. On the contrary, America often seemed mysterious to them; its inchoate ungraspability inspired a range of vertiginous sensations in the observer, both painful and pleasurable. Indeed, American mysteriousness and the will to explicate it through clarifying generalization were opposite sides of the same coin: see Tocqueville on "that strange melancholy which often haunts the inhabitants of democratic countries in the midst of their abundance" (2: 147). Additional light is shed on this fusion of opposites by Conrad's study of British travelers from Frances Trollope to Christopher Isherwood. Conrad shows that they resolutely created America in the image of their own fantasies, but that the fantasies often sprang from their own baffled malaise (e.g., 7–15).

7. Green oversimplifies in diagnosing the Leatherstocking saga as "the next great stage," after the Daniel Boone myth, "of the WASP adventure tale and adventure hero" (133), but he is right to place Cooper in the context of the history of the imperial adventure tale. The limitation of Green's approach to Cooper is that he does not apply to Cooper his good insight concerning Scott's ambivalence toward the absorption of Scotland into Great Britain: "If anyone could have written the serious novel of adventure, it probably would have been a Scotsman, because of the mode of Scots participation in the Empire — the disengagement (compared to England) despite the deep involvement" (121). Cooper manifests, it seems to me, even deeper reservations about the march of civilization than Scott; indeed, this note of reservation seems to me to be one of the motifs Cooper took over from Scott and extended.

8. Egejuru is not justified in concluding from this and other statements that "the African writer is very much controlled by an external audience whose existence he consciously tries to erase" (36), but it is clear that the writers she interviewed were somewhat hard-pressed to reconcile their Africanist commitments with the fact of being published and (often) more widely read abroad. Part of their dilemma must be political, part the result of the impossibility of bringing unconscious motives to full consciousness. Nineteenth-century American writers faced a similar if less intense set of pressures.

9. My thanks to Eric Haralson for first calling my attention to signs of dual audience consciousness in *Typee.*

10. Though they seldom raise the issue as a subject of direct remark, American writers of the Renaissance period must have been acutely aware of being vulnerable to both European and nativist scrutiny and criticism whenever they penned a scene that suggested a value judgment one way or another on national traits. In *Martin Chuzzlewit,* Dickens registers both sensitivities at once in his caricature of the egregious Mrs. Hominy, the American "literary" person who builds her reputation by purveying jingoistic cliché. Mrs. Hominy is the Tocquevillean democratic writer, the "independent" American constrained to speak in the voice of the majority; Dickens's narrator is the cosmopolitan Britisher recoiling against American boorishness. Postcolonial writers in other cultures have experienced similar pressures. Rajan wittily remarks on an Indian counterpart to Mrs. Hominy: "Countries which are newly independent can attach undue importance to the image of themselves which their literatures present, thus degrading the writer into a public relations officer. 'You have been unfair to the South Indian mother-in-law,' a critic told me indignantly at a railway station. It was well that I restrained my inclination to laugh. He was deadly serious and not unrepresentative in his seriousness" (84).

11. Nkosi proceeds to quote from Abioseh Nicol's "African Easter," which begins with a nursery rhyme ("Ding, dong bell") and juxtaposes this with "matin bells," the cry of the muezzin, and "pagan drums" (qtd. in 151–52). An intercultural salad considerably more diverse than Cooper's Templeton.

12. Lawson-Peebles borrows this term from art critic Harold Rosenberg (23).

13. Leslie Fiedler and Wright Morris have both written rather severely about American pastoralism as a form of cultural immaturity, in *Love and Death in the American Novel* and *The Territory Ahead,* respectively (Fiedler in particular being indebted to Lawrence), but formulating their position as a critique of social pathology without regard to America's postcolonial history.

WORKS CITED

Achebe, Chinua. *Things Fall Apart.* 1958. Greenwich, CT: Fawcett, 1959.

Amuta, Chidi. *The Theory of African Literature.* London: Zed, 1989.

Anozie, Sunday. *Christopher Okigbo: Creative Rhetoric.* London: Evans, 1972.

Ashcroft, Bill, Gareth Griffiths, and Helen Tiffin. *The Empire Writes Back: Theory and Practice in Post-Colonial Literatures.* London: Routledge, 1989.

Baird, James. *Ishmael: A Study of the Symbolic Mode in Primitivism.* New York: Harper, 1956.

Berger, Max. *The British Traveler in America, 1785–1835.* New York: Columbia UP, 1922.

Bridgman, Richard. *The Colloquial Style in America.* New York: Oxford UP, 1966.

Bryant, William Cullen. "Sonnet — to an American Painter Departing for Europe." *The Norton Anthology of American Literature.* Ed. Nina Baym, et al. 3rd ed. Vol. 1. New York: Norton, 1989. 893–94. 2 vols.

Coleridge, Samuel Taylor. *The Poems of Samuel Taylor Coleridge.* Ed. Ernest Hartley Coleridge. London: Oxford UP, 1931.

Conrad, Peter. *Imagining America.* New York: Oxford UP, 1980.

Cooper, James Fenimore. *Letters and Journals.* Ed. James Franklin Beard. 6 vols. Cambridge: Belknap–Harvard UP, 1960–68.

Cowan, James C. *D. H. Lawrence's American Journey.* Cleveland: P of Case Western Reserve U, 1970.

Dickens, Charles. *American Notes and Pictures from Italy.* London: Oxford UP, 1957.

———. *Martin Chuzzlewit.* London: Oxford UP, 1966.

Dobson, Joanne A. "'Oh, Susie, it is dangerous': Emily Dickinson and the Archetype." *Feminist Critics Read Emily Dickinson.* Ed. Suzanne Juhasz. Bloomington: Indiana UP, 1983. 80–97.

Duchac, Joseph. *The Poems of Emily Dickinson: An Annotated Guide to Commentary Published in English.* Reference Publication in Literature. Boston: Hall, 1979.

Egejuru, Phanuel. *Towards African Literary Independence: A Dialogue with Contemporary African Writers.* Contributions in Afro-American and African Studies 53. Westport, CT: Greenwood, 1980.

Emerson, Ralph Waldo. *The Collected Works of Ralph Waldo Emerson.* Ed. Robert E. Spiller and Alfred R. Ferguson. Vol. 1. Cambridge: Belknap-Harvard UP, 1971. 4 vols. 1971–87.

Ezekiel, Nissim. *Latter-Day Psalms.* Delhi: Oxford UP, 1982.

Fernández Retamar, Roberto. *Caliban and Other Essays.* Trans. Edward Baker. Minneapolis: U of Minnesota P, 1979.

Gilbert, Sandra M. "The Wayward Nun beneath the Hill: Emily Dickinson and the Mysteries of Womanhood." *Feminist Critics Read Emily Dickinson.* Ed. Suzanne Juhasz. Bloomington: Indiana UP, 1983. 22–44.

Gilbert, Sandra M., and Susan Gubar. *The Madwoman in the Attic: The Woman Writer and the Nineteenth-Century Literary Imagination.* New Haven: Yale UP, 1979.

Green, Martin. *Dreams of Adventure, Deeds of Empire.* New York: Basic, 1979.

Kipling, Rudyard. *American Notes.* New York: Arcadia, 1950.

Lawrence, D. H. *Studies in Classic American Literature.* 1923. Garden City, NY: Doubleday, 1951.

Lawson-Peebles, Robert. *Landscape and Written Expression in Revolutionary America: The World Turned Upside Down.* Cambridge: Cambridge UP, 1988.

Lyell, Charles. *A Second Visit to the United States of North America.* 3 vols. New York, 1849.

McWilliams, John P., Jr. *The American Epic: Transforming a Genre: 1770–1860.* Cambridge Studies in American Literature and Culture. Cambridge: Cambridge UP, 1989.

Martineau, Harriet. *Society in America.* 2 vols. New York, 1837.

Marx, Leo. *The Machine in the Garden: Technology and the Pastoral Ideal in America.* New York: Oxford UP, 1964.

Melville, Herman. *Moby-Dick.* Ed. Harrison Hayford, Hershel Parker, and G. Thomas Tanselle. Evanston: Northwestern UP; Chicago: Newberry Library, 1988.

———. *Typee.* Ed. Harrison Hayford, Hershel Parker, and G. Thomas Tanselle. Evanston: Northwestern UP; Chicago: Newberry Library, 1968.

———. *White-Jacket.* Ed. Harrison Hayford, Hershel Parker, and G. Thomas Tanselle. Evanston: Northwestern UP; Chicago: Newberry Library, 1970.

Memmi, Albert. *The Colonizer and the Colonized.* Trans. Howard Greenfield. Boston: Beacon, 1965.

Mesick, Jane Louise. *The English Traveler in America, 1836–1860*. New York: Columbia UP, 1922.

Mills, Nicolaus. *American and English Fiction in the Nineteenth Century: An Antigenre Critique and Comparison*. Bloomington: Indiana UP, 1974.

Murphy, Francis, ed. *Walt Whitman: A Critical Anthology*. Baltimore: Penguin, 1970.

Naipaul, V. S. *An Area of Darkness*. New York: Vintage, 1964.

——. *The Enigma of Arrival: A Novel in Five Sections*. New York: Viking, 1987.

Nandy, Ashis. *The Intimate Enemy: Loss and Recovery of Self Under Colonialism*. Delhi: Oxford UP, 1983.

Ngugi wa Thiong'o. *Decolonizing the Mind: The Politics of Language in African Literature*. London: Currey, 1986.

Nkosi, Lewis. *Tasks and Masks: Themes and Styles of African Literature*. Essex: Longman, 1981.

Novak, Barbara. *Nature and Culture: American Landscape and Painting, 1825–1875*. New York: Oxford UP, 1980.

Phillips, Elizabeth. *Emily Dickinson: Personae and Performance*. University Park: Pennsylvania State UP, 1988.

Rajan, Ballachandra. "The Indian Virtue." *Journal of Commonwealth Literature* 1 (1965): 79–85.

Rich, Adrienne. "Vesuvius at Home: The Power of Emily Dickinson." *Parnassus* 5 (1976): 49–74.

Said, Edward W. *Orientalism*. New York: Vintage, 1978.

Simpson, David. *The Politics of American English, 1776–1850*. New York: Oxford UP, 1986.

Snead, James. "European Pedigrees/African Contagions: Nationality, Narrative, and Communality in Tutuola, Achebe, and Reed." *Nation and Narration*. Ed. Homi K. Bhabha. London: Routledge, 1990. 231–49.

Soyinka, Wole. *Art, Dialogue and Outrage: Essays on Literature and Culture*. Ed. Biodun Jeyifo. Ibadan, Nigeria: New Horn, 1988.

Spengemann, William C. *A Mirror for Americanists: Reflections on the Idea of American Literature*. Hanover, NH: UP of New England, 1989.

Thoreau, Henry David. *Walden*. Ed. J. Lyndon Shanley. Princeton: Princeton UP, 1973.

Tocqueville, Alexis de. *Democracy in America*. Trans. Henry Reeve. Ed. Phillips Bradley. 2 vols. New York: Vintage, 1945.

Tuckerman, Henry T. *America and Her Commentators*. New York, 1864.

Warren, James Perrin. *Walt Whitman's Language Experiment*. University Park: Pennsylvania State UP, 1990.

Whitman, Walt. *Leaves of Grass*. Ed. Harold W. Blodgett and Sculley Bradley. Comprehensive Reader's Ed. New York: New York UP, 1965.

5   *Approaches in the Classroom*

I have found that I get my best teaching ideas from other instructors. In fact, I have a file called, "Other People's Class Stuff." This file contains syllabi, assignments, handouts, and various resources. When I came across someone's great idea, I used to say something along the lines of, "That sounds great, let me have a copy, so I can steal that for my class." I have been a blatant thief, but I have now turned over a new leaf and, rather than stealing unabashedly from my colleagues, I engage in a process known as "sharing best practices." I must thank my former dean, Toby Parcel, for passing along this phrase — it sounds so much nicer than the outright thievery I had practiced. Sharing best practices allows teachers to learn from the trial and error of others.

The essays collected here represent some instructors' best practices, providing concrete, practical examples of activities that teachers can use in their classrooms. Lois Tucker's "Liberating Students through Reader-Response Pedagogy in the Introductory Literature Course" discusses providing students with the tools needed for an active encounter with literature. Instructors may be particularly interested in Tucker's use of a student-driven syllabus in which students select the readings for the second part of the course.

Margaret Faye Jones's essay, "Bringing New Historicism into the American Literature Survey," provides both a definition of New Historicism and practical advice regarding how to use it in the classroom. Jones discusses the value of parallel reading of literary and nonliterary texts by using Benjamin Franklin's *Autobiography* and diary entries by Anne Shippen Livingston as examples. She notes that diaries and letters are particularly effective because they give students a glimpse into the private side of a particular subject. Other valuable nonliterary sources include legal documents, speeches, newspapers, and government documents.

William J. Scheick provides insight into the teaching of poetry in his essay, "Early Anglo-American Poetry: Genre, Voice, Art, and Representation." Scheick helps students understand poetry by first addressing issues of genre, voice, and art before discussing issues of representation. Scheick notes that his approach is designed to allow students to understand contextual implications, artistic techniques, and subtextual subtleties, as well as conceptual limitations.

"Portrait of the Artist as a Young Slave: Douglass's Frontispiece Engravings" by Ed Folsom is an excellent example of using New Historicism in the classroom. Folsom describes having his students "read" the 1845 frontispiece portrait alongside Frederick Douglass's narrative. He then compares the Douglass portrait to Walt Whitman's engraving from the first edition of *Leaves of Grass* and Douglass's later engraving included with *My Bondage and My Freedom,* both published in 1855. Folsom contends that Douglass's portraits reveal the relationship between the author and the slave.

Each of the foregoing essays provides wonderful examples of exercises that can be used as described or adapted to suit particular class settings. I expect to make use of many of them in my own teaching. I have never been one to make use of journals in my classes — I tried it once unsuccessfully — but having read Tucker's detailed instructions, I plan to give journals another try. Jones's essay reinforces my own thoughts about the value of using nonliterary texts in literature classes. I actually do a good bit of dabbling with New Historicism in my classes already. For example, I frequently incorporate music and essays from the period, but I have yet to incorporate more personal material such as letters or diaries. I often teach Zora Neale Hurston's "How It Feels to Be Colored Me" alongside her stories, but it would be interesting also to have students read some of her letters from the late 1920s, which are readily available in a collection edited by Carla Kaplan, *Zora Neale Hurston: A Life in Letters.* Scheick and Folsom not only provide specific examples of how to approach particular texts, but they also provide a road map for instructors to use in their discussions of other works. For example, instructors who find Folsom's discussion of portraiture valuable might also want to expand on this idea and pair literature with artwork of the period. Whether one thinks of utilizing the ideas included here as thievery or the sharing of best practices, they are clearly a great resource for teachers.

Liberating Students through Reader-Response Pedagogy in the Introductory Literature Course

LOIS P. TUCKER

In an essay which initially appeared in a 2000 issue of Teaching English in the Two-Year College, *Tucker discusses the value of reader-response pedagogy in college classes. This pedagogy involves the use of icebreakers, journals, and both individual and collaborative writing assignments. Tucker also provides practical advice for creating a student-driven syllabus, for which students work in groups to select readings for the second half of the course.*

INTRODUCTION

I can still remember the poems and stories that excited me and made me determine that I would become an English teacher. However, once I actually got to teach an introductory literature class, I realized that many of the students were not interested in reading the assigned literature. They could not have cared less whether Robert Frost was bending birches or mending walls. William Wordworth's "London 1802" was too far removed from them. If Hester Prynne was stupid enough to actually wear that scarlet letter on her person, then she deserved whatever happened to her. T. S. Eliot could continue to measure his life in teaspoons, and Alice Walker could go on searching for her mother's gardens all by herself. And worse than the students' lack of interest were the writing assignments they submitted that evidenced it. The papers generally lacked thought, depth of understanding, and a sense of commitment to a literary response.

Trying to remedy student's apathy so that reading and discussing literature could become enjoyable for both teacher and students, I sought to connect the students to the literary experience through a reader-response approach. I have had success with this approach by incorporating regular reader-response activities that validate students as literary critics in their own right and by allowing them to assist with selecting course readings.

From *Teaching English in the Two-Year College,* 28.2 (2000): 199–206.

THE VALUE OF A READER-RESPONSE APPROACH

Reader-response criticism allows students more latitude in responding to what they read and encourages varied responses. According to Ross C. Murfin, "[it] focuses on what texts do to — or in — the mind of the reader, rather than regarding a text as something with properties exclusively its own" (253). Employing a reader-response approach in the introductory literature course helps maintain the student interest and involvement necessary for a good course. This approach

- enables students to experience relevance in the reading task,
- involves them in an active, not passive, encounter with the literature,
- validates them as critical readers who are capable of determining meaning in texts, and
- provides them with the opportunity to express themselves freely.

The issue of relevance for the introductory literature student is major, as many critical theorists attest. Patricia Prandini Buckier asserts that "the most valuable pedagogical application of reader-response criticism creates a link between real-life experience and the work — helping the student to connect — and then builds on that connection" (38). Norman N. Holland avows that

> all of us, as we read, use the literary work to symbolize and finally to replicate ourselves. We work out through the text our own characteristic patterns of desire and adaptation. We interact with the work, making it part of our own psychic economy and making ourselves part of the literary work — as we interpret it ("UNITY" 816).

He also claims that reading literature meets personal human needs: "the need to impose oneself on the world; or the need to find certainties; or the need to be able to read; or the need to be read; or the need for human acceptance and understanding of all one's pivots and flourishes" ("Stanley" 440–41). And finally, Louise Rosenblatt posits that "a *poem* is what the reader lives through under the guidance of the text and experiences as relevant to the text" (qtd. in Murfin 253).

These theoretical positions apply to readers, in general, and to introductory literature students, in particular. For so many, the text and the process has precluded them. They have just been carried along for the ride in previous classroom encounters with literary works, and no one has demonstrated that the students' own experience is germane to the course reading assignments.

Students need to be involved in active encounters with literature. When the comfort of relevance is achieved, they can begin to appreciate literature the way Stanley Fish describes it — as "an event" (386), as an "activity, something [*they*] *do*" (383), in which they, according to Wolfgang Iser, actively participate and transact with the writer (30). This perspective on reading transforms the literature course from one in which the teacher is the proverbial "sage on the stage." Instead, the students actively engage in reading, extracting meaning that is released through their experiential involvement in the process.

The third benefit of the reader-response approach is that the students are validated as critical readers who are capable of determining meaning in texts. In this approach, the reader is key. In fact, Wolfgang Iser describes literature as full of "gaps" (Mailloux 425), which readers fill as they read. Readers, Iser continues, are "forced to explain [the gaps], to connect what the gaps sepa-rate, literally to create in [their minds] a poem or novel or play that isn't in the text but that the text incites" (Murfin 256). This approach is reassuring to the students. They realize that their interpretations are appreciated. They are not wrong. They did not miss the point.

Once the students feel that what they understand and what they write is respected, they begin to take ownership of literary perspectives. They are then comfortable enough to express themselves freely. Literature then takes on significance for them — in the class and in their lives.

ACTIVITIES WHICH LIBERATE STUDENTS: ICEBREAKERS

I keep in mind that the students in introductory literature are those who would prefer to be someplace else. Therefore, I resist the urge to jump right in and "cover the syllabus" as quickly as possible. I break the ice first by using some techniques that draw the students into the literary experience and allow them to let down their guard. Since many students are resistant to literature at the outset, I invite them to share orally with the class a memorable experi-ence, positive or negative, that they have previously had in studying or read-ing literature. Not only does this activity provide an overview of the students, but they feel that I am interested in them and what they have to say, and it also gives them the opportunity to identify with others who have had similar experiences.

It also helps to break the ice by starting the course with a literary work that is short, easy to read, and relevant to the group. With a group of adult learners, I begin with "The Story of an Hour" by Kate Chopin. This story works because it is only three pages long and lends itself to a variety of responses without students having to work hard on extracting meaning from the text. Before teaching the short story, I divide the class into groups and have them prepare a role-play activity to illustrate different responses to "bad" news. Each group decides what their bad news will be and who the receiver of the bad news will be. This activity involves the students, first of all, in a collaborative activity in which they become a little better acquainted with each other and also taps into their more creative, dramatic, and humor-ous selves. Discussion of the story can then begin in an atmosphere of laugh-ter and relaxation, making students feel more comfortable about sharing their responses to literature.

JOURNAL ENTRIES

Journal entries can be used to great advantage in making students feel comfortable in the classroom. In one variation of the journal, I structure a four-point framework which includes the following response activities:

1. *Responding to the Text:* Write a journal entry in which you note an observation from the story which made you feel something (something you liked or disliked; agreed with or disagreed with).

2. *Sharing Your Perspectives:* Share your observations in a group.

3. *Evaluating Your Perspectives:* How did your journal entry differ from those of your colleagues? What were the differences based on (gender, occupation, age, ethnicity, geography, social status, values, family backgrounds, personal experiences, background knowledge, other)?

4. *Refining Your Perspectives:* Broaden your understanding of how literature affects the reader by looking at the responses from other writers outside the class. Consider the responses to the work written by professional critics. How do they compare with your own perspectives? For example, do they confirm, support, extend, complement, refute, or differ from your ideas? Begin by using general critical indexes, such as *Twentieth Century Literary Criticism* (TCLC), *Nineteenth Century Literary Criticism* (NCLC), *Short Story Criticism* (SSC), *Contemporary Literary Criticism* (CLC), *Drama Criticism* (DC), and *Poetry Criticism* (PC). Other sources may be suggested to you by the "How to Use this Index" page in *NCLC* or *TCLC* or by the college librarian.

This fourth task of having students review the criticism actually takes us outside the strict boundaries of reader-response theory into reception theory, in which students are able to expand their collaborations to include historical perspectives. This review complements the reader-response process by including three features articulated by Louise Z. Smith: "its capacities to integrate formal with social analyses, to construct an intergenerational chain of receptions based upon real readers' experiences, and to reveal the socially formative nature of literature" (75). By incorporating this element of reception theory, I introduce students to some of the necessary rudiments of literary analysis and review in a manner that is painless and nonthreatening.

Other journal questions can be structured to derive specific objectives. Some that have worked for me include the following:

1. Cite three specific passages you enjoyed in the text. Explain what they mean to you. Why did you enjoy them?

2. When was the text written? What was going on historically at the time? Do you see any connection?

3. Write a plot summary of your reading. Do you know a similar piece with this plot or theme? Compare and contrast the two.

4. Put your magnifying glass on a character. Choose a favorite character in the text, either because you like or dislike him or her or because you can relate to the character through personal experience. Describe what you like or dislike about that character and tell why.

5. How do you see? Do you see people? Do you see events or circumstances (time, place, atmosphere, plot)? Write about the significance of what you see.

6. Assume the role of the writer. If you could change part of the story, what word, phrase, scene, character, or whatever, would you change? Why?

7. Analyze your feelings. How did the text make you feel? Did it sharpen your view on something? Did it challenge an existing belief? Did it confuse you? What did it make you feel?

In class, I incorporate the journal responses into the discussion of the literature so that the students see its relevance. They again can identify a sense of self in the context of these class discussions.

WRITING ASSIGNMENTS

I vary the writing assignments to allow the students to express the ideas that emerge in the journal entries and in the sharing of their perspectives.

Individual Writing Assignments

1. Write an essay in which you advance a particular point about the literary text from the course anthology that has been assigned to the whole class to read. (This very traditional assignment allows students to articulate their own perspective in a structured and well-considered framework amidst the experience of assessing the various perspectives that their colleagues have shared.)

2. Write an essay in which you advance a particular point about a literary text from the course anthology not assigned to the whole class. Share your essay with the class. (In this assignment, students apply their learning and sharing experiences beyond the assigned literary pieces. They can draw connections and identify contrasting stances among literary artists and literary pieces, using the skills of analysis and synthesis.)

Collaborative Writing Assignments

1. In groups of three or four, write a collaborative essay advancing a particular point which the whole group agrees to about an assigned literary text from the anthology. (In the small group activity, students get another opportunity to express their perspectives. With a common task at hand, they assess and refine their thoughts and contributions to come to consensus on a group project which usually concludes as an enjoyable give-

and-take experience. The idea of submitting a joint paper is also appealing to students who are already juggling various assignments due in other courses.)

2. In groups of three or four, select a work that has not been assigned to the whole class, but which complies with the theme or author which the class has been studying. Write a collaborative essay advancing a particular point on which the whole group agrees.

THE STUDENT-DRIVEN SYLLABUS

In the introductory literature course, far too often students are bombarded by the seemingly impenetrable "canon." I see two main problems with this. The first is the same issue of relevance. Since students need to be interested in what they're spending their time reading, I allow them to help choose the reading list for the semester. This practice proves successful in creating a socially and culturally comfortable learning environment. The second problem is the probability of their being turned off literature before they are turned on to it. To underscore this view, Douglas Lanier has suggested that teaching introductory literature through the study of the traditional canon usually constitutes what Gerald Graff calls a "coverage" model (qtd. in Lanier 199), which merely "exposes" students to a literary canon. This approach, Lanier continues, "can mislead students about the nature of literature and literary interpretation" (200).

In contrast, there are definite benefits derived from a student-driven syllabus. First, texts that the students select themselves will be meaningful to them. James J. Sosnoski alleges that "one of the major advantages of having students make their own anthologies is that the texts they choose are ones they can relate to" (280). Second, the opportunity of choosing their own texts encourages the students to review the reasons for enjoying them and further obligates them to assess the reasons why those works should be included for class study. This approach carries with it the further benefit of, according to M. H. Dunlop, "overcoming the frustrating passivity" that exists in typical introductory literature courses. By including "accessible" literature, the teacher makes the students "feel culturally at home [. . .] in these texts, and they read them rapidly with considerable interest and pleasure" (252). Hence, when students can connect with what they read, they are more interested in writing about it.

I propose two ways in which the student-driven syllabus can be adopted. The first is a modified implementation that takes place after the midterm break. Couched in the framework of the reader-response approach from the beginning of the course, the introductory literature course is a bearable experience for most students if the instructor selects accessible and relevant works. These works, along with the ice-breaking activities and focused journal responses, help the students to maintain interest for at least half of the semester. After midterm break, when the students understand the parameters and course guidelines, they then can select additional literary works to study.

It works best to have the students select their reading suggestions in groups. Groups provide them with a forum for justifying a piece of literature, first to their small group, then to the teacher, and then to the class as a whole. Since we can't read what everyone wants to read, I allow a slot on the reading list designated for individual choices. While the whole class reads most of the work, each student can read a text that he or she alone is reading. The accompanying writing assignment can be shared with the whole class.

I also use groups to present the theoretical elements of the chosen genre. We study the short story, nonfiction essays, drama, and poetry. I encourage the students to use PowerPoint demonstrations, overhead projections, or whatever other creative means they choose to explain the genre in presentations spread over the semester.

At the time for studying a particular genre, the groups assemble, beginning during the class period, to choose from the anthology the specific pieces that they wish to study. This works especially well if the class periods are longer than one hour. For shorter periods, the exercise may continue beyond the class period as a homework activity or for another period. After a designated amount of time, we regroup and hear the suggestions from each group. Through group consensus and class vote, the reading list for that particular genre is constituted. Though I may have decided that we were going to study, for example, twelve short stories for the semester, the students invariably read more than twelve to make their decision and in the process, share their feelings about what they have read — those pieces accepted for class study and those that were not.

Pragmatic Concerns

If one chooses to use literature outside of a required anthology, the teacher needs to keep in mind the basic logistics of ordering texts. Many times the books that the students prefer are those that are easily accessible and less costly. If such is not the case, Amazon.com is many a student's or teacher's answer when books are needed in a hurry.

Then there is the issue of how to fit all the students' interests into the syllabus. This calls for creative scheduling. However, since this is a collaborative exercise between teacher and students, they will help schedule what they want to cover. Here, also, in a role of allowing for a variety of reading and writing activities, you may (1) group the selected works for comparative study, (2) designate some reading as supplementary for extra credit, or (3) require that students complete a minimum number of texts from the final list. Having the students report on texts not covered in class enables students who have not read them the opportunity of deciding whether or not they want to add those texts to their personal reading lists. These reports are also a means of encouraging students to expand their reading activities by instituting "reading-and-sharing" communities outside of class.

Groups work well for covering a variety of works. I allow the students to group themselves according to interest and meet in discussion groups during class times. In so doing, my role changes. Dunlop enunciates this new role:

> [. . .] the teacher is not needed to certify anything about the texts or to guide student readers into or through their mysteries; the teacher is instead required to articulate the textual theory that will allow the students to begin decoding, interrogating, and manipulating the texts. In the text-based classroom, the teacher, like the students, is situated as a reader, and by articulating ways to read becomes a helpful guide on *how* to read instead of a forbidding guardian of meaning, a watchdog over *what* to read. (252–53)

At this point I let the students go and I wander from group to group, learning from them and sharing with them. I express confidence in their ability to encounter texts and attempt to validate them as critical readers.

CONCLUSION

Reader-response approaches to teaching literature can assist in making the literary experience of introductory literature students more meaningful and enjoyable, because in the words of Elizabeth Freund,

> reader-response criticism attempts to grapple with questions generally ignored by schools of criticism which teach us how to read; questions such as *why* do we read and what are the deepest sources of our engagement with literature: What does reading have to do with the life of the psyche, or the imagination, or our linguistic habits; what happens — consciously or unconsciously, cognitively or psychologically — during the reading process? Reader-response criticism probes the practical or theoretical consequences of the event of reading by further asking what the relationship is between the private and the public, or how and where meaning is made, authenticated and authorized, or why readers agree or disagree about their interpretations. (5–6)

Many theories exist on how to read, interpret, and analyze literature, but for reaching the students in introductory literature classes — to take them beyond mere passivity — the reader-response approach is invaluable. It enables the teacher to liberate the students and regard them as vital stakeholders in the process. By allowing students to assist in determining the reading list for the course, they become actively involved. Then when I follow with activities that encourage their own literary interpretation, that reassure them that they have a perspective worth sharing, and that validate their responses as part of that body of work which we call literary criticism, they invest more of themselves in the process. They want to see it work. They leave the class remembering the stances they passionately defended and the perspectives they accepted from their colleagues. The literary experience emerges as a more memorable one for them and for me.

WORKS CITED

Buckler, Patricia Prandini. "Combining Personal and Textual Experience: A Reader-Response Approach to Teaching American Literature." Cahalan and Downing 36–46.

Cahalan, James M., and David B. Downing, eds. *Practicing Theory in Introductory College Literature Courses.* Urbana: NCTE, 1991.

Dunlop, M. H. "Textual Theory and Formula Fiction." Cahalan and Downing 251–60.

Fish, Stanley. "Literature in the Reader: Affective Stylistics." *Self-Consuming Artifacts.* Berkeley: U of California P, 1972. 383–427.

Freund, Elizabeth. *The Return of the Reader: Reader-Response Criticism.* London: Methuen, 1987.

Holland, Norman N. "Stanley Fish, Stanley Fish." *Genre* 10 (1977): 433–41.

———. "UNITY IDENTITY TEXT SELF." *PMLA* 90 (1975): 813–22.

Iser, Wolfgang. *The Implied Reader.* Baltimore: Johns Hopkins UP, 1975.

Lanier, Douglas. "Less is More: Coverage, Critical Diversity, and the Limits of Pluralism." Cahalan and Downing 199–212.

Mailloux, Steven. "Reader-Response Criticism?" *Genre* 10 (1977): 413–31.

Murfin, Ross C. "Reader-Response Criticism and *The Scarlet Letter.*" *The Scarlet Letter.* By Nathaniel Hawthorne. Case Studies in Contemporary Criticism. Ed. Ross C. Murfin. Boston: Bedford, 1991. 252–61.

Smith, Louise Z. "In Search of Our Sisters' Rhetoric: Teaching through Reception Theory." Cahalan and Downing 72–84.

Sosnoski, James J. "Collaborative Hypertextbooks." Cahalan and Downing 271–90.

Bringing New Historicism into the American Literature Survey

MARGARET FAYE JONES

*J*ones *begins her Introduction to American Literature course by asking, "What does it mean to be an American?" as a means of illustrating that "American-ness" is not as clear-cut as one might think. In an attempt to provide a fuller picture answer to this question, she utilizes a modified New Historicism in her class. Jones notes that she follows Peter Barry's definition of New Historicism as a parallel reading of literary and nonliterary texts rather than merely as providing historical context for literature. She finds that students are often particularly interested in the nonliterary texts when they relate to their interests or majors. Jones provides specific examples of her teaching of Benjamin Franklin's* Autobiography *alongside diary entries by Anne Shippen Livingston to illustrate her methods in the classroom. She also suggests other possible approaches before addressing student and faculty concerns related to the incorporation of nonliterary texts. Jones's essay was published in 2000 in* Teaching English in the Two-Year College.

INTRODUCTION

"What does it mean to be an American?" I ask this question of students at the first class meeting of an Introduction to American Literature course. The answers are usually predictable and positive: "Being an American means we care about people's rights and freedoms." "We believe in educating everyone and that all people with motivation can succeed in this country." "We're the greatest country in the world." "Family and God are what we care the most about." Occasionally, the responses are not so complimentary: "All we care about is money." "We're too superficial and materialistic." "Americans want to take over the world."

That first class period, I simply record the responses on the board and ask students to write them down in their notebooks. I return to that same question frequently during the semester and ask the students to reconsider and modify, if necessary, any of their initial responses. The goal is to help them see that U.S. literary history consists of many voices, voices that may contradict

From *Teaching English in the Two-Year College* 28.2 (2000): 186–91.

some of their perceived impressions about what it means to be an American, voices that may have been silenced or diminished during the country's history. I don't belittle the students' definitions or the works of the canonical figures we read; I simply want the students to understand that the issue of "American-ness" is not as straightforward as they (and numerous politicians) sometimes believe. If they critique their own definitions of what it means to be an American, I believe the students will come to a deeper understanding of their literary and cultural heritage. Therefore, I construct the syllabus purposefully to include voices from a variety of ethnic groups and social classes during each of the historical periods we study.

However, I have never quite been able to meet my goal of inclusion when teaching eighteenth-century American literature, especially in regard to women. Of course, the textbook anthology (Baym, et al.) includes Mary Rowlandson and Phillis Wheatley, but the emphasis remains on men and political writings that preceded and followed the American Revolution. Because I wanted the students to get a fuller picture of the time period, I decided to use a modified New Historicism by adding the private journals and letters of eighteenth-century women.

NEW HISTORICISM

In his very useful overview of modern critical theory, Peter Barry defines New Historicism as a "method based on the *parallel* reading of literary and nonliterary texts, usually of the same time period" (172). While many of us provide historical backgrounds to the texts students read for our courses, that is not the same as "doing" New Historical work. New Historicism does not "privilege" the literary work over the nonliterary one (Barry 172). The two texts work off each other equally and provide a larger cultural picture of the historical period.

Aram Veeser lists some assumptions which underlie New Historicism's heterogeneous practices:

1. Every expressive act is embedded in a network of material practices;
2. Every act of unmasking, critique, and opposition uses the tools it condemns and risks falling prey to the practice it exposes;
3. Literary and nonliterary "texts" circulate inseparably;
4. No discourse, imaginative or archival, gives access to unchanging truths nor expresses inalterable human nature; and
5. A critical method and a language adequate to describe culture under capitalism participate in the economy they describe (xi).

New Historicism recognizes that all writings take place within specific historical periods and that literary artists and their texts can no more escape being affected and influenced by that culture than can the authors of more "prosaic" writings such as legal documents, letters, travel books, etc. Therefore, by looking at literary works in juxtaposition with these other texts, it becomes easier to find those underlying cultural influences. However, New Historicism reminds us that we (readers and critics) also work within a cultural milieu that we cannot shed to examine these texts with objectivity.

Using New Historicism in the classroom has benefits for both instructor and student. New Historical criticism is often much more accessible and interesting than some other theoretical approaches (Barry 178). New Historical practices also work well in conjunction with other theoretical approaches such as Marxist, feminist, postcolonial, and cultural studies. Finally, students often find this sort of analysis interesting because the non-literary texts — such as business, legal and scientific writings — can relate to their own interests or majors.

CLASSROOM ACTIVITIES

The major canonical text I teach for the eighteenth-century is Benjamin Franklin's *Autobiography*. I choose Franklin for several reasons. Students are familiar with him and usually like him. He also appeals to the working class and working students by being a self-made man. Finally, his work is a good example of what Larzer Ziff calls "the represented self as representative history" (118). As Ziff points out, Franklin's aim in this work is not to correct misconceptions or necessarily to present the "truth" about his past. The incidents in his life have been carefully chosen as lessons for his readers. Franklin's chief message in *The Autobiography* is that individuals have the ability to determine what kind of people they will be, and this ability is not due to intelligence or natural abilities, but learning specific habits (119). It certainly can be argued that Franklin single-handedly developed the American myth of the rags-to-riches potential of anyone who is willing to work hard enough to achieve success. It is an appealing myth, and many if not most of the students accept it.

We start by looking at the way Franklin carefully develops his persona. We discuss the incidents he chooses to relate. I point out his use of the term "errata" to refer to his mistakes (a printing term that implies correction). We pay special attention to the section where he develops his thirteen virtues and shares his daily schedule with the reader (90–96). After this discussion, I ask students to consider whether Franklin is truly representative of the American experience, and we move into a discussion of the lives of others during Franklin's time.

I bring to class some diary entries by Anne Shippen Livingston that were written in 1783. She was a woman who had fallen in love with a Frenchman but was persuaded by her father into a more economically providential match with an American, Colonel Henry Beekman Livingston. The marriage was a disaster, and after her husband turned abusive, she moved back in with her family. Her father ordered her to send her daughter to live with her in-laws for a time so that the child's inheritance would be assured. The diary entries deal with this ordeal, and it was also during this time that she made a list of "Some Directions Concerning a Daughter's Education" (Harris 64).

These directions seem to provide a parallel to Franklin's list of virtues. Some typical directions include the following:

> *6th* Observe strictly the little seeds of reason in her & cultivate the first appearance of it diligently.

> *13th* Seem not to admire her wit, but rather study to rectify her judgment.

> *18th* Show her the deformity of anger and rage.

> *25th* Particularly inform her in the duties of a single & married state.

> *28th* Discreetly check her desires after things pleasant & use her to frequent disappointments.

> *35th* Use her to rise betimes in the morning & set before her in the most winning manner an order for the whole day. (in Harris 67–68)

After reading this entry, we compare it to Franklin's *Autobiography*. First, we focus on the similarities. Both are types of autobiographical writing; both believe that by assuming certain types of behaviors, life can be successful (Franklin) or at least manageable (Livingston). Both also exhibit a typically eighteenth-century belief in reason. In a way, they are both didactic works. Franklin's purpose is to be a role model for his reader, to provide an example that the reader can emulate. Livingston is also concerned with teaching, but she limits herself to listing directions for her daughter.

Next, we discuss the differences between the two works. Students quickly point out that Franklin's is a public document; Livingston never had any idea that her entries would be read by anyone but herself. Then I ask the students how we can be sure of this. As Suzanne Bunkers points out, the locked diary is a twentieth-century invention. In previous centuries, women sometimes wrote diaries in collaboration. Other diaries were kept as family records (17). Therefore, we can't assume the private intentions of any diary writer, and as a class, we explore the possible purposes of Livingston. (Of course, at this point, I also point out the difficulty of ever knowing for sure an author's intention. What we consider is how the style and content of a work may change due to the writer's perception of an audience.)

Second, Franklin's remembrances of the past are told with a certain detachment, if with some regret about his "errata." Of course, he wrote years after the events had occurred and with a clear didactic purpose. Confession was not his major goal. Livingston's entries, on the other hand, are immediate and full of anguish at the likely loss of her daughter and her inability to have any power or voice in the decision. Students also discover quickly that Franklin's text, while specifying hard work and good morals, has a sense of freedom and autonomy about it. Livingston's directions for raising her daughter have a much more circumscribed feel to them.

However, for me, the most important thing about this exercise is that students begin to realize that no single text can represent any time period of a culture and that sometimes you have to look beyond literary works to see a truer picture and put canonical works into context.

Diaries and personal letters work well for this sort of project. Students like them because they provide a private side to the public world they are studying. Women's issues of childcare, spousal abuse, and financial concerns are often a surprise to the students. Some of the younger ones have a hard time believing that women haven't always had choices. Some of the more conservative are a little nonplused to discover that these were women's issues long before modern times.

The brevity of the diary entries and letters is an advantage as well. There is only one survey course in our curriculum, so we have to cover everything from Native American creation myths to John Updike in fifteen weeks. Time is always an issue, and shorter works take less course time. Students also tend to feel overwhelmed by the amount of reading they must do for the course. A diary entry or letter can have a great impact because it requires only a small investment of students' time.

Obviously, there are many texts that would work just as well, depending on the instructor's purpose. Sometimes, we read Deborah Read Franklin's letters to her husband in conjunction with his autobiography. These almost illiterate texts can be quite instructive. Not only do students make the contrast between the writing styles, they also see the difference in opportunities between the sexes. Furthermore, these letters also give modern readers a glimpse into the responsibilities of the eighteenth-century housewife. It can also be instructive to compare sections from autobiographies of members from various marginalized groups, such as Samson Occam's story of his life as a Native American preacher (Baym, et al. 286) or Olaudah Equiano's *Interesting Narrative* (Baym, et al. 343).

An instructor can also move out of narrative form altogether and bring in legal documents, speeches, newspaper articles, and government reports from the same time period. All of these work well in the classroom. Once again, using Franklin as an example, his *Autobiography* can be compared to a speech by Benjamin Rush on the education of women (*The Microbook*) or business letters from women.

Finally, students can be assigned to find such documents as part of research projects. In a recent class, a student brought in a report on almshouses by a state committee in Massachusetts in the 1850s as a counterpoint to a Mary Wilkins Freeman story, "Sister Liddy," which is set in a poorhouse. By looking at these texts together, students started to understand that there has been a debate in this country from its very beginning about what to do with the poor. I don't claim that any major insights were gained here, but I do believe some students came away from that class with the idea that the poverty question is older and more complicated than they first realized.

STUDENT AND FACULTY CONCERNS

While most students enjoy looking at documents that correlate with the texts in the anthology, occasionally they express some concern. The first has to do with a perception of political correctness on my part, and the second relates to the definition of literature in the first place.

When I use journals and letters in the classroom, sometimes a question indicates that a student believes I have a political agenda by bringing in these works. I try to deal with this issue by explaining at the beginning of the semester that everyone is influenced by some sort of theory or agenda, that there is no such thing as an objective and dispassionate study of literature. I also explain that all literature takes place within a culture and history that simply can't be removed from the text. Therefore, the more we know about that history and culture, the better we can interpret and appreciate literary works in general. I also make it clear that I am not making any claims for superior aesthetic qualities of some of these works, but I also point out how hard it is to decide exactly what makes something aesthetically superior.

Even after those explanations, some student will still ask in a puzzled tone after we have read a diary entry or letter, "Is this literature?" I actually welcome the question because it gives the class an opportunity to reflect on what exactly can be considered literature. We brainstorm together, and many of the suggestions return to aesthetic concerns. Then we look up the definition of "literature" in a dictionary. For example, in *The American Heritage Dictionary,* the first definition is "imaginative or creative writing." Students quickly note that this definition doesn't help them very much. Then I read from the preface of Larzer Ziff's *Writing in the New Nation.* "In that day [the late 1700s], most who thought about the matter defined literature as all of written knowledge, which is to say that belles lettres constituted a very small part of what they regarded as literary" (ix). Students can then see that the definition of literature itself (just like judging the quality of literary works) changes according to the needs and wants of the time and the cultures doing the defining.

The very fact that students ask these questions and we discuss them in class shows them, I hope, that literature is a living field of study and one that is relevant to them as individuals and citizens.

Some instructors have concerns about using New Historicism in their literature classrooms. These concerns include not being trained as a historian, not having time to do the amount of historical preparation necessary, and finding nonliterary texts that are accessible to the students and relevant to the subject. While trying a new theoretical technique always requires time and energy, these obstacles are not insurmountable.

First, most instructors of American and British literature survey courses are already quite knowledgeable about the general historical periods. What is really necessary is the willingness to critique and question the values of a literary work in juxtaposition to nonliterary texts.

Second, finding appropriate nonliterary texts does require forethought and planning. However, there are numerous resources to help. Colleagues from the history department and librarians can provide useful ideas. In the field of early American literature, many works by marginalized groups have been published. *The World Turned Upside Down,* edited by Colin Calloway, provides a variety of Native American voices, including speeches, myths, letters, autobiographies, treaties, deeds, and wills. Sharon Harris's *American*

Women Writers to 1800 provides many short excerpts from the writings of a variety of women in early America. One especially helpful resource is *The Microbook Library of American Civilization,* which is a microfiche collection of materials relating to American life and literature from the country's beginnings to the beginning of World War I. Materials include poetry, fiction, autobiography, biography, pamphlets, periodicals, as well as rare books that are often unavailable elsewhere. Using this resource, I have found an eighteenth-century informational handbook for Germans considering moving to the United States, a self-help book for new wives, and letters from a European monarch commanding that the native peoples be treated well.

CONCLUSION

Throughout the history of America, certain groups have been marginalized and denied full access to the publishing world that would have allowed their voices to be heard in a public arena. Such nonliterary writing that gives us a picture of these marginalized groups and their lives is appropriate material for the classroom. These works provide a wider context that will allow readers a new sense of the cultural milieu in which texts are written and read. By studying these works in conjunction with the ones in their course anthologies, students can begin to learn that literature is not a dead art with no relevance to them, but a living cultural artifact that arises out of the conflicts and contexts of people's lives.

WORKS CITED

Barry, Peter. *Beginning Theory: An Introduction to Literary and Cultural Theory.* Manchester: Manchester UP, 1995.
Baym, Nina, et al. eds. *The Norton Anthology of American Literature: Shorter 5th ed.* New York: Norton, 1999.
Bunkers, Suzanne. "Diaries: Public and Private Records of Women's Lives." *Legacy* 7.2 (1990): 17–26.
Calloway, Colin G., ed. *The World Turned Upside Down: Indian Voices from Early America.* Boston: Bedford, 1994.
Franklin, Benjamin. *The Autobiography.* 1791. Ed. Louis Masur. Boston: Bedford, 1993.
Harris, Sharon M. *American Women Writers to 1800.* New York: Oxford UP, 1996.
Livingston, Anne Shippen. Journal Entry. Harris 65–68.
The Microbook Library of American Civilization. Chicago: Library Resources, 1972.
Veeser, H. Aram. ed. *The New Historicism.* New York: Routledge, 1989.
Ziff, Larzer. *Writing in the New Nation: Prose, Print, and Politics in the Early United States.* New Haven: Yale UP, 1991.

Early Anglo-American Poetry: Genre, Voice, Art, and Representation

WILLIAM J. SCHEICK

*O*riginally *appearing in 1999 in* Teaching the Literatures of Early America, *edited by Carla Mulford, Scheick's essay argues that the diversity of early Anglo-American poetry requires "attention to historical context and such notions as the chain of being, universal order, sin, common sense, and reason." As an instructor, his goal is gradually to deepen his students' understanding of the verse by addressing issues of genre, voice, art, and representation. Scheick notes that the order of these perspectives is immaterial with the exception of representation, which he views as a counterbalance to the others and thus reserves for last. Scheick illustrates his approach to each of these issues through a variety of poetry such as Edward Taylor's meditations, Anne Bradstreet's "To My Dear Children," Philip Freneau and Hugh Henry Brackenridge's* A Poem on the Rising Glory of America, *Gaspar Pérez de Villagrá's* Historia de la Nueva México, *and Phillis Wheatley's "On Being Brought from Africa to America." Scheick's essay is particularly helpful for instructors seeking to have students make connections among poets.*

The subject and cultural matter of British American poetry from Anne Bradstreet's *The Tenth Muse* (1650) to Phillis Wheatley's *Poems on Various Subjects, Religious and Moral* (1773) is diverse. This matter, ranging from late-Renaissance and Reformed traditions to Neoclassical standards, necessitates attention to historical context and such notions as the chain of being, universal order, sin, common sense, and reason. Brief books by E. M. W. Tillyard and Peter Gay are helpful in introducing students to this pertinent information. Of course, even as a pedagogical prop any historical approach is at best contingent, one version among alternatives (White). So from time to time I mention problems inherent in all acts of historicizing, including several indeterminacies in my own approach to early Anglo-American poetry.

I present these poems in terms of a tiered axis of chronological perspectives, including genre, voice, art, and representation, capped with some post-structural considerations. The order of these perspectives is not crucial to my

From *Teaching the Literatures of Early America,* ed. Carla Mulford (New York: MLA, 1999) 187–99.

goal of incrementally deepening my students' perspectives on this verse, except for representation, which I position last because it provides a cautionary counterbalance to the other three.

GENRE

That many students can identify various genres is one advantage to the literary-model approach. Selecting a representative type of early American verse is difficult, and the choice is often determined by what has previously succeeded with students. Since I have found the elegy, a complex form rich for pedagogical purposes, to be unappealing even to graduate students, I tend to prefer the meditative poem. Meditative verse does not evince a single pattern, for its European antecedents are many; but in general, and as practiced by the Puritans, it focuses on a religious topic germane to the interior spiritual drama of the poet (Martz).

The richest examples of early colonial meditative poetry show the influence of the emblem tradition, such as exhibited in the English verse of Francis Quarles and George Herbert. Images (candles, wings, skulls, hearts, children) from Quarles's seventeenth-century bestseller *Emblems* and from a hieroglyphic poem such as Herbert's "Easter-Wings" (which visually converts the fallen-over hourglass of mortality into a butterfly of redemptive ascent) show that meditative verse often expresses religious concepts through verbal pictures. Such a poem may focus on the sea to represent humanity's helplessness in a turbulent world, as in Philip Pain's *Daily Meditations,* or on trees and rivers to represent, respectively, humanity's former Edenic posture and present temporal condition, as in Anne Bradstreet's frequently reprinted "Contemplations." In the unusual instance of "Meditation 2.3" Edward Taylor presents his own face as an emblem of mortality; students, urged to discern the fifty-one-year-old poet's facial features as well as the significance of these features in the poem, detect such details as his hirsute cheeks, blemished skin, and graying blond hair. This poem, related to early Puritan emblematic interpretations of human names and bodies, dramatizes how intensely personal meditative verse is.

Emblems such as these are concrete instances of how Puritans read nature as *liber mundi* (creation as a divinely inspired text that reiterates Scripture). Emblems tend to have layers of signification, and so students with some knowledge of the Bible might be encouraged to think further about verticality (the trees) and horizontalness (the river) in "Contemplations." In this poem, with the same number of stanzas as Christ's age at his crucifixion, the two natural types of river and trees emblematically suggest the intersection of the divine (eternal) and the human (temporal) on Christ's cross (Scheick). Similarly, Taylor's often anthologized "Meditation 1.8" offers such emblems as a caged bird, which represents, at the microcosmic level, the famished soul confined within the body and, at the macrocosmic level, inept humanity confined beneath the dome of nature. The proliferation of natural and domestic

SCHEICK: *Early Anglo-American Poetry: Genre, Voice, Art, and Representation*   357

types in Taylor's poem — horizon, cage, barrel, bread loaf, inverted bowl — at first seems free-associative; but all share the emblematic shape of the half circle. After students recall the traditional symbolism of the circle (unity, perfection) and its religious significance, I ask them to consider the value of the half circle for the poet, who laments that he can only write crookedly (produce marred meditations) because he is in the dark while the sun (Son, i.e., Christ) is beyond the arched horizon. Exemplifying how Puritans viewed nature emblematically, the half-circle natural types in Taylor's late-seventeenth-century meditation intimate the scriptural prophecy of Christ's second coming.

If such types give Taylor hope rather than assurance concerning his own personal redemption, a century later similar images usually convey a far more secular and presumptive prophecy. During the eighteenth century's revival of classical aesthetic models meditation lost its status as a predominant cultural art form. The epic, narrative verse in elevated style celebrating episodes historically and prophetically important to a people, became a popular classical mode in the new republic, dating from such early epic gestures as *A Poem, on the Rising Glory of America* by Philip Freneau and Hugh Henry Brackenridge. The epic traces in this work refer to Columbus's discovery of America, the settlers' feats, and the heroes' sacrifices during the French and Indian War — each embedded in another classical type, the dialogic pastoral mode celebrating agriculture.

As students contrast the imagery of this 1772 poem with the late-seventeenth-century emblems in Bradstreet's "Contemplations" and Taylor's "Meditation 1.8," they can be directed toward the following observations. Rather than symbolize scriptural meanings in the Christian *liber mundi* tradition, the natural types in *Rising Glory* reinforce historical meanings in the British imperial tradition. Whereas the meditative poets a century earlier rehearse the scriptural version of human events in the hope that the divine prophecies include them as individuals, Freneau and Brackenridge collapse the millennial prediction of the Book of Revelation into a rehearsal of Western history and recent New World settlement. They announce, at least in this youthful phase of their careers, that America, the "final stage" of empire, is destined to fulfill Old World history. In *Rising Glory* nature symbolizes not spiritual admonition but secular fulfillment, specifically fortune through commodification: "Much wealth and pleasure agriculture brings"; "Nor less from golden commerce flow the streams / Of richest plenty on our smiling land" (lines 356, 374–75).

When concluding the comparison I ask students whether a Puritan meditator would likely have written in the manner of the later poem. Most say no, but several indicate that certain images and the sentiment of the 1772 poem could have been meditatively applied to the imagined regenerative state of the elect in heaven. This point reminds students that the religious energy of the Puritan meditation and the secular energy of the later dialogic pastoral are subtly related despite evident generic differences.

VOICE

In contrasting the seventeenth-century meditation and the eighteenth-century epic-pastoral, including their nature imagery, my students are often quick to notice a related difference concerning voice. They are struck by the apparent loneliness of the Calvinistic meditative authors, who write as if no fellow human being could help them satisfy their primary spiritual desires. They detect Bradstreet's attraction to the beauty of nature in "Contemplations" and her affection for her spouse and children in such poems as "A Letter to Her Husband" and "Upon My Son Samuel." But they also acknowledge her isolation as "[s]ilent alone" her life follows "pathless paths" in a world that is at best a "lonely place, with pleasures dignifi'd" (lines 50–51, 144). Students likewise observe that in "Meditation 1.8" Taylor stands alone beneath the night sky, which is as beautiful to him as are the woods to Bradstreet and as insufficient to meet his spiritual needs. Like Bradstreet, Taylor presents nature, however much its splendor and plenitude fill his eyes, as "[a]n Empty Barrell": the "Creatures field" (nature) provides "no food for Souls" (14–16).

For meditative poets like Bradstreet and Taylor the beauty of nature does not invite proto-Romantic sentiment. This beauty, instead, is a divine goad indicting them as fallen descendants of Adam and Eve. Musing on the grandeur of nature as the artwork of the Logos, Bradstreet is struck "mute," her poem virtually discontinued after stanza 9; and Taylor, dizzy from starvation (the lack of Eucharistic manna), struggles with "puzzled thoughts" virtually depleted, "pore[d]" out, in the first stanza of his poor and porous poem (line 5). At such points, typical of Puritan meditative manner, both poets turn away from the book of nature, which only reminds them of what humanity has lost, and toward Holy Writ, as collective Christian memory, to recall the Old Testament account of the fall from grace and the New Testament gospel of redemption. Taylor's meditation ends with an authorized fantasy of his conceivable election to salvation; and Bradstreet's meditation ends with *memento mori* devices, including an allusion to the heavenly antithesis of the gravestone, designed to counter her vanity, a personal proclivity she confesses in "To My Dear Children." Neither meditator presumes redemption; indicted by nature, each remains a humble voice actively disposed to wait passively for the revelation of divine will after death.

Transatlantic comparisons may help students understand this unfamiliar attitude toward voice. While the meditative poem reveals a Renaissance ancestry, especially in its display of verbal agility, the Reformed version practiced by the Puritans downplays the value of the self, especially in typological terms. Typology, the correspondence between foreshadowing Old Testament matter and consummating New Testament matter, might or might not include the meditator, and that has considerable consequences concerning a poet's voice. When, for example, Herbert's Low Anglican "Aaron" is matched with Taylor's Congregationalist "Meditation 2.23," some students notice that the English poet concludes with a confident and affirmative sense of his share in the Old Testament high priest's fulfillment in Christ, whereas the New England poet (who occasionally alludes to Herbert's verse) finds no comfort in the Aaron type and instead only hopes that he might somehow be found worthy of redemption as one of the high priest's cups. Similar comparisons can be made between Herbert's "Affliction V" (on Noah's ark) and "The Altar" (on the Hebrew sacrificial table) and Taylor's "Meditation 2.29" and "Meditation 2.82." Here my students have seen, without much prompting, that Herbert's orderliness and neat resolution are in distinct contrast to Taylor's apparent disorder and irresolution.

Nearly a century later the swains in *Rising Glory* provide an even greater contrast. Their dialogic exchange and celebration of the common good (at least as they understood it) demonstrate an appreciation of community not evident in the meditative monologues. The voices of these country youths convey self-possession, not helplessness, and in nature they find incentive to speak rather than indictment and curtailment of speech. They share the meditators' regard for the rich plenitude of nature, but they do not draw biblical parallels from natural signs. They express a millennial and utilitarian vision of a "Paradise a new" where the commodification of natural riches fulfills human aspirations (line 754).

Sometimes a few students seem supportive of this essentially Deistic, exuberant voice prophesying the domination of nature for human benefit. I ask them to compare the sentiment of *Rising Glory* and Gaspar Pérez de Villagrá's seventeenth-century epic *Historia de la Nueva México,* which the class sampled earlier in the semester. Since students usually criticize Villagrá's celebration of unmitigated conquest, the comparison encourages a fuller awareness of the social and environmental implications of the 1772 poem.

My students even more often prefer the optimism of *Rising Glory* over the self-deprecation of Calvinistic meditations. On such occasions I ask them to determine which voice exhibits a greater appreciation of beauty. The ensuing debate touches on the question of what we mean by beauty, but finally students delve again into the poems. I consider the debate particularly successful if certain subtleties emerge — when, say, someone argues that the meditators' sense of dispossession increased their valuation of nature's beauty whereas the pastoralists' relentless stress on utilization and commodification may have blinded them to that perception.

However, this differentiation of voice risks the suggestion that seventeenth- and eighteenth-century authors were either strict Calvinists or implicit Deists. Phillis Wheatley's late-eighteenth-century verse, especially the widely available "On Being Brought from Africa to America," counters this misperception effectively because it mingles a Congregationalist sensitivity to the Bible and an Enlightenment awareness of politics. To highlight Wheatley's regard for personal liberty and her esteem for Holy Writ, I ask students to interpret the elliptical last two lines: "Remember, *Christians, Negroes,* black as *Cain* / May be refin'd, and join th' Angelic train" (lines 7–8). Some read the lines as "Remember, *Christians,* [that] *Negroes,*" whereas others read them as "Remember [that] *Christians,* [and] *Negroes.*" Does the final line refer only to intellectual and aesthetic refinement, such as the poet's careful management of metrics and rhyme, or does it also possibly refer to the management of the ambiguous syntax of the preceding line to imply the equality of both races as mutually "benighted soul[s]" (line 2)? To ask these related questions is to inquire into Wheatley's religiopolitical voice, which performs and proves her argument that an African American can be taught to understand the refinements of both religion and art. Advanced students might further be asked to consider whether the final line tactfully alludes to images from Isaiah, the poet's favorite prophetic scriptural book, specifically Isaiah 6.1 and 48.10. If so, then her voice simultaneously defers to scriptural authority (like the seventeenth-century meditative poets) while it subtly asserts its authority (like the eighteenth-century epic-pastoral poets) by making an unprecedented racial application of two biblical passages.

Art

Wheatley's poem is basically an encomium, the classical verse of praise revived by the eighteenth-century English authors she admired. In typical neoclassical manner, her poem is presented in rhymed couplets of nearly perfect iambic pentameter. In comparison to such model precision, the slight irregularities of the last two lines, including the ambiguous syntax and possible truncated allusions, appear to draw attention to themselves, particularly since they are emphatically introduced by the direct address "Remember." Are these irregularities the product of the young author's cunning or her lack of skill? Students who see these effects as intentional tend to value the poet's voice as empowered in its Enlightenment insistence on social revision. Students who see these effects as unintentional tend to assess her voice as inherently alienated from the religious and cultural paradigms it unsuccessfully attempts to assimilate and mimic.

Questions concerning intention apply as well to Puritan meditative verse. Bradstreet's "Contemplations," for instance, breaks into uneven units: stanzas 1–9 (on the book of nature), stanzas 10–20 (on biblical history), 21–23 (on human life in New Testament terms), 24–28 (on emblematic birds and fish), and 29–33 (on the mariner soul in the prone vessel of the body). Oddities occur, such as the echo of the first unit at the start of the third; and the fourth unit is structurally more a lateral swelling than a linear development of the gist of the poem, which is perhaps why some anthologists delete it. Is such fragmentation the product of Bradstreet's amateurishness or of her humility? Does it express her artistic refusal to vainly construct a poetic monument to herself in a world defined by time's "fatal wrack," which (as the poet observes) crumbles "into th' dust" all "sumptuous monuments" (lines 225, 229)?

Taylor's meditations, seemingly so free-associative and nonsequential, are likewise open to questions concerning intention. Does Taylor consciously revise the patterns of such metaphysical poets as Herbert, or is he a pale, inept version of them? Possibly Taylor practices a "decorum of imperfection," a poetic mode that recognizes the depravity of art, the impropriety of celebrating human life, and the human inability to glorify God (Mignon). As we saw in "Meditation 1.8," beneath the surface chaos of a poetic voice that presents itself as benighted, malnourished, feverish, sick, and maladroit, there is a semicircle emblem that engenders hope by intimating a divine order potentially encompassing and redeeming the poet's temporal disorder. Taylor's concern with salvation affects his art in another manner: He vacillates between despair and presumption just as the soul-bird in "Meditation 1.8" is depicted in various postures of fall and ascent. The Puritan meditative poet usually tries neither to presume nor to despair but to await disclosure of divine will; hence the series of poem-suspending questions in the penultimate stanzas of "Meditation 1.8" and "Meditation 2.3," which both end with a hope for redemption rather than with an optimistic personal redress typical of, say, Herbert's poetry.

For Wheatley, as students should see by now, salvation is far more imminent, not only spiritually but politically, especially regarding abolition. For Freneau and Brackenridge, personal salvation lies in the utilization of natural and human resources, in the temporal and secular fulfillment of American millennial prospects, "richly stor'd with all / The luxuries of life" (line 787). *Rising Glory* includes religious tradition and imagery, such as the poets' wish for Isaiah's power of prophecy and their claim that the star of Bethlehem now shines on America. But in contrast to Wheatley's presentation of religious and historical matters as integral concerns, Freneau and Brackenridge's religious allusions are hollow reeds, mere stage properties, in an ebullient secular forecast. Students readily sense that *Rising Glory*, unlike Puritan meditative verse and Wheatley's poetry, emphasizes the surfaces of life, at least overtly. If the 1772 poem does not quite replicate the catalogs of earlier New World advertisements (Richard Rich's poem *Newes from Virginia*, for example), it delights in the material world as commodity. Even the pronunciation of the names of things is delightful, as if artfully fashioned words were physical objects rather than representations.

REPRESENTATION

At this point I urge my class to delve beneath the surface representations and the design of *Rising Glory* to discover less evident features of the poem and the colonial enterprise it celebrates. If time permits, the sanguine vision of this poem can be instructively compared with the jaundiced satire of Ebenezer Cook(e)'s *The Sot-Weed Factor*. Or students can focus on the admission in *Rising Glory* that "the mysteries of future days" are unknowable, which remark may stimulate class scrutiny of the limitations in the author's awareness (line 594). My students, many of them Hispanic, notice the poem's chauvinism, including its anti-Spanish sentiment. Some notice that the iterated claim that "merciful" Britain did not, like "cruel Spain," shed "seas of Indian blood" is challenged when the poem elsewhere mentions "heroes"

"from Canada / To Georgia" who slew "Indian hosts" (lines 51–52, 259–60). I
then ask whether the poem's silence about the future presence of Native
Americans implicitly participates in the racial displacement and extermina-
tion overtly depicted in Villagrá's epic. Some hesitate to make that indictment, but others sense how cultural oversights and silence can also be
powerful instruments of suppression.

Students may need more help detecting still other problems in these
poems, such as how the derivativeness of *Rising Glory* undermines its
authors' claims for a new American art or how the diffusion of its focus — it
nervously flits from one thing to another as if fearful of looking too closely —
fails to impart a substantial identity to the colonies. In this poem America
seems more a reification of abundant energy than the momentous culmina-
tion of history. In short, the poem accidentally somewhat reflects the instability of the polymorphous society of late-eighteenth-century America. *Rising
Glory* omits more than a future for Native Americans; it is also silent about
slaves, who Wheatley knew were not "by freedom blest" (line 787). But is
Wheatley's nuanced representation of herself as a religiously and spiritually
refined person who politely raises Cain similarly compromised? I urge students to consider the potential cost of the poet's burying the resistant aesthetics of "Being Brought" — its possible appropriation of ministerial
authority in suggesting unprecedented racial readings of Isaiah's prophesies
— beneath an outward acquiescence to conventional religious and literary
authorization. Even if Wheatley hoped to instill her revisionary message deep
within the reader's mind, does her positioning of her resistance below the
conventional surface merely reenact the slave's daily experience of oppression? Class responses tend to be sharply divided.

Some students argue that the Puritan meditative poets were reenacting a
form of enslavement too, particularly through an early Calvinistic devaluation of human capability, the very capacity Freneau and Brackenridge later
exalt. Although, as I said, my students prefer the optimism of *Rising Glory* to
the self-deprecation of Calvinistic meditations, they tend to distrust as exaggeration Freneau and Brackenridge's representation of "America" and to
trust as genuine the Puritans' representation of their humble submission to
divine authority. When they do I ask them to differentiate between the preoccupation with the personal fulfillment that is prophesied in *Rising Glory*
and the preoccupation with personal salvation featured in the Puritan meditations.

I also remind students that the meditators assumed personae in a culturally authorized sinner-saint drama, not only by envisaging redemption but
also by addressing specific audiences (Hammond). Moreover, if Bradstreet
and Taylor practiced a decorum of imperfection, then they composed and
evaluated their verse in relation to a humanly constructed paradigm.
Therefore they valued their art, even if only as an expression of their incapa-
bility, potentially blurring the boundary between humility and pride.

In, say, Bradstreet's 1666 poem on the burning of her house and in
Taylor's 1683 poem on a sweeping flood, both of which seesaw between

resentment toward and acceptance of divine will, my students encounter other indications that submission to divine authority might not have been easy for Puritans. Bradstreet interrupts the recollection of lost prized material possessions with "Adieu, Adieu; All's Vanity" (line 36), a safe, conventional ventriloquising of Ecclesiastes 1.14. I ask my students, Since there is no personal poetry in this formulaic line, no detail, does Bradstreet's declaration inhabit the same emotion-laden, well-furnished house as the previous lines of the poem? Does the disruptiveness of this line signal her flight from a potentially rebellious sentiment, as if the house of her emotion-filled verse were also dangerously on fire? Here, as throughout my effort, I am content if students plumb such questions from various angles and discover diverse, even antithetical, grids of *represented* meanings.

Although my approach privileges depth over breadth of perception, it is designed to enlarge student appreciation of contextual implications, artistic techniques, subtextual subtleties, and finally conceptual limitations. This last goal — acknowledging the enigmatic elusiveness of certainty and hence viewing resolute determination skeptically — is personally important to me. To appreciate the persistence of mystery at the edge of human understanding is implicitly to urge a profound communal humility and tolerance.

WORKS CITED

Primary Works

Bradstreet, Anne. *The Works of Anne Bradstreet*. Ed. Jeannine Hensley. Cambridge: Harvard UP, 1967.

Cook(e), Ebenezer. *The Sot-Weed Factor*. 1708. *Colonial American Poetry*. Ed. Kenneth Silverman. New York: Hafner, 1968. 282–301.

Freneau, Philip, and Hugh Henry Brackenridge. *A Poem, on the Rising Glory of America*. 1772. *Colonial American Poetry*. Ed. Kenneth Silverman. New York: Hafner, 1968. 423–43.

Herbert, George. *The Works of George Herbert*. Ed. F. E. Hutchinson. Oxford: Clarendon, 1941.

Pain, Philip. *Daily Meditations*. 1668. Excerpted in *American Poetry of the Seventeenth Century*. Ed. Harrison T. Meserole. University Park: Pennsylvania State UP, 1985. 287–91.

Quarles, Francis. *The Complete Works of Francis Quarles*. Ed. A. B. Grosart. 3 vols. New York: AMS, 1967.

Rich, Richard. *Newes from Virginia*. 1610. *American Garland*. Ed. Charles A. Firth. Oxford: Clarendon, 1915. 9–16.

Taylor, Edward. *The Poems of Edward Taylor*. Ed. Donald E. Stanford. New Haven: Yale UP, 1960.

Wheatley, Phillis. *Phillis Wheatley and Her Writings*. Ed. William H. Robinson. New York: Garland, 1984.

Villagrá, Gaspar Pérez de. *Historia de la Nueva México*. 1610. Excerpted in *The Heath Anthology of American Literature*. Ed. Paul Lauter. Vol. 1. Lexington: Heath, 1998. 163–72.

Secondary Works

Gay, Peter. *The Age of Enlightenment*. New York: Time-Life, 1966.

Hammond, Jeffrey A. *Sinful Self, Saintly Self: The Puritan Experience of Poetry*. Athens: U of Georgia P, 1993.

Martz, Louis. *The Poetry of Meditation: A Study of English Literature in the Seventeenth Century*. New Haven: Yale UP, 1962.

Mignon, Charles W. "Edward Taylor's *Preparatory Meditations:* A Decorum of Imperfection." *PMLA* 83 (1968): 1423–28.

Scheick, William J. *Design in Puritan American Literature*. Lexington: UP of Kentucky, 1992.

Tillyard, E. M. W. *The Elizabethan World Picture*. London: Chatto, 1943.

White, Hayden. *Metahistory: The Historical Imagination in Nineteenth-Century Europe*. Baltimore: Johns Hopkins UP, 1973.

Portrait of the Artist as a Young Slave: Douglass's Frontispiece Engravings

ED FOLSOM

*W*hen teaching Douglass's narrative, Folsom asks his students to read the 1845 frontispiece portrait and to consider how it functions as part of Douglass's text. He argues that engraved portraits were particularly well suited to opening slave narratives because of "their emphasis on the process of creating verisimilitude, their habit of incorporating in the same image various stages of composition (from rough sketch to finished portrait). . . ." These attributes made them "more effective vehicles than photographs or paintings would have been in representing identity as an act of labor and artistry." Folsom compares Douglass's portrait with the engraving of Walt Whitman from the first edition of Leaves of Grass. Throughout his career, Whitman "coordinated illustrations of himself with the song of himself." In 1855, the same year as the first Leaves of Grass, Douglass published My Bondage and My Freedom, illustrated with another engraving. Folsom concludes that Douglass's portraits work to illustrate the relationship between the author and the slave. This essay originally appeared in Approaches to Teaching Narrative of the Life of Frederick Douglass, edited by James C. Hall.

I most often teach *Narrative of the Life of Frederick Douglass, an American Slave, Written by Himself* in an advanced undergraduate course on the literature and culture of nineteenth-century America. After students have completed their reading of the *Narrative* and we have spent at least one class period talking about the historical and political issues surrounding Douglass's text, I begin the next class by projecting a slide of the 1845 frontispiece portrait (Fig. 1). I tell the students I'd like them to *read* this portrait, to view it not only as a key physical element of the *book* that appeared in 1845 but also as an important component of the *text*, an image that has meaning in relation to the patterns of verbal imagery in Douglass's narrative. How, I ask my students, does this visual representation of Douglass correspond to his verbal self-representation in the narrative proper? How, in fact, does it function as part of the narrative?

From *Approaches to Teaching* Narrative of the Life of Frederick Douglass, ed. James C. Hall (New York: MLA, 1999) 55–65.

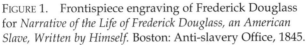

FIGURE 1.   Frontispiece engraving of Frederick Douglass for *Narrative of the Life of Frederick Douglass, an American Slave, Written by Himself.* Boston: Anti-slavery Office, 1845.

The portrait, I remind them, would have been very much a part of the original readers' experience of the text — the first representation of Douglass that they would have encountered and one that they no doubt returned to as they read and thought about the book. I quote Douglass's own statements about the importance of visual art: "Man is the only picture making and picture appreciating animal in the world," he wrote, going on to observe that visual art spans our individual lifetimes ("for childhood delights in pictures") and our history (art rises "with the first dawnings of [. . .] civilization, lifting the thoughts and sentiments of men higher by every one of its triumphs") and thus must be "diligently cultivated" (qtd. in Wheat [iii]). Douglass, then, would have been keenly aware of the impact the frontispiece picture of himself would have on readers.

I show my class a few slides of other examples of contemporary authors' portraits — Lowell and Whittier and Emerson and Longfellow (I save Whitman for later) — all of them framing the head and shoulders only, all of them presenting the author in formal dress, as the exemplar of decorum. These are portraits of the artist as a privileged man. Then I show the class some of the painful J. T. Zealy daguerreotypes of slaves taken in 1850 — naked or half-naked, stripped of their right to dignity even as their eyes register defiance, the very emblems of violated civilized decorum. I explain to my students that few contemporary visual representations exist of individual slaves and that these Zealy portraits were taken to serve as specimens to support the scientist Louis Agassiz's racist polygenesis theories.[1]

Coming back to Douglass's portrait, I ask my students what they see now and how what they see relates to what they've read, and then I stand back and let the responses come. Someone always mentions the clothes, how the dress and fashion seem too formal for a former slave and affiliate him too closely with the privileged white authors. If I'm lucky, someone else will respond that that's just what some white people in the mid-nineteenth century said about Douglass's manner of speaking and manner of writing — that it was too "white," too "learned" and refined to sound authentic. One abolitionist friend told Douglass he needed "a little of the plantation speech" in his writing to give it a realistic edge: "it is not best that you seem too learned" (qtd. in Foner, *Frederick Douglass* 59). And it was not only whites who felt this way: Douglass recalled that Sojourner Truth always considered it "her duty [. . .] to ridicule my efforts to speak and act like a person of cultivation" (qtd. in McFeely 97).

Questions follow: Could part of the impact of Douglass's portrait, then, be a shock of recognition for white readers, a sudden and surprising realization that an African American could assume the status and dress (and voice) of the privileged white author? Is the portrait a conservative gesture that tries to reassure a white readership by portraying Douglass as safe and familiar (a black man certifying white dominance by playing at being white), or is it a radically disorienting gesture that makes Douglass seem dangerously insurgent (a black man essentially altering the power hierarchy by claiming an identity previously reserved for whites)? Has the institution of white authorship usurped Douglass and co-opted his identity, or has Douglass, the black slave, invaded and undermined the all-white establishment of privileged authorship? Could the portrait have functioned for antebellum readers as a kind of optical illusion, at one moment comforting them with an image of assimilation, at the next challenging them with an image of inversion and invasion?

I try to raise questions that broaden the discussion into issues of cultural identity: What range of possibilities for identity formation do the visual representations we've looked at suggest for people living in mid-nineteenth-century America? Do the Zealy portraits of South Carolina slaves and the various portraits of America's successful white male authors in some way set the poles of social identity in America — from the powerless to the powerful, from those denied any education to those who enjoy the privileges of a Harvard education, from those whose portraits were made for "scientific" categorizing and who thus remain nameless or recalled only with a first name to those whose portraits were signs of their fame, familiar faces that accompanied their famous names? If these are the poles of identity in antebellum America, how far could a black man travel from the Zealy slave portraits toward the Boston Brahmin portraits? Does Douglass make the complete journey?

Some students will note that while at first glance Douglass's portrait looks more like those of the successful authors than like those of the slaves, his portrait actually unsettles the bipolar sense of separate and even opposite identities that one assumes when looking at the two sets of images. Douglass's portrait seems to enact an impossible melding of the slave portrait with the successful author portrait. His face and hair join him to the slave portraits, but his clothing and his manner and his firm and elegant signature — the sign of his self-authoring — tie him to the author portraits. It's as if Douglass was demonstrating the fluidity of self-fashioning, literally posing the possibility that one's race could no longer prevent an ascent to cultural power and influence.

I ask students to consider, too, the way this portrait fits into the developing notions of cultural celebrity. The 1840s were the period of America's first celebrity authors, the decade that marked the appearance of what Michael Newbury has called "the mixed feelings about celebrity and exposure in the cultural sphere that simultaneously gave prominent figures power over while leaving them vulnerable to" their new fans (182). Newbury discusses the ways that "celebrity-as-slave figurations" (162) appear at this time, as celebrities become not those who produce commodities but instead commodities themselves. Douglass's striking portrait makes him the first "slave-as-celebrity," and his fame made him identifiable on the street, an obviously dangerous result for an escaped slave. In the warped mirror world of slavery, even celebrity was distorted: America's first celebrity stalkers may have been slave catchers. Douglass's growing celebrity, in fact, led him to flee the country for England, where he purchased his freedom. But by becoming a freed man he entered a new kind of enslavement, an enslavement to a fetishized image of himself that the portrait helped create. That problematic developing dynamic of former-slave/current-celebrity suggests some promising approaches to reading Douglass's 1892 *Life and Times of Frederick Douglass,* where we see the author struggling with what fame has brought and made him.

At this point I invite my class to examine the portrait even more closely. I tell them the 1845 engraving was based on an oil portrait of Douglass completed in the early 1840s by an unidentified artist (Voss 22). The anonymous engraver managed to stiffen and strengthen the gentler face that appears in the painting, but the major change the engraver made was to empty out or half-erase the bottom half of the portrait. Instead of making an engraving that pretended to be a copy of the oil portrait, the engraver emphasized (rather than disguised) the artificial and constructed nature of his steelcut image.

While the engraving renders Douglass's face in photographic detail, its intensity of realistic detail quickly fades as our eyes descend; verisimilitude evaporates and we're left with a rough sketch. The total effect of the portrait emerges, then, from an intriguing tension between a half-sketched quality that emphasizes the artificial, constructed nature of the image and a finished, highly detailed quality that approaches photographic realism. I ask students to think about the implications of this oddly bifurcated image.

I explain that the emphasis on process, on the artifice of constructing detailed identity out of initial bare sketches, is part of the tradition of portrait engraving. Most portrait engravings in the nineteenth century emphasize to some extent the artifice of the engraving by leaving some part of the image unfinished or barely sketched in. The Douglass engraving, however, exaggerates this convention of having a detailed portrait arise out of a rough sketch; from the shoulders down Douglass is represented only by a bare, primitive line drawing, while from the shoulders up he emerges suddenly into a fully realized presence. Peter Dorsey describes the engraving as representing "a disappearing body" (445), but the dynamics of this portrait (mirroring the narrative) actually make it a self in the process of *appearing*. Like all visual art for Douglass, this portrait is about "lifting the thoughts and sentiments of men higher" by "rising" from the primitive to the "cultivated" (qtd. in Wheat [iii]).

At this point, students can begin to draw the connections between visual text and written text and to see how such a portrait enhances the pattern of Douglass's narrative, where Douglass the successful author and orator emerges from a slave who is prevented from having any access to his own personal history, whose ability to learn and form an identity is stunted by slavery's restrictions on movement and education. Douglass's book traces his rise from a generic "American slave" with an empty identity to "Frederick Douglass," a newly named and fully realized individual who has taken control of his life and is now the agent of his narrative instead of a faceless product of the slavery system, a servant in someone else's master narrative. His ability to gain access to writing and reading, to learn to "write by himself," brings his past under his own guidance and control, and his signature under his half-sketched, half-realized portrait is ink affirming a literacy that creates and verifies identity; for a significant part of Douglass's life, that signature was impossible, because the name and the ability to sign it were absent. His page was blank; his narrative is the story of learning to sign his name, at first literally and later figuratively, and to fill the blank pages with his identity. His book is his signature, and it ends with the act of signing his name, a full circle back to the frontispiece page. The visual emblem of himself imitates his emergence from blank, absent, or sketchy beginnings into a distinctive and distinguished selfhood.

If we look at the title page that appears opposite the portrait in the 1845 *Narrative,* we can see that the placement of the words underscores the significance of the portrait: The words "Frederick Douglass" appear in large type across from the singular, fully delineated face, while, in smaller type,

"American Slave" appears opposite the part of the portrait that is not fleshed out. The words "Written by Himself" appear opposite Douglass's verifying signature. The pattern of words on the title page mirrors the portrait. Douglass's barely visible hands resting on the single line of his leg form the fade-out lower border of the portrait, but those hands are affirmed as active by the signature, which appears clearly just below and which is, along with the entire narrative, the visible work of those hands. A student once suggested that in reading "up" the portrait, we move from a nondescript outline of a body through more fully realized imitative clothing — the white man's uniform of success — and on up to the most detailed and individualized part of the portrait — the face and hair that distinguish this from all previous portraits of authors. The imitativeness (of dress, style, manner, voice) ultimately yields distinction, and the portrait emphasizes the irony of cultural identity that one must embrace imitation to emerge as an individual. As Dorsey notes in his fine study of Douglass's "self-fashioning process," any attempt at "acquiring mastery — whether of human material, or textual resources — presupposes mimesis." Thus, Dorsey says, "Douglass emphasizes that resistance to oppression requires a degree of imitation; to change their position, the oppressed must at some level copy the metaphors, the behaviors, and even the thought processes of the oppressor" — only through such imitation can the oppressed gain "access to political exchanges that can alter social structures" (436–37).

Engraved portraits, then, served as particularly appropriate openings to slave narratives, a genre centered on confirmations of identity and celebrations of free individuals emerging from an institution that strove to keep such individuality invisible, blank, and unformed. Engravings — with their emphasis on the process of creating verisimilitude, their habit of incorporating in the same image various stages of composition (from rough sketch to finished portrait) — were thus more effective vehicles than photographs or paintings would have been in representing identity as an act of labor and artistry.

After the class finishes discussing the 1845 image, I show students another slide, this one of Walt Whitman, the writer we will study after Douglass. All the effects we've talked about in portrait engravings are famously captured in Samuel Hollyer's 1855 frontispiece engraving of Whitman for the first edition of *Leaves of Grass* (Fig. 2). (I discuss this portrait in more detail and compare it with Douglass's 1845 portrait in Folsom 135–45. I offer a summary of that discussion here.)

All through his poetic career, Whitman carefully coordinated illustrations of himself with the song of himself: every portrait, he once noted, "has some relation to the text" (Traubel 2: 536); "the portrait," Whitman said, "in fact is involved as part of the poem" (Kennedy 248). For Whitman the inclusion of his portrait was not a decoration or badge but, rather, a challenge to the reader to work, to struggle for meaning, to respond. As with Douglass's portrait, it was as essential a part of the book as the written text was and demanded the same kind of involvement from the reader, who was required

FIGURE 2.   Frontispiece engraving of Walt
Whitman for *Leaves of Grass*. Brooklyn, 1855.

to actively interpret not only the words but the visual images as well.

This 1855 frontispiece portrait has become the most familiar of all the images of Whitman — hat on, shirt open, head cocked, arm akimbo. Early reviewers often commented on Whitman's oddly *un*cultivated self-presentation: "The damaged hat, the rough beard, the naked throat, the shirt exposed to the waist, are each and all presented to show that the man to whom these articles belong scorns the delicate art of civilization" (Leaves of Grass *Imprints* 42). The 1855 portrait makes its point in a number of ways: It is in sharp contrast to the expected iconography of authors' portraits, portraits that conventionally emphasized formality and the face instead of this rough informality where arms, legs, and body diminish the centrality of the head. Authors' portraits in the nineteenth century indicated that writing was a function of the intellect, a formal business conducted in book-lined rooms where ideas fed the head through words. Whitman, of course, was out to undermine this conception, to move poetry to the streets, to deformalize it, to yank it away from the authority of tradition, and to insist that poetry emerges from the heart, lungs, genitals, and hands, as much as from the head. He wanted the representative democratic poet to speak in his poems, and the absence of his own name from the title page allowed the representative portrait to speak to authorship. These were poems written by a representative democratic person living life in the world and experiencing life through the five senses — a self that found authority in experience, that doffed its hat to no one, that refused to follow the decorum of removing one's hat indoors or even in books. Just as the appearance of Douglass's name in large type and his signature in a firm hand was crucial for the identity formation Douglass needed to represent, so is the absence of these nominal signs crucial for Whitman's quite different needs. As a white man speaking for the culture as a whole, Whitman could luxuriate in the absorption of his individual self into the communal identity of "America."

The engraved portrait, in one sense, works very much like Douglass's 1845 portrait. While Hollyer's engraving renders Whitman's face and upper torso in photographic detail, the intensity of its realistic detail fades toward the bottom of the image; Whitman's legs are rendered with less and less detail until they diminish to simple sketch lines, then fade into the blankness of the paper itself. The image advertises its constructedness. As with Douglass's portrait, Whitman's emerges from an intriguing tension between a rough, half-sketched quality that emphasizes the artificiality of the image and a finished, highly detailed quality that imitates the verisimilitude of the original daguerreotype on which it is based. It is as if Hollyer (and Whitman) want to underscore the process, the labor involved in making ink turn into identity, in making lines turn into humanity, in making a book turn into a man.

Whitman was familiar with Douglass's work, and the poems of the 1855 *Leaves* were in some ways based on what Whitman learned from slave narratives like Douglass's. Whitman's 1855 poems in fact incorporate a slave narrative, from the "runaway slave [who] came to my house and stopped outside" and "staid with me a week, before he was recuperated and passed north, / I had him sit next me at the table" (36) to the moments when Whitman speaks as the slave: "I am the hounded slave . . . . I wince at the bite of the dogs" (65) and "I hate him that oppresses me, / [. . .] How he informs against my brother and sister and takes pay for their blood, / How he laughs when I look down the bend after the steamboat that carries away my woman" (*Complete Poetry* 113). Whitman appropriated aspects of slave narratives to make concrete the expression of desire for freedom and equality in his poetry. Like a slave narrative, *Leaves* was the record of a human being seeking a new name, an unfettered identity, an open road that would lead away from all forms of enslavement — whether social conventions, literary traditions, or actual institutions of slavery.

Fittingly, Whitman's frontispiece portrait echoes certain aspects of Douglass's even as it differs from Douglass's in other ways: For Douglass, the escape was from work clothes to formal clothing, a change that signaled success and the acquisition of education and manners; for Whitman, the escape was in the opposite direction. Whitman, the white man, seeking democratic expression, could profitably fashion himself *down,* could take on the garb of the worker and seek to imaginatively identify with the slave's experience; Douglass, the black man, seeking cultural authority, had to fashion himself *up*, discovering identity in an escape from slavery. The same social conventions that marked an achievement of identity for Douglass threatened identity for Whitman. An African American posing as a distinguished writer was every bit as singular in the culture of mid-nineteenth-century America as a white poet posing as a day laborer. Just as Douglass's portrait undermined the generally expected image of a slave, Whitman's portrait undermined the expectations that his readers would have brought to an engraving of an author.

The same year that Whitman's *Leaves of Grass* appeared, Douglass published *My Bondage and My Freedom* and included a new frontispiece portrait, by J. C. Battre (Fig. 3). At the end of our class discussion about *Narrative*, I show my students a slide of this engraving. Like Whitman's portrait, Douglass's 1855 engraving was based on a daguerreotype, and an intense photographic realism is apparent in this image. True to the engraving tradition, however, the lower part of the portrait fades into simple lines, though the rough-to-finished effect is much more subtle than in the 1845 frontispiece. Here Douglass's clothes — more elegant and formal than those in the earlier engraving — are emphasized even more and given a finish that the clothing in the 1845 image lacked. Also emphasized is Douglass's rigid bearing: It is not a formal rigidity so much as stiff discomfort, as if the clothes are forcing a manner on a body that resists it. As in the 1845 image, Douglass's hands are muted, faded, but unlike the earlier portrait, here they are fisted and tensed. Douglass's narration of his life moves from his use of his fists to enforce his freedom and "rekindle in [his] breast the smouldering embers of liberty" (246) to his discovery of how to use words as his weapons of freedom. In *My Bondage and My Freedom*, Douglass apologizes for the roughness of his physical fight with Covey and the roughness of his writing about the fight — "undignified as it was, and as I fear my narration of it is" (246) — but at the same time he expands his description of the encounter. He is both beyond that roughness and essentially formed by it, and his portrait captures this quality precisely. The faded but fisted hands are subdued but still visible and are vital parts of Douglass's newer, more refined identity: The fully realized face, intelligent and serious and black, unites the clothes and the fists and gives coherence to the author and the slave. Peter Dorsey observes:

> The title of *My Bondage and My Freedom* [. . .] contains the poles of a metaphorical equation: a self inevitably bound by the figures he and others used but simultaneously liberated from those chains, not just by the realization that he was (and is) always more than the metaphors attached to him but by his own mastery of the possibilities of self-figuration. (447)

So, too, Douglass's title serves as a fitting caption for his frontispiece image. His pose and his costume represent both his bondage and his freedom, the brute physicality of his slave past and the straitened refinement of his

FIGURE 3. Frontispiece engraving of Frederick Douglass for *My Bondage and My Freedom*. New York: Miller, Orton, and Mulligan, 1855.

celebrity present. In his bondage Douglass found freedom, and in his freedom he finds other kinds of bondage. His frontispiece portraits, read as textual images, represent these tensions and ambiguities and serve as visual analogues of Douglass's narratives. By 1855, Douglass had become, as William L. Andrews says, "an accomplished man of letters, a sophisticated journalist as well as orator" (*To Tell* 218), but this accomplishment and erudition rose from and remained attached to a life that began in denial of accomplishment and learning. Douglass's portraits manifest these tensions of origin and result, of what Dorsey calls "becoming the other" (435). When a reporter for the *Herald of Freedom* in 1844 tried to describe Douglass's "impressive speech," his analysis breaks at the seams of these very tensions:

> It was not what you could describe as oratory or eloquence. It was sterner, darker, deeper than these. It was a storm of insurrection. [. . .] He stalked to and fro on the platform, roused up like the Numidian lion. [. . .] There was great oratory in his speech. [. . .] He was not up as a speaker, performing. He was an insurgent slave, taking hold on the right of speech, and charging on his tyrants the bondage of his race. [. . .] He is a surprising lecturer. I would not praise him, or describe him; but he is a colored man, a slave, of the race who can't take care of themselves — our inferiors, and therefore to be kept in slavery. [. . .] He is one of the most impressive and majestic speakers I have ever heard. [. . .] I have never seen a man leave the platform, or close a speech, with more real dignity, and eloquent majesty. (qtd. in Foner, *Frederick Douglass* 58)

Here once again is Douglass as a maddening, shifting optical illusion — not an orator, a great orator; not eloquent, majestically eloquent; a wild animal, a dignified man; an ignorant slave, an accomplished speaker. Douglass's emergence into eminence and accomplishment and fame always carried with it the ragged and rugged delineations of his past. His portraits are always about the relationship of the author to (and as) the young slave.

NOTE

1. Instructors can make slides of the Douglass portraits from public-domain copies of the 1845 *Narrative* and the 1855 *My Bondage and My Freedom*, available in the special collections departments of many public and university libraries. (The illustrations for this essay are from the University of Iowa Special Collections.) The portraits are reproduced in several modern editions of Douglass's work and are also available in Dorsey and in Voss. The Zealy daguerreotypes are in the Peabody Museum at Harvard University, and several are reproduced and discussed by Trachtenberg (52–60), in Reichlin, and in Wallis.

WORKS CITED

Andrews, William L. *To Tell a Free Story: The First Century of Afro-American Autobiography, 1760–1865*. Urbana: U of Illinois P, 1986.

Dorsey, Peter A. "Becoming the Other: The Mimesis of Metaphor in Douglass's *My Bondage and My Freedom*." *PMLA* 111 (1996): 435–50.

Douglass, Frederick. *My Bondage and My Freedom*. New York, 1855.

Foner, Philip S. *Frederick Douglass*. New York: Citadel, 1969.

Kennedy, William Sloane. *The Fight of a Book for the World*. West Yarmouth: Stonecroft, 1926.

Leaves of Grass Imprints. Boston, 1860.

McFeely, William S. *Frederick Douglass*. New York: Norton, 1991.

Newbury, Michael. "Eaten Alive: Slavery and Celebrity in Antebellum America." *ELH* 61 (1994): 159–87.

Traubel, Horace. *With Walt Whitman in Camden*. Vols. 1–3. 1906–14. New York: Rowman, 1961.

Voss, Frederick S. *Majestic in His Wrath: A Pictorial Life of Frederick Douglass*. Washington: Smithsonian, 1995.

Wheat, Ellen Harkins, ed. *Jacob Lawrence: The "Frederick Douglass" and "Harriet Tubman" Series of 1938–1940*. Seattle: U of Washington P, 1991.

Whitman, Walt. *Complete Poetry and Collected Prose*. New York: Lib. of Amer., 1982.

ADDITIONAL READINGS

Alberti, John. *The Canon in the Classroom: The Pedagogical Implications of Canon Revision in American Literature.* New York: Garland, 1995.

Allen, Paula Gunn. *Studies in American Indian Literature: Critical Essays and Course Designs.* New York: MLA, 1983.

Ammons, Elizabeth, and Susan Belasco. *Approaches to Teaching Stowe's* Uncle Tom's Cabin. New York: MLA, 2000.

Amory, Hugh, and David D. Hall, *The History of the Book in America.* New York: Cambridge UP, 1999.

Anderson, Danny J., and Jill S. Kuhnheim. *Cultural Studies in the Curriculum: Teaching Latin America.* New York: MLA, 2003.

Aranda, José, Jr. *When We Arrive: A New Literary History of Mexican America.* Tucson: U of Arizona P, 2003.

Augenbraum, Harold, and Margarite Fernández Olmos. *U.S. Latino Literature: A Critical Guide for Students and Teachers.* Westport, CT: Greenwood P, 2000.

Baker, Houston A., Jr. *Three American Literatures: Essays in Chicano, Native American, and Asian-American Literature for Teachers of American Literature.* New York: MLA, 1982.

Baym, Nina. *Feminism and American Literary History: Essays.* Piscataway, NJ: Rutgers UP, 1992.

Beach, Richard. *A Teacher's Guide to Reader-Response Theories.* Urbana, IL: NCTE, 1993.

Bercovitch, Sacvan. *The American Jeremiad.* Madison: U Wisconsin P, 1980.

———, Sacvan, ed. *The Cambridge History of American Literature.* 8 vols. New York: Cambridge UP, 1997.

Brooker, Jewel Spears. *Approaches to Teaching Eliot's Poetry and Plays.* New York: MLA, 1988.

Burt, Daniel S. *The Chronology of American Literature: America's Literary Achievements from the Colonial Era to Modern Times.* Boston: Houghton Mifflin, 2004.

Cahalan, James M., and David B. Downing, eds. *Practicing Theory in Introductory College Literature Courses.* Urbana, IL: NCTE, 1991.

Dimock, Wai Chee, and Michael T. Gilmore, eds. *Rethinking Class: Literary Studies and Social Formations.* New York: Columbia UP, 1994.

Eddins, Dwight, ed. *The Emperor Redressed: Critiquing Critical Theory.* Tuscaloosa: U of Alabama P, 1995.

Fast, Robin Riley, and Christine Mack Gordon. *Approaches to Teaching Dickinson's Poetry.* New York: MLA, 1989.

Fiedler, Leslie. *Love and Death in the American Novel.* First Dalkey Archive ed. Normal, IL: Dalkey Archive, 1998.

Fisher, Dexter, and Robert B. Stepto, eds. *Afro-American Literature: The Reconstruction of Instruction.* New York: MLA, 1979.

Foley, John Miles. *Teaching Oral Traditions.* New York: MLA, 1998.

Goebel, Bruce A., and James C. Hall. *Teaching a "New Canon"?: Students, Teachers, and Texts in the College Literature Classroom.* Urbana, IL: NCTE, 1995.

Graff, Gerald. *Beyond the Culture Wars: How Teaching the Conflicts Can Revitalize American Education.* New York: Norton, 1992.

Graff, Gerald, and Michael Warner, eds. *The Origins of Literary Studies in America: A Documentary Anthology.* New York: Routledge, 1989.

Graham, Maryemma, et al. *Teaching African American Literature.* Oxford: Routledge, 1998.

Haggerty, George, and Bonnie Zimmerman, eds. *Professions of Desire: Lesbian and Gay Studies in Literature.* New York: MLA, 1995.

Hall, James C. *Approaches to Teaching* Narrative of the Life of Frederick Douglass. New York: MLA, 1999.

Hoeveler, Diane Long, and Tamar Heller. *Approaches to Teaching Gothic Literature: The British and American Traditions.* New York: MLA, 2003.

Hoffmann, Leonore, and Deborah Rosenfelt. *Teaching Women's Literature from a Regional Perspective.* New York: MLA, 1982.

Hoffmann, Leonore, and Margo Culley. *Women's Personal Narratives: Essays in Criticism and Pedagogy.* New York: MLA, 1985.

Holifield, E. Brooks. *Era of Persuasion: American Thought and Culture, 1521–1680.* Woodbridge, CT: Twayne, 1989.

Hune, Shirley, et al., eds. *Asian Americans: Comparative and Global Perspectives.* Pullman: Washington State UP, 1991.

Knight, Denise D., and Cynthia J. Davis. *Approaches to Teaching Gilman's "The Yellow Wallpaper" and* Herland. New York: MLA, 2003.

Knippling, Alpana Sharma. *New Immigrant Literatures in the United States: A Sourcebook to Our Multicultural Literary Heritage.* Westport, CT: Greenwood P, 1996.

Koloski, Bernard. *Approaches to Teaching Chopin's* The Awakening. New York: MLA, 1988.

Kummings, Donald D. *Approaches to Teaching Whitman's* Leaves of Grass. New York: MLA, 1990.

Landsman, Ned C. *From Colonials to Provincials: American Thought and Culture, 1680–1760.* Woodbridge, CT: Twayne, 1997.

Lauter, Paul. *Canons and Contexts.* New York: Oxford UP, 1991.

Leonard, James S., ed. *Making Mark Twain Work in the Classroom.* Durham, NC: Duke UP, 1999.

Lewis, R. W. B. *The American Adam: Innocence, Tragedy, and Tradition in the Nineteenth Century.* Chicago: U Chicago P, 1959.

Lim, Shirley Geok-lin. *Approaches to Teaching Kingston's* The Woman Warrior. New York: MLA, 1991.

Lim, Shirley Geok-lin, and Amy Ling. *Reading the Literatures of Asian America.* Philadelphia: Temple UP, 1992.

Maitino, John R., and David R. Peck, eds. *Teaching American Ethnic Literatures.* Albuquerque: U of New Mexico, 1996.

Martín-Rodriguez, Manuel M. *Life in Search of Readers: Reading (in) Chicano/a Literature.* Albuquerque: U of New Mexico P, 2003.

Matthews, Jean. *Toward a New Society: American Thought and Culture, 1800–1830.* Woodbridge, CT: Twayne, 1991.

Matthiessen, F. O. *The American Renaissance: Art and Expression in the Age of Emerson and Whitman.* 1941. New York: Oxford UP, 1968.

Mayberry, Katherine J. *Teaching What You're Not: Identity Politics in Higher Education.* New York: New York UP, 1996.

McDowell, Deborah E., and Arnold Rampersad. *Slavery and the Literary Imagination.* Baltimore: Johns Hopkins UP, 1989.

Michaels, Walter Benn, and Donald E. Pease. *The American Renaissance Reconsidered.* Baltimore: Johns Hopkins UP, 1989.

Miller, Perry. *Errand into the Wilderness.* Cambridge, MA: Belknap, 1975.

Mulford, Carla. *Teaching the Literatures of Early America.* New York: MLA, 2000.

Palumbo-Liu, David, ed. *The Ethnic Canon: Histories, Institutions, and Interventions.* Minneapolis: U of Minnesota P, 1995.

Poey, Delia. *Latino American Literature in the Classroom: The Politics of Transformation.* Gainesville: UP of Florida, 2002.

Reising, Russell. *The Unusable Past: Theory and the Study of American Literature.* New York and London: Methuen, 1986.

Richter, David H. *Falling into Theory: Conflicting Views on Reading Literature.* Boston: Bedford/St. Martin's, 2000.

Rose, Anne C. *Voices of the Marketplace: American Thought and Culture, 1830–1860*. Woodbridge, CT: Twayne, 1997.

Ruoff, A. LaVonne Brown, and Jerry W. Ward, Jr., eds. *Redefining American Literary History*. New York: MLA, 1990.

Saldívar, José David. *Border Matters: Remapping American Cultural Studies*. Berkeley: U of California P, 1997.

Schneider, Richard J. *Approaches to Teaching Thoreau's* Walden *and Other Works*. New York: MLA, 1996.

Selden, Raman. *Practicing Theory and Reading Literature: An Introduction*. Lexington: UP of Kentucky, 1989.

Shalhope, Robert. *The Roots of Democracy: American Thought and Culture, 1760–1800*. Woodbridge, CT: Twayne, 1990.

Shirley, Carl R., and Paula W. Shirley. *Understanding Chicano Literature*. Columbia: U of South Carolina P, 1988.

Showalter, Elaine. *Teaching Literature*. Malden, MA: Blackwell, 2002.

Smith, Henry Nash. *Virgin Land: The American West as Symbol and Myth*. Cambridge, MA: Harvard UP, 1971.

Stevenson, Louise L. *The Victorian Homefront: American Thought and Culture, 1860–1880*. Woodbridge, CT: Twayne, 1991.

Sundquist, Eric, *American Realism: New Essays*. Baltimore: Johns Hopkins UP, 1982.

Taylor, Alan. *American Colonies: The Settling of North America*. New York: Penguin, 2002.

Tompkins, Jane. *Sensational Designs: The Cultural Work of American Fiction, 1790–1860*. New York: Oxford UP, 1986.

Yancey, Kathleen Blake. *Teaching Literature as Reflective Practice*. Urbana, IL: NCTE, 2004.

Wright, Louis B. *The Cultural Life of the American Colonies*. Mineola, NY: Dover, 2002.

ABOUT THE
VOLUME EDITOR

Venetria K. Patton is the director of African American Studies at Purdue University. She earned her Ph.D. from the University of California at Riverside. Patton's research interests include African American literature, diasporic women's literature, nineteenth-century American literature, and feminist discourse. She is the author of several essays as well as the book *Women in Chains: The Legacy of Slavery in Black Women's Fiction* (2000). Patton is the co-editor of *Double Take: A Revisionist Harlem Renaissance Anthology* (2001) and of the Spring 2004 issue of *The Black Scholar*. She is currently studying elders and ancestors in African American women's fiction.

ABOUT THE
CONTRIBUTORS

Charlene Avallone is an independent scholar working in Kailua, Hawai'i. A native New Yorker, she received her M.A. and Ph.D. from SUNY-Binghamton. Recent published essays of Avallone's include "The 'Red Roots' of White Feminism in Margaret Fuller's Writings" (1997) and "Catherine Sedgwick and the Art of Conversation" (2003). Her current project studies the feminization of conversation in the United States and the ideologies, educational discipline, rhetorical principles, and oratorical and literary practices of 1770 through 1870.

Sacvan Bercovitch was born and raised in Montreal, Canada. He received his Ph.D. from Claremont Graduate University. In 2002 and 2003 Bercovitch received two successive Fulbright grants that allowed him to travel and teach in Moscow and the Czech Republic. In these countries Bercovitch was able to deepen his understanding of the relationship between American literature and American popular culture. Several of his essays have been published on this topic in *The Puritan Origins of the American Self* (1975). Bercovitch is currently the Powell M. Cabot Research professor at Harvard University and also serves as the general editor of the eight-volume *Cambridge History of American Literature*.

Lawrence Buell is the Powell M. Cabot Professor of American Literature at Harvard University where he has been teaching since 1990. He completed his undergraduate degree at Princeton University and received his Ph.D. from Cornell University. Buell's extensive academic research over the past two decades has resulted in numerous published articles and five books, including *Emerson* (2003) and *Writing for an Endangered World: Literature, Culture, and Environment in the United States and Beyond* (2001). He is currently in the process of writing several books on such diverse topics as the future of environmental criticism, the aesthetics of displacement, and a cultural and critical history of "The Great American Novel."

Philip Fisher received his Ph.D. from Harvard University and currently teaches in the English department there. His academic interests include the

American novel, the English novel, cultural theory, modernism, and American art and its cultural institutions. Fisher has published several books on these topics, such as *Making and Effacing Art* (1991) and *New American Studies* (1991).

Ed Folsom is the Carver Professor of English at the University of Iowa. He has edited the *Walt Whitman Quarterly Review* since 1983 and has published several books on the poet, including *Re-Scripting Walt Whitman* (2005), *Whitman East and West* (2002), and *Walt Whitman and the World* (1995). In addition, Folsom has published over forty essays in journals like *American Literature* and *Studies in the American Renaissance*.

Trudier Harris is the J. Carlyle Sitterson Professor of English at the University of North Carolina at Chapel Hill. She received her M.A. and her Ph.D. from Ohio State University and years later, the university presented her with its first annual Award of Distinction for the College of Humanities. Harris is a specialist on African American literature and folklore and has lectured throughout the United States as well as in Europe, Jamaica, and Canada. She has published numerous articles and written eight books, one of which, *Black Women in the Fiction of James Baldwin* (1985), received the College Language Association Creative Scholarship Award. In 2003 Beacon Press published her memoir, *Summer Snow: Reflections from a Black Daughter of the South*.

Maureen Honey received her M.A. and her Ph.D. from Michigan State University and upon graduating accepted a job at the University of Nebraska, where she continues to teach English and women's studies. She has been interviewed on women's roles in World War II by national media giants such as PBS, NPR, CNN, NBC, the *Wall Street Journal,* and *U.S. News and World Report.* Harris has published a book on the subject entitled *Creating Rosie the Riveter: Class, Gender, and Propaganda during World War II* (1984).

Gregory S. Jay received his Ph.D. in English from the State University of New York in Buffalo. He has authored three books, entitled *American Literature and the Culture Wars* (1997), *America the Scrivener: Deconstruction and the Subject of Literary History* (1990), and *T. S Eliot and the Poetics of Literary History* (1983). He has also edited several books and published many essays and articles. Jay currently teaches English at the University of Wisconsin where he offers his students helpful writing tips such as "Be more or less specific" and "Exaggeration is a billion times worse than understatement."

Margaret Faye Jones was born in England and spent much of her childhood in rural Alabama. She has two master's degrees, in education and in English, and she received her Ph.D. in English from Indiana University of Pennsylvania. For the past nineteen years she has taught at Nashville Community College, and in January 2005 she was named dean of learning resources. Faye Jones's main academic interest is British and American working women of the Victorian age.

Amy Kaplan received her Ph.D. from Johns Hopkins University. She is currently the Edmund J. and Louise W. Kahn Endowed Term Professor in the Humanities at the University of Pennsylvania, where she teaches courses on the culture of imperialism; comparative perspectives on the Americas; and mourning, memory, and violence. Kaplan wrote *The Social Construction of American Realism* (1988) and most recently *The Anarchy of Empire in the Making of U.S. Culture* (2002). She has published essays on September 11 and Guantanamo Bay and is currently writing about the language and culture of empire today. Her essay *Manifest Domesticity* won the Norman Forster Prize for the best essay in American literature in 1988.

AnnLouise Keating spent much of her early life in Chicago. After receiving her M.A. and Ph.D. from the University of Illinois, Keating left for the southwest and a job at Eastern New Mexico University. She is currently a professor at Texas Woman's University, where she continues to break new ground teaching and researching transformative multiculturalism. Keating has been published extensively in various books and journals. In 1996 her book *Women Reading Women Writing: Self-Invention in Paula Gunn Allen, Gloria Anzaldúa, and Audre Lorde* was selected as an outstanding academic book.

Elaine H. Kim teaches Asian American studies and comparative ethnic studies at the University of California at Berkeley, where she received her Ph.D. Kim is the co-founder of Asian Women United of California, Asian Immigrant Women Advocates, and the Korean Community Center. She has worked as a video producer for the documentaries *Labor Women, Art to Art, Sa-I-Gu: From Women's Perspectives*, and *Slaying the Dragon: Asian Women in U.S. Television and Film*. In addition, Kim has published many books and articles on Asian American studies.

David Leverenz received his B.A. from Harvard University and his M.A. and Ph.D. from the University of California at Berkeley. His major publications include *The Language of Puritan Feeling: An Exploration in Literature, Psychology, and Social History* (1980), *Manhood and the American Renaissance* (1989), and *Paternalism Incorporated: Fables of American Fatherhood* (2003). Leverenz is also the father of four children who, he asserts, helped to raise him.

David Palumbo-Liu is professor of comparative literature and director of the Program in Modern Thought and Literature at Stanford University. He completed both his undergraduate and graduate work at the University of California at Berkeley, receiving his Ph.D. in 1988. Palumbo-Liu helped establish the Asian American Studies Department at Stanford University and is the author of several books and articles concerning Asian American pedagogy. His books include *The Poetics of Appropriation: The Literary Theory and Practice of Huang Tingjian* (1993); *The Ethnic Canon: History, Institutions, Interventions* (1995); *Streams of Cultural Capital: Transnational Cultural Studies* (1997); and *Asian/American: Historical Crossings of a Racial Frontier* (1999). Palumbo-Liu has also been interviewed by National Public Radio, the *Los Angeles Times*, the *New York Times*, and ABC.

Donald Pizer is the Pierce Butler Professor of English emeritus at Tulane University. He is the author of over forty books, including *The Novels of Frank Norris* (1966) and *The Novels of Theodore Dreiser: A Critical Study* (1976). He is especially interested in late nineteenth- and early twentieth-century American literature.

Lillian S. Robinson began her academic career in France studying at the Sorbonne before she returned to the United States to receive her M.A. from Brown University and her Ph.D. from Columbia University. After serving as the chair at several colleges and universities, she moved to a French-speaking institution in Montreal, Canada, where she is a professor of women's studies and the principal-directrice of the Simone de Beauvoir Institute at Concordia University. In 2001 a scholarship in women's studies was established in Robinson's name in commemoration of her contributions to the field. Robinson has published several books on the topic of women's issues in literature, among them *Wonder Women: Feminisms and Superheroes* (2004), *Monstrous Regiment: The Lady Knight in the Sixteenth-Century Epic* (1985), and *Sex, Class, and Culture* (1978). She has also published poetry, a literary mystery, and several scholarly articles.

John Carlos Rowe completed his undergraduate work at the Johns Hopkins University and received his Ph.D. from the State University of New York at Buffalo. He is currently an Associates' Professor of the Humanities, English, and a professor in the Program in American Studies and Ethnicity at the University of Southern California. In addition to over one hundred scholarly essays and critical reviews, Rowe is the author of *Henry Adams and Henry James: The Emergence of a Modern Consciousness* (1976), *Through the Custom-House: Nineteenth-Century American Fiction and Modern Theory* (1982), *The Theoretical Dimensions of Henry James* (1984), *At Emerson's Tomb: The Politics of Classic American Literature* (1997), *The Other Henry James* (1998), *Literary Culture and U.S. Imperialism: From the Revolution to World War II* (2000) and *The New American Studies* (2002).

A. LaVonne Brown Ruoff is a professor emerita of English at the University of Illinois in Chicago and a pioneer in Native American studies. Her personal relationships (her former husband was Menominee and her adopted daughter is Ojibwe) sparked an interest in Native American literature, which she began teaching thirty years ago. Her work in the field led to the publication of *American Indian Literatures: An Introduction, Bibliographic Review, and Selected Bibliography* (1990) and the Lifetime Scholarly Achievement Award of the Modern Language Association. Since retiring, Ruoff, with the help of her husband, restored a Victorian home in Oak Park, Illinois, and it won the Oak Park Historical Preservation Award for interior restoration.

Michael Ryan was born in Ireland and came to America in 1960. Currently, he is a professor at Northeastern University in Boston. His publications include *Marxism and Deconstruction: A Critical Articulation* (1982), *Politics and Culture: Working Hypotheses for a Post-Revolutionary Society* (1989), and *Camera Politica:*

The Politics and Ideology of Contemporary Hollywood Film (1988). Presently Ryan is working on an anthology of cultural studies and an introduction to a book on interpreting film.

Ada Savin is a Romanian-French scholar who teaches American studies at the University de Versailles Saint-Quentin-en-Yvelines in France. She has been widely published; her book *Journey into Otherness: Essays in North American History, Culture, and Literature* came out in 2005. Savin's academic interests include the peopling of North America, immigration, exile, ethnicity, multiculturalism, and boundaries represented in autobiographical writings.

William J. Scheick is the J. R. Millikan Centennial Professor at the University of Texas. From 1975 to 1992 he edited *Texas Studies in Literature and Language*, and he continues to edit *The Society of Early Americanists Newsletter*. His extensive list of publications includes creative work, professional articles, horticultural essays, and book reviews. He was awarded the Pushcart Prize for creative writing, the Choice Award for Outstanding Academic Book, and the Center for Humanities Research Prize in literary and cultural studies. Scheick's other interests include gardening, creating stained-glass panels, and photographing flowers for local and statewide publications.

Daniel Joseph Singal grew up in Boston and graduated from Harvard University. He received his M.A. and Ph.D. from Columbia University and began his teaching career at Tulane University. In 1980 he joined the faculty of Hobart and William Smith College, where he teaches American historiography and political history. His books include *The War Within: From Victorian to Modernist Thought in the South* (1982) and William Faulkner: The Making of a Modernist (1997). Singal is currently at work on a book that explores modernist culture in the United States from the late nineteenth century to the 1970s.

Cecelia Tichi is the William R. Kenan Jr. Professor of English at Vanderbilt University. She completed her undergraduate work at Penn State University, and received her master's degree from Johns Hopkins and her Ph.D. from the University of California at Davis. Her primary academic focus is on the nineteenth- and twentieth-century American novel, but her interests encompass everything from technology and the environment to country music. Tichi's diverse interests are evident in her published articles and books which include *Reading Country Music: Steel Guitars, Opry Stars, and Honky-Tonk Bars* (1998) and *Exposés and Excess: Muckracking in America* (2004). She is also the author of three novels that she published under the name Cecelia Tishy.

Lois P. Tucker was born and raised in Bermuda. She returned to the island after completing her undergraduate and graduate work in the United States to teach high school English. Recently Tucker received her Ph.D. from Indiana University of Pennsylvania. She is currently the principal of the Bermuda Institute and adjunct lecturer at Bermuda College, where she served as the associate dean on the faculty of arts and sciences for ten years.

Acknowledgments *(continued from page iv)*

Ed Folsom, "Portrait of the Artist as a Young Slave: Douglass's Frontispiece Engravings." From *Approaches to Teaching: Narrative of the Life of Frederick Douglass* by Ed Folsom. Copyright © 1999. Reprinted by permission of the Modern Language Association of America. Page 365, Frontispiece engraving of Frederick Douglass for *Narrative of the Life of Frederick Douglass, an American Slave, Written by Himself.* Boston: Anti-slavery Office, 1845. Yale Collection of American Literature, Beinecke Rare Book and Manuscript Library, Yale University. Page 370, Frontispiece engraving of Walk Whitman for *Leaves of Grass.* Brooklyn, 1855. Rare Book and Special Collections Department of the Library of Congress. Page 373, Frontispiece engraving of Frederick Douglass for *My Bondage and My Freedom.* New York: Miller, Orton and Mulligan, 1855. Courtesy of Yale University Library.

Trudier Harris. "African-American Literature: A Survey." From *Africana Studies: A Survey of Africa and the African Diaspora,* Second Edition, edited by Mario Azevedo. Copyright © 1998 Carolina Academic Press. Reprinted by permission of the publisher.

Gregory S. Jay. "The End of 'American' Literature: Toward a Multicultural Practice." From *College English* 3 (1991). Copyright © 1991 by the National Council of Teachers of English.

Margaret Faye Jones. "Bringing New Historicism into the American Literature Survey." From *Teaching English in the Two-Year College,* 28:2, December 2000. Copyright © 2000 by the National Council of Teachers of English. Reprinted with permission.

Amy Kaplan. "Manifest Domesticity." From *Teaching America,* Vol. 70, No. 3, September 1998. Copyright © 1998 by Duke University Press. Reprinted with permission of the publisher.

AnnLouise Keating. "Interrogating 'Whiteness,' (De)Constructing 'Race.'" From *Teaching African American Literature: Theory and Practice,* edited by Maryemma Graham, Sharon Pineault-Burk, and Marinna White Davis. Copyright © 1998. Reproduced by permission of Routledge/Taylor & Francis Books, Inc.

Elaine H. Kim. "Asian American Literature." From *Columbia Literacy History of the United States* by Emory Elliot, (p. 811–21). Copyright © 1988. Reprinted by permission of Columbia University Press.

David Leverenz. "Manhood, Class, and the American Renaissance." From *American Literature, Culture, and Ideology: Essays in Memory of Henry Nash Smith,* edited by Beverly R. Voloshin. *American University Studies:* series, Vol. 8. Copyright © 1990 Peter Lang Publishing, Inc., New York. Reprinted with permission of the publisher.

David Palumbo-Liu. "Assumed Identities." From *New Literary History,* Vol. 31, No. 4, Autumn, 2000. Reprinted by permission of the author.

Venetria K. Patton and Maureen Honey. "Revisioning the Harlem Renaissance." Excerpt from "Introduction" to *DOUBLE TAKE: A Revisionist Harlem Renaissance Anthology* by Venetria K. Patton and Maureen Honey. Copyright © 2002. Reprinted with permission of Rutgers University Press.

Donald Pizer. "Realism and Naturalism: The Problem of Definition." From *The Cambridge Companion to American Realism and Naturalism* by Donald Pizer. Copyright © 1995. Reprinted by permission of Cambridge University Press.

Lillian S. Robinson. "Treason Our Text: Feminist Challenges to the Literature" from *Tulsa Studies in Women's Literature*, vol. 2, no. 1, Spring 1982, the University of Tulsa. Reprinted by permission of the publisher.

John Carlos Rowe. "Nineteenth-Century United States Literary Culture and Transnationality." From *PMLA* 118.1, January 2003: 78–89. Copyright © 2002. Reprinted by permission of the Modern Language Association of America.

A. LaVonne Brown Ruoff. "Introduction to American Indian Literatures." From *American Indian Literatures: An Introduction, Bibliographic Review, and Selected Bibliography* by A. LaVonne Brown Ruoff. Copyright © 1990. Reprinted by permission of the Modern Language Association of America.

Michael Ryan. "Gender Studies, Queer Theory, Gay/Lesbian Studies." From *Literary Theory: A Practical Introduction* by Michael Ryan. Copyright © 1999. Reprinted by permission of Blackwell Publishing.

Ada Savin. "Mexican-American Literature." From *New Immigrant Literatures in the United States: A Sourcebook to Our Multicultural Literary Heritage*, edited by Alpana Sharma Knippling. Copyright © 1996 Greenwood Press. Reproduced with permission of Greenwood Publishing Group, Inc., Westport, CT.

William J. Scheick. "Early Anglo-American Poetry: Genre, Voice, Art, and Representation." From *Teaching the Literatures of Early America,* edited by Carla Mulfod. Copyright © 1999. Reprinted by permission of the Modern Language Association of America.

Daniel Joseph Singal. "Towards a Definition of American Modernism." From *American Quarterly* 39:1 (1987): 7–26. Copyright © the American Studies Association. Reprinted with permission of the Johns Hopkins University Press.

Cecelia Tichi. "American Literary Studies to the Civil War" from *Redrawing the Boundaries: The Transformation of English and American Literary Studies,* edited by Stephen Greenblatt and Giles Gunn. Copyright © 1995. Reprinted by permission of the Modern Language Association of America.

Lois P. Tucker. "Liberating Students Through Reader-Response Pedagogy in the Introductory Literature Course." From *Teaching English in the Two Year College,* 28:2, December 2000. Copyright © 2000 by the National Council of Teachers of English. Reprinted with permission.